Managing Climate Risks, Facing up to Losses and Damages

OECD
BETTER POLICIES FOR BETTER LIVES

Please cite this publication as:
OECD (2021), *Managing Climate Risks, Facing up to Losses and Damages*, OECD Publishing, Paris, *https://doi.org/10.1787/55ea1cc9-en*.

ISBN 978-92-64-34439-6 (print)
ISBN 978-92-64-43966-5 (pdf)
ISBN 978-92-64-38563-4 (HTML)
ISBN 978-92-64-95181-5 (epub)

Photo credits: Cover © Maro Haas

Corrigenda to publications may be found on line at: *www.oecd.org/about/publishing/corrigenda.htm*.

Preface

Time is running out to address the impacts of climate change. The Intergovernmental Panel on Climate Change's latest scientific assessment makes the severity of the climate hazards we face very clear; even large-scale, high-impact events such as ice sheet collapse and abrupt ocean circulation changes cannot be ruled out. We are in an increasingly perilous situation. A large share of the Earth's current and future populations will face more frequent and intense climate events. The number of governments adopting net-zero goals is encouraging. However, this needs to be translated into real action and real outcomes. In the short term, actions are in many cases not reducing climate risks, rather the opposite.

Building the transparency, trust and solidarity needed to achieve the goals set out in the Paris Agreement is critically important. The Paris Agreement itself provides transparency and review mechanisms to encourage increasingly ambitious and effective climate action. Individual governments have the critical responsibility to deliver on their commitments towards the Paris Agreement. But success will require solidarity across and within nations, effective institutions, coherent policies that set the right incentives across the economy, innovative partnerships, new technologies and transformative approaches as well as investments into increasing resilience.

Precisely how climate change will play out in different regions in the coming decades remains uncertain, but this is not an excuse to delay action. This OECD report explores the uncertainties associated with climate risks and examines in detail the three main types of climate hazard: namely, slow onset changes, extreme weather events and tipping points. It then analyses the policy, financial and technological approaches needed to reduce and manage the risks of losses and damages from climate change.

The OECD is scaling up its support to countries in navigating the climate challenges ahead. This report is part of that effort. It makes a number of important recommendations. As well as limiting warming to 1.5°C, governments should carefully consider uncertainties associated with climate risks to guide policy and investment decisions. Developed countries need to scale up both financial and technical support to developing countries and make such support more accessible and predictable. I hope that this report helps to inform discussions within the UN climate process on Loss and Damage. Further, it aims to inform policy, financial and technological responses on the ground to enhance the effectiveness of efforts to reduce and manage the risks of losses and damages related to climate change.

Mathias Cormann
Secretary-General, OECD

Foreword

This report addresses the urgent issue of already occurring and future climate-related losses and damages. It approaches climate-related losses and damages from a risk management perspective. It explores how climate change currently is and in the future will play out in different geographies, over time, focusing on the three types of hazards: slow-onset changes such as sea-level rise; extreme events including heatwaves, heavy rainfall and drought; and the potential for large-scale non-linear changes within the climate system itself. The report explores approaches to reduce and manage risks with a focus on policy action and finance and the role of technology in supporting effective risk governance processes. Drawing on experiences from around the world, Least Developed Countries and Small Island Developing States in particular, the report highlights a number of good practices and points to ways forward.

The report was largely completed before the release of the report by Working Group I (WGI) of the Intergovernmental Panel on Climate Change (IPCC) as part of its Sixth Assessment Report (AR6). Nevertheless it was informed by the same (and some more recent) research literature that is assessed in the WGI report. This report also benefited throughout a year-long project, from advice and bespoke inputs on specific issues from leading climate change scientists. It has also been able to draw on a wide range of expertise, both of research (e.g. economics, social science) and senior-level policy, finance and disaster risk and recovery experts from international organisations, national governments and think tanks. A series of workshops bringing together policy and science communities and a High Level Advisory Group established to provide input and feedback on the development of this report have been particularly valuable in ensuring that the report was informed by a diverse set of perspectives and expertise.

This report is aimed at policy makers responsible for exploring and assessing potential actions to reduce and manage the risks of losses and damages from climate change. Many key insights also apply more widely across society including on environment and disaster risk management and for ministries such as finance, infrastructure, water and agriculture that increasingly need to consider the adverse impacts of climate change. The report distils information and enhances understanding of some important issues regarding these risks. In so doing, it hopes to inform (international and domestic) political and public dialogue, and to stimulate action indirectly through stakeholders in the private sector and civil society.

Acknowledgements

The report *Managing climate risks, facing up to losses and damages* was prepared under the supervision of Simon Buckle, Head of the Environment, Transitions and Resilience Division at the OECD Environment Directorate, who has also contributed to writing the report. The co-ordinating lead authors for the report are Nicolina Lamhauge, Marcia Rocha, Balazs Stadler and Bopha Chhun from the OECD Environment Directorate. The following experts have contributed to the individual chapters, sections and boxes:

- *Chapter 2: Types of uncertainties and understanding of risks of losses and damages*
  - Lead authors: Erica L. Thompson (London School of Economics) (entirety of Chapter 2); Friederike Otto (Oxford University, now Grantham Institute, Imperial College London) and Luke Harrington (Victoria University of Wellington, New Zealand) (Section 2.2.1); Chandra Sekhar Bahinipati (Indian Institute of Technology Tirupati, India) (Box 2.6);
- *Chapter 3: Climate change impacts and their cascading effects: implications for losses and damages*
  - Lead authors: Jochen Hinkel (Global Climate Forum) (Box 3.2 and Section 3.4); Friederike Otto (Oxford University, now Grantham Institute, Imperial College London) and Luke Harrington (Victoria University of Wellington, New Zealand) (Section 3.5); Timothy M. Lenton, Jesse F. Abrams, Paul D. L. Ritchie, Chris A. Boulton, Mark Williamson (Global Systems Institute, University of Exeter) (Sections 3.2.1 and 3.6);
  - Contributing author: Leigh Wolfrom (OECD Directorate for Financial and Enterprise Affairs) (Section 3.2.1);
- Chapter 4: *Policy, governance and institutions for reducing and managing losses and damages*
  - Lead authors: Jochen Hinkel (Global Climate Forum) (Section 4.5); Rosalind Cornforth, Lindsay Todman, Ross Fairgreave, Heather Plumpton, Theodore Shepherd, Elena Tarnavsky, Celia Petty (Walker Institute, University of Reading) (Box 4.3);
  - Contributing author: James Acidri (Evidence for Development) (perspectives that informed the framing of the chapter);
- *Chapter 5: Finance and financial risks in the face of growing losses and damages*
  - Lead authors: Leigh Wolfrom (OECD Directorate for Financial and Enterprise Affairs) (Section 5.3.3); Juan Casado-Asensio and Alberto Agnelli (OECD Development Co-operation Directorate) (Section 5.4).

The report also benefited from valuable strategic guidance provided by members of a High-Level Advisory Group established for the preparation of this report, as well as members of their teams. The High-Level Advisory Group was co-chaired by Mr. Masamichi Kono, OECD Deputy Secretary-General and Dr. Maria Flachsbarth, Parliamentary State Secretary, German Federal Ministry for Economic Cooperation and Development (BMZ). Members of the High-Level Advisory Group are (in alphabetical order): Mr. Christoph Bals, Policy Director, Germanwatch and Vice-Chair of Munich Climate Insurance Initiative (MCII); H.E. Mrs. Janine Coye Felson, Ambassador and Deputy Permanent Representative for the Permanent Mission of Belize to the United Nations; Dr. Arunabha Ghosh, Founder and Chief Executive Officer, Council on

Energy, Environment and Water (CEEW); Prof. Saleemul Huq, Director, International Centre for Climate Change and Development (ICCCAD); Ms. Ekhosuehi Iyahen, Secretary-General, Insurance Development Forum (IDF); Ms. Maria Carolina Urmeneta Labarca, Head of Climate Change Divisions, Ministry of the Environment, Chile; Prof. Jürg Luterbacher, Director, Science and Innovation, and Chief Scientist, World Meteorological Organization (WMO); Mr. Ricardo Mena, Director, United Nations Office for Disaster Risk Reductions (UNDRR) in Geneva; Ambassador Seyni Nafo, High Representative for Climate Change to the Malian President and Coordinator of the African Adaptation Initiative; Prof. Mari Elka Pangestu, Managing Director of Development Policy and Partnerships, World Bank; Prof. Johan Rockström, Director, Postdam Institute for Climate Impact Research (PIK); The Rt Hon Aiyaz Sayed-Khaiyum, Attorney-General and Minister for Economy, Civil Service and Communications, Republic of Fiji; The Rt Hon Anne-Marie Trevelyan, United Kingdom International Champion on Adaptation and Resilience for the COP26 Presidency and Secretary of State for International Trade and President of the Board of Trade; Mr. German (Jerry) Velasquez, Director for Mitigation and Adaptation Division, Green Climate Fund (GCF).

The comments and suggestions from external reviewers are also gratefully acknowledged, including from: Annette Detken, InsuResilience Solutions Fund; Christian Otto, Potsdam Institute for Climate Impact Research (PIK); Roger Pulwarty, National Oceanic and Atmospheric Administration (NOAA); Debra Roberts, Intergovernmental Panel on Climate Change (IPCC) and eThekwini Municipality in Durban; Theodore Shepherd, University of Reading; Erica Thompson, London School of Economics; and Koko Warner, Secretariat of the United Nations Framework Convention on Climate Change (UNFCCC).

The authors would also like to thank the speakers and participants of the three workshops that were organised to inform the preparation of the report:

- *Assessing the socio-economic losses and damages from climate change*, 13 January, 2021;
- *Approaches to reduce and manage the risks of losses and damages*, 15 April, 2021;
- *Methodological challenges in assessing the socio-economic losses and damages from climate change in India*, 25 May, 2021, organised in collaboration with the Indian Institute of Technology Tirupati (IITT) and the Indian National Institute of Disaster Management (NIDM).

The authors are grateful for the oversight, review, information and comments provided by the Environment Policy Committee (EPOC) and its Working Party on Climate, Investment, and Development (WPCID) and the Network on Environment and Development Co-operation (ENVIRONET) of the Development Assistance Committee (DAC).

The project has benefitted from the overall guidance of Rodolfo Lacy, Director, and Ingrid Barnsley, Deputy Director of the Environment Directorate, OECD. The authors would also like to thank the following OECD colleagues for their insightful comments and review: Aimée Aguilar-Jaber, Marta Arbinolo, Juan Casado-Asensio, Mario Cervantes, Antoine Dechezleprêtre, Kathleen Dominique, John Dulac, Jane Ellis, Catherine Gamper, Raphael Jachnik, Sirini Jeudy-Hugo, Takayoshi Kato, Fatos Koc, Eliza Lanzi, Xavier Leflaive, Catriona Marshall, Mireille Martini, Mariana Mirabile, Michael Mullan, Shashwati Shankar Padmanabhan, Robert Patalano, Edward Perry, Mikaela Rambali, Delia Sanchez-Trancon, Jens Sedemund, Leigh Wolfrom, Robert Youngman.

The report was prepared for publication with support from Nassera Belkhiter, Dominique Haleva and Ines Reale from the OECD Environment Directorate, with editorial support provided by Mark Foss.

Financial support from and collaboration with the German Federal Ministry for Economic Cooperation and Development (BMZ) and input provided by various programmes of the Deutsche Gesellschaft für Internationale Zusammenarbeit (GIZ) GmbH, in particular from Marting Kipping, Christoph von Stechow, Manuel Friedlein, Nicola Hanke, Joana Helms, Lea Sarah Kulick, Daniel Stadtmüller and Britta Horstmann is gratefully acknowledged.

Table of contents

Tables

Figures

Boxes

Executive summary

Changes in the climate are rapid, widespread and intensifying. Human influence on this change is unequivocal. The heatwaves, wildfires, floods and tropical storms that have affected many parts of the world in recent years provide a foretaste of the future. Unchecked, climate change will affect all aspects of human life and the natural world, leading to increasing losses and damages. Lives, livelihoods and the social and economic stability of countries and regions are at risk along with the natural environment on which we all depend.

The impacts of climate change are not evenly distributed. Developing countries – especially Least Developed Countries (LDCs) and Small Island Developing States (SIDS) – are disproportionately affected by the impacts of climate change. This is due both to their geographic location and high-levels of exposure and vulnerability to climate-related hazards. Marginalised populations and communities, within and across countries, are particularly vulnerable.

There is high confidence on the aspects of climate change directly related to warming of the climate system and the severity of the associated impacts. There are, however, uncertainties in relation to where, when and how climate-related hazards will occur and how they will interact with future socio-economic developments that determine levels of exposure and vulnerability. Using a medical analogy, scientists have now diagnosed the nature and cause of the "warming disease" and have a good understanding of the prognosis, even if they cannot precisely predict the timing and severity of its effects or how exactly it might interact with other pre-existing conditions, such as extreme poverty or biodiversity loss.

These uncertainties are not a reason to delay action. Quite the opposite. Yet the nature of the uncertainties has important implications for how to approach the challenge of reducing and managing the risks. The context for action is also complex and challenging. This report argues that responsibilities for reducing and managing the risks are shared across different stakeholder groups, nationally and internationally. Large emitting countries have a responsibility to lead the net zero transition. Developed countries must scale up both financial and technical support to developing countries and make such support more accessible and predictable. Ambitious and bold climate action today will reduce future losses and damages; a failure to act means transferring the burden and risks to future generations.

In different ways and with different resources and levels of ambition, governments, the private sector, researchers, civil society organisations and individual citizens – often in partnerships – are taking action. These different stakeholders have complementary roles that offer areas for further action and collaboration. Recommended actions put forward in the report to reduce and manage both economic and non-economic losses and damages are summarised below, with a focus on the role of governments:

1. **Take a precautionary approach by aiming to limit the temperature increase to 1.5°C**: Accelerate strategies to achieve net zero globally by mid-century, supported by shorter-term targets and plans, while rapidly scaling up finance, technology and capacity development.
2. **Create a more effective international development finance landscape supporting efforts to reduce and manage current impacts and projected risks of losses and damages**: Scale-up

finance, improve access to finance and reduce transaction costs to decrease future risks, while fostering country ownership and better aligning international development finance with national priorities, circumstances and needs.

3. **Strengthen the global architecture for climate and disaster risk finance**: Enhance availability and access to financial protection, particularly for the most vulnerable and increase the coherence of international support for climate and disaster risk finance.
4. **Enhance fiscal resilience to deal with increasingly adverse impacts**: Implement a comprehensive approach to risk management to reduce, retain and transfer risks of losses and damages, limit contingent liabilities and review the implications of climate risks for fiscal sustainability.
5. **Protect livelihoods, reduce precarity through insurance, social protection and humanitarian assistance**: Develop insurance markets to make available coverage for climate risks, ensure protection of the most vulnerable segments of society through enhanced social protection, and reduce losses and damages through anticipatory and predictable humanitarian action.
6. **Adopt approaches to decision making that account for uncertainties in climate risks**: Manage risks across different time and spatial scales, enhance capacities within the decision-making process to plan under uncertainty, adopt iterative and adaptive decision-making processes, and identify and manage risks that may overwhelm local capacities.
7. **Integrate climate and sustainable development objectives and improve policy coherence**: Approach decisions on climate risks as an integral component of sustainable development and increase coherence across national and international policy communities.
8. **Improve data, capabilities and processes for climate risk governance:** Enhance international support for observational and forecasting capabilities, particularly in developing countries and including for collection and interpretation of data on extreme events and impacts; further strengthen weather and climate information services and establish an international mechanism to monitor tipping elements in the climate system to provide early warning for strategies and actions.
9. **Facilitate inclusive stakeholder engagement that builds on the knowledge, expertise and values of different actors and gives due recognition to intangible losses and damages**. Develop partnerships to enhance coordination and collaboration across communities of policy and practice, nationally and internationally, improve awareness and understanding on the risk and strengthen approaches to reduce and manage the risks of losses and damages, and leverage private sector expertise.

1 Losses and damages from climate change: A critical moment for action

Losses and damages are happening now and the risks of future losses and damages will increase with climate change. This chapter briefly summarises the observed and projected physical changes due to climate change. It sets out both the framework for the analysis of climate risks and the associated risks of losses and damages that underpin this report. Some illustrative ways that climate risks manifest are presented and responsibilities for reducing and managing them discussed. The chapter also summarises the key messages and recommendations emerging from this report, including on the policy, financial and technological toolkits that can be used to reduce and manage the risks of losses and damages.

In Brief

A critical moment for climate action with losses and damages from climate change mounting

Climate-related hazards are having devastating and widespread impacts on lives; they are also directly impacting peoples' livelihoods. This is especially the case when they occur in conjunction with broader social, economic and political stressors. Unchecked, climate change will cause increasingly severe economic and social impacts. These impacts relate, for example, to changes in labour and agricultural productivity, health effects, loss of capital assets, displacement of people and changes to ecosystems. In an interconnected world, climate impacts experienced in one country – and the responses to those impacts – can impose threats beyond its borders.

Beyond the effects on economic production, people and communities are also vulnerable to intangible or non-economic losses and damages. These include the psychological or mental health impacts of extreme and slow-onset events, the loss of cultural artefacts and places, and loss of sense of identity and security. Intangible effects are not easily quantifiable and hence rarely feature in socio-economic assessments. However, many people consider vulnerabilities of some intangible aspects (e.g. health of family members, sense of safety) more important than the benefits of consumption associated with higher incomes.

Climate risk is a function of hazard, the exposure of people and assets, and their vulnerability to that particular hazard. It may be compounded by other unanticipated challenges (e.g. as many countries experienced during the COVID-19 pandemic). The extent of climate risks therefore will vary depending on a range of underlying factors. These include income and wealth, economic (including fiscal) and institutional structure, and geographic location. Different factors will also influence how people experience climate risks, including: i) values and worldviews; ii) a sense of place and the identities, cultures and values attached to places and landscapes; iii) perceptions of justice and accountability (e.g. distributive and procedural); and iv) discourses and power.

Developing countries, including Least Developed Countries and Small Island Developing States, are disproportionately affected by the impacts of climate change. Within countries, segments of the population marginalised by, for example, their socio-economic status, gender, race, age, disability, income, and class identities or geographic locations are particularly at risk. Future generations will carry the burden for inadequate climate action by current and past generations, especially those of large emitting economies and fossil-fuel exporting countries.

In this report, the ***risk of losses and damages*** refers to the harm that may result from the interactions of climate-related hazards, exposure and vulnerability. These can be reduced and managed through mitigation and adaptation efforts, as well as other interventions including disaster risk reduction, disaster risk finance and humanitarian assistance. Losses and damages are occurring now and will grow over time without urgent action to manage climate risks. In addition to rapid and deep cuts in greenhouse gas emissions to achieve climate neutrality globally, efforts should be scaled up to address the other two components of risk: exposure and vulnerability in their specific contexts.

The precise impacts of climate change on human and natural systems are subject to varying degrees of uncertainty. Given the nature and scale of the observed and projected natural and socio-economic impacts, some of which can lead to irreversible damages, these uncertainties have important implications for efforts to reduce and manage climate risks.

The context for action is complex and challenging. First, even at the temperature range set out in the Paris Agreement, a large share of current and future populations will face increasingly frequent and intense hazards, with some regions experiencing hazards not seen before, e.g. as disease vectors shift their range. This will all things being equal, drive increases in the losses and damages currently experienced for populations that may have contributed hardly at all to climate change.

Reducing exposure and vulnerability to climate change is also challenging. Complex historical processes have contributed to current exposures and vulnerabilities. Choices made today can further drive changes in these components that may be hard to reverse. Examples include expansion of urban and suburban developments, persistent inequality and increasing pressures on the environment (e.g. water resources). The capacity of countries to respond to climate change will also be subject to factors such as a strong and diversified economy, institutional and human capacity as well as ready access to finance and technology and effective governance structures.

Responsibilities for losses and damages are shared across many different actors, nationally and internationally. The level of climate hazard is driven by large greenhouse gas emitting countries. The scale and effectiveness of action to reduce and manage the risks will depend on several factors. These comprise the availability of financial resources (domestic and international, public and private); the availability of specific technical capacities; and the effectiveness and coherence of policy interventions designed to increase resilience and reduce exposure and vulnerabilities to climate-related hazards. In many developing countries, actions to reduce and manage the risks of losses and damages will rely on support from the international level. This is an active area of discussion and negotiation within the UN climate process, particularly in relation to current and future levels of climate finance.

A broad range of national policies and international support for sustainable development or disaster risk reduction, recovery and reconstruction will also be important. Indeed, decisions on climate action are not made in isolation. Rather, they are an integral component of countries' development objectives. As such, they must be assessed in relation to the broader spectrum of socio-economic risks and the associated uncertainties relevant for decision making. If not carefully managed, some measures intended to reduce and manage the risk of losses and damages may increase the risks for other segments of society or across countries.

1.1. Introduction

The lives and livelihoods of hundreds of millions of people, their cultures, development gains, economic prosperity and equality are at risk due to already occurring and future climate-related losses and damages. Temperatures continue to rise and climate-related hazards that cause major losses and damages in both developed and developing countries are becoming more frequent and intense.

The COVID-19 pandemic has demonstrated the potential scale and impact of global disruptions. At the same time, it has shown that decisive action is possible in the face of an urgent threat, initially to save lives but subsequently also livelihoods. This has contributed to calls for using the recovery to chart a new economic and ecological path that includes the net-zero transition, efforts to strengthen societal resilience, including related to climate change, and to integrate climate action with efforts to improve wider well-being, including on natural capital (Buckle et al., 2020[1]).

Early assessments of COVID-19 measures announced by OECD countries and major emerging economies suggest that just over 20% include an explicit focus on environmental objectives. The remaining share either does not consider environmental dimensions, or worse, reverses progress on some of them (OECD, 2021[2]). Important progress has nonetheless been made in recent years to address the challenges posed by climate change. Countries and other actors are committing to more rapid and ambitious action than might not have seemed possible a decade ago. Since 2019, a large number of countries have put forward commitments to reach by mid-century net-zero carbon dioxide or greenhouse gas (GHG) emissions (UNFCCC, 2015[3]). In May 2021, such commitments covered more than 70% of global emissions (CAT, 2021[4]). Climate action in line with these net-zero goals is, however, heterogeneous, and countries' shorter-term commitments are not yet always consistent with longer-term goals.

By March 2021, 126 developing countries were formulating and implementing National Adaptation Plans (NAPs), with 22 countries having completed the preparation of their first NAP (UNFCCC, 2021[5]). However, with mounting losses and damages, countries are recognising the need to strengthen the coherence of their approaches to climate change with that on disaster risk reduction (UNDRR, 2021[6]; OECD, 2020[7]). Meanwhile, the humanitarian community now considers climate change one of the greatest threats facing communities around the world (IFRC, 2021[8]).

This report provides analysis, insights, discussion and recommendations on the risks of losses and damages from climate change. It also highlights approaches to reduce and manage those risks that can inform relevant national and international policy and processes. This topic has been subject to much discussion under the United Nations Framework Convention on Climate Change (UNFCCC). Of particular importance in this context is Article 8 of the Paris Agreement, which encourages Parties to the Agreement to "enhance understanding, action and support [...] with respect to loss and damage associated with the adverse effects of climate change". Through its analysis and recommendations, this report aims to contribute to that objective. The report takes a global perspective but highlights the diversity of circumstances in which people find themselves, with a particular focus on Least Developed Countries (LDCs) and Small Island Developing States (SIDS).

The rest of this chapter is structured around five sections. Section 1.2 summarises the observed and projected physical changes due to climate change. Section 1.3 sets out the framework for the analysis of climate risks, impacts, and losses and damages that underpins this report. This includes a discussion on the losses and damages related to climate change that are already occurring, some illustrative ways climate risks are manifested, and the interrelationship between climate change and biodiversity. Section 1.4 provides context for action in reducing and managing the risks of losses and damages. Section 1.5 sets out the structure and intended audience for this report before Section 1.6 summarises key recommendations from the entire report.

1.2. Observed and projected climate change

This section briefly summarises observed and projected future changes in the climate. It also highlights some uncertainties inherent in projections of future climate change due to a range of different sources. This provides some illustrative insights without aiming to be complete. More comprehensive material can be found in the Intergovernmental Panel on Climate Change (IPCC) Working Group I contribution to the Sixth Assessment Report (AR6) (IPCC, 2021[9]) and the forthcoming contributions of Working Groups II and III, expected in 2022. Deep dives on different types of hazards are provided in subsequent chapters of this report.

1.2.1. Observed climate change

Human influence on the warming of the climate system is unequivocal (IPCC, 2021[9]). Average global surface temperature was 1.09°C higher in 2011-20 than over 1850-1900, with larger increases over land (1.59°C) than the ocean (0.88°C) (IPCC, 2021[9]). There are significant variations over the Earth's surface.

Polar regions and the land surface have experienced greater absolute warming than tropical regions and the sea surface, a pattern expected to continue (IPCC, 2021[9]). As well as increases in global surface temperatures, the physical impacts of climate change include increases in sea-level rise (SLR) (Frederikse et al., 2020[10]), and ice melt, as well as land degradation exacerbated by changes in the climate (IPCC, 2019[11]), among others.

Oceans absorbed over 90% of the additional heating due to climate change over 1971-2018 (IPCC, 2021[9]). This has warmed the oceans, particularly the upper layers since it takes a long time for the ocean as a whole to reach thermal equilibrium. The consequent thermal expansion was responsible for half of the increases in SLR over 1971-2018, with sea levels rising about 3.7 millimetres (mm) per year over 2006-18 (IPCC, 2021[9]). Other factors also increasingly contribute to accelerating mean SLR, such as the widespread shrinking of the cryosphere, i.e. frozen regions of the Earth system, though only ice melt on land contributes to SLR.

Climate is naturally variable, due to factors such as solar radiation, volcanic activity and complex interactions between the atmosphere and ocean. The temperature increase during the 20th century, however, far exceeded increases that could be attributed to natural variability (Crowley, 2000[12]). Indeed, the World Meteorological Organization (WMO) recently warned that, due to such variability, there was about a 40% chance that temporarily this temperature measure could increase to as much as 1.5°C in at least one of the next five years (WMO, 2020[13]). Natural variability and feedbacks in the climate system mean that the range of best estimates of the climate's response to anthropogenic GHG emissions – known as the climate sensitivity – remain uncertain. This uncertainty remains despite significant scientific advances in reducing the range (Sherwood et al., 2020[14]; IPCC, 2021[9]).

The scale of changes in the climate system and the current state of many of its aspects are unprecedented over centuries to millennia (IPCC, 2021[9]). Climate change is also contributing to increases in the severity, variety and frequency of some extreme weather events, such as heatwaves (Vautard et al., 2020[15]) and wildfires (Kirchmeier-Young et al., 2019[16]). The IPCC (2021[9]) is increasingly confident in the attribution of observed extremes (e.g. heatwaves, heavy precipitation, droughts) to human activity. Confidence in such attribution is greatest for hot extremes.

The ocean and the cryosphere have long response times to climate forcing by GHGs. The deep ocean will continue to warm and sea level to rise over the next several centuries, even if GHG concentrations stabilised today (IPCC, 2019[17]). This means that GHG emitted by humans – particularly carbon dioxide that has a long residence time in the atmosphere – will drive future climate change in these systems over several centuries. This points to the need to consider the potentially long-time scales in current evaluation of climate risks (Clark et al., 2016[18]).

Climate change is also altering the geographical distribution of species at an accelerating rate (Pecl et al., 2017[19]). Some species are moving towards the Poles, while others are moving to cooler, higher altitudes. On average, terrestrial populations are moving 17 km per decade, while marine ones are moving 72 km per decade. The range of others subject to intolerable levels of heat is shrinking. Established species interactions are being disrupted and new relationships formed.

1.2.2. Projections of future climate change

Future emissions pathways will be determined by the complex and rapidly evolving range of societal, technological, economic and political choices made by governments, countries and citizens in the short-, mid- and long-term. Climate models since the 1970s have performed well in predicting global mean surface temperature rise using scenarios of atmospheric concentrations of GHGs (Hausfather et al., 2020[20]). There is a good understanding of how different choices will influence future emissions, even if there is some uncertainty about how these will translate into atmospheric concentrations of GHGs due to changing interactions between different components of the climate system as the planet warms.

The IPCC has established five central Representative Concentration Pathways (RCPs), bounded by a low-carbon mitigation scenario (RCP1.9) and a carbon-intensive baseline scenario (RCP8.5). Each pathway represents a potential future of climate forcing, with higher atmospheric GHG concentrations leading to higher levels of global mean surface temperature increase. Figure 1.1 shows illustrative pathways for different future worlds, based on the RCPs.

Figure 1.1. Future annual emissions of CO_2 and of a subset of key non-CO_2 across five illustrative RCP pathways

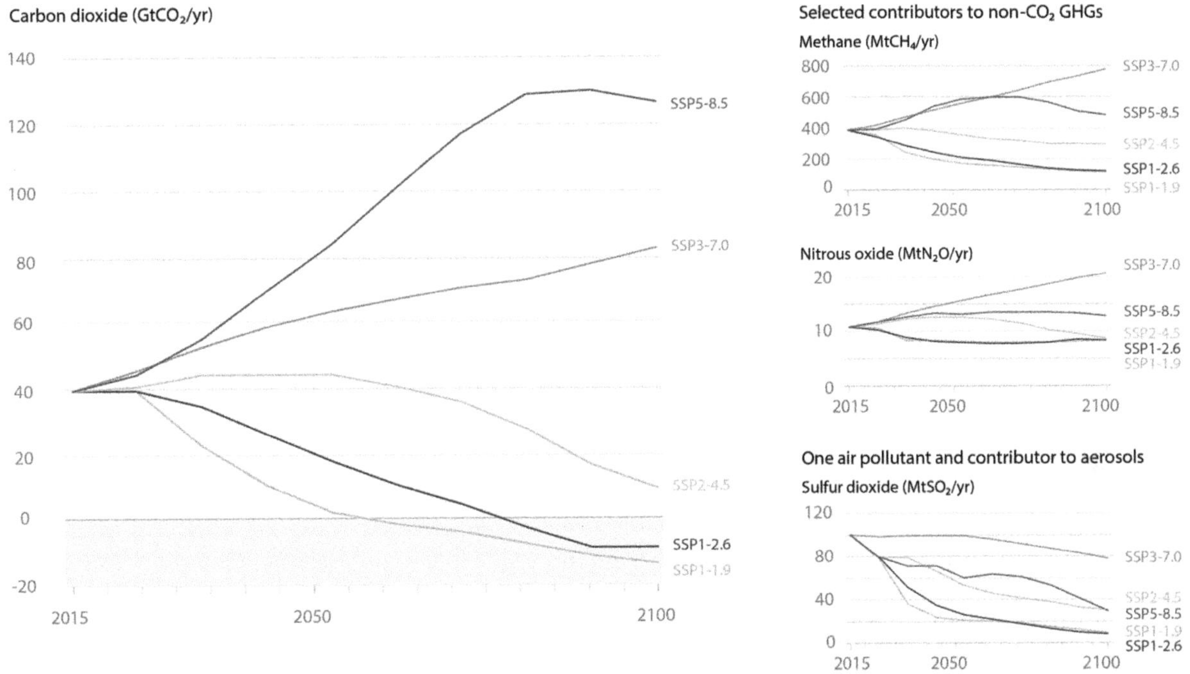

Note: Emissions of carbon dioxide (CO_2) alone, selected contributors to non-CO_2 and one air pollutant and contributor to aerosols. The scenario categories summarise the wide range of emission scenarios published in the scientific literature. The trajectories provided refer to a RCP scenario coupled with a Shared Socioeconomic Pathway (SSP) (see Chapter 2 for details). These provide the socio-economic and technological factors that result in different emissions and thus concentration pathways. SSP1-1.9, SSP1-2.6, SSP2-4.5, SSP3-7.0 and SSP5-8.5 refer respectively to RCP/SSP scenario combinations RCP1.9/SSP1, RCP2.6/SSP1, RCP4.5/SSP2, RCP7/SSP3 and RCP8.5/SSP5. These form a basis for the physical study of different future worlds, with different levels of warming and climate change impacts.
Source: (IPCC, 2021[9]).

The projected increases of global mean surface temperatures for selected 20-year time periods in the near-, mid- and long-term relative to the end of the 19th century (1850-1900) are provided in Table 1.1. As shown in the table, only the low (SSP1-2.6) and very low (SSP1-1.9) GHG emissions scenarios are unlikely and extremely unlikely, respectively, not to exceed 2°C during this century. Between 2021 and 2040, all scenarios are projected to at least reach or exceed the 1.5°C level. Climate change is projected to continue to lead to changes in the frequency, intensity, spatial extent, duration, variety and timing of many weather extremes that may result in unprecedented extremes (IPCC, 2021[9]). Indeed, temperature records in many places of North America, for example, were recently broken by several degrees.

Table 1.1. Changes in global surface temperature resulting from different RCP scenarios

	Near term, 2021-40		Mid term, 2041-60		Long term, 2081-2100	
Scenario	Best estimate (ºC)	Very likely range (ºC)	Best estimate (ºC)	Very likely range (ºC)	Best estimate (ºC)	Very likely range (ºC)
SSP1-1.9	1.5	1.2 to 1.7	1.6	1.2 to 2.0	1.4	1.0 to 1.8
SSP1-2.6	1.5	1.2 to 1.8	1.7	1.3 to 2.2	1.8	1.3 to 2.4
SSP2-4.5	1.5	1.2 to 1.8	2.0	1.6 to 2.5	2.7	2.1 to 3.5
SSP3-7.0	1.5	1.2 to 1.8	2.1	1.7 to 2.6	3.6	2.8 to 4.6
SSP5-8.5	1.6	1.3 to 1.9	2.4	1.9 to 3.0	4.4	3.3 to 5.7

Note: Changes in global surface temperature (relative to 1850-1900), assessed based on multiple lines of evidence, for selected 20-year time periods and the five illustrative emissions scenarios considered. The figures provided refer to the RCP scenario coupled with an SSP (see Chapter 2 for details). These provide the socio-economic and technological factors that result in different emissions and thus concentration pathways. SSP1-1.9, SSP1-2.6, SSP2-4.5, SSP3-7.0 and SSP5-8.5 refer respectively to RCP/SSP scenario combinations RCP1.9/SSP1, RCP2.6/SSP1, RCP4.5/SSP2, RCP7/SSP3 and RCP8.5/SSP5. These form a basis for the physical study of different future worlds, with different levels of warming and climate change impacts. The "very likely" range refers to the range between the 5th to 95th percentiles.
Source: Table SPM1 in (IPCC, 2021[9]).

Multiple emissions pathways are consistent with each RCP scenario. Non-constant factors influence GHG concentrations in the atmosphere. including the uptake of atmospheric carbon by plants and the ocean and the share and trajectory of different GHGs and other climate forcers. Projections of the temperature increase at lower levels of emissions such as those consistent with RCP1.9 and RCP2.6 are likely to be more precise and more accurate than forecasts of the impacts of higher levels of emissions. Current trajectories in line with emissions reductions commitments seem consistent with warming of around 2.4°C by the end of the century (CAT, 2021[4]).

Climate-related hazards will continue to increase in severity with increasing warming levels (IPCC, 2021[9]). These include SLR (Frederikse et al., 2020[10]), ice melt and land degradation exacerbated by changes in the climate (IPCC, 2019[11]), among others. Climate change is projected to continue to lead to changes in the frequency, intensity, spatial extent, duration, variety and timing of weather extremes, potentially resulting in unprecedented extremes (Seneviratne et al., 2012[21]; Kirchmeier-Young et al., 2019[16]; Vautard et al., 2020[15]).

Climate change also has the potential to push components of the Earth system past critical thresholds. Evidence is mounting on the risk of exceeding such tipping points of the climate system, including some during this century (Lenton et al., 2019[22]; IPCC, 2019[17]). Tipping points consist of thresholds of abrupt, often irreversible long-term changes that cannot be avoided once the threshold is crossed. Tipping elements of the Earth system include ice sheet and glacier mass loss and permafrost degradation. These effects are expected to be irreversible on time scales relevant to human societies and ecosystems.

Another tipping element of the ocean is the Atlantic Meridional Overturning Circulation (AMOC), which is at its weakest in the last millennium. A collapse, or even slowdown, could have potentially large impacts on regional weather patterns that support human and ecological systems (Caesar et al., 2021[23]). This could affect ecosystems, as well as human health, livelihoods, food security, water supply and economic growth at a global scale. For example, Europe would become colder and drier, which would reduce agricultural productivity. Changes in sea-surface temperature and rainfall patterns in the tropical Atlantic would impact the stability of the Amazon and could lead to the disruption of West African and Indian Monsoons. As Earth's systems are interconnected, passing one climate tipping point could also trigger others (Rocha et al., 2018[24]). Such a global cascade of tipping points would constitute a clear emergency (Lenton et al., 2019[22]). The implications are examined in detail in Chapter 3.

1.3. Climate risks, impacts and losses and damages

Climate risks are a key starting point for any analysis of losses and damages. This report uses the IPCC's conceptualisation of climate risk that frames it as a function of the climate-related hazard; the exposure of people and assets; and their vulnerability to that particular hazard (IPCC, 2014[25]) (see Figure 1.2). At the intersection of hazard, exposure and vulnerability the consequences of climate risks materialise with "effects on lives, livelihoods, health and well-being, ecosystems and social and cultural assets; services (including ecosystem services); and infrastructure" (IPCC, 2018[26]). While the impacts can be both adverse and beneficial, the focus in this report is on the former.

Figure 1.2. Illustration of the core aspects underlying the IPCC framework concept of risk

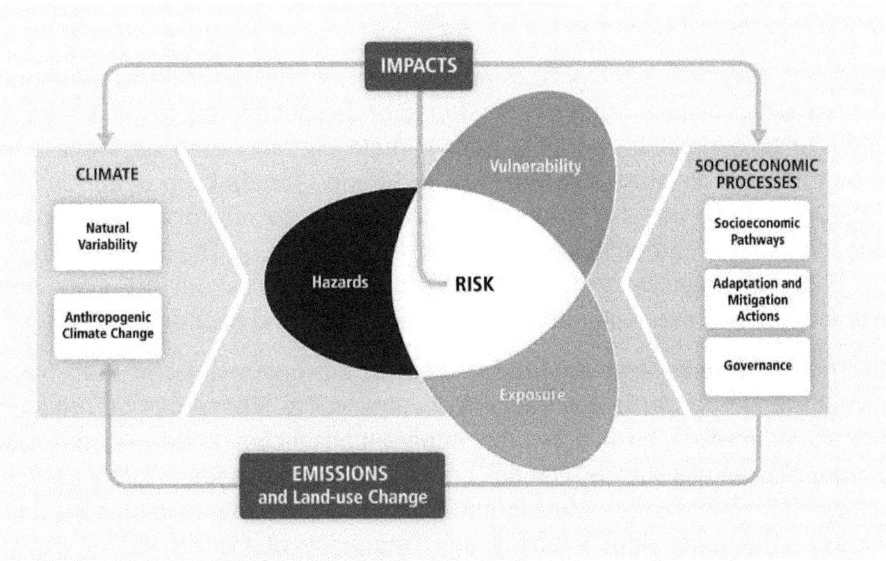

Note: Climate risks result from the interaction between hazards resulting from changes in the physical climate, the exposure of people or assets to those hazards and the vulnerability of those exposed elements. Changes in the climate system (left-hand side), including anthropogenic climate change, and in socio-economic processes (right-hand side), including socio-economic pathways, mitigation and adaptation actions, influence hazards, exposure and vulnerability.
Source: (IPCC, 2014[25]).

Hazard refers to the potential occurrence of a natural or human-induced physical event or trend. It may lead to the loss of lives, livelihoods and natural or produced assets, among others. Climate-related hazards range from extreme weather events (e.g. heat waves, cold spells, droughts, floods and storms) to slow-onset changes (e.g. SLR). Hazards also include tipping points in the climate system that will be triggered and unfold on different time and spatial scales and at different intensities if certain thresholds are crossed. Humans may never have experienced some hazards (e.g. some of the tipping points); hazards that are more familiar may, now and in the future, occur in places they did not before. In other words, risk management needs to consider novel hazards.

Exposure describes the lives, livelihoods, natural and economic assets that are geographically and temporally exposed to the effects of particular hazards of a given intensity. The nature and extent of exposure will depend on the hazard, as well as the characteristics of the relevant area. A more severe hurricane or tropical cyclone, for example, is likely to affect more people and assets in a coastal area than a weaker hurricane. Moreover, exposure will change with time: SLR is expanding the areas exposed to potential storm surges for a given intensity of hurricane. Additionally, urbanisation and development change the number of people and value of assets exposed. The exposed people and assets are far greater in a major city than in a sparsely populated coastal area. As noted above, the geographical extent and nature of hazards are likely to change, leading to novel exposures.

Vulnerability refers to the multifaceted ways people and assets are sensitive to, and can be adversely impacted, by climate-related hazards. Vulnerability to hazards is driven by socio-economic assets, structures and circumstances. These shape, support or constrain the ability of people to access the tangible and intangible resources needed to reduce exposure to the hazards and manage the impacts. Vulnerability varies across geographic regions, across economic sectors, within segments of the population (e.g. based on gender, class or ethnicity). It also depends on individual characteristics such as age and health. Responses to hazards may be gradual, such as refurbishment of houses or changes in construction material. However, given a sufficiently intense hazard, some transitions may be irreversible (e.g. relocation of an entire community after an intense wildfire). Another important aspect of vulnerability is whether systems can recover after the occurrence of an intense hazard. Both the speed and extent of recovery are important to reduce losses and damages.

Although humans live in very diverse climatic regimes, each society has culturally adapted over millennia to the climate of a particular location, from which change or deviations may result in losses and damages. While some regions may experience benefits from climate change, such as the expansion of certain agricultural regions to higher altitudes and latitudes in Siberia (Tchebakova et al., 2011[27]) and Canada (Hannah et al., 2020[28]), these benefits would be accompanied by environmental impacts, including on water, nature conservation and carbon storage (Hannah et al., 2020[28]). The benefits are therefore minimal compared to the potential negative climate impacts globally. At risk are the lives and livelihoods of hundreds of millions of people, their cultures, development gains and economic prosperity.

In this report, the ***risk of losses and damages*** refers to the potential harm that may result from the interactions of climate-related hazards, exposure and vulnerability. These can be reduced and managed through mitigation and adaptation, as well as other interventions including disaster risk reduction, disaster risk finance and humanitarian assistance. The risks of losses and damages will vary depending on a range of underlying factors that influence the nature of the hazards and countries' exposure and vulnerability to them. This includes: i) the (changing) intensity and frequency of the hazard; ii) geographic location; iii) exposure of people and assets; iv) vulnerability of people and assets to that hazard; and v) the extent to which the immediate losses and damages have longer-term implications for livelihoods and larger-scale development outcomes.

Developing countries, including LDCs and SIDS, are disproportionately affected by the impacts of climate change. This is due to their geographic location at low latitudes, generally lower levels of development and economic diversification, fiscal constraints and their physical characteristics. Within countries, some segments of the population are particularly at risk. These include segments marginalised by, for example, their socio-economic status, gender, race, age, disability, income and class identities (Eriksen et al., 2021[29]). In many developing countries, women may be more vulnerable to climate hazards than men within the same household. This is the result of social practices, such as less extensive social networks for women or less accumulation of human capital, which lead to less awareness about the risks and available responses (Alhassan, Kuwornu and Osei-Asare, 2019[30]; Rahman, 2013[31]). Estimates suggest that climate change could pull more than 130 million people into poverty by 2030 (Jafino et al., 2020[32]). In several regions, this can degrade political stability and weaken social cohesion (Sofuoğlu and Ay, 2020[33]).

1.3.1. Current losses and damages

Climate-related hazards are already having devastating and widespread impacts on lives and livelihoods, particularly when they occur in conjunction with broader social, economic and political stressors. In 2018, for example, droughts, floods and storms in India caused around USD 6.1 billion in damages (Guha-Sapir, Below and Hoyois, 2021[34]). When Hurricane Dorian made landfall in the Bahamas in 2019, it caused at least 70 deaths, with losses and damages estimated at a quarter of the Bahamas' GDP (Zegarra et al., 2020[35]). The 2019-20 Australia wildfire season resulted in 19 million hectares (ha) of land being burned and at least 33 deaths. The economic impacts were estimated at AUD 20 billion (Filkov et al., 2020[36]). There is robust scientific evidence that climate change made these events more likely (Shultz et al., 2020[37]; Hunt and Menon, 2020[38]; van Oldenborgh et al., 2021[39]).

The extraordinary weather events during the northern hemisphere summer of 2021 showed that no one is immune from the effects of extreme events. Record-breaking heat over Europe, the west of North America and the northeast of the Russian Federation (hereafter "Russia") triggered deadly heatwaves and devastating fires. Some scientists considered the heatwave in North America virtually impossible without human-induced climate change (Sofuoğlu and Ay, 2020[33]). Lytton, a village in British Columbia, Canada, recorded a maximum temperature of 49.6ºC, a staggering 4.6°C higher than the previous maximum temperature ever observed in Canada. Shortly thereafter, a wildfire largely destroyed the village (WMO, 2021[40]). In July, some parts of Europe saw two months of normal rainfall in just two days. This led to floods, around 200 deaths and significant damage to key economic infrastructure (World Weather Attribution, 2021[41]). Extreme heat in eastern Mediterranean in July and early August 2021 led to severe wildfires in Turkey and Greece. Later in the month, the heatwave extended further west, leading to fires in other European and African countries, such as Italy and Algeria. Heavier than normal monsoon rains in India and the rest of South Asia, and incessant and prolonged rainfall in the People's Republic of China, also led to significant economic losses, deaths and injuries.

Over 1970 to 2019, disasters from weather, climate and water extremes represented 50% of all recorded disasters, 45% of deaths related to disasters and 74% of related economic losses (WMO, 2021[42]). Improvements in early warning are saving lives, with deaths from these disasters falling to about 40% of their level in the 1970s by the 2010s. More than 91% of the deaths occurred in developing countries. The WMO assessment reported an almost eightfold increase in average daily economic losses between 1970-79 and 2010-19. However, the absolute value of reported economic losses is likely to underrepresent the impact of such disasters on development and livelihoods. It may also reflect reporting gaps in developing countries. For example, Africa saw 35% of the deaths related to weather, climate and water extremes but just 1% of reported global economic losses (WMO, 2021[42]).

1.3.2. Transmission mechanisms and factors influencing the experience of risk

This section sets out some illustrative ways or transmission mechanisms through which climate change can cause economic and non-economic losses and damages. Climate change is putting lives at risk and directly impacting peoples' livelihoods, for example, through changes in labour and agricultural productivity, certain health effects, the loss of capital assets and the functioning of ecosystems. Other, more indirect impacts on livelihoods include changes in the demand of goods and services, disruption of supply chains, faster spread of certain infectious diseases and negative effects on broader well-being. Examples below illustrate socio-economic impacts observed in empirical assessments for relatively small deviations in past climate:

- ***Health:*** The physiological limit of human survival is 35°C with 100% humidity (or 35°C wet-bulb temperature; equivalent to 45°C with 50% humidity). Accordingly, high temperature levels are strongly associated with high mortality rates across countries (Deschênes and Greenstone, 2011[43]; Carleton et al., 2019[44]). Rising temperatures also contribute to increased morbidity from vector-borne diseases. For example, mosquitoes can reproduce faster around warming waters. This, in turn, could increase spread of malaria (Linthicum et al., 1999[45]; Luque Fernández et al., 2009[46]; Makin, 2011[47]). At the same time, fertility decreases with rising temperatures affecting the health of reproductive cells (Lam and Miron, 1996[48]; Fisch et al., 2003[49]; Barreca, Deschênes and Guldi, 2018[50]).

- ***Production:*** Climate change may cause severe and more chronic food insecurity, increasing the propensity of malnutrition (Jankowska et al., 2012[51]; Grace et al., 2012[52]). This could occur through disruption of agricultural production, storage, supply chains and the nutritional value of crops. When climatic events destroy crops and cattle or reduce agricultural yields, they also impact food prices. The 2010 Russian heatwaves, for example, led to export ban of grains in Russia. This, in turn, raised grain prices around the world (Welton, 2011[53]) (see Chapter 4, Box 4.1).
- ***Productivity:*** In light of the health effects of heat stress, high temperature levels also decrease general labour productivity for both manual and cognitive tasks (Cai, Lu and Wang, 2018[54]) (Graff Zivin et al., 2020[55]). For example, one study observed that worker productivity in the Chinese manufacturing sector declined by 2% for every Celsius degree increase above 25°C for the day (Cai, Lu and Wang, 2018[54]). Temperature rise is also associated with decreased GDP growth. The magnitude of the decline depends on the geography of the country, the approach and assumptions for assessing the effect (Dell, Jones and Olken, 2012[56]; Burke, Hsiang and Miguel, 2015[57]).

Extreme events can have strong negative effects on economic growth that can last years or decades as the effect of disaster dissipates slowly (Botzen, Deschênes and Sanders, 2019[58]; Hsiang, 2010[59]; Loayza et al., 2012[60]) (see Chapter 5). The slow recovery of New Orleans after Hurricane Katrina in 2005 illustrates the potentially long-lasting and non-linear impacts of extreme events. Sixteen years after the event, employment in New Orleans has not recovered to pre-Katrina levels due to out-migration (Bureau of Labor Statistics, 2021[61]). Reconstruction and recovery are burdens on the budget and depend on the economic capacity of the affected region, among other factors. This underlines the importance of adequate emergency relief and support for reconstruction and recovery after such events. With particularly strong or repeated extreme events, full recovery may not always be possible. This can lead to short or longer term displacement of people (see Chapter 4, Box 4.6).

In an interconnected world, the climate impacts in one country – and the responses to those impacts – can impose threats beyond its borders. These impacts can occur through global supply chains that disrupt the price, quality and availability of goods and services (IPCC, 2019[11]), the spread of infectious diseases (Liang and Gong, 2017[62]), and the movement of people responding to the impacts of environmental and climate change (McLeman, 2019[63]). For example, Hurricane Katrina damaged a significant portion of the oil refinery capacity of the United States. This caused energy prices to shoot up by 40% around the world, which then decreased demand for cars (Kilian, 2008[64]).

Climate risk is compounded by the potential for losses to cascade across interconnected socio-economic systems and impose intolerable burdens on countries (UNDRR, 2019[65]; Zscheischler et al., 2020[66]). The nature of such compound events varies with three types highlighted here (see discussion in Chapter 3):

- Two or more extreme events occurring simultaneously or successively, e.g. Tropical Cyclone Harold affected several Pacific island states during 2020, while people and systems were responding to COVID-19.
- Combinations of extreme events with underlying conditions that amplify the impact of the events, e.g. Hurricane Harvey leading to floods in Texas during 2017, amplified by land subsidence.
- Combinations of events that would not in themselves be considered extreme but which cumulatively lead to a large impact. With climate change, such mutually reinforcing slow-onset changes and extreme events could cause diverse potential impacts, such as large disruptions of food production around the world (Kummu et al., 2021[67]).

Beyond the effects on economic production, the population will also be vulnerable to intangible or non-economic losses and damages. These include loss of cultural artefacts, places, and loss of sense of identity and security due, for example, to displacement (Graham et al., 2013[68]; Barnett et al., 2016[69]; Adger et al., 2012[70]). These effects are not easily quantifiable and hence rarely feature in socio-economic assessments. However, many people consider vulnerabilities of some intangible aspects (e.g. health of family members, sense of safety) more important than vulnerabilities of consumption associated with higher incomes (Tschakert et al., 2019[71]). The psychological or mental health impact of extreme and slow-onset events is one example of an intangible effect (Rataj, Kunzweiler and Garthus-Niegel, 2016[72]; Hayes et al., 2018[73]). The 2018 California wildfires, for instance, have shown to have a large impact on severity of depression, post-traumatic stress disorder (PTSD) and anxiety; direct exposure is associated with 30% worse PTSD symptoms than no exposure (Silveira et al., 2021[74]). However, such quantification will be partial. Lived experiences within and across communities due to occupation or other identities, for example, also determine the perception of climate risks. This, in turn, determines the response to the risks constructed (Rühlemann and Jordan, 2020[75]; Eriksen et al., 2021[29]).

Factors that influence how climate risks are experienced at the household and community levels include (Granderson, 2014[76]):

- ***Values and worldviews***, including standards, assumptions, beliefs, preferences and interests that guide peoples' perceptions of themselves in the world and their views on what is worth protecting and doing. Values and worldviews further highlight certain risks, informing decision-making processes. Other risks may be hidden.
- ***Sense of place,*** and the values attached to places or landscapes, shape perceptions of climate risks. The impacts of climate variability and change are manifested in places and landscapes. However, these contexts also anchor identities, values and institutions. When places are disrupted or lost (e.g. due to SLR, fires or loss of glaciers), cultural beliefs and practices often tied to places and landscapes will guide options being considered.
- ***Perceptions of justice and accountability*** vary over space and time, and can be examined in two ways. A distributive perspective looks at equity and fairness of outcomes, while a procedural perspective is concerned with inclusive, deliberative, accountable and transparent decision-making processes. Marginalised segments of society, within and across national borders, have often contributed little to climate variability and change. Yet they will often be more vulnerable to the impacts of these changes due to their available resources. Future generations similarly carry the burden of inadequate climate action by current and past generations reluctant to act on climate risks often perceived as too uncertain to take ambitious action.
- ***Discourses and power*** will determine whose constructions of risks, and whose responses, count in decision making. They are further a reflection of politics and power dynamics, empowering some as experts and legitimising specific responses.

1.3.3. Climate change and biodiversity

Unchecked, climate change will cause increasingly severe economic and social impacts. These include through its impact on biodiversity and the ecosystem services on which societies and individuals depend (IPBES, 2019[77]). For example, wildfire has been important in biological evolution and in shaping ecosystems for millennia. However, due to climate change and other human drivers, it is now threatening species with extinction and radically changing terrestrial ecosystems that have never been exposed or adapted to such hazards (Kelly et al., 2020[78]). The changing distribution of species driven by climate change discussed above will exacerbate biodiversity loss, affect ecosystem functions, impact human health and ecosystem-based livelihoods, and even feedback onto climate change (Pecl et al., 2017[19]).

Policy makers need to consider these significant interdependencies between climate change and biodiversity in formulating strategies and actions. For example, ecosystems are vital to livelihoods for many communities. Through nature-based solutions, ecosystem approaches may help reduce both the vulnerability of communities to climate hazards and the severity of hazards themselves by carbon sequestration. There are risks however, if such approaches are implemented without the full engagement and consent of local communities and Indigenous people, do not integrate both climate change and biodiversity goals, or distract from other vital climate and biodiversity policy priorities (Seddon et al., 2021[79]).

1.4. Reducing and managing the risk of losses and damages: Context for action

Section 1.3 highlights that losses and damages are happening now and the risks of future losses and damages will increase with climate change. The complexity and pace of change are stretching the ability of human and natural systems to cope with current impacts, and to reduce and manage risks. These risks threaten development gains.

Losses and damages can materialise even where risks are well understood and potentially avoidable. This might be due to the cost of reducing the risks; failure to mitigate GHG emissions (collectively) and adapt (nationally or locally); economic, social or technological barriers or inequalities; the effectiveness and coherence of policy interventions; physical limits to adaptation; the contribution of compounding factors such as diseases; or factors other than climate change (see Box 1.1). Efforts to reduce and manage the risks of losses and damages therefore need to consider actions in relation to all three components of climate risks. Specifically:

- limit the increase in the frequency and intensity of hazards through deep and urgent reductions in GHG emissions and actions to protect and enhance natural carbon sinks
- minimise the exposure of lives, livelihoods and assets to those hazards
- reduce the vulnerabilities of exposed human and natural systems to these hazards.

Science shows that any delay to mitigate GHG emissions and actions to protect and enhance natural carbon sinks such as forests and peatland increases the risks of adverse and increasingly severe climate impacts (IPCC, 2021[9]). Therefore, increases in the intensity and frequency of damaging climate-related hazards should be urgently limited. This can happen through rapid and far-reaching emission reductions from developed countries, as well as large, rapidly growing emissions-intensive developing economies aligned with the temperature goal of the Paris Agreement (UNFCCC, 2015[3]). The level of hazard is not something that can be influenced by individual developing countries, other than the largest, emissions-intensive ones.

Even if the temperature range in the Paris Agreement is attained, a large share of the Earth's current and future population will face increasingly frequent, intense and even novel (i.e. new to that region) climate-related hazards. For example, SLR will continue long after global temperatures have been stabilised. This will, all things being equal, drive increases in losses and damages currently experienced for populations that may have contributed little or not at all to climate change. Efforts must therefore also be scaled up to address the other two components of risk: exposure and vulnerability.

Exposure and vulnerability are the result of complex processes, endowments and choices. These include historic patterns of economic and social development (such as colonial influences), as well as individual and policy choices. Some drivers of exposure and vulnerability can be addressed through domestic processes (e.g. through land-use management or infrastructure standards). Others may be subject to international co-operation and changes, such as in today's global markets.

Box 1.1. Summary of discussion on limits to adaptation in the IPCC Fifth Assessment Report

Research has explored the issues of barriers and limits to adaptation determined by, for example, actors' values, objectives and planning horizons. Perceptions of the risks will influence risk management approaches. Some risks will be considered routine or with limited impact and therefore acceptable. Other risks will be seen as intolerable since they pose fundamental threats to actors' objectives or the sustainability of natural systems. Risk management aims to avoid such intolerable risks or reduce them to a tolerable level through various interventions. However, the capacity of societal actors and natural systems to reduce and manage the risks is finite due to biophysical, institutional, financial, social and cultural factors. These factors create limits to adaptation as do real or perceived deficiencies in human, social and financial capital.

Limits to adaptation have been exemplified by thresholds related to different features of climate change. Beyond these thresholds, non-linear responses are possible for agricultural crops, species of fish and forest, and marine communities, such as coral reef. This phenomenon is related to the concept of climate tipping points; triggering these points may cause large, non-linear changes in the climate system (see Chapter 3). Across most regions and sectors, however, it remains challenging to quantify magnitudes of climate change that would constitute future adaptation limits. In addition, economic and technological developments, as well as changes in cultural norms and values, will determine the capacity of a system to avoid such limits. This has led to the differentiation between "soft" and "hard" adaptation limits with the argument that there is scope to alleviate soft limits over time but no prospects for avoiding intolerable risks for hard limits.

Source: (IPCC, 2014[25]).

Reducing exposure can be challenging and, in some cases, undesirable for wider socio-economic reasons. Despite (rather than because of) the increasing concentration of people and assets, urbanisation rates continue to be high. Further examples include the continuing development in areas of high climate-related hazard. For example, urban and suburban development have expanded into forested areas, even with climate strategies to address vulnerability in place (Goss et al., 2020[80]). In addition, enhancing the resilience of infrastructure to more intense hazards will eventually become prohibitively expensive. In some situations, building such protective infrastructure could fundamentally change the character of the place it is designed to protect (see Chapter 4 for a discussion related to SIDS). Some adaptation actions may be relatively low cost, such as placing houses on stilts in coastal areas prone to floods. However, they may not make systems resilient to all physically possible levels of hazard intensity.

Reducing vulnerabilities to climate change also poses challenges. Many of the most vulnerable countries lack key elements of adaptive capacity to respond to climate change (Hallegatte, Fay and Barbier, 2018[81]). These include a strong and vibrant economy, ready access to finance and technology (including information dissemination systems) and strong governance with well-defined roles and responsibilities for adaptation. Capacity and resource constraints in any country will only make the risks of losses and damages more difficult to reduce and manage. This is especially true in a context of still increasing climate change and where there is rapid urbanisation.

In addition, managing and reducing losses and damages must be informed by a good understanding of the risks. Human action is driving climate change. However, the precise impacts of climate change on human and natural systems, which will vary over space and time, also have varying degrees of uncertainty (see Chapter 2). Even physical changes stemming from altered dynamics of the atmosphere or ocean are exceptionally difficult to model. It is more challenging still to model how these changes then interact with and affect human and natural systems, where uncertainties may be at least as great. Some observed and projected natural and socio-economic impacts can lead to irreversible damages. Given the nature and scale of these impacts, uncertainties have important implications for efforts to reduce and manage climate risks.

In many developing countries, these actions will need to be supported adequately by the international community. This is an active area of discussion and negotiation within the UN climate process, particularly in relation to current and future levels of climate finance. A broader range of national policies and international support for sustainable development or disaster recovery and reconstruction will also be needed. These can help determine a country's resilience to climate risks, as well as the humanitarian assistance provided in anticipation of or in response to an extreme event.

Indeed, decisions on climate change are not made in isolation. Rather, they are an integral component of countries' development objectives. As such, they must be assessed in relation to the broader spectrum of socio-economic risks and the associated uncertainties relevant for decision making. Such an assessment can be direct or indirect. Direct assessment, for example, would look at land-use management, agricultural practices and infrastructure standards. Indirect assessment could examine livelihoods development, social protection and basic health care provision. In addition to addressing the drivers of change in the three components of climate risk, the process could assess the coherence of approaches across policy domains beyond climate change. If not carefully managed, some measures intended to reduce and manage the risk of losses and damages may increase the risks for segments of society or across countries (Eriksen et al., 2021[29]).

Many different actors, nationally and internationally, therefore share responsibilities for losses and damages that occur now and in the future. The scale and effectiveness of action to reduce and manage the risks of losses and damages depends on several factors. These include the availability of financial resources (domestic or international) and specific technical capacities. Equally important are the effectiveness and coherence of policy interventions to increase resilience, and reduce exposure and vulnerabilities to climate-related hazards. The balance of these different factors will vary over time in each geographical context. The relative responsibilities of major emitters – developed and developing – for the GHG emissions driving the level of hazard is relatively uncontentious scientifically and open to quantitative analysis. However, responsibility for exposure and vulnerability is more open to debate. Determinations of relative responsibility for these risk components would require careful analysis and deliberation. Further, it requires judgements about respective roles and capabilities at different points in time across the range of relevant actors. Box 1.2 sets out some further issues around the responsibility for losses and damages, focusing on the policy debate on Loss and Damage within the UN climate process.

Ultimately, the OECD cannot provide answers to these questions, or even propose them. The issue of responsibility for losses and damages goes to the political heart of the multilateral process on climate change, disaster risk reduction as well as the broader context of sustainable development and must be resolved through those processes. Most important perhaps, those involved should aim to ensure that the effort leads to enhanced levels of international co-operation, solidarity and support, and not the reverse.

Box 1.2. Negotiations on Loss and Damage within the UN climate process

The Alliance of Small Island States initiated discussions on Loss and Damage from climate change within the UN climate process in the early 1990s. This discussion emerged in the context of compensation for losses in these countries from sea-level rise and other climate change impacts. The Warsaw International Mechanism (WIM) was established in 2013 with a mandate to "address loss and damage associated with impacts of climate change, including extreme events and slow-onset events in developing countries that are particularly vulnerable to the adverse effects of climate change" (UNFCCC, n.d.[82]). The Paris Agreement in its Article 8 further states that "Parties recognize the importance of averting, minimising and addressing loss and damage associated with the adverse effects of climate change [….]" (UNFCCC, 2015[3]).

The discussions on Loss and Damage within the UN climate process focus on developing countries. They have been politically contentious as they touch upon issues of equity and fairness. At the core of this debate is the question of proving historical responsibility of developed countries for the climate hazards and associated losses and damages that occur in developing countries. Some of the most vulnerable countries, including some Small Island Developing States and Least Developed Countries, have called for compensation from developed countries for those losses and damages. However, the Paris Decision "agrees that Article 8 of the Agreement does not involve or provide a basis for any liability or compensation" (UNFCCC, 2016[83]).

As these discussions evolve as part of the international climate negotiations, they will involve difficult scientific, political and legal judgements on the extent to which climate change has caused or amplified the adverse impacts related to a specific climate hazard. The impacts due to climate change are conditional on exposure and vulnerability, which primarily depend on historical processes and national decision making. Given the political difficulties that surround the issue of responsibility for Loss and Damage, this report does not attempt to define or provide direct guidance on this issue. It does, however, provide analytical insights and recommendations that could inform discussions within the WIM and the wider negotiation process.

1.5. Structure of report and intended audience

This chapter presented the climate risk framing as conceptualised by the IPCC and summarised climate change and its observed and projected impacts on natural and socio-economic systems. Climate change is happening and anthropogenic GHG emissions are unequivocally driving it. This is enough to justify urgent emissions reductions to achieve the goal set out in the Paris Agreement but it is not sufficient to inform efforts to reduce and manage climate risks. This is set out in ***Chapter 2***, which examines the different levels of confidence and associated uncertainties influencing understanding of these risks that decision makers need to understand and adopt. ***Chapter 3*** describes the types of hazards from climate change. It provides new analyses examining the impacts of slow-onset changes (with a focus on SLR), extreme events (heatwaves) and tipping points (AMOC), their associated risks of losses and damages, and the potential for cascading impacts spanning over different sectors and regions. The rest of the report focuses on the ways in which the risks of losses and damages from climate change can be reduced and managed through policy (***Chapter 4***), finance (***Chapter 5***) and technology (***Chapter 6***). The final section of the present chapter sets out the recommendations emerging from this analysis.

This report is primarily aimed at policy makers responsible for exploring and assessing potential actions to reduce and manage the risks of losses and damages from climate change. However, many key insights apply more widely across society. Key audiences include officials in ministries of environment and disaster risk management organisations at national and local levels involved in developing or informing countries' climate action commitments and plans. However, the report may equally be of interest for their counterparts in other ministries such as finance, infrastructure, water and agriculture that increasingly need to consider the adverse impacts of climate change. The report distils information and enhances understanding of some important issues regarding these risks. In so doing, it hopes to inform (international and domestic) political and public dialogue, and to stimulate action indirectly through stakeholders in the private sector and civil society.

1.6. Taking the agenda forward

The call for urgent action on climate change is at or near the top of most political agendas, despite the continuing pandemic and related economic dislocation. This is true in the context of the international climate negotiations and also at local, regional and national levels. In different ways and with different resources and levels of ambition, governments, the private sector, researchers, civil society organisations and individual citizens – often in partnerships – are taking action. These different stakeholders have complementary roles that offer areas for further action and collaboration. Recommended actions to reduce and manage both economic and non-economic losses and damages are highlighted below, with a focus on the role of governments:

1. **Take a precautionary approach by aiming to limit the temperature increase to 1.5°C:**
    - *Accelerate the transition to net-zero*, recognising that different countries will follow different pathways and developed countries should aim to reach net-zero earlier than 2050.
    - *Rapidly scale up finance, technology, capacity development,* and other support for mitigation and adaptation action in developing countries, delivering on developed country commitments.
    - Put in place credible, ambitious and adequately resourced *shorter-term targets and plans* that generate wider socio-economic benefits and deliver on longer-term or net-zero commitments.
2. **Create a more effective international development finance landscape supporting efforts to reduce and manage current impacts and projected risks of losses and damages:**
    - *Scale-up climate-related development finance* to support communities and countries already experiencing losses and damages, and to reduce and manage future risks, particularly for LDCs and SIDS.
    - *Improve access to finance and reduce transaction costs* by streamlining multiple accreditation and reporting requirements and s*trengthen complementarities* across financing mechanisms.
    - *Develop local and national capacity*, foster country ownership and better align international development finance with national priorities, circumstances and needs.
    - *Enhance the predictability* of international support for efforts to reduce and manage the risks of losses and damages.
3. **Strengthen the global architecture for climate and disaster risk finance:**
    - *Enhance the availability and access to financial protection* that is comprehensive (i.e. to different hazards) and systematic (e.g. different layers of risk), particularly for the most vulnerable.
    - *Increase the coherence of international support* for climate and disaster risk finance through enhanced exchange, co-operation and agreement on joint principles by providers of support.
4. **Enhance fiscal resilience to deal with increasingly adverse impacts:**
    - *Implement a comprehensive approach to risk management,* using a set of complementary financial mechanisms to *reduce, retain and transfer* risks of losses and damages.

- *Limit contingent liabilities*, incentivise and enable private actors to reduce and manage their own risks, including through disclosures, understanding and awareness of climate risks.
- *Review the implications of climate risks for debt sustainability* and identify options for addressing these, including the eligibility of countries highly vulnerable to climate risks to international financial support.

5. **Protect livelihoods, reduce precarity through insurance, social protection and humanitarian assistance:**
   - *Develop insurance markets* to make available coverage for climate risks and incentivise those with the financial capacity to do so to manage them.
   - *Enhance social protection for the most marginalised segments of society* that do not have the financial means to access formal insurance markets to reduce vulnerability to climate-related hazards and subsequent losses and damages.
   - Reduce losses and damages through *anticipatory humanitarian action* and improve the predictability of humanitarian assistance.
6. **Adopt approaches to decision making that account for uncertainties in climate risks:**
   - *Manage risks across different time and spatial scales* and understand how they can compound and cascade across systems and borders.
   - *Enhance capacities* within the decision-making process to incorporate quantitative and qualitative assessments of the *implications of uncertainty* for options and outcomes.
   - *Adopt iterative and adaptive decision-making processes*, guided by learning and evolving understanding of the risks and take a strict precautionary approach when choices may lock-in long-term changes to risks.
   - *Identify and manage* risks that may overwhelm local capacities by anticipating future thresholds and decision points where alternative responses may be needed.
7. **Integrate climate and sustainable development objectives and improve policy coherence:**
   - *Approach decisions on climate risks as an integral component of sustainable development* and assess options in relation to the broader spectrum of socio-economic risks and uncertainties relevant for decision making.
   - *Increase coherence across national and international policy communities*, including climate change adaptation and risk management, humanitarian and the broader development communities, building on their respective strengths and areas of expertise.
8. **Improve data, capabilities and processes for climate risk governance:**
   - *Enhance international support* for access to observational and forecasting capabilities, technology and capacity building in developing countries, prioritising *high quality, high resolution observational data collection* and management.
   - Prioritise international action to enhance the *collection and interpretation of data on extreme events and impacts* in developing countries, including to underpin attribution studies and climate policy.
   - *Further strengthen weather and climate information services,* particularly in LDCs and SIDS, ensuring they are demand-driven, usable and useful.
   - *Establish an international mechanism to monitor climate tipping elements* to enhance understanding on their potential impacts and to develop techniques to detect and, where feasible, provide early warning for strategies and actions.

9. **Facilitate inclusive stakeholder engagement that builds on the knowledge, expertise and values of different actors and gives due recognition to intangible losses and damages:**
   - *Develop partnerships to enhance coordination and collaboration* nationally and internationally, across policy, science, and other expertise, including Indigenous and local communities.
   - *Improve awareness and understanding* of how climate change threatens what people value and develop context-specific approaches to reducing and managing intangible, as well as economic, losses and damages.
   - *Leverage private sector expertise* to support broader societal efforts to reduce and manage the risks of losses and damages.

References

Adger, W. et al. (2012), “Cultural dimensions of climate change impacts and adaptation”, *Nature Climate Change*, Vol. 3/2, pp. 112-117, http://dx.doi.org/10.1038/nclimate1666. [70]

Alhassan, S., J. Kuwornu and Y. Osei-Asare (2019), “Gender dimension of vulnerability to climate change and variability: Empirical evidence of smallholder farming households in Ghana”, *International Journal of Climate Change Strategies and Management*, Vol. 11/2, pp. 195-214, http://dx.doi.org/10.1108/IJCCSM-10-2016-0156. [30]

Añel, J. (ed.) (2020), “The environmental consequences of climate-driven agricultural frontiers”, *PLOS ONE*, Vol. 15/2, p. e0228305, http://dx.doi.org/10.1371/journal.pone.0228305. [28]

Barnett, J. et al. (2016), “A science of loss”, *Nature Climate Change*, Vol. 6/11, pp. 976-978, http://dx.doi.org/10.1038/nclimate3140. [69]

Barreca, A., O. Deschênes and M. Guldi (2018), “Maybe next month? Temperature shocks and dynamic adjustments in birth rates”, *Demography*, Vol. 55/4, pp. 1269-1293, http://dx.doi.org/10.1007/s13524-018-0690-7. [50]

Botzen, W., O. Deschênes and M. Sanders (2019), “The economic impacts of natural disasters: A review of models and empirical studies”, *Review of Environmental Economics and Policy*, Vol. 13/2, pp. 167-188, http://dx.doi.org/10.1093/reep/rez004. [58]

Buckle, S. et al. (2020), “Addressing the COVID-19 and climate crises: Potential economic recovery pathways and their implications for climate change mitigation, NDCs and broader socio-economic goals”, *OECD/IEA Climate Change Expert Group Papers*, No. 2020/04, OECD Publishing, Paris, https://dx.doi.org/10.1787/50abd39c-en. [1]

Bureau of Labor Statistics (2021), *Employment in New Orleans-Metairie, LA Metropolitan Statistical Area (Series Id: LAUMT223538000000003)*, (database), https://www.bls.gov/oes/current/oes_35380.htm (accessed on 12 April 2021). [61]

Burke, M., S. Hsiang and E. Miguel (2015), “Global non-linear effect of temperature on economic production”, *Nature*, Vol. 527/7577, pp. 235-239, http://dx.doi.org/10.1038/nature15725. [57]

Caesar, L. et al. (2021), “Current Atlantic Meridional Overturning Circulation weakest in last millennium”, *Nature Geoscience*, Vol. 14, pp. 118-120, http://dx.doi.org/10.1038/s41561-021-00699-z. [23]

Cai, X., Y. Lu and J. Wang (2018), “The impact of temperature on manufacturing worker productivity: Evidence from personnel data”, *Journal of Comparative Economics*, Vol. 46/4, pp. 889-905, http://dx.doi.org/10.1016/j.jce.2018.06.003. [54]

Carleton, T. et al. (2019), “Valuing the global mortality consequences of climate change accounting for adaptation costs and benefits”, *Working Paper*, No. 2018-51, University of Chicago, Becker Friedman Institute for Economics, https://ssrn.com/abstract=3224365. [44]

CAT (2021), *Warming Projections Global Update*, May, Climate Action Tracker, https://climateactiontracker.org/documents/853/CAT_2021-05-04_Briefing_Global-Update_Climate-Summit-Momentum.pdf. [4]

Clark, P. et al. (2016), "Consequences of twenty-first-century policy for multi-millennial climate and sea-level change", *Nature Climate Change*, Vol. 6/4, http://dx.doi.org/10.1038/nclimate2923. [18]

Crowley, T. (2000), "Causes of climate change over the past 1000 years", *Science*, Vol. 289/5477, http://dx.doi.org/10.1126/science.289.5477.270. [12]

Dell, M., B. Jones and B. Olken (2012), "Temperature shocks and economic growth: Evidence from the last half century", *American Economic Journal: Macroeconomics*, Vol. 4/3, pp. 66-95, http://dx.doi.org/10.1257/mac.4.3.66. [56]

Deschênes, O. and M. Greenstone (2011), "Climate change, mortality, and adaptation: Evidence from annual fluctuations in weather in the US", *American Economic Journal: Applied Economics*, Vol. 3/4, pp. 152-185, http://dx.doi.org/10.1257/app.3.4.152. [43]

Eriksen, S. et al. (2021), "Adaptation interventions and their effect on vulnerability in developing countries: Help, hindrance or irrelevance?", *World Development*, Vol. 141, p. 105383, http://dx.doi.org/10.1016/j.worlddev.2020.105383. [29]

Filkov, A. et al. (2020), "Impact of Australia's catastrophic 2019/20 bushfire season on communities and environment. Retrospective analysis and current trends", *Journal of Safety Science and Resilience*, Vol. 1/1, pp. 44-56, http://dx.doi.org/10.1016/j.jnlssr.2020.06.009. [36]

Fisch, H. et al. (2003), "The relationship of long term global temperature change and human fertility", *Medical Hypotheses*, Vol. 61, pp. 21-28, http://dx.doi.org/10.1016/S0306-9877(03)00061-6. [49]

Frederikse, T. et al. (2020), "The causes of sea-level rise since 1900", *Nature*, Vol. 584/7821, pp. 393-397, http://dx.doi.org/10.1038/s41586-020-2591-3. [10]

Goss, M. et al. (2020), "Climate change is increasing the likelihood of extreme autumn wildfire conditions across California", *Environmental Research Letters*, Vol. 15/9, p. 094016, http://dx.doi.org/10.1088/1748-9326/ab83a7. [80]

Grace, K. et al. (2012), "Child malnutrition and climate in Sub-Saharan Africa: An analysis of recent trends in Kenya", *Applied Geography*, Vol. 35/1-2, pp. 405-413, http://dx.doi.org/10.1016/j.apgeog.2012.06.017. [52]

Graff Zivin, J. et al. (2020), "Temperature and high-stakes cognitive performance: Evidence from the national college entrance examination in China", *Journal of Environmental Economics and Management*, Vol. 104, p. 102365, http://dx.doi.org/10.1016/j.jeem.2020.102365. [55]

Graham, S. et al. (2013), "The social values at risk from sea-level rise", *Environmental Impact Assessment Review*, Vol. 41, pp. 45-52, http://dx.doi.org/10.1016/j.eiar.2013.02.002. [68]

Granderson, A. (2014), "Making sense of climate change risks and responses at the community level: A cultural-political lens", *Climate Risk Management*, Vol. 3, pp. 55-64, http://dx.doi.org/10.1016/j.crm.2014.05.003. [76]

Guha-Sapir, D., R. Below and P. Hoyois (2021), *EM-DAT: The CRED/OFDA International Disaster Database*, (database), http://www.emdat.be (accessed on 7 April 2021). [34]

Hallegatte, S., M. Fay and E. Barbier (2018), "Poverty and climate change: Introduction", *Environment and Development Economics*, Vol. 23/3, pp. 217-233, http://dx.doi.org/10.1017/s1355770x18000141. [81]

Hausfather, Z. et al. (2020), "Evaluating the performance of past climate model projections", *Geophysical Research Letters*, Vol. 47/1, http://dx.doi.org/10.1029/2019GL085378. [20]

Hayes, K. et al. (2018), "Climate change and mental health: Risks, impacts and priority actions", *International Journal of Mental Health Systems*, Vol. 12, http://dx.doi.org/10.1186/S13033-018-0210-6. [73]

Hsiang, S. (2010), "Temperatures and cyclones strongly associated with economic production in the Caribbean and Central America", *Proceedings of the National Academy of Sciences of the United States of America*, Vol. 107/35, pp. 15367-15372, http://dx.doi.org/10.1073/pnas.1009510107. [59]

Hunt, K. and A. Menon (2020), "The 2018 Kerala floods: A climate change perspective", *Climate Dynamics*, Vol. 54/3-4, pp. 2433-2446, http://dx.doi.org/10.1007/s00382-020-05123-7. [38]

IFRC (2021), *Strategy 2030: Platform for Change; Global Reach, Local Action*, International Red Cross and Red Crescent Movement, Geneva, https://www.ifrc.org/media/13322. [8]

IPBES (2019), *Summary for Policymakers of the Global Assessment Report on Biodiversity and Ecosystem Services*, Intergovernmental Science-Policy Platform on Biodiversity and Ecosystem Services, Bonn, http://dx.doi.org/10.5281/zenodo.3553579. [77]

IPCC (2021), *Climate Change 2021: The Physical Science Basis. Contribution of Working Group I to the Sixth Assessment Report of the Intergovernmental Panel on Climate Change*, Masson-Delmotte, V. et al. (eds.), Cambridge University Press, Cambridge, United Kingdom, and New York, in press. [9]

IPCC (2019), *Climate Change and Land: An IPCC Special Report on Climate Change, Desertification, Land Degradation, Sustainable Land Management, Food Security, and Greenhouse Gas Fluxes in Terrestrial Ecosystems*, Intergovernmental Panel on Climate Change, Geneva, https://www.ipcc.ch/srccl/. [11]

IPCC (2019), "Summary for Policymakers", in H.-O. Pörtner et al. (eds.), *IPCC Special Report on the Ocean and Cryosphere in a Changing Climate*, Intergovernmental Panel on Climate Change, Geneva. [17]

IPCC (2018), "Annex 1: Glossary", in *Global Warming of 1.5°C*, Masson-Delmotte, V. et al. (eds.), Intergovernmental Panel on Climate Change, Geneva. [26]

IPCC (2014), *Climate Change 2014: Impacts,Adaptation, and Vulnerability. Part A: Global and Sectoral Aspects. Contribution of Working Group II to the Fifth Assessment Report of the Intergovernmental Panel on Climate Change*, University of Cambridge, Cambridge, United Kingdom, and New York. [25]

Jafino, B. et al. (2020), *Revised Estimates of the Impact of Climate Change on Extreme Poverty by 2030*, World Bank, Washington, DC, http://dx.doi.org/10.1596/1813-9450-9417. [32]

Jankowska, M. et al. (2012), "Climate change and human health: Spatial modeling of water availability, malnutrition, and livelihoods in Mali, Africa", *Applied Geography*, Vol. 33/1, pp. 4-15, http://dx.doi.org/10.1016/j.apgeog.2011.08.009. [51]

Kelly, L. et al. (2020), "Fire and biodiversity in the Anthropocene", *Science*, Vol. 370/6519, http://dx.doi.org/10.1126/science.abb0355. [78]

Kilian, L. (2008), "The economic effects of energy price shocks", *Journal of Economic Literature*, Vol. 46/4, pp. 871-909, http://dx.doi.org/10.1257/jel.46.4.871. [64]

Kirchmeier-Young, M. et al. (2019), "Attribution of the influence of human-Induced climate change on an extreme fire season", *Earth's Future*, Vol. 7/1, pp. 2-10, http://dx.doi.org/10.1029/2018ef001050. [16]

Kummu, M. et al. (2021), "Climate change risks pushing one-third of global food production outside the safe climatic space", *One Earth*, Vol. 4/5, pp. 720-729, http://dx.doi.org/10.1016/j.oneear.2021.04.017. [67]

Lam, D. and J. Miron (1996), "The effects of temperature on human fertility", *Demography*, Vol. 33/3, pp. 291-305, http://dx.doi.org/10.2307/2061762. [48]

Lenton, T. et al. (2019), "Climate tipping points – too risky to bet against", *Nature*, Vol. 575, pp. 592-595, http://dx.doi.org/10.1038/d41586-019-03595-0. [22]

Liang, L. and P. Gong (2017), "Climate change and human infectious diseases: A synthesis of research findings from global and spatio-temporal perspectives", *Environment International*, Vol. 103, pp. 99-108, http://dx.doi.org/10.1016/j.envint.2017.03.011. [62]

Linthicum, K. et al. (1999), "Climate and satellite indicators to forecast Rift Valley fever epidemics in Kenya", *Science*, Vol. 285/5426, pp. 397-400, http://dx.doi.org/10.1126/SCIENCE.285.5426.397. [45]

Loayza, N. et al. (2012), "Natural disasters and growth: Going beyond the averages", *World Development*, Vol. 40/7, pp. 1317-1336, http://dx.doi.org/10.1016/j.worlddev.2012.03.002. [60]

Luque Fernández, M. et al. (2009), "Influence of temperature and rainfall on the evolution of cholera epidemics in Lusaka, Zambia, 2003–2006: Analysis of a time series", *Transactions of the Royal Society of Tropical Medicine and Hygiene*, Vol. 103/2, pp. 137-143, http://dx.doi.org/10.1016/j.trstmh.2008.07.017. [46]

Makin, J. (2011), "Implications of climate change for skin cancer prevention in Australia", *Health Promotion Journal of Australia : Official Journal of Australian Association of Health Promotion Professionals*, Vol. 22 Spec No, http://dx.doi.org/10.1071/HE11439. [47]

McLeman, R. (2019), "International migration and climate adaptation in an era of hardening borders", *Nature Climate Change*, Vol. 9/12, pp. 911-918, http://dx.doi.org/10.1038/s41558-019-0634-2. [63]

OECD (2021), *Key findings from the update of the OECD Green Recovery Database*, OECD Publishing, Paris, https://dx.doi.org/10.1787/55b8abba-en. [2]

OECD (2020), *Common Ground Between the Paris Agreement and the Sendai Framework: Climate Change Adaptation and Disaster Risk Reduction*, OECD Publishing, Paris, https://dx.doi.org/10.1787/3edc8d09-en. [7]

Pecl, G. et al. (2017), "Biodiversity redistribution under climate change: Impacts on ecosystems and human well-being", *Science*, Vol. 355/6332, p. eaai9214, http://dx.doi.org/10.1126/science.aai9214. [19]

Rahman, M. (2013), "Climate change, disaster and gender vulnerability: A study on two divisions of Bangladesh", *American Journal of Human Ecology*, Vol. 2/2, pp. 72-82, http://dx.doi.org/10.11634/216796221302315. [31]

Rataj, E., K. Kunzweiler and S. Garthus-Niegel (2016), "Extreme weather events in developing countries and related injuries and mental health disorders - a systematic review", *BMC Public Health*, Vol. 16/1, p. 1020, http://dx.doi.org/10.1186/s12889-016-3692-7. [72]

Rocha, J. et al. (2018), "Cascading regime shifts within and across scales", *Science*, Vol. 362/6421, pp. 1379-1383, http://dx.doi.org/10.1126/science.aat7850. [24]

Rühlemann, A. and J. Jordan (2020), "Risk perception and culture: Implications for vulnerability and adaptation to climate change", *Disasters*, Vol. 45/2, pp. 424-452, http://dx.doi.org/10.1111/disa.12429. [75]

Seddon, N. et al. (2021), "Getting the message right on nature-based solutions to climate change", *Global Change Biology*, Vol. 27/8, pp. 1518-1546, http://dx.doi.org/10.1111/gcb.15513. [79]

Seneviratne, S. et al. (2012), "Changes in climate extremes and their impacts on the natural physical environment.", in Field, C. et al. (eds.), *Managing the Risks of Extreme Events and Disasters to Advance Climate Change Adaptation. A Special Report of Working Groups I and II of the Intergovernmental Panel on Climate Change*, Cambridge University Press, Cambridge, United Kingdom, and New York. [21]

Sherwood, S. et al. (2020), "An assessment of Earth's climate sensitivity using multiple lines of evidence", *Reviews of Geophysics*, Vol. 58/4, http://dx.doi.org/10.1029/2019rg000678. [14]

Shultz, J. et al. (2020), "Double environmental injustice – Climate change, Hurricane Dorian, and the Bahamas", *New England Journal of Medicine*, Vol. 382/1, pp. 1-3, http://dx.doi.org/10.1056/nejmp1912965. [37]

Silveira, S. et al. (2021), "Chronic mental health sequelae of climate change extremes: A case study of the deadliest Californian wildfire", *International Journal of Environmental Research and Public Health*, Vol. 18/4, p. 1487, http://dx.doi.org/10.3390/ijerph18041487. [74]

Sofuoğlu, E. and A. Ay (2020), "The relationship between climate change and political instability: The case of MENA countries (1985:01–2016)", *Environmental Science and Pollution Research*, Vol. 27/12, pp. 14033-14043, http://dx.doi.org/10.1007/s11356-020-07937-8. [33]

Tchebakova, N. et al. (2011), "Agroclimatic potential across central Siberia in an altered twenty-first century", *Environmental Research Letters*, Vol. 6/4, p. 045207, http://dx.doi.org/10.1088/1748-9326/6/4/045207. [27]

Tschakert, P. et al. (2019), "One thousand ways to experience loss: A systematic analysis of climate-related intangible harm from around the world", *Global Environmental Change*, Vol. 55, pp. 58-72, http://dx.doi.org/10.1016/j.gloenvcha.2018.11.006. [71]

UNDRR (2021), *Promoting Synergy and Alignment: Between Climate Change Adaptation and Disaster Risk Reduction in the Context of National Adaptation Plans*, United Nations Office for Disaster Risk Reduction, Geneva. [6]

UNDRR (2019), *Global Assessment Report on Disaster Risk Reduction*, United Nations Office for Disaster Risk Reduction, Geneva, https://gar.undrr.org/report-2019. [65]

UNFCCC (2021), *National Adaptation Plans 2020: Progress in the Formulation and Implementation of NAPs*, United Nations Framework Convention on Climate Change, Bonn, https://unfccc.int/documents/273920. [5]

UNFCCC (2016), *Decision 1/CP.21: Adoption of the Paris Agreement*, United Nations Framework Convention on Climate Change, Bonn. [83]

UNFCCC (2015), *Paris Agreement*, United Nations Framework Convention on Climate Change, Bonn, https://treaties.un.org/pages/ViewDetails.aspx?src=TREATY&mtdsg_no=XXVII-7-d&chapter=27. [3]

UNFCCC (n.d.), "Warsaw International Mechanism for Loss and Damage associated with Climate Change Impacts (WIM)", webpage, https://unfccc.int/topics/adaptation-and-resilience/workstreams/loss-and-damage-ld/warsaw-international-mechanism-for-loss-and-damage-associated-with-climate-change-impacts-wim (accessed on 13 April 2021). [82]

van Oldenborgh, G. et al. (2021), "Attribution of the Australian bushfire risk to anthropogenic climate change", *Natural Hazards and Earth System Sciences*, Vol. 21/3, pp. 941-960, http://dx.doi.org/10.5194/nhess-21-941-2021. [39]

Vautard, R. et al. (2020), "Human contribution to the record-breaking June and July 2019 heatwaves in Western Europe", *Environmental Research Letters*, Vol. 15/9, p. 094077, http://dx.doi.org/10.1088/1748-9326/aba3d4. [15]

Welton, G. (2011), "The impact of Russia's 2010 grain export ban", *Research Reports*, June, Oxfam, Oxford, United Kingdom, https://www-cdn.oxfam.org/s3fs-public/file_attachments/rr-impact-russias-grain-export-ban-280611-en_3.pdf. [53]

WMO (2021), *Atlas of Mortality and Economic Losses from Weather, Climate and Water Extremes*, World Meteorological Organization, Geneva. [42]

WMO (2021), "North America heatwave almost impossibe without climate change", 8 July, World Meteorological Organization, Geneva, https://public.wmo.int/en/media/news/north-america-heatwave-almost-impossible-without-climate-change. [40]

WMO (2020), *WMO Global Annual to Decadal Climate Update*, World Meteorological Organization, Geneva. [13]

World Weather Attribution (2021), "Heavy rainfall which led to severe flooding in Western Europe made more likely by climate change", 23 August, World Weather Attribution, https://www.worldweatherattribution.org/heavy-rainfall-which-led-to-severe-flooding-in-western-europe-made-more-likely-by-climate-change/. [41]

Zegarra, M. et al. (2020), "Impact of Hurricane Dorian in the Bahamas: A view from the sky", *Technical Note*, No. DB-TN-1857, Inter-American Development Bank, Washington, DC, https://publications.iadb.org/publications/english/document/Impact_of_Hurricane_Dorian_in_The_Bahamas_A_View_from_the_Sky.pdf. [35]

Zscheischler, J. et al. (2020), "A typology of compound weather and climate events", *Nature Reviews Earth & Environment*, Vol. 1/7, pp. 333-347, http://dx.doi.org/10.1038/s43017-020-0060-z. [66]

2 Types of uncertainties and understanding of risks of losses and damages

This chapter explores the different levels of confidence and associated uncertainties influencing understanding of risks of losses and damages from climate change. Specifically, it looks at different levels of confidence in projections of the physical climate and in expectations of future vulnerability and exposure. These include and/or relate to uncertainties on emissions trajectories; on how the climate system responds to those emissions; climate variability and uncertainty about socio-economic development patterns. The chapter includes worked analytical examples that unpack and illustrate the different types of uncertainties. It ends by examining how these uncertainties need to be considered together for an effective communication of climate risk.

In Brief

Different levels of confidence on different types of risks of losses and damages from climate change

Human influence on the warming of the climate system is unequivocal. There is very high confidence on the thermodynamic aspects of climate change and the severity of the associated impacts. There are deep uncertainties in relation to important aspects of the physical climate response to climate forcing, and to vulnerability and exposure of socio-economic systems. However, these uncertainties are not a reason for delaying action.

Climate change is a result of complex physical processes. Deep scientific understanding about these processes is reserved to a limited group of highly specialised experts and scholars. While policy makers in the area of climate change do not require such understanding, they do often need to link science and policy. Therefore, they must deal with a number of different types and forms of uncertainties. A policy maker well-informed about the nuances of climate risk is one well-placed to identify effective and robust courses of action to reduce and manage that risk. These different types of uncertainties include:

- ***Uncertainties in relation to quality and quantity of observational data***: Earth is more extensively and systematically observed today than at any other time. Yet, there is still a long way to go before establishing a comprehensive, systematic global climate monitoring system. Any progress in monitoring is a step forward with potential short-term benefits.
- ***Uncertainties in equilibrium climate sensitivity (ECS) and transient climate response (TCR)***: A first-order question about a climate plan or strategy is how effective it will be in mitigating climate change. The ranges of ECS and TCR estimates represent the uncertainties around the scale of the response of the climate to greenhouse gas emissions. The urgent need for stringent emissions reductions becomes even more evident in light of these uncertainties.
- ***Uncertainties in projections of global and regional climate change***: Despite high confidence in the thermodynamic aspects of climate change and the severity of the associated impacts, there is far less confidence in the detail of when, where and how these hazards will occur. However, short-term projected regional changes are still useful. They provide a range of potential changes to which human and natural systems can be subject to, even if the exact date and extent of those changes are not accurately predicted. Therefore, from a policy-making perspective, climate modelling informs on broad patterns and the potential for how climate change could unfold locally. This information can feed directly into the shaping of policies dealing with climate-related risks, including physical, behavioural and cultural adaptation to expected changes.
- ***Uncertainties related to socio-economic data***: Socio-economic data should underlie every policy decision to help infer the possible consequences of the policy. Often, however, crucial data are unavailable. In these cases, policy makers may rely instead on proxy variables and regression estimations among other approaches, introducing further uncertainties. Broader and deeper understanding of the issues can be achieved by jointly conducting quantitative and qualitative analyses.
- ***Uncertainties related to socio-economic projections***: Another important source of uncertainty is that related to the socio-economic outcomes. Integrated assessment models are the most influential approach in the climate policy arena to analysing alternative futures. These

models integrate relevant components of the climate system and the economy in a single model. While they are useful to compare the future effects of different policies, they are constrained because they rarely model physical and socioeconomic uncertainty, especially the way the uncertainties interact. Therefore, other models need to complement integrated assessment models. These alternatives include agent-based models or resample and reweighting models. Projections are also sensitive to the role of nature in socio-economic systems, such as the intrinsic value of nature and its role in economic production and human well-being. These elements, therefore, should be carefully considered.

- ***Other socio-economic uncertainties***: There are other socio-economic uncertainties, such as those relating to socio-economic tipping points and social discount rates. Socio-economic tipping points are abrupt changes in society out of proportion to their origin (non-linear). Such tipping points could enhance or threaten the effectiveness of climate policy; by nature, they are extremely difficult to predict. Policies should aim to encourage the crossing of tipping points that help enhance the resilience of societies. The social discount rates need to reflect local values and cultures. They essentially describe the weight of the future in relation to the present: uncertain settings or high damages imply low social discount rates.

Uncertainties underlying the risks of losses and damages have decreased in the past decades. However, they remain an important factor in the perception of risk and in how climate change action responds to that perception. Given the compelling accumulation of scientific evidence about climate change and its potential consequences, lack of confidence in for example how, when and where a hazard will occur cannot be a reason for inaction. Indeed, this chapter shows that larger uncertainties can lead to a larger range of potential climate risk. The uncertainties and ambiguities surrounding some aspects of climate change projections should therefore amplify – not weaken – the case for strong climate action.

2.1. Introduction

Chapter 1 summarises understanding of climate change, highlighting key aspects of how the physical climate responds to anthropogenic greenhouse gas (GHG) emissions and how vulnerability and exposure can contribute to higher climate risk and socio-economic impacts. The Sixth Assessment Report (AR6), Working Group 1 (WG1) of the Intergovernmental Panel on Climate Change (IPCC) concluded that, "it is unequivocal that human influence has warmed the atmosphere, ocean and land". Additionally it assessed that "the scale of recent changes across the climate system as a whole and the present state of many aspects of the climate system are unprecedented over many centuries to many thousands of years" (IPCC, 2021[1]).

Given these assessments, there is extremely high confidence about the thermodynamic aspects of climate change relating to the balance of energy flows into and out of the Earth system. Higher emissions, for example, lead to higher concentrations of greenhouse gases in the atmosphere and therefore a higher climate forcing. This, in turn, leads to higher mean surface temperature (IPCC, 2013[2]; Hausfather et al., 2020[3]). These thermodynamic changes also drive far-reaching changes in the dynamics of the ocean and atmosphere. Such changes notably affect the water cycle and precipitation patterns. These changes, in turn, lead to increased frequency and magnitude of many extreme weather events, such as heavy precipitation and floods, as well as droughts and heat waves.

Increased climate forcing of the Earth system due to enhanced GHG concentrations also drives irreversible long-term changes in sea level (mainly due to both thermal expansion and the ice loss from glaciers and ice sheets) (IPCC, 2021[1]). If it continues unchecked, climate change will also eventually activate tipping points, which would completely change the behaviour of the climate system. Chapter 3 explores one such potential change: the shutting off of the Atlantic Meridional Overturning Circulation (AMOC), a major ocean circulation that transfers heat from the tropics to high northern latitudes which is very likely to weaken in the 21st century (IPCC, 2021[1]).

There is high confidence these physical changes in the climate will cause different types of socio-economic impacts and associated losses and damages, including direct impacts on peoples' livelihoods. These could occur, for example, through changes in rainfall patterns, temperatures and the distribution of biodiversity and ecosystem services. More indirect impacts on livelihoods are also possible through, for example, changes in the demand for goods and services (Granderson, 2014[4]).

There is also evidence that disadvantageous socio-economic conditions worsen vulnerability and exposure within countries through various channels. These could lead to more severe losses and damages (Hallegatte, Bangalore and Vogt-Schilb, 2016[5]). Impacts from climate change can also translate into loss of personal safety, place-based practices, identities and cultural heritage, and lead to displacement (Barnett et al., 2016[6]) (Adger et al., 2012[7]). These losses and damages are less easily quantifiable but may be equally or more important, as non-economic losses and damages occur at varying degrees and are perceived very differently by different societies.

There is high confidence on the thermodynamic aspects of climate change and the severity of the associated impacts. However, there is far less confidence in the detail of when, where and how these hazards will occur. This is due to the enormous challenges of modelling the highly complex and non-linear climate system. Compounding this challenge (and perhaps in some circumstances dominating this), there is also uncertainty regarding the future socio-economic conditions under which the hazards will manifest, which are key to understanding the levels of vulnerability and exposure to future climate change, and hence the risks of losses and damages on different timescales (Riahi et al., 2017[8]).

According to the IPCC, "uncertainty denotes a cognitive state of incomplete knowledge that results from a lack of information and/or from disagreement about what is known or even knowable" (Kunreuther et al., 2014[9]). Some aspects of uncertainty about a given future climate or socio-economic variable may be quantifiable and have a well-defined probability distribution. Other aspects of uncertainty may not be quantifiable. Both kinds of uncertainty are discussed in this chapter. Given the compelling evidence about the scale of the climate challenge, these uncertainties are no reason to delay action. On the contrary, climate-related damages are likely to increase in a non-linear manner away from present conditions with the magnitude of climate change. Therefore, uncertainty about the future climate on these regional to local scales is actually a reason for greater, not lesser concern.

Model projections of future precipitation illustrate this uncertainty. In some spatial regions, climate models have a high degree of agreement on the direction of change (Zappa, Bevacqua and Shepherd, 2021[10]). In some regions, however, models either disagree on the direction of change or project only a small change. The nature of the uncertainties has different policy implications for adaptation. In one region, the direction of change could be uncertain (e.g. a range of climate model projections on either side of a mean outcome of zero). Such a region faces different choices than one with a high level of confidence in the direction of change and where that change is relatively small and close to zero. In other words, the absence of confidence in how a change will happen is not the same as confidence in the absence of a change.

Indeed, in dealing with uncertainty in climate risk, one must strike a balance in guarding against two types of potential errors. The first error is the possibility of false positives (i.e. avoiding the possibility of overestimating the risk that an impact will happen). The second error is the possibility of false negatives [i.e. avoiding the possibility of underestimating that same risk (Shepherd, 2019[11])]. Finding this balance is not trivial. It requires a good understanding of different levels and types of uncertainties and how to best use this uncertainty to inform decision making.

The following sections explore uncertainties in relation to the physical climate response to forcing and to vulnerability and exposure of socio-economic systems (Figure 2.1). They aim to characterise information available to policy makers in light of uncertain knowledge, and how policy makers can more accurately shape the communication of risk to help spur action. Section 2.2 looks at the confidence in projections of the physical climate. Section 2.3 explores confidence in expectations of future vulnerability and exposure. Finally, Section 2.4 discusses how these uncertainties need to be considered together for an effective communication of climate risk.

Figure 2.1. Types of uncertainties influencing understanding of risks of losses and damages

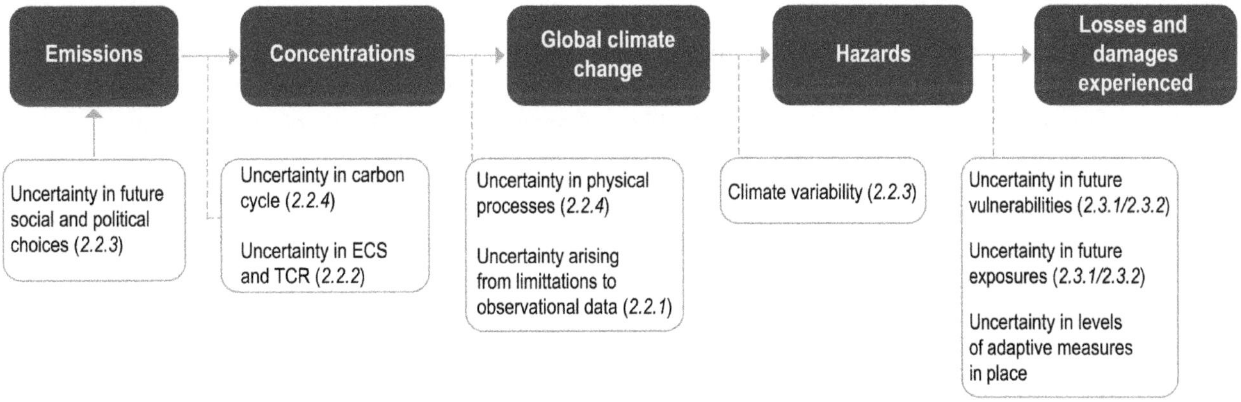

2.2. Confidence and uncertainties in projections of the physical climate

Climate change is a result of complex physical processes. Deep scientific understanding of these processes is largely limited to a small group of highly specialised experts and scholars. While such understanding is not required, policy makers in the area of climate change often need to link science and policy. Therefore, they must deal with a number of different types and forms of uncertainties. A policy maker well-informed about nuances in understanding climate risk is one well-placed to identify effective and robust action to reduce and manage that risk.

This subsection sets out understanding of risks of losses and damages to motivate ambitious climate action from policy makers. It explores uncertainties of different nature, including those pertaining to the climate system itself and those arising from unknown future social and political choices determining climate forcing. These include those arising from availability of observational data and related to climate sensitivity, as well as future emissions projections and uncertainties in regional and global climate change projections. Some uncertainties may be reduced by better scientific tools including observation and modelling; others may be reduced only by political commitment or by the passage of time.

2.2.1. Quality and quantity of observational data

Past and present weather and climate observations

Data and observations of past and present weather and climate are key to understanding variability and change in the climate system and provide a benchmark against which to monitor changes. High-quality data and observations are also key in supporting research, which informs understanding of present and future climate change.

Observations of past behaviour of a number of climate-related variables are used to develop and improve the climate models that provide projections of the future climate system (Flato, 2013[12]). Based on the premise that if models are not able to predict the past well, then they cannot be expected to predict the future, a direct approach to evaluate the effectiveness of a climate model is to compare model output with historical observations. Data from the deep past (from millions to hundreds of years ago) – so-called paleoclimate data – are also important in evaluating climate models outside of the range of more recent climate observations that were used to develop them (Braconnot et al., 2012[13]).

Such an approach reveals that climate models reproduce well general features and aspects of global mean surface temperature from the past. Conversely, they perform less well for the patterns of precipitation at large scale and not well for precipitation at regional scale (Flato, 2013[12]). In analysing the difference between model output and observations, a good knowledge and understanding is needed of uncertainties and potential errors.

Global climate monitoring is costly. It is therefore important to consider the need for climate monitoring in light of societal goals (Goody et al., 2002[14]). There are broadly three different timescales at which climate monitoring is needed. Each has implications for different societal goals (Goody et al., 2002[14]):

- First, the monitoring of present climate serves a number of societal goals. For example, it can support business activities in the agricultural or industrial sectors leading to short-term successes and gains. It can also inform action to protect and avoid losses of lives, livelihoods and assets.
- Second, climate monitoring can inform prediction of short-term (e.g. one-two years) future climate, such as predictions of the El Niño phenomenon. This type of phenomena is linked to a number of natural disasters potentially at global scale, which means their monitoring is well motivated and linked to societal goals.
- Third, climate data and monitoring indirectly informs projections of future climate at longer temporal scales. (50-100 years and beyond) as it allows for calibration and evaluation of models. Model results inform judgements on the long-term implications of human interference with the climate system. They have had significant implications for the international climate process, amplified by their central role in IPCC assessments (e.g. informing the adoption of long-term global temperature goals of the Paris Agreement).

Earth is more extensively and systematically observed today than at any other time. The ability to observe the climate has greatly improved in recent years thanks to improved technology. These include advances in measurements of, for example, sea level and temperatures, and Earth information technology such as satellite remote sensing (Guo, Zhang and Zhu, 2015[15]).

Improved methodology for analysing climate observations from meteorological stations has also led to better and more accurate climate observations over the past century (Mitchell and Jones, 2005[16]). Multiple datasets for global mean temperature have been constructed using different methods and a variety of proxies, with high agreement. This confirms the overall picture of increasing global surface temperatures (Rahmstorf, Foster and Cahill, 2017[17]). The emergence and successes of big data analytics have also been increasingly applied to both weather and climate science (Hassani, Huang and Silva, 2019[18]).

Monitoring weather provides valuable information on key climate variables, such as temperature. However, monitoring climate requires tracking a larger number of variables with more accuracy and low bias (National Research Council, 2012[19]). Many nations around the world recognise the need to maintain and improve climate observations in order to better understand how climate change is unfolding today and in support of better climate change predictions. This is evidenced by acceptance of the World Meteorological Organization (WMO)'s Global Climate Observing System (GCOS) Implementation plan (GCOS, 2016[20]), submitted to the COP22 in Marrakesh.

The GCOS Implementation plan "sets out a way forward for scientific and technological innovations for the Earth observation programmes of space agencies and for the national implementation of climate observing systems and networks". In particular, the plan identifies actions needed for climate monitoring. It considers the increasing requirements of scientific research, the United Nations Framework Convention on Climate

Change (UNFCCC) and other multilateral agreements. In short, it identifies a number of Essential Climate Variables (ECVs), summarised in Table 2.1, and defines target requirements for measuring them.

Table 2.1. Essential Climate Variables as defined by GCOS

Measurement domain	Essential Climate Variables (ECVs)
Atmospheric	***Surface*** **-** air temperature, wind speed and direction, water vapour, pressure, precipitation, surface radiation budget. Upper-air: temperature, wind speed and direction, water vapour, cloud properties, Earth radiation budget, lightning. Composition: carbon dioxide (CO_2), methane (CH_4), other long-lived GHGs, ozone, aerosol, precursors for aerosol and ozone.
Oceanic	***Physics*** **-** temperature: sea surface and subsurface. Salinity: sea surface and subsurface; currents, surface currents, sea level, sea state, sea ice, ocean surface stress, ocean surface heat flux. Biogeochemistry: inorganic carbon, oxygen, nutrients, transient tracers, nitrous oxide (N_2O), ocean colour. Biology/ecosystems: plankton, marine habitat properties.
Terrestrial	***Hydrology*** **-** river discharge, groundwater, lakes, soil moisture. Cryosphere: snow, glaciers, ice sheets and ice shelves, permafrost. Biosphere: albedo, land cover, fraction of absorbed photosynthetically active radiation, leaf area index, above-ground biomass, soil carbon, fire, land surface temperature. Human use of natural resources: water use, GHG fluxes.

Source*:* (GCOS, 2016[20]).

In addition to this effort, the WMO has provided updated information since 1993 in its Status of the Global Climate series (for the most recent, (Kennedy et al., 2021[21]). It provides these data through the Commission for Climatology that guides the World Climate Programme, and in co-operation with its members. The publication provides key information on the so-called global climate indicators (Trewin et al., 2021[22]), which represent a subset of the ECVs. In so doing, it provides credible scientific information on climate and its variability.

This monitoring shows that levels of uncertainties, quality and extent of data vary highly for different indicators. For example, global mean surface temperature changes can be determined with low levels of uncertainties and for long periods into the past. In contrast, ocean acidification has limited underlying observational data with only a low number of stations monitoring this indicator worldwide and for a limited number of years. Meanwhile, sea ice extent observations depend on satellite data, which are available over the last 40 years.

Climate reanalysis, which combines models with observations, has also made an important contribution in the past decades. It has provided globally complete estimates of many key climate variables with high frequency and spatial resolutions. Different climate centres produce several reanalyses using different models (Kalnay et al., 1996[23]; Dee et al., 2011[24]; Kobayashi et al., 2015[25]; Randles et al., 2017[26]). Among estimates in these models are atmospheric parameters. These range from air temperature, pressure and wind to surface parameters such as rainfall, soil moisture and sea-surface temperature. Such datasets are valuable in that they produce consistent time series of gridded data that would be virtually impossible to measure and analyse directly.

Reanalyses are a cleaned, standardised and interpolated form of past data used as input for many studies of historical climatic change. The limitations and biases in observational data and models used as input for creating these datasets are inevitably passed on to the final reanalysed dataset. In other words, the reliability of the dataset will be as good as its inputs and should not be taken as historical truth.

Systems and networks for gathering climate information are increasing and becoming more efficient. However, there is still a long way to go before establishing a comprehensive, systematic global climate monitoring system. Any progress in monitoring is a step forward with potential short-term benefits.

Since many gaps remain in the system, priorities must be assigned. In particular, quality and availability of data are highly heterogeneous geographically and temporally as well as for different types of climate variables. This problem results in differing quality of weather forecasts in different regions, often among the most vulnerable, as well as limiting climate research. Unequal data coverage, stemming from a range of political and economic issues, leads inevitably to larger uncertainties. For example, estimating future climate change in areas that are less represented has implications for climate justice (Brönnimann and Wintzer, 2018[27]).

Improvements in climate monitoring can have a direct impact on decision making related to climate risk management and resilience measures, among other issues. This is because these decisions need to answer questions relating to placement of infrastructure or areas to prioritise for soil or water conservation measures – questions that climate observations can directly inform. Better data, over long periods, may also inform the testing and development of models that can provide better predictions in the mid and longer term.

Observational records of specific impactful events

High-quality observational data are needed to do statistics of different types of extreme events and for detecting and attributing climate change (Otto, 2016[28]). This then enables researchers to draw conclusions (with varying degrees of confidence) about whether a given hazard occurred or was made more intense by human-made climate change overlaid on current climate variability. Such climate attribution studies are most often initiated on the basis of an event causing significant negative impacts for local communities (Philip et al., 2020[29]). Yet the monitoring and reporting of impacts associated with different classes of extreme weather can often be sparse and inconsistent between poorer and wealthier countries (Visser, Petersen and Ligtvoet, 2014[30]; Noy, 2015[31]; Noy and duPont IV, 2018[32]; Tschumi and Zscheischler, 2019[33]). Valid concerns exist about the mixed quality of impact data between different classes of extreme weather within high income countries (Tschumi and Zscheischler, 2019[33]). However, many other regions of the world fail to record *any impacts whatsoever* for entire classes of extreme weather (Noy, 2015[31]), such as heatwaves (Harrington and Otto, 2020[34]).

Observational data for impactful events are also important for calibration and evaluation of models for the future prediction of such events. Global Climate Models (GCMs) are effective in accurately predicting global increases in mean surface temperature increase as a result of GHG emissions. For example, at the global scale, these models are not meant to and cannot predict singular extreme events, such as a heatwave (see Section 2.2.4) or a flooding at a particular location (at least yet).

Secondary models connect global change projections from GCMs with local, specific events. Downscaling models, for example, aim mainly to improve the numerical resolutions. Impact models may additionally model the effect on other physical or human variables. Impact models also take in the outputs (e.g. projected changes in temperature, precipitation or sea-level rise) from GCMs. They then explore possible impacts of these environmental changes on various sectors of the economy (e.g. agriculture, water resources, forestry). Like for GCMs, both impact and downscaling models need to be tested and calibrated against observations from the past to make better predictions (Xu, Han and Yang, 2018[35]). Good observational data about small-scale and local climatic extremes and climate impacts therefore provide key information to these models.

Table 2.2. Quantifying impacts for different categories of extreme weather

Event type	Easy-to-measure impacts	Difficult-to-measure impacts	Rarely-measured impacts
Heatwave	N/A	Excess mortality from heat, heat-related hospitalisations, infrastructure damage.*	Productivity and other indirect economic losses.
Flooding	Insured asset damage, direct mortality.	Uninsured asset damage. Crop losses.	Mental health impacts, disease outbreaks.
Drought	Crop losses.	Food insecurity and malnutrition.	Heat-related impacts during drought. Other indirect economic losses.
Wildfire	Insured asset damage, direct mortality.	Uninsured asset damage. Adverse health outcomes from related air pollution.	Productivity and other indirect economic losses.
Reporting coverage	All countries	High income countries only	Bespoke studies only

Note: A schematic representation of how uncertainties in quantifying the impacts of extreme weather differs depending on the category of extreme weather considered (rows), alongside the frequency with which different categories of impacts are reported by different countries (colours). The four event classes have been ordered on the basis of how often they are the subject of an attribution analysis.

*Because floods are experienced more frequently and by a larger fraction of the global population than wildfires[1], more information is available about which impacts are well measured or poorly quantified in different settings. This explains the different levels of "impact reporting coverage" between the two categories in the table.

Blue boxes show event impacts commonly reported by all countries.

Orange boxes show event impacts typically reported only by high income countries.

Red boxes show extreme event impacts not routinely reported, and that require bespoke analyses (often published in peer-reviewed literature) to yield an impact estimate.

The next sub-sections attempt to summarise the different dimensions of uncertainty that exist when quantifying the impacts of on different classes of extreme weather, as an example of physical hazards (Table 2.2). Gaps in the assessment of other types of hazards, such as slow-onset events and tipping points (see Chapter 3), also exist but are not covered in this section. In addition, this discussion is not intended to provide a comprehensive review of the many publications within the disaster impact literature. Rather, it seeks to understand the *relative* magnitude of reporting gaps in extreme weather impact databases.

Flooding

Of the types of extreme weather most commonly analysed from an attribution perspective (see Table 2.2), the impacts associated with extreme rainfall events and subsequent flooding are the most well-defined in available databases (Tschumi and Zscheischler, 2019[33]). One reason why flooding events – either due to "storms" or "tropical cyclones" – are so well-represented in databases like EM-DAT, Sigma Explorer or DesInventar relates to the characteristics of their impacts. Physical assets, like property, roads or other infrastructure, are most commonly damaged during floods (Hallegatte et al., 2013[36]). Such damages share the beneficial qualities of having:

- well-defined economic value (and insurance coverage, in the case of wealthier countries)
- definitive spatial boundaries within which most impacts took place (i.e. locations that become inundated)
- little-to-no time lag in the emergence of impacts post-event peak.

When combined with satellite and other data products, these characteristics enable relatively rapid assessments of most impacts associated with extreme floods (Ward et al., 2017[37]). Many other significant impacts of flooding are known to be poorly captured in extreme event impact databases. These include the mental health impacts of repeat events (English National Study of Flooding and Health Study Group,

2019[38]), flood-related displacement (Tong, 2017[39]), or the well-documented disease burden of floods (Brown and Murray, 2013[40]; Marcheggiani et al., 2010[41]; English National Study of Flooding and Health Study Group, 2019[38]). The studies that have identified these impacts are constrained by the need for high-quality health data covering multiple different floods to improve statistical power. Estimates of these more diffuse or difficult-to-quantify impacts of flood events are rarely available until years afterward, and often for bespoke cases only.

Wildfires

Wildfire impact profiles share at least three similarities with flooding. First, they expose well-defined economic assets, which are often insured in wealthier countries. Second, definitive spatial boundaries often disaggregate where most impacts take place (i.e. buildings burnt down versus those that did not). Third, there are smaller temporal lags in the emergence of impact.

Uncertainties similarly exist around the wider health impacts of wildfires. Preliminary analysis of the air pollution from the 2019/20 Australian bushfires, for example, found approximately 400 excess deaths and over 1 000 hospitalisations attributed to bushfire smoke exposure (Borchers Arriagada et al., 2020[42]).

Floods are experienced more frequently and by a larger fraction of the global population than wildfires.[1] Therefore, more information is available about which impacts are well measured or poorly quantified in different settings. This explains the different levels of "impact reporting coverage" between the two categories of event in Table 2.2.

Heatwaves

Unlike for flooding events, directly observable impacts from heatwaves rarely exist. Previous well-studied events, however, offer insight into impacts that arise during heatwaves. Of special note are exceptional heatwaves affecting southeast Australia in January 2009 (Steffen et al., 2019[43]). Re-assessment of the Australian heatwaves over subsequent years identified at least four significant categories of impacts (Zander et al., 2015[44]):

- excess mortality associated with extreme heat (estimates of more than 500 deaths)
- excess morbidity, with another estimated 3 000 hospitalisations from people suffering heat-related illnesses
- economic losses from electricity and transport infrastructure impacts totalled AUD 800 million, with heat-related blackouts affecting half a million people, widespread transport disruption from rail infrastructure malfunctions and road closures due to bitumen melting
- wider labour productivity losses estimated at hundreds of millions of Australian dollars.

Unfortunately, even the most comprehensive heatwave impact reports offered to disaster databases like EM-DAT are typically limited to one of the four factors: excess-mortality calculations. Moreover, only countries in Western Europe routinely provide such numbers (Guha-Sapir, Hargitt and Hoyois, 2004[45]; Guha-Sapir, Hoyois and Below, 2016[46]). Meanwhile, for the majority of low- and lower-middle income countries, no real-time monitoring mechanisms are in place for *any* of these four (or more) categories of heatwave impacts. As a consequence, heatwave impacts are often not reported at all, despite clear meteorological evidence and longer-term retrospective analyses pointing to the opposite conclusions (Russo et al., 2016[47]; Ozturk, Saygili-Araci and Kurnaz, 2021[48]; Zittis et al., 2021[49]).

In short, robust evidence suggests that any instances of extremely high relative temperatures that persist for more than several days – in other words, a heatwave (Perkins and Alexander, 2013[50]) – can cause substantive social, health and economic impacts, irrespective of the location considered (Gasparrini et al., 2015[51]; Ebi et al., 2021[52]). The direct and indirect economic costs of a truly unprecedented heatwave (akin to the 2003 Europe event) affecting an unprepared (Fouillet et al., 2008[53]; Hess et al., 2018[54]) megacity in the Global South, for example, would likely approach hundreds of millions of dollars (Steffen et al., 2019[43]). In such an event, thousands of people could die from heat stress (Whitman et al., 1997[55]; Robine et al., 2008[56]; Mora et al., 2017[57]) and tens of thousands more could suffer from heat-related morbidity (Vaidyanathan et al., 2019[58]).

As it stands, few countries of the world have the capacity to provide real-time or near-real-time reports of the economic or morbidity impacts of heatwaves to impact databases (Tschumi and Zscheischler, 2019[33]). Indeed, many of the world's most vulnerable countries lack any monitoring capability to detect impacts of heatwaves. This results in no heatwave "events" being reported to disaster databases (Harrington and Otto, 2020[34]). These reporting deficits contribute to mistaken perceptions. They suggest that extreme heatwaves either do not occur, or do not cause significant economic or health impacts in lower income or climatologically hot regions (Tschumi and Zscheischler, 2019[33]; Otto et al., 2020[59]). Until such reporting gaps are closed, thousands of excess deaths due to extreme heat will likely continue to go unreported every year. Despite forecasts a week in advance, clear warnings and community actions in a developed country region, the province of British Columbia alone reported that excess deaths had tripled to 719 during the heatwave of June/July 2021 (Government of British Columbia, 2021[60]).

Drought

Many lower income countries have detailed monitoring frameworks for direct crop losses from drought. This is due to the importance for non-governmental organisations to identify food insecurity and subsequent humanitarian concerns (Benson and Clay, 1998[61]; Clay and Stokke, 2000[62]; Harrington and Otto, 2020[63]).

Beyond the monitoring of direct crop losses and potential water scarcity in vulnerable regions, many economic impacts associated with drought are highly diffuse. Indirect economic losses can sometimes take several years to emerge. This lag creates problems when trying to compile a catalogue of impacts soon after an event occurs. In addition, complex macroeconomic modelling tools are often needed to successfully quantify such losses (Kamber, McDonald and Price, 2013[64]; Edwards, Gray and Hunter, 2019[65]). This creates further disparities in reporting quality between those countries that can routinely identify these impacts, and those that cannot.

2.2.2. Variation in modelled climate sensitivity

Equilibrium climate sensitivity (ECS) refers to the change in global mean temperature following a doubling of atmospheric CO_2-equivalent (CO_2-eq[2]) concentration (Kattenberg et al., 1996[66]). In other words, if one doubles the amount of CO_2-eq concentration in the atmosphere and waits for the climate to respond, the resulting temperature increase once the climate reaches equilibrium again is the ECS.

Another type of sensitivity of the Earth system is the so-called transient climate response (TCR). TCR differs from ECS as it refers to the amount of warming that occurs *at the time* the CO_2-eq concentration doubles following a linear and steady increase in emissions (having increased gradually by 1% each year), as opposed to when the system has reached equilibrium. TCR is more closely related to the way cumulative GHG emissions have changed in the more recent past.[3]

The ECS and the TCR are not simple metrics. Rather, they are the result of complex response within the Earth system and have been the subject of research over many decades. For the last 40 years, there has been high confidence that ECS is somewhere between 1.5-4.5°C (Ad Hoc Study Group on Carbon Dioxide and Climate et al., 1979[67]; IPCC, 2013[2]). The most recent IPCC Assessment updates this to a likely range of 2.5-4°C (high confidence), with a best estimate of ECS of 3°C. This update is based on improved knowledge of climate processes, paleoclimate evidence and the response of the climate system to increasing radiative forcing. In other words, a doubling of CO_2-eq emissions concentrations in the atmosphere would result in an increase of 2.5-4°C in surface mean temperature of the planet (IPCC, 2021[1]).

TCR is lower than ECS within a likely range as 1.0°C to 2.3°C (that is, each1000 PgC of cumulative CO_2 emissions is assessed to likely cause a increase in global surface temperature with a best estimate within that range), with a best estimate of 1.65°C (IPCC, 2021[1]). This reflects delays and lags in the climate system such as the time required to transfer heat to the deeper levels of the ocean and reach a new equilibrium. The size of the temperature increase these emissions determines the extent and severity of climate change associated with anthropogenic emissions. Consequently, ECS and TCR are key metrics for understanding present and future human-made climate change.

A first-order question about a climate plan or strategy is its likely effectiveness. Uncertainties surrounding ECS and TCR have direct consequences for the scale of the response of the climate to GHG emissions (Figure 2.1). The place of ECS within the 1.5-4.5ºC range will have a direct consequence on the severity, timing and scale of climate impacts with important societal ramifications.

Pledges by countries to reduce emissions are inadequate to achieve the long-term temperature goal of the Paris Agreement (UNFCCC, 2015[68]). If realised ECS falls within the high end of the distribution of current ECS estimates, then, resulting emissions levels could lead to even higher warming (and impacts) than currently projected in the second half of the century. In that case, emissions reductions would need to be accelerated or carbon dioxide reduction (CDR) technologies deployed earlier and at a greater scale than might otherwise have been the case. Some recent literature suggests that even considering these uncertainties, the 1.5ºC temperature goal of the Paris Agreement is physically achievable (Holden et al., 2018[69]; CONSTRAIN, 2020[70]), though immense effort and luck would both be required. A good understanding of ECS uncertainty is therefore crucial for any climate risk assessment and policy making in relation to both mitigation and adaptation. Despite many efforts to narrow the ECS uncertainty range, it has remained large over the past four decades.

There are many ways and lines of evidence used to determine ECS and TCR, each based on multiple studies, models and data sets. These include data from the deep past (paleoclimate), recent observations and outputs of climate models.[4] A recent study, using these multiple lines of evidence, has narrowed the range down in a meaningful way (Sherwood et al., 2020[71]). The study concludes that values on the low-end of the ECS uncertainty range (i.e. below 1.5 degrees), where the climate response to anthropogenic emissions is lower, are very unlikely. It suggests less than a 5% chance of an ECS lower than 2 degrees. By contrast, it concludes there is a more than 5% chance of values above the higher end of the AR5 range (over 4.5 degrees). As in previous assessments, the warming by the end of the century could be higher than the upper range of warming levels expected today for any given scenario for GHG concentrations over the course of the century.[5]

Other studies also suggest the response of the climate to increases in GHG concentration is "fat-tailed". In other words, there is a slim, but sufficiently large, probability of extreme warming (Ackerman, Stanton and Bueno, 2010[72]; Wagner and Weitzman, 2018[73]; Weitzman, 2009[74]). ECS uncertainties have been partially quantified from ensembles of climate model runs. These assess the robustness of the results given different available models and plausible parameter ranges. The shape of the distribution of ECS estimates from such methods indicates the levels of uncertainty. It also indicates the chance that ECS will be realised on the high end of the range. However, the tails of the distribution are sensitive to assumptions. Box 2.1 explores the implications of different ECD distributions. ECS, rather than an input, is an outcome of a model run. It depends on and changes across models based on how complex climate system dynamics are modelled.

Box 2.1. Implications of different ECS distributions

One way to estimate ECS is through climate models. Deterministic projections (i.e. cause and effect predictions) of changes in the climate are subject to a large number of uncertainties. These arise from incomplete understanding of the climate system, as well as imprecise models and the sensitivity of models and model runs to initial conditions set by the modeller (Collins et al., 2013[75]). There are also only a relatively small number of models and they disagree significantly. This is relevant for the way ECS is estimated.

To illustrate the understanding of uncertainties in ECS arising from models, Figure 2.2a compares the probability distribution of ECS as per Sherwood et al. (2020[71]). The most recent ECS estimates are under CMIP6 (Meehl et al., 2020[76]). First, Figure 2.2a shows that CMIP6 ECS estimates from climate models are higher than the AR5 1.5-4.5°C range, with only very few values falling below 1.5°C and many values surpassing the upper limit of 4.5°C. This increase is well documented in the literature. It stems mainly from stronger positive cloud feedbacks from decreasing extratropical low cloud coverage and albedo in models (Zelinka et al., 2020[77]).

Beyond the absolute values of ECS, a visual interpretation of the histogram in Figure 2.2a and b shows fewer lower values of ECS than higher values. This suggests the shape of the distribution fitting those values is fat-tailed towards higher estimates. Figure 2.2b fits, for illustrative purpose only, two types of naïve distributions to the CMIP6 ECS data. Figure 2.2b shows that assuming a fat-tailed, lognormal distribution would lead to higher probabilities of higher values. Conversely, assuming a Gaussian curve (normal distribution) would decrease the probability of these higher values. Therefore, the assumed shape of this distribution influences the estimated probability of higher levels of warming, an understanding important for informing measures dealing with climate risk.

This distribution fitting is by no means proposed as alternative estimations of ECS distributions to the one presented in Sherwood et al. (2020[71]). The Sherwood study uses multiple lines of evidence and constitutes state-of-art estimates of ECS. The difference between the two panels reflects the effect of the additional data available to a more sophisticated (Sherwood) method, in particular the effect on the tails. Any such distribution is an attempt to visualise our present uncertainty and (lack of) knowledge, reflecting a summary of many expert judgements rather than a quantification of some physical truth ((Jebeile and Crucifix, 2020[78])).

Figure 2.2. Distribution fitting of CMIP6 Equilibrium Climate Sensitivity estimates

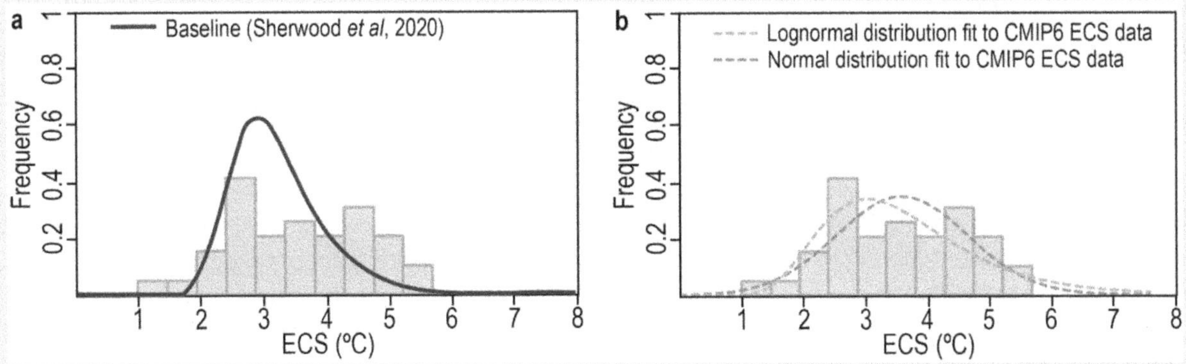

Note: CMIP6 estimates were obtained from (Meehl et al., 2020[76]) and span over 1.1-5.6°C. Distribution fitting in panel b was performed using R, package "fitdist" by maximum likelihood estimation over variable parameters (mean, standard deviation) within the class of models.

Estimated ECS and TCR levels have direct implications for estimates of the remaining carbon budgets consistent with different long-term temperature goals. Uncertainties in ECS and TCR, which are properties of the climate system as a whole, introduce high levels of uncertainty for mitigation pathways globally and for implications regionally/locally.

The need for urgent and stringent emissions reductions at all levels becomes even more evident in light of these uncertainties. This is especially true as the most recent research rules out low (less-damaging) values while maintaining the possibility of high (more-damaging) ones. As a result of continued research into climate sensitivity, understanding of emissions budgets and the physical processes that could lead to high-end outcomes have evolved and improved substantially.

Given the above, working emissions scenarios and their implication for global mitigation and local adaptation are not really independent from an understanding of ECS and TCR. Closely monitoring changes in emissions and changes in temperatures and impacts is therefore crucial. This monitoring can allow for emissions scenarios to be incrementally improved to match the reality of climate change and for action to swiftly respond to the improvement of knowledge.

A slow response time in climate politics is a high-risk approach, which assumes the lower end of possible carbon budgets in the hope that the lower end could become the higher end with further information. But it could go the other way. Budgets set at a 66% chance, or even 50% chance, of meeting the global temperature goal, are more vulnerable to changes than those that take a more robust attitude towards the need to meet the target.

2.2.3. Uncertainties in future emissions projections and climate forcing

In addition to the uncertainties on how the climate responds to climate forcing, detailed prediction of future climate change is also limited by i) uncertainties in the projection of future GHG emissions levels; and ii) uncertainties in how those emissions translate into GHG concentrations in the atmosphere, which will determine the amount of climate forcing (Figure 2.1).

First, uncertainties in projected emissions stem from the imperfect ability to predict future activities around the world and therefore the resulting emissions. This is due to the complex interplay of rapidly changing societal, technological, economic and other political choices for governments, countries and citizens in the short-, mid- and long-term.

Second, uncertainties related to how emissions will ultimately translate into climate forcing are directly linked to the current understanding of carbon cycle. In other words, they are linked to the series of processes by which carbon compounds, including CO_2, are interconverted and incorporated in the environment and returned to the atmosphere (see Box 2.2)

Estimation of future emissions of GHGs, aerosols and their precursors is crucial for any analysis of future climate change. However, the prediction of future anthropogenic emissions is mainly governed by political, economic and societal choices. Therefore, the exercise of predicting short-, mid- and long-term emissions is inherently speculative, based on understanding of socio-economic systems and assumptions about potential choices. Because politically-determined targets and aspirations do not necessarily translate into perfect regulation of human activities, the question is not simply to predict what kind of future will result from each action, select the future most wanted and determine emissions accordingly. Instead, there is a messy interface between the predictions of science, the aspirations of politics, and the real-world actions of individuals and organisations. Nevertheless, one should beware of treating social change as a problem of prediction rather than action: leadership will be required to orient the social and economic world towards emission reductions, and the assumption that no leadership exists may be an unfortunately self-fulfilling prophecy.

Climate modelling of future GHG emissions relies therefore on building “scenarios”, each associated with different plausible narratives describing how societies may evolve. Scenarios will then be used to estimate different climate change futures that can inform action and actual choices of societies and governments.

Box 2.2. Carbon cycle uncertainties and RCP scenarios

The RCP scenarios are emissions concentrations pathways. While strongly correlated, GHG emissions and GHG concentrations in the atmosphere are not the same. As such, there is not one emissions pathway that is linked to one RCP scenario.

Figure 2.3. Time series of annual emissions compatible with RCP scenarios

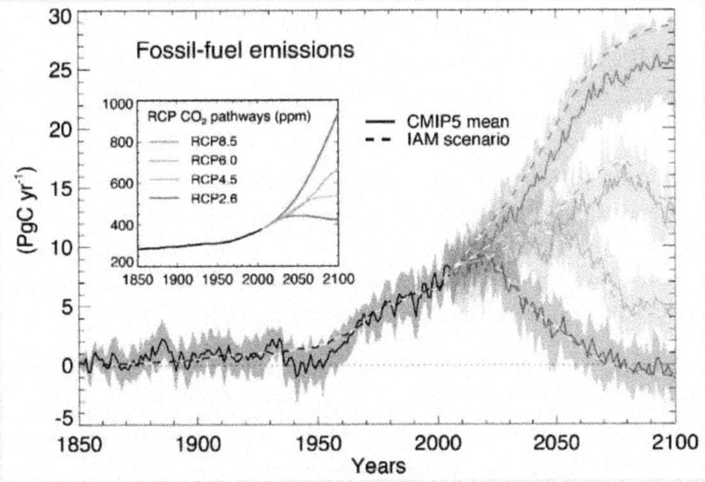

Note: Compatible fossil fuel emissions simulated by the CMIP5 models for the four RCP scenarios. Time series of annual emission (PgC yr–1). Dashed lines represent the historical estimates and RCP emissions calculated by the IAMs used to define the RCP scenarios; solid lines and plumes show results from CMIP5 Earth System Models (model mean, with one standard deviation shaded).
Source: (Stocker et al., 2013[79]).

Indeed, projections of GHG concentrations over the 21st century rely on simplifying assumptions about biogeochemical cycles, including the carbon cycle. Uncertainties about the carbon cycle include the relation between increased CO_2 emissions and terrestrial carbon uptake and storage and the role of “tipping point” feedback processes such as permafrost thawing, forest dieback and the weakening of land and ocean carbon sinks (Steffen et al., 2018[80]). Considering these uncertainties, a range of possible emissions trajectories could lead to a certain level of concentration (Figure 2.3). These uncertainties have implications for policy making (and not concentrations) as human activities lead to emissions. Climate policy and action can therefore only directly regulate emissions.

Uncertainties about the carbon cycle are potentially much larger than assumed (Higgins and Harte, 2012[81]). This could effectively mean that carbon cycle responses could lead to higher levels of warming than expected. In this sense, using concentrations instead of emissions may lead to an underestimation of warming and neglect research and understanding of possible feedback processes. It is important to assess these ranges of emissions systematically so they can be narrowed over time.

In turn, how these emissions will translate into concentrations will determine the extent of climate change. From a physical point of view, and for the purpose of climate modelling, a focus on concentration pathways makes sense as it reduces one level of uncertainties. However, these uncertainties can have important implications for policy making and cannot be ignored.

Climate policy commitments and pledges worldwide indicate where emissions are headed over time. Nationally Determined Contributions (NDCs) under the Paris Agreement often include emissions reductions commitments. These limit emissions (or emissions intensity of, for example, economic output) to a target emissions range at a target year or period. In addition to NDCs, a large number of countries have put forward commitments to reach net-zero CO_2 or GHG emissions by mid-century. Such commitments also serve as a signpost for where emissions are heading.

Emissions levels in line with those commitments do not necessarily need to directly inform the development of scenarios. However, they provide important information in relation to the plausibility of different existing scenarios. In May 2021, analysis showed that NDCs and longer-term climate targets put forward by countries would lead to warming of about 2.4°C (1.9-3°C) by the end of the century (CAT, 2021[82]).

The IPCC Fifth Assessment Report developed four Representative Concentration Pathways (RCPs). The low-carbon mitigation scenario comprises stringent climate and energy system interventions, while a high-carbon scenario assumes continued growth in emissions. These were later complemented with an additional scenario in line with the goal to pursue "efforts to limit the temperature increase to 1.5°C above pre-industrial levels", adopted in the Paris Agreement (UNFCCC, 2015[68]) (see Chapter 1, section 1.2.2 and Figure 1.1).

Integrated Assessment Models (IAMs) produce global emissions scenarios. These models consider the potential evolution of energy system, population growth, economic development and other drivers of emissions such as agriculture and land use. IAMs are traditionally used to examine the cost-effectiveness of achieving mitigation goals. Overall, they are useful and widely used tools for answering policy-relevant questions at different levels although they also have blind spots and limitations which require consideration e.g. (Gambhir, 2019[83]).

Based on results from IAMs, a second set of scenarios, the Shared Socio-economic Pathways (SSPs), have been constructed. The SSPs show in more detail the socio-economic and technological factors that result in different emissions and thus concentration pathways (see also Section 2.3.2). Importantly, the different SSP scenarios provide critical information on potential global socio-economic and technological choices. These can be put into the context of NDCs and longer-term net-zero targets. Figure 2.4 shows global trajectories for nine RCP/SSP scenario combinations for CO_2 emissions that form a basis for the physical study of different future worlds, with different levels of warming and climate change impacts.

Figure 2.4. Global CO_2 emissions in different RCP/SSP scenario combinations

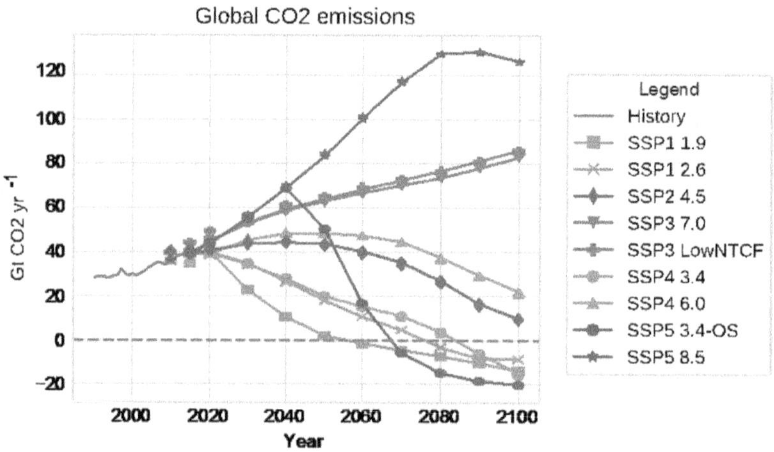

Note: Harmonised trajectories of Global CO_2. Scenario names refer to combination of SSP/RCP scenarios as such: SSP1 1.9 denotes SSP1/RCP1.9 scenario combination and so forth. OS stands for "overshoot" and LowNTCF for low near-term climate forcing species emission.
Source: (Gidden et al., 2019[84]).

There are no probabilities attached to the scenarios as they rely on a number of choices and assumptions (e.g. spread of a technology), which are not describable as probabilities. In this sense, there are no right or wrong scenarios. Instead; they can be more or less plausible based on, for example, real world policy, socio-economic and technological choices and describe potential implications of those. Recent work has questioned the plausibility of the highest scenario (Hausfather and Peters, 2020[85]). RCP8.5, the highest concentration pathway in the scenario set, would be unlikely on the basis of emissions alone. It would require major players to walk away from their commitments and burn fossil fuels beyond the likely economic availability of the resource.

In general, as time advances the scenario space becomes more constrained. In future, therefore, new sets of scenarios will reflect the new dominant axes of social and political uncertainty. These scenarios should be constructed in a way that is useful for policy makers. For example, they could distinguish feasible social and political choices or outcomes, by highlighting barriers, opportunities, synergies and trade-offs across different pathways, or by incorporating the systemic effects of losses and damages. A wider range of futures analysis techniques may be required to complement information from energy and integrated assessment models (Gambhir, 2019[83])

It is impossible to know what choices governments and societies in general will make in the short-, mid- and long-term. However, RCP and SSP scenarios together provide policy makers with important insights on how these choices determine the type of transition for the world in the next decades. In so doing, they can help inform these choices. For example, there are different ways to achieve the goal of limiting warming to 1.5°C by 2100 (IPCC, 2018[86]). These depend on choices of different socio-economic potential trajectories, resource efficiency measures, and societal and technological developments. They also consider trade-offs between early, deep reductions and the use of atmospheric CDR technologies. Pathways relying on low energy demand and low material consumption use only a limited amount of CDR. On the other end, scenarios with high levels of future energy demand show lower levels of CO_2 emissions reductions to 2030; they rely to a much greater extent on the use of CDR technologies later in the century [(IPCC, 2018[86]), and Figure 6.4)].

Put another way, the assumed extensive use of large-scale CDR is the only way for high-consumption pathways to meet the Paris ambition of limiting warming to 1.5ºC. There is no certainty these technologies can be deployed at reasonable costs or risks. Therefore, the high emissions growth pathways carry higher implementation risk for the Paris goal.

Scenarios frameworks, such as the SSP/RCP scenarios and their predecessor SRES scenarios (IPCC, 2000[87]), can be useful frameworks. They can shape policy makers' understanding of global transformation trends over long time horizons needed to avoid the most dangerous impacts from climate change. At the international level, the RCP scenario framework informed the work of international policy makers. For example, in the context of international climate negotiations, the framework contributed to adoption of common and global temperature goals of the Paris Agreement.

The usability of such scenarios is less direct and evident for policy makers at the national level. For example, a national group that plays the crucial role of turning objectives into actual emissions reductions can act in their jurisdictions and localities, such as cities or states. However, information provided by these global scenarios is not directly fit for their purpose. First, temporal and spatial scales in these are too coarse for policy making at finer scales. In addition, climate policy action will depend on a range of factors that go beyond what these scenarios consider and capture even though efforts are underway to include more areas of relevance for decision making at national level.

The use of scenarios is intended to broaden a debate and capture the most important feasible axes of uncertainty. This is useful in simplifying the wide range of possible outcomes to a tractable plausible set. These scenarios inform and frame debates about socio-economic and technological development over the next century, identifying trade-offs and the most crucial elements of the low-carbon transition.

In collapsing the range of plausible futures to a handful of possible outcomes, however, other uncertainties are necessarily disregarded that may turn out to be significant. For example, the emissions implied by RCP8.5 are now thought to be implausible (Hausfather and Peters, 2020[85]). However, carbon cycle feedbacks could one day result in RCP8.5-like concentrations with lower anthropogenic emissions (see also Section 2.2.2 and Box 2.2). On the socio-economic side, some researchers consider that systematic effects of abrupt social, political or technological changes should be more directly incorporated into energy modelling approaches (McCollum et al., 2020[88]). Indeed, to inform policies most effectively, decision makers must keep in mind the possibility of higher impact, lower probability unfolding of climate change.

There are also a number of well-known shortcomings associated with IAMs in failing to model certain key aspects of the real world. For example, IAMs only implicitly considers politics as a driver for emissions reductions or delay of action (Peng et al., 2021[89]). A range of political and socio-economic aspects determines the extent and types of action of countries, businesses and societies that global scenarios do not currently capture. For example, a central challenge in the world today is reducing economic inequality. How countries achieve that societal objective may have important implications for decarbonisation. Peng et al. (2021[89]) explore concrete areas that could improve these models, as for example the inclusion of public opinion or how trade and investment policies can be captured.

Projections based on real world drivers can indeed help shape action at the local, subnational and national levels. These projections are made in the context of emissions reductions needed globally to avoid the most dangerous impacts of climate change. In addition to global scenarios, confident information about where emissions are heading can answer a number of questions relevant to policy makers.

First, confident information can provide a good indication of whether a policy or a strategy will be effective in reducing emissions in line with national commitments. This can be a crucial step in leveraging buy-in of the policy plan by decision makers and by the public. Second, a roadmap towards commitments, in particular long-term commitments, provides concrete policy options that clarifies how the country plans to achieve the target. This makes them more credible (Rogelj et al., 2021[90]). Such roadmaps can support the formulation of concrete implementation plans. As such, they rely on the projection of emissions and explore policy options leading to needed levels of reductions. Lastly, such roadmaps are also the basis for evaluation of fairness and adequacy of commitments from a country perspective. This can help advance discussions around the issue of equity (Rogelj et al., 2021[90]).

2.2.4. Uncertainties in projections of global and regional climate change

As highlighted in Chapter 1, climate risk is a function of hazards, vulnerability and exposure. In order to better characterise the climate risk, and the risk of losses and damages, an important effort is to better characterise how, where and by when different types of potential hazards (e.g. extreme weather events such as heatwaves, flooding or droughts) may occur. As discussed in previous sections, this work is done using different models. These range from Global Circulation Models (GCMs) to downscaled models, regional models and models focusing on particular sectors of the economy and types of impacts.

At the global level, much of that exercise involves many academic and operational institutions around the world in the context of model intercomparison projects. These include the Coupled Model Intercomparison Project (CMIP), co-ordinated by the World Climate Research Programme (for details see to Box 2.3).

These projects have helped construct a consistent and policy-relevant knowledge base and a foundation for the IPCC assessments. They compare the outputs of different models and show how, for different future warming scenarios (see Section 2.2.3), climate change may unfold around the globe for different regions and timeframes. The level of confidence in these different projections depends on a range of factors. Effective and accountable model-informed decision making needs to consider the varying degrees of confidence and value of the information for different types of decisions (Nissan et al., 2019[91]).

The next sub-sections explore different levels of confidence in GCM data in two ways. First, they examine different spatial and time resolutions. Second, they look at type of processes and hazards to examine where larger uncertainties can lead to a larger range of potential climate risk.

Different levels of confidence in projections at different temporal and spatial scales: The case of extreme temperature projections

With mounting impacts from climate change threatening human and natural systems, there is an increasing need for information on future climate change to support policy planning and climate risk management strategies (Wang et al., 2016[92]; Donatti et al., 2016[93]; Giuliani et al., 2017[94]; Finn, 2020[95]). The varying temporal and spatial scales at which this planning is necessary require different types of information, informing different types of responses. For example, long-term mitigation strategies at the global level require information in substantially longer temporal and larger spatial scales than responses to immediate localised threats. Using an illustrative example of temperature projections from state-of-the-art climate models (CMIP6), this subsection explores how the information from these models can best inform climate action and strategies.

Chapter 1 discussed the high confidence in the relationship between human-made emissions and the rise of average global temperatures. Indeed, climate models have performed well in predicting global mean surface temperature rise on the basis of anthropogenic emissions scenarios for the last five decades (Hausfather et al., 2020[96]). This suggests that climate models capture well the key underlying physical processes driving the rise in temperatures (Hausfather et al., 2020[96]). This gives confidence in the ability of climate models to project temperature increase resulting from different future emissions levels, albeit with some uncertainty.

Climate change will not unfold uniformly around the planet. Warming will be larger over land than oceans and at Arctic latitudes, for example (Collins et al., 2013[75]). However, climate-related risks in general increase with degrees of average warming of the planet.

Indeed, climate risks for natural and human systems are higher for warming at 1.5°C than at present at 0.87°C[6], and higher again at 2°C (IPCC, 2018[97]). Global average temperature increase is therefore a key metric for the approximate magnitude of climate change impacts in different potential worlds of changed climate. The timing of potential crossing of thresholds of increased risks of physical hazards, such as extreme or slow-onset events or tipping points, is a simple metric to discuss with policy makers and stakeholders. These thresholds could include, for example, crossing tipping points and the increased frequency and severity of extreme weather events.

Global average temperature, however, is not a metric that can directly inform policy makers of specific localised temperature events for reasons discussed earlier. These events are related to the less well-understood climate dynamics that are driven by the increased energy flow into the climate system overlaid on local weather patterns.

Indeed, while the frequency and severity of many of such events, including hot extremes, marine heatwaves, and heavy precipitation, increase with average warming of the planet, severe heatwaves affecting human lives and livelihoods happen already at current – relatively low – levels of average warming (Stott, Stone and Allen, 2004[98]; Vautard et al., 2020[99]; Le Tertre et al., 2006[100]). In the last days of June 2021, for example, Pacific coast areas of the United States and Canada experienced record temperatures. A recent study shows these heatwaves were virtually impossible without human-induced climate change: the event was statistically estimated to be about a 1 in 1 000 year event in the current climate (Sjoukje Philip et al., 2021[101]).

Yet global average temperature projections in models are calculated as the average of a number of discrete projections of temperature made at the grid-level of the models[7] at much higher temporal and spatial resolutions. Thus, a focus on the global average temperature change alone would obscure the wealth of more granular information available from model projections at these higher resolutions.

The section uses the most recent projections for extreme temperatures from GCMs in the CMIP6 database (Box 2.3) to explore these underlying model projections. Specifically, it explores the level of variability and agreement across models. Ultimately, it examines the confidence in these projections at different temporal and spatial scales for a subset of the models comprising the CMIP6 database. In so doing, it aims to shed light on the value of these climate projections for guiding short-term decisions to reduce those risks through, for example, adaptation measures.

Box 2.3. Overview of climate model intercomparison projects

The overall goal of the Coupled Model Intercomparison Project (CMIP) is to better understand the past, present and future of the climate system resulting from natural factors or from changes in climate forcing in the atmosphere caused by human and other activities. To that end, it uses a number of coupled atmosphere-ocean General Circulation Models (GCMs). GCMs represent physical processes in the atmosphere, ocean, cryosphere, biosphere and land, considering the interactions between them, for predicting climate at near-(next decades) or long-term (next centuries). CMIP, established in 1995 and in its sixth phase (CMIP6 – https://pcmdi.llnl.gov/CMIP6/), involves a large number of research institutions. They run their climate models under a standard experimental framework or use a common set of input parameters (Eyring et al., 2016[102]) to study and compare their outputs. This means that outputs from different models can be directly compared.

The CMIP exercise enables assessment of model performance, including by evaluating models' strengths and weaknesses, to foster development and review of GCMs. CMIP also makes the resulting multi-model output datasets available for analysis and application in a variety of impact studies. The climate projections produced in the context of CMIPs underpin IPCC assessments on climate change.

For its part, CMIP6 provides the basis for scientific assessment on climate change in the IPCC's Sixth Assessment Reports (AR6). CMIP6 uses over 100 models from 50 institutions to estimate how the climate will respond to different concentration scenarios, based on different socio-economic scenarios. GCMs project a range of climate variables around the globe at varying temporal and spatial resolutions, which can be analysed collectively in the CMIP context. Approaches have been developed to distil the most credible information on impacts and risks for stakeholders and policy makers (Eyring et al., 2019[103]).

CMIP is the largest and most comprehensive intercomparison project, but there are dozens of others. They range from the official and highly-coordinated to small unofficial projects. The others have similar aims and take a systematic approach to comparing different aspects of model inputs, outputs and performance.

Figure 2.5 shows extreme temperature projections for the cities of Hyderabad (India) and Paris (France) for three different scenarios of warming. These are: i) a low-carbon scenario in line with the 1.5°C in the Paris Agreement (RCP 1.9); ii) a middle scenario (RCP 4.5); and iii) a very high-carbon scenario assuming continued growth in emissions (RCP 8.5). The locations explored in this section were chosen as broadly representative of different types of climates and levels of socio-economic vulnerabilities. The Indian State capital, for example, has higher vulnerability than the French capital (Kadiyala et al., 2020[104]). In addition, both cities experience more than global average impacts of climate change. For example, average yearly temperature in the French territory increased by 0.95°C between 1901 and 2000 – about 20% higher than the global average of 0.74°C (MEEDDM, 2009[105]).

Figure 2.5. Projected annual maximum temperatures and decadal averages for Paris and Hyderabad

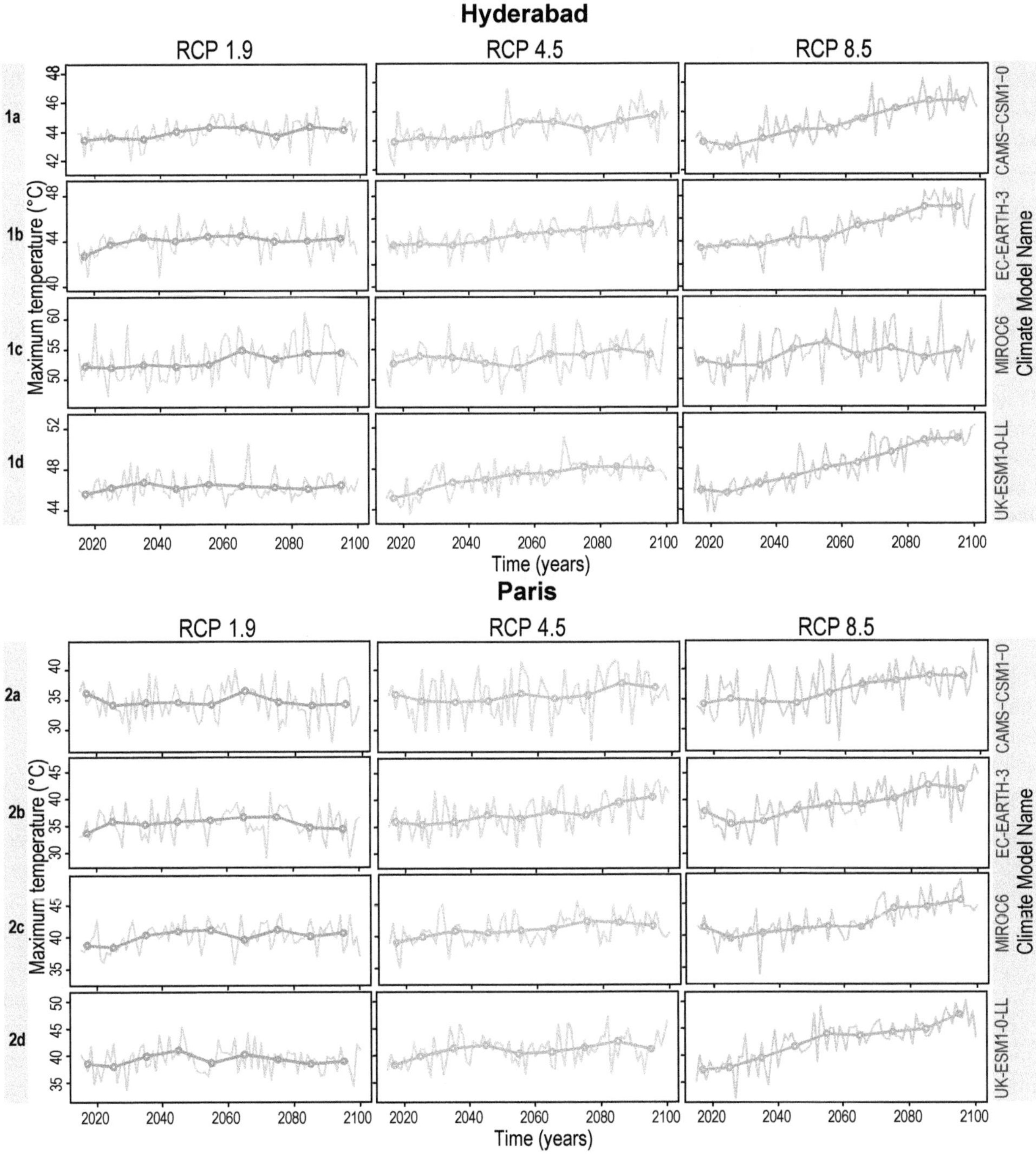

Note: Annual surface temperature extreme and their decadal averages in Paris (yearly maximum extreme average in 48-49ºN 2-3ºE) and Hyderabad (annual maximum extreme average in 17-18ºN 78-79ºE). Data were obtained from CMIP6 database (https://esgf-node.llnl.gov/projects/esgf-llnl/) for daily extreme temperature (variable "tasmax"); for scenario combinations RCP1.9 (SSP1), RCP 4.5 (SSP2) and RCP 8.5 (SSP5); and for models CAMS-CSMi-0 (variant 'r2i1p1f1'), EC-Earth-3 (variant 'r4i1p1f1'), MIROC6 (variant 'r1i1p1f1') and UK-ESM1-0-LL (variant 'r1i1p1f2'). Note that first decadal average point is calculated using only 5 data points (2015-2019).

Figure 2.5 shows, for all three scenarios, that annual maximum temperatures for both locations vary considerably on an annual time scale throughout the century. This is familiar from most people's everyday experience: some summers are hotter than others. The average maximum annual temperature, however, increases over time as average global temperature increases. The trend is much clearer for the higher concentration scenarios RCP4.5 and RCP8.5. Different models show more or less change for each scenario for a number of reasons. These relate to how each of the models portrays the global climate historically and into the future. This section does not explore these implications, but policy makers should be aware of the high degree of variability in the annual data.

The models realistically show that extreme temperatures can already happen at lower levels of warming and in the near term. Because of this annual variability (Box 2.4) and the initial conditions used in the model runs, the precise timing of occurrence of heatwave events is expected to differ across different realisations of the same model and across different models. Despite these differences, trends should be reasonably consistent. Indeed, Figure 2.6 (panels 1a and 2a) shows a large spread and no correlation in the timing of yearly maxima anomalies when considering models together. This indicates that climate models cannot predict the exact timing of individual heatwave events with any skill.

Moving towards coarser temporal resolutions, such as the smoother decadal averages, reveals much greater agreement between models (see Figure 2.5 and the decadal average anomalies in Figure 2.6, panels 1d and 2d). With the large annual variability removed, the long-term trend is clearer and consistent between models. The decadal temperature extreme averages rise over time along with global average warming. In the highest warming scenario (RCP8.5) towards the end of the century, the severity of heat in even the coolest years could exceed the severity of the most extreme heat experienced today. In the strong-mitigation scenario (RCP1.9), modelled extreme heat remains similar to or only a little above the present climate. This provides an opportunity to reduce risks of physical hazards through stringent emissions reductions.

Figure 2.6 (panels 1a and 2a) draws a picture of scenarios in terms of temperature anomalies.[8] It shows that in higher warming scenarios (RCP4.5 and RCP8.5) temperature extremes can exceed the average extremes in the 20-year baseline period by up to roughly 10°C for both cities studied here. The same difference in anomaly may, however, mean different things for both cities. This is due to their different geographical locations and overall climate.

Paris has an oceanic and tropical wet climate. In recent years, the city has been hit by severe heat waves [most notably the deadly heatwave in 2003 (Le Tertre et al., 2006[100])]. An increase in the severity and frequency of those events can undoubtedly lead to high impacts. This is especially the case in the absence of continuous improvements in resilience.

Hyderabad has a dry climate with temperatures already significantly higher than in Paris due to its location. The same anomaly increase, then, could result in levels of temperatures that human and natural systems cannot physiologically endure. This could lead to the crossing of physical adaptation limits or major transformations in human societies and ecosystems (Hanna and Tait, 2015[106]; Andrews et al., 2018[107]; Stillman, 2019[108]). The relationship of geographic location and overall climate has important implications for the understanding of climate risk in these regions and for the risk of losses and damages.

Figure 2.6. Extreme temperature anomalies at different spatial and temporal scales

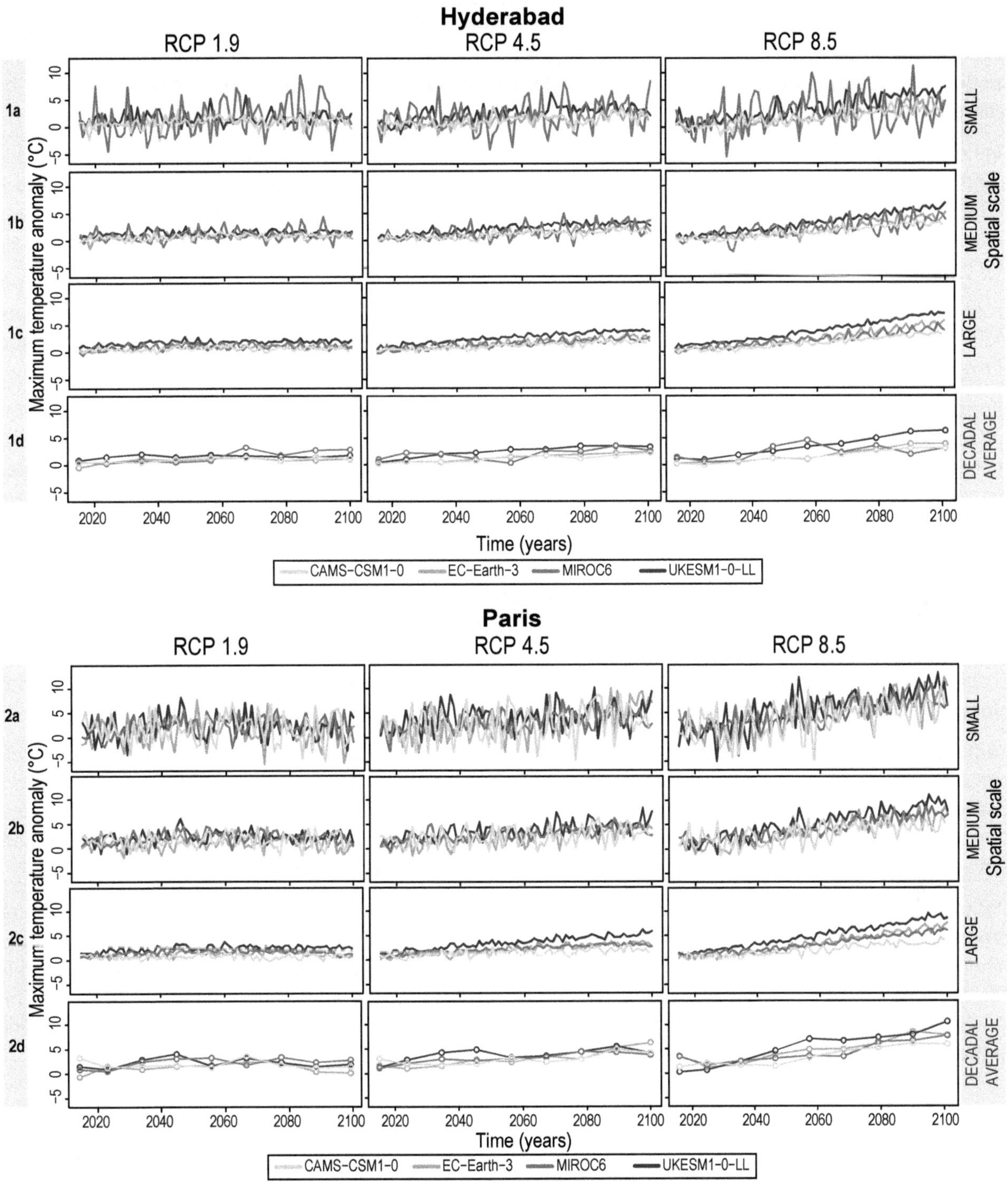

Note: Yearly surface temperature extreme anomalies (increase above baseline) at different spatial resolutions around Paris (France) and Hyderabad (India). Small, medium and large-scale temperatures result from average extreme temperature over a 1x1, 15x15 and 50x50-degree cells (48-49°N 2-3°E, 41-56°N 5°W-10°E and 24-73°N 22°W-27°E for Paris, respectively; 17-18°N 78-79°E, 10-25°N 71-86°E and 7°S-42°N 54-103°E for Hyderabad, respectively). Data were obtained from CMIP6 database (https://esgf-node.llnl.gov/projects/esgf-llnl/) for daily extreme temperature (variable "tasmax"); for scenario combinations RCP1.9 (SSP1), RCP4.5 (SSP2) and RCP8.5 (SSP5); for models CAMS-CSMi-0 (variant r2i1p1f1); EC-Earth-3 (variant r4i1p1f1); MIROC6 (variant r1i1p1f1); and UK-ESM1-0-LL (variant r1i1p1f2). Extreme temperature anomalies were calculated as the difference of yearly maximum at any given year from the long-term average of yearly maxima for the period of 1986-2005. The choice of the baseline period is in line with baseline period used for temperature anomalies presented in AR5. Note that first decadal average point is calculated using only 5 data points (2015-19).

As with temporal scales, confidence in temperature extreme projections is lower at higher spatial resolution. Figure 2.6 shows that for both regions, the variability in projections is lower if spatial scales are larger. Like for temporal scales, climate variability determines the detail of *where* extreme temperatures occur at the small scale (Box 2.4). In this way, each model run is just one potential realisation of this (model-dependent) climate variability. The model can be different from how these heat events will be realised in the real world.

Figure 2.6 also shows that for larger temporal scales (panels 1d and 2d) and spatial scales (panels 1b and c and 2b and c), patterns in temperature are smoothed (i.e. they are flattened and less spikey). There is higher confidence in these smoother patterns to describe average features of the climate system. However, because they result from averaging, the patterns cannot be considered as direct indications of local climate at a certain point in time.

From a policy-making perspective therefore, high-resolution modelling shows the potential for many regions to experience episodes of extreme heat over the next century. However, it cannot predict the detail of exactly when and where they will occur beyond a timescale of weeks (Nissan et al., 2019[91]).

Information at more detailed temporal scales is still valuable for policy making. It informs on broad patterns and the potential for how climate change could unfold locally. As such, it can feed directly into the shaping of policies dealing climate-related risks including physical, behavioural and cultural adaptation to expected changes. Projections of extreme temperature *per se* do not completely determine impact. This is also a function of humidity, duration of heatwave, minimum overnight temperatures, wind speed and so on, plus any adaptation measures (Nissan et al., 2019[91]).

The prospects for improvement of such information are mixed. There is no likelihood of anything other than estimates of statistical risk for longer-term projections (decades to centuries). However, improvements to modelling can improve estimates of that statistical risk. This is especially true for specific geographical locations and quantifying more accurately the risk of extreme events that are rarely observed. This may inform adaptation plans, climate risk assessments, insurance provision and infrastructure planning.

Medium-range initialised climate projections (months to several years) may benefit from large-scale investments in climate model improvements, improving the ability to produce medium-range and more locally informative climate projections. Preliminary results from such initialised climate model runs suggest the potential availability of a small amount of statistical skill in forward prediction on seasonal to interannual and even decadal timescales (Smith et al., 2019[109]; Dunstone et al., 2020[110]).

Statistical skill, however, cannot be directly translated into predictive utility. For example, seasonal forecasts that offer a "40% chance of a hotter than average summer" are of quantitative use only to a small minority of stakeholders. For short-term forecasts (weeks to months), increasing the time scale of accurate weather forecasting by model improvement is of potentially immense benefit (Nissan et al., 2019[91]). This allows rapid measures to be taken in advance of forecasted events by, for example, setting up cooling centres or distributing information and water.

Box 2.4. Climate variability

Climate is defined as long-term average characteristics of weather in a given area over decades (usually 30 years). Climate variability refers to natural variations in the statistics of climate occurring on all timescales. The IPCC notes that "variability may be due to natural internal processes within the climate system (internal variability), or to variations in natural or anthropogenic external forcing (external variability)" (IPCC, 2018[111]). In everyday experience, one winter may be cold and wet and another mild and dry. However, this only represents actual climatic change when the average trend is sustained over many years. This also means, perhaps counter-intuitively, that colder years may occur "randomly" even in a warmer climate. Similarly, extreme rainfall may occur sometimes even if the climatic trend is towards drying.

The most well-known example of natural variability due to internal processes of the climate system is the rapid periodic warming of the eastern Pacific Ocean known as El Niño. El Niño and its "opposite", La Niña, are patterns of changes to temperature, rain and wind patterns in many regions that last for months or years. An example of external natural variability is a major volcanic eruption, like Mount Pinatubo in 1991. This eruption led to the injection of large quantities of sulphur dioxide (SO_2), into the stratosphere, causing a period of cooler than average global temperatures (Council, 2001[112]). In general, external factors are estimated separately and then given to models as an input. Conversely, internal factors are generated dynamically by models themselves. Some factors may be treated in one model as external, and in other models as internal. In either case, they are an additional source of variation between models.

Climate variability is sometimes referred to aleatoric or random uncertainty. This is the actual realisation of the climate, either in model simulations or in nature, which is subject to internal variability and the chaotic nature of atmospheric and oceanic dynamics. Each model will generate a different pattern of internal variability.

The scale of internal variability is relatively consistent and can be compared with observations of real-world variability. Nevertheless, the variability implies that each model run may predict differently how the climate will be realised. This means that even if one had complete knowledge of the physics and statistics of an event, it is still a long way from being able to predict exactly when they will occur.

Variability, then, has important implications for losses and damages. For example, as a result of climate variability, an area that is prone to hurricanes could be hit by no hurricanes in ten years or be hit by three hurricanes in one year. This would have consequences for adaptation policy measures or insurance.

Figure 2.5 and Figure 2.6, panels a and b, compare internal variability in four state-of-the-art climate models. When averaged over larger areas (panel c) and longer timescales (panel d) or over multiple models (coloured lines), natural variability is "averaged out". Instead, the overall trend is visible. Both the trend and the superimposed variability are of high importance for the actual realised climate and weather experienced in any given location.

Different levels of confidence on projections of different types of processes: Temperature vs. rainfall

As discussed in the previous section, there is a high level of agreement and important features that are robust across climate models when projecting temperature at sufficiently large temporal and spatial scales. For example, global warming continues in the 21st century for all of the RCP scenarios. Temperature increase levels are similar during the decade after 2015. Warming rates increase significantly faster for higher concentration scenarios thereafter (IPCC, 2021[1]). In addition, temperature change will not be regionally uniform. There are also robust features in large-scale warming patterns across models. These include larger warming over land than seas; amplified surface warming in Arctic latitudes; and minima in surface warming in the North Atlantic and Southern Ocean [(Collins et al., 2013[75]; IPCC, 2021[1]) and Figure 2.7]. This means that average land surface temperatures and those in the far North, in general, can be expected to increase by significantly more than the global average. Since the world's human population live on land rather than in the ocean, the increase in average land temperatures is particularly important. In addition, almost half of the population lives in coastal areas or in close proximity to the coast, being directly or indirectly dependent on the ocean. Ocean warming can also therefore have devastating consequences, including through not only sea level rise but also, for example, by strongly intensified cyclones and changes to marine ecosystems.

Figure 2.7. Annual mean temperature change (°C) relative to 1850-1900 for different warming worlds

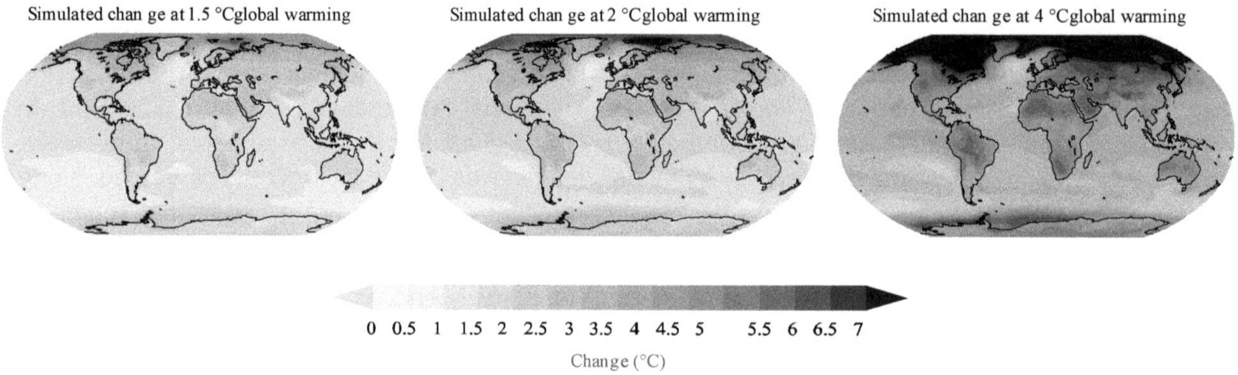

Note: Simulated annual mean temperature change (°C) at global warming levels of 1.5°C, 2°C and 4°C (20-yr mean global surface temperature change relative to 1850–1900), based on CMIP6 multi-model mean change.
Source: (IPCC, 2021[1])

Climate models predict that global precipitation will increase with global mean surface temperature. These predictions are made in accordance with the basic physics of increased moisture held by warmer air. Estimates suggest the magnitude of this effect could be an increase of around 1-3% for every degree of warming (Siler et al., 2018[113]). In temperature projections, climate models show a general agreement about the above broad patterns of regional temperature change. However, there is less confidence on how changes in precipitation will be distributed spatially around the globe. Robust patterns emerge from projections of ensembles of models only in certain regions, with large areas and low latitudes in particular showing a lack of model agreement on even on the direction of precipitation changes (Figure 2.8).

The response of the climate in terms of precipitation involves more complex physical processes than that of surface temperature response to forcing. This includes, for example, the increase of the atmospheric concentration in water vapour with global warming, and cloud formation. Significant differences in cloud physics between models are partly responsible for the variation in climate sensitivity (Zelinka et al., 2020[77]). Other factors such as changes in atmospheric dynamics and water availability must also be considered (Collins et al., 2013[75]).

Due to these multiple interacting drivers, changes are not regionally uniform. What is less well understood is the considerably higher level of disagreement across models and the main reasons for the spread in precipitation projections for different regions of the world (Collins et al., 2013[75]; Shepherd, 2014[114]; Bony et al., 2015[115]; Zappa, Bevacqua and Shepherd, 2021[10]). Figure 2.8 shows where large changes in precipitation as a result of climate change are projected for different regions of the world. The plot distinguishes regions where models agree on the direction of change (full stippling) or those where a large response is projected but there is less agreement about the direction of change (open stippling).

To make use of the available information, multiple possibilities must be considered simultaneously. Different models can project changes in precipitation of different signs. In other words, the same region may be projected to become wetter or drier in a warmer world according to different models (Collins et al., 2013[75]). These discrepancies can be due to a number of reasons, including differences across models or, in some cases, a result of small ensemble size from each model (Rowell, 2011[116]).

Taking averages across models reduces the variation but hides important uncertainties. For precipitation projections of different signs, averaging could lead to a misleading picture of change. Specifically, it could result in values close to zero. This could lead to a false confidence on the absence of change, whereas large changes are actually being projected, only in different directions (Zappa and Shepherd, 2017[117]; Zappa, Bevacqua and Shepherd, 2021[10]). In addition, in a number of regions, changes in precipitation can also vary in sign within a year. For instance, the UK Climate Projections (Lowe et al., 2018[118]) project "hotter, drier summers and warmer, wetter winters". Considering only annual mean values may hide some of these seasonal changes (Collins et al., 2013[75]), which are particularly important for loss and damage and for adaptation planning.

Figure 2.8. Projections of precipitation change based on CMIP6 model

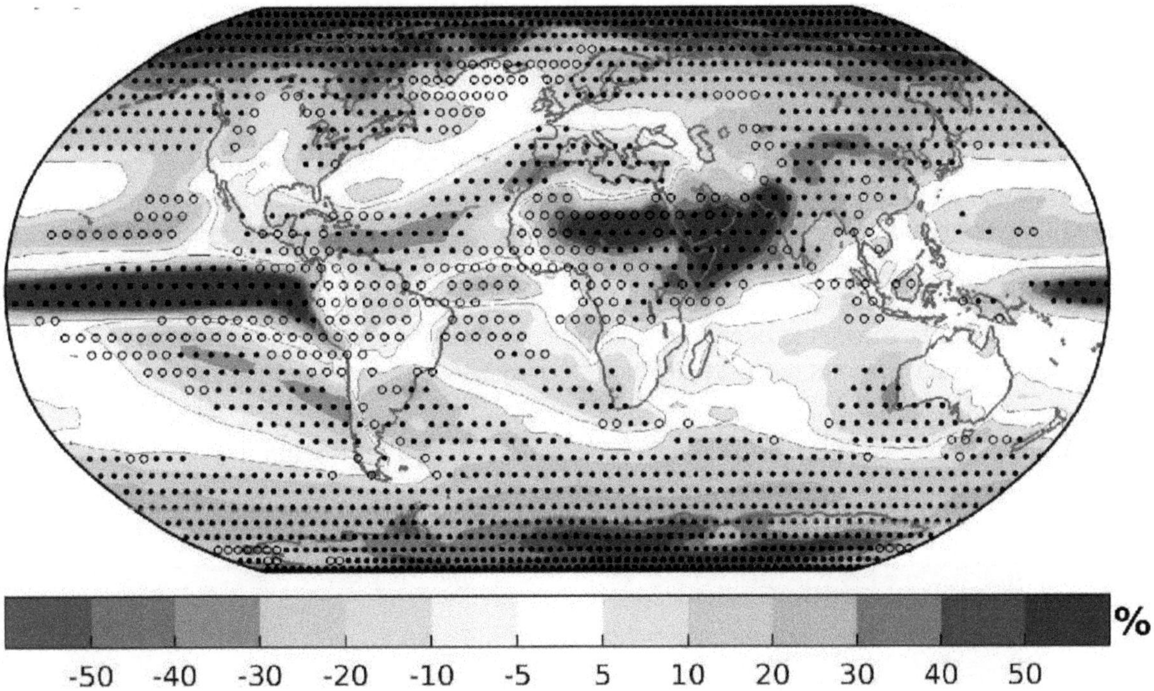

Note: Projected change (percentage) in the annual mean precipitation by 2081-2100 in the SSP5-8.5 scenario as portrayed. Projected changes are quantified as the mean of the signal-to-noise of individual model responses (noting that "signal" refers to the mean response to climate change whereas "noise" refers to the unforced internal variability), rather than the signal-to-noise of the mean response. This aims to avoid the compensation arising from discordant individual model responses on the multi-model mean. Projected changes based on CMIP6 are shown as full stippling to indicate a robust response (≥90% of models agree on the direction of precipitation change). Conversely, the open stippling indicates a plausibly large response in a non-robust projection, that is, in either direction of precipitation change.
Source: (Zappa, Bevacqua and Shepherd, 2021[10]).

Comparing temperature and rainfall projections in GCMs is useful for policy makers and stakeholders. It helps illustrate the implications of using scientific information to support decision making in terms of quantitative regional and local climate predictions. While projections are available, they are subject to different types and considerable amounts of uncertainties. Efforts have been made in trying to unpack and better understand these uncertainties for temperature and precipitation (Hawkins and Sutton, 2009[119]; Hawkins and Sutton, 2010[120]):

- Uncertainty in future emissions and therefore future radiative forcing, due to uncertainty over decisions affecting the future such as socio-economic and political choices (as discussed in Section 2.2.3).
- Randomness in internal variability of the climate system, or realisation uncertainty, which is the natural variability of the climate system. This can arise even in the absence of changes to radiative forcing. Such variability is thought to be largely independent from future anthropogenic emissions but is superimposed onto the underlying anthropogenic trend (Box 2.4). Initialisation of models to present conditions may render the first months to years of internal variability marginally predictable.
- Disagreement between models: as seen in Figure 2.5 and Figure 2.6, individual climate models will model somewhat different changes for the same radiative forcing because of how they treat the physical features of the climate system differently.
- Discrepancy between models and real world: the set of climate models available share common assumptions and biases. This means the real outcome may not be perfectly represented by any of the models. It does not mean the models are worthless, only that model-derived information needs to be treated with care and be consistent with other evidence.

For both temperature and precipitation projections, the relative importance of the first three of the above sources of uncertainties in climate change projections varies significantly with region, time horizon of predictions and the temporal scale over which projections are being averaged (Hawkins and Sutton, 2009[119]; Hawkins and Sutton, 2010[120]).

Interestingly, for the two climate variables, the relative importance of these uncertainties over time varies in different ways. Figure 2.9 shows climate internal variability and model uncertainties are the dominant sources of uncertainties of temperature and precipitation for roughly two decades' lead time of projections. Thereafter, scenario uncertainty plays a dominant role in projections of temperature. Conversely, for precipitation, model uncertainty remains the main source of uncertainty. Although these plots show changing fractional contributions to uncertainty, the absolute magnitude of all uncertainties increases with lead time. The analysis does not measure any discrepancy between models and real world.

Figure 2.9. Different types of uncertainties in global mean temperature and precipitation projections

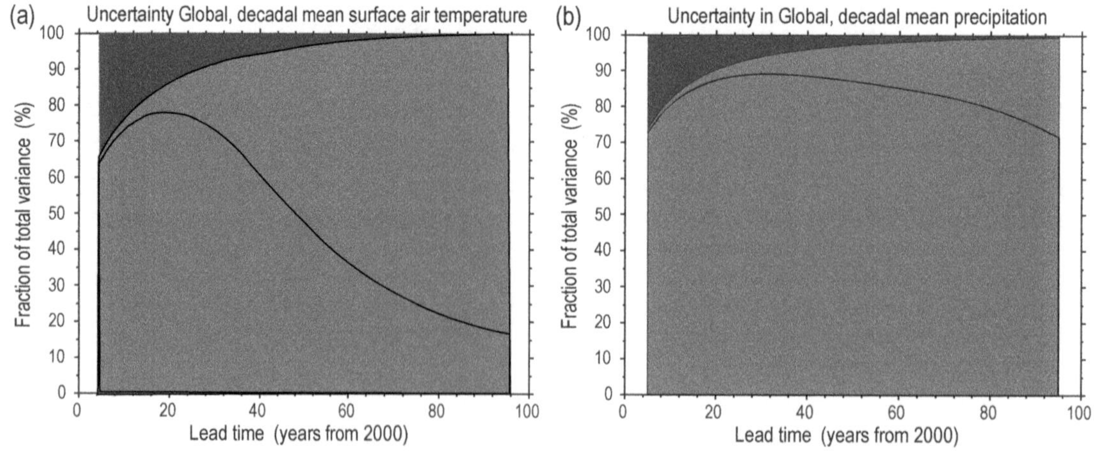

Note: Fraction of total variance in decadal mean projections explained by internal variability (brown), model uncertainty (blue) and scenario uncertainty (green), for global mean surface air temperature (a) and precipitation (b)

Source: (Hawkins and Sutton, 2009[119]; Hawkins and Sutton, 2010[120]).

The relative importance in the sources of uncertainties – more so than their exact quantification – is relevant for how climate change projections can best inform decision making. If mostly influenced by climate internal variability, climate projections over the next two decades need to be considered carefully. Impacts will be exacerbated by forcing resulting from emissions already in the system. However, how impacts will be realised still depends strongly on highly complex chaotic dynamics of the climate system that are difficult, if not impossible, to predict (Box 2.4).

The unexpected nature of recent climatic events, such as extreme rainfall in the People's Republic of China and Germany, and extreme heat in Canada, underlines this unpredictability and the high importance of the variability superimposed on the trend. Short-term projected regional changes are therefore useful to provide a range of potential changes that might affect communities and ecosystems. The exact date and extent of changes or of extreme events cannot, however, be derived from these models.

State-of-the-art initialised climate models give only low (albeit statistically significant) levels of skill. They will be of interest mainly to highly quantitative, portfolio-averaged stakeholders such as large insurance companies. However, they will not likely be useful for individual adaptation decisions. To respond to these impacts, a focus on the resilience and adaptability of human and natural systems to possible changes and events, rather than on seeking to predict in detail, would better serve policy measures for losses and damages.

Over longer time horizons (about four decades), the main source of uncertainty in global and regional projections of temperatures lies in the emissions or concentration scenarios assumed. In considering these potential changes, policy makers could usefully consider the full plausible range of changes, including all evidence and not solely derived from numerical models. This, in turn, would permit an understanding of the minimum and maximum amount of change the system may have to adapt to.

The bounding scenarios, reflecting the decision makers' tolerance for risk, can inform the time horizon from and over which the decision and policy measure need to be operational (Kotamarthi et al., 2016[121]). A city planner may treat emissions scenarios as fully external to her operational boundaries. Conversely, an international climate policy negotiator may treat them as a yet-to-be-determined choice.

For precipitation in many regions, disagreement between models remains the main source of uncertainty of regional and global change projections, with implications for policy making. Future changes in the frequency and intensity of drought and flood events are, however, critical to the resilience of many communities and ecosystems. Planning for a drought or for a flood entail different policy measures. As a result, projections remain difficult for regions where different models project different types of change altogether. It is important to note that for some regions such as the UK (Lowe et al., 2018[118]) both increased drought and increased flooding may be projected at different times of the year and seasons. In this case, measures need to tackle both types of hazards.

GCMs are thus indispensable tools for the understanding of the climate change phenomenon. However, while many qualitative results are highly robust and confident, many regional projections of detailed change are inherently uncertain in differing ways. The exploration and understanding of the remaining uncertainty is therefore in itself a highly policy-relevant output of modern climate science. Certainly, modellers have deep but incomplete understanding of the complex climate system. Furthermore, those models are limited by the extent of that knowledge. The uncertainty in future choices of societies and governments, which are actually the main driver of climate risk, is considerably more important for policy makers.

In light of this latter type of uncertainty, GCMs can be highly effective tools. They can strengthen collective understanding of potential different futures and of how decisions today can influence the risk of climate change tomorrow. Greater and more co-ordinated investment in climate modelling capability could help tackle these uncertainties directly. In so doing, they could improve the relevance of scientific programmes

(Palmer and Stevens, 2019[122]). The presumption that simply increasing computational effort will necessarily improve the reliability of modelling output is, however, disputed (Stainforth and Calel, 2020[123]). Other approaches based on narratives (Dessai et al., 2018[124]) and storylines (Shepherd et al., 2018[125]), which treat uncertainty in less rigid frameworks, are also active research areas with direct application to adaptation planning (Bhave et al., 2018[126])where model-based methods are subject to high levels of uncertainty.

2.3. Uncertainties relating to socio-economic exposure and vulnerability

The hazard component of risk is associated with uncertainties around the sensitivity of climate to GHG emissions (see Section 2.2). However, other components of risk – exposure and vulnerability[9] – are influenced by socio-economic, institutional, political and cultural characteristics. Therefore, they are associated with the uncertainty underlying these characteristics. As opposed to physical hazards, socio-economic processes do not obey the laws of physics because they are a result of human choices. This makes it easier to influence these processes through policy and economy. However, it also makes it immensely more difficult to project them, compared to hazards.

While uncertainties in the physical climate and those pertaining to socio-economic systems are usually discussed separately, they interact in complex ways to determine risks of losses and damages. A better understanding is essential of the different levels and types of uncertainties underlying the vulnerability and exposure components of climate risk. This can inform policy makers' decisions on how to manage those risks and take the right action. This section explores five broad types of uncertainties related to socio-economic vulnerability and exposure. It also introduces methods to characterise and possibly alleviate these uncertainties, while exploring implications for policy makers.

Different sources of uncertainties limit the understanding of how climate change will unfold. This complicates the assessment of the appropriate mitigation and adaptation actions to address it (Congressional Budget Office, 2005[127]; Gillingham et al., 2015[128]). Policy makers inevitably face uncertainties in making decisions. It is key to evaluate policies in light of that uncertainty. One can alleviate, but never eliminate uncertainties; the future, especially of socio-economic outcomes, will always be uncertain to an extent. The far future is even more uncertain. Examination of uncertainties, however, can still be productive. Better characterising – and potentially even decreasing – uncertainties informs on the potential outcomes of a policy action. More or better quality of information relating to uncertainties enables policies to be less risky and more effective.[10] In addition, understanding uncertainties serves as a communication tool for the political process. Once uncertainties are characterised, there is common ground for policy disputes on how to act in light of them. Without characterisation, disputes are less likely to be transparent and, as a consequence, less likely to be fruitful.

There are potentially different methodologies to address different types of socio-economic uncertainties. Table 2.3 summarises the types of uncertainties included in this section with ways to address them and implications for policies. The characterisation of different types of uncertainties requires different methods and provides different types of information, ranging from quantitative to qualitative. Box 2.5 provides a selective overview of the estimated losses and damages from climate change with diverse range of methodologies, which also illustrates the impact of uncertainty on projected losses and damages. It is key to consider and meaningfully combine these different information types and methods without imposing a hierarchy. For example, qualitative information should not be secondary to quantitative information.

Table 2.3. Uncertainties and their methodological and policy implications

Source of uncertainty	Methods to address it	Policy implications
Quantitative data	Statistical, econometrical approaches	Update surveys with climate vulnerability and exposure questions. Use innovative data sources to complement traditional measures. Where there is lack of knowledge, use proxy variables, interpolation or statistical estimation. Use the estimated uncertainty in policy making process.
Qualitative data	Place-based approaches	Complement quantitative analyses with qualitative ones to improve the design, targeting and implementation of policies.
Projections of economic damages	Computational models, such as integrated assessment models (IAMs), agent-based models, and reweight and resample techniques	IAMs are immensely useful to compare the costs of different policies in the long run, but they do not examine uncertainty in detail. Complementing IAM analyses with models that explicitly assess the uncertainty of projections would help broaden policy making.
Socio-economic role of nature	Mix of methods: econometrics, place-based approaches, computational models	The estimated costs of climate change are sensitive to the non-market value of nature and the role of nature in production. Each of these should be carefully considered in welfare and in the economy when designing policies. High uncertainty warrants precautionary approaches.
Other	Theoretical reflection, place-based approaches	Policies should encourage triggering socio-economic tipping points, as they are needed for a long-term transformation to increase resilience. Social discount rates need to reflect the local values and cultures. Uncertain settings and sufficiently high damages imply low social discount rates.

Note: The table summarises subsections 2.3.1, 2.3.2 and 2.3.3.

Box 2.5. Illustration of the effect of methodological choice through selected estimates

As an indication of the associated uncertainties, Table 2.4 shows a very selective overview of the impacts of climate change estimated in the literature. These pieces all look at different aspects of climate change, examining different hazards, sectors, regions or outcomes, and accordingly approaching the question with different methods and assumptions. As such, it is impossible to aggregate or average these numbers even if they aim to estimate similar outcomes. For example, both OECD (2015[129]) and Burke, Hsiang and Miguel (2015[130]) aim to look at the economic effects of climate change. However, Burke et al. (2015[130]) takes a top-down approach using econometric modelling, and examining how temperature changes are associated with GDP, and based on that association how changing temperatures would impact GDP. OECD (2015[129]), on the other hand, uses a computable general equilibrium model, which allows the inclusion of multiple types of hazards, and for a detailed examination of the mechanisms through which the impacts take place (e.g. decreasing labour productivity). However, both approaches have shortcomings, for example, they do not include the effects of possible droughts, nor indirect impacts through the effect of climate on ecosystem services. Neither aimed at providing estimates of the impacts associated with crossing climate tipping points.

Since the methods covered by the literature are different, and differ considerably, e.g. which hazard they examine or how do they take into account adaptation, they cannot be considered equivalent, cannot be added and will overlap to an extent. Note that all of the estimates are uncertain and incomplete, and can be taken only as an indicative estimate of the lower boundary of impacts. They show considerable range of estimated impacts, which illustrates the extent of physical and socio-economic uncertainty. Taken together, they point to sizeable climate impacts, motivating ambitious climate action.

Table 2.4. Selection of projected losses and damage estimates

Source	Method	Hazard	Area of focus	Region	Estimate
Jafino et al. **(2020[131])**	Resampling and reweighing model	Temperature increase and extreme events	Levels of poverty	Global	In the range of 30 and 130 million additional people in extreme poverty until 2030
				Sub-Saharan Africa	In the range 10 and 50 million additional people in extreme poverty until 2030
				South Asia	In the range of 10 and 60 million people in extreme poverty until 2030
OECD **(2015[129])**	CGE modelling	Temperature rise, sea-level rise, cyclones and extreme temperatures	Economic effects	Global	Around 1.5% of GDP until 2050 (1-3%)
				Sub-Saharan Africa	Around 3% of GDP until 2050
				South and South-East Asia	Around 2.5% of GDP by 2050
Halegatte, Rentschler and Rozenberg **(2019[132])**	Econometric and modelling	Extreme weather events	Infrastructure damage	Selected developing countries in Africa, Asia and South-America	Around USD 1 trillion between 2020 and 2030

Burke, Hsiang and Miguel **(2015[130])**	Econometric	Temperature increase	Economic effects	Global	23% of GDP per capita until 2100, 10% until 2050
				Sub-Saharan Africa	Around 30% of GDP per capita until 2050, around 90% until 2100
				South-East Asia	Around 30% of GDP per capita by 2050, around 90% until 2100
Bastien-Olvera and Moore **(2020[133])**	IAM	Temperature increase	Non-economic damages to ecosystems	Global	Around USD 190 trillion of non-economic damages to ecosystems until 2050
Gasparrini et al **(2017[134])**	Statistics and computational projections	Extreme temperatures through heat-related mortality	Mortality	Selected areas of Europe, Asia, Oceania, Americas	Up to 10-15% increase in annual heat related mortality
WHO **(2014[135])**	Climate-health models	Temperature rise, variable rainfall patterns and extreme temperatures, affecting malnutrition, heat stress, diarrhoea and malaria	Healthcare costs	Global	USD 2-4 billion increase of annual healthcare costs between 2030 and 2050
			Mortality through malnutrition, heat stress, diarrhoea and malaria	Global	250,000 excess deaths per year between 2030 and 2050
Hayes et al **(2018[136])**	Literature review	Extreme events	Mental health	Global	Large effects on mental health, disproportionately affecting the most marginalised groups
Tschakert et al **(2019[137])**	Systematic case analysis	Climate change	Non-economic losses and damages	Global	Intangible losses and at-risk sentiments are pervasive across the world

Note: Percentages refer to the level of the shown year, i.e. a 90% decrease means in 2050 means that, if without climate change there the value would be 100 in 2050, with climate change it is purported to be 10 instead.
Source: (Bastien-Olvera and Moore, 2020[133]), (Burke, Hsiang and Miguel, 2015[130]), (Gasparrini et al., 2017[134]), (Hallegatte et al., 2015[138]), (Hallegatte, Rentschler and Rozenberg, 2019[132]), (Hayes et al., 2018[136]), (Jafino et al., 2020[131]), (OECD, 2015[129]) (Tschakert et al., 2019[137]), (WHO, 2014[135]) and author calculations.

2.3.1. Uncertainties related to the availability of socio-economic data

Data are a key component of the policy-making process. For example, data can be used to gauge past regularities and link the past with the future, providing a vantage point for projections (Haug et al., 2009[139]; Riahi et al., 2017[8]). Relevant data for exposure and vulnerability can be quantitative (unemployment rate or gross domestic product [GDP] growth) or qualitative (data from interviews or surveys and narratives). In addition, innovative data sources, such as satellite data or text-based data, can also advance knowledge on exposure and vulnerability. Where direct measurement is impossible, proxy variables, interpolation or statistical estimation can be used.

This subsection explores these different types of data. It looks at how they can contribute to better understanding of exposure and vulnerabilities. It also examines where remaining gaps and lack of information contribute to uncertainties.

Quantitative data

One source of uncertainty in understanding present and future vulnerability and exposure relates to availability of quantitative information. Specifically, the extent and quality of data on exposure or vulnerabilities are below average in regions where some types of hazards are projected to be harshest (IPCC, 2018[97]).[11] For example, there are no official subnational population data available in some of the least developed countries, which could be an indicator of exposure of lives and livelihoods (World Bank, 2021[140]). Similarly, up-to-date detailed vulnerability data – for example, on hospital capacities or income –are available only in developed countries (WHO, 2021[141]). Any data about vulnerabilities or exposure cannot be fully complete. As explained in Chapter 1, vulnerability and exposure are multifaceted concepts and may be both direct and indirect; it is impossible to be sure to have captured all of the rapidly evolving aspects.

Even when using multiple sources of data, physical, mental and cultural vulnerabilities cannot be fully captured because of their varied, ever-changing – and sometimes subjective – nature. Still, in managing climate risks, policy makers must strive to obtain as much information to make robust decisions. This can put climate policies on firmer ground, making climate policies better targeted, more effective and more efficient, which leads to improved socio-economic outcomes. Traditional data sources, such as surveys and administrative data, could be used to inform levels of exposures and vulnerabilities (Brouwer et al., 2007[142]; Hallegatte and Rozenberg, 2017[143]). A range of data routinely collected by governments can inform on vulnerability and exposure (Deschênes, Greenstone and Guryan, 2009[144]) and on policies aiming at reducing vulnerabilities and exposure. For example, tax records show the size and incomes of households, which indicate exposure of lives and livelihoods in a given area. Household surveys usually collect information on home ownership, for example, which provide information on vulnerability (Taupo, Cuffe and Noy, 2018[145]).

Information from surveys, however, is not comprehensive and there is room for improvement. For example, surveys can be complemented with direct questions on awareness of climate exposures and vulnerabilities of firms and households. One can formulate a range of specific questions for a survey that address vulnerability and exposure. However, the specificity and complexity of questions must be balanced with the potential for reaching the largest share of the population possible. Indeed, survey questions should be as simple as possible to discourage respondents from opting out (Blair, Czaja and Blair, 2014[146]). Household surveys are considered to be one of the great innovations of social science research in the past century, upon which many policies were and are based. However, they also show a decline in quality recently. Non-response rates, for example, have increased (Meyer, Mok and Sullivan, 2015[147]; Brown et al., 2014[148]).

Composite indices are a way to use traditional data in a more comprehensive way (Nardo et al., 2005[149]). These indices are built from components (usually relying on traditional data). Thus, they can be comprehensive and provide a useful ranking for the most or least resilient regions or countries. For instance, Climate Risk Index, developed by Germanwatch, uses a reinsurance data on past extreme events. This is useful to measure exposure and vulnerability (particularly to extreme events) (Eckstein, Künzel and Schäfer, 2021[150]). Different indices, such as the ND-GAIN index or The Hague Centre for Strategic Studies' Climate Vulnerability Index, include climate projections or potential readiness for various climate futures (Usanov and Gehem, 2014[151]; Chen et al., 2015[152]).

Index numbers tend to rely on ad hoc assumptions, such as what elements to include or the weighting of those elements. This leads to difficulty in interpretation. For example, it is not always clear what 10% difference between two countries means. For comparisons, all countries or regions should face the same weighing scheme for the index. In reality, different exposures and vulnerabilities might be important for different regions. Sea-level rise, for example, will be important for Small Island Developing States but less so for landlocked developed countries. Thus, index numbers are useful to provide a comprehensive snapshot and ranking but should be interpreted with caution.

Innovative data sources, such as satellite images, can complement traditional data. These sources often provide an option where traditional data are lacking or insufficient, enabling assessment of alternative measures of socio-economic exposure and vulnerabilities. For example, satellite data can provide subnational estimates of population and assets that are exposed. They can also inform on the level of vulnerabilities. For example, they can infer the area of affected crops and physical vulnerability of assets from the hues and shades of satellite images (Brown, de Beurs and Marshall, 2012[153]; Ceola, Laio and Montanari, 2014[154]). The World Bank also uses satellite images in cases where no adequate data are available about subpopulation from national statistical offices (World Bank, 2021[140]). Moreover, satellite data are usually freely available on the Internet (Turner, 2013[155]; LaJeunesse Connette et al., 2016[156]). These types of data enable a wide-ranging coverage of certain climate risks. However, again, they cannot be comprehensive, simply because exposure and vulnerability are multifaceted concepts.

Where direct data on vulnerability are unavailable, it can be estimated indirectly. Climate impact (risk) has three components: hazard, exposure and vulnerability (see Chapter 1). If the hazard is given, the remaining risk will describe the combination of exposure and vulnerability. In 2017, for example, Hurricane Maria caused estimated economic damage valued at more than 200% of the annual GDP in Dominica (Government of the Commonwealth of Dominica, 2017[157]). Thus, exposure and vulnerability of GDP to this hazard was quite large.

If exposure is also given, it is known the whole island was exposed to this hazard. If all of Dominica is exposed to a hazard like Hurricane Maria, for example, the economic costs exceed 200% of the GDP (IFRC, 2017[158]). This would be an indirect estimate of vulnerability for a given hazard and exposure. It can also work, the other way around: if there is information on vulnerability, it is possible to provide an indirect estimate of exposure.

A regression framework is a systematic way to make indirect assessment. In the case of Dominica, the framework would need data about the impact and exposure of similar events (e.g. Hurricanes David, Lenny and Erika). The multitude of data enables statistical abstraction from hazards, exposures and other relevant variables (e.g. macroeconomic conditions) to estimate vulnerability. For example, using a regression framework, the average hurricane strike is estimated to decrease the economic growth rate by at least 0.83 percentage points in Central America and the Caribbean (Strobl, 2012[159]). As another example, the annual cost of the Australian heatwaves during the end of 2013 and beginning 2014, has been estimated at USD 650 per person (Zander et al., 2015[44]); this estimates vulnerability of labour income to heatwaves. The hazards are given (the heatwave season of 2013/14); population exposure is abstracted away by examining the income *per person*.

As an advantage of this statistical approach, the only required variables are an impact variable (such as GDP or mortality), the hazards, and either exposures or vulnerabilities. In addition, statistical estimation of exposure of vulnerability is likely to be more comprehensive than using a direct measure. This is because it can capture all elements related to the impact variable but unrelated to hazards and exposures or vulnerabilities.

The approach also has disadvantages. First, the impact variable limits the indirect estimate. Impact on GDP, for example, will not capture non-economic vulnerabilities. The estimated impact of past climates on socio-economic outcomes is subject to statistical imprecision and sensitivity of results to assumptions (Newell, Prest and Sexton, 2021[160]). These statistical uncertainties can be explicitly assessed by statistical and econometric approaches. Knowledge on statistical uncertainties is often not used. Decision makers and academics tend to focus on the central results, even though statistical uncertainties carry important information for policy (Romer, 2020[161]). Finally, by nature, indirect estimate provides information on an aggregate level, with potentially low spatial and temporal resolutions than an individual data source. This makes its use difficult to assess local vulnerabilities and thus to tailor policies to local needs.

Other approaches are possible when direct measurement of vulnerability or exposure is impossible on the desired spatial or temporal scales. Interpolation techniques, for example, could support decision making. These techniques take exposure or vulnerability data on a more spatially or temporally aggregated scale, estimating exposure and vulnerability on finer scales. Information on finer scale could be important to accommodate local needs in policy making. For example, Uddin et al (2019[162]) create a risk map of the coastal region of Bangladesh on a fine spatial scale using interpolation. This could provide a roadmap for policies tackling flood risks. In Europe, similar methodology is used to monitor exposure to polluted air (EEA, 2008[163]). For policy makers, these methods help fine-tune policies to localities. However, interpolation makes more data based on existing sources. As such, it requires assumptions, which should be carefully assessed.

In other cases, a proxy variable may be preferable. This would not measure the variable of interest but rather a phenomenon that moves together (correlates) with the variable of interest. In the case of GDP, nightlight images from satellites were used to provide an approximation of subnational GDP levels in East Africa (Henderson, Storeygard and Weil, 2012[164]). Nightlight images were also used to estimate worldwide exposure to floods (Ceola, Laio and Montanari, 2014[154]) or to look at the short-term economic impacts of extreme weather events (Ishizawa, Miranda and Strobl, 2017[165]).

The frequency of certain words or phrases is another possible proxy variable to approximate vulnerabilities or exposure. Such words are found in official documents, journal articles, newspaper pieces, social media and other written communication. Here, the researcher compiling the data would search for expressions that indicate vulnerability or exposure in newspapers or Internet articles. How frequently are they mentioned at different times and places? In what contexts are they mentioned? What is their emotional connotation? Regions with higher climate vulnerability will have more discussion on the Internet and in newspapers about those issues (Archibald and Butt, 2018[166]; Bromley-Trujillo and Poe, 2020[167]).

The challenges posed by data availability are more pronounced in developing countries where a larger share of the economy tends to be informal. Generally, central and local governments have fewer resources and less capacity to conduct assessments. India, one of the countries most affected by extreme events, is projected to incur one of the highest costs from climate change (Kreft, Eckstein and Melchior, 2016[168]) and face specific challenges. Box 2.6 discusses these challenges, touching on migrant workers, informal economy, non-economic and indirect losses, and damages.

Box 2.6. Challenges of estimating losses and damages in India

Abundant evidence reveals that India has frequently experienced both extreme events and slow-onset processes induced by climate change. Such events affect lives and livelihoods, infrastructure, ecosystems, biodiversity and cultural heritage, among others (Government of India, 2011[169]). In fact, India is ranked among the ten worst countries affected by natural disasters. Three-fourths of its states and union territories are prone to disasters such as cyclonic storms, floods and droughts (Government of India, 2011[169]). Recently, both national and state governments have drafted climate change and disaster mitigation plans such as the National Action Plan on Climate Change and the State Action Plan on Climate Change. Disaster management plans have also been prepared at the district level. Risk-hazard mapping is one of the goals of the Prime Minister's ten-point agenda for disaster risk reduction.

Migrant workers

Both climatic and non-climatic factors are responsible for rural-urban migration in India (Viswanathan and Kavi Kumar, 2015[170]). Migrant workers, including permanent and seasonal ones, are living in highly susceptible regions and exposed to climatic change. The informal sector employs a large proportion of migrants. These informal workers do not have voting rights in the city since their native village is listed on their identity cards, i.e., Voter card, Aadhaar card, driver's' licence, bank passbook, etc. Hence, they are denied relief and compensation that follows an extreme event, such as the 2015 Chennai flood [see (Patankar, 2019[171])]. Thus, losses and damages incurred by migrant workers are not included in loss and damage assessments. Not surprisingly, reverse migration is rampant following an extreme event. Such a reverse flow creates a shortage of labour in urban areas and delays recovery for the business units in the city. For example, around 83% of textile owners in Surat reported that labour shortage was a major issue during the recovery period (Bahinipati et al., 2017[172]).

Informal economy

Estimating losses and damages for the informal sector is also challenging. Most micro, small and medium-sized enterprises operate informally in India and absorb a large number of migrant workers. The informality implies that pre-disaster information related to stock and flow of capital assets, employment or supply chain is not available for a particular location hit by an extreme event. In addition, the workers are unlikely to be covered insurance. Thus, insurance claims cannot be used as a proxy for losses and damages. For instance, according to Patankar (2019[171]), around 93% of business units in Mumbai do not have insurance coverage for floods. Meanwhile, Bahinipati et al. (2017[172]) find that only one-fourth of total losses and damages were covered through insurance and government supported compensation for textile units in Surat. The flood that occurred in Chennai during 2015 led to economic losses and damages to smaller firms in the ballpark of INR 8.4 billion per week (KPMG, 2016[173]). Further, a study found that around 14 000 micro industries and business units were badly affected by flooding in Uttarakhand in 2013. This led to an estimated USD 631 million (Singh, 2018[174]) in loss and damages.

Non-economic losses and damages

In the case of non-economic losses and damages, the major challenges are conceptualising, accounting for and, if possible, monetising them (IPCC, 2012[175]; Serdeczny, Waters and Chan, 2016[176]). Since the stock of non-economic goods is not recorded, it is difficult to attribute *ex post* non-economic losses and damages from a natural disaster perspective. Methodologically, it is a challenge to estimate non-economic losses and damages in monetary terms, i.e. to price non-economic goods. Since these goods are not traded on the market, stated preference methods such as contingent valuation and choice modelling could be adopted to estimate losses and damages. Banihipati (2020[177]) opted for contingent valuation to estimate non-economic losses and damages in the case of drought-affected households in western India. Surprisingly, it observed that households consider immediate economic losses and damages to be more important. Another challenge is attributing non-economic losses and damages to climatic or non-climatic causes. Some of these losses, such as school dropout rates, migration, loss of identity and psychosocial stress, are generic in nature. Most often, they are not perceived by an affected entity as an effect of climatic events. For instance, scarcity of water in the cities is perceived to be due to poor land-use practices, population increase and environmental degradation rather than climatic shocks (Singh et al., 2021[178]). Similarly, households in the drought-affected regions of western India are not able to relate seasonal migration, school dropout rates to the occurrence of droughts and instead view it as a regular outcome of the economic process (Banihipati, 2020[177]). Often, non-economic losses and damages can be better described by qualitative methods (explored in the next subsection).

Indirect losses and damages

There is also a challenge to estimate losses and damages associated with indirect impact or spill over effects (e.g. a drought causing crop damage that impacts food prices, and hence consumption expenditure and nutrition). To date, relatively few studies have estimated indirect losses and damages (Ranger et al., 2010[179]). Thus, such estimates are often missing in disaster assessment reports. Yet such losses can be sizeable. During the 2006 floods in Surat, the mean losses and damages for textile units were around INR 1.98 million as per 2013 prices – the direct effects were INR 0.98 million, and the indirect effects were INR 1 million (Bahinipati et al., 2017[172]).

Qualitative data

Some key aspects of losses and damages cannot be quantified, such as sense of place, identity or security (Barnett et al., 2016[6]). Such aspects require knowledge of local socio-economic or cultural contexts and qualitative approaches to assess them, with researchers often conducting fieldwork in the affected area. Here, the data are typically collected through in-depth interviews, surveys or focus group discussions. Data emerging from such assessments are often in the form of narratives or stories. They reveal aspects of the lives that people consider to be the most important. These are as relevant for climate policy making as quantitative data (Tschakert et al., 2019[137]).

The broad variety of qualitative methods can draw out the complexities of a given policy situation, which quantitative analyses hardly achieve with certainty. In providing objective data, quantitative analyses may provide a false sense of confidence and objectivity since morality numbers and the like are associated with high levels of uncertainty (see the first subsection of 2.3.1). Qualitative data are inherently different, answering equally important questions regarding losses and damages. Thus, both quantitative and qualitative data should be considered. Indeed, the two approaches should be integrated to avoid imposing a hierarchy between methods.

Generally, qualitative data can add depth and explanation to what can be observed quantitatively, thereby decreasing uncertainty related to interpretation. For example, two different studies found a positive quantitative association between precipitation and conflicts (Witsenburg and Adano, 2009[180]; De Juan, 2015[181]). However, their interpretation of this positive association is different. One study conducts interviews with locals and concludes that raids are easier to carry out in wet weather (Witsenburg and Adano, 2009[180]). The other study argues that rains provide valuable resource (water) during droughts, thus increasing competition and conflict (De Juan, 2015[181]). While the quantitative results are similar, the qualitative analysis shows that policy implications are completely different.

Narratives and other qualitative information can also influence decision makers, sometimes more so than only numbers or figures. For example, images of a marine biologist removing a plastic straw from a sea turtle's nostril inspired plastic straw bans around the world (Houck, 2018[182]). In the climate arena, the picture of a starving polar bear commanded more attention and sparked a larger interest than scientific studies on the same topic published in the same year (Rode et al., 2015[183]; Whiteman et al., 2015[184]).

However, any policy judgement will be inherently based on a comparison of implicit sets of values, as implementing a policy means not implementing another one with different effects. Therefore, decision makers and other stakeholders may prefer a vantage point that enables them to compare these trade-offs in policies. Often, this takes the form of figures or indices to justify the choice of one policy over another and motivate policy action.

Full quantification of the effects of climate change in monetary terms is impossible. This is due both to lack of sufficient knowledge but also the context-specific or idiosyncratic nature of some values (Tschakert et al., 2017[185]). Some social effects can be quantified but in different ways than economic damages. For example, lives lost and psychological scales of well-being [e.g. Grief Intensity Scale, PG-13 (Prigerson and Maciejewski, 2006[186])] present qualitative information in a comparable way. By considering these qualitative aspects, policy makers could have a fuller picture of the impacts of climate change and thus design more effective policies.

2.3.2. Uncertainty related to projections

Modelling future economic damages of climate change and uncertainties

How carbon emissions translate to damages has been a key question for climate economics for decades. It is a complex problem, in part, because there are different types and intensities of climate change hazards, ranging from heat waves, sea-level rise to the crossing of a climate tipping point (see Chapter 3). Additionally, the potential of damages from climate change spans different sectors of the economy. It also cascades over time, and from local to regional and global levels. Potentially, it also cascades from global to the local level; global food prices will have a local impact on availability (see Section 3.3).

Damage estimates will inevitably be uncertain, but they are still useful. The exercise allows direct comparison of the costs of not implementing climate policies – i.e. costs incurring from damages – with the costs of implementing policies that will reduce damage costs. Inquiries of this type have contributed to the wealthy body of literature on cost-benefit analysis of mitigation scenarios. For decades, these have been used to stimulate (or argue against) stringent action on climate change. There are different types of modelling tools and approaches that are used to assess this question. This subsection will explore some of these, highlighting their strengths and limitations.

IAMs are the most widely used type of model for estimating damages from climate change[12] (Wei, Mi and Huang, 2015[187]). IAMs provide a representation of economic, energy, land and climate systems. In so doing, they can help illustrate and analyse the interdependencies and trade-offs between choices made in these systems. The DICE and PAGE models are among the most influential IAMs used for estimating damages costs from climate change (Nordhaus, 1992[188]) (Stern, 2006[189]) . These models allow cost estimates for avoiding climate change for different levels of temperature increase, providing a cost-benefit analysis of mitigation scenarios. Given assumptions on GDP growth, population growth policies and technology, among other factors, IAMs inform researchers and policy makers about economic and environmental outcomes, as well as energy pathways and land use. This analysis is based on simplified firm and household decisions.

The climate module of an IAM describes climate impacts, which will be translated into economic damages through a damage function. A damage function in an IAM links carbon emissions and economic damages. It aims to capture all impacts of the carbon emission in a single function.

Over the years, formulations of damage functions have improved, which has contributed to more accurate descriptions and potentially better damage estimates. In early IAMs, damage functions often relied on ad hoc assumptions without much empirical basis. For example, Nordhaus (1992[188]) specified a squared damage function that multiplied economic output. This was based on early empirical work. Conversely, Kalkuhl and Wenz (2020[190]) use the latest advances in climate econometrics with detailed subnational data to provide updated estimates of Nordhaus' parameterisation. They find the damage caused by emission of a single tonne of CO_2 is around USD 70-140, more than twice the estimate provided by Nordhaus (1992[188]).

The severe damages caused by high temperatures have been supported by other empirical works (Burke, Hsiang and Miguel, 2015[130]) (Hsiang, 2016[191]). These empirical estimates are helpful guides to reduce the uncertainties around climate damages. Comparing damage functions across different IAMs may also be helpful in setting bounds.

However, the appropriate form for the damage function is still unclear. Most IAMs, starting from Nordhaus (1992[188]), a use a multiplicative function. This multiplies damages by level of consumption, implying consumption is impaired by damages but cannot be decreased to zero. In contrast, an additive function of damages can completely counteract the welfare provided by consumption (Weitzman, 2009[74]). Additive form is more appropriate for settings where environmental goods and services are difficult to substitute (see second subsection of 2.3.2 for a more detailed discussion of the socio-economic role of nature).

Damages, as estimated by IAMs, unquestionably vary widely and are attached to high levels of uncertainties. A single function cannot capture all of the wide range of economic impacts from climate change. Some critics argue the very concept of a damage function is misleading (Pindyck, 2017[192]).

Fundamentally, the exact damage function is not knowable. Each of the three components of risks (hazards, exposure and vulnerability) are uncertain in the future. They will become still more uncertain as estimates look further into the future (Neumann et al., 2020[193]).

As another potential limitation, IAM results use coarse temporal resolution (typically time steps of a decade or more). In addition, they cannot model the transition pathway between two subsequent time steps, which adds to the level of uncertainty associated with such damage estimates (Monasterolo, Roventini and Foxon, 2019[194]). The structure of IAMs also makes it difficult to use econometric or statistical tools to assess their validity (Nordhaus, 2018[195]).

Uncertainties attached with such damage estimates and functional form assumption, therefore, need to be considered carefully. In addition, policy makers need to understand what types of questions these models can usefully inform. They must also recognise where output from these models is not fit for policy making.

Using IAMs to estimate economic costs of climate change in the near term, say, for the length of a political cycle or a mandate, will most likely produce meaningless results. Comparing different IAMs for the cost-effectiveness analysis of different mitigation pathways can, beyond high levels of uncertainties, inform international climate policy where global temperature goals can drive action in countries. If used in the appropriate manner, these models can be informative. Uncertainties associated with results are by no means a barrier to action. While the exact damages are unknowable, they will not be zero; and accumulating evidence suggests they are likely to be sizeable.

IAMs will likely underestimate the vulnerability and exposure. This occurs because certain elements are difficult to include in economic models, such as ecosystem responses, extreme events or tipping points. Thus, these are often not treated within models, leading to an underassessment of risks (Stern, 2013[196]). There are exceptions, for example IAMs with stochastic damages (Cai, Lenton and Lontzek, 2016[197]).

Economic models have still not caught up to the latest climate models. For example, they assume too long of a delay between carbon emissions and warming (Dietz et al., 2021[198]). A model is a simplified version of reality, which means some aspects will be left out or streamlined. However, in IAMs the simplifying assumptions will lead to underestimation of climate risks. Therefore, for IAM estimates, the uncertainty will be the extent to which the true effect will exceed the modelled one.

Other modelling approaches can approach uncertainty of climate change and socio-economic interactions in a more flexible manner compared to IAMs (Farmer et al., 2015[199]; Hallegatte and Rozenberg, 2017[143]). These include models that start from the subcomponents to build up their structure (bottom-up models). Two such approaches are discussed here: agent-based models and resampling and reweighting models.

Agent-based models assume multiple different agents, such as firms, households or individual consumers, who interact with each other and with their environment. Each agent has its own decision problems and behaviour rules on how to approach them. The outcomes of the model arise from the complex interplay of the different agents. The interplay can be complex. Often, multiple runs of the same model leads to different outcomes, which can be regarded as a characterisation of uncertainty.

The flexibility of agent-based models allows modellers to examine the outcomes at different levels of aggregation. They can thus compare how simulated agent interactions at the micro-level give rise to macro-level outcomes. Disentangling at different levels is useful for locating the source of uncertainties surrounding exposure and vulnerability and assessing what influences them. Thus, for policy makers, agent-based models provide a comprehensive approach to elicit the effects of policy or climate shocks, and assess the surrounding uncertainties (Kniveton, Smith and Wood, 2011[200]; Rai and Henry, 2016[201]; Hailegiorgis, Crooks and Cioffi-Revilla, 2018[202]).

Moreover, these models can provide a detailed description of different uncertainties, impacts and how they interact. Thus, compared to IAMs, for example, they are more appropriate to examine the effects of compound events, the comprehensive mechanisms and transmission channels. The examination of transmission channels is often needed to fine-tune policies.

Agent-based models, however, are limited by their behavioural assumptions, which are difficult to verify. The same behavioural rules can lead to similar outcomes at the macro level, where the verification is easier. Because of this, they often require in-depth knowledge of the modelled situation to inform the model.

These models are mostly applied to well-defined local problems (Kniveton, Smith and Wood, 2011[200]; Hailegiorgis, Crooks and Cioffi-Revilla, 2018[202]). They also provide a stylised description of a wider, complex issue, which is difficult to do with other types of approaches. For example, an agent-based model has revealed the costs of global supply chain disruptions caused by natural disasters are comparable to the disasters' direct cost impacts (Otto et al., 2017[203]). This type of analysis enables policy makers to identify bottlenecks and make their supply chains more resilient.

The second modelling approach is to assess the impact of socio-economic effects and the uncertainty surrounding them in a resampling and reweighting model. First, the approach uses quantitative data to estimate the effects of climate change on multiple socio-economic outcomes, such as household income, labour productivity or food prices. In the second step, it simulates households' future vulnerability and exposure using the IPCC's Shared Socioeconomic Pathways as a basis (Hallegatte and Rozenberg, 2017[143]) (see subsection below). In the third step, the simulation is done for a world with severe and moderate climate change using the IPCC's Representative Concertation Pathways (see Section 2.2.3).

The difference between the severe and moderate climate change scenarios gives an estimate of the effect of climate change on each outcome (e.g. household income, labour productivity, food prices). To assess the uncertainty, the second and third steps are run several thousand times, each time changing the future composition of households and climate model used. This part enables assessment of the uncertainty associated with each socio-economic outcome modelled. For example, it has been shown that the expected effect of climate change on poverty through extreme events is projected to be three times higher than the effect through labour productivity.

The productivity effect is much larger than the effects of extreme events in some scenarios (Jafino et al., 2020[131]). Therefore, an extreme weather event will likely have a larger effect than productivity. However, it is not possible to rule out that the productivity effect will overwhelmingly dominate.

Hence, resampling and reweighting models perform well in assessing uncertainties. They approach scientific and socio-economic uncertainties in a single framework. This is often important because for some regions different climate models predict completely different hazards [e.g. droughts or floods in West Africa (World Bank, 2021[204])].

The drawback of these types of models is their lack of a consistent macroeconomic framework. This makes it difficult to assess how policies could alter outcomes in the longer run. As another drawback, they can only estimate the effects of individual channels rather than compound impacts. This is important because the total effect of climate change is likely to be more than the sum of individual impacts.

Uncertainties related to the socio-economic role of nature

The way computational models treat ecosystems, and the environment more broadly, profoundly affects the estimated impacts of climate change. Climate change puts several ecosystems at risk, which in turn affects socio-economic well-being (van der Geest et al., 2019[205]). In particular, if the global mean temperature were to rise 1.5°C or less instead of 2°C, significant ecosystem damaged is avoided (IPCC, 2018[86]).

However, how changes in ecosystems respond to climate change and how such changes subsequently affect socio-economic well-being are not always clear. There are two crucial issues, which give rise to uncertainty about exposure and vulnerability: the role of relative prices with respect to environmental services; and the non-economic value of nature.

First, the role of relative prices is important because it determines the difficulty of future access to environmental goods. Computational models need to make assumptions about the production process; how various goods can be substituted in production; and consumption. Investigations have shown that estimated impacts are sensitive to assumptions about substitutability of nature with other factors, even if climate impacts are temporary (Hoel and Sterner, 2007[206]; Sterner and Persson, 2008[207]). If substitution of environmental and other goods is not perfect, environmental services, such as access to clean water, will get more expensive relative to other goods such as mobile phones.

Estimated costs quickly rise with the difficulty of substitution but are severe even with modest assumptions. For example, Sterner and Persson (2008[207]) assume that the environmental and other goods are substitutable but not perfectly[13] in a simple DICE model. They find the world needs to be carbon neutral optimally before 2100. This finding contrasts with the original DICE model, which prescribes that carbon emissions should peak around the same time. Accordingly, economic damages are likely to be underestimated within most IAMs, which assume that environmental and other goods are perfectly substitutable.

Given these results, policy makers should carefully examine the use of environmental goods in the economy and if such goods can be substituted. Potential investments could decrease vulnerability by making it easier to substitute some environmental goods. For example, access to clean drinking water could be a serious problem to poorer households, due to rising water prices. Thus, investments in water infrastructure might alleviate uncertainties connected to relative prices and make populations more resilient. Such infrastructure could include wastewater treatment plants or desalination plants and processes. Other environmental goods and services might be more difficult to substitute, such as carbon sequestration from the Amazon rainforest.

The second important source of uncertainty is the non-economic value of ecosystems and environmental goods. As mentioned in Section 2.3.1, the most important impacts will likely be non-economic in nature. Many argue against putting a monetary value on ecosystems on principle (Costanza et al., 2017[208]; Des Jardins, 2013[209]). However, the needs of policy makers to conduct cost-benefit analyses of environmental policies prompted economists to devise methods of such valuation (Perman et al., 2011[210]). Thus, these impacts are essentially qualitative impacts, approximated with quantitative methods.

Several research papers have shown that ecosystems or even single species carry value to people who might not use or even see them (Bateman et al., 2002[211]; Fankhauser, Dietz and Gradwell, 2014[212]). For example, the average willingness-to-pay for the preservation of threatened species is around USD 400 per household, according to a recent review (Subroy et al., 2019[213]). However, these appraisals are quite uncertain and the results are sensitive to the choice of methodologies (Bastien-Olvera and Moore, 2020[133]).

Recent research finds that estimated non-economic impacts are about four times higher than economic impacts. For policy makers, this implies high uncertainty regarding how non-economic costs will affect the population. As the ultimate goal of policies is usually some form of welfare, policy makers must consider non-economic damages in their appraisals.

Conducting appraisals of non-economic damages using established methods (e.g. contingent valuation, choice experiments) would decrease uncertainties. In so doing, they would help tailor policies to population needs. An area might be economically resilient to certain types of hazards. However, it could be vulnerable to non-economic impacts such as forest dieback or species extinction. Therefore, investments should go beyond protecting ecosystems that contribute directly to economic production (e.g.agriculture, tourism, fishery): they should also protect ecosystems with no direct economic value. This point relates back to the qualitative impacts discussed in Section 2.3.1.

Shared Socioeconomic Pathways as a measure of uncertainty

As discussed in Section 2.2.3, IPCC has created a set of scenarios for socio-economic systems (similarly to RCPs). These will underlie some of the discussion in the forthcoming Sixth Assessment Report. The SSPs describe five consistent narratives of future developments in the world (Riahi et al., 2017[8]). The SSPs are not predictions, and do not aspire to describe the future. Rather, they provide consistent scenarios based on assumptions of trends.

In the same vein, since the pathways are not forecasts based on the current state, there are no probabilities attached to them. The future might not resemble the past or the present. SSPs explore a range of different futures to assess what these plausible worlds could mean for natural and human systems.

The SSPs were built by groups of experts by first creating five general storylines about the ways in which the world can develop (Riahi et al., 2017[8]). Then, to guide the interpretation and assumptions, the storylines were translated to quantitative input tables. Based on the input tables, the narratives were converted to quantitative projections about three socio-economic drivers: GDP, population and urbanisation. Each of these is difficult to project, especially in the longer term.

Figure 2.10. Main outcomes of the Shared Socioeconomic Pathways

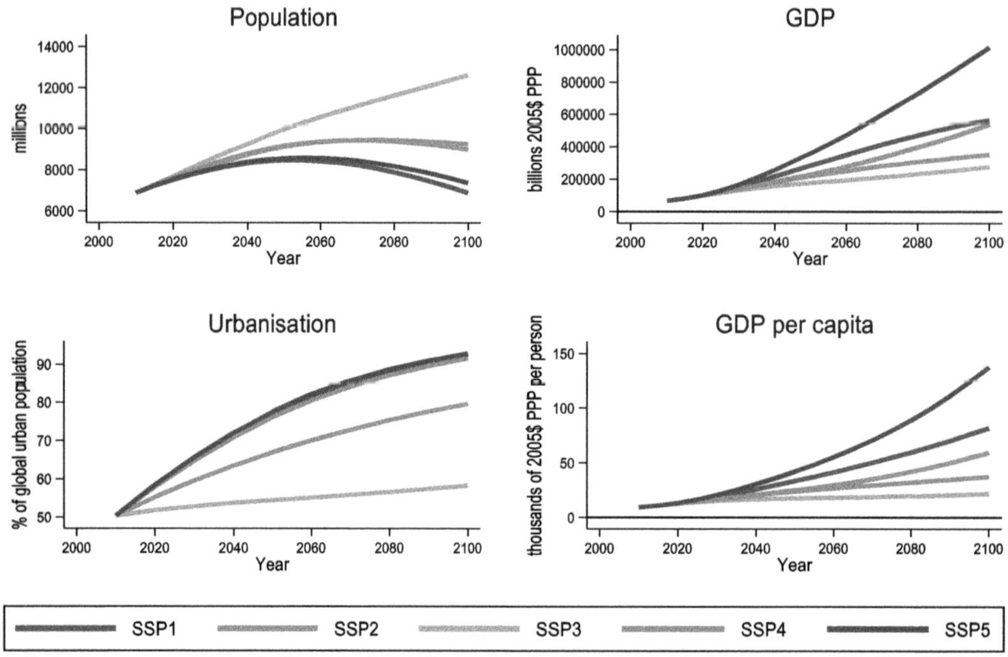

Note: The figure shows the (baseline marker) projections of population, GDP, urbanisation and GDP per capita.
Source: (Riahi et al., 2017[8]); Population: (Samir and Lutz, 2017[214]); GDP: (Dellink et al., 2017[215]); Urbanisation: (Jiang and O'Neill, 2017[216]).

The five pathways describe quite different worlds. Even within individual pathways, different models yield different outcomes, an indication of considerable uncertainty. While the exact projections of the five scenarios are uncertain, general trends are clear – see Figure 2.10 for projections principally used by the IPCC in discussions (baseline marker projections):

- ***SSP1*** (green) depicts a sustainable development pathway. It is a relatively optimistic scenario, where socio-economic systems (such as infrastructures and lifestyles) undergo a rapid shift to a less carbon-intensive operation, enabled by technology (see Chapter 6). This decreases the hazards and exposures considerably. Thus, GDP per capita and urbanisation are among the highest, and population growth is among the lowest of the SSPs (van Vuuren et al., 2017[217]).
- ***SSP2*** (brown) illustrates a world in which historical trends continue. Hazards and exposure increase gradually but are somewhat offset by more adaptation options, which decreases vulnerabilities slowly. This pathway is in the middle, compared to other SSPs, in terms of socio-economic outcomes (Fricko et al., 2017[218]).
- ***SSP3*** (grey) point to considerable increases in both exposure and vulnerabilities. This pathway is the worst overall in terms of global socio-economic outcomes; GDP levels are the lowest, population is the highest (Fujimori et al., 2017[219]).
- ***SSP4*** (red) describes a world with increasing hazards and exposure. It has decreasing vulnerabilities but only for developed countries. This worsens inequalities across and within countries, increasing poverty and generating political and social tensions. In this world, environmental problems are fundamentally local. Accordingly, GDP and GDP per capita is in the lower half of the SSPs (Calvin et al., 2017[220]).
- ***SSP5*** (purple), labelled "fossil-fuelled development", has the highest GDP and GDP per capita, and optimistic projections for high population growth and urbanisation. In this pathway, rapid

development takes place, which relies on the continuing exploitation of natural resources. Such rapid development could lead to decreased vulnerability in some places. However, it would uphold high-carbon status quo and necessarily lead to more impacts compared to pathways that encompass a transition towards low-carbon economies (Kriegler et al., 2017[221]).

Uncertainty also pervades each individual SSP. Recall that Figure 2.10 only depicts the baseline marker scenarios and that different modelling groups develop the scenarios in different ways. This includes in relation to the different mitigation scenarios used in physical climate models (see Section 2.2).

Accordingly, except for SSP3, all of the pathways could achieve warming below 1.5°C (compared to pre-industrial levels) (IPCC, 2018[86]). Figure 2.11 shows the net carbon emissions (emissions minus removal) associated with the SSPs, based on several models (Riahi et al., 2017[8]). Green lines show pathways where the 1.5°C target is achieved; blue lines show other pathways; and dark blue shows the baseline marker models.

The nature of uncertainties and risks is different for each. For example, achieving the 1.5°C target carries fewer risks in SSP1 than in SSP5. In SSP1, emissions decline swiftly slowing the warming, whereas they initially continue at the current levels or increase in SSP5. For SSP5 the target is achieved if sufficient carbon can be removed from the atmosphere (net carbon emissions are deeply negative).

Since the far future is more uncertain than the near future, edging towards a pathway that relies on technology in the far future is more uncertain and riskier. For policy makers, such a path implies that risks can be decreased by acting sooner rather than later. It also implies they favour policies that bring the world closer to one of the less risky worlds. The SSPs provide a common grounding for policy makers for discussions of socio-economic aspects and surrounding issues, which provides more clarity to these debates.

Figure 2.11. Carbon emissions in Shared Socioeconomic Pathways

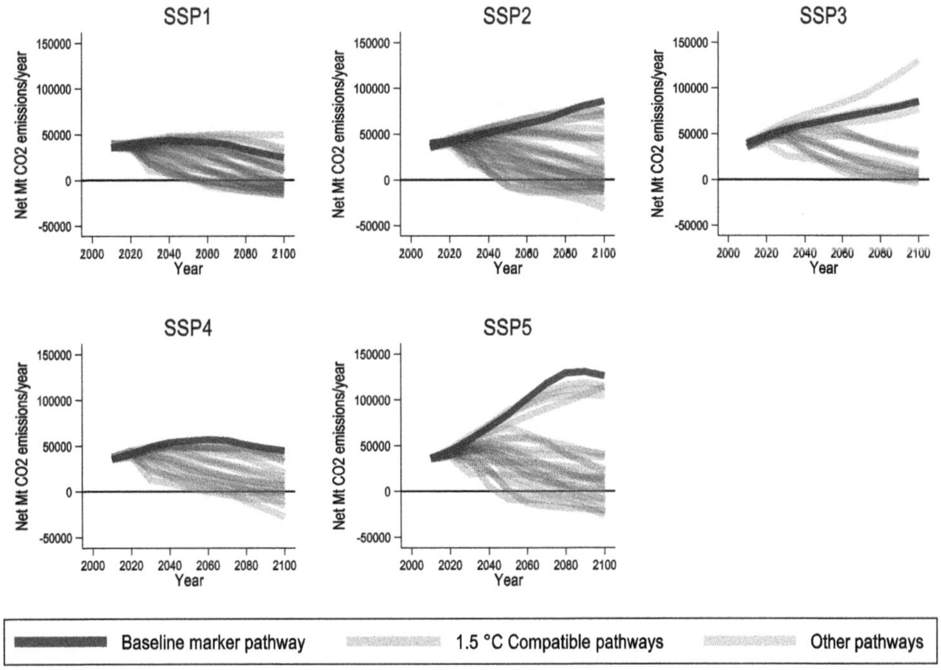

Note: The graph shows the net carbon emissions (Mt) in each year, according to the various simulations for each SSP scenario (Riahi et al., 2017[8]). Dark blue shows the baseline; green lines show the pathways compatible with 1.5°C warming; and light blue lines show other pathways.
Source: *IIASA SSP Public Database* (Riahi et al., 2017[8]).

2.3.3. Other uncertainties

Uncertainty arises from the complex nature of socio-economic systems. Thus, projections describe a possible future development. However, they cannot and will not be realised simply because of unforeseen random shocks. Projections cannot account or assign probabilities for all random shocks. This is equally true whether they are trade shocks (from the global economic systems) or exceptional circumstances (such as the COVID-19 pandemic). Thus, projections should be carefully considered but not taken as predictions. Resilience should be built to random shocks, for example, by diversifying supply chains.

An extreme case of uncertain shocks occurs when such shocks lead to impacts out of proportion with their origin (non-linear), especially socio-economic tipping points. Socio-economic tipping points are thresholds in socio-economic systems, which lead to abrupt changes and upset whole systems, leading to new equilibria.[14]

Socio-economic tipping points are discussed separately from projections because they are so difficult or impossible to project but have immense consequences. A projection may predict general trends perfectly, but a random shock from the world economy might trigger a socio-economic tipping point that could shift them.

Knowledge of when and how tipping points will be crossed is unknown. However, policy makers can encourage their tipping through comprehensive policies. For example, they could invest in renewable technologies but also remove fossil fuel subsidies (Otto et al., 2020[222]). According to experimental evidence, a roughly 25% committed minority in a group can tip the group majority to a different behaviour (Centola et al., 2018[223]).

Importantly, socio-economic tipping points can be tipped both ways. On the one hand, ground-breaking research in 1973 revealed ozone depletion in the atmosphere. This led to signing the Montreal Protocol only 14 years later, despite objections from affected industries. On the other, a new fuel tax in France in 2019 led to resistance and overturning of a policy.

Tipping points remain unknowable, even if it is possible to broadly categorise them. David Tábara et al. (2018[224]), for example, identify six types of tipping points relating to different parts of the socio-economic system. These are energy systems, governance, socio-cultural, technological systems, resource systems and economy. The number of tipping points increases with the complexity of societies. This means that multiple tipping points will likely need to be tipped for transformation (Otto et al., 2020[222]).

The social discount rate provides another uncertainty for policy design. The social discount rate determines the weight of future – compared to the present – in cost-benefit assessments. If future generations are just as important as current ones, the social discount rate is zero. If the next year counts for half as much as this year, the social discount rate is around 30%. As it increases, the well-being of future people carries less weight in these assessments. Social discount rates received special attention in the climate policy arena because actions taken today influence well-being in the coming decades or even centuries. Despite the scholarly attention, no clear consensus has been reached (Kelleher, 2017[225]; Varian, 2006[226]). Thus, the social discount rate is uncertain and it is likely to be different in different societies. However, research has provided a framework to consider social discount rates in a consistent way. For most, the social discount rate has two components: preference for the present and the inequality aversion across generations (Kolstad et al., 2015[227]).

First, preference for the present means that a given monetary is worth more today than it will be next year. Ultimately, this preference can be derived from forgone gains: a sum of money can be invested today, which will yield gains next year. This means the sum of money today is worth more than the same sum next year. This only holds for goods traded on the market. It does not hold for non-market goods, such as lives or livelihoods. It is unclear if ten lives lost next year are preferable to ten lives lost today.

Second, inequality aversion across generations refers to the expectation that economic growth will continue and people in the future are likely to be wealthier. Consequently, they can bear the economic costs more easily. This expectation is debatable. It is unclear whether the economy will continue to grow indefinitely and by how much is uncertain (Dellink et al., 2017[215]).

This uncertainty increases further out in the future. This implies the social discount rate will decline over time for two reasons. First, governments are risk-averse (see Chapter 1) and would prefer not to make overly strong assumptions about future wealth. This also relates to governments' general aversion of creating economic inequalities across generations; a high discount rate implies that future generations will bear the brunt of costs (Gollier, 2015[228]). It also relates to sustainability concerns that point to the possibility of future generations being worse off than current ones (Asheim and Mitra, 2010[229]). These considerations are ultimately political. Second, the mathematics of the expected value shows that discount rates need to be conservative under uncertainty (Gollier, 2002[230]).[15] Thus, without any value judgement, the discount rates should be declining as uncertainty increases.Uncertainty is likely to increase as projections go further into the future. Of course, this lesson also translates across countries: policy makers in countries facing more uncertainty should use lower discount rates than those in less uncertain countries.

2.4. The communication of climate-related risk and implications for policy processes

Sections 2.2 and 2.3 explore the high level of confidence in knowledge of climate change. At the same time, they highlight different levels and types of uncertainties in the understanding of certain features of the climate system. They also explore implications for the understanding of climate-related risk of losses and damages.

There are long-standing challenges in communicating climate change. In the face of climate scepticism, disputes over the integrity of climate scientists and heated debate on appropriate policy responses, the IPCC has always emphasised the degree of confidence associated with its statements. Its landmark Fourth Assessment Report (AR4) in 2007 concluded that warming of the climate system was unequivocal (IPCC, 2007[231]). Subsequent reviews have only strengthened levels of confidence around the reality of climate change and that it is driven by human activity.

Uncertainties underlying the risks of climate change have decreased in the past decades. This is evidenced by the shift towards higher confidence levels in IPCC Assessment reports' Summaries for Policy makers (Molina and Abadal, 2021[232]), for example. However, uncertainties remain an important factor in how the risk is perceived and in how action on climate change is taken as a consequence. Indeed, public acceptance (e.g. of climate scientists' predictions of sea-level rise) is influenced by how uncertainty is communicated and also to what extent. When scientists acknowledge the full extent of inevitable uncertainty, the public's level of trust in those predictions decreases (Howe et al., 2019[233]).

The profound understanding today of climate change is owed to years of climate research and advances in knowledge of the Earth's climate system. Hence, communication of climate change knowledge is subject to the practice of scientific communication. As such, it often involves efforts to be comprehensive, balanced and conservative. This may have the unintended consequence of eroding trust in the message among non-experts (Ho and Budescu, 2019[234]).

The predictability of the climate system especially at finer spatial and temporal scales remains limited, due to, among other factors, inherently variable and complex chaotic dynamics (Box 2.4). Climate projections can be improved with scientific advances. However, they will always be subject to types and levels of uncertainty. Further, their accurate communication will inevitably involve the consideration of these uncertainties.

As a summary of recent cutting-edge research, the IPCC assessment focuses on the most recent (and therefore most uncertain) results and on future research needed to tackle the remaining unknowns. The IPCC assessment does not spend thousands of pages summarising the extremely high confidence of scientists in the greenhouse effect. By definition, it is tasked to consider the more uncertain aspects of change. If uncertainty by itself is perceived as a reason for doubt, then this could lead to a mistrust of the whole message.

Issues around trust could suggest the climate change problem is facing an unsolvable dilemma: where there is uncertainty, there is little trust, and where there is little trust, there is little action. Other scientific communities have faced such problems in the past (Oreskes and Conway, 2010[235]). The climate change challenge, while informed by science, is not a purely scientific problem *per se*. Indeed, it is influenced by a series of other factors, such as vulnerability and exposure. Such factors fall outside the pure climate science domain. As such, they require action and answers that go beyond that which can be informed by science. Indeed, uncertainties associated with such factors may be far greater than uncertainties in physical climate projections.

This challenges the notion that more accurate scientific predictions of climate change impacts are a requirement for action on climate. Climate science informs policy makers on potential ways physical climate change can unfold for different parts of the world. It does this even if individual models do not always agree on the direction of important changes in a specific region. Yet solutions for climate change transcend the advances of scientific knowledge, however extremely valuable these are.

Indeed, the exact predictions of when and where hazards will occur is not a requirement in other areas of risk management. Governments do not expect to know when an individual or a group of people will be infected by a pathogen before they enact measures to counteract pandemics. Nor is it even necessary to assess probability to be high: one may buy fire insurance for a house even though the probability of fire is small.

The same rationale is applicable to the climate challenge. There is certainty that climate change is happening and good knowledge about how and what types of hazards can occur in different regions and over different timeframes. In other words, despite uncertainties, current knowledge of climate change is sufficient to support implementation of many risk management measures. Of course, as in the other cases, the availability of more detailed information would be highly valuable.

Since the likely damages increase disproportionately as one moves from the mean of potential responses, larger uncertainties can lead to a larger range of potential climate risk that are to be taken into account through management approaches. From a risk management perspective, when dealing with uncertainties, one needs to balance the possibilities and consequences of overestimating or underestimating the risk. In other words, one needs to minimise both false alarms and missed warnings (Shepherd, 2019[11]).

Finding a balance between these two extremes is not trivial. There is no single probabilistic threshold that can guarantee a risk is not being over- or underestimated, for example. Multiple factors, including value judgements and risk tolerance, can influence this threshold.

The IPCC terminology of likelihoods (Table 2.5) embeds an assessment of what probability levels mean in terms of certainty about an outcome. These levels have direct consequences for policy making. They imply different levels of “call for action” (Molina and Abadal, 2021[232]) and can be considered more or less important in risk management strategies.

However, likelihoods are not the same as risk. Since climate change is essentially a risk management problem, policy makers need to consider these likelihoods carefully and critically. Indeed, Sutton (2019[236]) argues that climate science must “take the needs of risk assessment much more seriously”.

Table 2.5. IPCC likelihood terminology

Likelihood terminology	Likelihood of the occurrence/outcome
Virtually certain	99-100% probability
Extremely likely	95-100% probability
Very likely	90-100% probability
Likely	66-100% probability
More likely than not	>50-100% probability
About as likely as not	33-66% probability
Unlikely	0-33% probability
Very unlikely	0-10% probability
Extremely unlikely	0-5% probability
Exceptionally unlikely	0-1% probability

Source: Box TS.1 in (Stocker et al., 2013[79]).

In working and considering the IPCC likelihoods in a risk management strategy, one could reasonably assume the projection of impacts for which probabilities are high. In other words, probabilities backed up by consistent, multiple and independent lines of high-quality evidence will be considered. In this case, terms such as "virtually certain", "extremely unlikely" or "very likely" will be usable directly as meaningful probabilities in a risk assessment.

As likelihoods in the projections decrease, inclusions in the risk assessment will depend on the relevant magnitude of the impact in question. For example, the Atlantic Meridional Overturning Circulation has an up to 10% probability of collapsing during the 21st century (IPCC, 2019[237]), with potentially impactful consequences. In this case, probability may be high enough for it to be considered in risk assessments. Conversely, a 50% probability of less rainfall in a deserted uninhabited area may be regarded as negligible, considering the lower potential for losses and damages.

Terminologies assigned to the middle and lower range of probabilities, therefore, need to be considered with care and are not always presented in a systematic manner. Given any probability distribution, one could frame a result with any degree of likelihood. A 1% chance of temperature above 40 degrees, a 10% chance of temperature above 35 degrees, a 50% chance of temperature above 30 degrees, and a 99% chance of temperature about 20 degrees may all refer to the same forecast in the same place on the same day. There is a subjective element to the presentation of likelihoods and the choice of what variables to communicate.

In many other areas of life and of decision making, a significantly more prudent approach is taken against the same odds the world faces with climate change. For example, if an aircraft had an up to 33% probability of not arriving at its destination, this would not be considered an unlikely outcome. Climate pathways that take carbon budgets with only a 66% chance of meeting the Paris "target" betray a loose interpretation of the word "target". This deserves greater scrutiny by policy makers as to whether that is truly the intended meaning.

Similarly, even though the probability of fire in an individual private home may be lower than 1%, the potential damage of such an event is high. Therefore, most people purchase insurance to protect their homes. The same rationale applies to government and societal decisions and action to address climate change. Uncertainty will always be present; decisions must be taken regardless.

Paradoxically, these uncertainties and ambiguities are the very aspects of climate change that are critical to understand better. More understanding can forge effective responses to climate risks and reduce sceptical reactions to the compelling accumulation of scientific evidence (Pidgeon, 2012[238]; Poortvliet et al., 2020[239]). Therefore, greater recognition is needed of both the strengths and limitations of current physical climate models.

Collectively, both the planet and human societies are driven to conditions never before observed in human history. There is also need for approaches to policy and decision making in relation to adaptation that can cope with inevitable uncertainties. These uncertainties arise from the dynamics of the physical climate system closely interacting with complex and equally dynamic social and economic systems. The uncertainties and ambiguities surrounding some aspects of climate change projections should also amplify – not weaken – the case for strong climate mitigation action, undoubtedly the safest and most effective way to reduce the risks of losses and damages.

References

Ackerman, F., E. Stanton and R. Bueno (2010), "Fat tails, exponents, extreme uncertainty: Simulating catastrophe in DICE", *Ecological Economics*, Vol. 69/8, pp. 1657-1665, http://dx.doi.org/10.1016/j.ecolecon.2010.03.013. [72]

Ad Hoc Study Group on Carbon Dioxide and Climate et al. (1979), *Carbon Dioxide and Climate*, National Academies Press, Washington, DC, http://dx.doi.org/10.17226/12181. [67]

Adger, W. et al. (2012), "Cultural dimensions of climate change impacts and adaptation", *Nature Climate Change*, Vol. 3/2, pp. 112-117, http://dx.doi.org/10.1038/nclimate1666. [7]

Álvarez, I. (ed.) (2016), "Locally downscaled and spatially customizable climate data for historical and future periods for North America", *PLOS ONE*, Vol. 11/6, p. e0156720, http://dx.doi.org/10.1371/journal.pone.0156720. [92]

Andrews, O. et al. (2018), "Implications for workability and survivability in populations exposed to extreme heat under climate change: A modelling study", *The Lancet Planetary Health*, Vol. 2/12, pp. e540-e547, http://dx.doi.org/10.1016/s2542-5196(18)30240-7. [107]

Archibald, C. and N. Butt (2018), "Using Google search data to inform global climate change adaptation policy", *Climatic Change*, Vol. 150/3-4, pp. 447-456, http://dx.doi.org/10.1007/s10584-018-2289-9. [166]

Asheim, G. and T. Mitra (2010), "Sustainability and discounted utilitarianism in models of economic growth", *Mathematical Social Sciences*, Vol. 59/2, pp. 148-169, http://dx.doi.org/10.1016/j.mathsocsci.2009.08.003. [229]

Bahinipati, C. et al. (2017), "Flood-induced loss and damage to textile industry in Surat City, India", *Environment and Urbanization ASIA*, Vol. 8/2, pp. 170-187, http://dx.doi.org/10.1177/0975425317714903. [172]

Banihipati, C. (2020), "Assessing the costs of droughts in rural India: A comparison of economic and non-economic loss and damage", *Current Science*, Vol. 118/11, pp. 1832-1841. [177]

Barnett, J. et al. (2016), "A science of loss", *Nature Climate Change*, Vol. 6/11, pp. 976-978, http://dx.doi.org/10.1038/nclimate3140. [6]

Bastien-Olvera, B. and F. Moore (2020), "Use and non-use value of nature and the social cost of carbon", *Nature Sustainability*, Vol. 4/2, pp. 101-108, http://dx.doi.org/10.1038/s41893-020-00615-0. [133]

Bateman, I. et al. (2002), *Economic Valuation with Stated Preference Techniques*, Edward Elgar Publishing, Cheltenham, UK, https://ideas.repec.org/b/elg/eebook/2639.html (accessed on 6 January 2021). [211]

Benson, C. and E. Clay (1998), "The impact of drought on sub-saharan African economies", *World Bank Technical Papers*, World Bank, Washington, DC, https://elibrary.worldbank.org/doi/abs/10.1596/0-8213-4180-4. [61]

Bhave, A. et al. (2018), "Water Resource Planning Under Future Climate and Socioeconomic Uncertainty in the Cauvery River Basin in Karnataka, India", *Water Resources Research*, Vol. 54/2, pp. 708-728, http://dx.doi.org/10.1002/2017wr020970. [126]

Blair, J., R. Czaja and E. Blair (2014), *Designing Surveys: A Guide to Decisions and Procedures*, SAGE Publications, Thousand Oaks, CA. [146]

Bony, S. et al. (2015), "Clouds, circulation and climate sensitivity", *Nature Geoscience*, Vol. 8/4, pp. 261-268, http://dx.doi.org/10.1038/ngeo2398. [115]

Borchers Arriagada, N. et al. (2020), "Unprecedented smoke-related health burden associated with the 2019-20 bushfires in eastern Australia", *Medical Journal of Australia*, Vol. 213/6, pp. 282-283, http://dx.doi.org/10.5694/mja2.50545. [42]

Braconnot, P. et al. (2012), "Evaluation of climate models using palaeoclimatic data", *Nature Climate Change*, Vol. 2/6, pp. 417-424, http://dx.doi.org/10.1038/nclimate1456. [13]

Bromley-Trujillo, R. and J. Poe (2020), "The importance of salience: Public opinion and state policy action on climate change", *Journal of Public Policy*, Vol. 40/2, pp. 280-304, http://dx.doi.org/10.1017/S0143814X18000375. [167]

Brönnimann, S. and J. Wintzer (2018), "Climate data empathy", *Wiley Interdisciplinary Reviews: Climate Change*, Vol. 10/2, http://dx.doi.org/10.1002/wcc.559. [27]

Brouwer, R. et al. (2007), "Socioeconomic vulnerability and adaptation to environmental risk: A case study of climate change and flooding in Bangladesh", *Risk Analysis*, Vol. 27/2, pp. 313-326, http://dx.doi.org/10.1111/j.1539-6924.2007.00884.x. [142]

Brown, L. et al. (2014), "The past, present, and future of federal surveys: Observations from the Committee on National Statistics", *Conference Proceedings from JSM (Joint Statistical Meeting) 2014 - Social Statistics Section)*, Committee on National Statistics, Washington, DC. [148]

Brown, L. and V. Murray (2013), "Examining the relationship between infectious diseases and flooding in Europe", *Disaster Health*, Vol. 1/2, pp. 117-127, http://dx.doi.org/10.4161/dish.25216. [40]

Brown, M., K. de Beurs and M. Marshall (2012), "Global phenological response to climate change in crop areas using satellite remote sensing of vegetation, humidity and temperature over 26 years", *Remote Sensing of Environment*, Vol. 126, pp. 174-183, http://dx.doi.org/10.1016/j.rse.2012.08.009. [153]

Burke, M., S. Hsiang and E. Miguel (2015), "Global non-linear effect of temperature on economic production", *Nature*, Vol. 527/7577, pp. 235-239, http://dx.doi.org/10.1038/nature15725. [130]

Cai, Y., T. Lenton and T. Lontzek (2016), "Risk of multiple interacting tipping points should encourage rapid CO2 emission reduction", *Nature Climate Change*, Vol. 6/5, pp. 520-525, http://dx.doi.org/10.1038/nclimate2964. [197]

Calvin, K. et al. (2017), "The SSP4: A world of deepening inequality", *Global Environmental Change*, Vol. 42, pp. 284-296, http://dx.doi.org/10.1016/j.gloenvcha.2016.06.010. [220]

CAT (2021), *Warming Projections Global Update*, Climate Action Tracker. [82]

Centola, D. et al. (2018), "Experimental evidence for tipping points in social convention", *Science*, Vol. 360/6393, pp. 1116-1119, http://dx.doi.org/10.1126/science.aas8827. [223]

Ceola, S., F. Laio and A. Montanari (2014), "Satellite nighttime lights reveal increasing human exposure to floods worldwide", *Geophysical Research Letters*, Vol. 41/20, pp. 7184-7190, http://dx.doi.org/10.1002/2014GL061859. [154]

Chen, C. et al. (2015), "University of Notre Dame Global Adaptation Index", *Technical Report*, https://gain.nd.edu/assets/254377/nd_gain_technical_document_2015.pdf. [152]

Clay, E. and O. Stokke (2000), *Food Aid and Human Security*, Frank Cass, Portland, OR. [62]

Collins, M. et al. (2013), "Long-term climate change: Projections, commitments and irreversibility", in Stocker, T. et al. (eds.), *Climate Change 2013: The Physical Science Basis. Contribution of Working Group I to the Fifth Assessment Report*, Intergovernmental Panel on Climate Change, Geneva. [75]

Congressional Budget Office (2005), "Uncertainty in analyzing climate change: Policy implications", *A CBO Paper*, Congressional Budget Office, Washington, DC. [127]

CONSTRAIN (2020), *A New Generation of Climate Models, COVID-19 and the Paris Agreement*, ZERO IN ON Reports, The CONSTRAIN Project. [70]

Costanza, R. et al. (2017), "Twenty years of ecosystem services: How far have we come and how far do we still need to go?", *Ecosystem Services*, Vol. 28, pp. 1-16, http://dx.doi.org/10.1016/J.ECOSER.2017.09.008. [208]

Council, N. (2001), *Climate Change Science: An Analysis of Some Key Questions*, National Academies Press, Washington, DC, http://dx.doi.org/10.17226/10139. [112]

David Tàbara, J. et al. (2018), *Positive Tipping Points in a Rapidly Warming World*, Elsevier B.V., http://dx.doi.org/10.1016/j.cosust.2018.01.012. [224]

De Juan, A. (2015), "Long-term environmental change and geographical patterns of violence in Darfur, 2003-2005", *Political Geography*, Vol. 45, pp. 22-33, http://dx.doi.org/10.1016/J.POLGEO.2014.09.001. [181]

Dee, D. et al. (2011), "The ERA-Interim reanalysis: Configuration and performance of the data assimilation system", *Quarterly Journal of the Royal Meteorological Society*, Vol. 137/656, pp. 553-597, http://dx.doi.org/10.1002/qj.828. [24]

Dellink, R. et al. (2017), "Long-term economic growth projections in the Shared Socioeconomic Pathways", *Global Environmental Change*, Vol. 42, pp. 200-214, http://dx.doi.org/10.1016/j.gloenvcha.2015.06.004. [215]

Des Jardins, J. (2013), *Environmental Ethics: An Introduction to Environmental Philosophy (Fifth Edition)*, Cengage Learning, Belmont, CA, https://digitalcommons.csbsju.edu/academic_books/5 (accessed on 6 January 2021). [209]

Deschênes, O., M. Greenstone and J. Guryan (2009), "Climate change and birth weight", *American Economic Review*, Vol. 99/2, pp. 211-217, http://dx.doi.org/10.1257/aer.99.2.211. [144]

Dessai, S. et al. (2018), "Building narratives to characterise uncertainty in regional climate change through expert elicitation", *Environmental Research Letters*, Vol. 13/7, p. 074005, http://dx.doi.org/10.1088/1748-9326/aabcdd. [124]

Dietz, S. et al. (2021), "Are economists getting climate dynamics right and does it matter?", *Journal of the Association of Environmental and Resource Economists*, Vol. 8/5, pp. 895-921, http://dx.doi.org/10.1086/713977. [198]

Donatti, C. et al. (2016), "What information do policy makers need to develop climate adaptation plans for smallholder farmers? The case of Central America and Mexico", *Climatic Change*, Vol. 141/1, pp. 107-121, http://dx.doi.org/10.1007/s10584-016-1787-x. [93]

Dunstone, N. et al. (2020), "Skilful interannual climate prediction from two large initialised model ensembles", *Environmental Research Letters*, Vol. 15/9, p. 094083, http://dx.doi.org/10.1088/1748-9326/ab9f7d. [110]

Ebi, K. et al. (2021), "Burning embers: Synthesis of the health risks of climate change", *Environmental Research Letters*, Vol. 16/4, p. 044042, http://dx.doi.org/10.1088/1748-9326/abeadd. [52]

Eckstein, D., V. Künzel and L. Schäfer (2021), *Global Climate Risk Index 2021*, Germanwatch, Bonn, https://germanwatch.org/sites/default/files/Global%20Climate%20Risk%20Index%202021_2.pdf. [150]

Edwards, B., M. Gray and B. Hunter (2019), "The social and economic impacts of drought", *Australian Journal of Social Issues*, Vol. 54/1, pp. 22-31, https://doi.org/10.1002/ajs4.52. [65]

EEA (2008), "European scale exceedance mapping for PM10 and ozone based on daily interpolation fields", *ETC/ACC Technical Paper*, No. 2007/08, European Environmental Agency, Copenhagen. [163]

English National Study of Flooding and Health Study Group (2019), "Impact of repeat flooding on mental health and health-related quality of life: A cross-sectional analysis of the English National Study of Flooding and Health", *BMJ Open*, Vol. 9/11, p. e031562, http://dx.doi.org/10.1136/bmjopen-2019-031562. [38]

Eyring, V. et al. (2016), "Overview of the Coupled Model Intercomparison Project Phase 6 (CMIP6) experimental design and organization", *Geoscientific Model Development*, Vol. 9/5, pp. 1937-1958, http://dx.doi.org/10.5194/gmd-9-1937-2016. [102]

Eyring, V. et al. (2019), "Taking climate model evaluation to the next level", *Nature Climate Change*, Vol. 9/2, pp. 102-110, http://dx.doi.org/10.1038/s41558-018-0355-y. [103]

Fankhauser, S., S. Dietz and P. Gradwell (2014), "Non-economic losses in the context of the UNFCCC work programme on loss and damage", *Technical Paper*, No. FCCC/TP/2013/2, United Nations Framework Convention on Climate Change, Geneva. [212]

Farmer, J. et al. (2015), "A third wave in the economics of climate change", *Environmental and Resource Economics*, Vol. 62/2, pp. 329-357, http://dx.doi.org/10.1007/s10640-015-9965-2. [199]

Finn, D. (2020), *How do we build collaborative science for better urban planning and climate change adaptation?*, American Geophysical Union, Washington, DC. [95]

Flato, G. (2013), "Evaluation of climate models", in Stocker, T. (ed.), *Climate Change 2013: The Physical Science Basis. Contribution of Working Group I to the Fifth Assessment Report of the Intergovernmental Panel on Climate Change*, Cambridge University Press, Cambridge, United Kingdom and New York, NY. [12]

Fouillet, A. et al. (2008), "Has the impact of heat waves on mortality changed in France since the European heat wave of summer 2003? A study of the 2006 heat wave", *International Journal of Epidemiology*, Vol. 37/2, pp. 309-317, http://dx.doi.org/10.1093/ije/dym253. [53]

Fricko, O. et al. (2017), "The marker quantification of the Shared Socioeconomic Pathway 2: A middle-of-the-road scenario for the 21st century", *Global Environmental Change*, Vol. 42, pp. 251-267, http://dx.doi.org/10.1016/j.gloenvcha.2016.06.004. [218]

Fujimori, S. et al. (2017), "SSP3: AIM implementation of Shared Socioeconomic Pathways", *Global Environmental Change*, Vol. 42, pp. 268-283, http://dx.doi.org/10.1016/j.gloenvcha.2016.06.009. [219]

Gambhir, A. (2019), "Planning a Low-Carbon Energy Transition: What Can and Can't the Models Tell Us?", *Joule*, Vol. 3/8, pp. 1795-1798, http://dx.doi.org/10.1016/j.joule.2019.07.016. [83]

Gasparrini, A. et al. (2015), "Mortality risk attributable to high and low ambient temperature: A multicountry observational study", *The Lancet*, Vol. 386/9991, pp. 369-375, http://dx.doi.org/10.1016/s0140-6736(14)62114-0. [51]

Gasparrini, A. et al. (2017), "Projections of temperature-related excess mortality under climate change scenarios", *The Lancet Planetary Health*, Vol. 1/9, pp. e360-e367, http://dx.doi.org/10.1016/s2542-5196(17)30156-0. [134]

GCOS (2016), *The Global Observing System for Climate: Implementation Needs*, GCOS, https://library.wmo.int/doc_num.php?explnum_id=3417 (accessed on 27 May 2021). [20]

Gidden, M. et al. (2019), "Global emissions pathways under different socioeconomic scenarios for use in CMIP6: A dataset of harmonized emissions trajectories through the end of the century", *Geoscientific Model Development*, Vol. 12/4, pp. 1443-1475, http://dx.doi.org/10.5194/gmd-12-1443-2019. [84]

Gillingham, K. et al. (2015), *Modeling Uncertainty in Climate Change: A Multi-Model Comparison*, National Bureau of Economic Research, Cambridge, MA, http://dx.doi.org/10.3386/w21637. [128]

Giuliani, G. et al. (2017), "Spatially enabling the Global Framework for Climate Services: Reviewing geospatial solutions to efficiently share and integrate climate data & information", *Climate Services*, Vol. 8, pp. 44-58, http://dx.doi.org/10.1016/j.cliser.2017.08.003. [94]

Gollier, C. (2015), "Discounting, inequality and economic convergence", *Journal of Environmental Economics and Management*, Vol. 69, pp. 53-61, http://dx.doi.org/10.1016/j.jeem.2014.10.005. [228]

Gollier, C. (2002), "Discounting an uncertain future", *Journal of Public Economics*, Vol. 85/2, pp. 149-166, http://dx.doi.org/10.1016/S0047-2727(01)00079-2. [230]

Goody, R. et al. (2002), "Why monitor the climate?", *Bulletin of the American Meteorological Society*, pp. 873-878, https://doi.org/10.1175/1520-0477(2002)083<0873:WWSMTC>2.3.CO;2 (accessed on 27 May 2021). [14]

Government of British Columbia (2021), "Chief coroner's updated statement on public safety during heat wave", 2 July, Statement, Public Safety and Solictor General, Government of British Columbia, Victoria, https://news.gov.bc.ca/releases/2021PSSG0062-001295. [60]

Government of India (2011), *Disaster Management in India*, Ministry of Home Affairs, New Delhi. [169]

Government of the Commonwealth of Dominica (2017), *PDNA: Post-Disaster Needs Assessment Hurricane Maria September 18, 2017*, Government of the Commonwealth of Dominica. [157]

Granderson, A. (2014), "Making sense of climate change risks and responses at the community level: A cultural-political lens", *Climate Risk Management*, Vol. 3, pp. 55-64, http://dx.doi.org/10.1016/j.crm.2014.05.003. [4]

Guha-Sapir, D., D. Hargitt and P. Hoyois (2004), *Thirty Years of Natural Disasters 1974-2003: The Numbers*, Centre for Research on the Epidemiology of Disasters, Brussels. [45]

Guha-Sapir, D., P. Hoyois and R. Below (2016), *Annual Disaster Statistical Review 2015: The Numbers and Trends*, Centre for Research on the Epidemiology of Disasters, Brussels. [46]

Guo, H., L. Zhang and L. Zhu (2015), "Earth observation big data for climate change research", *Advances in Climate Change Research*, Vol. 6/2, pp. 108-117, http://dx.doi.org/10.1016/j.accre.2015.09.007. [15]

Hailegiorgis, A., A. Crooks and C. Cioffi-Revilla (2018), "An agent-based model of rural households' adaptation to climate change", *Journal of Artificial Societies and Social Simulation*, Vol. 21/4, p. 4, http://dx.doi.org/10.18564/jasss.3812. [202]

Hallegatte, S. et al. (2015), *Shock Waves: Managing the Impacts of Climate Change on Poverty*, Washington, DC: World Bank, http://dx.doi.org/10.1596/978-1-4648-0673-5. [138]

Hallegatte, S., M. Bangalore and A. Vogt-Schilb (2016), *Socioeconomic Resilience: Multi-Hazard Estimates in 117 Countries*, World Bank, Washington, DC, http://dx.doi.org/10.1596/1813-9450-7886. [5]

Hallegatte, S. et al. (2013), "Future flood losses in major coastal cities", *Nature Climate Change*, Vol. 3/9, pp. 802-806, http://dx.doi.org/10.1038/nclimate1979. [36]

Hallegatte, S., J. Rentschler and J. Rozenberg (2019), *Lifelines: The Resilient Infrastructure Opportunity*, Washington, DC: World Bank, http://dx.doi.org/10.1596/978-1-4648-1430-3. [132]

Hallegatte, S. and J. Rozenberg (2017), "Climate change through a poverty lens", *Nature Climate Change*, Vol. 7/4, pp. 250-256, http://dx.doi.org/10.1038/nclimate3253. [143]

Hanna, E. and P. Tait (2015), "Limitations to thermoregulation and acclimatization challenge human adaptation to global warming", *International Journal of Environmental Research and Public Health*, Vol. 12/7, pp. 8034-8074, http://dx.doi.org/10.3390/ijerph120708034. [106]

Harrington, L. and F. Otto (2020), "Reconciling theory with the reality of African heatwaves", *Nature Climate Change*, Vol. 10/9, pp. 796-798, http://dx.doi.org/10.1038/s41558-020-0851-8. [34]

Harrington, L. and F. Otto (2020), "Reconciling theory with the reality of African heatwaves", *Nature Climate Change*, Vol. 10/9, pp. 796-798, http://dx.doi.org/10.1038/s41558-020-0851-8. [63]

Hassani, H., X. Huang and E. Silva (2019), "Big data and climate change", *Big Data and Cognitive Computing*, Vol. 3/1, p. 12, http://dx.doi.org/10.3390/bdcc3010012. [18]

Haug, C. et al. (2009), "Navigating the dilemmas of climate policy in Europe: Evidence from policy evaluation studies", *Climatic Change*, Vol. 101/3-4, pp. 427-445, http://dx.doi.org/10.1007/s10584-009-9682-3. [139]

Hausfather, Z. et al. (2020), "Evaluating the performance of past climate model projections", *Geophysical Research Letters*, Vol. 47/1, http://dx.doi.org/10.1029/2019GL085378. [3]

Hausfather, Z. et al. (2020), "Evaluating the performance of past climate model projections", *Geophysical Research Letters*, Vol. 47/1, http://dx.doi.org/10.1029/2019GL085378. [96]

Hausfather, Z. and G. Peters (2020), "Emissions – the 'business as usual' story is misleading", *Nature*, Vol. 577/7792, pp. 618-620, http://dx.doi.org/10.1038/d41586-020-00177-3. [85]

Hawkins, E. and R. Sutton (2010), "The potential to narrow uncertainty in projections of regional precipitation change", *Climate Dynamics*, Vol. 37/1-2, pp. 407-418, http://dx.doi.org/10.1007/s00382-010-0810-6. [120]

Hawkins, E. and R. Sutton (2009), "The potential to narrow uncertainty in regional climate predictions", *Bulletin of the American Meteorological Societ*, Vol. 90/8, pp. 1095-1107. [119]

Hayes, K. et al. (2018), "Climate change and mental health: risks, impacts and priority actions", *International Journal of Mental Health Systems*, Vol. 12/1, http://dx.doi.org/10.1186/s13033-018-0210-6. [136]

Henderson, J., A. Storeygard and D. Weil (2012), "Measuring economic growth from outer space", *American Economic Review*, Vol. 102/2, pp. 994-1028, http://dx.doi.org/10.1257/aer.102.2.994. [164]

Hess, J. et al. (2018), "Building resilience to climate change: Pilot evaluation of the impact of India's first heat action plan on all-cause mortality", *Journal of Environmental and Public Health*, Vol. 2018, pp. 1-8, http://dx.doi.org/10.1155/2018/7973519. [54]

Higgins, P. and J. Harte (2012), "Carbon cycle uncertainty increases climate change risks and mitigation challenges", *Journal of Climate*, Vol. 25/21, pp. 7660-7668, http://dx.doi.org/10.1175/jcli-d-12-00089.1. [81]

Ho, E. and D. Budescu (2019), "Climate uncertainty communication", *Nature Climate Change*, Vol. 9/11, pp. 802-803, http://dx.doi.org/10.1038/s41558-019-0606-6. [234]

Hoel, M. and T. Sterner (2007), "Discounting and relative prices", *Climatic Change*, Vol. 84/3-4, pp. 265-280, http://dx.doi.org/10.1007/s10584-007-9255-2. [206]

Holden, P. et al. (2018), "Climate–carbon cycle uncertainties and the Paris Agreement", *Nature Climate Change*, Vol. 8/7, pp. 609-613, http://dx.doi.org/10.1038/s41558-018-0197-7. [69]

Houck, B. (2018), "Why the world Is hating on plastic straws right now", 12 July, Eater. [182]

Howe, L. et al. (2019), "Acknowledging uncertainty impacts public acceptance of climate scientists' predictions", *Nature Climate Change*, Vol. 9/11, pp. 863-867, http://dx.doi.org/10.1038/s41558-019-0587-5. [233]

Hsiang, S. (2016), "Climate Econometrics", *Annual Review of Resource Economics*, Vol. 8/1, pp. 43-75, http://dx.doi.org/10.1146/annurev-resource-100815-095343. [191]

IFRC (2017), "Dominica: Hurricane Maria", *Information Bulletin*, International Federation of Red Cross and Red Crescent Societies, Geneva. [158]

IPCC (2019), "Summary for Policymakers", in H.-O. Pörtner et al. (eds.), *IPCC Special Report on the Ocean and Cryosphere in a Changing Climate*, Intergovernmental Panel on Climate Change, Geneva. [237]

IPCC (2018), "Annex I: Glossary [Matthews, J.B.R. (ed.)]", in Masson-Delmotte, V. et al. (eds.), *Global Warming of 1.5°C. An IPCC Special Report on the impacts of global warming of 1.5°C above pre-industrial levels and related global greenhouse gas emission pathways, in the context of strengthening the global response to the threat of climate change*, Intergovernmental Panel on Climate Change, Geneva. [111]

IPCC (2018), "Summary for Policymakers", in Masson-Delmotte, V. et al. (eds.), *Global Warming of 1.5°C. An IPCC Special Report on the impacts of global warming of 1.5°C above pre-industrial levels and related global greenhouse gas emission pathways, in the context of strengthening the global response to the threat of climate c [...]*, World Meteorological Organization, Geneva, Switzerland. [97]

IPCC (2013), "Summary for Policymakers", in Stocker, T. et al. (eds.), *Climate Change 2013: The Physical Science Basis. Contribution of Working Group I to the Fifth Assessment Report of the Intergovernmental Panel on Climate Change*, Cambridge University Press, Cambridge, United Kingdom and New York, NY. [2]

IPCC (2012), *Managing the Risks of Extreme Events and Disasters to Advance Climate Change Adaptation. A Special Report of Working Groups I and II of the Intergovernmental Panel on Climate Change*, Cambridge University Press, Cambridge, United Kingdom, https://www.ipcc.ch/pdf/special-reports/srex/SREX_Full_Report.pdf. [175]

IPCC (2007), "Summary for Policymakers", in Solomon, S. (ed.), *Climate Change 2007: The Physical Science Basis. Contribution of Working Group I to the Fourth Assessment Report of the Intergovernmental Panel on Climate Change*, Cambridge University Press, Cambridge, United Kingdom and New York, NY. [231]

IPCC (2000), *IPCC Special Report Emissions Scenarios – Summary for Policymakers*, Intergovernmental Panel on Climate Change, Geneva. [87]

Ishizawa, O., J. Miranda and E. Strobl (2017), *The Impact of Hurricane Strikes on Short-Term Local Economic Activity: Evidence from Nightlight Images in the Dominican Republic*, World Bank, Washington, DC, http://dx.doi.org/10.1596/1813-9450-8275. [165]

Jafino, B. et al. (2020), "Revised estimates of the impact of climate change on extreme poverty by 2030", *Policy Research Working Paper*, No. 9417, World Bank, Washington, DC, https://openknowledge.worldbank.org/handle/10986/34555. [131]

Jebeile, J. and M. Crucifix (2020), "Multi-model ensembles in climate science: Mathematical structures and expert judgements", *Studies in History and Philosophy of Science Part A*, Vol. 83, pp. 44-52, http://dx.doi.org/10.1016/j.shpsa.2020.03.001. [78]

Jiang, L. and B. O'Neill (2017), "Global urbanization projections for the Shared Socioeconomic Pathways", *Global Environmental Change*, Vol. 42, pp. 193-199, http://dx.doi.org/10.1016/j.gloenvcha.2015.03.008. [216]

Kadiyala, M. et al. (2020), “Assessment of climate change and vulnerability in Indian state of Telangana for better agricultural planning”, *Theoretical and Applied Climatology*, Vol. 143/1-2, pp. 309-325, http://dx.doi.org/10.1007/s00704-020-03425-8. [104]

Kalkuhl, M. and L. Wenz (2020), “The impact of climate conditions on economic production. Evidence from a global panel of regions”, *Journal of Environmental Economics and Management*, Vol. 103, p. 102360, http://dx.doi.org/10.1016/j.jeem.2020.102360. [190]

Kalnay, E. et al. (1996), “The NCEP/NCAR 40-year reanalysis project”, *Bulletin of the American Meteorological Society*, Vol. 77/3, http://dx.doi.org/10.1175/1520-0477(1996)077<0437:TNYRP>2.0.CO;2. [23]

Kamber, G., C. McDonald and G. Price (2013), *Drying out: Investigating the economic effects of drought in New Zealand*, Reserve Bank of New Zealand, Wellington, https://www.nzae.org.nz/wp-content/uploads/2014/05/price.pdf. [64]

Kattenberg, A. et al. (1996), “Climate models - Projections of future climate”, in *Climate Change 1995: The Science of Climate Change, Contribution of Working Group I to the Second Assessment Report of the Intergovernmental Panel on Climate Change*, Cambridge University Press, Cambridge, United Kingdom. [66]

Kelleher, J. (2017), “Descriptive versus prescriptive discounting in climate change policy analysis”, *Georgetown Journal of Law & Public Policy*, Vol. 15, https://heinonline.org/HOL/Page?handle=hein.journals/geojlap15&id=972&div=&collection= (accessed on 28 April 2021). [225]

Kennedy, J. et al. (2021), *State of the Global Climate 2020*, World Meteorological Organization, Geneva. [21]

Kniveton, D., C. Smith and S. Wood (2011), “Agent-based model simulations of future changes in migration flows for Burkina Faso”, *Global Environmental Change*, Vol. 21/SUPPL. 1, pp. S34-S40, http://dx.doi.org/10.1016/j.gloenvcha.2011.09.006. [200]

Kobayashi, S. et al. (2015), “The JRA-55 Reanalysis: General Specifications and Basic Characteristics”, *Journal of the Meteorological Society of Japan. Ser. II*, Vol. 93/1, pp. 5-48, http://dx.doi.org/10.2151/jmsj.2015-001. [25]

Kolstad, C. et al. (2015), “Social, economic, and ethical concepts and methods”, In *Intergovernmental Panel of Climate Change Working Group 3*, Cambridge University Press, Cambridge, United Kingdom, http://dx.doi.org/10.1017/cbo9781107415416.009. [227]

Kotamarthi, R. et al. (2016), *Use of Climate Information for Decision-Making and Impacts Research: State of Our Understanding*, prepared for the Department of Defense, Strategic Environmental Research and Development Program. [121]

KPMG (2016), “Preparing MSMEs for effective disaster management”, April, KPMG, Amstelveen, The Netherlands, https://assets.kpmg/content/dam/kpmg/pdf/2016/05/Disaster-Management-Preparedness-SME.pdf. [173]

Kreft, S., D. Eckstein and I. Melchior (2016), *Global Climate Risk Index 2017: Who Suffers Most From Extreme Weather Events? Weather-related Loss Events in 2015 and 1996 to 2015*, Germanwatch, Bonn. [168]

Kriegler, E. et al. (2017), "Fossil-fueled development (SSP5): An energy and resource intensive scenario for the 21st century", *Global Environmental Change*, Vol. 42, pp. 297-315, http://dx.doi.org/10.1016/j.gloenvcha.2016.05.015. [221]

Kunreuther, H. et al. (2014), "Integrated risk and uncertainty assessment of climate change response policies", in Edenhofer, O. et al. (eds.), *Climate Change 2014: Mitigation of Climate Change. Contribution of Working Group III to the Fifth Assessment Report of the Intergovernmental Panel on Climate Chang*, Cambridge University Press, Cambridge, United Kingdom and New York, NY. [9]

LaJeunesse Connette, K. et al. (2016), "Assessment of mining extent and expansion in Myanmar based on freely-available satellite imagery", *Remote Sensing*, Vol. 8/11, p. 912, http://dx.doi.org/10.3390/rs8110912. [156]

Le Tertre, A. et al. (2006), "Impact of the 2003 heatwave on all-cause mortality in 9 French cities", *Epidemiology*, Vol. 17/1, pp. 75-79, http://www.jstor.org/stable/20486164. [100]

Lowe, J. et al. (2018), *UKCP18 Science Overview Report*, MET Office. [118]

Marcheggiani, S. et al. (2010), "Risks of water-borne disease outbreaks after extreme events", *Toxicological & Environmental Chemistry*, Vol. 92/3, pp. 593-599, http://dx.doi.org/10.1080/02772240903252140. [41]

Masson-Delmotte, V. et al. (eds.) (2021), *Climate Change 2021: The Physical Science Basis. Contribution of Working Group I to the Sixth Assessment Report of the Intergovernmental Panel on Climate Change*, Cambridge University Press, In press. [1]

Masson-Delmotte, V. et al. (eds.) (2018), *Global Warming of 1.5°C. An IPCC Special Report on the impacts of global warming of 1.5°C above pre-industrial levels and related global greenhouse gas emission pathways, in the context of strengthening the global response to the threat of climate change, sustainable development, and efforts to eradicate poverty.* [86]

McCollum, D. et al. (2020), "Energy modellers should explore extremes more systematically in scenarios", *Nature Energy*, Vol. 5/2, pp. 104-107, http://dx.doi.org/10.1038/s41560-020-0555-3. [88]

MEEDDM, G. (2009), *Evaluation du coût des impacts du changement climatique et de l'adaptation en France*, http://www.onerc.gouv.fr (accessed on 4 July 2021). [105]

Meehl, G. et al. (2020), "Context for interpreting equilibrium climate sensitivity and transient climate response from the CMIP6 Earth system models", *Science Advances*, Vol. 6/26, p. eaba1981, http://dx.doi.org/10.1126/sciadv.aba1981. [76]

Meyer, B., W. Mok and J. Sullivan (2015), "Household Surveys in Crisis", *Journal of Economic Perspectives*, Vol. 29/4, pp. 199-226, http://dx.doi.org/10.1257/jep.29.4.199. [147]

Mitchell, T. and P. Jones (2005), "An improved method of constructing a database of monthly climate observations and associated high-resolution grids", *International Journal of Climatology*, Vol. 25/6, pp. 693-712, http://dx.doi.org/10.1002/joc.1181. [16]

Molina, T. and E. Abadal (2021), "The evolution of communicating the uncertainty of climate change to policymakers: A study of IPCC synthesis reports", *Sustainability*, Vol. 13/5, p. 2466, http://dx.doi.org/10.3390/su13052466. [232]

Monasterolo, I., A. Roventini and T. Foxon (2019), "Uncertainty of climate policies and implications for economics and finance: An evolutionary economics approach", *Ecological Economics*, Vol. 163, pp. 177-182, http://dx.doi.org/10.1016/j.ecolecon.2019.05.012. [194]

Mora, C. et al. (2017), "Global risk of deadly heat", *Nature Climate Change*, Vol. 7/7, pp. 501-506, http://dx.doi.org/10.1038/nclimate3322. [57]

Nardo, M. et al. (2005), *Handbook on Constructing Composite Indicators*, OECD, Paris, https://www.oecd.org/sdd/42495745.pdf. [149]

National Research Council (2012), "Integrated climate observing system and Earth system analysis", in *A National Strategy for Advancing Climate Modeling*, National Academies Press, Washington, DC, http://dx.doi.org/10.17226/13430. [19]

Neumann, J. et al. (2020), "Climate damage functions for estimating the economic impacts of climate change in the United States", *Review of Environmental Economics and Policy*, Vol. 14/1, pp. 25-43, http://dx.doi.org/10.1093/reep/rez021. [193]

Newell, R., B. Prest and S. Sexton (2021), "The GDP-Temperature relationship: Implications for climate change damages", *Journal of Environmental Economics and Management*, p. 102445, http://dx.doi.org/10.1016/j.jeem.2021.102445. [160]

Nissan, H. et al. (2019), "On the use and misuse of climate change projections in international development", *Wiley Interdisciplinary Reviews: Climate Change*, Vol. 10/3, p. e579, http://dx.doi.org/10.1002/wcc.579. [91]

Nordhaus, W. (2018), "Evolution of modeling of the economics of global warming: Changes in the DICE model, 1992-2017", *Climatic Change*, Vol. 148/4, pp. 623-640, http://dx.doi.org/10.1007/s10584-018-2218-y. [195]

Nordhaus, W. (1992), "An optimal transition path for controlling greenhouse gases", *Science*, Vol. 258/5086, pp. 1315-1319, http://dx.doi.org/10.1126/SCIENCE.258.5086.1315. [188]

Noy, I. (2015), "Natural disasters in the Pacific Island Countries: new measurements of impacts", *Natural Hazards*, Vol. 84/S1, pp. 7-18, http://dx.doi.org/10.1007/s11069-015-1957-6. [31]

Noy, I. and W. duPont IV (2018), "The long-term consequences of disasters: What do we know, and what we still don't", *International Review of Environmental and Resource Economics*, Vol. 12/4, pp. 325-354, http://dx.doi.org/10.1561/101.00000104. [32]

OECD (2015), *The Economic Consequences of Climate Change*, OECD Publishing, Paris, https://dx.doi.org/10.1787/9789264235410-en. [129]

Oreskes, N. and E. Conway (2010), *Merchants of Doubt: How a Handful of Scientists Obscure The Truth on Issues from Tobacco Smoke to Global Warming*, Bloomsbury Press, New York. [235]

Otto, C. et al. (2017), "Modeling loss-propagation in the global supply network: The dynamic agent-based model acclimate", *Journal of Economic Dynamics and Control*, Vol. 83, pp. 232-269, http://dx.doi.org/10.1016/J.JEDC.2017.08.001. [203]

Otto, F. (2016), "The art of attribution", *Nature Climate Change*, Vol. 6/4, pp. 342-343, http://dx.doi.org/10.1038/nclimate2971. [28]

Otto, F. et al. (2020), “Challenges to understanding extreme weather changes in lower income countries”, *Bulletin of the American Meteorological Society*, Vol. 101/10, pp. E1851-E1860, http://dx.doi.org/10.1175/bams-d-19-0317.1. [59]

Otto, I. et al. (2020), “Social tipping dynamics for stabilizing Earth’s climate by 2050”, *Proceedings of the National Academy of Sciences of the United States of America*, Vol. 117/5, pp. 2354-2365, http://dx.doi.org/10.1073/pnas.1900577117. [222]

Ozturk, T., F. Saygili-Araci and M. Kurnaz (2021), “Projected changes in extreme temperature and precipitation indices over CORDEX-MENA domain”, *Atmosphere*, Vol. 12/5, p. 622, http://dx.doi.org/10.3390/atmos12050622. [48]

Palmer, T. and B. Stevens (2019), “The scientific challenge of understanding and estimating climate change”, *Proceedings of the National Academy of Sciences*, Vol. 116/49, pp. 24390-24395, http://dx.doi.org/10.1073/pnas.1906691116. [122]

Patankar, A. (2019), “Impacts of natural disasters on households and small businesses in India”, *SSRN Electronic Journal*, http://dx.doi.org/10.2139/ssrn.3590902. [171]

Peng, W. et al. (2021), “Climate policy models need to get real about people — here’s how”, *Nature*, Vol. 594/7862, pp. 174-176, http://dx.doi.org/10.1038/d41586-021-01500-2. [89]

Perkins, S. and L. Alexander (2013), “On the Measurement of Heat Waves”, *Journal of Climate*, Vol. 26/13, pp. 4500-4517, http://dx.doi.org/10.1175/jcli-d-12-00383.1. [50]

Perman, R. et al. (2011), *Natural Resource and Environmental Economics* -, Addison Wesley, https://www.amazon.fr/Natural-Resource-Environmental-Economics-Perman/dp/0321417534 (accessed on 6 January 2021). [210]

Philip, S. et al. (2020), “A protocol for probabilistic extreme event attribution analyses”, *Advances in Statistical Climatology, Meteorology and Oceanography*, Vol. 6/2, pp. 177-203, http://dx.doi.org/10.5194/ascmo-6-177-2020. [29]

Pidgeon, N. (2012), “Climate change risk perception and communication: Addressing a critical moment?”, *Risk Analysis*, Vol. 32/6, pp. 951-956, http://dx.doi.org/10.1111/j.1539-6924.2012.01856.x. [238]

Pindyck, R. (2017), “The use and misuse of models for climate policy”, *Review of Environmental Economics and Policy*, Vol. 11/1, pp. 100-114, http://dx.doi.org/10.1093/reep/rew012. [192]

Poortvliet, P. et al. (2020), “Communicating Climate Change Risk: A Content Analysis of IPCC’s Summary for Policymakers”, *Sustainability*, Vol. 12/12, p. 4861, http://dx.doi.org/10.3390/su12124861. [239]

Prigerson, H. and P. Maciejewski (2006), *Prolonged Grief Disorder (PG-13)*, Weill Cornell Medicine Center for Research on End-of-Life Care, New York. [186]

Rahmstorf, S., G. Foster and N. Cahill (2017), “Global temperature evolution: Recent trends and some pitfalls”, *Environmental Research Letters*, Vol. 12/5, p. 054001, http://dx.doi.org/10.1088/1748-9326/aa6825. [17]

Rai, V. and A. Henry (2016), *Agent-based Modelling of Consumer Energy Choices*, Nature Publishing Group, http://dx.doi.org/10.1038/nclimate2967. [201]

Randles, C. et al. (2017), "The MERRA-2 Aerosol Reanalysis, 1980 onward. Part I: System description and data assimilation evaluation", *Journal of Climate*, Vol. 30/17, pp. 6823-6850, http://dx.doi.org/10.1175/jcli-d-16-0609.1. [26]

Ranger, N. et al. (2010), "An assessment of the potential impact of climate change on flood risk in Mumbai", *Climatic Change*, Vol. 104/1, pp. 139-167, http://dx.doi.org/10.1007/s10584-010-9979-2. [179]

Riahi, K. et al. (2017), "The Shared Socioeconomic Pathways and their energy, land use, and greenhouse gas emissions implications: An overview", *Global Environmental Change*, Vol. 42, pp. 153-168, http://dx.doi.org/10.1016/j.gloenvcha.2016.05.009. [8]

Robine, J. et al. (2008), "Death toll exceeded 70,000 in Europe during the summer of 2003", *Comptes Rendus Biologies*, Vol. 331/2, pp. 171-178, http://dx.doi.org/10.1016/j.crvi.2007.12.001. [56]

Rode, K. et al. (2015), "Can polar bears use terrestrial foods to offset lost ice-based hunting opportunities?", *Frontiers in Ecology and the Environment*, Vol. 13/3, pp. 138-145, http://dx.doi.org/10.1890/140202. [183]

Rogelj, J. et al. (2021), "Net-zero emissions targets are vague: Three ways to fix", *Nature*, Vol. 591/7850, pp. 365-368, http://dx.doi.org/10.1038/d41586-021-00662-3. [90]

Romer, D. (2020), "In praise of confidence intervals", *AEA Papers and Proceedings*, Vol. 110, pp. 55-60, http://dx.doi.org/10.1257/pandp.20201059. [161]

Rowell, D. (2011), "Sources of uncertainty in future changes in local precipitation", *Climate Dynamics*, Vol. 39/7-8, pp. 1929-1950, http://dx.doi.org/10.1007/s00382-011-1210-2. [116]

Russo, S. et al. (2016), "When will unusual heat waves become normal in a warming Africa?", *Environmental Research Letters*, Vol. 11/5, p. 054016, http://dx.doi.org/10.1088/1748-9326/11/5/054016. [47]

Samir, K. and W. Lutz (2017), "The human core of the Shared Socioeconomic Pathways: Population scenarios by age, sex and level of education for all countries to 2100", *Global Environmental Change*, Vol. 42, pp. 181-192, http://dx.doi.org/10.1016/j.gloenvcha.2014.06.004. [214]

Serdeczny, O., E. Waters and S. Chan (2016), "Non-economic loss and damage in the context of climate change", *Discussion Paper*, No. 3, German Development Institute, Bonn. [176]

Sharpe, S. and T. Lenton (2021), "Upward-scaling tipping cascades to meet climate goals: Plausible grounds for hope", *Climate Policy*, Vol. 21/4, pp. 421-433, http://dx.doi.org/10.1080/14693062.2020.1870097. [240]

Shepherd, T. (2019), "Storyline approach to the construction of regional climate change information", *Proceedings of the Royal Society A: Mathematical, Physical and Engineering Sciences*, Vol. 475/2225, p. 20190013, http://dx.doi.org/10.1098/rspa.2019.0013. [11]

Shepherd, T. (2014), "Atmospheric circulation as a source of uncertainty in climate change projections", *Nature Geoscience*, Vol. 7/10, pp. 703-708, http://dx.doi.org/10.1038/ngeo2253. [114]

Shepherd, T. et al. (2018), "Storylines: an alternative approach to representing uncertainty in physical aspects of climate change", *Climatic Change*, Vol. 151/3-4, pp. 555-571, http://dx.doi.org/10.1007/s10584-018-2317-9. [125]

Sherwood, S. et al. (2020), "An Assessment of Earth's Climate Sensitivity Using Multiple Lines of Evidence", *Reviews of Geophysics*, Vol. 58/4, http://dx.doi.org/10.1029/2019rg000678. [71]

Siler, N. et al. (2018), "Revisiting the surface-energy-flux perspective on the sensitivity of global precipitation to climate change", *Climate Dynamics*, Vol. 52/7-8, pp. 3983-3995, http://dx.doi.org/10.1007/s00382-018-4359-0. [113]

Singh, C. (2018), *Assessing India's Mounting Climate Losses to Financial Institutions*, Action on Climate Today, http://www.indiaenvironmentportal.org.in/files/file/climate-losses-revised.pdf. [174]

Singh, C. et al. (2021), "Losses and damages associated with slow-onset events: Urban drought and water insecurity in Asia", *Current Opinion in Environmental Sustainability*, Vol. 50, pp. 72-86, http://dx.doi.org/10.1016/j.cosust.2021.02.006. [178]

Sjoukje Philip, C. et al. (2021), "Rapid attribution analysis of the extraordinary heatwave on the Pacific Coast of the US and Canada June 2021", World Weather Attribution, https://www.worldweatherattribution.org/wp-content/uploads/NW-US-extreme-heat-2021-scientific-report-WWA.pdf. [101]

Smith, D. et al. (2019), "Robust skill of decadal climate predictions", *npj Climate and Atmospheric Science*, Vol. 2/1, http://dx.doi.org/10.1038/s41612-019-0071-y. [109]

Stainforth, D. and R. Calel (2020), "New priorities for climate science and climate economics in the 2020s", *Nature Communications*, Vol. 11/1, http://dx.doi.org/10.1038/s41467-020-16624-8. [123]

Steffen, W. et al. (2019), *Compound Costs: How Climate Change is Damaging Australia's Economy*, Climate Council of Australia, Potts Point. [43]

Steffen, W. et al. (2018), "Trajectories of the Earth System in the Anthropocene", *Proceedings of the National Academy of Sciences*, Vol. 115/33, pp. 8252-8259, http://dx.doi.org/10.1073/pnas.1810141115. [80]

Sterner, T. and U. Persson (2008), "An even Sterner Review: Introducing relative prices into the discounting debate", *Review of Environmental Economics and Policy*, Vol. 2/1, pp. 61-76, http://dx.doi.org/10.1093/reep/rem024. [207]

Stern, N. (2013), "The structure of economic modeling of the potential impacts of climate change: Grafting gross underestimation of risk onto already narrow science models", *Journal of Economic Literature*, Vol. 51/3, pp. 838-859, http://dx.doi.org/10.1257/jel.51.3.838. [196]

Stern, N. (2006), *The Economics of Climate Change : The Stern Review*, Cambridge University Press, Cambridge, United Kingdom. [189]

Stillman, J. (2019), "Heat waves, the new normal: Summertime temperature extremes will impact animals, ecosystems, and human communities", *Physiology*, Vol. 34/2, pp. 86-100, http://dx.doi.org/10.1152/physiol.00040.2018. [108]

Stocker, T. et al. (2001), "Physical climate processes and feedbacks", in Houghton, J. et al. (eds.), *Climate Change 2001: The Scientific Basis – Contribution of Working Group I to the Third Assessment Report of the Intergovernmental Panel on Climate Change*, Cambridge University Press, Cambridge, United Kingdom and New York, NY. [241]

Stocker, T. et al. (2013), "Technical summary", in Stocker, T. et al. (eds.), *Climate Change 2013: The Physical Science Basis. Contribution of Working Group I to the Fifth Assessment Report of the Intergovernmental Panel on Climate Change*, Intergovernmental Panel on Climate Change, Geneva. [79]

Stott, P., D. Stone and M. Allen (2004), "Human contribution to the European heatwave of 2003", *Nature*, Vol. 432/7017, pp. 610-614, http://dx.doi.org/10.1038/nature03089. [98]

Strobl, E. (2012), "The economic growth impact of natural disasters in developing countries: Evidence from hurricane strikes in the Central American and Caribbean regions", *Journal of Development Economics*, Vol. 97/1, pp. 130-141, http://dx.doi.org/10.1016/j.jdeveco.2010.12.002. [159]

Subroy, V. et al. (2019), "The worth of wildlife: A meta-analysis of global non-market values of threatened species", *Ecological Economics*, Vol. 164, p. 106374, http://dx.doi.org/10.1016/j.ecolecon.2019.106374. [213]

Sutton, R. (2019), "Climate science needs to take risk assessment much more seriously", *Bulletin of the American Meteorological Society*, Vol. 100/9, pp. 1637-1642, http://dx.doi.org/10.1175/bams-d-18-0280.1. [236]

Taupo, T., H. Cuffe and I. Noy (2018), "Household vulnerability on the frontline of climate change: the Pacific atoll nation of Tuvalu", *Environmental Economics and Policy Studies*, Vol. 20/4, pp. 705-739, http://dx.doi.org/10.1007/s10018-018-0212-2. [145]

Tong, S. (2017), "Flooding-related displacement and mental health", *The Lancet Planetary Health*, Vol. 1/4, pp. e124-e125, http://dx.doi.org/10.1016/s2542-5196(17)30062-1. [39]

Trewin, B. et al. (2021), "Headline indicators for global climate monitoring", *Bulletin of the American Meteorological Society*, Vol. 102/1, pp. E20-E37, http://dx.doi.org/10.1175/bams-d-19-0196.1. [22]

Tschakert, P. et al. (2017), "Climate change and loss, as if people mattered: Values, places and experiences", *WIREs Climate Change*, Vol. 8/5, http://dx.doi.org/10.1002/wcc.476. [186]

Tschakert, P. et al. (2019), "One thousand ways to experience loss: A systematic analysis of climate-related intangible harm from around the world", *Global Environmental Change*, Vol. 55, pp. 58-72, http://dx.doi.org/10.1016/j.gloenvcha.2018.11.006. [137]

Tschumi, E. and J. Zscheischler (2019), "Countrywide climate features during recorded climate-related disasters", *Climatic Change*, Vol. 158/3-4, pp. 593-609, http://dx.doi.org/10.1007/s10584-019-02556-w. [33]

Turner, W. (2013), "Satellites: Make data freely accessible", *Nature*, Vol. 498/7452, pp. 37-37, http://dx.doi.org/10.1038/498037c. [155]

Uddin, M. et al. (2019), "Mapping of climate vulnerability of the coastal region of Bangladesh using principal component analysis", *Applied Geography*, Vol. 102, pp. 47-57, http://dx.doi.org/10.1016/j.apgeog.2018.12.011. [162]

UNFCCC (2015), *Paris Agreement*, United Nations Framework Convention on Climate Change, Paris, https://treaties.un.org/pages/ViewDetails.aspx?src=TREATY&mtdsg_no=XXVII-7-d&chapter=27. [68]

Usanov, A. and M. Gehem (2014), *Innovation in a Waming World*, The Hague Centre for Strategic Studies and TNO, https://hcss.nl/report/innovation-in-a-warming-world-research-tackling-the-grand-challenge-of-climate-change-in-europe/. [151]

Vaidyanathan, A. et al. (2019), "Assessment of extreme heat and hospitalizations to inform early warning systems", *Proceedings of the National Academy of Sciences*, Vol. 116/12, pp. 5420-5427, http://dx.doi.org/10.1073/pnas.1806393116. [58]

van der Geest, K. et al. (2019), "The impacts of climate change on ecosystem services and resulting losses and damages to people and society", in Mechler, R. et al. (eds.), *Loss and Damage from Climate Change. Climate Risk Management, Policy and Governance*, Springer, Cham, http://dx.doi.org/10.1007/978-3-319-72026-5_9. [205]

van Vuuren, D. et al. (2017), "Energy, land-use and greenhouse gas emissions trajectories under a green growth paradigm", *Global Environmental Change*, Vol. 42, pp. 237-250, http://dx.doi.org/10.1016/j.gloenvcha.2016.05.008. [217]

Varian, H. (2006), "Economist seeks to recalculate the costs of global climate change", *New York Times*, 14 December, https://www.nytimes.com/2006/12/14/business/worldbusiness/14iht-climate.3896788.html (accessed on 31 March 2021). [226]

Vautard, R. et al. (2020), "Human contribution to the record-breaking June and July 2019 heatwaves in Western Europe", *Environmental Research Letters*, Vol. 15/9, p. 094077, http://dx.doi.org/10.1088/1748-9326/aba3d4. [99]

Visser, H., A. Petersen and W. Ligtvoet (2014), "On the relation between weather-related disaster impacts, vulnerability and climate change", *Climatic Change*, Vol. 125/3-4, pp. 461-477, http://dx.doi.org/10.1007/s10584-014-1179-z. [30]

Viswanathan, B. and K. Kavi Kumar (2015), "Weather, agriculture and rural migration: Evidence from state and district level migration in India", *Environment and Development Economics*, Vol. 20/4, pp. 469-492, http://dx.doi.org/10.1017/s1355770x1500008x. [170]

Wagner, G. and M. Weitzman (2018), "Potentially large equilibrium climate sensitivity tail uncertainty", *Economics Letters*, Vol. 168, pp. 144-146, http://dx.doi.org/10.1016/j.econlet.2018.04.036. [73]

Ward, P. et al. (2017), "A global framework for future costs and benefits of river-flood protection in urban areas", *Nature Climate Change*, Vol. 7/9, pp. 642-646, http://dx.doi.org/10.1038/nclimate3350. [37]

Weitzman, M. (2009), "Additive damages, fat-tailed climate dynamics, and uncertain discounting", *Economics: The Open-Access, Open-Assessment E-Journal*, Vol. 3/2009-39, p. 1, http://dx.doi.org/10.5018/economics-ejournal.ja.2009-39. [74]

Wei, Y., Z. Mi and Z. Huang (2015), "Climate policy modeling: An online SCI-E and SSCI based literature review", *Omega*, Vol. 57, pp. 70-84, http://dx.doi.org/10.1016/j.omega.2014.10.011. [187]

Whiteman, J. et al. (2015), “Summer declines in activity and body temperature offer polar bears limited energy savings”, *Science*, Vol. 349/6245, pp. 295-298, http://dx.doi.org/10.1126/science.aaa8623. [184]

Whitman, S. et al. (1997), “Mortality in Chicago attributed to the July 1995 heat wave”, *American Journal of Public Health*, Vol. 87/9, pp. 1515-1518, http://dx.doi.org/10.2105/ajph.87.9.1515. [55]

WHO (2021), “Hospital beds (per 10 000 population)”, *Global Health Observatory*, (database), https://www.who.int/data/gho/data/indicators/indicator-details/GHO/hospital-beds-(per-10-000-population) (accessed on 10 September 2021). [141]

WHO (2014), *Quantitative risk assessment of the effects of climate change on selected causes of death, 2030s and 2050s*, https://apps.who.int/iris/bitstream/handle/10665/134014/9789241507691_eng.pdf?sequence=1&isAllowed=y. [135]

Witsenburg, K. and W. Adano (2009), “Of rain and raids: Violent livestock raiding in northern Kenya”, *Civil Wars*, Vol. 11/4, pp. 514-538, http://dx.doi.org/10.1080/13698240903403915. [180]

World Bank (2021), *Climate Change Knowledge Portal*, website, https://climateknowledgeportal.worldbank.org/ (accessed on 10 September 2021). [204]

World Bank (2021), “Subnational population”, *DataBank*, (database), https://databank.worldbank.org/source/subnational-population (accessed on 10 September 2021). [140]

Xu, Z., Y. Han and Z. Yang (2018), “Dynamical downscaling of regional climate: A review of methods and limitations”, *Science China Earth Sciences*, Vol. 62/2, pp. 365-375, http://dx.doi.org/10.1007/s11430-018-9261-5. [35]

Zander, K. et al. (2015), “Heat stress causes substantial labour productivity loss in Australia”, *Nature Climate Change*, Vol. 5/7, pp. 647-651, http://dx.doi.org/10.1038/nclimate2623. [44]

Zappa, G., E. Bevacqua and T. Shepherd (2021), “Communicating potentially large but non-robust changes in multi-model projections of future climate”, *International Journal of Climatology*, Vol. 41/6, pp. 3657-3669, http://dx.doi.org/10.1002/joc.7041. [10]

Zappa, G. and T. Shepherd (2017), “Storylines of atmospheric circulation change for European regional climate impact assessment”, *Journal of Climate*, Vol. 30/16, pp. 6561-6577, http://dx.doi.org/10.1175/jcli-d-16-0807.1. [117]

Zelinka, M. et al. (2020), “Causes of higher climate sensitivity in CMIP6 models”, *Geophysical Research Letters*, Vol. 47/1, http://dx.doi.org/10.1029/2019gl085782. [77]

Zittis, G. et al. (2021), “Business-as-usual will lead to super and ultra-extreme heatwaves in the Middle East and North Africa”, *npj Climate and Atmospheric Science*, Vol. 4/1, http://dx.doi.org/10.1038/s41612-021-00178-7. [49]

Notes

[1] The Flood Observatory, https://floodobservatory.colorado.edu/.

[2] A carbon dioxide equivalent or CO_2 equivalent (CO_2-eq) is a metric used to compare the emissions from various GHG to CO_2 emissions. It is calculated by converting amounts of other gases to the equivalent amount of carbon dioxide on the basis of their global-warming potential (GWP).

[3] For assessment of losses and damages while atmospheric concentrations of GHGs continue to rise and the climate is still changing, the TCR is the more useful metric to understand levels of global change such as climatic responses in the mid-21st century. For assessment of the long-term "new normal" resulting from a given level of climate change, after the Earth system has stabilised, the ECS is more useful to understand changes such as the long-term sea level rise commitment.

[4] The uncertainty in the ECS range arises from the multiple processes and feedbacks in the climate system. These can amplify or dampen the amount of warming resulting from a direct increase in emissions and thus forcing. Atmospheric feedbacks, which largely control ECS, include water vapour in the atmosphere and clouds and their interaction with radiation. In addition, uncertainties in oceanic processes determining the transports of air-sea fluxes of heat and surface reflectivity, such as albedo of clouds, snow or land surfaces, are also at the origin of the uncertainty range in ECS (Stocker et al., 2001[241]). There is high confidence that in combination these feedbacks will lead to an amplification (rather than dampening) of the warming that would be expected by simple physics, especially over long-term scales (Flato, 2013[12]).

[5] Note this is not inconsistent with the AR5 "likely" (66-100% probability) range being 1.5-4.5ºC, since there was up to a 34% chance of the outcome being outside the bounds.

[6] Observed global mean surface temperature (GMST) provided for the decade 2006-15 relative to the average over the 1850-1900 period (IPCC, 2018[97]). The likely range is between 0.75°C and 0.99°C.

[7] A GCM model divides up the Earth into slices, a so-called grid, at which a high number of complex processes of the Earth's dynamics are modelled and projected. The spatial resolution of state-of-the-art GCMs is about 100 km.

[8] Temperature anomalies mean a deviation from a baseline reference value. A positive anomaly means the temperature in question is above the baseline and a negative anomaly means the temperature is below that baseline. "Anomaly" is a scientific term and does not mean that anything is unexpected or unexplainable. The use of temperature anomalies minimises biases introduced by models and the effect of climate variability. This allows for more meaningful comparisons between locations and models, as well as more accurate calculations of temperature trends.

[9] Exposure describes the assets and livelihoods that are exposed to climatic hazards, such as people living in low lying coastal areas. Vulnerability describes the propensity of exposed assets and livelihoods to be adversely affected by hazards, such as physical durability of buildings in low lying coastal areas (see Section 1.4 in Chapter 1).

[10] There are exceptions, of course, such as the insurance market, where more information may collapse the market: for example, if an insurance provider knows exactly which households will be hit with floods in the next couple of years, it will refuse to provide insurance to those households. In turn, households that will not be affected will not take insurance. They know they are only being offered insurance because they will not be hit. This is because insurance essentially creates a market for uncertainty (see Chapter 5). Once

uncertainty is sufficiently alleviated, they will not work. However, even these markets cannot work with a sufficient amount of information, which enables a risk transfer through the market. This is one reason why governments must strive to balance privacy of insureds and information that insurance companies can access.

12 There are different types of IAMs and different models for each type of IAM, developed by a number of institutions and research entities over the years. Full-scale IAMs describe the potential evolution of energy-system, population growth, economic development and other drivers of emissions such as agriculture and land use. These are traditionally used to examine the cost-effectiveness of achieving mitigation goals. Another type of IAMs, which are the focus of this section, are reduced-complexity. They make simplified assumptions around socio-economic drivers of emissions, costs of mitigations, while including costs of avoiding climate impacts.

13 Sterner and Persson (2008[207]) assume 0.5 for elasticity of substitution, meaning a 10% increase in environmental goods' price would increase the demand for the other good by 5% – with perfect substitution the figure would be 10%.

14 "Abrupt" is difficult to define, especially in the social sciences. Some papers do not even consider the temporal aspects of socio-economic tipping points (David Tàbara et al., 2018[224]). Sharpe and Lenton (2021[240]) consider a length of 20 years as a tipping point. Otto et al. (2020[222]) define it as 30 years.

15 For example, if there is a 50% chance the 10% discount rate is appropriate, and a 50% chance the 0% discount rate is appropriate, then the expected value in 100 years is: $0.5 \times (1-0.1)^{100} + 0.5 \times (1-0)^{100} \approx 0.5$. The implied certainty-equivalent social discount rate is r: $0.5 = (1-r)^{100}$. Thus, $r = 0.01$ or 1%, which is below 5% (the average of 10% and 0%).

3 Climate change impacts and their cascading effects: implications for losses and damages

This chapter characterises observed and projected physical and socio-economic losses and damages, highlighting the interconnectedness of risks across societies. It aims at elucidating the potential cascading effects of impacts from climate change and how these add complexity to the evaluation of risks. The nature and potential scale of climate risks are illustrated by analysis of impacts of sea-level rise in Small Island Developing States; the potential impact of and attribution of extreme events to human-made climate change; and the implications of crossing a tipping threshold for the Atlantic Meridional Overturning Circulation.

In Brief

Climate-related hazards are widespread and intensifying rapidly, leading to cascading impacts across sectors and international borders.

This chapter analyses three broad categories of physical climate hazard: i) ***extreme weather events,*** including higher frequency and severity of heatwaves, droughts, extreme rainfall and floods; ii) ***slow-onset events***, including sea-level rise, ocean acidification, glacial retreat, loss of biodiversity and desertification; and iii) ***tipping points,*** including Atlantic Meridional Overturning Circulation (AMOC) collapse and the Amazon rainforest dieback.

Natural, social and economic systems around the world are interconnected and interdependent. Consequently, climate change impacts may propagate internationally through, for example, global trade, financial flows and supply networks. These cascading effects of climate change across sectors and international borders pose particular challenge to risk assessments.

This chapter provides a discussion and novel analysis of three specific instances of climate-related hazards, one from each of the three broad categories above. These hazards pose serious threats to human and natural systems, leading to losses and damages already today for extreme and slow-onset events. The severity of these hazards, summarised below, is projected to increase.

Sea-level rise in Small Island Developing States

- Small Island Developing States (SIDS) comprise a heterogeneous group of island territories most of which are situated in the Caribbean, the Pacific and the Indian Ocean. Irrespective of this diversity, all SIDS are vulnerable to climate change, and in particular sea-level rise (SLR) for four reasons: i) the most habitable area of SIDS is the low-lying coastal zone; ii) SIDS are disproportionally affected by weather-related disasters; iii) SIDS have fragile economies and a limited range of natural resources; and iv) many are far away from markets.
- Impacts, losses and damages in SIDS as a result of SLR are manifold: coastal flooding; coastal erosion and loss of land; loss of ecosystems, which enhances coastal flooding and erosion; and loss of freshwater resources.

Quantifying the adverse impacts of climate change with extreme event attribution

- Assessing and quantifying the real-world impacts of climate change as they manifest themselves represents an enduring challenge for scientists. "Attribution science" represents a "bottom-up" methodology to disentangle the different physical drivers of these costly disasters. It also helps quantify the exacerbating effect of climate change on individual extreme weather events.
- Novel analysis reveals that heat-related extremes are becoming more frequent and severe by orders of magnitude more rapidly than any other type of extreme weather. It also shows tropical oceans are, by far, witnessing the most rapid relative changes in high-temperature extremes. The next most rapid changes occur in North African and Middle East arid regions, and then other tropical land areas. In addition, the average relative change in extreme heat is 50% higher for a person in a Least Developed Country (LDC) compared to global average increase. Meanwhile, OECD members experience relative changes in extreme heat slower than the global average.
- The severity of a climate-related hazard is an imperfect proxy for the severity of impacts; vulnerability and exposure also play a crucial role in determining the magnitude of losses and

damages. Indeed, relatively common and/or frequent weather hazards can still cause significant and detrimental impacts if they strike vulnerable, exposed communities. The opportunities to reduce vulnerability are largest in poorer countries.

- Attribution science offers many benefits, particularly a method to causally link the recent extreme weather events with climate change. However, it too often produces an inconclusive result when considering weather extremes that impact lower income countries. Specific impediments to raising the quality and quantity of event attribution studies for lower income countries have been identified. These include poor observational records, the inadequacy of lower-resolution climate models and differences in extreme event impact reporting mechanisms.
- There is an urgent need to develop a quantitative inventory of the impacts of extreme weather due to anthropogenic climate change. This chapter proposes a preliminary framework for an inventory of the impacts of climate change from extreme weather.

Tipping points

- The abrupt weakening or collapse of the AMOC would result in a climatic shift with profound regional, and even global, implications. Europe would become colder and drier, which would reduce agricultural productivity and render most land unsuitable for arable farming. Boreal forests in northern Europe and Asia would likely die back, mostly due to regional drying. Conversely, boreal forests in North America could benefit from increased precipitation and cooler summers.
- The reorganisation of the climate system induced by the AMOC collapse would affect ecosystems, as well as human health, livelihoods, food security, water supply and economic growth at a global scale. Changes in sea-surface temperature and rainfall patterns in the tropical Atlantic would impact the stability of the Amazon. The future climate of the Amazon region after an AMOC shutdown would resemble the climate of African regions where savannah and grasslands are the dominant biome, suggesting the loss of the rainforest. Even without the AMOC collapse, northern Africa is projected to experience the largest decrease in rainfall on the planet due to climate change. A collapse of the AMOC would disrupt the West African monsoon, leading to further reduction in precipitation.
- The AMOC collapse explored in depth in this report is just one of the many parts of the Earth system that have the potential to display a tipping point. The Intergovernmental Panel on Climate Change (IPCC) assesses the shutdown of the AMOC as "very unlikely" within this century i.e. 0-10% likelihood. However, such a collapse cannot be ruled out. Recent research shows the AMOC is at its weakest in a millennium and that this slowdown will likely continue. Given the potentially far-reaching cascading impacts, such high-impact low-likelihood events must be included in risk assessments, as the IPCC recommends.
- Climate change continues to reshape the global socio-economic structure. This is likely to impact on progress towards Sustainable Development Goals, disrupt global trade and amplify social conflict, inequalities and human security. As well as rapid and deep reductions in greenhouse gas emissions, measuring and monitoring of key tipping elements, such as the AMOC, will provide countries with time to develop strategies (including through adaptation and preventive measures) to deal with the consequences of these abrupt changes of the climate systems.

3.1. Introduction

Losses and damages are the outcome of complex and linked physical and socio-economic processes over many decades and even centuries. As highlighted in Chapter 1, it is useful to think about climate risks in terms of climate-related ***hazards*** of a given intensity, ***exposure*** and ***vulnerability*** to that hazard (IPCC, 2014[1]). This means that risk depends on the scale of anthropogenic climate change at a global level. Together with the geographical location of the country, this anthropogenic change determines the nature and intensity of the climate-related hazards it faces. The risk also depends on exposure of human and natural systems to that hazard. Finally, it depends on vulnerability to the different hazards to which the country is subjected.

The interaction of these three elements acting on interconnected systems may lead to key risks cascading through sectors and regions. Storm surges, coastal flooding or sea-level rise (SLR), for example, may disrupt livelihoods. Systemic risks due to extreme weather events may also lead to breakdown of infrastructure networks and critical services; risk of food and water insecurity; and loss of rural livelihoods and income, particularly for poorer populations (IPCC, 2014[2]).

Chapter 1 highlighted, among others, that climate change leads to significant changes in natural and human systems on all continents and across oceans. Chapter 2 examined in detail the different types and levels of uncertainties in all three elements of risk, namely hazards, exposure and vulnerability. These uncertainties must be considered when formulating approaches to reducing and managing the risks of losses and damages from climate change. Chapter 3 provides in-depth analysis of three types of climate-related hazards as well their associated impacts. Section 3.2 provides a summary description of climate-related hazards, including extreme weather events, slow-onset events and tipping points. Section 3.3 discusses the potential for cascading impacts spanning over different sectors and regions. The chapter then discusses three specific types of climate-related hazards likely to give rise to losses and damages. First, it looks at sea-level rise (SLR) with a specific focus on the situation of Small Island Developing States (SIDS) (Section 3.4). Second, it examines extreme events and their attribution to anthropogenic climate change, with a specific focus on heatwaves (Section 3.5). Finally, the chapter discusses the implications of climatic tipping points for losses and damages (Section 3.6). It takes a deep dive on one specific tipping point, the weakening of the Atlantic Meridional Overturning Circulation (AMOC) that transfers heat from the equator to high latitudes in the Atlantic. These three types of hazards pose serious threats to human and natural systems. They have already led to losses and damages; the severity of these hazards are projected to increase in the future.

3.2. Climate change impacts: From climate-related hazards to economic losses

3.2.1. Climate-related hazards

The accumulation of greenhouse gas (GHG) emissions in the atmosphere will cause further warming and long-lasting changes in many components of the Earth system, amplifying current risks and creating new ones. The Intergovernmental Panel on Climate Change (IPCC) is the most authoritative source on projections of climate-related hazards from climate change. It projects with confidence that impacts of climate change will increase in severity, frequency and magnitude with continued global warming and that these impacts may become irreversible. These climate-related hazards are diverse, occur at different timescales and manifest at different speeds (IPCC, 2014[2]). Article 8 of the Paris Agreement recognises these distinct temporal scales and their potential different consequences for losses and damages. It states that "Parties recognize the importance of averting, minimising and addressing loss and damage associated with the adverse effects of climate change, including extreme weather events and slow-onset events" (Paris Agreement, 2015[3]).

In addition to extreme weather events and slow-onset events, climate change also has the potential to push components of the Earth system past critical thresholds – the "climate tipping points". This will lead to qualitatively new climatic states with potentially large-scale impacts on human and ecological systems (Lenton et al., 2008[4]). Based on a range of definitions accepted by Parties to the United Nations

Framework Convention on Climate Change (UNFCCC) or provided by the IPCC and the body of climate science literature, this chapter considers three broad categories of climate-related hazards for characterising the impacts of climate change:

- ***Extreme weather events***: IPCC defines an extreme weather event as "an event that is rare at a particular place and time of year. [...] By definition, the characteristics of what is called extreme weather may vary from place to place in an absolute sense" (IPCC, 2018[5]). Typically, an extreme weather event is associated with timeframes of less than a day to a few weeks[1] (Seneviratne et al., 2012[6]). Extreme weather events include higher frequency and severity of heatwaves, droughts, cyclones, extreme rainfall, extreme sea levels (surges, waves; Box 3.2), flooding (resulting from extreme rainfall, extreme sea levels and glacier melting) and wildfires (resulting from multivariate drivers, including heat, lack of rainfall and winds), for example.
- ***Slow-onset events***: At the time of writing, there was no official definition of slow-onset event under the IPCC. Schäfer et al. (2021[7]) define slow-onset processes "as phenomena caused or intensified by anthropogenic climate change that take place over prolonged periods of time – typically decades, or even centuries – without a clear start or end point." The UNFCCC, in its Cancun Agreements, acknowledges that slow-onset events include SLR, increasing temperatures, ocean acidification, glacial retreat and related impacts, salinisation, land and forest degradation, loss of biodiversity and desertification (UNFCCC, 2010[8]).
- ***Tipping points***: The IPCC defines tipping point as a "level of change in system properties beyond which a system reorganises, often in a nonlinear manner, and does not return to the initial state even if the drivers of the change are abated. For the climate system, the term refers to a critical threshold when global or regional climate changes from one stable state to another stable state." The IPCC introduced the idea of climate tipping points about two decades ago when they were considered likely only at high rates and magnitudes of warming between 5-6ºC by 2100 (IPCC, 2001[9]). More recent IPCC reports recognise the risk of crossing tipping points at much lower levels of warming (IPCC, 2018[10]; IPCC, 2019[11]). Examples of climate tipping elements are collapse of the West Antarctic ice sheet, the AMOC collapse, coral reef die-off and Amazon rainforest dieback.

The following sub-sections briefly analyse the most recent literature on these three distinct phenomena. As much as possible, they assess the likelihood of human influence on observed past changes (e.g. of the occurrence of different types of extreme weather events) or of the crossing of a tipping point in different potential warming futures. These likelihood assessments are based on the IPCC's well-established likelihood scale and terms as described in Chapter 2. That chapter also discussed how a risk management strategy needs to avoid the possibility of overestimating or underestimating the risk of an event (Shepherd, 2019[12]). Climate change is a problem of risk management for policy makers in national contexts (see also Chapter 2). Sutton (2019[13]), for example, considers the focus of climate science on likelihoods unhelpful as likelihoods are not the same as risk. The likelihoods presented here for projected changes therefore need to be considered critically from a policy-making perspective and when formulating risk management strategies.

Additionally, the risk of a certain event is determined by more than its likelihood. Other key factors are where and when it will occur, the levels of vulnerability and exposure of the systems impacted, as well as the severity of the hazard itself. Large singular disasters may only occur once in a few years. However, hazardous events of smaller intensity may occur far more frequently. Indeed, the cumulative impact of such high frequency, low impact events can be as or more devastating than major disasters (refer to Chapter 5 for a discussion on the impact of recurring impacts on fiscal sustainability of countries).

Extreme weather events

Climate change leads to changes in the frequency, intensity, spatial extent, duration and timing of weather extremes, potentially resulting in unprecedented extremes (IPCC, 2021[14]). Changes in many extreme weather events have been observed since the mid-20th century. Every increment of global warming causes clearly discernible increases in the intensity and frequency of hot extremes, including heatwaves, heavy precipitation and marine heatwaves. It also includes increases in the proportion of intense tropical cyclones (IPCC, 2021[14]). Figure 3.1 displays a synthesis of the number of regions where climatic impact-drivers are projected to change between 1.5-2°C. "Change" is understood as physical climate system conditions, such as means, events and extremes, that affect an element of society or ecosystems. The figure shows that changes in several climatic impact-drivers would be more widespread at 2°C relative to 1.5°C. This trend would be even more pronounced globally for higher warming levels.

Figure 3.1. Synthesis of the number of regions where climatic impact-drivers are projected to change

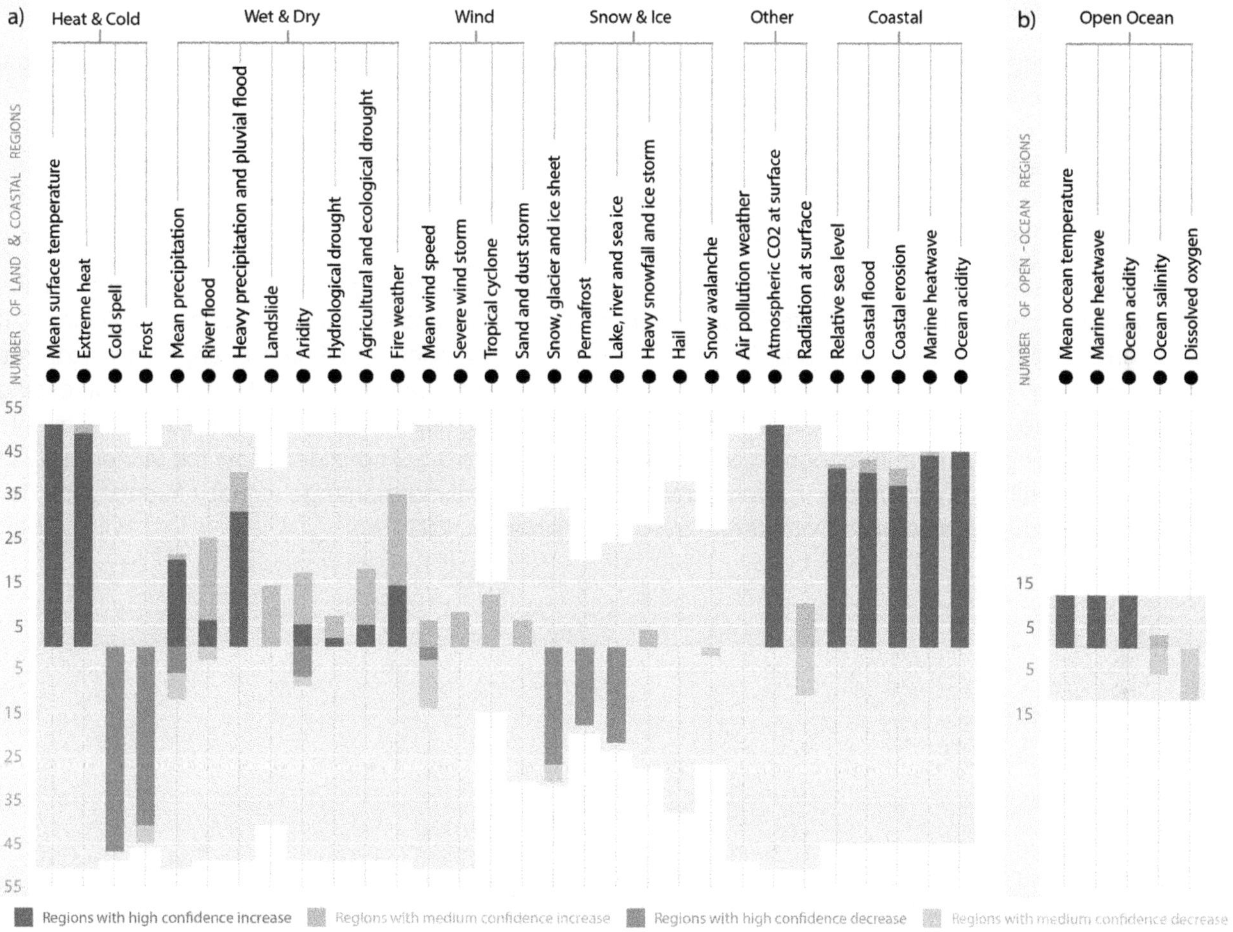

Note: Number of land and coastal regions (a) and open-ocean regions (b) where each climatic impact-driver is projected to increase or decrease with high confidence (dark shade) or medium confidence (light shade). The height of the lighter shaded "envelope" behind each bar represents the maximum number of regions for which each climatic impact-driver is relevant. The envelope is symmetrical about the x-axis showing the maximum possible number of relevant regions for climatic impact-driver increase (upper part) or decrease (lower part).
Source: Figure SPM.9 from (IPCC, 2021[14]).

Rising temperatures and more frequent heatwaves and droughts are expected to extend fire weather seasons i.e. periods of time where weather conditions are conducive to the outbreak of wildfires. The extension of fire weather seasons therefore increases the potential for wildfires (Jolly et al., 2015[15]; Ross, 6 August 2020[16]; Gomes Da Costa et al., 2020[17]).

In recent years, several major wildfires have occurred around the world. In 2017, extreme wildfires burned 1.4 million acres in Chile, which represented a cost of USD 362.2 million, including combat of wildfires, housing reconstruction and support for productive sectors, among others (González et al., 2020[18]). Extreme bushfires burned more than 46 million acres [18.6 million hectares (ha)] in Australia during the 2019-20 season, with losses estimated at about USD 1.3 billion (CDP, 2020[19]). The extreme heat in the eastern Mediterranean in early August 2021 led to severe wildfires in Greece and Turkey. Later in the month, the heatwave extended farther west, leading to fires in other European and African countries, such as Italy, France and Algeria (Frost, 2021[20]; Mezahi, 2021[21]; Frost, 2021[22]). In 2020, California wildfires burned a record-breaking 4.2 million acres (1.7 million ha). At the time of writing, fires in the 2021 season had already burned 2.2 million acres (0.9 million ha). This posed a threat to the Giant Forest, which harbours more than 2 000 Sequoia trees (Reuters, 2021[23]; Keeley and Syphard, 2021[24]). Box 3.1 describes recent impacts from record temperatures experience in the Pacific coast areas of the United States and Canada and their relation with climate change.

Peak wind speeds of the most intense tropical cyclones, as well as the proportion of intense tropical cyclones (categories 4-5), are projected to increase globally with increasing global warming (IPCC, 2021[14]). More frequent or more intense cyclonic or convective storms will also increase the frequency of extreme precipitation events (Witze, 2018[25]). Coastal flooding risk is likely to increase as a result of rising sea levels, which can lead to increased tidal flooding. This, in turn, can increase erosion rates, as well as lead to greater inundation (and salt water intrusion) as a result of storm surge.

Section 3.5 presents an in-depth analysis of the quantification of the impacts of climate change using extreme event attribution. The chapter focuses on methods and uncertainties in attribution science. It reflects on how to improve current and future estimates of the impacts of climate change from extreme weather. Extreme event attribution has evolved primarily to assess changes in the likelihood of witnessing a specific extreme weather event. It aims to provide understanding of how today's extreme weather events might be worsening due to anthropogenic climate change. Section 3.5.3 considers how the vulnerability of exposed communities to past extreme events containing a strong climate-change signal influences the risk of losses and damages associated with these events (Philip et al., 2021[26]).

Box 3.1. Recent heatwaves in the Pacific coast areas of the United States and Canada

The 2021 Pacific Northwest heat wave impacted the United States and western Canada for a four-day period, June 26-29. A large mass of high pressure air called a "heat dome" settled over regions not known for extreme heat, including Portland, Oregon and Seattle, Washington in the United States, and Vancouver, British Columbia in Canada. Temperatures rose far above 40°C in many regions. Moreover, they occurred one whole month before the climatologically warmest part of the year, normally occurring at end of July or early August (Philip et al., 2021[26]) The region's peak temperature was recorded in Lytton, British Columbia at 49.6°C, setting a new record for the entire country (Di Liberto, 2021[27]). Shortly after setting the record, wildfire spread across Lytton.

According to the National Center for Environmental Information Climate Extreme Index, the Pacific Northwest has experienced more extreme temperatures over the last 20 years (Di Liberto, 2021[27]). A study in a growing body of research termed "rapid attribution" analysis predicted the heat wave would have been extremely unlikely without human-induced climate change: the event was statistically estimated to be about a 1 in 1 000 year event in the current climate (Philip et al., 2021[26]).

The high temperatures were particularly harmful for the region as it is not adapted to this type of extreme heat. More than 500 reported deaths and 180 wildfires were recorded in British Columbia (Schiermeier, 2021[28]) and about 200 related deaths in Oregon and Washington (Popovich and Choi-Schagrin, 2021[29]). An analysis reported a sharp rise in emergency department visits. Nearly 3 000 in the Pacific Northwest visited an emergency department between June 25-30 for heat-related illness – seven times higher than in June 2019 (Schramm et al., 2021[30]).

The 2021 heat wave caused shoreline temperatures to rise above 50°C, leading to mass deaths of marine life and restructuring of entire marine ecosystems. Preliminary estimates show that billions of marine animals died from the extreme heat. These included mussels that live on the shoreline and sea creatures that live in the mussel beds. This loss can lead to cascading effects to other animals. Sea stars, for example, feed on mussels; sea ducks also feast on mussels before migrating to their summer breeding grounds in the Arctic (Einhorn, 2021[31]).

Examples of economic losses from extreme weather events

This sub-section provides data on economic losses and damages from past extreme weather events. Non-economic losses and damages are equally important albeit less easily quantifiable. These are discussed in Chapter 1 and further explored in terms of their uncertainties in Chapter 2.

Extreme weather events, especially storms, floods, droughts, wildfires, heatwaves, and cold and frost,[2] can result in economic losses; significant damage; and loss of income and livelihoods. These losses touch both private and public spheres. They can damage privately-owned buildings and infrastructure, such as homes and businesses. Publicly-owned buildings and infrastructure at risk include schools, hospitals, roads and power generation and distribution infrastructure. Reported economic losses from climate-related events are highly volatile from year-to-year. However, they have been increasing on a global basis since 2000 at a much faster rate than gross domestic product (GDP) (see Figure 3.2).[3]

Figure 3.2. Economic losses from climate-related catastrophes by type (USD bn)

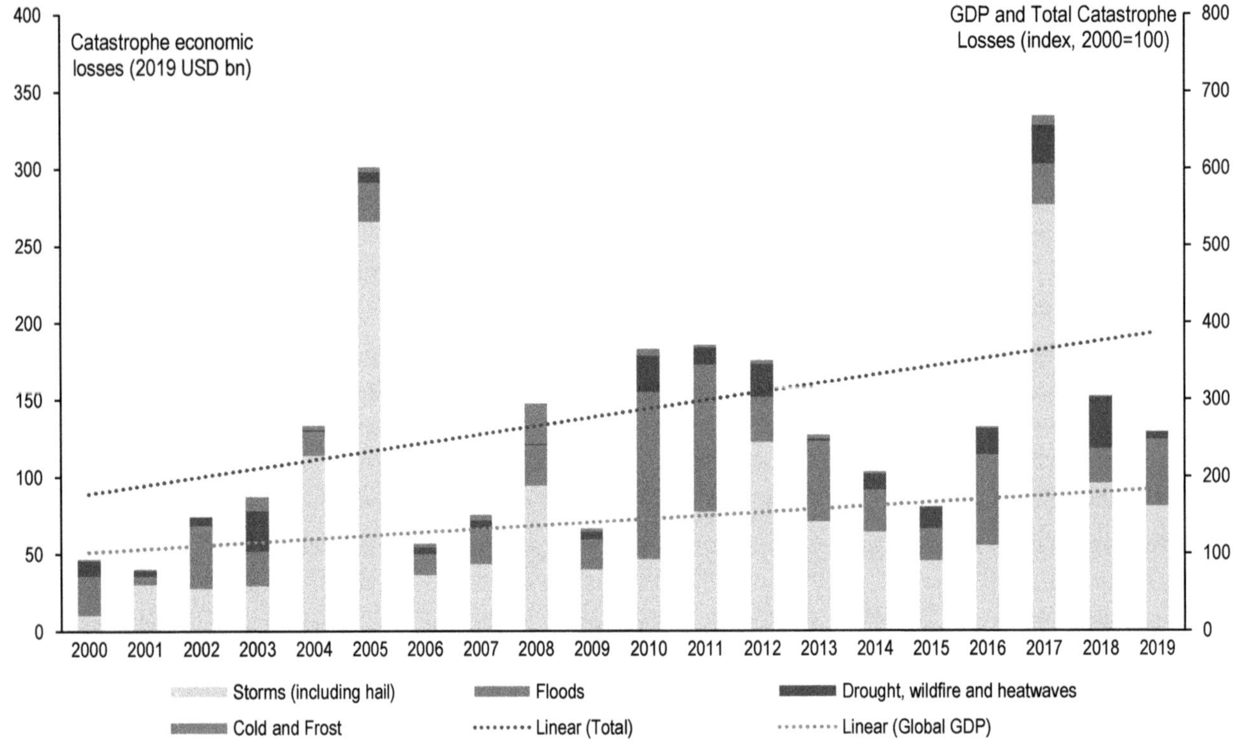

Source: OECD calculations based on data on economic losses provided by Swiss Re sigma and data on gross domestic product from *World Economic Outlook* (database) (April 2021).

There is significant uncertainty about the trajectory of future climate changes and the impact of these changes on economic losses in specific countries or locations. Nevertheless, several analyses have examined potential impacts. For example, S&P Global Ratings (2015[32]) with support from Swiss Re estimated the level of damage from a 1-in-250 year (i.e. an event with 0.4% likelihood of occurring in any given year) flood or cyclone would increase significantly in many countries by 2050 (see Figure 3.3). Increasing severity of extreme weather events, along with continued development in hazard-prone locations, will almost certainly lead to rising climate-related catastrophe losses in the future.

Figure 3.3. Increase in expected damage from a 1-in-250 year cyclone or flood in 2050 (percentage)

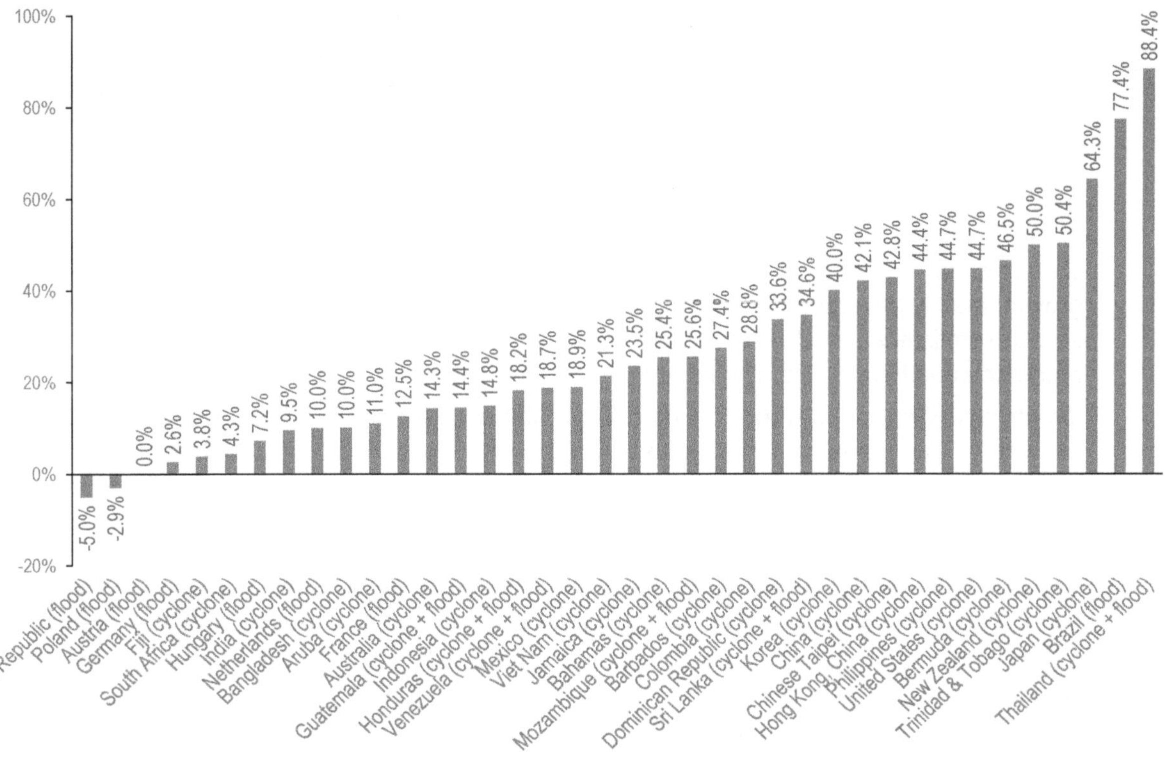

Note: The S&P Global Ratings estimates for future tropical cyclone damage are based on: i) an increase in maximum wind speed of 1% to 5%; ii) no change in frequency of cyclone formation; iii) sea-level rise of +25 cm to +40 cm across different basins; and iv) increased cyclone-related precipitation. The estimates for flood are based on estimates of changes in return periods for a 100-year flood developed by Hirabayashi et al. (2013[33]).
Source: OECD calculations based on estimates of direct damage from a 1-in-250 year flood (14 sovereign issuers) or cyclone (30 sovereign issuers) provided by S&P Global Ratings (2015[32]).

Slow-onset events

The Cancun Agreements (dating from UNFCCC COP16) include the following different types of climate-related hazards under the category of "slow-onset events": SLR, increasing temperatures, ocean acidification, glacial retreat and related impacts, salinisation, land and forest degradation, loss of biodiversity and desertification (UNFCCC, 2010[8]). As opposed to extreme weather events, slow-onset events unfold over decades or centuries. This sub-section provides a short overview of the state-of-art knowledge on slow-onset events, based on IPCC's Special Report on Climate Change and Land (IPCC, 2019[34]), the Special Report on the Ocean and Cryosphere in a Changing Climate (IPCC, 2019[35]), their review and summary provided in van der Geest and van den Berg (2021[36]) and the contribution of Working Group I to the IPCC Sixth Assessment Report (IPCC, 2021[14]).

- ***Increasing temperatures***: The global surface temperature was 1.09°C higher in 2011-20 than 1850-1900[4], but not all areas experience the average amount of warming. Over land, significantly greater rises in temperature have been measured (1.59°C on average) than over the ocean (0.88°C on average). Polar regions also experience greater warming than tropical zones, with Arctic temperatures rising by more than double the global average. Changes due to higher temperatures include heatwaves and changes to ecosystem functioning (especially in high latitudes).
- ***Sea-level rise***: Current levels of human-induced SLR are mainly from thermal expansion of seawater due to higher temperatures with increasing contributions from glacier and ice sheet melt.

Over the 20th century, SLR amounted to 1-2 millimetres (mm) per year in most regions; this rate has now accelerated to 3.7 mm per year (from 2006 to 2018). Projections of annual SLR by the end of the 21st century are of 4-9 mm and 10-20 mm per year under a low-(RCP2.6) and high-(RCP 8.5) GHG emissions scenario, respectively. Adverse effects of SLR include the exacerbation of extreme sea-level events such as storm surge and waves, and associated coastal flooding. Under high existential risk to SLR are, of course, SIDS and low-lying coastal deltas such as southern Bangladesh. Risks and uncertainties of mean SLR and extreme sea-level rise events are discussed in Box 3.2. Section 3.4 explores the potential impacts and associated losses and damages of SLR and sea-level extremes, with a particular focus on SIDS.

- ***Salinisation***: In salinisation, non-saline soil becomes saline enough to negatively affect plant growth, mainly driven by SLR and irrigation. Main impacts of salinisation include land degradation and desertification, biodiversity loss and adverse effects on agricultural production, freshwater resources and health. It is estimated that salt affects 7.4% of land globally.
- ***Ocean acidification***: Carbon dioxide (CO_2) in the atmosphere forms a weak acid as it dissolves in seawater. This leads to a decrease in pH as atmospheric CO_2 concentrations increase, with negative consequences for marine life. One notable consequence of ocean acidification is coral bleaching. Over the past three decades, seawater pH declined by 0.017-0.027 per decade as a result of rising concentrations of CO_2 in the atmosphere, a change assessed by the IPCC as "unusual in the last 2 million years"; such a decline could be up to 90% faster under an extremely high-emissions scenario (RCP8.5). Impacts of ocean acidification include loss of biodiversity, for example, by reducing the calcification of organisms and by affecting fish species, invertebrates and corals.
- ***Glacial retreat***: Glacial retreat occurs when the snow and ice mass of glaciers melt at a faster rate than they accumulate. This leads to the alteration of the flow of meltwater rivers, with adverse effects on water availability for irrigation and contributing to SLR. Ice loss on land, particularly the vast Greenland and Antarctic Ice Sheets and high mountain areas in the Andes, Himalayas and Alps, contribute with about 1.81 mm to SLR each year. Glacial retreat can lead to local and regional impacts involving river and stream flow, ecosystems and agricultural livelihoods. A loss of 36% of glacier mass is projected to occur under an extremely high-emission scenario (RCP8.5) by 2100, in comparison to 18% in a low-emission scenario (RCP2.6).
- ***Land and forest degradation***: Land degradation consists of a negative trend in land properties and conditions, often expressed as reduction or loss of biological productivity, ecological integrity and/or value to humans. Land degradation affects about 3.2 billion people worldwide. Land and forest degradation can have a wide range of impacts on the natural environment and society (e.g. loss of ecosystem services).
- ***Desertification***: This consists in degradation of land into arid, semi-arid and dry-subhumid areas and results from the interaction of different human and environmental processes, notably drought. Main impacts are related to the loss of ecosystem services and resulting implications for livelihoods of natural resource-dependent populations.
- ***Loss of biodiversity***: Biodiversity is the variability among living organisms from terrestrial, marine, and other aquatic ecosystems. Biodiversity includes variability at the genetic, species and ecosystem levels (CBD, 1992[37]). Biodiversity declines when the variability in any one of these levels decreases. Loss of biodiversity can lead to the loss of ecosystem functions. This, in turn, leads to declined ecosystem services, such as carbon sequestration and the capacity to adapt to further climate change. The main drivers of biodiversity loss are land-use change, over-exploitation of animals and plants (including illegal trade), pollution, invasive non-native species and, increasingly, climate change (Pecl et al., 2017[38]). Indeed, approaches to deal with biodiversity loss have many synergies with approaches considered by the climate agenda worldwide (See Chapter 1).

Box 3.2. Uncertainty in sea-level rise and extreme sea-level events

The Sixth Assessment Report of the IPCC (AR6) projects a ***mean sea level*** to rise by *likely* 0.6-1.0 m by 2100 if GHG emissions rise unabated (i.e. under the very high-emissions scenario RCP8.5) (Oppenheimer et al., 2019[39]; Fox-Kemper et al., 2021[40]). If emissions are reduced to meet the goal of the Paris Agreement to limit global warming "well below 2°C" (i.e. under the low-emissions scenario RCP2.6), global mean sea level would likely rise by 0.3-0.6m in 2100 (Oppenheimer et al., 2019[39]; Fox-Kemper et al., 2021[40]).

Four aspects are important for managing risks of losses and damages from sea-level rise (SLR) (Chapter 4). First, the above-named sea-level ranges are *likely ranges*, which means a 17% chance of SLR exceeding this range for a given emission scenario. The scientific uncertainty about such potential ***high-end mean SLR*** is higher than about the likely range due to ***deep uncertainty*** (Chapter 4, Section 4.2) about the possible, but unlikely, rapid melting of the ice sheets of Greenland and Antarctica. Under RCP8.5, an SLR of 2 m by 2100 cannot be ruled out (Fox-Kemper et al., 2021[40]).

Second, SLR will continue for centuries to millennia, even when GHG concentrations are stabilised due to continued ocean warming and ice sheet melt. IPCC AR6 projects that global mean sea levels will rise by 2-6 m if warming is limited to 2°C and 19-22 m with 5°C warming over the next 2 000 years.

Third, sea levels do not rise uniformly across the globe but are regionally differentiated mainly due to three factors: i) changes in ocean circulation and regionally differentiated rates of thermal expansion; ii) redistribution of mass within the cryosphere (due to the melting of the ice sheets) and hydrosphere (due to changes in land water storage); and iii) vertical land movement (Lowe et al., 2009[41]; Nicholls et al., 2013[42]; Bamber et al., 2019[43]; Hinkel et al., 2019[44]; Stammer et al., 2019[45]).

Fourth, mean SLR is a slow-onset hazard, but most impacts of mean SLR will not be felt directly. Instead, gradual mean SLR will raise the heights of ***extreme sea-level events*** such as tides, surges and waves (Oppenheimer et al., 2019[39]; Wahl et al., 2017[46]; Woodroffe, 2008[47]). Through this effect, extreme sea-level events that are rare (e.g. once per century) will become common by 2100 (e.g. annual) under every emission scenario (Menéndez and Woodworth, 2010[48]; Oppenheimer et al., 2021[49]).

The uncertainties in today's extreme sea level are thereby often larger than those associated with 21st century climate change and SLR (Wahl et al., 2017[46]). This is mostly because sufficiently long local observation of extreme sea level is lacking (e.g. for SIDS) (Nurse et al., 2014[50]). Tide-surge and wave models can provide the missing information. For example, global datasets of extreme sea level produced with numeric models are increasingly becoming available (Muis et al., 2020[51]; Muis et al., 2016[52]; Vousdoukas et al., 2017[53]). These data can be used for local analysis in SIDS if local data are lacking. While these models can generally reproduce observed extreme sea level reasonably well, they often perform badly in areas threatened by tropical cyclones. This is because climate model input data lack the spatial/temporal resolution necessary to fully include the strong winds of tropical cyclones. They also lack a sufficient number of tropical cyclones for reliable statistics of extreme values (Appendini et al., 2017[54]; Hodges, Cobb and Vidale, 2017[55]; Mentaschi et al., 2020[56]; Mentaschi, 2018[57]; Muis et al., 2020[51]).

For wave modelling, another major uncertainty is the lack of high resolution bathymetry data. These are necessary to assess how offshore waves propagate onto the shore and cause damage (Athanasiou et al., 2019[58]).

Note: In IPCC terms, *likely* means a 66% chance. Here and in the context of SLR science, likely range refers to the 17th to 83rd percentiles of the probability distribution of future SLR. This means that experts judge a 66% chance that sea levels will be within the likely range and a 17% chance that sea levels will be above this likely range.

Tipping points

In popular understanding, a "tipping point" is where a small change makes a big difference to the future state of a system (Gladwell, 2000[59]). In the context of climate change, a "climate tipping point" is where a small change in climate (e.g. global temperature) makes a big difference to a large part of the climate system, changing its future state (Lenton et al., 2008[4]). The crossing of tipping points typically triggers accelerating change and is usually inherently hard to reverse. The resulting transition to a different state can appear fast or slow from a human perspective. This perception occurs because its rate depends on the system in question (e.g. the atmosphere changes fast, the biosphere at an intermediate rate, and ice sheets typically change slowly).

Crucial to the existence of a tipping point is the presence of strongly reinforcing positive feedback within a system (Levermann et al., 2011[60]). This can amplify a small initial change and turn it into a large consequence. It can also be self-propelled without further forcing once tipped (Scheffer et al., 2012[61]). Essentially, the relative strength of positive (amplifying) and negative (damping) feedback loops within some part of the climate system can change as the overall climate changes and affects that sub-system. Climate tipping points arise when the balance of feedback loops within a part of the climate system shifts. In such a shift, positive (amplifying) feedback loops dominate over negative (damping) feedback loops. This supports self-propelling change within that part of the climate system (Lenton and Williams, 2013[62]). The relevant positive feedback loops may also act to amplify global temperature change. However, they do not have to do so for a tipping point to occur.

Climate "tipping elements" (Figure 3.4) are defined as at least sub-continental scale parts (or subsystems) of the climate system that can pass a climate tipping point (Lenton et al., 2008[4]). When near a tipping point, these elements can be tipped into a qualitatively different state by small external perturbations or by internal climate variability (Lenton, 2011[63]). However, to bring them near to a tipping point usually requires significant forcing of the climate. Policy-relevant tipping elements are defined here as those that may pass a tipping point this century due to anthropogenic climate forcing.

Figure 3.4. Candidate tipping elements in the climate system

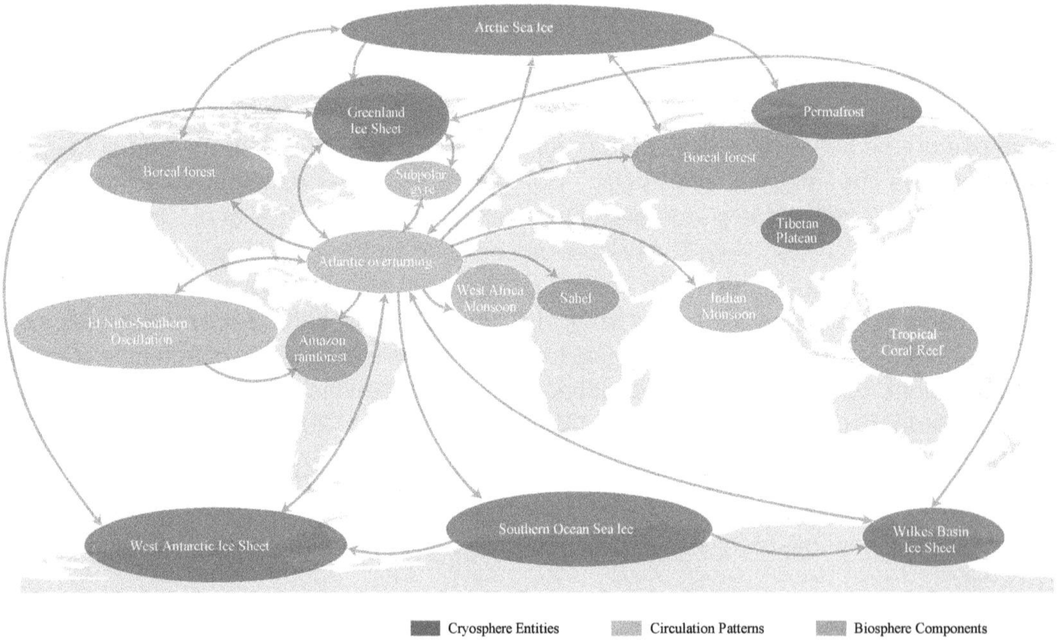

Note: Global map of candidate tipping elements of the climate systems and potential tipping cascades. Arrows show the potential interactions among the tipping elements that could generate tipping cascades, based on expert elicitation.
Source: World map obtained from Peel, M. C., Finlyson, B. L., and McMahon, T. A. (University of Melbourne).

Recently, evidence that climate tipping points may be approaching – and at least one in West Antarctica may have been crossed – has underpinned declarations of a climate and ecological emergency (Lenton et al., 2019[64]). Table 3.1 summarises different policy-relevant climate tipping points and assesses the likelihood of crossing them at different levels of global warming (above pre-industrial). The assessment is based on paleo-climate and observational evidence, future projections from different models [e.g. (Drijfhout, 2015[65])], and expert elicitation of probabilities at different levels of warming (Kriegler et al., 2009[66]). Once a threshold is crossed, the speed at which the implications unfold will be different for different tipping elements (Ritchie et al., 2021[67]). Some might impact within decades, others only over centuries.

Table 3.1. Likelihood of crossing climate tipping points at different levels of global warming

	Global warming (above pre-industrial)				
Tipping point	≤1.5°C	>1.5°C to <2°C	2°C to <3°C	3°C to 5°C	>5°C
Greenland ice sheet meltdown	Unlikely	As likely as not	Likely	Very likely	Virtually certain
West Antarctic ice sheet collapse	Unlikely	As likely as not	Likely	Very likely	Virtually certain
Wilkes Basin ice sheet collapse	Exceptionally unlikely	Exceptionally unlikely	As likely as not	Likely	Virtually certain
Arctic summer sea-ice loss	Very unlikely	As likely as not	Virtually certain		
Year-round loss of Arctic sea ice	Exceptionally unlikely	Exceptionally unlikely	Exceptionally unlikely	Very unlikely	Likely
Southern Ocean sea-ice abrupt loss	Very unlikely		Unlikely		
Subpolar gyre convection collapse	Unlikely	As likely as not	As likely as not	Likely	Likely
Atlantic overturning (AMOC) collapse	Very unlikely	Very unlikely	Unlikely	As likely as not	Likely
El Niño-Southern Oscillation shift	Exceptionally unlikely	Very unlikely	Unlikely	As likely as not	As likely as not
Tibetan plateau abrupt snow melt	Very unlikely	Unlikely	As likely as not	As likely as not	As likely as not
Permafrost abrupt collapse	Exceptionally unlikely	Exceptionally unlikely	Exceptionally unlikely	Very unlikely	Unlikely
Boreal forest dieback	Exceptionally unlikely	Very unlikely	Very unlikely	Unlikely	Unlikely
Amazon rainforest dieback	Exceptionally unlikely	Very unlikely	Unlikely	Unlikely	As likely as not
Sahel abrupt greening	Exceptionally unlikely	Exceptionally unlikely	Very unlikely	Very unlikely	Very unlikely
Tropical coral reef degradation	Very likely	Very likely	Virtually certain	Virtually certain	Virtually certain

Note: This likelihood assessment uses IPCC's well-established likelihood scale and terms (see also Chapter 2, Section 2.4): "Virtually certain"=99-100% probability; "Very likely"=90-100% probability; "Likely"=66-100% probability; "About as likely as not"=33-66% probability; "Unlikely"=0-33% probability; "Very unlikely"=0-10% probability; "Exceptionally unlikely"=0-1% probability. Probabilities are treated cumulatively with respect to temperature rise, thus for a given temperature range (e.g. >1.5°C to <2°C) the probability given for a specific tipping point is the cumulative probability of passing it at all levels of global warming up to the upper end of that range (here <2°C). The probabilities are given for each tipping point as an independent event, i.e. neglecting causal interactions between them. Overall, such contingent interactions are expected to make other tipping events more likely (although there are a few specific counterexamples) (Kriegler et al., 2009[66]; Cai, Lenton and Lontzek, 2016[68]; Wunderling et al., 2021[69]).

The tipping points probability assessment shown in Table 3.1 can be summarised as follows: Below or at 1.5°C above pre-industrial levels, it is unlikely (0-33% probability) or very unlikely (0-10% probability) that cryosphere or ocean-atmosphere tipping points will be passed. That part of the West Antarctic ice sheet may have passed a tipping point is an exception. However, between 1.5°C and 2°C above pre-industrial levels (i.e. in the Paris Agreement range) key ice sheet tipping points have a 33-66% probability of being passed. The same probability exists for complete loss of Arctic summer sea ice and a collapse of deep convection in the Labrador Sea. Between 2°C and 3°C above pre-industrial levels, it is likely (66-100% probability) that major ice sheet tipping points will be passed. It is also virtually certain (99-100% probability) that Arctic summer sea ice and tropical coral reefs will be lost. Between 3°C and 5°C above pre-industrial levels, it is very likely that major ice sheet tipping points will be passed. As likely as not (33-66% probability), there will be major reorganisations of oceanic and atmospheric circulation.

Given this probability assessment, biophysical impacts of passing particular tipping points should be assessed, as well as how these impacts translate into social impacts and economic costs. Table 3.2 summarises biophysical climate impacts for a subset of tipping points, updated from Lenton and Ciscar (2012[70]). These impacts span effects on temperature, sea level, precipitation, atmospheric circulation, ocean circulation, biogeochemical cycles, modes of climate variability and extreme weather events. In so doing, they aim to give a non-exhaustive flavour of the interconnectedness of the climate system. Effects on temperature can come both directly via changes in surface albedo (reflectivity). They can also come indirectly via changes in GHG emissions, such as CO_2 and methane (CH_4) emissions generated by permafrost thaw. Most of the listed temperature effects are positive feedback loops that will further increase global temperatures.

Table 3.2. Potential physical climate impacts of crossing different climate tipping points

Tipping event	Temperature	Sea level	Precipitation	Biogeochemical cycles	Extreme events
Greenland ice sheet meltdown	Local ↑	≤7 m global ≤0.5 m/century uneven	Local shift to rainfall, WAM disruption	Flooding of permafrost, ↑CO_2, CH_4	Storm surges, icebergs
West Antarctic ice sheet collapse	Local ↑	≤3.3 m abrupt ≤1 m/century uneven	Local shift	(as above)	Storm surges, icebergs
Wilkes Basin ice sheet collapse	Local ↑	≤4 m abrupt uneven	Local shift	(as above)	Storm surges, icebergs
Arctic summer sea-ice loss	↑Arctic & N. Hem.	(minimal effect)	Local shift snow to rainfall	↑Permafrost thawing, ↑CO_2, CH_4	Extreme European snowfall
SPG convection collapse	↓N. Atlantic	Regional shifts ↑0.3 m in parts of N. Atlantic			Amplified cold winter blocking events Europe
AMOC collapse	↓N. Hem. ↑S. Hem.	Regional shifts ↑0.8 m in parts of N. Atlantic	Sahel drying, ↓WAM, ↓ISM, ↓EAM, Amazon	↑CO_2 from ocean and land, biome changes	Cold winters in Europe, S ward hurricanes shift
ENSO shift	↑S Asia, S Australia…↓New Zealand	Regional effects	↓SE Asia, E Australia, Amazon…	↑CO_2, reduced land C storage	Droughts, floods
Boreal forest dieback	↓winter local, ↑global	–	↓regional?	↑CO_2, biodiversity loss	Fires, insect outbreaks
Amazon dieback	↑regional, ↑global	–	↓regional	↑CO_2, biodiversity loss	Droughts, fires, teleconnections

Note: WAM=West African Monsoon; ISM=Indian Summer Monsoon; EAM=East Asian Monsoon; NAO=North Atlantic Oscillation; AMO=Atlantic Multidecadal Oscillation; PDO=Pacific Decadal Oscillation; SO=Southern Oscillation.
Source: updated from (Lenton and Ciscar, 2012[70]).

3.3. Cascading impacts of climate change

The "cascading effects" of climate change are a result of the interconnectedness and interdependencies of natural, social and economic systems. Impacts propagate through international processes, such as global trade, financial flows and supply networks (Acemoglu et al., 2012[71]). These systemic climate risks pose particular challenges to risk assessment. This is especially the case when risks are transmitted in complex ways through sectors and international borders, which remain today poorly understood (Koks, 2018[72]; Challinor et al., 2018[73]).

Figure 3.5 illustrates one such complex risk transmission chain, which took place in 2010 and led to rise in food prices globally. As a result of droughts, a decline in grain yield in the Russian Federation (hereafter "Russia") led to a shortfall in cereals in the international market (also see Box 4.1). At the same time, excess rainfall in Pakistan led to a rise in food prices globally. These higher prices led to a 50% higher use of food banks in the United Kingdom. In Egypt, higher food prices became one trigger for riots leading to a change of government (Hildén et al., 2020[74]). As another example, the cascading effects of flood risk could pose global economic risks of the same order of magnitude as asset damages within and outside the affected region, due to dependencies in infrastructure systems (Koks, 2018[72]).

Figure 3.5. An example of cross-border impacts: Drought and food prices

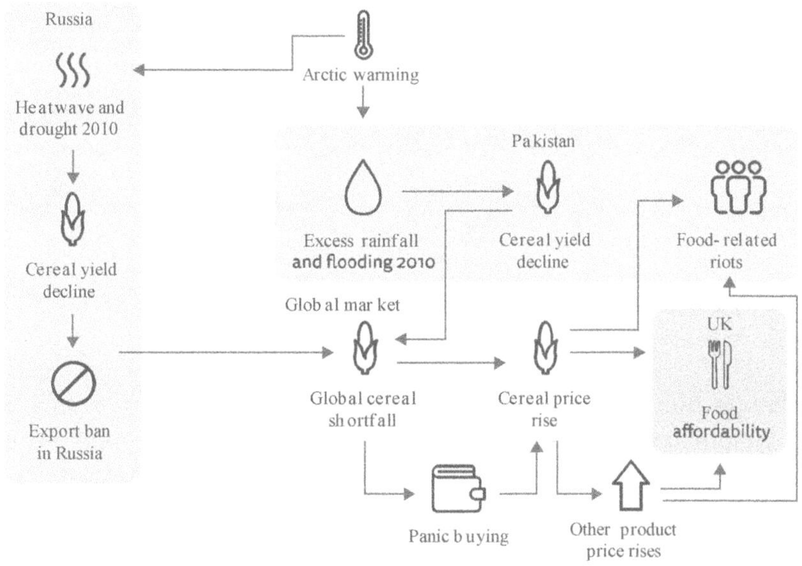

Source: (Hildén et al., 2020[74])

A cascade takes place as a result of a significant change to a key system variable or variables. This induces the breach of "multiple thresholds across scales of space, time, social organization and across ecological, social, and economic domains" (Kinzig et al., 2006[75]). These thresholds are not easy to understand or analyse, let alone to address. The 2018 Global Risks Report acknowledges it remains a challenge for humanity to deal with "complex risks in systems characterised by feedback loops, tipping points and opaque cause-and-effect relationships that can make intervention problematic" (World Economic Forum, 2018[76]).

Progress on understanding cascading impacts from climate change has been evolving mainly along three axes: socio-ecological resilience, disaster risk reduction (UNDRR, 2015[77]) and systems dynamics (Lawrence, Blackett and Cradock-Henry, 2020[78]). In this sense, work relating to cascades covers a broad range of topics and thematic areas. These include human-ecosystems dynamics, ecology, natural and climate-related hazards research and systems theory.

Box 3.3 analyses the potential impacts and implications of cascades in New Zealand. It seeks to gain insight into how different types of climate change hazards (e.g. extreme events, SLR or "surprise" elements of the climate system) play concurrently across diverse linked systems and domains (Lawrence, Blackett and Cradock-Henry, 2020[78]). This highlights the importance of understanding the different types of climate-related hazards, and their potential consequences in time and space as a basis for exploring the more complex cascading impacts from climate change.

Box 3.3. Cascading climate change impacts and implications – a case study

Lawrence, Blackett and Cradock-Henry, (2020[78]) investigated cascading impacts and implications in New Zealand. According to the analysis, the framework "systematises the interaction between cascades, who and how cascades affect the system of interest, where interdependencies and co-dependencies occur, and how far impacts and implications might extend across multiple geographic locations, scales, and sectors". Figure 3.6 summarises the process of data collection and analysis.

Figure 3.6. The process of data collection and analysis

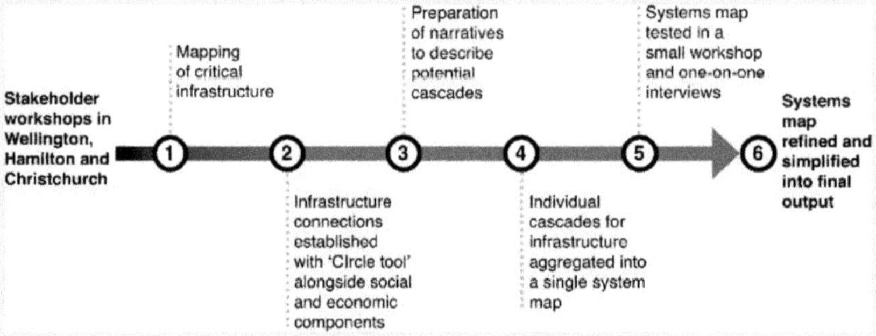

Source: (Lawrence, Blackett and Cradock-Henry, 2020[78]).

Physical climate change hazards were characterised into typologies. In this way, different types of hazards could be systematically represented for different regions. The different impacts included: i) slowly emerging and ongoing (e.g. sea-level rise and rising groundwater tables); ii) widening climate variability (e.g. increased drought, flood frequency and duration); iii) extremes (e.g. coastal storm surge and intense rainfall); iv) combined impacts (e.g. coastal and river flooding); and v) surprises (e.g. unknown impacts from atmospheric changes). A dynamic systems framework is used to examine the implications of the combination of such impacts, providing a richer assessment of the risks than traditional linear risk assessment. It analysed both the impacts on water and urban infrastructure systems and financial services, and the implications of cascading climate change impacts for governance.

The study demonstrates that close consideration of the combined effects of diverse types of linked impacts can promote better understanding of the scope and scale of climate change impacts. It examines the dependencies and feedback loops between the different systems studied, namely water and urban infrastructure and financial services. In so doing, it allows for "stress-testing" risk assumptions. The authors conclude this approach "can facilitate the design of adaptation responses that are flexible, yet robust under different future conditions, and thus avoid reaching thresholds that are beyond the ability of communities and physical systems to cope" (see also Chapter 4). For example, understanding linkages and dependencies between the financial sector and human well-being outcomes can make adaptation responses more transparent. More generally, it can inform adaptive planning and governance arrangements in delivering more effective adaptation alongside mitigation policy and practice.

Note: "The sites were: Hamilton, a landlocked city adjacent to rural areas with flood risk, and conservation and tourism demands; Wellington, a capital city constrained by geography for access and egress, and surrounded by coasts; and Christchurch, a city set around low-lying estuaries and coast, recently lowered by earthquake subsidence, with significant flood and storm water challenges."

The next sections present three separate novel studies. They focus on the impacts and, where possible, the potential cascading effects of three types of climate-related hazards: SLR, heatwaves and the tipping point resulting from the collapse of the AMOC. Using state-of-art science in these areas, the studies aim to shed light on the level of climate-related risks; reflect on how this scientific knowledge can inform policy making; and identify remaining gaps and limitations.

3.4. SLR: Impacts and associated risks of losses and damages in SIDS

SIDS comprise a heterogeneous group of island territories situated in the Caribbean, the Pacific, the Atlantic and the Indian Ocean, and the South China Sea. The UN Office of the High Representative for the Least Developed Countries, Landlocked Developing Countries, and Small Island Developing States lists 58 SIDS (UN-OHRLLS, 2021[79]), which are the territories considered in this discussion. [5]

3.4.1. While diverse in character, all SIDS are vulnerable

SIDS are diverse in terms of size, coastal characteristics, culture and geography (Nurse et al., 2014[50]; Ratter, 2018[80]; UN-OHRLLS, 2015[81]). In terms of physical geography, some SIDS are volcanic islands characterised by mountains and steep slopes. Others are tectonically raised limestone islands that generally have a flat tabular surface. Still others are coral reef islands composed of unconsolidated sediments sourced from adjacent coral reefs with elevations of usually no more than 3 m (Nunn et al., 2016[82]; Ratter, 2018[80]). Dome SIDS are archipelagos that consist of many small islands scattered across the ocean, with often large distances between them. However, not all SIDS are small islands. This category also includes Papua New Guinea, Cuba, Haiti and the Dominican Republic. Finally, not all SIDS are complete island territories, as this category also includes continental countries like Belize, Guyana, Surinam and Guinea-Bissau. SIDS are also diverse socio-economically. Island population ranges from about 1 600 (Niue) to 11 million (Cuba) (OECD, 2018[83]). Meanwhile, per capita incomes range from USD 2 300 in the Solomon Islands to USD 60 000 in Singapore (World Bank, 2021[84]).

Low elevations, exposure to hazards and fragile economies enhance vulnerability of SIDS

Irrespective of this diversity, all SIDS are vulnerable to climate change, and in particular SLR and its consequences (e.g. higher surges and waves). This vulnerability has long been recognised by international institutions such as the United Nations Agenda 21, the United Nations Framework Convention on Climate Change (UNFCCC, 1992[85]), the UN General Assembly and many subsequent policy documents including the Paris Agreement.

This recognition is mainly due to three reasons (Leatherman and Beller-Simms, 1997[86]; Nurse et al., 2014[50]; Robinson, 2020[87]; UN-OHRLLS, 2015[81]):

- First, the only habitable area of SIDS is the low-lying coastal zone. This includes atoll islands where the entire island is part of the coastal zone. Elevations are rarely higher than 2-3 m above mean sea levels (Woodroffe, 2008[47]). However, this also includes steep sloped volcanic islands, where the only habitable area is the narrow coastal fringe surrounding those islands. Hence, these places are highly threatened by SLR with limited on-island relocation opportunities (Nurse et al., 2014[50]; UN-OHRLLS, 2015[81]).
- Second, SIDS are disproportionally affected by weather-related disasters because of their location. SIDS are located in the oceans, which exposes them to various climate-related hazards. These include ocean-atmosphere interactions such as tropical cyclones, storm surges, wind waves and high climate variability (e.g. due to El Niño-Southern Oscillation; ENSO). For example, mean sea levels in some Pacific SIDS can be 20-30 cm higher during La Niña events (IPCC, 2014[88]). In addition, many SIDS are located near tectonically active zones. They are thus threatened by

earthquakes, volcanic eruptions and associated tsunamis. Adding to this challenge, many SIDS have long coastlines per unit area, which make protecting against ocean hazards expensive.

- Third, SIDS have fragile economies and a limited range of natural resources. The economies of many SIDS are not very diversified, relying on a few sectors such as tourism and fisheries that are vulnerable to external shocks. For example, fish export makes up nearly 60% of national GDP in Kiribati and the Marshall Islands. Meanwhile, tourism makes up between 50-80% of the national economies of the Bahamas, the Maldives, Palau, Vanuatu, the Seychelles, the Cook Islands and Antigua & Barbuda (UN-OHRLLS, 2015[81]). A low resilience of subsistence economies and the relative isolation and great distance to markets add to this socio-economic fragility.

In face of these vulnerabilities, SLR threatens SIDS with a range of impacts (see Figure 3.7). This includes enhanced coastal flooding causing damages to people, their livelihoods, their physical assets and resources, specifically the salinisation of surface and groundwater bodies. SLR also leads to enhanced coastal erosion leading to a loss of land. If this erosion affects natural or artificial coastal defences, it can also exacerbate coastal flooding. In addition, SLR can lead to a loss of coastal ecosystems and associated biodiversity. This, in turn, has adverse effects on livelihoods depending on these ecosystems. The loss of ecosystems further exacerbates coastal flooding and erosion because ecosystems such as corals and mangroves protect islands from these hazards.

Figure 3.7. Most important impacts of sea-level rise and associated climate drivers on SIDS

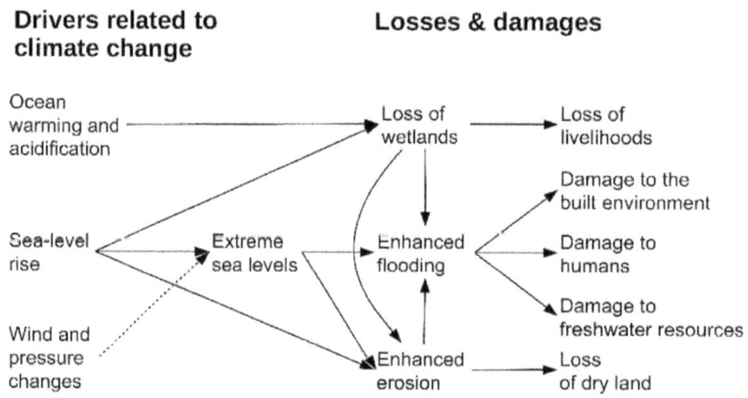

SLR is not the only factor driving increasing risks of losses and damages from climate change. Other climate drivers of great importance for SIDS are ocean warming and ocean acidification. These phenomena threaten the survival of coral reefs that protect SIDS against SLR and extreme sea-level events (Box 3.2).

The risks are compounded by a range of other anthropogenic pressures associated with rapid human development, urbanisation and mass tourism facing many SIDS today. This includes water pollution, reef destruction through fishing and diving, and the conversion of mangrove forest into other land uses. Finally, climate risks and potential impacts can only be understood in light of the many ongoing and possible human responses to manage SLR risks (see Chapter 4, Section 4.5).

3.4.2. Losses and damages

Coastal flooding

Extreme sea-level events such as waves and surges may lead to coastal flooding. The extent of these events is shaped by how extreme sea levels interact with the coastal profile. This profile is made up of both natural flood barriers (e.g. coral reefs, mangroves) and artificial ones (e.g. dykes, sea walls). If no barriers exist, extreme sea levels propagate inland where they exceed land elevation. If barriers exist, flooding can occur under several conditions: if waves overtop, or surges overflow, the barriers (i.e. if their heights exceed the height of the barriers); or if waves and surges destroy the barriers.

Coastal floods are among the most devastating natural disasters. They cause loss of lives; damage human health, buildings, infrastructure, freshwater systems and agricultural land; and interrupt livelihoods, economic activities and supply chains (Kron, 2012[89]). SIDS are, for reasons previously noted, vulnerable to coastal flooding. Cumulative total damages caused by tropical cyclones (due to both extreme sea level and extreme wind) from 1990 to 2013 amounted to over 10% of cumulative GDP for nine SIDS. Damages were as high as about 40% for the Maldives, 50% for Samoa, 80% for Saint Kitts and Nevis, and 90% for Grenada (UNEP, 2014[90]). Overall, Pacific SIDS have the highest per capita disaster risk globally (Edmonds and Noy, 2018[91]).

Dedicated comparative assessments of future coastal flood risks to SIDS under SLR are not available. However, several global assessments have produced results at a national level, including for SIDS (Bisaro et al., 2019[92]). Several general messages can be drawn from these studies. First, if SIDS do not adapt to SLR, the impacts will be devastating (Lincke and Hinkel, 2018[93]; Oppenheimer et al., 2019[39]; Wong et al., 2014[94]). Second, it is unlikely or even implausible to assume that SIDS will not adapt to SLR (Hinkel et al., 2014[95]) because coastal adaptation is widespread today. It also has a long history (Charlier, Chaineux and Morcos, 2005[96]), including in SIDS (Klöck and Nunn, 2019[97]). Third, in densely populated areas, also including those on SIDS, adaptation is generally cost-efficient. In other words, it costs much less than the losses and damages experienced without adaptation (Aerts et al., 2014[98]; Hallegatte et al., 2013[99]; Hinkel et al., 2018[100]; Lincke and Hinkel, 2018[93]; Oppenheimer et al., 2019[39]; Bisaro et al., 2019[92]). However, adaptation is also costly, amounting to several percent of national GDP for many SIDS towards the end of the century. Hence, it may not by affordable, highlighting the existential risk that SLR poses for SIDS (Wong et al., 2014[94]; Oppenheimer et al., 2019[39]).

Coastal erosion and loss of land

Independent of SLR, erosion of land at coasts is widespread. Erosion is influenced by a range of natural and anthropogenic drivers. Natural drivers of coastal erosion include currents, tides, waves, surges and natural relative sea-level change (due to vertical land movements). These induce a permanent loss of land, usually associated with a gain of land where the eroded sediment is deposited.

Widespread human modifications of the coast have altered these natural erosion, sediment transport and sediment accretion processes. It is not possible to attribute erosion to precise natural or human drivers. However, it is estimated about 24% of the world's sandy coastline is eroding, 28% is accreting (gaining land) and the rest is stable (Luijendijk et al., 2018[101]).

Rises in mean sea levels are expected to lead to enhanced erosion. The same is true for higher surges and waves as they bring more energy onto the shore (Ranasinghe, 2016[102]; Wong et al., 2014[94]). In absolute terms, global modelling efforts have found that Caribbean SIDS are the most affected by coastal retreat due to erosion (without protective measures). They have a median shoreline recession of 300 m until 2100 under RCP8.5, about 70% of which is caused by SLR (Vousdoukas et al., 2020[103]).

Processes of eroding and accreting land are specifically pronounced in coral islands. Unconsolidated biogenic material from coral reefs are deposited by currents and waves onto coral islands and their lagoons (Duvat, 2018[104]; Holdaway, Ford and Owen, 2021[105]; Kench, 2012[106]; Kumar et al., 2018[107]). This has led to the concern that SLR may soon lead to the disappearance of coral islands.

Recent studies have somewhat alleviated concerns about the disappearance of coral islands. Studies have looked at a large number of coral islands in the Pacific and Indian Oceans, either by meta-analysing case studies or through analysing satellite images. These studies found about 90% of these islands were either stable or have increased in area over the last decades of SLR (Duvat, 2018[104]; Holdaway, Ford and Owen,

2021[105]). This includes islands in regions where sea level rose by over three to four times the global average (McLean and Kench, 2015[108]).

These studies also highlight diverse drivers that are contributing to change on the islands. These drivers include natural currents, variability and extreme sea-level events. In addition, humans alter sediment transport patterns by destroying coral reefs and constructing coastal infrastructure such as sea walls, harbours and breakwaters. Anthropogenic SLR plays a minor role (McLean and Kench, 2015[108]).

While the findings are encouraging, SLR may well threaten these islands in the future. This underscores the importance of one aspect for adaptation: coral islands can withstand and grow with SLR under several conditions. First, the reef needs to produce sufficient sediment. Second, natural sediment transportation dynamics must be kept alive. Third, islands must be allowed to be flooded episodically so they can grow vertically through the sediment deposited by the flood. This ability to adapt, however, is threatened by other climate drivers as discussed further below.

Loss of ecosystems

In combination with other drivers, SLR also threatens coastal ecosystems such as corals and mangroves. These ecosystems naturally protect coasts from extreme sea level that erodes shores and causes floods. Loss of these ecosystems, then, exacerbates erosion and flooding impacts.

Coral reefs are particularly important for protecting coasts from extreme waves – the main coastal hazard for many Pacific and Indian Ocean SIDS. The reef crest and reef flat both dissipate wave energy. As a result, the wave arriving at the coastline is smaller than outside of the reef. On global average, it has been estimated that coral reefs reduce wave energy by 97% (Ferrario et al., 2014[109]). This, in turn, means that taking away the corals has a disastrous effect on these coasts in terms of enhancing coastal flooding. Furthermore, corals support local livelihoods in many ways. For example, they provide the basis for tourism (which is the biggest economic sector in many SIDS). They also serve as an important habitat for local fisheries. Globally, the value of corals for tourism has been estimated to USD 36 billion (Spalding et al., 2017[110]).

The main climate driver of coral loss is not SLR but rather ocean warming. To some extent, corals can even grow upwards with SLR. However, warmer than normal temperatures can lead to mass coral bleaching and subsequent dieback (Hughes et al., 2017[111]). Corals throughout the world are already severely stressed under today's level of global warming (Hughes et al., 2018[112]). By 2070, more than 75% of corals are expected to be experiencing annual severe bleaching even under intermediate levels of global warming (i.e. RCP4.5) (van Hooidonk et al., 2016[113]). Ocean acidification adds to the challenge facing corals. Acidification can reduce the rate at which corals build up their calcareous structures. However, the long-term effects of this process are only beginning to be understood (Kroeker et al., 2013[114]).

The loss of corals significantly increases risk of both erosion and floods. Unhealthy or dead reefs cannot produce the sediment required for coral islands to grow and keep up with SLR. Similar to corals, mangroves protect the coastline of SIDS from extreme sea-level events. They provide a number of important ecosystem services such as support for fisheries and carbon sequestration. Generally, mangroves can keep up with high rates of SLR by migrating inland and upwards the coastal slope if sufficient accommodation space and sediment supply are available (Lovelock et al., 2015[115]; Schuerch et al., 2018[116]).

Accommodation space refers to the inland migration not prohibited by steep coastal slopes or human infrastructures (e.g. dykes, roads, human settlements, etc.). However, the coastal zone is small, and/or heavily used by humans (Sasmito et al., 2015[117]). This can often limit the availability of such accommodation space in SIDS. Similarly, the availability of sediment that mangroves need to grow upwards with SLR is heavily constrained. Anthropogenic pressures such as the damming of rivers, for example, bring sediment to the coast. This process is expected to worsen over the 21st century (Dunn et al., 2019[118]). A comparative analysis in 2015 looked at mangrove sites, including on SIDS in the Indo-Pacific region. In about 70% of the study sites, sediment unavailability already constrains mangroves' ability to adjust to SLR today (Lovelock et al., 2015[115]).

Loss of freshwater resources

Many SIDS are already characterised by limited fresh water supply and SLR. Extreme sea-level events and associated enhanced coastal flooding and coastal erosion put additional pressures on these limits (Nurse et al., 2014[50]). Many studies have found that SLR alone does not necessarily threaten freshwater lenses. Two conditions protect against this threat. First, sufficient vertical accommodation space must allow the freshwater lenses to move upwards with SLR. Second, coastal erosion must not reduce island size (Falkland and White, 2020[119]).

SLR that leads to more frequent surge or wave flooding of islands, however, has adverse consequences for freshwater availability on SIDS. This is particularly true for coral islands, which have a freshwater lens that is only a few metres thick. With such a thin lens, small amounts of salt water intrusion from above can render the freshwater not potable for months to years (Gingerich, Voss and Johnson, 2017[120]; Holding and Allen, 2015[121]).

With SLR, wave-induced flooding will become more intense and frequent. This increases the recovery time of freshwater lenses. This, in turn, can lead to freshwater no longer being potable. Some studies argue the risk of losing potable water is inevitable in some cases. Storlazzi et al. (2018[122]) suggest the coral islands of Roi-Namur in the Republic of Marshall Islands will lose potable water in 2030-40 under RCP8.5 and 2055-65 under RCP4.5. This leads the authors to conclude that "most atolls will be uninhabitable by the mid-21st century."

The conclusions of Storlazzi et al. (2018[122]) fail to consider human adaptation. Many atolls are already heavily threatened by water stress. Hence, they de-salinate sea water for potable water, or import and use brackish groundwater for non-potable water needs (Falkland and White, 2020[119]). While de-salinisation is technically feasible in most cases, it is also an expensive and technologically complex option. It requires effective operation and maintenance (Falkland and White, 2020[119]).

3.5. Quantifying the impacts of climate change with extreme event attribution

The costs of extreme weather are rising (Barthel and Neumayer, 2012[123]; Smith and Katz, 2013[124]; Smith and Matthews, 2015[125]; NOAA National Centers for Environmental Information (NCEI), 2021[126]). Examples of these increasing costs, like the frequency of "billion-dollar disasters" in the United States, are frequently cited in public discourse as evidence of anthropogenic climate change. For many, such anecdotes represent "real-world impacts of climate change". However, such claims could be considered premature. Other factors unrelated to climate change also drive increases in event damages. These include the increasing exposure of physical assets or improvements in reporting event-related costs (Smith and Katz, 2013[124]). A more rounded assessment of the costs of human-caused climate change instead requires a disentangling of these different factors. Notably, it should identify the role of exposure and vulnerability in the context of the extreme event. It also isolates the role of climate change in the extreme event itself.

While deemed impossible by scientists themselves for decades, the advent of the science of extreme event attribution offers a quantitative method to answer the question of whether and to what extent climate change is responsible for worsening the impacts of individual extreme weather events today. Extreme event attribution therefore represents a critical conceptual bridge. It links today's extreme weather with long-term increases in global-mean temperatures that are driven by human-induced climate change (see Box 3.4).

Box 3.4. What is extreme event attribution?

Event attribution literature is rapidly growing. In so doing, it is providing a deeper understanding of how climate change is impacting natural and human systems at the local level. It is also indicating how higher levels of greenhouse gas emissions, combined with other pollutants and a changing land surface, alter the likelihood and intensity of extreme events (Stott et al., 2015[127]; Otto, 2017[128]). Climate change not only affects the overall temperature of the planet but also the atmospheric circulation (Vautard et al., 2016[129]). Hence, climate change can affect extreme weather in three possible ways. It can i) increase the likelihood of an event occurring; ii) it can decrease the likelihood of an event occurring; or iii) it can have no effect on the likelihood of an event occurring.

The approach most widely used, illustrated in Figure 3.8, uses the example of the 2010 Russian heat wave (Otto et al., 2012[130]). First, it assesses the probability of the observed intensity of the extreme event in question (horizontal dotted line) to occur in the current climate (red dots), all human-induced (non-climate) drivers included. It then compares it with the probability of its occurrence in a world without human-induced climate change (blue dots). This enables the isolation and quantification of the effect of climate change (horizontal arrow) on the probability of occurrence of an event of a given magnitude, as well as the change in intensity of an event of an observed likelihood (small vertical arrow).

Figure 3.8. Attribution analysis of the 2010 Russia heatwave

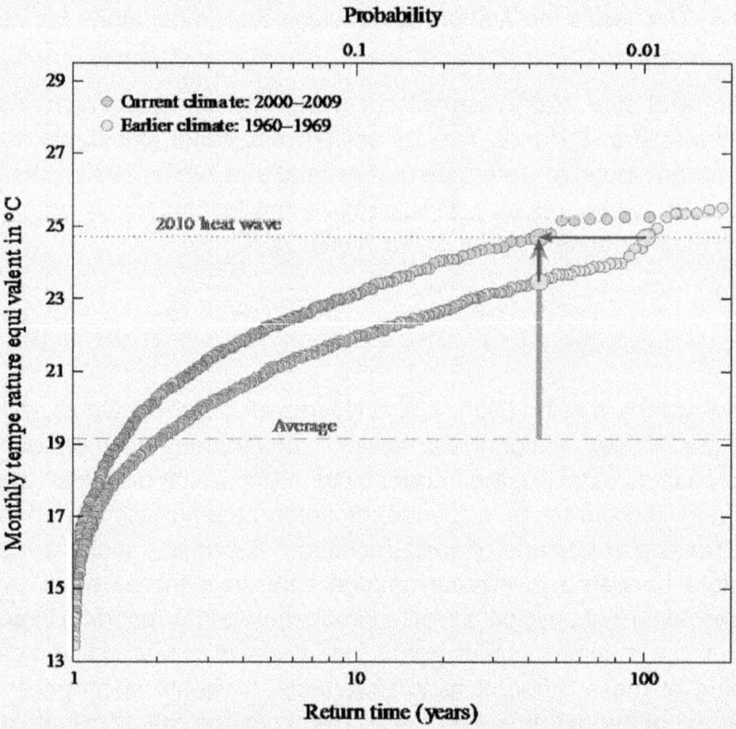

Note: Return time of extremely high monthly mean temperatures in Western Russia in the current climate (red) and an earlier climate (blue). The dashed line shows monthly average temperatures, and the dotted line shows the magnitude of the heat wave in 2010. The grey arrow shows the departure from the average in the magnitude, and the red vertical arrow depicts the role of climate change in that departure. The red horizontal arrow shows the increase in frequency of a 2010-like heat wave due to anthropogenic climate change.
Source: (Otto, 2017[128]).

For today's climate, observations of weather and climate can help estimate the likelihood of an event. Observations of a hypothetical, counterfactual world without anthropogenic climate change do not exist. Furthermore, only weather that has *occurred* can be observed; it is not possible to observe all weather events possible in a given climate. Event attribution thus relies on climate models to simulate possible weather, including the extreme event in question, in a given region and season accurately enough to draw conclusions on the role of climate change. Early studies applying the probabilistic event attribution approach employed a single climate model (Stott, Stone and Allen, 2004[131]); thus, the results depend heavily on that model's reliability (Bellprat and Doblas-Reyes, 2016[132]; Otto et al., 2020[133]). A more robust approach has since been developed that includes both observation-based statistical analysis and multiple models of varying complexity. A whole new field of climate science has thus emerged, and the methods are constantly improving (Philip et al., 2020[134]; van Oldenborgh et al., 2021[135]).

Two aspects of the methodology are important. First, the definition of an extreme event is a crucial part of the analysis and determines the outcome. In the most commonly used approach, the event is always defined as a type of weather that leads to an impact. This could be, for example, extreme rainfall above a certain threshold in a particular area or season that causes flooding. Other methodologies favour highly-conditioned (or storyline) approaches, which are not probabilistic and consider a much narrower event definition [(Shepherd et al., 2018[136]; Hegdahl et al., 2020[137]) and Box 4.2]. Second, attribution of extreme events relies on the availability of climate models realistically simulating the type of event. For example, the impacts of extreme tornado or hailstorm events will remain unassessed while current-generation models fail to meaningfully simulate the relevant physical processes.

In addition, the best available impact data relating to a given class of extreme weather affecting a specific region are often only one single data point – the impacts of that recently-observed event. Consequently, attribution statements work within the constraints of one impact observation. In the context of framing attribution statements, scientists have a limited understanding of the specific shape of the hazard-impact relationship. In other words, they are often unable to quantitatively resolve whether a slightly less-intense event would have resulted in slightly fewer impacts, or perhaps no impacts whatsoever. Climate models can look at the probability of witnessing meteorological characteristics equal to or worse than the recently-observed, knowingly-impactful event. They can quantify what fraction of this probability would not have occurred in a pre-industrial climate. In this way, the attribution methodology sidesteps the need to resolve other details in the hazard-impact relationship. Instead, it frames the estimated attributable change in impacts solely around the one observed data point. There must be confidence in this point being directly relevant to the communities who suffered from that event (Frame et al., 2020[138]; Clarke, E. L. Otto and Jones, 2021[139]).

The science of extreme event attribution has received high scrutiny by peers. Some claim that scientists are too confident in their attribution statements (Bellprat and Doblas-Reyes, 2016[132]). Others argue they are too cautious (Lloyd and Oreskes, 2018[140]; Lloyd et al., 2021[141]). Within the probabilistic attribution community, this scrutiny led to a rather fast development of transparent and more robust methods of estimating changing hazards. These methods are detailed in van Oldenborgh et al. (2021[135]). They consist of careful considerations of the event definition; a standardised evaluation of whether to include climate models in a study; and assessment of structural uncertainties in climate models and due to observational data constraints.

3.5.1. Robust features of worsening extreme weather due to climate change

Attribution science has helped to identify many robust features of worsening extreme weather due to climate change (despite the methodological challenges and uncertainties discussed in Box 3.4 and Box 3.5 respectively). First and foremost, there is high confidence that heat-related extremes are becoming more frequent and severe by orders of magnitude more rapidly than any other type of extreme weather (Fischer and Knutti, 2015[142]), and that changes in marine heatwaves emerge even faster than land-based heatwaves (Oliver et al., 2017[143]; Frölicher, Fischer and Gruber, 2018[144])[6]. This is important to emphasise, as significant differences around future risk management exist when one class of extreme weather is *only* being made twice as likely due to current levels of warming (e.g. flooding in the UK (Otto et al., 2018[145]), while another class of event might be becoming hundreds of times more common (like heatwaves in the Tropics (Perkins-Kirkpatrick and Gibson, 2017[146]). This is especially true when risk assessments on national levels are primarily driven by the insurance industry, who generally do not insure against heat-related losses, thereby ignoring the class of extremes where climate change has the largest impacts.

Second, there is high confidence in the projected rates of intensification for both extreme heatwaves and extreme rainfall events. These rates of change are well-simulated in climate models, and the physical processes which contribute to these changes are also well-understood. As shown in Figure 3.9, future projections of both mean temperatures and extreme high temperatures can be expressed as a simple linear response to anthropogenic increases in global-mean warming. Over land, mean temperatures are found to warm faster than the global average, which in turn relates to differences in the speed of projected warming over land versus oceans (Joshi et al., 2007[147]) and has been explained largely as a result of atmospheric dynamics (Joshi et al., 2007[147]; Byrne and O'Gorman, 2013[148]; Byrne and O'Gorman, 2018[149]). For the case of high-temperature extremes (bottom row of Figure 3.9), there is an additional amplification factor found for moisture-limited regions like the Mediterranean (Seneviratne et al., 2016[150]; Vogel et al., 2017[151]; Vogel, Zscheischler and Seneviratne, 2018[152]). For example, (Vautard et al., 2020[153]) found that "without human-induced climate change", heatwaves as exceptional as the European events of June and July 2019 would have had "temperatures about 1.5 to 3 degrees lower". Synthesizing the evidence places the rates of intensification of high temperature extremes at between 1 and 3 degrees per degree of global warming – though it is emphasised that this range intends to represent all populated land regions, and any individual region would likely have a narrower range of uncertainty.

Figure 3.9. Change in local temperatures per degree of global warming

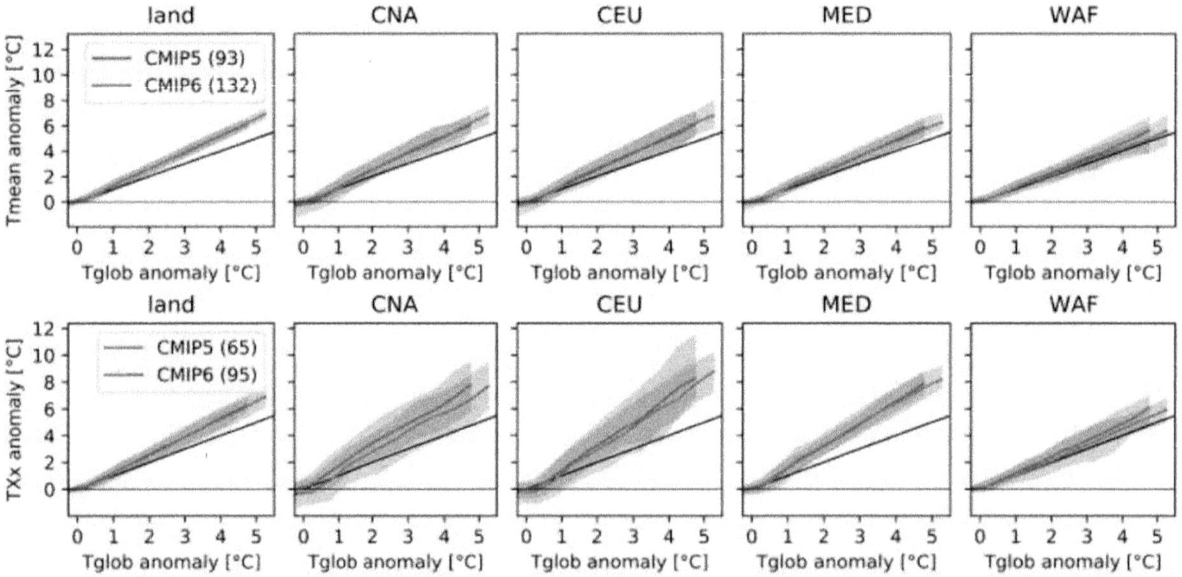

Note: Projected changes in average temperatures (top row) and annual maximum daily maximum temperatures (bottom row) under future warming scenarios, for a range of selected regions (CNA = central North America; CEU = Central Europe; MED = Mediterranean; WAF = Western Africa). Results are presented as changes relative to corresponding increases in global mean temperature; the black line denotes a 1:1 relationship

Source: (Seneviratne and Hauser, 2020[154])

With respect to the physical processes driving the intensification of rainfall extremes, there is more moisture in a warmer atmosphere, which increases the intensity of all precipitation events if one assumes that atmospheric circulation does not otherwise change (Allen and Ingram, 2002[155]; Allan and Soden, 2008[156]). However, other physical factors not explored in detail here may reduce (Pendergrass, 2018[157]) or intensify events (Meredith et al., 2015[158]; Meredith et al., 2015[159]; Prein et al., 2015[160]; Prein et al., 2016[161]; Fowler et al., 2021[162]). A synthesis of the rates of intensification for extreme rainfall span the range of 5% - 15% per degree of global warming: differences of course exist depending on what region of the world and duration of events (Westra et al., 2014[163]; Prein et al., 2016[161]; Hodnebrog et al., 2019[164]) are considered or how extreme the events of interest are (Fischer and Knutti, 2015[142]; Kharin et al., 2018[165]; Pendergrass, 2018[157]).

Third, several attribution studies (Freychet et al., 2019[166]) have shown that large swathes of Asia (particularly India) and parts of the US exhibit a suppressed GHG signal of heatwave intensification, because of the cooling effects of aerosol emissions associated with local air pollution and/or large scale irrigation. Consequently, there exists high confidence that efforts to improve air pollution or modify irrigation practices in the future would affect these temporary dampening effects, thereby risking a potentially sudden worsening of relative heatwave severity over the regions in question. So seemingly paradoxically, one of the effects of reduced burning of fossil fuels might be to increase temperatures in some parts of the world, since the cooling effect of atmospheric aerosols would rapidly dissipate.

Fourth, many extreme events with multivariate drivers (like heat stress, agricultural drought or wildfires) often result in attribution statements which are more uncertain when compared with a univariate extreme event. This is in part due to the lack of high-resolution, high-quality observations for variables beyond rainfall and temperature. Climate models and event attribution tools can however still usefully selectively identify and decompose the *relative* importance of individual variables to otherwise complex signals of change (Uhe et al., 2017[167]; Philip et al., 2018[168]; Kew et al., 2021[169]). For example, multi-month or multi-year precipitation deficits rarely show changes in response to current levels of global warming (Otto et al., 2015[170]), except for some specific regions (Otto et al., 2018[171]). And while this absence of any change in the frequency of low-rainfall years was also found for California, (Diffenbaugh, Swain and Touma, 2015[172]) demonstrated that concurrent temperature increases meant the overall risks of drought were still in fact rising. In addition, since 2010, Chile has been affected by a 'mega-drought', name given to an extraordinary drought phenomenon affecting the countries' most populated areas, which is unprecedented in historical and/or instrumentally recorded logs or paleo-climate records covering the last 1000 years. Attribution studies have shown that approximately 25% of the precipitation deficit during the years 2010 to 2015 can be attributed to anthropogenic climate change, and that this factor will continue in the future, favoring the occurrence of these events and increasing the rate of aridification in central and southern areas of the country (CR2, 2015[173]).

Box 3.5. Known sources of uncertainties in event attribution studies

Uncertainties in quantifying the impacts of different classes of extreme weather

Better understanding of losses and damages from climate change requires better quantification of the impacts caused by extreme weather events. However, the monitoring and systematic reporting of climate impacts associated with different classes of extreme weather – let alone of the underlying exposures and vulnerabilities – is often sparse and inconsistent between poorer and wealthier countries (Guha-Sapir, Hargitt and Hoyois, 2004[174]; Visser, Petersen and Ligtvoet, 2014[175]; Noy, 2016[176]; Noy and duPont IV, 2018[177]; Tschumi and Zscheischler, 2019[178]). Chapter 2 (Section 2.2.1.) summarises the different dimensions of uncertainty that exist when quantifying the impacts of different classes of extreme weather, namely flooding, wildfires, heatwaves and droughts.

Different aspects of attribution uncertainty for different classes of extreme weather

The most important limiting constraint when quantifying the role of anthropogenic climate change on any extreme weather event relates to whether available climate models can meaningfully simulate the physical drivers of the event in question (Box 3.4). Attribution scientists consider other factors for those classes of event where evaluation identifies high confidence in climate models (e.g. large-scale extreme rainfall events or land-based heatwaves) (van Oldenborgh et al., 2021[135]).

One source of uncertainty concerns the choice of spatial and temporal scale considered when defining the extreme event in question (Angélil et al., 2014[179]). Attribution scientists typically choose the scale based on isolating the most significant impacts of the event e.g. where/when temperature anomalies were most extreme. Such a choice is necessary, but is made with the knowledge that an alternative selection can sometimes change the severity of both the observed 'event' itself, as well as the estimated influence of climate change on the event (Cattiaux and Ribes, 2018[180]). This is not because of any real-world difference in how much climate change has strengthened the intensity of that heatwave. Rather, it is because translating that intensification into a "change in recurrence frequency" considers how much a given signal has emerged from background variability and the noise associated with heat extremes increases at smaller spatio-temporal scales. Indeed, for heat-related extremes, systematically reanalysing the same heatwave event at increasingly finer spatial or temporal scales typically reduces the magnitude of any *frequency*-based attribution metrics (Angélil et al., 2014[179]). For example, a study shows climate change made the extreme heat in Europe in 2018 between 2 and 100 times more likely, depending on choices of spatial and temporal scales for analysing the event (Leach et al., 2020[181]).

For rain-related extremes, topographic features and other local effects mean that opposing signals of future precipitation change can also be found in nearby locations (Caloiero, 2014[182]). Similarly, opposing signals of climate change can also be found when considering changes in wintertime and summertime rainfall for the same location (Guillod et al., 2017[183]). As a consequence, there is significant potential for cancellation of otherwise-robust climate change signals when looking at precipitation-related extremes over increasingly large spatial or temporal scales. Thus, any attempt to quantify drying or wettening signals under climate change requires careful treatment of climatological rainfall characteristics over the region in question.

These considerations lead to three general rules for analysis. Choosing spatio-temporal scales that map closest to impacts means that extreme rainfall analyses consider short timeframes (days) and smaller spatial scales (cities to regions). Heatwave analyses consider a range of spatial scales (cities to continents) but often small temporal scales (days to weeks). Finally, drought analyses consider large spatial (regions to continents) and temporal scales (months to years).

Note: Chapter 2 considers uncertainties in more detail.

3.5.2. Expected emergence of unprecedented changes in extreme heat

There are often questions of when certain regions of the world might become 'uninhabitable' due to change extreme heat or heat stress in the future. This section attempts to demonstrate the patterns and relative speed of change associated with distributional shifts in the hottest day per year for different parts of the world. It also tries to explain why there will never be a simple, binary disaggregation of future regions on the basis of where humans can or cannot continue to live.

Relative change in hottest day of the year as proxy for extreme high temperatures

Figure 3.10, panel (a), considers the signal of relative change in the hottest day of the year (TXx) as a proxy for extreme high temperatures. These changes are normalised to show the signal of change per degree of global-mean warming (under a high-emissions RCP8.5 scenario). TXx has been analysed extensively in the past (Sillmann et al., 2013[184]; King et al., 2015[185]; King et al., 2016[186]; Harrington et al., 2018[187]). It maps well to changes in extreme heatwaves over multi-day timescales, too (Perkins and Alexander, 2013[188]; Cowan et al., 2014[189]; Russo, Sillmann and Fischer, 2015[190]; Russo et al., 2016[191]; Angélil et al., 2017[192]).

Results show an unambiguous signal over land of warming signals in TXx. This outpaces corresponding changes in global mean temperature by a factor of up to 1.8 in some locations. As explained earlier, these patterns of change are very well understood. They relate primarily to two differences. First, they relate to the factors determining mean warming rates over land versus oceans (Joshi et al., 2007[147]). Second, they relate to an additional acceleration over moisture-limited continental areas where further intensification of the hottest days of the year are driven by soil moisture feedback mechanisms (Vogel et al., 2017[151]).

Figure 3.10. The "new normal": Future extreme heat and changes relative to past experiences

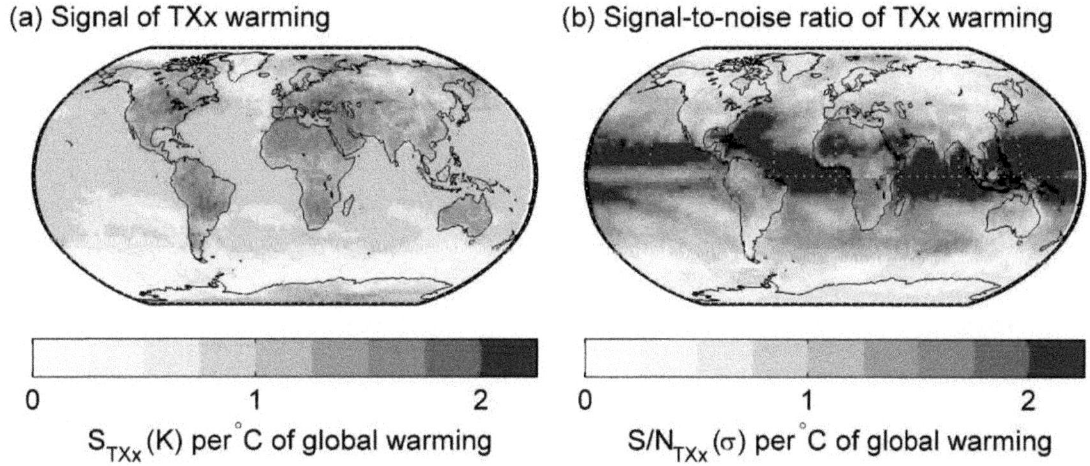

Note: (a) Multi-model medial spatial patterns of the change in TXx per °C of warming under future warming scenarios. (b) Same as panel (a) but showing the spatial patterns of signal-to-noise ratios (S/N ratios) of TXx. Future changes in TXx are normalised on the basis of year-to-year variations experienced in the historical record (S/N ratios). An S/N ratio of 1 means that projected increases in temperatures on the hottest day of the year will equal the standard deviation of year-to-year variations in TXx in the present climate.

A new "average" hottest day of the year based on historical year-to-year variations

Figure 3.10, panel b considers future changes in TXx normalised on the basis of year-to-year variations in the historical record. Specifically, the signal of warming in TXx is divided by the local standard deviation of

TXx. This is calculated using linearly detrended historical data from all years in the 20th century (hereafter "signal-to-noise" or S/N ratios). An S/N ratio of 1 means the future change (increase) in the average temperature of the hottest day of the year is the same as the standard deviation of the temperature of the hottest day of the year in the present climate. In other words, the new "average" hottest day would previously have been about a 1-in-6 year event. This enables a globally comparable assessment that measures whether future changes in heat extremes are *unusual* relative to the range of experiences common to individual locations (and ecosystems or societies therein) (Hawkins and Sutton, 2012[193]; Frame et al., 2017[194]; Hawkins et al., 2020[195]).

When viewed through this lens, Figure 3.10 panel (b) reveals that tropical oceans are, by far, witnessing the most rapid *relative* changes in high-temperature extremes. They are followed by North African and Middle East arid regions, and then other tropical land areas. These patterns also align with results elsewhere that show marine heatwaves are already becoming more intense and frequent. These reports show speeds of change are unrivalled when considering climate extremes elsewhere in the climate system (Oliver et al., 2017[143]; Frölicher, Fischer and Gruber, 2018[144]). These extremes are, however closely, followed by the worsening of tropical land-based heatwaves (Perkins-Kirkpatrick and Gibson, 2017[146]) and heat stress waves (Mora et al., 2017[196]).

To further highlight the diversity in relative changes in extreme heat between different regions of the world, Table 3.3 presents the median S/N ratio of changes in TXx for different warming levels. It presents for the globe, for LDCs and for the OECD as of June 2021. Globally, the average relative change in extreme heat is found to follow global mean temperature changes at a near 1:1 ratio. OECD member states experience slower than average relative changes in extreme heat. By contrast, the average changes experienced by LDCs are some 50% faster than the global average. This pattern of lower income countries experiencing faster relative changes in extreme heat has also been corroborated extensively in previous research (Mahlstein et al., 2011[197]; Harrington et al., 2016[198]; Frame et al., 2017[194]; Harrington et al., 2018[187]; King and Harrington, 2018[199]).

Table 3.3. Population exposure to future extreme heat outside the norms of past experiences

	Signal-to-noise ratio (σ) of TXx experienced by median person		
Global warming since 1861-80	**Worldwide**	**LDC members**	**OECD members**
+ 1.0°C	1.0 (0.3/1.7)	1.5 (0.3/2.2)	0.8 (0.3/1.5)
+ 1.5°C	1.5 (0.6/2.3)	2.2 (0.6/3.3)	1.3 (0.6/2.1)
+ 2.0°C	2.0 (1.0/3.1)	3.0 (1.1/4.4)	1.8 (1.0/2.8)
+ 2.5°C	2.6 (1.3/3.8)	3.8 (1.4/5.4)	2.3 (1.3/3.5)
+ 3.0°C	3.2 (1.5/4.6)	4.5 (1.6/6.5)	2.9 (1.6/4.1)
+ 3.5°C	3.7 (1.8/5.2)	5.2 (1.9/7.4)	3.3 (1.8/4.7)

Note: Model projections of the signal to noise (S/N) ratios of TXx experienced by the median person under future warming thresholds (using RCP8.5), for three population groupings: the global population, the combined population of 46 Least Developed Countries, and the combined population of 38 OECD member countries. Gridded population data are fixed at 2015 levels and taken from (Center for International Earth Science Information Network - CIESIN, 2005[200]). The main numbers show the multi-model median TXx S/N ratio experienced by the median person of each population grouping. The bracketed values show climate model uncertainty (multi-model 10th and 90th percentiles) associated with S/N ratios for the median individual in response to the specified level of warming.

Every tonne of carbon released will make the future increasingly unrecognisable

Figure 3.11 shows the levels of global mean warming required to locally exceed future thresholds of extreme heat emergence. These thresholds are represented by levels of change +3σ and +6σ. The +3σ levels approximate when the hottest day of an average year in the new climate would be considered rare in the past. Meanwhile, +6σ represents levels when the hottest day of even the coolest year in the future would still exceed the hottest temperatures ever experienced in the past.

The worsening patterns of change that accompany warming everywhere in Figure 3.10 strengthens the conclusion that every additional tonne of carbon emissions released into the atmosphere will only make the future more and more unrecognisable. This is especially the case when comparing the experiences of extreme future heat with those of the past several decades. A comparison with a pre-industrial climate would be even more dramatic.

Figure 3.11. Warming required to exceed future thresholds of extreme heat beyond past experiences

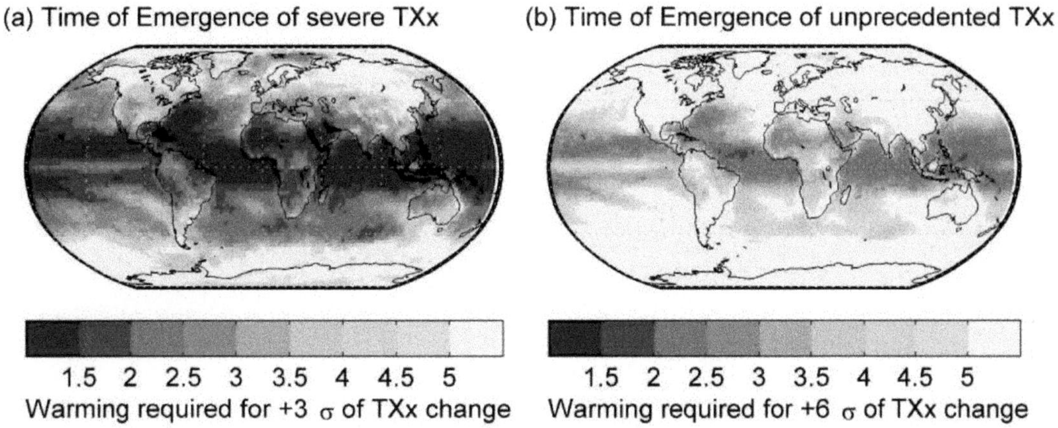

Note: Panels (a) and (b) use the results presented in panel 4.1b to estimate the global mean temperature increase required to witness signal-to-noise ratios in excess of 3 and 6, respectively, at each grid cell. Panel (a), +3σ, approximates levels when the hottest day of an average year in the new climate would be considered rare in the past. Panel (b), +6σ, approximates levels when the hottest day of even the coolest year in the future would still exceed the hottest temperatures ever experienced in the past.

No singular definition or threshold is precise enough to identify when a location will no longer be suitable for "human habitability". Different countries, as well as communities therein, have developed significantly different levels of tolerance to unusual heat over time (whether via cultural, technological or physiological change). No one index of extreme heat (or heat stress) can capture this myriad of regional and sub-regional differences in susceptibility to future change (Matthews, 2018[201]; Vanos et al., 2020[202]). Any choice of climate metric, or threshold to define "catastrophic changes", will therefore emphasise some regions over others. Too often, it will also mischaracterise the differing levels of resilience within individual communities and countries, or indeed potential to adapt.

3.5.3. The importance of exposure and vulnerability when assessing the future impacts of extreme weather

Extreme event attribution has evolved to primarily assess probabilistic changes in the likelihood of witnessing extreme meteorological hazards. It thereby offers a quantitative framework to understand how the impacts of today's extreme weather events might be worsening due to anthropogenic climate change.

However, it is equally crucial to assess how non-hazard factors (i.e. exposure and vulnerability) modulate the severity of extreme weather impacts, as well as their potential for change over time. This is crucial for decision makers to understand how the risks and impacts from extreme weather might improve or worsen.

This section considers several non-hazard determinants of extreme weather impacts, as well as the range of possible changes expected over the 21st century.

The share of vulnerable populations is projected to grow

Figure 3.12 presents projected changes in two categories of vulnerable people – those aged over 65 and over 85 years. In so doing, it creates five alternative storylines of socio-economic outcomes over the 21st century (the Shared Socio-economic Pathways, or SSPs). Each circle represents a new decade, as global elderly populations grow from 2020 levels (set to equal 1).

Figure 3.12. Population ageing scenarios

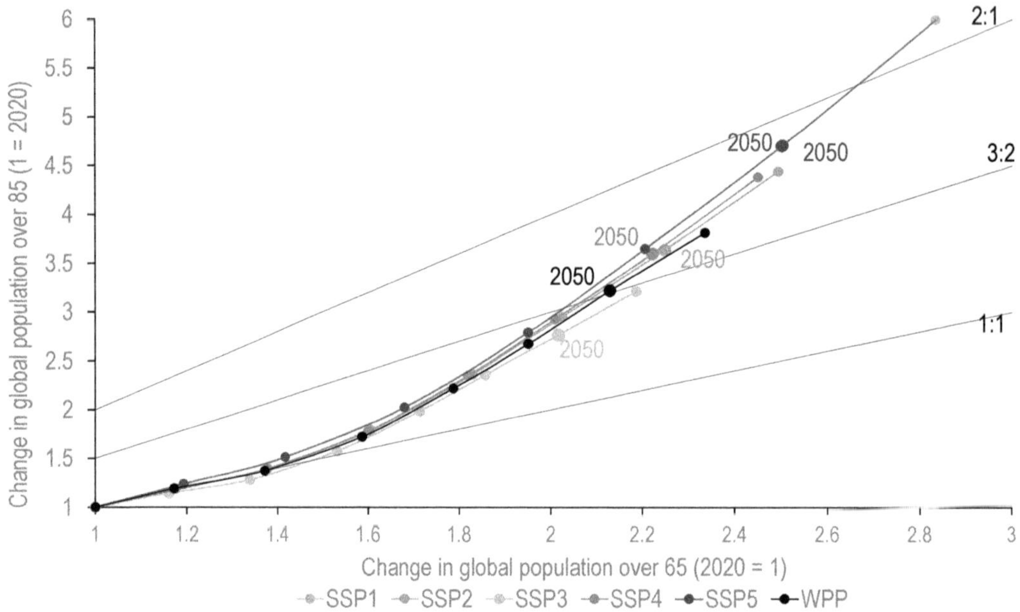

Note: Projected changes (relative to 2020) in the global population aged over 65 years (horizontal axis) and 85 years (vertical axis) for each decade between 2020 and 2070 under the five Shared Socio-economic Pathways and the population scenarios developed for the UN World Population Prospects 2019. Each circle denotes a new decade; larger filled circles show the values for 2050. Note that the pathways for SSPs 1 and 5 overlap one another.

Two clear patterns emerge related to global population growth and the most vulnerable populations. First, the rates of global population growth in the age group most often assessed as "vulnerable" – those over 65 – are significant. They will increase by a factor of between 2 and 2.5 by 2050 depending on the scenario considered.

Second, and more concerning, the rates of growth when isolating only the most vulnerable (Whitty and Watt, 2020[203]) within this grouping (those over 85 years old) are even more rapid. By mid-century, 3- to 4-fold increases in population size are expected, which will shift to 5- to 20-fold increases by the end of the century (not shown in Figure 3.12). The rate of growth accelerates beyond corresponding changes in the over-65 group with every successive decade under all scenarios.

These projected rates of change are driven by an ageing global population and improving health-care outcomes. They clearly indicate the collective risks posed by extreme weather, and particularly extreme heatwaves (Whitty and Watt, 2020[203]), could increase significantly. This will be the case even if the climate-related hazards themselves remain unchanged. Chapters 1, 2 and 5 explore other socio-economic factors potentially at the origin of exposure and vulnerability of human and natural systems.

The severity of the hazard is an imperfect proxy for the severity of impacts

The impacts of an extreme weather event can be different depending on the vulnerability of exposed communities (Quigley et al., 2020[204]). Indeed, the rarity of the meteorological hazard in question can often fail as a proxy for how impactful the weather event might be. Consider two examples of recent extreme weather events that were the subject of event attribution analyses. The first case examines how persistent heavy rainfall caused flooding in the southern United Kingdom in the winter of 2013-14 (Schaller et al., 2016[205]); the second case looks at how extreme rainfall caused flooding over Southern China during the March-July rainy season of 2019 (Li et al., 2021[206]), both summarised in Figure 3.13.

Figure 3.13. Extreme weather hazards versus impacts

	Severity of Weather Hazard	Severity of Event Impacts
China Floods Spring 2019	1-in-10 years	-USD 3 billion in damage -19,000 houses collapsed -83,000 houses damaged -420,000 ha of crop damage -91 deaths
South UK Floods 2013/14	1-in-250 years	-USD 1.5-2.2 billion in damage -11,000 houses damaged -45,000 ha of farmland flooded

Note: Schematic representation of the two case study extreme events: the Southern China floods of spring 2019, and floods in the southern United Kingdom of the winter of 2013-14. The size of the coloured circles and boxes respectively represent the relative severity of the weather event itself, and the magnitude of the social, economic or health impacts associated with the event. The event severity is described as a return period, which denotes the probability of witnessing an event of equal or greater severity within any given year.

Floods in southern United Kingdom, 2013-14

The magnitude of the rainfall that fell over southern United Kingdom during the winter of 2013-14 was exceptional (Schaller et al., 2016[205]). According to the UK Met Office (2014[207]), 12 storms passed over the UK region between mid-December 2013 and mid-February 2014, marking the stormiest period in over 20 years. The UK Environment Agency estimated total costs and impacts of the winter 2013-14 floods at USD 1.5-2.2 billion, equivalent to GBP 1.0-1.5 billion in 2014 (Chatterton et al., 2016[208]). Of this, most costs were associated with the 11 000 damaged residential properties. Meanwhile, an estimated 45 000 ha of farmland were flooded during the event. The sequence of back-to-back storm systems was unusual: the rainfall anomalies were described as a 1-in-250 year event for those most heavily affected southern regions (UK Met Office, 2014[207]).

While the impacts resulting from the flooding were significant, they were nevertheless smaller than other UK floods in the previous decade. Indeed, although the autumn floods in 2000 were less severe from a meteorological standpoint (UK Met Office, 2014[207]), their total costs were higher than those of the 2013-14 event (Pall et al., 2011[209]). Meanwhile, the summer floods of 2007 resulted in almost three times the economic impacts as the 2013-14 event. Much of the reduced costs was attributed to improved flood defences and early warning systems in the intervening period (Chatterton et al., 2016[208]).

Floods in China, 2019

During March to July of 2019, Southern China also experienced the impacts of severe weather. A protracted, intense rainy season produced widespread flooding impacts over a highly populated region of the country (Li et al., 2021[206]). While the "first rainy season" typically spans from April to June in this area of China, the onset was some 28 days early in 2019 and also finished 22 days later than usual (Li et al., 2021[206]). This persistent, above-average rainfall culminated in severe flooding impacts during the second week of June. According to the China Ministry of Emergency Management, flooding and landslides directly affected 6 million people. They also led to 91 deaths, the damage or collapse of over 100 000 houses, and damage to some 419 000 ha of crops. In total, the direct costs of the event were estimated at USD 3 billion (Li et al., 2021[206]).

However, a multi-method assessment of the meteorological drivers of the event found it was actually comparably unremarkable, from a statistical perspective. Indeed, Li et al. (2021[206]) estimate the recurrence frequency in today's climate from a 1-in-6 to a 1-in-28 year event, with a central estimate of a 1-in-10 year event. This qualitatively corroborates with a similarly impactful flooding event that affected the same region in 2008.These examples highlight the inherent vulnerability of those exposed to the impacts of extreme weather. In particular, it reveals how relatively common weather hazards can still cause significant and detrimental impacts if they strike vulnerable, exposed communities.

Fortunately, the improved outcomes associated with recurrent floods in the United Kingdom also point to the significant potential for resilience-building measures in climate-vulnerable nations. That is, for many types of extreme weather and regions, the potential for targeted disaster risk reduction measures over the medium term can often counteract any climate change-induced worsening of the hazard over the same period [(Jongman et al., 2015[210]; Kreibich et al., 2017[211]) and explored in Chapter 5].

The opportunities to reduce vulnerability are largest in poorer countries

As highlighted above, the impacts of future extreme weather can often be reduced – even if climate change is making the hazards themselves worse. Targeted measures can improve climate resilience, often via wider improvements in living standards and economic prosperity (Schleussner et al., 2021[212]). These include poverty alleviation health care, social safety and adaptation measures, among others.

Supporting evidence can be found in the widespread reduction in deaths associated with climate extremes as economic prosperity grew over the 20th century (Ritchie and Roser, 2014[213]). The potential for resilience-building measures to alleviate the otherwise-worsening impacts of extreme weather is therefore significant. This is especially true for countries most vulnerable to extreme weather impacts today (Schleussner et al., 2021[212]). Barriers to implementing these measures exist, however, primarily related to governance and finance (Andrijevic et al., 2019[214]).

3.5.4. Developing an inventory of extreme weather impacts attributable to anthropogenic climate change

An inventory of the impacts of extreme weather caused by anthropogenic climate change is urgently needed. Such an effort would complement disaster databases, which compile extreme weather impacts without considering whether they were influenced by a warming climate. This disaggregation will help inform future adaptation priorities at the local decision scale (Otto et al., 2015[215]). They will also strengthen the evidence base informing wider policy discussions relating to losses and damages from climate change and climate finance more broadly.

Figure 3.14 proposes a preliminary framework for an inventory of the impacts of climate change from extreme weather in three parts. First, it identifies all possible impacts associated with the extreme weather event in question. Second, it determines the fraction of attributable risk associated with the extreme weather event known to have caused these impacts. Third, it multiplies the two to yield an estimate of the event-related impacts that would have not occurred if an equally rare event occurred in a "world without climate change" (Allen, 2003[216]; Frame et al., 2020[138]; Clarke, E. L. Otto and Jones, 2021[139]).

This framework, of course, abstracts from any consideration of the exposure and vulnerability to that particular hazard. It also does not consider whether earlier policies and decisions influencing these factors could have reduced impacts. Further development of such an inventory could track the evolution of exposure and vulnerability to specific types of hazard to inform efforts to reduce the overall risk of losses and damages.

Figure 3.14. An inventory framework for extreme weather impacts due to climate change

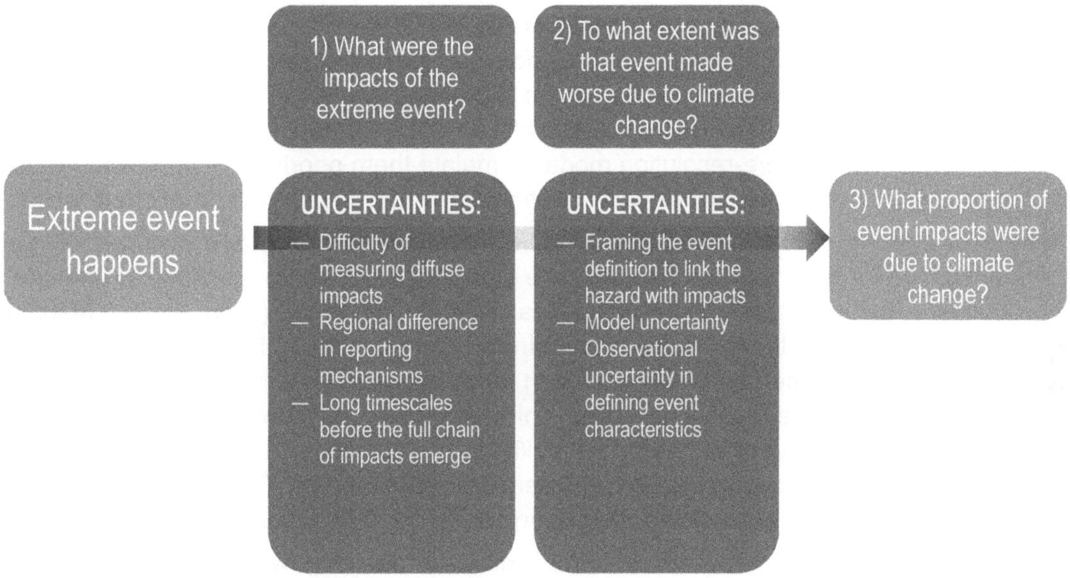

Note: Schematic representation of applying attribution science to develop an estimate of the impacts from extreme weather attributable to anthropogenic climate change. The list of uncertainties associated with each of steps (1) and (2) is discussed further in Sections 2.2 and 2.3, respectively.

As with other branches of climate science, any method to quantify how large-scale, time-averaged signals of climate change translate to the finer scales most relevant for decision making introduces uncertainty (Maraun et al., 2017[217]; Shepherd and Sobel, 2020[218]). This truism applies to the attribution step of the inventory framework conceptualised in Figure 3.14. Moreover, uncertainties are further compounded by other factors relating to the quantification of impacts associated with an extreme event. However, uncertainty alone does not represent a definitive barrier to useful, actionable information (Shepherd, 2019[12]), particularly if that uncertainty is well understood and its drivers separated (Marotzke et al., 2017[219]).

3.5.5. Barriers to understanding impacts and drivers of extreme weather in lower income countries

The benefits of probabilistic attribution are manifold, particularly in offering a method to causally link the impacts of recent extreme weather events with climate change. However, the same methods too often end up with an inconclusive result when considering weather extremes that impact lower income countries. Multiple factors combine to explain why the geographic coverage of attribution studies is heavily skewed towards higher income countries and are discussed elsewhere (Otto et al., 2020[133]; Otto et al., 2020[220]).

Specific impediments to raising the quality and quantity of event attribution studies over lower income countries are detailed below.

1. ***Poor observational records***: Attribution studies are more successful in regions where scientists can quantify the severity of the extreme weather event relative to historical records. The capacity to perform attribution analyses is therefore always going to be limited in regions where observational records either do not exist, are not publicly available, or have short record lengths. In many lower income countries, the limited observational coverage of past weather, both in space and time, fundamentally limits the ability to contextualise the severity of the event, or readily validate the quality of any climate models used.
2. ***Climate model deficiencies***: Many low income countries are located in tropical regions, where extreme weather events are heavily influenced by physical processes (like convection or ocean-atmosphere interactions). These processes are significantly more difficult to adequately simulate in climate models. As an alternative interpretation, climate model simulations require a much higher spatial resolution to achieve comparable levels of quality in the tropics (when compared with higher latitude regions). This is because processes affecting the formation of extreme weather are both more uncertain, and coarse-resolution models simulate them poorly. This adds a further barrier to successfully performing the same quality of attribution study in different parts of the world.
3. ***Modes of internal climate variability affecting extreme flooding and drought***: The signal of climate change for hydrological extremes (like drought and flooding) affecting low-latitude nations is modulated by important modes of natural climate variability (such as the Madden-Julian Oscillation, El Niño-Southern Oscillation and Indian Ocean Dipole). Even if a hypothetical climate change signal in extreme rainfall were uniform for all countries, it would take longer for that signal to be detectable in these tropical countries – of which many are disproportionally low income – by virtue of these large drivers of natural variability in the climate system. These modes of climate variability are also notoriously difficult to simulate in climate models. This places a further constraint on which models can be considered "fit-for-purpose" for an attribution analysis.
4. ***Selection biases***: No systematic method exists for deciding which extreme weather event warrants an attribution analysis. Most attribution studies are initiated on the basis of identifying impactful events that scientists know about. This leads to a preferential focus on those regions for which the impact reporting structures are most robust, information flows immediate and for which weather-related impacts generate international media attention. Moreover, attribution scientists in wealthy countries often derive funding from a national government or meteorological service, which often leads to an emphasis on extreme events within the country of the funder. These factors result in a systematic oversampling of attribution studies for events in wealthy countries, irrespective of whether the data and modelling tools are more suited to that region.
5. ***The detectability of extreme weather impacts***: The most easily-reported extreme weather impacts are damage to insured physical assets post-event – particularly from flooding, wildfires and tropical cyclones/hurricanes. Lower income countries also have lower rates of insurance coverage for the types of physical assets susceptible to extreme weather. This translates to a mismatch in the magnitude of impacts recorded in disaster databases. Similarly, many of the worst outcomes from extreme weather in lower income nations – like droughts – come in the form of diffuse impacts. Such impacts both emerge over time and require more sophisticated monitoring tools to quantify. Combined, these issues further exacerbate the selection biases and inequities in the regional coverage of attribution studies.
6. ***Differences in extreme event impact reporting mechanisms***: Finally, the institutions that report extreme weather impact data to natural disaster databases also differ between lower and higher income nations. Well-resourced governments tend to perform this role directly for higher income countries. By contrast, non-governmental organisations (NGOs) and other aid agencies typically fill this role in lower income nations. The work is by-product of monitoring systems to identify

locations with the greatest need for humanitarian aid. This, however, leads to disparities in the classes of climate event and types of information monitored and subsequently reported. European governments, for example, have developed robust mechanisms to quantify the impacts of extreme heatwaves soon after the event. However, similarly severe events occurring in sub-Saharan Africa often go undetected (Harrington and Otto, 2020[221]) because NGOs can only identify the humanitarian impacts of floods and droughts. As a consequence, most databases of heatwave impacts over the 20th and 21st centuries place an artificial emphasis on European events. This mistakenly implies that no heat-related impacts have occurred whatsoever in many low income nations.

A multitude of research, data and funding gaps need to be addressed to fully understand, quantify and monitor the worsening impacts of extreme weather from climate change. First, extremely large information gaps exist when it comes to quantifying what impacts were actually generated by extreme weather. Targeted support is needed to reduce geographic disparities in the coverage of on-the-ground monitoring programmes. This is equally true for the meteorological characteristics of extreme weather, and the subsequent social, health and economic impacts of these extreme events.

There is an equally urgent need for a systematic, bottom-up reporting system to record the meteorological characteristics of all extreme weather events. Such recordings should have enough detail for a subsequent attribution analysis. A step-change is needed in the way science is resourced, particularly in lower income countries. The barriers to completing an attribution study will always be in these countries. Therefore, higher income countries need to offer both scientific expertise and financial support to ensure robust applications of event attribution science (broadly understood) can be accessible for all countries.

3.6. Cascading impacts of crossing a climate tipping point: Collapse of the Atlantic Meridional Overturning Circulation

Passing tipping points in the climate system, leading to widespread, abrupt and/or irreversible damages, are among the largest risks from climate change (Lenton et al., 2008[4]; Lenton et al., 2019[64]). The IPCC defines a tipping point as an irreversible "level of change in system properties beyond which a system reorganises, often in a non-linear manner, and does not return to the initial state even if the drivers of the change are abated. For the climate system, the term refers to a critical threshold at which global or regional climate changes from one stable state to another stable state." (IPCC, 2018[5]). Passing tipping points could cause severe social and economic impacts (Lenton and Ciscar, 2012[70]; Lontzek et al., 2015[222]; Cai, Lenton and Lontzek, 2016[68]).

There are multiple subsystems of the Earth's climate system – termed "tipping elements" (Lenton et al., 2019[64]) – that could pass a tipping point this century under climate change. Examples include a collapse of the AMOC, irreversible shrinkage of the Greenland or West Antarctic ice sheets, disruption of major monsoon systems or dieback of the Amazon rainforest (Lenton et al., 2008[4]; Lenton et al., 2019[64]).

For over a decade, scientific assessment has agreed that several tipping points have significant (~10s of a percentage) probabilities even at low levels of warming. This rises to "more likely than not" (>50%) under unmitigated global warming (Kriegler et al., 2009[66]). The effectiveness of collective action to avoid crossing climate tipping points may still depend on reducing uncertainty about where the tipping points lie (Barrett and Dannenberg, 2014[223]). However, the latest scientific evidence is clear that some tipping points could be crossed within the 1.5-2°C Paris climate target range, with many more at risk under 3-4°C of warming [(Lenton et al., 2019[64]) and Table 3.1]. The diverse impacts of crossing different climate tipping points remain seriously understudied (Table 3.2).

Recent work has also emphasised the risk that crossing one tipping point can increase the likelihood of crossing another, potentially leading to a "cascade" of impacts (Cai, Lenton and Lontzek, 2016[68]; Lenton et al., 2019[64]). In the worst case scenario, such a cascade might lead to a new, less habitable, “hothouse” climate state (Steffen et al., 2018[224]). Interactions could happen through ocean and atmospheric circulation or through feedbacks that increase GHG levels and global temperature (Table 3.2).

Given this context, this chapter focuses on the cascading impacts of a potential collapse of the AMOC, and its cascading effects on other tipping elements. It has chosen the AMOC collapse because it is the most studied tipping element, it connects together the climate system and it could have huge impacts.

3.6.1. Why is the collapse of the AMOC of concern?

A collapse of the AMOC represents a fundamental reorganisation of ocean circulation. It would redistribute heat around the planet and lead to a corresponding coupled response from sea ice and the atmosphere (Box 3.6 explains the AMOC and how its collapse could occur). In the past, the AMOC collapse has resulted in a drastically colder Europe. It has shifted rainfall patterns that made parts of Europe and northern Africa and India drier, and areas in the southern hemisphere wetter. It also profoundly affected marine and terrestrial ecosystems (physical impacts are explored in Table 3.2).

In AMOC weakening scenarios (without total collapse) where deep convection shuts off in the Labrador Sea region, the impacts are still significant (Table 3.2). They can unfold faster than a full AMOC collapse (Drijfhout et al., 2015[225]; Sgubin et al., 2017[226]). These include dynamic effects on sea level, with increases down the eastern seaboard of the United States of around 20 cm in the regions around Boston, New York and Washington, DC (Yin, Schlesinger and Stouffer, 2009[227]). A rise in sea level along the northeast coast of North America was, in fact, observed between 2009-10 – time in which the AMOC had a marked turndown – with the sea level rising 128 mm in New York (Yin, Schlesinger and Stouffer, 2009[227]).

The climate effects may be likened to the Little Ice Age (LIA), a period of significantly colder weather patterns in the northern hemisphere between the 15 and 19 centuries (Moreno-Chamarro et al., 2016[228]). This was one of several centennial-scale climatic oscillations during the present interglacial period. As the most commonly accepted explanation for the LIA, volcanically triggered changes in the AMOC helped amplify internal climate variability (Schleussner and Feulner, 2013[229]). Specifically, changes in freshwater forcing may have reduced the formation of Labrador Sea Water and contributed towards the onset of LIA cooling (Moffa-Sánchez et al., 2014[230]). The AMOC collapse, or the abrupt weakening associated with subpolar gyre (SPG) collapse, could therefore have cascading effects far beyond the parts of the globe where it occurs (Wunderling et al., 2021[69]).

Global warming can slow down the overturning circulation and could trigger a tipping point collapse of the AMOC (Lenton et al., 2008[4]). There are two relevant effects – thermal and haline (salinity). Warming, which is greater in the high latitudes than the tropics, makes high-latitude surface waters less dense. This weakens circulation but is unlikely to collapse it. The bigger risk comes from increased freshwater input making the North Atlantic less salty (Hawkins et al., 2011[231]). Warming tends to increase atmospheric moisture content and high-latitude precipitation that falls directly on the North Atlantic. It also drains off the land into the Arctic basin and North Atlantic. Warming is also causing accelerating melt of the Greenland ice sheet, adding freshwater close to the regions of deep convection.

Box 3.6. What is the AMOC and why does it have a tipping point?

The Atlantic Meridional Overturning Circulation (AMOC) is the Atlantic branch of the thermohaline circulation (THC), which transports heat and salt around the global ocean. The THC, sometimes referred to as the ocean's "great conveyor belt", carries some 30 times more water than all the world's freshwater rivers combined. The AMOC is a system of currents in the Atlantic Ocean that transports heat from the southern hemisphere and the tropics to the northern mid-high latitudes, bringing warm surface water up to Europe (red arrows in Figure 3.15). In the North Atlantic, one arm of the Gulf Stream breaks towards Iceland, forming part of the AMOC that transports heat far northward. As that warm water heads north, it loses heat to the atmosphere, cooling it down. It also evaporates freshwater to the atmosphere, leaving it saltier. Both effects make the surface water denser.

Figure 3.15. The Atlantic Meridional Overturning Circulation

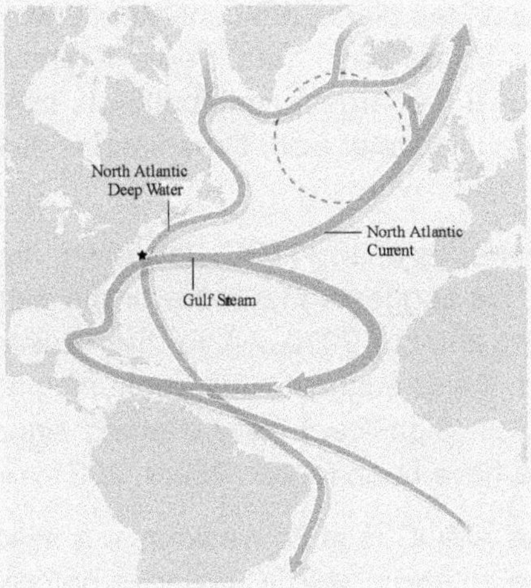

Source: (Praetorius, 2018[232])

On either side of Greenland, the surface waters get cold enough, salty enough, and therefore dense enough to sink to great depth in the ocean through a process known as deep convection. This North Atlantic Deep Water (NADW) formation propels a southward return flow of cold water at depth (blue arrow in Figure 3.15). These cold deep waters eventually return to the surface in the Southern Ocean, completing the loop of the overturning circulation.

The AMOC is self-sustaining due to a process known as the salt-advection (positive) feedback (Cheng et al., 2018[233]). In essence, the circulation itself maintains the salty dense North Atlantic surface waters that can sink to the depths and drive the circulation. The circulation can be shut down, such that the AMOC moves to another stable state (Stommel, 1961[234]). If the AMOC draws in salt at its southern boundary (around 34S in latitude), it is in a regime of "bi-stability" where both "on" and "off" states are stable. Current observational evidence suggests the AMOC is bi-stable at present. Conversely, many climate models are biased too stable in that they do not show net salt input and hence are in a "mono-stable" regime.

The tipping point between "on" and "off" states can be triggered if sufficient freshwater enters the NADW formation there. Once the AMOC has collapsed and is in the "off" state, there is a different tipping point at which the AMOC can be switched back "on". These two tipping points bound the region of "bi-stability" where both states are stable under the same global climate boundary conditions.

Current concern about an AMOC tipping point stems in part from understanding tens of thousands of years of the prehistoric climate record (Barker and Knorr, 2016[235]). In the past, the AMOC has switched on and off repeatedly, triggering rapid changes in temperatures and precipitation patterns around the North Atlantic and beyond (Barker and Knorr, 2016[235]). During the last ice age, there were more than 20 "Dansgaard-Oeschger events" (named after their discoverers) in which the AMOC abruptly strengthened. Some thousand or more years later, it abruptly collapsed, with associated abrupt changes in sea-ice cover and atmospheric circulation patterns (Buizert and Schmittner, 2015[236]). Proxy evidence suggests the subpolar gyre and the AMOC are not completely stable in the current interglacial period, even absent anthropogenic climate change. Section 3.6.2 explores whether and how global warming could affect their stability.

The Greenland ice sheet is melting at the upper end of projections, or about six times faster than in the 1990s. According to one study, the subpolar North Atlantic recently became less salty than at any time in the past 120 years (Holliday et al., 2020[237]). Recent studies have inferred the AMOC has weakened by 15% since the 1950s (Rahmstorf et al., 2015[238]). This manifests itself as a "cold spot" in the ocean to the South of Greenland – the only place on the planet not consistently warming (Caesar et al., 2018[239]). This AMOC slowdown is unprecedented in the past 1 000 years (Rahmstorf et al., 2015[238]; Caesar et al., 2021[240]). Freshwater budgets suggest the largest contribution is coming from increased precipitation in the high northern latitudes. However, meltwater from Greenland is also making a significant and growing contribution (Bamber et al., 2018[241]).

Additional evidence supports the inference of an AMOC slowdown, including an increase in salinity of the South Atlantic in recent decades. This suggests that more of the salt that once travelled north with the AMOC is remaining in the tropics (Zhu and Liu, 2020[242]). Further research has argued that the Gulf Stream along Florida's coast has weakened. It also suggests this weakening has been particularly strong over the past two decades (Piecuch, 2020[243]). Significant early warning signals in multiple independent AMOC indices based on observational data have been found (Boers, 2021[244]).

Although recent research shows the AMOC is at its weakest in a millennium, the latest IPCC AR6 gives medium confidence there will not be an abrupt AMOC collapse before 2100 (IPCC, 2021[14]). The AMOC is "very likely" to further weaken this century. However, collapse within the 21st century is deemed very unlikely, but physically plausible (Douville et al., 2021[245]). This is partly limited by the clause that collapse must complete during this century. There is a different interpretation to model results used by IPCC. Collapse of the AMOC occurs in one model at 1.4°C warming relative to pre-industrial global temperatures, in two additional runs of the same model at 1.6-1.9°C, and in two runs of a different model at 2.2-2.5°C (Drijfhout et al., 2015[225]; Sgubin et al., 2017[226]). Furthermore, IPCC models have been found to be biased too stable with respect to observational constraints. Correcting for this bias leads to the AMOC collapse under a doubling of CO_2 in one model (Liu et al., 2017[246]).

The present report considers the possibility of an AMOC collapse at 2-3°C global warming above pre-industrial temperature to be a significant risk worthy of assessment. Such a collapse is consistent with earlier expert elicitation (Kriegler et al., 2009[66]). Furthermore, the impacts of expected AMOC weakening are a scaled down version of those from total collapse. Hence, an impact assessment is useful for both eventualities. Even if a complete AMOC collapse does not occur, a collapse of deep convection in the North Atlantic SPG, and associated abrupt weakening of the AMOC, would still have major impacts (Sgubin et al., 2017[226]; Swingedouw et al., 2021[247]). In this scenario, deep convection shuts off in the Labrador Sea region and is left only in the Greenland–Iceland–Norwegian Seas.

This analysis assesses the above scenario to be "as likely as not" (33-66% probability) at 1.5-2°C global warming above pre-industrial temperatures. The assessment is based on this probability occurring in three climate models at 1.1-1.4°C, in five additional runs across four models at 1.6-1.9°C and with a further instance at 2.0°C (Drijfhout et al., 2015[225]; Sgubin et al., 2017[226]). In this section, state-of-the-art climate model experiments (refer to Annex 3.A for detailed methodology) are used to examine the impacts of an

AMOC collapse and how it interacts globally with other tipping elements in the climate system to either increase or decrease their likelihood.

3.6.2. Climatic impacts of an AMOC collapse and cascading effects on other tipping elements

Surface air temperature and precipitation

A collapse of the AMOC on its own (without underlying warming) would lead to large-scale climatic impacts globally (Jackson et al., 2015[248]; Mecking et al., 2016[249]). The left column of Figure 3.16 provides temperature and precipitation responses. The top left panel illustrates that an AMOC collapse (without underlying warming) would lead to widespread cooling across the northern hemisphere, with the more extreme consequences farther north. Specifically, Europe would observe a drop of 3°C to 8°C in annual mean surface air temperature. For its part, North America would experience a less severe decline of 1°C to 3°C. In contrast, there is little temperature change in the southern hemisphere – only a small increase in temperature in the Atlantic Ocean off the southwestern coast of Africa.[7]

Large equatorial anomalies in precipitation correspond to a southward shift of the Intertropical Convergence Zone (ITCZ) under a collapse of the AMOC (Figure 3.16, bottom left panel). Most of the northern hemisphere experiences a drying with the exception of North America, which becomes slightly wetter on average. India would lose more than half of its current rainfall if the AMOC were to collapse. This suggests a significant disruption to the Indian summer monsoon, affecting the livelihood of millions of people as well as the regional economy (Gadgil and Gadgil, 2006[250]). The bottom left panel of Figure 3.16 also indicates a significant drying in the Amazon basin.

Figure 3.16. Surface air temperature and precipitation response to an AMOC collapse alone and an AMOC collapse after 2.5ºC warming above pre-industrial

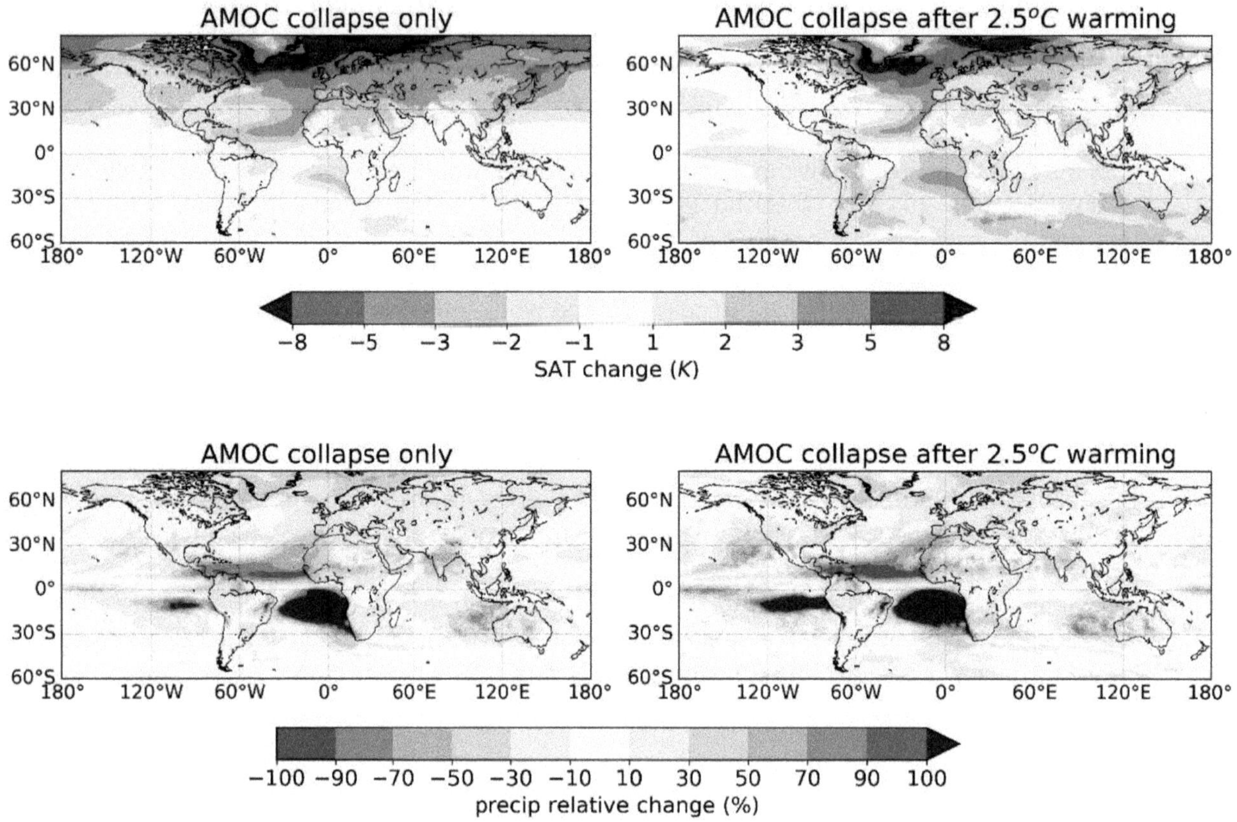

Note: Surface air temperature (SAT, top row) and precipitation (bottom row) response to AMOC-collapse scenarios. Left column, the climatic impacts of just an AMOC collapse without the additional global warming most likely to accompany a collapse in any realistic future scenario is isolated. The isolated impacts of an AMOC collapse are analysed by taking the difference of 30-year means of the control run and the AMOC-off run, once the simulation is approximately stationary, performed by the HadGEM3-GC2 model. Right column, the analysis is expanded to include the impacts of an AMOC collapse against a more realistic future climate state, accounting for the additional effects of global warming using the future scenario SSP1-2.6 in the model HadGEM3-GC31-MM. The forcing scenario SSP1-2.6 refers to Shared Socio-economic Pathway SSP1 and Regional Concentration Pathway RCP2.6 - a low-emissions pathway with high sustainability. Under the SSP1-2.6 scenario, HadGEM3-GC31-MM reaches a mean global warming of 2.5°C above pre-industrial levels by the end of the century (2071-2100). This warming pattern is overlaid to the impacts of an AMOC collapse to establish the overall impact if the AMOC were to collapse after 2.5°C global warming relative to the present-day climate (2006-35).

The left column of Figure 3.16 highlighted the direct impacts from an AMOC collapse alone. Conversely, the right column shows the impacts in a more realistic scenario of an AMOC collapse after 2.5ºC warming since pre-industrial conditions relative to the present-day climate (see Annex 3.A). Overlaying this warming trend (top right panel) shows contrasting temperature responses between the northern and southern hemispheres. The northern hemisphere still displays a widespread cooling (particularly over the North Atlantic) although mitigated partly due to the underlying warming.

Conversely, the southern hemisphere continues to experience widespread warming due to the underlying warming trend, largely unaffected by an AMOC collapse. Interestingly, the precipitation patterns and size of anomalies are mainly unchanged from just considering an AMOC collapse alone. The main differences are less drying over Asia, but more drying in the tropics of the Atlantic Ocean for an AMOC collapse after 2.5ºC warming.

Climate niche

The results of Xu et al. (2020[251]) provide an illustrative indication of impacts of an AMOC collapse on climate "suitability" for humans. The study showed that humans, like all species, have an "apparent climate niche". In this niche, population density peaks (both now and at different times in the past). The climate niche is characterised by a major mode centred on ~11 °C to 15 °C mean annual temperature (MAT) and ~1 000 mm mean annual precipitation (MAP), with a secondary mode at ~25 °C (Xu et al., 2020[251]). Many other social factors influence human population density. Further, there is remarkable consistency in the distribution of population density with respect to climate over millennia (Xu et al., 2020[251]). This may in part reflect historical contingency – people simply live where others have lived before. Nevertheless, food production clearly depends on climate. Moreover, the density of crop production and animal rearing with respect to climate is strikingly similar to the density of people (Xu et al., 2020[251]).

As discussed above, a collapse or weakening, of the AMOC will lead to changes in temperature and precipitation, geographically shifting the apparent climate niche for humans. Previously, Xu et al. (2020[251]) examined the effect of global warming moving the apparent climate niche. The analysis here considers the effects of an AMOC collapse in isolation, and on top of global warming. The pre-industrial population density distribution is used as a baseline for constructing the human climate niche. The population density distribution with respect to MAT and precipitation is assumed to sum to unity, providing a normalised measure.

Figure 3.17. The modelled change in the human climate niche following the simulated collapse of the AMOC

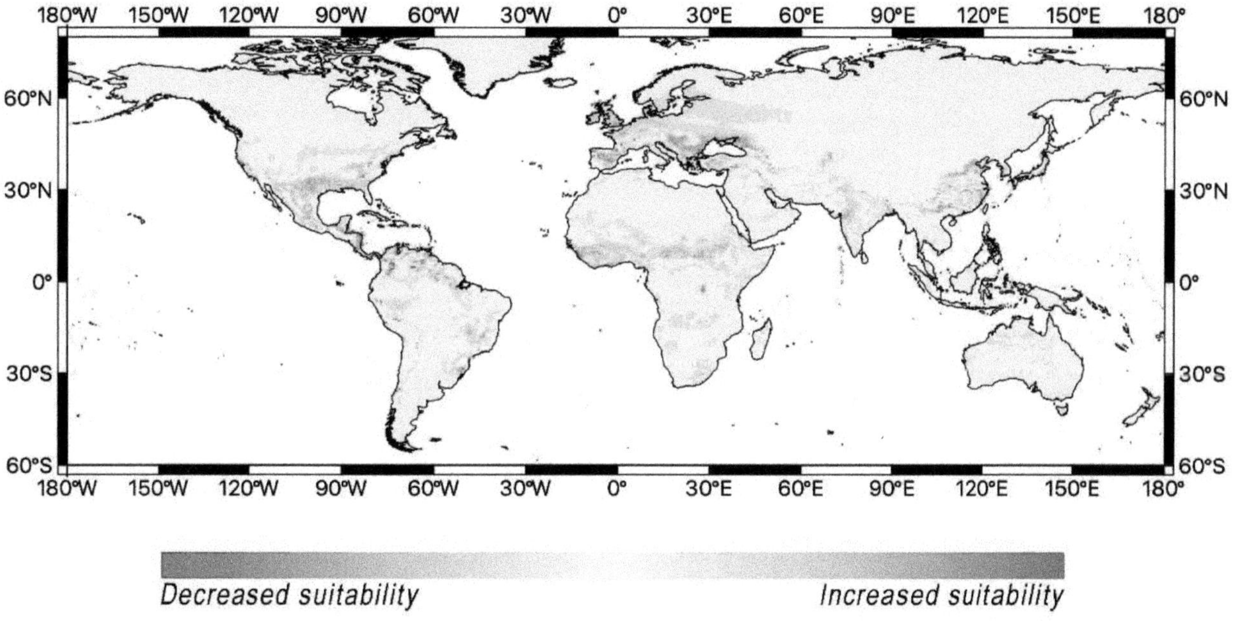

Note: The isolated impacts of the AMOC collapse without any additional warming. This is a theoretical simulation as additional warming would be necessary to trigger the collapse of the AMOC. The change in the human climate niche is presented as the difference between the calculated climate niche for the AMOC-on control run and the climate niche after the simulated collapse of the AMOC. The control scenario is representative of a pre-industrial world. The climate niches are calculated using 30-year means of the control run and the AMOC-off run, once the simulation is approximately stationary, performed by the HadGEM3-GC2 model.

Changes in climate "suitability" are then calculated as the proportions of summed niche gain or loss. The global "suitability" for human populations in AMOC-on and AMOC-off scenarios (Figure 3.17) are then mapped. The projected geographical shift of "suitable" conditions is substantial. Conditions deteriorate in some regions but improve in others (Figure 3.17). Regions south of the equator would mostly become more "suitable". Sub-Saharan Africa, as well as Central and South America, would see the largest gain in "suitability". On the other hand, a collapse of the AMOC would result in a reduction in "suitability" in the Global North: across Europe, the United States and northern Africa.

The SSP1-2.6 low-carbon emissions pathway reaches a mean global warming of 2.5°C above pre-industrial levels by the end of the century. If these impacts are added to those of the AMOC collapse, the results show some marked differences to the effect of the AMOC collapse in isolation. Europe, the region most influenced by the warming effect and the precipitation brought by the Gulf Stream, would have the largest decrease in climate "suitability". While North America would mostly become more "suitable", large chunks of South America, particularly Brazil, would become less suitable. The decrease in suitability in Brazil is largely due to two factors: a change in precipitation patterns and the effect of global warming, which is further amplified by the AMOC collapse in the Global South. Much of Africa would have only a mild increase or decrease in "suitability". However, including warming markedly changes the picture for central Africa. There, SSP1-2.6 warming would lead to a decrease in suitability. This effect is amplified by the southern hemisphere warming due to a collapse of the AMOC (Figure 3.18).

Figure 3.18. The modelled change in the human climate niche following the simulated collapse of the AMOC after 2.5°C warming above pre-industrial temperatures according to SSP1-2.6

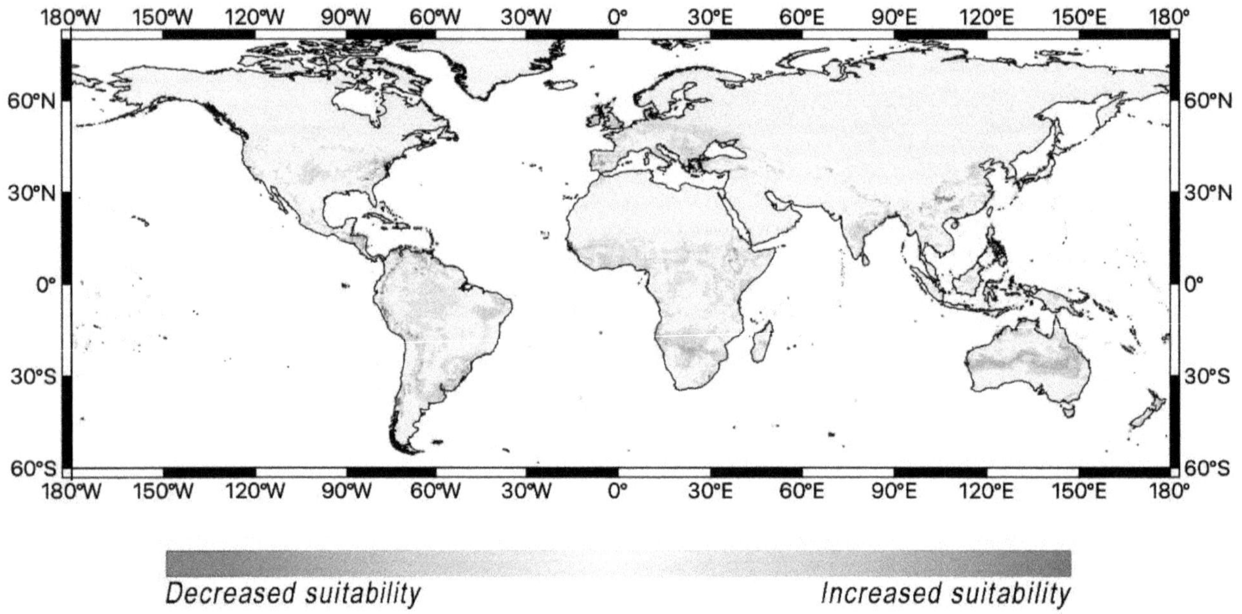

Note: The impacts on the suitability of climate for human populations for a more realistic scenario involving the AMOC collapse triggered by 2.5°C warming above pre-industrial according to scenario SSP1-2.6. The change in the human climate niche is presented as the difference between the calculated climate niche for the AMOC-on control run and the climate niche after the simulated collapse of the AMOC. The control scenario is representative of a pre-industrial world. The climate niches are calculated using 30-year means of the control run and the AMOC-off run, once the simulation is approximately stationary, performed by the HadGEM3-GC2 model. The effects of the AMOC collapse are overlaid over the additional effects of global warming according to the SSP1-2.6 scenario run in the HadGEM3-GC31-MM model. The forcing scenario SSP1-2.6 refers to Shared Socio-economic Pathway SSP1 and Regional Concentration Pathway RCP2.6 – a low-emissions pathway with high sustainability. Under the SSP1-2.6 scenario, HadGEM3-GC31-MM reaches a mean global warming of 2.5°C above pre-industrial levels by the end of the century (2071-2100). This warming pattern is overlaid to the impacts of an AMOC collapse to establish the overall impact if the AMOC were to collapse after 2.5°C global warming relative to the present-day climate (2006-35).

The simplicity of this approach is appealing but has inherent limitations. While the success of human societies is linked in complex ways to climate (Carleton and Hsiang, 2016[252]), climate alone cannot predict where and which societies will thrive. Furthermore, populations in a location are historically adapted to climate. Changes thus pose their own challenges, even if the climate is nominally becoming more "suitable" in a particular location. Therefore, the geographical shift in the human climate niche shown here should not be taken as a prediction of human migration or loss of the ability for humans to thrive in a particular region. Rather, it illustrates the potential large-scale impacts of the collapse of the AMOC both in isolation and in the context of a global warming scenario.

Effect on agriculture

In this sub-section, a more detailed "niche" based approach assesses effects on climate suitability for the major staple crops of wheat, maize and rice. The major staple crops of wheat, maize and rice provide over 50% of global calories (FAOSTAT, 2021[253]). The growth suitability of these crops is assessed with ECOCROP data on the optimal temperature, precipitation and growing season length. A location is deemed suitable for crop growth for a given year if it has temperature and precipitation within the ECOCROP bounds for the growing season length of the crop. The proportion of the 150 years with climate suitable for crop growth for the growing season length is examined. The same is then performed for the AMOC-off run, and the AMOC-off run with the added warming. The analysis shows that an AMOC collapse reduces suitability for wheat, although there are areas of increase (see Figure 3.19 and Figure 3.20). Maize suitably declines across Europe and Russia and the higher latitudes of North America, but increases in parts of South America, southern Africa and Australia. Changes in rice suitability follow a similar pattern but over a smaller area.

Figure 3.19. Differences in crop growing suitability between AMOC-on and AMOC-off, and AMOC-off plus warming

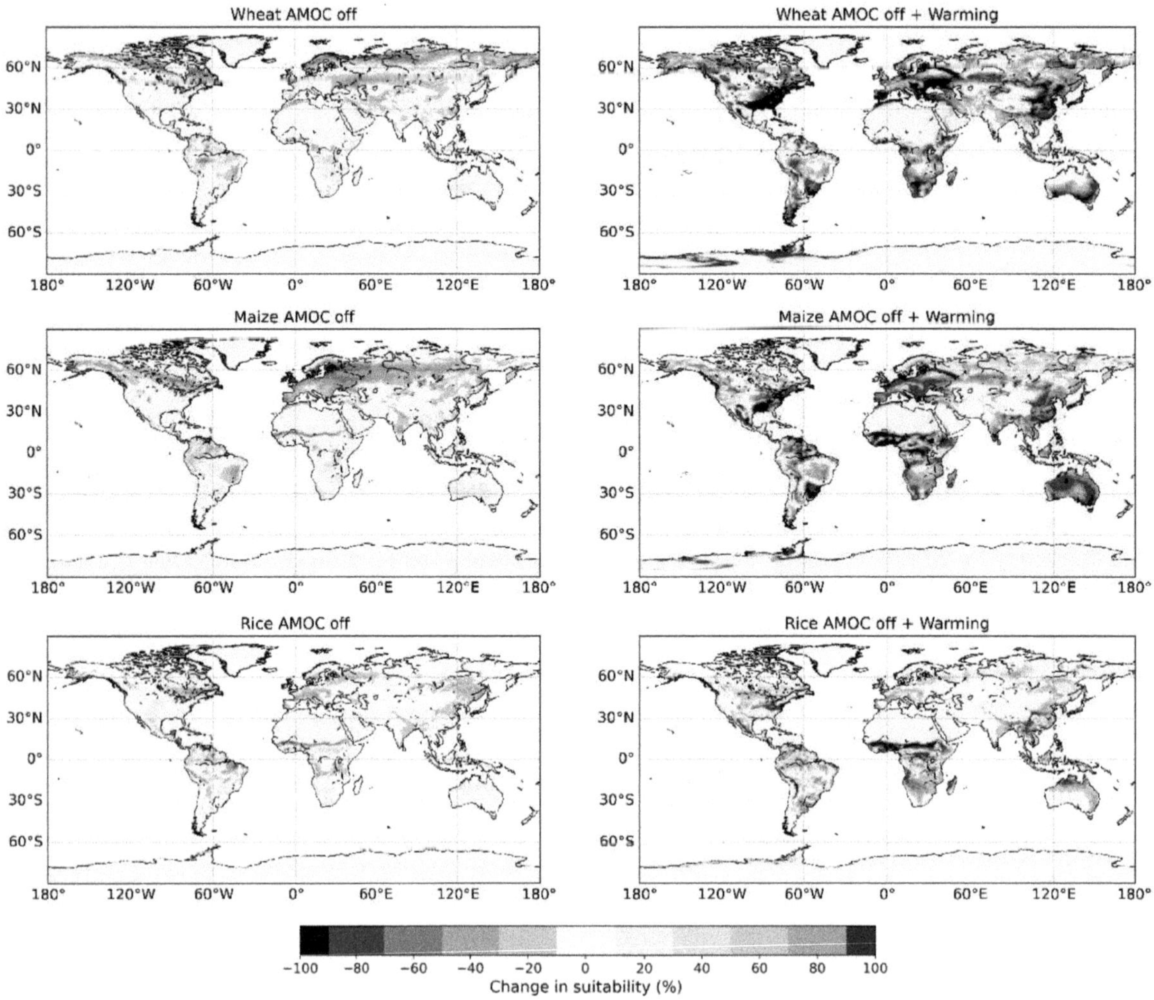

Note: Differences shown here are the AMOC-on suitability (percentage) minus either the AMOC-off or AMOC-off plus warming suitability.

To summarise these changes, the percentage of land that would have a suitability greater than 90% in each of the three cases is calculated (see Figure 3.19 and Figure 3.20). With AMOC-off but no warming, ~5% of the land loses suitability for wheat. This corresponds to a loss of nearly a quarter of the current suitable area. Meanwhile, ~2% of the land becomes unsuitable for maize (a loss of 16% of the currently suitable area). Rice experiences a smaller change. When climate change is also considered, approximately half of the remaining suitable land is lost for wheat and maize. For rice, there is a modest increase in suitable area, exceeding that in the baseline state. However, gains in suitable area for rice cultivation are dwarfed by losses in suitable area from wheat and maize. This analysis does not overlay the subset of areas where each crop is actually grown. However, an AMOC collapse would clearly pose a critical challenge to food security. Such a collapse combined with climate change would have a catastrophic impact.

Figure 3.20. Bar chart showing the percentage of total land grid boxes suitable for crop growth in each simulation

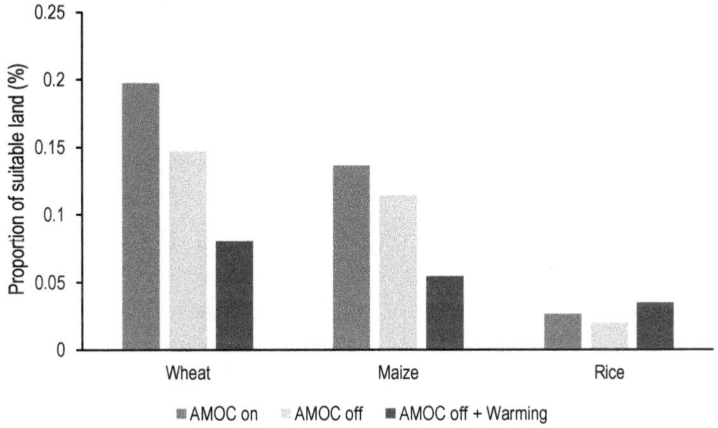

Note: Here, a location is considered suitable for crop growth if more than 90% of the 150 years analysed are suitable, as detailed in the main text. AMOC off refers to AMOC-off without warming included.

Climate analogues

The change induced by a collapse or slowing down of the AMOC can also be quantified. A number can be identified by comparing the projected climate of some major cities to the current climate to find climate analogues (Table 3.4). The statistical technique of "climate analogues" quantifies the similarity of a location's climate relative to the climate of another place and/or time. Similarity is calculated using the mean temperature and total precipitation for averaged monthly values. Using climate analogue analysis, the 14 selected cities generally shift towards colder climates. There is a much larger impact on cities in the northern hemisphere than in the southern hemisphere. European cities are more impacted than North American cities with a high degree of cooling.

With the inclusion of the SSP1-2.6 warming, some cities shift towards warmer analogues. Conversely, in the AMOC collapse-only scenario, all cities examined shifted towards colder climates. However, many of the cities show a similar climate shift both with and without warming. This is largely due to the influence of changes in precipitation on which the AMOC exerts the dominant influence.

Table 3.4. Climate analogues for the isolated effects of a simulated AMOC collapse for 14 major cities

	AMOC-on control		Analogue – AMOC collapse		
City	$\underline{T}$(°C)	$\underline{P}$(mm yr-1)	Nearest city	$\underline{T}$(°C)	$\underline{P}$(mm yr-1)
Amsterdam	10.3	798.0	Aleutian Islands, Alaska, US	6.0	725.9
Bangkok	29.0	889.4	Addis Ababa, Ethiopia	28.2	890.7
Berlin	9.3	651.2	Stockholm, Sweden	5.6	534.9
Cape Town	18.0	551.7	Cape Town, South Africa	18.9	813.8
Istanbul	14.7	963.0	Ghent, Brussels	11.5	773.1
London	10.4	717.1	Aleutian Islands, Alaska, US	6.1	607.4
Miami	24.5	1135.7	Jacksonville, Florida, US	23.5	1 191.8
Nairobi	20.1	1228.6	Nairobi, Kenya	20.0	1 339.6
New York	12.1	1562.3	Providence, Rhode Island, US	10.3	1 617.4
Paris	10.8	748.5	Copenhagen, Denmark	7.2	626.1
Rio de Janeiro	23.3	1258.2	Rio de Janeiro, Brazil	22.8	1 341.3
San Francisco	16.2	1291.1	San Francisco, California, US	14.9	1 401.5

Note: Climate analogues are calculated employing a statistical model that quantifies the similarity of climates based on average monthly temperatures and precipitation rates. Analogues are calculated by comparing the climate of the target city in the AMOC-collapse run with the climate of cities in the AMOC-on control run to determine an AMOC-on analogue for each target city in the collapsed AMOC scenario. This generates a set of co-ordinates for the closest climate analogue. Analogue cities are picked as the closest large city to the set of analogue co-ordinates. Temperatures are presented as the average annual temperatures for each target city for the AMOC-on control run and for the analogues in the AMOC-collapse run. Precipitation is presented as the average annual cumulative precipitation for each target city for the AMOC-on control run and for the analogues in the AMOC-collapse run.

Potential cascading effects – triggering other tipping points

As the AMOC is the "great connector" in the climate system, its collapse could trigger tipping cascades (Wunderling et al., 2021[69]). This sub-section examines the impact of an AMOC collapse on other recognised tipping elements, namely the Amazon rainforest, boreal forests, and the monsoon systems of India and West Africa [for the effect on ENSO see Williamson et al. (2017[254])].

Amazon rainforest

The AMOC collapse would have a cascading effect on the Amazon rainforest, which has been suggested as another climate tipping point (Lenton et al., 2008[4]). Dieback of the rainforest would have global implications due to the loss of carbon storage, as well as other considerations. These include loss of biodiversity and a change in precipitation patterns (Cox et al., 2004[255]). As seen previously, changes in climate can be found within the Amazon basin. In particular, a shift in the ITCZ caused a southward shift in precipitation. The following sub-section looks in more detail on the potential effect of this shift on the rainforest.

Figure 3.21. Impacts of an AMOC collapse on the Amazon rainforest

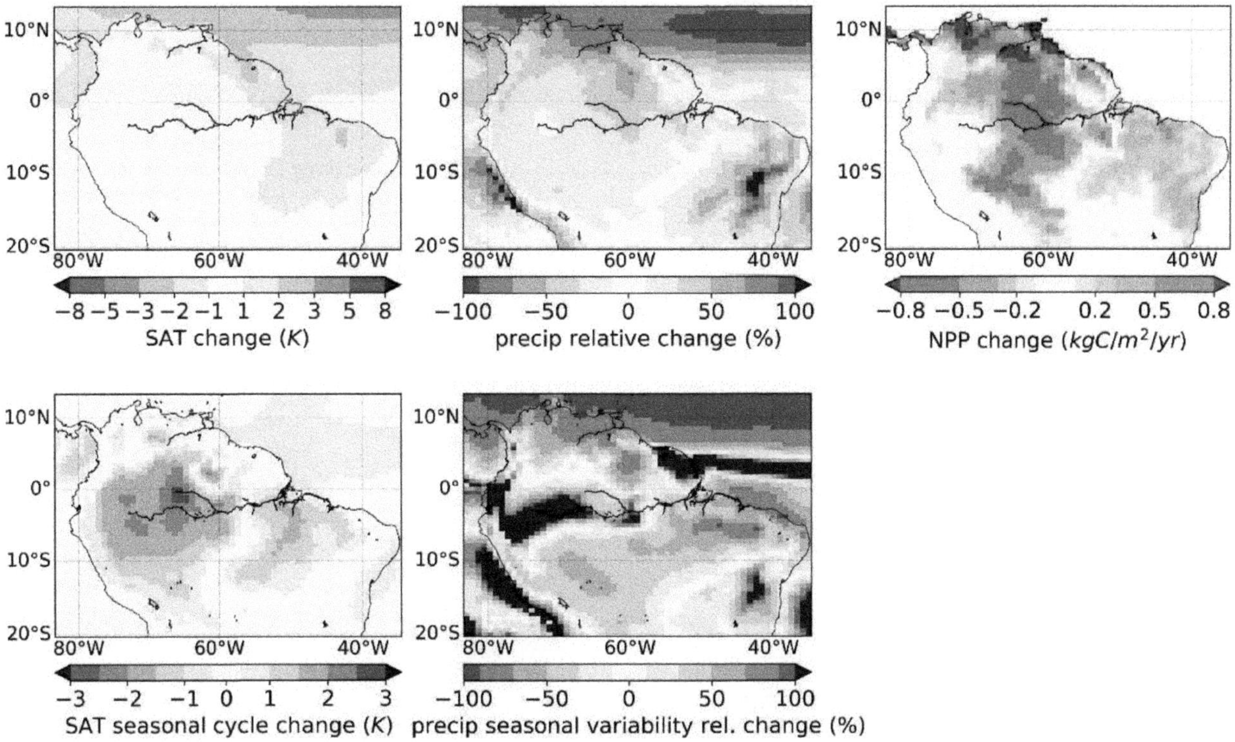

Note: Climatic impacts on the Amazon rainforest following an AMOC collapse without the additional global warming most likely to accompany a collapse in any realistic future scenario is isolated. The isolated impacts of an AMOC collapse are analysed by taking the difference of 30-year means of the control run and the AMOC-off run, once the simulation is approximately stationary, performed by the HadGEM3-GC2 model. Climatic impacts include surface air temperature (SAT, left column) anomaly (top) and seasonal cycle amplitude anomaly (bottom); precipitation (middle column) anomaly (top) and seasonal variability change (bottom); 8°C anomaly (NPP, right).

Figure 3.21 indicates the impact of an AMOC collapse alone on the Amazon rainforest without any underlying warming trend applied. Despite little change to the annual mean surface air temperature over the Amazon basin, the seasonal cycle increases by up to 2°C after a collapse of the AMOC. Additionally, precipitation reduces by up to 50% as does the seasonal variability in the precipitation. These changes indicate an extension to the dry season combined with more extreme temperatures, which would ultimately cause large-scale dieback. Although there is no dynamic vegetation within the model run,[8] the net primary productivity (NPP) would suggest that dieback tipping is likely. Specifically, NPP decreases by more than 0.5kgC/m^2/yr over much of the Amazon. It even approaches a drop of 1kgC/m^2/yr in northern regions of the Amazon. On the other hand, the NPP increases east of the Amazon, largely due to more precipitation and a small drop in annual mean temperature in the region.

The climate analogue of the AMOC is analysed to help determine what sort of vegetation will be found in the Amazon with an AMOC collapse. To that end, the analysis examines the land grid boxes in the AMOC-on run that most closely match the precipitation and temperature mean annual cycles from the Amazon basin. Because of the change in seasonality across the equator, the analysis is run separately for the northern and southern hemispheres.

Figure 3.22. Climate analogue analysis for temperature and precipitation, for the northern hemisphere and southern hemisphere Amazon basin

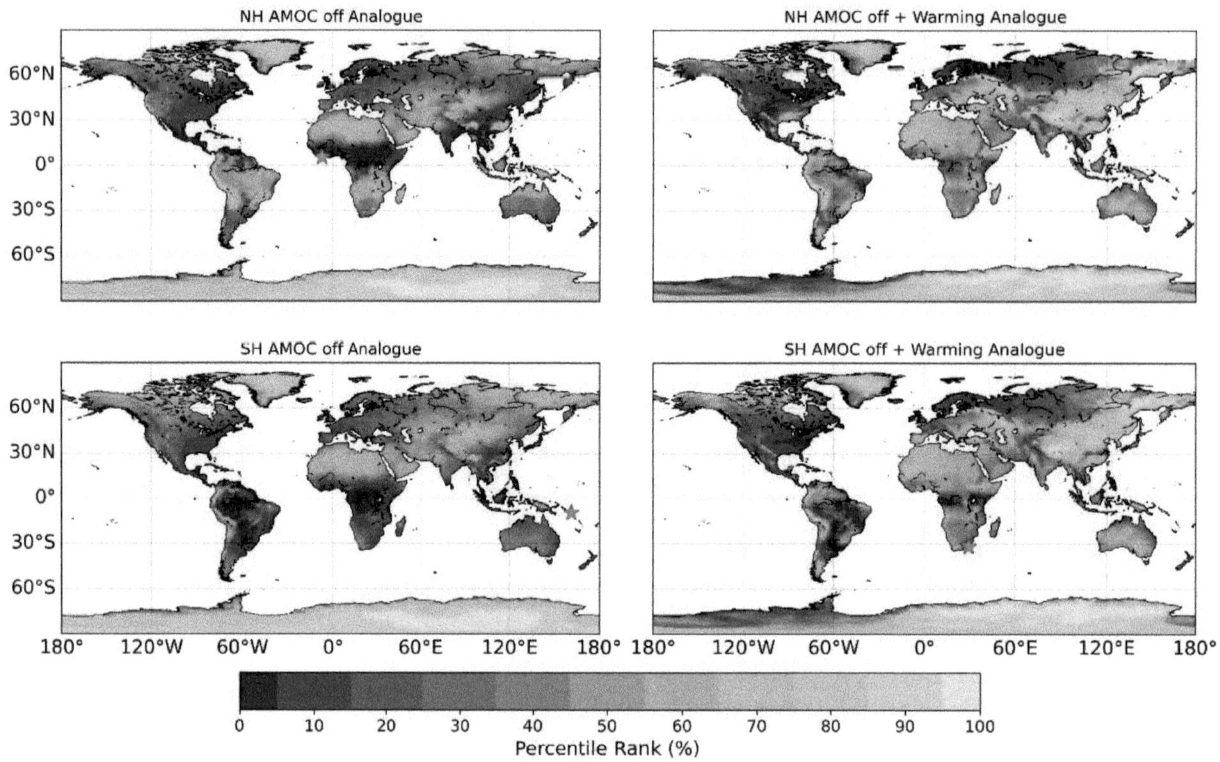

Note: Climate analogue analysis for temperature and precipitation, for the northern hemisphere (NH; top row) and southern hemisphere (SH; bottom row) Amazon basin; NH: northern hemisphere; SH: southern hemisphere. Red stars show the closest climate to the AMOC-on Amazon NH/SH climate.

Figure 3.22 shows the climate analogue analysis for both the northern hemisphere (top) and southern hemisphere (bottom) for an AMOC collapse in isolation (left) and combined with climate change (right). Darker colours refer to grid boxes that have a closer AMOC-on climate to Amazon AMOC-off climate, with the red star showing the closest climate in each instance. With an AMOC collapse in isolation there is not much change in temperature in the Amazon, but precipitation patterns are very different.

When combining the above effects, this analysis finds the Sahel is the closest climate analogue for the northern hemisphere, and the Solomon Islands for the southern hemisphere. When future climate change is combined with an AMOC collapse, the overall pattern of climate analogue ranking remains broadly similar. However, the closest analogue moves to East Africa for the northern hemisphere Amazon and to South Africa for the southern hemisphere Amazon. This analysis supports the inferences made above that the biome would be transformed away from a rainforest state.

Boreal forests

The boreal forests in North America and north Europe/Asia remove carbon from the atmosphere and help limit global warming. Under an AMOC-collapse scenario without underlying warming (Figure 3.23), the boreal forests over Europe and Asia respond differently to those in North America. As previously discussed, there is a widespread cooling over the northern hemisphere, though Europe and Asia will experience stronger cooling compared to North America. The amplitude of the seasonal cycle increases in Europe and Asia, pointing towards greater cooling to winter temperatures than to summer temperatures.

Conversely, the amplitude of the seasonal cycle decreases in North America, resulting in bigger impacts to summer temperatures.

Opposite responses between the two regions are also observed in the precipitation. There would be widespread drying across Europe and Asia, but in North America precipitation would increase. This leads to a negative impact on the NPP of boreal forests in Europe and Asia and therefore a possible tipping event. In eastern Canada, NPP also declines, but productivity increases further south in the United States. This would suggest a stabilising effect to the boreal forests with the possibility of a southward advance.

Figure 3.23. Potential impacts of an AMOC collapse on boreal forests

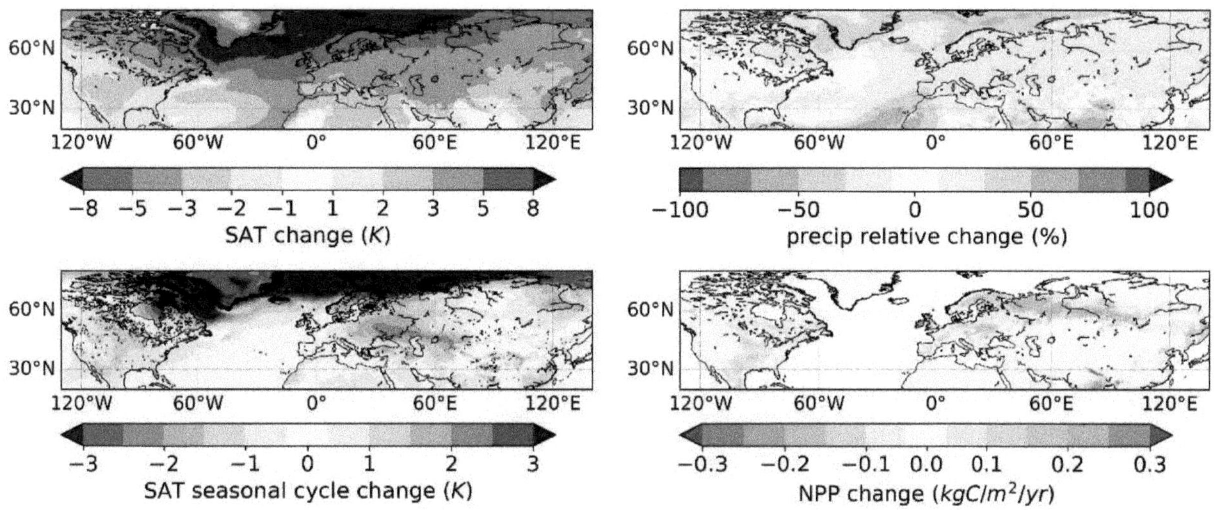

Note: Climatic impacts on boreal forests following an AMOC collapse without the additional global warming most likely to accompany a collapse in any realistic future scenario is isolated. The isolated impacts of an AMOC collapse are analysed by taking the difference of 30-year means of the control run and the AMOC-off run, once the simulation is approximately stationary, performed by the HadGEM3-GC2 model. Climatic impacts include surface air temperature (left column) anomaly (top) and seasonal cycle amplitude anomaly (bottom); precipitation relative change (top right); net primary productivity anomaly (NPP, bottom right)

Monsoon systems

As the main driver of the Indian summer monsoon, the land warms faster than the ocean during the summer, creating a temperature gradient that generates winds. These winds, emanating from the Indian Ocean, contain moisture that falls as precipitation once over land. Precipitation releases latent heat that increases the temperature over land and therefore amplifies the monsoon winds (Levermann et al., 2009[256]). The African monsoon is strengthened when northern hemisphere summer insolation is high (Rossignol-Strick, 1985[257]). A collapse of the AMOC would result in reduced northern hemisphere temperatures and therefore a weakening of the African monsoon.

Figure 3.24 suggests a collapse of the AMOC alone would disrupt both the Indian summer monsoon and the African monsoon. The summer (JJA) wind speeds over the Indian Ocean and western Atlantic will be significantly reduced. Weaker winds coming off the oceans will consequently carry less moisture and therefore summer precipitation over the land is vastly reduced – in north India, summer precipitation decreases by more than 70%. Weaker winds and less rainfall also negatively affect productivity. Reduced productivity, in turn, impacts the ability of farmers to grow crop. Therefore, a disruption to the monsoon season would have negative implications for millions of livelihoods.

Figure 3.24. Summer (JJA) impacts of an AMOC collapse on the West African and Indian monsoons

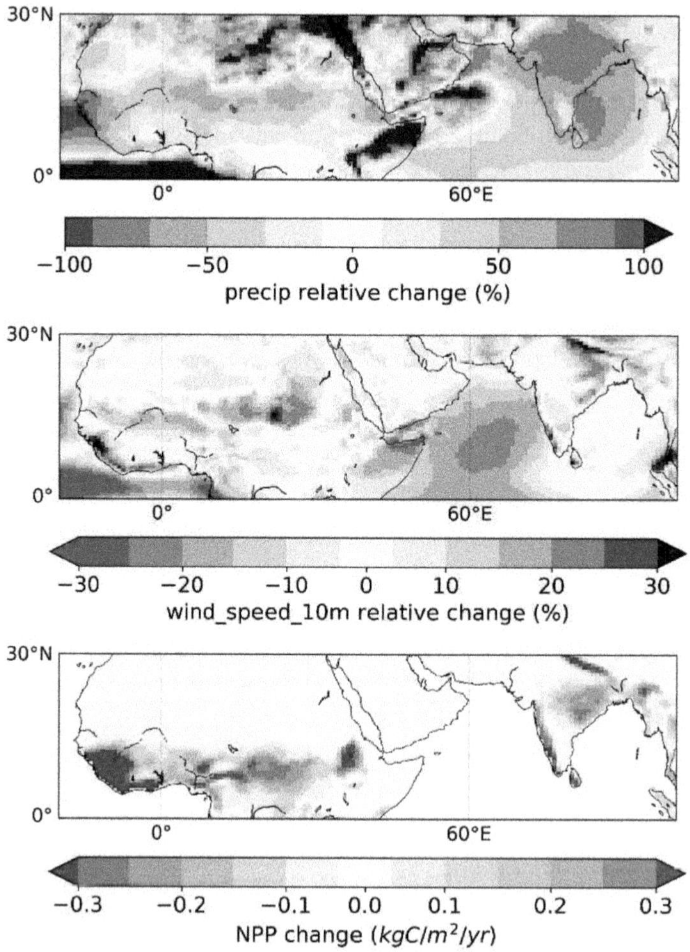

Note: Summer (JJA, June-July-August) climatic impacts on the West African and Indian monsoons following an AMOC collapse without the additional global warming most likely to accompany a collapse in any realistic future scenario is isolated. The isolated impacts of an AMOC collapse are analysed by taking the difference of 30-year means of the control run and the AMOC-off run, once the simulation is approximately stationary, performed by the HadGEM3-GC2 model. Climatic impacts include precipitation relative change (top); wind speed at 10 m relative change (middle); net primary productivity anomaly (NPP, bottom).

3.6.3. Summary findings

Socio-economic implications and impacts

Serious weakening or the shut-off of the AMOC and the resulting climatic shift would have profound implications. This is especially the case for the landmasses and the people occupying those landmasses around the North Atlantic. The climate changes induced by an AMOC collapse (and global warming) would affect ecosystems, as well as human health, livelihoods, food security, water supply and economic growth in many ways. These changes are summarised below.

Economic shocks

A collapse of the AMOC may lead to a substantial reduction in global economic output and exacerbate global economic inequalities. As detailed above, a possible shutdown of the AMOC would have global impacts on climate "suitability". Burke, Hsiang and Miguel (2015[258]) show how overall economic productivity depends nonlinearly on temperature. It gives a peak in productivity at an annual average temperature of 13.6°C. This is comparable to the peak of population density identified by Xu et al. (2020[251]).

However, the impact of an AMOC collapse cannot be adequately characterised by a derived relationship of current temperature to current productivity. This relationship only considers economic activities directly exposed to the weather (Keen et al., 2021[259]). Several studies have taken such an approach [e.g. (Tol, 2009[260]; Link and Tol, 2010[261]; Anthoff, Estrada and Tol, 2016[262])]. They consider only the overall change in temperature from global warming and an AMOC collapse combined. However, one would follow the other, each with its own impacts. Many impacts are associated with changes in other aspects of climate than temperature, notably the water cycle.

Some studies have even argued that an AMOC collapse would have a net economic benefit. For the reasons detailed above, this seems untenable. Other research has speculated on the past influence of the AMOC on the concentration of geopolitical power and wealth in the North Atlantic region (Railsback, 2017[263]). However, such "climate determinism" is widely contested.

An exploration of the potential economic impacts of the collapse of the AMOC (or the tipping of any other climate tipping point) centres not on theoretical effects on human productivity due to climate, but on the physical drivers. In passing tipping elements, the spatial patterns and modes of temporal variability of the climate could change drastically (Lenton and Ciscar, 2012[70]; Rodgers et al., 2021[264]). If such drastic changes were to happen, drawing on inferences from the current spatial-temporal pattern (which societies have had centuries to adapt to) would be useless (Keen et al., 2021[259]).

Effect on agriculture

The collapse of the AMOC would have a huge impact on agriculture globally. Much of the northern hemisphere would become less suitable for growth of many staple crops. However, Europe would be particularly affected. The AMOC makes Europe both warmer and wetter than it would be otherwise. If the AMOC weakened or collapsed in the coming decade as a consequence of further warming, Europe's seasonality would strongly increase. This, in turn, would lead to harsher winters, and hotter and drier summers.

This shift in Europe's climate is projected to reduce agricultural productivity and render most land unsuitable for arable farming. Consequently, the climate would be less suitable for the growth of maize and wheat (with the exception of wheat growth in the United Kingdom). This may lead to an increase in food prices. Conversely, the southern hemisphere would have an increase in suitability for rice growth. This would be especially the case in South East Asia, where rice is one of the main staple crops produced in the region. However, this growth is not analysed within the context of a potential failure of the Asian monsoon, which could have detrimental effects on agriculture throughout Asia.

Amazon rainforest

Changes in sea-surface temperature and rainfall patterns in the tropical Atlantic will impact the stability of the Amazon. Previous research found the global warming and an AMOC collapse processes are likely to have competing impacts on the rainfall in the Amazon (Ciemer et al., 2021[265]). The study further concludes that the tipping of the AMOC from the strong to the weak mode may have a stabilising effect on the Amazon rainforest. Changes in precipitation in the data used in the present analysis reveals a general decrease across the basin.

In terms of the effect from an AMOC collapse alone, Ciemer et al. (2021[265]) find significant decreases in rainfall. These decreases are not countered by changes in climate. However, without dynamic vegetation used in the model, local hydrological effects cannot be ruled out. Climate analogues that consider both temperature and precipitation find the future climatology of the Amazon region to match current savannah or grasslands type regions in Africa. This suggests loss of the rainforest. A conversion of 40% of the Amazon rainforest to savannah would result in a loss of approximately 90 gigatonnes (Gt) of CO_2 stored in the vegetation. Conversely, full conversion could lead to losses up to 255 Gt CO_2 (Steffen et al., 2018[224]).

Boreal forests

Similar to the Amazon rainforest, boreal forests are a key component in regulating Earth's climate by sequestering carbon. Boreal forest dieback will cause the transition to steppe grasslands, which store less carbon than boreal forests (Koven, 2013[266]). Consequently, dieback of the boreal forests could release over 100 Gt CO_2 to the atmosphere (Steffen et al., 2018[224]) and therefore amplify global warming further.

This analysis finds that an AMOC collapse alone would likely cause dieback to the boreal forests in northern Europe and Asia. On the other hand, an enhanced boreal forest in North America (about one-third of current global boreal forests) will increase carbon storage (Steffen et al., 2018[224]). However, there is no dynamic vegetation in the model. Using net primary productivity as an indicator instead makes it difficult to determine the overall impact to boreal forests under an AMOC-collapse scenario.

Monsoon systems

The Indian summer monsoon, which occurs from May to September, is instrumental to the Indian economy and agriculture (Bhat, 2006[267]). The monsoon has been identified as a potential future tipping element due to climate change (Lenton et al., 2008[4]). Using a simple box model for the Indian monsoon Zickfeld et al. (2005[268]) suggests that an increase to the planetary albedo, such as sulphur emissions and/or land-use changes, could disrupt the monsoon. There have been indications in the second half of the 20th century that the monsoon may be in decline with decreased summer rainfall. This has led to more frequent droughts (Ramanathan et al., 2005[269]) and reduced rice harvests (Auffhammer, Ramanathan and Vincent, 2006[270]). One major drought in 2002 (Bhat, 2006[267]), is estimated to have cost the Indian government USD 340 million in drought relief programmes. It has also caused an increased number of suicides among farmers (Liepert and Giannini, 2015[271]). Weakening of the Indian summer monsoon following a collapse of the AMOC would most likely have detrimental impacts on Indian farmers' rice harvests.

This analysis finds that, under global warming projections, West Africa will experience the largest decreases in rainfall on the planet. A collapse of the AMOC will exacerbate this effect, disrupting the African monsoon and leading to further reduction in precipitation. This, in turn, will potentially lead to widespread drought over much of the region. The lack of adaptive capacity to climate change across the region will compound the problem. As an area with high rates of poverty, individuals do not have the means to prepare for or adapt to ongoing climate change. Meanwhile, governance fails to act to mitigate the negative impacts of climate change.

Further socio-economic effects

In addition to the socio-economic impacts explored above, other knock-on effects will result from an AMOC collapse:

- A decrease in ocean NPP for the AMOC-collapse scenario seems related to a reduction in north-eastward nutrient transport through the Faroe-Shetland region associated with a retarded North Atlantic Current.
- SLR will occur at rates up to 20-25 mm/yr (Levermann et al., 2005[272]).
- Additional SLR will occur around European and North American coasts of up to 50 cm (Vellinga and Wood, 2007[273]; Levermann et al., 2009[256]).

- European land protection and population relocation would require an additional EUR 1.4 billion per year, based on calculations from Vousdoukas et al. (2020[274]).
- Energy demand and consumption will change due to changing temperature patterns. In a scenario that combines global warming and an AMOC collapse, some parts of Europe may remain warmer than pre-industrial conditions. However, the cooling effect of AMOC in winters would win out over global warming, cooling some regions to below pre-industrial temperatures.

The potential tipping point explored here is just one of the many parts of the Earth system that could produce this effect. Recent research shows the AMOC is at its weakest in a century. However, according to the latest IPCC AR6, there is medium confidence that the projected decline in the AMOC will not involve an abrupt collapse before 2100 (IPCC, 2021[14]). Still, this timeline cannot be ruled out.

A slowing down of the AMOC is already detected and likely to continue. The results presented here are specific to the model and scenario chosen; a more comprehensive assessment would require an ensemble of models. Despite these limitations, results agree with previous research. They show the potential for far-reaching impacts of crossing the tipping threshold of one of the planet's most important systems.

Climate change is reshaping the global socio-economic structure, and will continue to do so. This is likely to impact on progress towards the Sustainable Development Goals, disrupt global trade and amplify social conflict, inequalities and human security. Rapid and deep reductions in GHG emissions are needed to prevent crossing critical thresholds of the climate system.

An international effort for measuring and monitoring key tipping elements, such as the AMOC, is key. This will provide countries with time to develop strategies (including through adaptation and preventive measures) to deal with the consequences of these abrupt changes of climate systems.

References

Acemoglu, D. et al. (2012), “The network origins of aggregate fluctuations”, *Econometrica*, Vol. 80/5, pp. 1977-2016, http://dx.doi.org/10.3982/ecta9623. [71]

Aerts, J. et al. (2014), “Evaluating Flood Resilience Strategies for Coastal Megacities”, *Science*, Vol. 344/6183, pp. 473-475, http://dx.doi.org/10.1126/science.1248222. [98]

Allan, R. and B. Soden (2008), “Atmospheric Warming and the Amplification of Precipitation Extremes”, *Science*, Vol. 321/5895, pp. 1481-1484, http://dx.doi.org/10.1126/science.1160787. [156]

Allen, M. (2003), “Liability for climate change”, *Nature*, Vol. 421/6926, pp. 891-892, http://dx.doi.org/10.1038/421891a. [216]

Allen, M. and W. Ingram (2002), “Constraints on future changes in climate and the hydrologic cycle”, *Nature*, Vol. 419/6903, pp. 224-232, http://dx.doi.org/10.1038/nature01092. [155]

Andrijevic, M. et al. (2019), “Governance in socioeconomic pathways and its role for future adaptive capacity”, *Nature Sustainability*, Vol. 3/1, pp. 35-41, http://dx.doi.org/10.1038/s41893-019-0405-0. [214]

Angélil, O. et al. (2017), “On the nonlinearity of spatial scales in extreme weather attribution statements”, *Climate Dynamics*, Vol. 50/7-8, pp. 2739-2752, http://dx.doi.org/10.1007/s00382-017-3768-9. [192]

Angélil, O. et al. (2014), “Attribution of extreme weather to anthropogenic greenhouse gas emissions: Sensitivity to spatial and temporal scales”, *Geophysical Research Letters*, Vol. 41/6, pp. 2150-2155, http://dx.doi.org/10.1002/2014gl059234. [179]

Anthoff, D., F. Estrada and R. Tol (2016), “Shutting down the thermohaline circulation”, *American Economic Review*, Vol. 106/5, pp. 602-606, http://dx.doi.org/10.1257/aer.p20161102. [262]

Appendini, C. et al. (2017), “On the role of climate change on wind waves generated by tropical cyclones in the Gulf of Mexico”, *Coastal Engineering Journal*, Vol. 59/2, pp. 1740001-1-1740001-32, http://dx.doi.org/10.1142/s0578563417400010. [54]

Athanasiou, P. et al. (2019), “Global distribution of nearshore slopes with implications for coastal retreat”, *Earth System Science Data*, Vol. 11/4, pp. 1515-1529, http://dx.doi.org/10.5194/essd-11-1515-2019. [58]

Auffhammer, M., V. Ramanathan and J. Vincent (2006), “Integrated model shows that atmospheric brown clouds and greenhouse gases have reduced rice harvests in India”, *Proceedings of the National Academy of Sciences*, Vol. 103/52, pp. 19668-19672, http://dx.doi.org/10.1073/pnas.0609584104. [270]

Bamber, J. et al. (2019), “Ice sheet contributions to future sea-level rise from structured expert judgment”, *Proceedings of the National Academy of Sciences*, Vol. 116/23, pp. 11195-11200, http://dx.doi.org/10.1073/pnas.1817205116. [43]

Bamber, J. et al. (2018), “Land ice freshwater budget of the Arctic and North Atlantic Oceans: 1. Data, methods, and results”, *Journal of Geophysical Research: Oceans*, Vol. 123/3, pp. 1827-1837, http://dx.doi.org/10.1002/2017jc013605. [241]

Barker, S. and G. Knorr (2016), "A paleo-perspective on the AMOC as a tipping element", *Past Global Change Magazine*, Vol. 24/1, pp. 14-15, http://dx.doi.org/10.22498/pages.24.1.14. [235]

Barrett, S. and A. Dannenberg (2014), "On the sensitivity of collective action to uncertainty about climate tipping points", *Nature Climate Change*, Vol. 4, pp. 36-39. [223]

Barros, V. et al. (eds.) (2014), *Climate Change 2014: Impacts, Adaptation, and Vulnerability. Part B: Regional Aspects. Contribution of Working Group II to the Fifth Assessment Report of the Intergovernmental Panel on Climate Change*, Cambridge University Press, Cambridge, United Kingdom and New York, NY, USA, pp. 688. [88]

Barthel, F. and E. Neumayer (2012), "A trend analysis of normalized insured damage from natural disasters", *Climatic Change*, Vol. 113/2, pp. 215-237, http://dx.doi.org/10.1007/s10584-011-0331-2. [123]

Bellprat, O. and F. Doblas-Reyes (2016), "Attribution of extreme weather and climate events overestimated by unreliable climate simulations", *Geophysical Research Letters*, Vol. 43/5, pp. 2158-2164, http://dx.doi.org/10.1002/2015gl067189. [132]

Bhat, G. (2006), "The Indian drought of 2002 – a sub-seasonal phenomenon?", *Quarterly Journal of the Royal Meteorological Society*, Vol. 132/621, pp. 2583-2602, http://dx.doi.org/10.1256/qj.05.13. [267]

Bisaro, A. et al. (2019), "Leveraging public adaptation finance through urban land reclamation: Cases from Germany, the Netherlands and the Maldives", *Climatic Change*, Vol. 160/4, pp. 671-689, http://dx.doi.org/10.1007/s10584-019-02507-5. [92]

Boers, N. (2021), "Observation-based early-warning signals for a collapse of the Atlantic Meridional Overturning Circulation", *Nature Climate Change*, Vol. 11/8, pp. 680-688, http://dx.doi.org/10.1038/s41558-021-01097-4. [244]

Buizert, C. and A. Schmittner (2015), "Southern Ocean control of glacial AMOC stability and Dansgaard-Oeschger interstadial duration", *Paleoceanography*, Vol. 30/12, pp. 1595-1612, http://dx.doi.org/10.1002/2015pa002795. [236]

Burke, M., S. Hsiang and E. Miguel (2015), "Global non-linear effect of temperature on economic production", *Nature*, Vol. 527/7577, pp. 235-239, http://dx.doi.org/10.1038/nature15725. [258]

Byrne, M. and P. O'Gorman (2018), "Trends in continental temperature and humidity directly linked to ocean warming", *Proceedings of the National Academy of Sciences*, Vol. 115/19, pp. 4863-4868, http://dx.doi.org/10.1073/pnas.1722312115. [149]

Byrne, M. and P. O'Gorman (2013), "Link between land-ocean warming contrast and surface relative humidities in simulations with coupled climate models", *Geophysical Research Letters*, Vol. 40/19, pp. 5223-5227, http://dx.doi.org/10.1002/grl.50971. [148]

Caesar, L. et al. (2021), "Current Atlantic Meridional Overturning Circulation weakest in last millennium", *Nature Geoscience*, Vol. 14/3, pp. 118-120, http://dx.doi.org/10.1038/s41561-021-00699-z. [240]

Caesar, L. et al. (2018), "Observed fingerprint of a weakening Atlantic Ocean overturning circulation", *Nature*, Vol. 556/7700, pp. 191-196, http://dx.doi.org/10.1038/s41586-018-0006-5. [239]

Cai, Y., T. Lenton and T. Lontzek (2016), "Risk of multiple interacting tipping points should encourage rapid CO2 emission reduction", *Nature Climate Change*, Vol. 6/5, pp. 520-525, http://dx.doi.org/10.1038/nclimate2964. [68]

Caloiero, T. (2014), "Analysis of rainfall trend in New Zealand", *Environmental Earth Sciences*, Vol. 73/10, pp. 6297-6310, http://dx.doi.org/10.1007/s12665-014-3852-y. [182]

Carleton, T. and S. Hsiang (2016), "Social and economic impacts of climate", *Science*, Vol. 353/6304, pp. aad9837-aad9837, http://dx.doi.org/10.1126/science.aad9837. [252]

Cattiaux, J. and A. Ribes (2018), "Defining Single Extreme Weather Events in a Climate Perspective", *Bulletin of the American Meteorological Society*, Vol. 99/8, pp. 1557-1568, http://dx.doi.org/10.1175/bams-d-17-0281.1. [180]

CBD (1992), *The Convention of Biological Diversity*, (1760 U.N.T.S. 69). [37]

CDP (2020), "2019-2020 Australian Bushfires", 9 September, Center for Disaster Philanthropy, Washington, DC, https://disasterphilanthropy.org/disaster/2019-australian-wildfires/ (accessed on 21 September 2021). [19]

Center for International Earth Science Information Network - CIESIN (2005), *Gridded Population of the World, Version 3 (GPWv3): Population Count Grid, Future Estimates.Palisades,NY:NASA Socioeconomic Data and Applications Center (SEDAC).*, Columbia University, United Nations Food and Agriculture Programme - FAO, and Centro Internacional de Agricultura Tropical - CIAT, https://doi.org/10.7927/H42B8VZZ (accessed on 8 October 2021). [200]

Challinor, A. et al. (2018), "Transmission of climate risks across sectors and borders", *Philosophical Transactions of the Royal Society A: Mathematical, Physical and Engineering Sciences*, Vol. 376/2121, p. 20170301, http://dx.doi.org/10.1098/rsta.2017.0301. [73]

Charlier, R., M. Chaineux and S. Morcos (2005), "Panorama of the history of coastal protection", *Journal of Coastal Research*, Vol. 211, pp. 79-111, http://dx.doi.org/10.2112/03561.1. [96]

Chatterton, J. et al. (2016), *The Costs and Impacts of the Winter 2013 to 2014 Floods*, Environment Agency, Bristol, United Kingdom, https://assets.publishing.service.gov.uk/media/603549118fa8f5480a5386be/The_costs_and_impacts_of_the_winter_2013_to_2014_floods_-_report.pdf. [208]

Cheng, W. et al. (2018), "Can the salt-advection feedback be detected in internal variability of the Atlantic Meridional Overturning Circulation?", *Journal of Climate*, Vol. 31/16, pp. 6649-6667, http://dx.doi.org/10.1175/jcli-d-17-0825.1. [233]

Ciavarella, A. et al. (2021), "Prolonged Siberian heat of 2020 almost impossible without human influence", *Climatic Change*, Vol. 166/1-2, http://dx.doi.org/10.1007/s10584-021-03052-w. [283]

Ciemer, C. et al. (2021), "Impact of an AMOC weakening on the stability of the southern Amazon rainforest", *The European Physical Journal Special Topics*, http://dx.doi.org/10.1140/epjs/s11734-021-00186-x. [265]

Clarke, B., F. E. L. Otto and R. Jones (2021), "Inventories of extreme weather events and impacts: Implications for loss and damage from and adaptation to climate extremes", *Climate Risk Management*, Vol. 32, p. 100285, http://dx.doi.org/10.1016/j.crm.2021.100285. [139]

Cowan, T. et al. (2014), "More frequent, longer, and hotter heat waves for Australia in the twenty-first century", *Journal of Climate*, Vol. 27/15, pp. 5851-5871, http://dx.doi.org/10.1175/jcli-d-14-00092.1. [189]

Cox, P. et al. (2004), "Amazonian forest dieback under climate-carbon cycle projections for the 21st century", *Theoretical and Applied Climatology*, Vol. 78/1-3, http://dx.doi.org/10.1007/s00704-004-0049-4. [255]

CR2 (2015), *Report to the Nation. The 2010-2015 mega-drought: A lesson for the future.*, Center for Climate and Resilience Research ,, https://www.cr2.cl/megasequia/#1513260570409-9738626d-983a. [173]

Di Liberto, T. (2021), "Astounding heat obliterates all-time records across the Pacific Northwest and Western Canada in June 2021", 30 June, Climate.gov, https://www.climate.gov/news-features/event-tracker/astounding-heat-obliterates-all-time-records-across-pacific-northwest (accessed on 10 Sep 2021). [27]

Diffenbaugh, N., D. Swain and D. Touma (2015), "Anthropogenic warming has increased drought risk in California", *Proceedings of the National Academy of Sciences*, Vol. 112/13, pp. 3931-3936, http://dx.doi.org/10.1073/pnas.1422385112. [172]

Douville, H. et al. (2021), "Water cycle changes", in Masson-Delmotte, V. et al. (eds.), *Climate Change 2021: The Physical Science Basis. Contribution of Working Group I to 45 the Sixth Assessment Report of the Intergovernmental Panel on Climate Change*, Cambridge University Press, Cambridge, United Kingdom. [245]

Drijfhout, S. (2015), "Competition between global warming and an abrupt collapse of the AMOC in Earth's energy imbalance", *Scientific Reports*, Vol. 5/1, http://dx.doi.org/10.1038/srep14877. [65]

Drijfhout, S. et al. (2015), "Catalogue of abrupt shifts in Intergovernmental Panel on Climate Change climate models", *Proceedings of the National Academy of Sciences*, Vol. 112/43, pp. E5777-E5786, http://dx.doi.org/10.1073/pnas.1511451112. [225]

Dunn, F. et al. (2019), "Projections of declining fluvial sediment delivery to major deltas worldwide in response to climate change and anthropogenic stress", *Environmental Research Letters*, Vol. 14/8, p. 084034, http://dx.doi.org/10.1088/1748-9326/ab304e. [118]

Duvat, V. (2018), "A global assessment of atoll island planform changes over the past decades", *Wiley Interdisciplinary Reviews: Climate Change*, Vol. 10/1, p. e557, http://dx.doi.org/10.1002/wcc.557. [104]

Edmonds, C. and I. Noy (2018), "The economics of disaster risks and impacts in the Pacific", *Disaster Prevention and Management: An International Journal*, Vol. 27/5, pp. 478-494, http://dx.doi.org/10.1108/dpm-02-2018-0057. [91]

Einhorn, C. (2021), "Like in 'postapocalyptic movies': Heat wave killed marine wildlife en masse", 9 July, The New York Times, https://www.nytimes.com/2021/07/09/climate/marine-heat-wave.html. [31]

Falkland, T. and I. White (2020), "Freshwater availability under climate change", in *Springer Climate, Climate Change and Impacts in the Pacific*, Springer International Publishing, Cham, http://dx.doi.org/10.1007/978-3-030-32878-8_11. [119]

FAOSTAT (2021), "Food Balance Sheets", https://www.fao.org/faostat/en/#data/FBS (accessed on 13 October 2021). [253]

Ferrario, F. et al. (2014), "The effectiveness of coral reefs for coastal hazard risk reduction and adaptation", *Nature Communications*, Vol. 5/1, http://dx.doi.org/10.1038/ncomms4794. [109]

Fischer, E. and R. Knutti (2015), "Anthropogenic contribution to global occurrence of heavy-precipitation and high-temperature extremes", *Nature Climate Change*, Vol. 5/6, pp. 560-564, http://dx.doi.org/10.1038/nclimate2617. [142]

Fowler, H. et al. (2021), "Anthropogenic intensification of short-duration rainfall extremes", *Nature Reviews Earth & Environment*, Vol. 2/2, pp. 107-122, http://dx.doi.org/10.1038/s43017-020-00128-6. [162]

Fox-Kemper, B. et al. (2021), "Ocean, cryosphere and sea level change", in *Climate Change 2021: The Physical Science Basis. Contribution of Working Group I to the Sixth Assessment Report of the Intergovernmental Panel on Climate Change*, Cambridge University Press, Cambridge, United Kingdom. [40]

Frame, D. et al. (2017), "Population-based emergence of unfamiliar climates", *Nature Climate Change*, Vol. 7/6, pp. 407-411, http://dx.doi.org/10.1038/nclimate3297. [194]

Frame, D. et al. (2020), "Climate change attribution and the economic costs of extreme weather events: A study on damages from extreme rainfall and drought", *Climatic Change*, Vol. 162/2, pp. 781-797, http://dx.doi.org/10.1007/s10584-020-02729-y. [138]

Freychet, N. et al. (2019), "The Local Aerosol Emission Effect on Surface Shortwave Radiation and Temperatures", *Journal of Advances in Modeling Earth Systems*, Vol. 11/3, pp. 806-817, http://dx.doi.org/10.1029/2018ms001530. [166]

Frölicher, T., E. Fischer and N. Gruber (2018), "Marine heatwaves under global warming", *Nature*, Vol. 560/7718, pp. 360-364, http://dx.doi.org/10.1038/s41586-018-0383-9. [144]

Frost, R. (2021), "Turkey, Greece and Italy: Which countries are being affected by wildfires and why?", 13 August, euronews.travel, https://www.euronews.com/travel/2021/08/12/european-heatwave-which-countries-face-the-biggest-risk-from-wildfires. [20]

Frost, R. (2021), "Wildfire near French resort of Saint-Tropez kills two people", 12 August, euronews.travel, https://www.euronews.com/travel/2021/08/12/european-heatwave-which-countries-face-the-biggest-risk-from-wildfires. [22]

Gadgil, S. and S. Gadgil (2006), "The Indian monsoon, GDP and agriculture", *Economic and Political Weekly*, Vol. 41/47, pp. 4887-4895, http://www.jstor.org/stable/4418949. [250]

Gingerich, S., C. Voss and A. Johnson (2017), "Seawater-flooding events and impact on freshwater lenses of low-lying islands: Controlling factors, basic management and mitigation", *Journal of Hydrology*, Vol. 551, pp. 676-688, http://dx.doi.org/10.1016/j.jhydrol.2017.03.001. [120]

Gladwell, M. (2000), *The Tipping Point: How Little Things Can Make a Big Difference*, Little Brown, Boston. [59]

Gomes Da Costa, H. et al. (2020), "European wildfire danger and vulnerability under a changing climate: Towards integrating risk dimensions", No. EUR 30116 EN, Publications Office of the European Union, Luxembourg, http://dx.doi.org/doi:10.2760/46951. [17]

González, M. et al. (2020), *Incendios forestales en Chile: causas, impactos y resiliencia*, Centro de Ciencia del Clima y la Resiliencia (CR)2, Universidad de Chile,Universidad de Concepción y Universidad Austral de Chile. [18]

Guha-Sapir, D., D. Hargitt and P. Hoyois (2004), *Thirty Years of Natural Disasters 1974-2003: The Numbers*, Centre for Research on the Epidemiology of Disasters, Brussels. [174]

Guillod, B. et al. (2017), "A large set of potential past, present and future hydro-meteorological time series for the UK", Hydrology and Earth Systems Sciences, http://dx.doi.org/10.5194/hess-2017-246. [183]

Hallegatte, S. et al. (2013), "Future flood losses in major coastal cities", *Nature Climate Change*, Vol. 3/9, pp. 802-806, http://dx.doi.org/10.1038/nclimate1979. [99]

Harrington, L. et al. (2016), "Poorest countries experience earlier anthropogenic emergence of daily temperature extremes", *Environmental Research Letters*, Vol. 11/5, p. 055007, http://dx.doi.org/10.1088/1748-9326/11/5/055007. [198]

Harrington, L. et al. (2018), "How uneven are changes to impact-relevant climate hazards in a 1.5 °C world and beyond?", *Geophysical Research Letters*, Vol. 45/13, pp. 6672-6680, http://dx.doi.org/10.1029/2018gl078888. [187]

Harrington, L. and F. Otto (2020), "Reconciling theory with the reality of African heatwaves", *Nature Climate Change*, Vol. 10/9, pp. 796-798, http://dx.doi.org/10.1038/s41558-020-0851-8. [221]

Hawkins, E. et al. (2020), "Observed emergence of the climate change signal: From the familiar to the unknown", *Geophysical Research Letters*, Vol. 47/6, http://dx.doi.org/10.1029/2019gl086259. [195]

Hawkins, E. et al. (2011), "Bistability of the Atlantic overturning circulation in a global climate model and links to ocean freshwater transport", *Geophysical Research Letters*, Vol. 38/10, http://dx.doi.org/10.1029/2011gl047208. [231]

Hawkins, E. and R. Sutton (2012), "Time of emergence of climate signals", *Geophysical Research Letters*, Vol. 39/1, http://dx.doi.org/10.1029/2011gl050087. [193]

Hegdahl, T. et al. (2020), "An Event-Based Approach to Explore Selected Present and Future Atmospheric River–Induced Floods in Western Norway", *Journal of Hydrometeorology*, Vol. 21/9, pp. 2003-2021, http://dx.doi.org/10.1175/jhm-d-19-0071.1. [137]

Hewitt, H. et al. (2011), "Design and implementation of the infrastructure of HadGEM3: the next-generation Met Office climate modelling system", *Geoscientific Model Development*, Vol. 4/2, pp. 223-253, http://dx.doi.org/10.5194/gmd-4-223-2011. [276]

Hildén, M. et al. (2020), "Cascading climate impacts: A new factor in European policy-making", *Policy Brief*, CASCADES, https://www.sei.org/wp-content/uploads/2020/03/cascades-policy-brief-1-1.pdf. [74]

Hinkel, J. et al. (2018), "The ability of societies to adapt to twenty-first-century sea-level rise", *Nature Climate Change*, Vol. 8/7, pp. 570-578, http://dx.doi.org/10.1038/s41558-018-0176-z. [100]

Hinkel, J. et al. (2019), "Meeting user needs for sea level rise information: A decision analysis perspective", *Earth's Future*, Vol. 7/3, pp. 320-337, http://dx.doi.org/10.1029/2018ef001071. [44]

Hinkel, J. et al. (2014), “Coastal flood damage and adaptation costs under 21st century sea-level rise”, *Proceedings of the National Academy of Sciences*, Vol. 111/9, pp. 3292-3297, http://dx.doi.org/10.1073/pnas.1222469111. [95]

Hirabayashi, Y. et al. (2013), *Global flood risk under climate change*, Nature Publishing Group, https://www.nature.com/articles/nclimate1911. [33]

Hodges, K., A. Cobb and P. Vidale (2017), “How well are tropical cyclones represented in reanalysis datasets?”, *Journal of Climate*, Vol. 30/14, pp. 5243-5264, http://dx.doi.org/10.1175/jcli-d-16-0557.1. [55]

Hodnebrog, Ø. et al. (2019), “Intensification of summer precipitation with shorter time-scales in Europe”, *Environmental Research Letters*, Vol. 14/12, p. 124050, http://dx.doi.org/10.1088/1748-9326/ab549c. [164]

Holdaway, A., M. Ford and S. Owen (2021), “Global-scale changes in the area of atoll islands during the 21st century”, *Anthropocene*, Vol. 33, p. 100282, http://dx.doi.org/10.1016/j.ancene.2021.100282. [105]

Holding, S. and D. Allen (2015), “From days to decades: Numerical modelling of freshwater lens response to climate change stressors on small low-lying islands”, *Hydrology and Earth System Sciences*, Vol. 19/2, pp. 933-949, http://dx.doi.org/10.5194/hess-19-933-2015. [121]

Holliday, N. et al. (2020), “Ocean circulation causes the largest freshening event for 120 years in eastern subpolar North Atlantic”, *Nature Communications*, Vol. 11/1, http://dx.doi.org/10.1038/s41467-020-14474-y. [237]

Hughes, T. et al. (2018), “Spatial and temporal patterns of mass bleaching of corals in the Anthropocene”, *Science*, Vol. 359/6371, pp. 80-83, http://dx.doi.org/10.1126/science.aan8048. [112]

Hughes, T. et al. (2017), “Global warming and recurrent mass bleaching of corals”, *Nature*, Vol. 543/7645, pp. 373-377, http://dx.doi.org/10.1038/nature21707. [111]

IPCC (2021), *Climate Change 2021: The Physical Science Basis. Contribution of Working Group I to the Sixth Assessment Report of the Intergovernmental Panel on Climate Change*, Masson-Delmotte, V. et al. (eds), Cambridge University Press, United Kingdom, In press. [14]

IPCC (2019), *IPCC Special Report on Climate Change and Land*, Intergovernmental Panel on Climate Change, Geneva. [34]

IPCC (2019), *IPCC Special Report on the Ocean and Cryosphere in a Changing Climate*, Intergovernmental Panel on Climate Change, Geneva. [35]

IPCC (2019), “Summary for Policymakers”, in H.-O. Pörtner et al. (eds.), *IPCC Special Report on the Ocean and Cryosphere in a Changing Climate*, Intergovernmental Panel on Climate Change, Geneva. [11]

IPCC (2018), “Annex I: Glossary [Matthews, J.B.R. (ed.)]”, in Masson-Delmotte, V. et al. (eds.), *Global Warming of 1.5°C. An IPCC Special Report on the impacts of global warming of 1.5°C above pre-industrial levels and related global greenhouse gas emission pathways, in the context of strengthening the global response to the threat of climate change…*, Intergovernmental Panel on Climate Change, Geneva. [5]

IPCC (2018), "Summary for Policymakers", in Masson-Delmotte, V. et al. (eds.), *Global Warming of 1.5°C. An IPCC Special Report on the impacts of global warming of 1.5°C above pre-industrial levels and related global greenhouse gas emission pathways, in the context of strengthening the global response to the threat of climate....*, Intergovernmental Panel on Climate Change, Geneva. [10]

IPCC (2014), *Climate Change 2014: Synthesis Report. Contribution of Working Groups I, II and III to the Fifth Assessment Report of the Intergovernmental Panel on Climate Change*, R.K. Pachauri; L.A. Meyer (eds.), Intergovernmental Panel on Climate Change, Geneva. [2]

IPCC (2014), "Summary for policymakers", in Field, C. et al. (eds.), *Climate Change 2014: Impacts,Adaptation, and Vulnerability. Part A: Global and Sectoral Aspects. Contribution of Working Group II to the Fifth Assessment Report of the Intergovernmental Panel on Climate Change*, Cambridge, United Kingdom, and New York. [1]

IPCC (2001), *Climate Change 2001: Synthesis Report. A Contribution of Working Groups I, II, and III to the Third Assessment Report of the Integovernmental Panel on Climate Change*, Watson, R.T. et al. (eds.), Cambridge University Press, Cambridge, United Kingdom, and New York. [9]

Jackson, L. et al. (2015), "Global and European climate impacts of a slowdown of the AMOC in a high resolution GCM", *Climate Dynamics*, Vol. 45/11-12, pp. 3299-3316, http://dx.doi.org/10.1007/s00382-015-2540-2. [248]

Jacob, D. et al. (2005), "Slowdown of the thermohaline circulation causes enhanced maritime climate influence and snow cover over Europe", *Geophysical Research Letters*, Vol. 32/21, http://dx.doi.org/10.1029/2005gl023286. [279]

Jolly, W. et al. (2015), "Climate-induced variations in global wildfire danger from 1979 to 2013", *Nature Communications*, Vol. 6/1, pp. 1-11, http://dx.doi.org/10.1038/ncomms8537. [15]

Jongman, B. et al. (2015), "Declining vulnerability to river floods and the global benefits of adaptation", *Proceedings of the National Academy of Sciences*, Vol. 112/18, pp. E2271-E2280, https://www.pnas.org/content/112/18/E2271.short. [210]

Joshi, M. et al. (2007), "Mechanisms for the land/sea warming contrast exhibited by simulations of climate change", *Climate Dynamics*, Vol. 30/5, pp. 455-465, http://dx.doi.org/10.1007/s00382-007-0306-1. [147]

Keeley, J. and A. Syphard (2021), "Large California wildfires: 2020 fires in historical context", *Fire Ecology*, Vol. 17/1, http://dx.doi.org/10.1186/s42408-021-00110-7. [24]

Keen, S. et al. (2021), "Economists' erroneous estimates of damages from climate change", *arXiv*, Vol. 2108.07847v1, https://arxiv.org/abs/2108.07847v1. [259]

Kench, P. (2012), "Compromising reef island shoreline dynamics: Legacies of the engineering paradigm in the Maldives", in *Pitfalls of Shoreline Stabilization, Coastal Research Library*, Springer Netherlands, Dordrecht, http://dx.doi.org/10.1007/978-94-007-4123-2_11. [106]

Kew, S. et al. (2021), "Impact of precipitation and increasing temperatures on drought trends in eastern Africa", *Earth System Dynamics*, Vol. 12/1, pp. 17-35, http://dx.doi.org/10.5194/esd-12-17-2021. [169]

Kharin, V. et al. (2018), "Risks from Climate Extremes Change Differently from 1.5°C to 2.0°C Depending on Rarity", *Earth's Future*, Vol. 6/5, pp. 704-715, http://dx.doi.org/10.1002/2018ef000813. [165]

King, A. et al. (2016), "Emergence of heat extremes attributable to anthropogenic influences", *Geophysical Research Letters*, Vol. 43/7, pp. 3438-3443, http://dx.doi.org/10.1002/2015gl067448. [186]

King, A. et al. (2015), "The timing of anthropogenic emergence in simulated climate extremes", *Environmental Research Letters*, Vol. 10/9, p. 094015, http://dx.doi.org/10.1088/1748-9326/10/9/094015. [185]

King, A. and L. Harrington (2018), "The inequality of climate change from 1.5 to 2°C of global warming", *Geophysical Research Letters*, Vol. 45/10, pp. 5030-5033, http://dx.doi.org/10.1029/2018gl078430. [199]

Kinzig, A. et al. (2006), "Resilience and regime shifts: Assessing cascading effects", *Ecology and Society*, Vol. 11/1. [75]

Klöck, C. and P. Nunn (2019), "Adaptation to climate change in Small Island Developing States: A systematic literature review of academic research", *The Journal of Environment & Development*, Vol. 28/2, pp. 196-218, http://dx.doi.org/10.1177/1070496519835895. [97]

Koks, E. (2018), "Moving flood risk modelling forwards", *Nature Climate Change*, Vol. 8/7, pp. 561-562, http://dx.doi.org/10.1038/s41558-018-0185-y. [72]

Koven, C. (2013), "Boreal carbon loss due to poleward shift in low-carbon ecosystems", *Nature Geoscience*, Vol. 6/6, pp. 452-456, http://dx.doi.org/10.1038/ngeo1801. [266]

Kreibich, H. et al. (2017), "Adaptation to flood risk: Results of international paired flood event studies", *Earth's Future*, Vol. 5/10, pp. 953-965, http://dx.doi.org/10.1002/2017ef000606. [211]

Kriegler, E. et al. (2009), "Imprecise probability assessment of tipping points in the climate system", *Proceedings of the National Academy of Sciences*, Vol. 106/13, pp. 5041-5046, http://dx.doi.org/10.1073/pnas.0809117106. [66]

Kroeker, K. et al. (2013), "Impacts of ocean acidification on marine organisms: Quantifying sensitivities and interaction with warming", *Global Change Biology*, Vol. 19/6, pp. 1884-1896, http://dx.doi.org/10.1111/gcb.12179. [114]

Kron, W. (2012), "Coasts: The high-risk areas of the world", *Natural Hazards*, Vol. 66/3, pp. 1363-1382, http://dx.doi.org/10.1007/s11069-012-0215-4. [89]

Kumar, L. et al. (2018), "An indicative index of physical susceptibility of small islands to coastal erosion induced by climate change: An application to the Pacific islands", *Geomatics, Natural Hazards and Risk*, Vol. 9/1, pp. 691-702, http://dx.doi.org/10.1080/19475705.2018.1455749. [107]

Lawrence, J., P. Blackett and N. Cradock-Henry (2020), "Cascading climate change impacts and implications", *Climate Risk Management*, Vol. 29, p. 100234, http://dx.doi.org/10.1016/j.crm.2020.100234. [78]

Leach, N. et al. (2020), "Anthropogenic Influence on the 2018 Summer Warm Spell in Europe: The Impact of Different Spatio-Temporal Scales", *Bulletin of the American Meteorological Society*, Vol. 101/1, pp. S41-S46, http://dx.doi.org/10.1175/bams-d-19-0201.1. [181]

Leatherman, S. and N. Beller-Simms (1997), "Sea-level rise and Small Island States: An overview", *Journal of Coastal Research*, http://www.jstor.org/stable/25736084 (accessed on 8 July 2021). [86]

Lenton, T. (2011), "Early warning of climate tipping points", *Nature Climate Change*, Vol. 1/4, pp. 201-209, http://dx.doi.org/10.1038/nclimate1143. [63]

Lenton, T. and J. Ciscar (2012), "Integrating tipping points into climate impact assessments", *Climatic Change*, Vol. 117/3, pp. 585-597, http://dx.doi.org/10.1007/s10584-012-0572-8. [70]

Lenton, T. et al. (2008), "Tipping elements in the Earth's climate system", *Proceedings of the National Academy of Sciences*, Vol. 105/6, pp. 1786-1793, http://dx.doi.org/10.1073/pnas.0705414105. [4]

Lenton, T. et al. (2019), "Climate tipping points — too risky to bet against", *Nature*, Vol. 575/7784, pp. 592-595, http://dx.doi.org/10.1038/d41586-019-03595-0. [64]

Lenton, T. and H. Williams (2013), "On the origin of planetary-scale tipping points", *Trends in Ecology & Evolution*, Vol. 28/7, pp. 380-382, http://dx.doi.org/10.1016/j.tree.2013.06.001. [62]

Levermann, A. et al. (2011), "Potential climatic transitions with profound impact on Europe", *Climatic Change*, Vol. 110/3-4, pp. 845-878, http://dx.doi.org/10.1007/s10584-011-0126-5. [60]

Levermann, A. et al. (2005), "Dynamic sea level changes following changes in the thermohaline circulation", *Climate Dynamics*, Vol. 24/4, pp. 347-354, http://dx.doi.org/10.1007/s00382-004-0505-y. [272]

Levermann, A. et al. (2009), "Basic mechanism for abrupt monsoon transitions", *Proceedings of the National Academy of Sciences*, Vol. 106/49, pp. 20572-20577, http://dx.doi.org/10.1073/pnas.0901414106. [256]

Liepert, B. and A. Giannini (2015), "Global warming, the atmospheric brown cloud, and the changing Indian summer monsoon", *Bulletin of the Atomic Scientists*, Vol. 71/4, pp. 23-30, http://dx.doi.org/10.1177/0096340215590802. [271]

Lincke, D. and J. Hinkel (2018), "Economically robust protection against 21st century sea-level rise", *Global Environmental Change*, Vol. 51, pp. 67-73, http://dx.doi.org/10.1016/j.gloenvcha.2018.05.003. [93]

Link, P. and R. Tol (2010), "Estimation of the economic impact of temperature changes induced by a shutdown of the thermohaline circulation: An application of FUND", *Climatic Change*, Vol. 104/2, pp. 287-304, http://dx.doi.org/10.1007/s10584-009-9796-7. [261]

Li, R. et al. (2021), "Anthropogenic Influences on heavy precipitation during the 2019 extremely wet rainy season in Southern China", *Bulletin of the American Meteorological Society*, Vol. 102/1, pp. S103-S109, http://dx.doi.org/10.1175/bams-d-20-0135.1. [206]

Liu, W. et al. (2017), "Overlooked possibility of a collapsed Atlantic Meridional Overturning Circulation in warming climate", *Science Advances*, Vol. 3/1, p. e1601666, http://dx.doi.org/10.1126/sciadv.1601666. [246]

Lloyd, E. and N. Oreskes (2018), "Climate change attribution: When is it appropriate to accept new methods?", *Earth's Future*, Vol. 6/3, pp. 311-325, http://dx.doi.org/10.1002/2017ef000665. [140]

Lloyd, E. et al. (2021), "Climate scientists set the bar of proof too high", *Climatic Change*, Vol. 165/3-4, http://dx.doi.org/10.1007/s10584-021-03061-9. [141]

Lontzek, T. et al. (2015), "Stochastic integrated assessment of climate tipping points indicates the need for strict climate policy", *Nature Climate Change*, Vol. 5/5, pp. 441-444, http://dx.doi.org/10.1038/nclimate2570. [222]

Lovelock, C. et al. (2015), "The vulnerability of Indo-Pacific mangrove forests to sea-level rise", *Nature*, Vol. 526/7574, pp. 559-563, http://dx.doi.org/10.1038/nature15538. [115]

Lowe, J. et al. (2009), "Marine and coastal projections", in *UK Climate Projections Science Report*, Met Office Hadley Centre and Exeter, United Kingdom. [41]

Luijendijk, A. et al. (2018), "The state of the world's beaches", *Scientific Reports*, Vol. 8/1, http://dx.doi.org/10.1038/s41598-018-24630-6. [101]

Mahlstein, I. et al. (2011), "Early onset of significant local warming in low latitude countries", *Environmental Research Letters*, Vol. 6/3, p. 034009, http://dx.doi.org/10.1088/1748-9326/6/3/034009. [197]

Maraun, D. et al. (2017), "Towards process-informed bias correction of climate change simulations", *Nature Climate Change*, Vol. 7/11, pp. 764-773, http://dx.doi.org/10.1038/nclimate3418. [217]

Marotzke, J. et al. (2017), "Climate research must sharpen its view", *Nature Climate Change*, Vol. 7/2, pp. 89-91, http://dx.doi.org/10.1038/nclimate3206. [219]

Matthews, T. (2018), "Humid heat and climate change", *Progress in Physical Geography: Earth and Environment*, Vol. 42/3, pp. 391-405, http://dx.doi.org/10.1177/0309133318776490. [201]

McLean, R. and P. Kench (2015), "Destruction or persistence of coral atoll islands in the face of 20th and 21st century sea-level rise?", *WIREs Climate Change*, Vol. 6/5, pp. 445-463, http://dx.doi.org/10.1002/wcc.350. [108]

Mecking, J. et al. (2016), "Stable AMOC off state in an eddy-permitting coupled climate model", *Climate Dynamics*, Vol. 47/7-8, pp. 2455-2470, http://dx.doi.org/10.1007/s00382-016-2975-0. [249]

Menéndez, M. and P. Woodworth (2010), "Changes in extreme high water levels based on a quasi-global tide-gauge data set", *Journal of Geophysical Research: Oceans*, Vol. 115/C10, http://dx.doi.org/10.1029/2009jc005997. [48]

Mentaschi, L. (2018), *The Effect of Changing Spatial Resolution in Global Dynamic Wave Models*, Wiley, Hoboken, United States, http://dx.doi.org/10.1002/essoar.10500014.1. [57]

Mentaschi, L. et al. (2020), "Assessment of global wave models on regular and unstructured grids using the Unresolved Obstacles Source Term", *Ocean Dynamics*, Vol. 70/11, pp. 1475-1483, http://dx.doi.org/10.1007/s10236-020-01410-3. [56]

Meredith, E. et al. (2015), "Evidence for added value of convection-permitting models for studying changes in extreme precipitation", *Journal of Geophysical Research: Atmospheres*, Vol. 120/24, pp. 12500-12513, http://dx.doi.org/10.1002/2015jd024238. [158]

Meredith, E. et al. (2015), "Crucial role of Black Sea warming in amplifying the 2012 Krymsk precipitation extreme", *Nature Geoscience*, Vol. 8/8, pp. 615-619, http://dx.doi.org/10.1038/ngeo2483. [159]

Mezahi, M. (2021), "Algeria's desperate wildfire fight: Buckets and branches", 22 August, BBC, https://www.bbc.com/news/world-africa-58269789. [21]

Moffa-Sánchez, P. et al. (2014), "Surface changes in the eastern Labrador Sea around the onset of the Little Ice Age", *Paleoceanography*, Vol. 29/3, pp. 160-175, http://dx.doi.org/10.1002/2013pa002523. [230]

Mora, C. et al. (2017), "Global risk of deadly heat", *Nature Climate Change*, Vol. 7/7, pp. 501-506, http://dx.doi.org/10.1038/nclimate3322. [196]

Moreno-Chamarro, E. et al. (2016), "An abrupt weakening of the subpolar gyre as trigger of Little Ice Age-type episodes", *Climate Dynamics*, Vol. 48/3-4, pp. 727-744, http://dx.doi.org/10.1007/s00382-016-3106-7. [228]

Muis, S. et al. (2020), "A high-resolution global dataset of extreme sea levels, tides, and storm surges, including future projections", *Frontiers in Marine Science*, Vol. 7, http://dx.doi.org/10.3389/fmars.2020.00263. [51]

Muis, S. et al. (2016), "A global reanalysis of storm surges and extreme sea levels", *Nature Communications*, Vol. 7/1, http://dx.doi.org/10.1038/ncomms11969. [52]

Nicholls, R. et al. (2013), "Sea-level scenarios for evaluating coastal impacts", *WIREs Climate Change*, Vol. 5/1, pp. 129-150, http://dx.doi.org/10.1002/wcc.253. [42]

NOAA National Centers for Environmental Information (NCEI) (2021), ".S. Billion-Dollar Weather and Climate Disasters". [126]

Noy, I. (2016), "The socio-economics of cyclones", *Nature Climate Change*, Vol. 6/4, pp. 343-345, http://dx.doi.org/10.1038/nclimate2975. [176]

Noy, I. and W. duPont IV (2018), "The long-term consequences of disasters: What do we know, and what we still don't", *International Review of Environmental and Resource Economics*, Vol. 12/4, pp. 325-354, http://dx.doi.org/10.1561/101.00000104. [177]

Nunn, P. et al. (2016), "Classifying Pacific islands", *Geoscience Letters*, Vol. 3/1, http://dx.doi.org/10.1186/s40562-016-0041-8. [82]

Nurse, L. et al. (2014), *Small isla*, Cambridge University Press, Cambridge, United Kingdom, and New York. [50]

OECD (2018), *Making Development Co-operation Work for Small Island Developing States*, OECD Publishing, Paris, https://dx.doi.org/10.1787/9789264287648-en. [83]

Oliver, E. et al. (2017), "The unprecedented 2015/16 Tasman Sea marine heatwave", *Nature Communications*, Vol. 8/1, http://dx.doi.org/10.1038/ncomms16101. [143]

Oppenheimer, M. et al. (2021), "Sea level rise and implications for low-lying islands, coasts and communities", in H.-O. Pörtner et al. (eds.), *IPCC Special Report on the Ocean and Cryosphere in a Changing Climate*, Cambridge University Press, Cambridge, United Kingdom. [49]

Oppenheimer, M. et al. (2019), *Sea Level Rise and Implications for Low Lying Islands, Coasts and Communities*, Oxford University Press. [39]

Otto, F. (2017), "Attribution of weather and climate events", *Annual Review of Environment and Resources*, Vol. 42/1, pp. 627-646, http://dx.doi.org/10.1146/annurev-environ-102016-060847. [128]

Otto, F. et al. (2015), "Attribution of extreme weather events in Africa: A preliminary exploration of the science and policy implications", *Climatic Change*, Vol. 132/4, pp. 531-543, http://dx.doi.org/10.1007/s10584-015-1432-0. [215]

Otto, F. et al. (2020), "Toward an inventory of the impacts of human-induced climate change", *Bulletin of the American Meteorological Society*, Vol. 101/11, pp. E1972-E1979, http://dx.doi.org/10.1175/bams-d-20-0027.1. [133]

Otto, F. et al. (2020), "Challenges to understanding extreme weather changes in lower income countries", *Bulletin of the American Meteorological Society*, Vol. 101/10, pp. E1851-E1860, http://dx.doi.org/10.1175/bams-d-19-0317.1. [220]

Otto, F. et al. (2015), "Factors Other Than Climate Change, Main Drivers of 2014/15 Water Shortage in Southeast Brazil", *Bulletin of the American Meteorological Society*, Vol. 96/12, pp. S35-S40, http://dx.doi.org/10.1175/bams-d-15-00120.1. [170]

Otto, F. et al. (2012), "Reconciling two approaches to attribution of the 2010 Russian heat wave", *Geophysical Research Letters*, Vol. 39/4, pp. n/a-n/a, http://dx.doi.org/10.1029/2011gl050422. [130]

Otto, F. et al. (2018), "Climate change increases the probability of heavy rains in Northern England/Southern Scotland like those of storm Desmond—a real-time event attribution revisited", *Environmental Research Letters*, Vol. 13/2, p. 024006, http://dx.doi.org/10.1088/1748-9326/aa9663. [145]

Otto, F. et al. (2018), "Anthropogenic influence on the drivers of the Western Cape drought 2015–2017", *Environmental Research Letters*, Vol. 13/12, p. 124010, http://dx.doi.org/10.1088/1748-9326/aae9f9. [171]

Pall, P. et al. (2011), "Anthropogenic greenhouse gas contribution to flood risk in England and Wales in autumn 2000", *Nature*, Vol. 470/7334, pp. 382-385, http://dx.doi.org/10.1038/nature09762. [209]

Paris Agreement (2015), *15 December 2015*, United Nations Treaty Collection Certified True Copies (CTCs) of Multilateral Treaties Deposited with the Secretary-General Chapter XXVII.7.d, https://treaties.un.org/pages/ViewDetails.aspx?src=TREATY&mtdsg_no=XXVII-7-d&chapter=27 (accessed on 28 April 2020). [3]

Pecl, G. et al. (2017), "Biodiversity redistribution under climate change: Impacts on ecosystems and human well-being", *Science*, Vol. 355/6332, p. eaai9214, http://dx.doi.org/10.1126/science.aai9214. [38]

Pendergrass, A. (2018), "What precipitation is extreme?", *Science*, Vol. 360/6393, pp. 1072-1073, http://dx.doi.org/10.1126/science.aat1871. [157]

Perkins-Kirkpatrick, S. and P. Gibson (2017), "Changes in regional heatwave characteristics as a function of increasing global temperature", *Scientific Reports*, Vol. 7/1, http://dx.doi.org/10.1038/s41598-017-12520-2. [146]

Perkins, S. and L. Alexander (2013), "On the measurement of heat waves", *Journal of Climate*, Vol. 26/13, pp. 4500-4517, http://dx.doi.org/10.1175/jcli-d-12-00383.1. [188]

Philip, S. et al. (2018), "Attribution Analysis of the Ethiopian Drought of 2015", *Journal of Climate*, Vol. 31/6, pp. 2465-2486, http://dx.doi.org/10.1175/jcli-d-17-0274.1. [168]

Philip, S. et al. (2021), "Rapid attribution analysis of the extraordinary heatwave on the Pacific Coast of the US and Canada June 2021", World Weather Attribution, https://www.worldweatherattribution.org/wp-content/uploads/NW-US-extreme-heat-2021-scientific-report-WWA.pdf. [26]

Philip, S. et al. (2020), "A protocol for probabilistic extreme event attribution analyses", *Advances in Statistical Climatology, Meteorology and Oceanography*, Vol. 6/2, pp. 177-203, http://dx.doi.org/10.5194/ascmo-6-177-2020. [134]

Piecuch, C. (2020), "Weakening of the Gulf Stream at Florida Straits over the past century inferred from coastal sea-level data", *Earth and Space Science Open7Archive*, http://dx.doi.org/10.1002/essoar.10502506.1. [243]

Popovich, N. and W. Choi-Schagrin (2021), "Hidden toll of the northwest heat wave: Hundreds of extra deaths", 11 August, The New York Times, https://www.nytimes.com/interactive/2021/08/11/climate/deaths-pacific-northwest-heat-wave.html. [29]

Praetorius, S. (2018), "North Atlantic circulation slows down", *Nature*, Vol. 556/7700, pp. 180-181, http://dx.doi.org/10.1038/d41586-018-04086-4. [232]

Prein, A. et al. (2015), "A review on regional convection-permitting climate modeling: Demonstrations, prospects, and challenges", *Reviews of Geophysics*, Vol. 53/2, pp. 323-361, http://dx.doi.org/10.1002/2014rg000475. [160]

Prein, A. et al. (2016), "The future intensification of hourly precipitation extremes", *Nature Climate Change*, Vol. 7/1, pp. 48-52, http://dx.doi.org/10.1038/nclimate3168. [161]

Quigley, M. et al. (2020), "A multi-hazards earth science perspective on the COVID-19 pandemic: The potential for concurrent and cascading crises", *Environment Systems and Decisions*, Vol. 40/2, pp. 199-215, http://dx.doi.org/10.1007/s10669-020-09772-1. [204]

Rahmstorf, S. et al. (2015), "Exceptional twentieth-century slowdown in Atlantic Ocean overturning circulation", *Nature Climate Change*, Vol. 5/5, pp. 475-480, http://dx.doi.org/10.1038/nclimate2554. [238]

Railsback, L. (2017), "Rain, riches, and empire: The relationship between nations ruling distant lands, nations of great wealth, and regions of regular moderate atmospheric precipitation", *Weather, Climate, and Society*, Vol. 9/3, pp. 455-469, http://dx.doi.org/10.1175/wcas-d-16-0143.1. [263]

Ramanathan, V. et al. (2005), "Atmospheric brown clouds: Impacts on South Asian climate and hydrological cycle", *Proceedings of the National Academy of Sciences*, Vol. 102/15, pp. 5326-5333, http://dx.doi.org/10.1073/pnas.0500656102. [269]

Ranasinghe, R. (2016), "Assessing climate change impacts on open sandy coasts: A review", *Earth-Science Reviews*, Vol. 160, pp. 320-332, http://dx.doi.org/10.1016/j.earscirev.2016.07.011. [102]

Ratter, B. (2018), *Geography of Small Islands*, Springer International Publishing, Cham, http://dx.doi.org/10.1007/978-3-319-63869-0. [80]

Reuters (2021), "California's giant sequoias remain safe from growing wildfire", 20 September, Reuters, https://www.reuters.com/business/environment/californias-giant-sequoias-remain-safe-growing-wildfire-2021-09-20/. [23]

Riahi, K. et al. (2017), "The Shared Socio-economic Pathways and their energy, land use, and greenhouse gas emissions implications: An overview", *Global Environmental Change*, Vol. 42, pp. 153-168, http://dx.doi.org/10.1016/j.gloenvcha.2016.05.009. [278]

Ritchie, H. and M. Roser (2014), "Natural disasters", *Our World in Data*, https://ourworldindata.org/natural-disasters. [213]

Ritchie, P. et al. (2021), "Overshooting tipping point thresholds in a changing climate", *Nature*, Vol. 592/7855, pp. 517-523, http://dx.doi.org/10.1038/s41586-021-03263-2. [67]

Robinson, S. (2020), "Climate change adaptation in SIDS : A systematic review of the literature pre and post the IPCC Fifth Assessment Report", *WIREs Climate Change*, Vol. 11/4, http://dx.doi.org/10.1002/wcc.653. [87]

Rodgers, K. et al. (2021), "Ubiquity of human-induced changes in climate variability", *Earth System Dynamics Discussion [preprint]*, http://dx.doi.org/10.5194/esd-2021-50. [264]

Rossignol-Strick, M. (1985), "Mediterranean Quaternary sapropels, an immediate response of the African monsoon to variation of insolation", *Palaeogeography, Palaeoclimatology, Palaeoecology*, Vol. 49/3-4, pp. 237-263, http://dx.doi.org/10.1016/0031-0182(85)90056-2. [257]

Ross, L. (6 August 2020), "Climate change and wildfires: Projecting future wildfire potential", Four Twenty Seven blog, http://427mt.com/2020/08/06/projecting-future-wildfire-potential/. [16]

Russo, S. et al. (2016), "When will unusual heat waves become normal in a warming Africa?", *Environmental Research Letters*, Vol. 11/5, p. 054016, http://dx.doi.org/10.1088/1748-9326/11/5/054016. [191]

Russo, S., J. Sillmann and E. Fischer (2015), "Top ten European heatwaves since 1950 and their occurrence in the coming decades", *Environmental Research Letters*, Vol. 10/12, p. 124003, http://dx.doi.org/10.1088/1748-9326/10/12/124003. [190]

Sasmito, S. et al. (2015), "Can mangroves keep pace with contemporary sea level rise? A global data review", *Wetlands Ecology and Management*, Vol. 24/2, pp. 263-278, http://dx.doi.org/10.1007/s11273-015-9466-7. [117]

Schäfer, L. et al. (2021), *Slow-onset Processes and Resulting Loss and Damage – An introduction*, Germanwatch e.V, Bonn, Germany. [7]

Schaller, N. et al. (2016), "Human influence on climate in the 2014 southern England winter floods and their impacts", *Nature Climate Change*, Vol. 6/6, pp. 627-634, http://dx.doi.org/10.1038/nclimate2927. [205]

Scheffer, M. et al. (2012), “Anticipating critical transitions”, *Science*, Vol. 338/6105, pp. 344-348, http://dx.doi.org/10.1126/science.1225244. [61]

Schiermeier, Q. (2021), “Climate change made North America’s deadly heatwave 150 times more likely”, *Nature*, http://dx.doi.org/10.1038/d41586-021-01869-0. [28]

Schleussner, C. and G. Feulner (2013), “Was the Little Ice Age the result of a volcanically-triggered regime shift in the North Atlantic ocean circulation?”, p. 6980. [229]

Schleussner, C. et al. (2021), “Pathways of climate resilience over the 21st century”, *Environmental Research Letters*, Vol. 16/5, p. 054058, http://dx.doi.org/10.1088/1748-9326/abed79. [212]

Schramm, P. et al. (2021), “Heat-related emergency department visits during the northwestern heat wave – United States, June 2021”, *Morbidity and Mortality Weekly Report*, No. 70, 23 July, US Centers for Disease Control and Prevention, Washington, DC, https://www.cdc.gov/mmwr/volumes/70/wr/pdfs/mm7029e1-H.pdf. [30]

Schuerch, M. et al. (2018), “Future response of global coastal wetlands to sea-level rise”, *Nature*, Vol. 561/7722, pp. 231-234, http://dx.doi.org/10.1038/s41586-018-0476-5. [116]

Seneviratne, S. et al. (2016), “Allowable CO2 emissions based on regional and impact-related climate targets”, *Nature*, Vol. 529/7587, pp. 477-483, http://dx.doi.org/10.1038/nature16542. [150]

Seneviratne, S. and M. Hauser (2020), “Regional Climate Sensitivity of Climate Extremes in CMIP6 Versus CMIP5 Multimodel Ensembles”, *Earth’s Future*, <p>e2019EF001474 2019EF001474</p>, p. e2019EF001474, https://doi.org/10.1029/2019EF001474. [154]

Seneviratne, S. et al. (2012), “Changes in climate extremes and their impacts on the natural physical environment.”, in Field, C. et al. (eds.), *Managing the Risks of Extreme Events and Disasters to Advance Climate Change Adaptation. A Special Report of Working Groups I and II of the Intergovernmental Panel on Climate Change*, Cambridge University Press, Cambridge, United Kingdom, and New York. [6]

Sgubin, G. et al. (2017), “Abrupt cooling over the North Atlantic in modern climate models”, *Nature Communications*, Vol. 8/1, http://dx.doi.org/10.1038/ncomms14375. [226]

Shepherd, T. (2019), “Storyline approach to the construction of regional climate change information”, *Proceedings of the Royal Society A: Mathematical, Physical and Engineering Sciences*, Vol. 475/2225, p. 20190013, http://dx.doi.org/10.1098/rspa.2019.0013. [12]

Shepherd, T. et al. (2018), “Storylines: an alternative approach to representing uncertainty in physical aspects of climate change”, *Climatic Change*, Vol. 151/3-4, pp. 555-571, http://dx.doi.org/10.1007/s10584-018-2317-9. [136]

Shepherd, T. and A. Sobel (2020), “Localness in climate change”, *Comparative Studies of South Asia, Africa and the Middle East*, Vol. 40/1, pp. 7-16, http://dx.doi.org/10.1215/1089201x-8185983. [218]

Sillmann, J. et al. (2013), “Climate extremes indices in the CMIP5 multimodel ensemble: Part 2. Future climate projections”, *Journal of Geophysical Research: Atmospheres*, Vol. 118/6, pp. 2473-2493, http://dx.doi.org/10.1002/jgrd.50188. [184]

Smith, A. and R. Katz (2013), "US billion-dollar weather and climate disasters: Data sources, trends, accuracy and biases", *Natural Hazards*, Vol. 67/2, pp. 387-410, http://dx.doi.org/10.1007/s11069-013-0566-5. [124]

Smith, A. and J. Matthews (2015), "Quantifying uncertainty and variable sensitivity within the US billion-dollar weather and climate disaster cost estimates", *Natural Hazards*, Vol. 77/3, pp. 1829-1851, http://dx.doi.org/10.1007/s11069-015-1678-x. [125]

Spalding, M. et al. (2017), "Mapping the global value and distribution of coral reef tourism", *Marine Policy*, Vol. 82, pp. 104-113, http://dx.doi.org/10.1016/j.marpol.2017.05.014. [110]

Spinoni, J. et al. (2013), "World drought frequency, duration, and severity for 1951-2010", *International Journal of Climatology*, Vol. 34/8, pp. 2792-2804, http://dx.doi.org/10.1002/joc.3875. [280]

Stammer, D. et al. (2019), "Framework for High-End Estimates of Sea Level Rise for Stakeholder Applications", *Earth's Future*, Vol. 7/8, pp. 923-938, http://dx.doi.org/10.1029/2019ef001163. [45]

Standard & Poor's Ratings Service (2015), *The Heat Is On: How Climate Change Can Impact Sovereign Ratings*, https://www.agefi.com/uploads/media/S_P_The_Heat_Is_On_How_Climate_Change_Can_Impact_Sovereign_Ratings_25-11-2015.pdf. [32]

Steffen, W. et al. (2018), "Trajectories of the Earth system in the Anthropocene", *Proceedings of the National Academy of Sciences*, Vol. 115/33, pp. 8252-8259, http://dx.doi.org/10.1073/pnas.1810141115. [224]

Stommel, H. (1961), "Thermohaline convection with two stable regimes of flow", *Tellus*, Vol. 13/2, pp. 224-230, http://dx.doi.org/10.1111/j.2153-3490.1961.tb00079.x. [234]

Storlazzi, C. et al. (2018), "Most atolls will be uninhabitable by the mid-21st century because of sea-level rise exacerbating wave-driven flooding", *Science Advances*, Vol. 4/4, p. eaap9741, http://dx.doi.org/10.1126/sciadv.aap9741. [122]

Stott, P. et al. (2015), "Attribution of extreme weather and climate-related events", *WIREs Climate Change*, Vol. 7/1, pp. 23-41, http://dx.doi.org/10.1002/wcc.380. [127]

Stott, P., D. Stone and M. Allen (2004), "Human contribution to the European heatwave of 2003", *Nature*, Vol. 432/7017, pp. 610-614, http://dx.doi.org/10.1038/nature03089. [131]

Sutton, R. (2019), "Climate science needs to take risk assessment much more seriously", *Bulletin of the American Meteorological Society*, Vol. 100/9, pp. 1637-1642, http://dx.doi.org/10.1175/bams-d-18-0280.1. [13]

Swingedouw, D. et al. (2021), "On the risk of abrupt changes in the North Atlantic subpolar gyre in CMIP6 models", *Annals of the New York Academy of Sciences*, http://dx.doi.org/10.1111/nyas.14659. [247]

Swingedouw, D. et al. (2009), "Impact of freshwater release in the North Atlantic under different climate conditions in an OAGCM", *Journal of Climate*, Vol. 22/23, pp. 6377-6403, http://dx.doi.org/10.1175/2009jcli3028.1. [282]

Swiss Re Institute (2021), *Natural catastrophes in 2020: secondary perils in the spotlight, but don't forget primary-peril risks*, https://www.swissre.com/institute/research/sigma-research/sigma-2021-01.html. [281]

Tol, R. (2009), "The economic effects of climate change", *Journal of Economic Perspectives*, Vol. 23/2, pp. 29-51, http://dx.doi.org/10.1257/jep.23.2.29. [260]

Tschumi, E. and J. Zscheischler (2019), "Countrywide climate features during recorded climate-related disasters", *Climatic Change*, Vol. 158/3-4, pp. 593-609, http://dx.doi.org/10.1007/s10584-019-02556-w. [178]

Uhe, P. et al. (2017), "Attributing drivers of the 2016 Kenyan drought", *International Journal of Climatology*, Vol. 38, pp. e554-e568, http://dx.doi.org/10.1002/joc.5389. [167]

UK Met Office (2014), "Winter storms, January to February 2014", (fact sheet), UK Met Office, https://www.metoffice.gov.uk/binaries/content/assets/metofficegovuk/pdf/weather/learn-about/uk-past-events/interesting/2014/winter-storms-january-to-february-2014---met-office.pdf. [207]

UNDRR (2015), *Sendai Framework for Disaster Risk Reduction 2015 - 2030*, United Nations Office for Disaster Risk Reduction, Geneva. [77]

UNEP (2014), *GEO Small Island Developing States Outlook*, United Nations Environment Programme, Nairobi. [90]

UNFCCC (2010), *Decision 1/CP.16: The Cancun Agreements: Outcome of the work of the Ad Hoc Working Group on Long-term Cooperative Action under the Convention*, United Nations Framework Convention on Climate Change, Geneva. [8]

UNFCCC (1992), *United Nations Framework Convention on Climate Change*, United Nations Framework Convention on Climate Change, Bonn. [85]

UN-OHRLLS (2021), *Country Profiles*, United Nations Office of the High Representative for the Least Developed Countries, Landlocked Developing Countries and the Small Island Developing States, New York, http://unohrlls.org/about-sids/country-profiles/ (accessed on 8 July 2021). [79]

UN-OHRLLS (2015), *Small Island Developing States in Numbers: Climate Change*, The United Nations Office of the High Representative for the Least Developed Countries, Landlocked Developing Countries and the Small Island Developing States, New York. [81]

van der Geest, K. and R. van den Berg (2021), "Slow-onset events: A review of the evidence from the IPCC Special Reports on Land, Oceans and Cryosphere", *Current Opinion in Environmental Sustainability*, Vol. 50, pp. 109-120, http://dx.doi.org/10.1016/j.cosust.2021.03.008. [36]

van Hooidonk, R. et al. (2016), "Local-scale projections of coral reef futures and implications of the Paris Agreement", *Scientific Reports*, Vol. 6/1, http://dx.doi.org/10.1038/srep39666. [113]

van Oldenborgh, G. et al. (2021), "Pathways and pitfalls in extreme event attribution", *Climatic Change*, Vol. 166/1-2, http://dx.doi.org/10.1007/s10584-021-03071-7. [135]

Vanos, J. et al. (2020), “Simplicity lacks robustness when projecting heat-health outcomes in a changing climate”, *Nature Communications*, Vol. 11/1, http://dx.doi.org/10.1038/s41467-020-19994-1. [202]

Vautard, R. et al. (2020), “Human contribution to the record-breaking June and July 2019 heatwaves in Western Europe”, *Environmental Research Letters*, Vol. 15/9, p. 094077, http://dx.doi.org/10.1088/1748-9326/aba3d4. [153]

Vautard, R. et al. (2016), “Attribution of human-induced dynamical and thermodynamical contributions in extreme weather events”, *Environmental Research Letters*, Vol. 11/11, p. 114009, http://dx.doi.org/10.1088/1748-9326/11/11/114009. [129]

Vellinga, M. and R. Wood (2007), “Impacts of thermohaline circulation shutdown in the twenty-first century”, *Climatic Change*, Vol. 91/1-2, pp. 43-63, http://dx.doi.org/10.1007/s10584-006-9146-y. [273]

Vellinga, M. and R. Wood (2002), “Global climatic impacts of a collapse of the Atlantic Thermohaline Circulation”, *Climatic Change*, Vol. 54/3, pp. 251-267, http://dx.doi.org/10.1023/a:1016168827653. [277]

Visser, H., A. Petersen and W. Ligtvoet (2014), “On the relation between weather-related disaster impacts, vulnerability and climate change”, *Climatic Change*, Vol. 125/3-4, pp. 461-477, http://dx.doi.org/10.1007/s10584-014-1179-z. [175]

Vogel, M. et al. (2017), “Regional amplification of projected changes in extreme temperatures strongly controlled by soil moisture-temperature feedbacks”, *Geophysical Research Letters*, Vol. 44/3, pp. 1511-1519, http://dx.doi.org/10.1002/2016gl071235. [151]

Vogel, M., J. Zscheischler and S. Seneviratne (2018), “Varying soil moisture–atmosphere feedbacks explain divergent temperature extremes and precipitation projections in central Europe”, *Earth System Dynamics*, Vol. 9/3, pp. 1107-1125, http://dx.doi.org/10.5194/esd-9-1107-2018. [152]

Vousdoukas, M. et al. (2020), “Economic motivation for raising coastal flood defenses in Europe”, *Nature Communications*, Vol. 11/1, http://dx.doi.org/10.1038/s41467-020-15665-3. [274]

Vousdoukas, M. et al. (2017), “Extreme sea levels on the rise along Europe’s coasts”, *Earth’s Future*, Vol. 5/3, pp. 304-323, http://dx.doi.org/10.1002/2016ef000505. [53]

Vousdoukas, M. et al. (2020), “Sandy coastlines under threat of erosion”, *Nature Climate Change*, Vol. 10/3, pp. 260-263, http://dx.doi.org/10.1038/s41558-020-0697-0. [103]

Wahl, T. et al. (2017), “Understanding extreme sea levels for broad-scale coastal impact and adaptation analysis”, *Nature Communications*, Vol. 8/1, http://dx.doi.org/10.1038/ncomms16075. [46]

Westra, S. et al. (2014), “Future changes to the intensity and frequency of short-duration extreme rainfall”, *Reviews of Geophysics*, Vol. 52/3, pp. 522-555, http://dx.doi.org/10.1002/2014rg000464. [163]

Whitty, C. and F. Watt (2020), “Map clusters of diseases to tackle multimorbidity”, *Nature*, Vol. 579/7800, pp. 494-496, http://dx.doi.org/10.1038/d41586-020-00837-4. [203]

Williams, K. et al. (2015), "The Met Office Global Coupled model 2.0 (GC2) configuration", *Geoscientific Model Development*, Vol. 8/5, pp. 1509-1524, http://dx.doi.org/10.5194/gmd-8-1509-2015. [275]

Williamson, M. et al. (2017), "Effect of AMOC collapse on ENSO in a high resolution general circulation model", *Climate Dynamics*, Vol. 50/7-8, pp. 2537-2552, http://dx.doi.org/10.1007/s00382-017-3756-0. [254]

Witze, A. (2018), "Why extreme rains are gaining strength as the climate warms", *Nature*, Vol. 563/7732, pp. 458-460, http://dx.doi.org/10.1038/d41586-018-07447-1. [25]

Wong, P. et al. (2014), "Coastal systems and low-lying areas", in Field, C. et al. (eds.), *Climate Change 2014: Impacts, Adaptation, and Vulnerability. Part A: Global and Sectoral Aspects. Contribution of Working Group II to the Fifth Assessment Report of the Intergovernmental Panel of Climate Change*, Cambridge University Press, Cambridge, United Kingdom, and New York. [94]

Woodroffe, C. (2008), "Reef-island topography and the vulnerability of atolls to sea-level rise", *Global and Planetary Change*, Vol. 62/1-2, pp. 77-96, http://dx.doi.org/10.1016/j.gloplacha.2007.11.001. [47]

World Bank (2021), *GDP per capita (current US$) | Data [WWW Document]*, https://data.worldbank.org/indicator/NY.GDP.PCAP.CD (accessed 7.2.21) (accessed on 2 July 2021). [84]

World Economic Forum (2018), *The Global Risks Report 2018*, World Economic Forum, Geneva. [76]

Wunderling, N. et al. (2021), "Interacting tipping elements increase risk of climate domino effects under global warming", *Earth System Dynamics*, Vol. 12/2, pp. 601-619, http://dx.doi.org/10.5194/esd-12-601-2021. [69]

Xu, C. et al. (2020), "Future of the human climate niche", *Proceedings of the National Academy of Sciences*, Vol. 117/21, pp. 11350-11355, http://dx.doi.org/10.1073/pnas.1910114117. [251]

Yin, J., M. Schlesinger and R. Stouffer (2009), "Model projections of rapid sea-level rise on the northeast coast of the United States", *Nature Geoscience*, Vol. 2/4, pp. 262-266, http://dx.doi.org/10.1038/ngeo462. [227]

Zhu, C. and Z. Liu (2020), "Weakening Atlantic overturning circulation causes South Atlantic salinity pile-up", *Nature Climate Change*, Vol. 10/11, pp. 998-1003, http://dx.doi.org/10.1038/s41558-020-0897-7. [242]

Zickfeld, K. (2005), "Is the Indian summer monsoon stable against global change?", *Geophysical Research Letters*, Vol. 32/15, http://dx.doi.org/10.1029/2005gl022771. [268]

Annex 3.A. Cascading impacts of crossing a climate tipping point: Collapse of the Atlantic Ocean Overturning Circulation – methodology

The model used for the study of the Atlantic Ocean Overturning Circulation (AMOC) is HadGEM3, the latest version of the UK Met Office's state-of-the-art climate model. The model and its performance have previously been described in detail elsewhere (Williams et al., 2015[275]) but briefly, it is the Global Coupled 2.0 model (GC2) configuration of the HadGEM3 model (Hewitt et al., 2011[276]) consisting of coupled atmosphere, ocean, sea-ice and land-surface models.

Details of the experimental design and of the runs analysed here have also been given previously (Jackson et al., 2015[248]; Mecking et al., 2016[249]; Williamson et al., 2017[254]). Two runs of the model are compared to isolate the effects of an AMOC collapse: a steady state control run (the AMOC is in its usual on state in this run) and an AMOC-off steady state run. The AMOC is collapsed using the methodology of Vellinga and Wood (2002[277]). This involves perturbing the salinity in the upper layers of the North Atlantic to inhibit deep convection and hence quickly shut down the AMOC (the absence of the sinking branch of the AMOC, referred to here as the AMOC-off state).

This method of collapsing the AMOC is unrealistic. The most likely cause of an AMOC shutdown in global warming projections, in fact, is progressively increasing freshwater addition from Arctic runoff and melt of the Greenland ice sheet. However, the method is useful for investigating the impacts of a shutdown.

The salinity perturbations are applied to the upper 536 m of the Atlantic and Arctic Ocean north of 20°N each December for only the first ten years. Each salinity perturbation is equivalent to continuously adding freshwater at a rate of 1Sv (1Sv=10^6 m^3/s) for ten years (total of 10 SvYr). To give an idea of the size of this annual perturbation, a freshwater flux from the Greenland ice sheet of 1Sv would melt it completely in nine years. The AMOC-off run is integrated for a total of 450 years from the start of the salinity perturbations. No external forcing is applied to the model apart from diurnal and annual cycles of the radiative fluxes and atmospheric CO_2 concentrations are fixed to 1978 levels.

As the perturbations are applied, the AMOC collapses from the steady ~15 Sv (maximum stream function at 26.5°N) in the control run and remains very weak for the full model simulation period of 450 years. As a result, meridional Atlantic Ocean heat transport at 30°N is halved from ~1 to ~0.5 PW and surface air temperature (SAT) is reduced by ~4°C in the North Atlantic (Jackson et al., 2015[248]). The AMOC-off simulation is approximately stationary 60 years after the salinity perturbations end. However, the maximum in the AMOC stream function at 26.5°N does have a very slow increasing trend reaching ~5 Sv at the end of the 450 years. Further North, however, the AMOC shows no signs of recovering (Mecking et al., 2016[249]).

First, the climatic impacts of just the AMOC-collapse without the additional global warming most likely to accompany a collapse in any realistic future scenario is isolated. The isolated impacts of an AMOC collapse are analysed by taking the difference of 30-year means of the control run and the AMOC-off run once the simulation is approximately stationary. Following a similar approach to that used by Vellinga and Wood (2007[273]), the analysis is expanded to include the impacts of an AMOC collapse against a more realistic future climate state. In so doing, it accounts for the additional effects of global warming using the future scenario SSP126 in the model HadGEM3-GC31-MM (Williams et al., 2015[275]). The model uses the Global Coupled model 3.1 (GC31) configuration of the HadGEM3 model and has the same atmospheric and ocean resolutions as used in the AMOC hosing experiments. The forcing scenario SSP126 refers to

Shared Socio-economic Pathway SSP1 and Regional Concentration Pathway RCP2.6 - a low-emissions pathway with high sustainability (Riahi et al., 2017[278]).

Under the SSP126 scenario, HadGEM3-GC31-MM reaches a mean global warming of 2.5°C above pre-industrial levels by the end of the century (2071-2100). This warming pattern is overlaid to the impacts of an AMOC collapse to establish the overall impact if the AMOC were to collapse after 2.5°C global warming relative to the present-day climate. As discussed in the previous section, this scenario is considered a plausible scenario with a significant, albeit "unlikely" (0-33%) probability in IPCC language.

Notes

[1] Droughts are an exception and may last from a few months to a few years (Spinoni et al., 2013[280]). Despite the potentially long duration of droughts, this chapter classifies them as extreme weather events (as opposed to slow-onset events).

[2] The economic loss data comprise "all financial losses directly attributable to a major event", including damage to buildings, infrastructure, motor vehicles and other physical assets, as well as "business interruption as a direct consequence of the property damage") (Swiss Re Institute, 2021[281]). The data include any event that resulted in insured losses of more than USD 52.7 million, economic losses of more than USD 105.4 million, 20 or more deaths, 50 or more injuries or 2 000 or more people made homeless. Weather-related extreme events refer to events primarily classified by Swiss Re as: (i) cold, frost; (ii) drought, bush fires heatwaves; (iii) flood; (iv) hail; or (v) storm.

[3] As governments and the insurance sector have improved post-disaster data capture over time, reporting of economic losses has likely also become more comprehensive. As a result, some portion of the growth in economic losses from catastrophes over time is likely due to improved data capture.

[4] The warming from 1850-1900 until 2011-20 has been assessed as 1.09°C, with a likely range of 0.95 to 1.20°C (IPCC, 2021[14]).

[5] There is no universal definition of SIDS; the list of territories belonging to this category differs across the literature.

[6] Considering globally aggregated numbers, for a 10-year return period, heat waves increase in likelihood by 9.4 times, whilst heavy precipitation and drought increase by 2.7 and 4.1 times (IPCC, 2021[14]). It has been shown, however, that for some individual events, such as the prolonged Siberian heat of 2020, the increase in likelihood is orders of magnitude higher than in a climate without human influence (Ciavarella et al., 2021[283]).

[7] The magnitude of temperature changes is model-dependent, but there is general agreement across models that there would be widespread cooling across the northern hemisphere (Vellinga and Wood, 2002[277]; Jacob et al., 2005[279]; Vellinga and Wood, 2007[273]; Swingedouw et al., 2009[282]; Drijfhout, 2015[65]).

[8] A caveat: there is no dynamic vegetation in the model, i.e. there is no interaction between vegetation and the atmosphere. Because of this, one cannot see if the vegetation is altered by the change in the precipitation. One can, however, assume the forest is stable under the conditions seen in the AMOC-on run, and then compare conditions when the AMOC collapses.

4 Policy, governance and institutions for reducing and managing losses and damages

This chapter examines the role of policy, governance and institutions in reducing and managing current and future risks of losses and damages from climate change. It first examines approaches to decision making under uncertainty. This is followed by a discussion of approaches to address the components of climate risks (hazards, exposure and vulnerability) before exploring the role of institutions, governance and norms. The final section focuses on the implications of sea-level rise on policy priorities and decision-making processes in Small Island Developing States.

In Brief

Policy, governance and institutions can help address the risks of losses and damages and their underlying drivers in a context of uncertainty

Climate variability and change are radically altering the conditions that societies and ecosystems need to thrive – a trend that will become more prevalent in the future. These changes are overlaid on demographic, economic, technological, political and social changes. Decision makers at all levels therefore must determine which risks to address, how, to what extent and when.

Many different types of uncertainties affect understanding of future climate hazards, exposure and vulnerability. Some cannot be described in terms of probabilities of the range of outcomes. Indeed, sometimes the full range of outcomes may not even be known. This level of uncertainty demands a shift in the nature of decision making. Traditional "predict then act" approaches must give way to decision-making models that make policy and investment choices more robust under a range of potential futures. Science must be complemented by an understanding of and engagement with diverse socio-economic contexts for decisions. Such a process requires effective partnerships that facilitate collaboration across policy and science communities and are inclusive to different types of knowledge, including local and Indigenous knowledge. Finally, they must be considered legitimate by the stakeholders involved.

The intensity and frequency of climate hazards will grow with continuing warming of the climate system. Approaches to reduce and manage these risks must include a focus on the three components of climate risk identified by the Intergovernmental Panel on Climate Change, namely hazards, exposure and vulnerability, as well as their drivers and interactions:

- ***Hazards:*** Limiting the severity of climate hazards requires rapid and deep reductions in global greenhouse gas (GHG) emissions and the protection and enhancement of natural sinks. Cumulative emissions of carbon dioxide need to be capped at a level consistent with efforts to limit temperature increase to 1.5°C. How these challenging goals are approached will have critically important implications for sustainable development and well-being outcomes, as well as implications for the other two components of climate risk (exposure and vulnerability).
- ***Exposure***: Exposure is dynamic, influenced by history; geography; economic, social and institutional context; and individual choices. Climate change itself will affect exposures as the location, frequency and intensity of hazards shift. Policy approaches include regulation (e.g. land use) and standards; pricing mechanisms (e.g. insurance cover) and early warning systems. While direct exposure of people to some hazards may decline with economic development, losses and damages related to livelihoods and assets may increase. Development in high-risk areas and poorly governed urbanisation can significantly increase exposures.
- ***Vulnerability***: The vulnerability of livelihoods, lives and assets is complex. It depends on individual, household, community and societal-level assets, capabilities, institutions (e.g. markets, political and justice system), policies and practices that determine how people and organisations can prepare for and respond to climate hazards. Moreover, practices, infrastructures and ecosystems that may once have been resilient to hazards may no longer be so; climate change will also create novel hazards. At an individual or household level, particularly important capacities are: i) economic (e.g. income diversity, savings, access to social protection and insurance); ii) institutional (e.g. access to, and awareness of, resources that can inform and

facilitate proactive and protective efforts); and iii) political (e.g. access to and active participation in decision-making processes).

The institutions in place will guide efforts to reduce and manage risks. Institutional structures shape the political context for decision making. They empower some interests, while reducing the influence of others. They also influence how risks are perceived, valued, prioritised and addressed. The political process can also change the relevant institutional structures. Approaches to climate risk therefore are inevitably political and a reflection of the diverse values and interests of stakeholders.

Risk governance focuses on processes and institutions that guide and facilitate the management of risks when decisions are made under uncertainty. This can be through adaptive or iterative approaches, highlighting mechanisms that facilitate continuous monitoring, evaluation and learning. Approaches can also build on the growing experience of countries in strengthening the coherence between their climate and disaster-risk communities.

Norms play an important role in determining the nature and scale of action across all three dimensions of climate risk. Some forms of climate action happen relatively rapidly, such as the response to a specific event or repeated events causing widespread losses and damages. However, institutional inertia, values and vested interests can prevent or delay others.

So-called norm entrepreneurs can contribute to the diffusion of new norms by identifying and promoting the implications of different choices. Young people are playing a vital role in bringing climate change to the attention of the broader public. They are pressuring governments to act, while highlighting the implications of individual consumption and lifestyle choices.

Sea-level rise (SLR) is one of several climate hazards threatening Small Island Developing States (SIDS). The policy response to SLR can be grouped in four categories, each with strengths and weaknesses:

- ***protect***, to reduce losses and damages through hard engineering structures or nature-based solutions
- ***advance***, to prevent the propagation of coastal hazards inland by building new land seawards and upwards
- ***accommodate***, to reduce the vulnerability of people, livelihoods and the built environment
- ***retreat***, to reduce or eliminate exposure by moving people, infrastructures and human activities out of the risk zone.

Policy responses to SLR in SIDS will depend on socio-economic circumstances that may transcend this context, e.g. use of early warning systems, emergency planning and contingency planning. However, given the deep uncertainty about future SLR, SIDS must implement flexible options that can be adjusted over time. They must thus determine which long-term decisions can be postponed until the level of uncertainty decreases. Long-term decisions that cannot be postponed, such as on critical infrastructure investments, must factor in SLR. In so doing, the uncertainty preferences of stakeholders will inform the choices made. Many technical options are available for adapting to even high levels of SLR. However, implementing these at significant scale would be costly and lead to radically different coastal landscapes. This would, in turn, threaten the rich cultural diversity and heritage of SIDS. International support to SIDS in the form of finance, technology and capacity should therefore be a policy priority. In addition, deep and rapid cuts in GHG emissions to limit the scale of hazards are urgently needed.

4.1. Introduction

Climate-related extreme events and slow-onset changes are already having devastating and widespread impacts on lives and livelihoods. This is especially true when these changes occur alongside broader social, economic and political stressors. To illustrate, while East Africa in 2020 had to deal with the COVID-19 pandemic and its associated crisis, it also coped with flooding from one of the wettest rainfall seasons in 40 years. Floods displaced hundreds of thousands of people. They also contributed to the loss of crop and livestock equivalent to 70 000 hectares (ha) and 96 000 animal deaths. Meanwhile, the region suffered through the worst locust outbreak in 25 years (Kassegn and Endris, 2021[1]). These concurrent disasters further exacerbated prevailing food insecurity in the region, threatening development gains. The Philippines was also hit by concurrent disasters in 2020. During the COVID-19 pandemic, 22 tropical cyclones hit the country, including the strongest ever recorded to have made landfall (Tropical Cyclone Goni). The cyclones caused widespread destruction, leaving thousands homeless (Rocha et al., 2021[2]). The intensity and frequency of climate hazards will grow with continuing warming of the climate system (IPCC, 2021[3]).

Decision makers at all levels are faced with climate variability interacting with current and projected future levels of climate change. As such, they must determine which risks to address, how, to what extent and when to act. At the household or community level, adaptation to weather and climate hazards may involve adjustments to, or a shift in, livelihood choices. This can entail a change in crops or a shift from farming into other income-generating activities. It may also lead to migration in search of new opportunities, either nationally or internationally, or even displacement (IPCC, 2014[4]). At the national level, damaging weather and climate hazards can reverse development gains. Such a reversal may increase income inequality and the vulnerability of already marginalised segments of society (World Bank, 2021[5]). Hazards directly affecting one country, segment of society or sector may spread to other parts of society. In some cases, hazards may cross local, regional or even national borders, as illustrated in Box 4.1.

Chapter 4 highlights approaches to reduce and manage the risks of losses and damages from climate change. The chapter focuses on the role of policy, governance and institutions. The role of finance and technology are covered in Chapters 5 and 6, respectively. The remainder of this chapter is structured in four sections. Section 4.2 examines approaches to decision making under uncertainty. Section 4.3 discusses approaches to address the components of climate risks (hazards, exposure and vulnerability). Section 4.4 explores the role of institutions, governance and norms. Section 4.5 discusses the implications of sea-level rise (SLR) on policy priorities and decision-making processes in Small Island Developing States (SIDS).

4.2. Decision making under uncertainty

Chapter 3 illustrated the currently serious and potentially devastating future impacts of climate change. These impacts become more likely if action to reduce and manage the risks is not commensurate with the goal of the Paris Agreement to limit temperature increase to 1.5°C. Following 10 000 years of a relatively stable climate, the Earth is now moving into a climatic regime that is rapidly changing (IPCC, 2021[3]; Marshall and Plumb, 2008[6]).

Box 4.1. Globally networked climate risks

The systemic, cross-border nature of many climate risks can be illustrated by their disruptive impacts on agricultural production processes and food security. Modern food systems are both dynamic and complex. They are comprised of formal and informal sectors across product value chains, which may involve international trade. Over 2008-18, the impact of hydrological, meteorological and geological disasters[1] on the agriculture sector[2] in Least Developed Countries (LDCs) and Lower-Middle Income Countries (LMICs) totalled USD 108 billion in damaged or lost crop and livestock production. Across all income groups, this amounted to USD 280 billion or 4% of potential crop and livestock production (FAO, 2021[7]). Such disruptions can fundamentally alter livelihoods and food security given the high dependency of many developing countries on agricultural income (FAO, 2021[7]; Naqvi, Gaupp and Hochrainer-Stigler, 2020[8]).

Production disruptions can also disrupt markets, especially when affecting one or more highly fertile agricultural regions known as "breadbasket" regions (UNDRR, 2019[9]). Around 60% of global grain production occurs in five regional breadbaskets: The People's Republic of China (hereafter "China"), the United States, India, Brazil and Argentina, and in a few regions within those countries. Only four grains account for almost half of the calories of the average global diet (Woetzel et al., 2020[10]).[3] This concentration of production, often in the form of monocultures, delivers economies of scale. However, it is vulnerable to pest infestation, localised extreme weather events and slow-onset changes. Such changes include temperature increases and desertification that can affect a considerable portion of global production (Woetzel et al., 2020[10]). Connections between distant weather phenomena, e.g. the relationship between the El Niño/Southern Oscillation and regional climate extremes such as Indian heatwaves, also increase the risk of simultaneous crop failure across regions (Gaupp et al., 2019[11]).

The unusually intense 2010 heatwave in the Russian Federation (hereafter "Russia") reduced the grain harvest by around a third. This contributed to an initial dramatic increase in international grain prices (up by over 60% between June and August 2010). In mid-August 2020, in response to concerns about the impact on domestic food security, the Russian government imposed an export ban on grain. The ban, which stayed in place until July 2011, further increased international grain prices (Challinor et al., 2018[12]). During the same period, the breadbasket region of Pakistan was affected by devastating floods that displaced over 20 million people, some for months (Naqvi, Gaupp and Hochrainer-Stigler, 2020[8]). The two events were connected meteorologically (Lau and Kim, 2012[13]; Trenberth and Fasullo, 2012[14]) Combined with other extreme weather events that year, they contributed to the price of wheat more than doubling (Challinor et al., 2018[12]).

The risk of such "Multiple Breadbasket Failures" is projected to increase with climate change for wheat, maize and soybean crops and decrease for rice (Gaupp et al., 2019[11]). International mechanisms are in place to reduce and manage these risks. These include monitoring and early warning of crop failures and co-ordination of food distribution based on humanitarian need in the event of shortages (Janetos et al., 2017[15]). Further policy proposals put forward include formalisation of grain reserve arrangements and binding agreements between a small set of grain traders (Headey and Fan, 2008[16]).

Notes:

1. Hydrological, meteorological and geological disasters (and the associated losses in LDCs and LMICs) include i) drought (34%); ii) floods (19%); iii) storms (18%); iv) earthquakes, landslides and mass movements (13%); v) crop and livestock pests, diseases and infestations (9%); vi) extreme temperatures (6%); and vii) wildfires (1%).

2. Including crops, livestock, forestry, fisheries and aquaculture.

3. The main breadbasket regions differ across crops (Woetzel et al., 2020[10]): ***For wheat***: China, European Union, India, Russia and the United States; ***for corn***: Argentina, Brazil, China, European Union and the United States; ***for soy***: Argentina, Brazil, China, India and the United States; ***for rice***: Bangladesh, China, India, Indonesia and Viet Nam.

4.2.1 The changing nature of risk and uncertainty

Areas that historically have had to manage floods may in the future face challenges associated with droughts for which there is little management experience. In high mountain regions, for example, snowmelt and glacier retreat are contributing to a short-term increase in water availability. This coincides with other risks, including glacier lake outburst floods. Following an increase in water supply in the short-term, water supply will start to diminish (Hock et al., 2019[17]). In the Himalayan region, uncertainties in climatic projections and glacier dynamics could have major implications for more than a billion people in the wider region that depend on this Asian "water tower" (Scott et al., 2019[18]; Mishra, 2015[19]).

Areas at risk of wildfires may see the frequency and magnitude of these events increase to unprecedented levels (Goss et al., 2020[20]). Slow-onset changes such as SLR will increasingly threaten livelihoods and lifestyles of coastal and island communities. These include threats to traditional belief and cultural systems (McNamara, Westoby and Chandra, 2021[21]). Crossing tipping points in the climate system could trigger major transformations to the climate system and significant disruptions to economies and societies, both regionally and globally. Thresholds at which such tipping points would be triggered are uncertain. However, some may already be close or even exceeded (Lenton et al., 2019[22]). This highlights the novelty of potential challenges for policy makers in identifying and implementing approaches to reduce and manage the risks of losses and damages from climate change.

Different types of uncertainties limit the applicability of historical data for understanding future climate hazards. As discussed in Chapter 2, this includes uncertainties stemming from i) future emissions linked to different demographic and socio-economic pathways; ii) uncertainty in the response of the global climate system to different levels of emissions and aerosols; and iii) the natural variability of the climate system (Zheng, Zhao and Oleson, 2021[23]). Additionally, there are uncertainties in the other components of climate risk (i.e. exposure and vulnerability), such as the sensitivity to a given change in climate of people, assets and activities. These uncertainties have called into question the traditional "predict then act" approach. Instead, given the high costs of inaction or delayed action, policy processes and decisions can usefully be guided by robust and flexible policy choices that make them suitable to a range of potential future climates (Vincent and Conway, 2021[24]).

A focus on robustness and flexibility in decision making needs to consider the values and perspectives of actors in the process (Marchau et al., 2019[25]). One key aspect is the level of uncertainty in the system about which a decision is needed (see also Chapter 2). If the extreme ends of the decision-making spectrum are defined as full certainty or total ignorance, four intermediate levels of uncertainty include (Marchau et al., 2019[25]) (see also Figure 4.1)

- ***Level 1***: There is not full certainty but decision makers generally do not consider it necessary to measure the degrees of uncertainty. This can apply to short-term decisions for a well-defined system where historical data are seen as a good indicator of the future.
- ***Level 2***: The parameters in the model used to describe the real-world system are used to estimate the probability distribution for a few alternative futures. Related policy processes can be informed by expected outcomes and levels of acceptable risk.
- ***Level 3***: There is a limited set of plausible futures, but the level of uncertainty is such that probabilities cannot be assigned to them. Instead, scenario analysis can point to policies that will produce more favourable outcomes. The "best" policy will produce the most favourable outcomes (a political/social choice) across the different scenarios.
- ***Level 4***: This level of deep uncertainty can apply to two situations. In the first, there are many plausible futures due, for example, to lack of knowledge or data about the functional relationships. In the second, the future is not even qualitatively known due, for example, to unpredictable high-impact events. It can either be difficult (first case) or impossible (second case) to describe

interactions among the variables, determine the probability distribution for different outcomes or even value the desirability of alternative outcomes.

Figure 4.1. Sample characteristics of different levels of uncertainty

	Full certainty	Level 1	Level 2	Level 3	Level 4 (deep) uncertainty		Total ignorance
					Level 4a	Level 4b	
Context (x)		A clear enough future	Alternate futures (with probabilities)	A few plausible futures	Many plausible futures	Unknown future	
		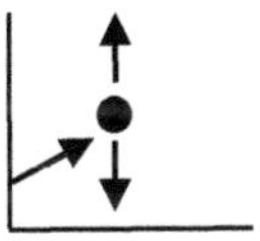	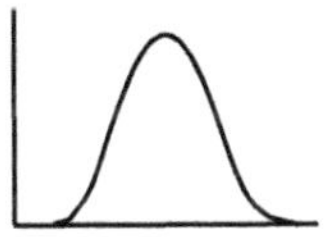	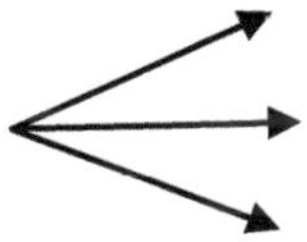		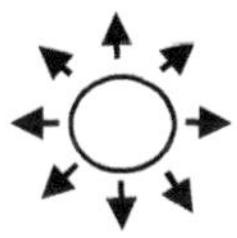	
System model (R)		A single (deterministic) system model	A single (stochastic) system model	A few alternative system models	Many alternative system models	Unknown system model; know we don't know	
System outcomes (O)		A point estimate for each outcome	A confidence interval for each outcome	A limited range of outcomes	A wide range of outcomes	Unknown outcomes; know we don't know	
Weights (W)		A single set of weights	Several sets of weights, with a probability attached to each set	A limited range of weights	A wide range of weights	Unknown weights; know we don't know	

Note: This table assumes four primary locations of uncertainty: external forces (X); the structure of the system mode and its parameters (R); the system outcomes (O); the relative importance of specific outcomes placed by the actors in the policy domain (W).
Source: Adjusted from (Walker, Lempert and Kwakkel, 2013[26]).

In terms of climate change, different hazards across different timescales will have different levels of uncertainty associated with them. For example, SLR rise is a slow-onset change that occurs over decades. Conversely, extreme events such as heavy precipitation can occur over hours or days. The uncertainty of these different types of hazards, and thus how to address them, varies widely. In the context of SLR over the coming decade, it may be sufficient to consider a small range of possible futures. These would revolve around a central estimate determined by the rate of thermal expansion of the upper sea surface and the additional water from glacier and ice-sheet melt. On longer timescales, there is arguably a limited number of different plausible futures. However, it is difficult to place credible probabilities on the occurrence of each possible outcome.

For extreme events, the occurrence of some can be predicted on a timescale of several days, such as the heavy precipitation event in Pakistan in 2010 (Webster, Toma and Kim, 2011[27]). On longer timescales, dynamic aspects of climate change, such as changes in average precipitation, are highly uncertain (Shepherd, 2014[28]). The potential crossing of tipping points in the climate system is at the high end of the uncertainty spectrum. It is not possible to attach probabilities to the activation of particular tipping points. Moreover, there is a wide range of potential outcomes from crossing a given tipping point. Some future states of the climate are unknown or very imperfectly known.

4.2.3 The rise in decision-driven approaches to uncertainty

The past few decades have seen a rise in decision-driven approaches that recognise the need for decisions to both reduce the risks and to strengthen resilience in the face of inherent uncertainties. Such decision-driven approaches typically rely on institutional structures that facilitate an iterative approach informed by learning and recognise the interconnectedness, complexity, feedbacks and thresholds across different systems and impacts. Box 4.2 briefly summarises three approaches to decision making under uncertainty that have received prominent attention in the academic literature and increasingly inform policy processes. Discussion on further approaches and additional details are available in Marchau et al. (2019[25]). Box 4.3 illustrates how different approaches combined can guide decision-making processes in the agricultural sector in Uganda, where future levels of precipitation are uncertain.

Box 4.2. Examples of approaches on decision making under uncertainty

Robust Decision Making (RDM)

RDM approaches provide a set of concepts, processes and tools that use computation to yield better decisions under conditions of uncertainty (Lempert, 2019[29]). RDM approaches combine decision analysis, scenarios and modelling to stress test different policy approaches against a wide range of plausible future pathways, rather than making predictions. Analysis of the model runs then help decision makers identify key features that distinguish those futures in which their plans meet or miss set policy goals (Lempert, 2019[29]). In developing countries, data requirements and resource constraints among others limit the uptake of RDM approaches (Bhave et al., 2016[30]). This results in research exploring how simplified modelling approaches can provide decision support, e.g. in the context of the Lake Tana basin in Ethiopia (Shortridge, Guikema and Zaitchik, 2016[31]).

Dynamic Adaptive Policy Pathways (DAPP)

The DAPP approach recognises the multitude of uncertainties that decision makers face (i.e. climate change and broader socio-economic factors). It calls on planners to establish a framework for action informed by a strategic vision of the future and guided by short-term, flexible actions that can be adjusted to reflect changing circumstances (Haasnoot et al., 2013[32]). In this way, the DAPP approach provides a decision space that helps overcomes policy paralysis in the context of uncertainty. Biophysical, cultural, socio-economic, and political-institutional dimensions determine why, how, when and who acts on climate. Decisions today may open up some options while foreclosing others; changes in the biophysical and socio-economic systems also determine the range of future available options (Haasnoot et al., 2020[33]). The DAPP approach has informed policy that focuses on water risk management in delta areas, such as in the Netherlands (Government of the Netherlands, 2020[34]), Bangladesh (Government of Bangladesh, 2018[35]), in the Murray-Darling Basin in Australia (Murray-Darling Basin Authority, n.d.[36]) and in the context of the Thames Barrier in the United Kingdom (UK Government, 2021[37]).

Storylines approach

The storylines approach aims to identify plausible climatic and socio-economic factors that drive risks to assess the impact of particular actions in a context where future changes in the climate are uncertain (Shepherd, 2019[38]). The approach may be informed by particular types of (historical or plausible) events with high societal impacts, or particularly dangerous physical pathways of the climate system (e.g. tipping points) (Shepherd et al., 2018[39]). The emphasis on plausibility and the event-based nature of the storyline approach makes it well suited for a variety of purposes. It can improve risk awareness; strengthen decision making; explore the boundaries of plausibility of certain climate projections; provide a physical basis for understanding the different components of uncertainty; and link physical climate information with human aspects of climate change (Shepherd et al., 2018[39]).

The technical complexity of some decision-driven approaches limits their applicability to developing countries. In some developing countries, for example, data availability may be sparse or unreliable and computing and technical capacities inadequate (Shortridge, Guikema and Zaitchik, 2016[31]). In such contexts, simplified analytical processes have been applied. For example, hydrologic models are replaced by simple relationships or assumptions about how climate conditions impact streamflow. They may also focus on individual variables rather than the broader systems (Shortridge, Guikema and Zaitchik, 2016[31]). Such simplifications require a good understanding of potential implications on outcomes. Alternatively, policy choices can be tested against explicit statements of causal relationships, or theories of causation, to guide reasoning over choices and outcomes (Popper, 2019[40]).

Uncertainty and long-lived infrastructure

This explicit treatment of uncertainty is particularly valuable in the context of large investments in long-lived infrastructure such as energy, transport, coastal protection and water management systems (Shortridge, Guikema and Zaitchik, 2016[31]). Failure to treat uncertainty risks locking in long-lived investments that may exacerbate the exposure of people and assets to future climate risks. A focus on uncertainty instead contributes to approaches that perform well under a set of different future conditions. This can then be more politically palatable than large and potentially irreversible decisions (Bhave et al., 2016[30]).

The Thames Barrier illustrates the treatment of uncertainty. The Barrier was designed to be adaptable to different SLR rates and change affecting the estuary up to around 2070. Different options have been identified for improving or replacing the Barrier. However, given the adaptive nature of the approach, a final decision will not likely be needed until around 2040 (UK Government, 2021[37]).

Where long-lived infrastructure is in place, and the focus is largely on maintenance and modification rather than construction, the resilience of the system to different climate futures should be assessed. This process may guide efforts to retrofit infrastructure or add redundancy. In this way, when extreme weather events bring down one component of the system, other components can take over (OECD, 2018[41]; OECD, 2020[42]). While adding redundancy to systems will increase initial costs, this can be seen as a form of insurance against extreme events.

Reconciling long-term investments with election cycles

The benefits of investments to address these risks of losses and damages may only materialise over time. This can pose a challenge for elected officials (Evans, Rowell and Semazzi, 2020[43]). Research has shown that voters are more likely to reward an incumbent presidential party for delivering disaster relief spending than for investing in disaster preparedness (Healy and Malhotra, 2009[44]). Most decision makers also respond to budgetary planning cycles that often do not favour a focus on long-term goals (Evans, Rowell and Semazzi, 2020[43]). Climate hazards must therefore be clearly communicated for advances in science to guide decision making (Jack et al., 2021[45]) (see Chapter 2).

Co-production approaches where producers and users of the information work together to translate science into actionable information can also guide policy processes (Vincent et al., 2021[46]). This can also facilitate a focus on local or sector perspectives (Cornforth, Petty and Walker, 2021[47]). Agreed and transparent processes for addressing the preferences and values of current and future generations are also important (Lawrence and Haasnoot, 2017[48]) (see Section 4.4.2). Unprecedented extreme events in 2021, such as the record temperatures over British Columbia, Canada, underline that damaging climate hazards are no longer for the distant future.

Box 4.3. Uncertainty and the use of decision-driven approaches in East Africa

Over Africa, and especially East Africa, future climate projections of precipitation are particularly uncertain. There is limited understanding of the physical processes that control the amount of rainfall during the rainy seasons. Recent drying in East Africa has caused many areas to suffer from droughts and food shortages. These impacts contrast with projections from most climate models of a wetter future. The divergence between projections and reality is referred to as the "East African climate paradox" (Wainwright et al., 2019[49]). The uncertainty in the region affects multiple aspects of society, including food security, water availability for crops and livestock, public health and infrastructure; impacts that are playing out against a broader set of socio-economic risks.

As part of the Future Climate for Africa (FCFA) programme, the HyCRISTAL (Integrating Hydro-Climate Science into Policy Decisions for Climate-Resilient Infrastructure and Livelihoods in East Africa) project has developed three future ***climate storylines*** for East Africa. These capture the diversity in climate projections for the region (Burgin et al., 2019[50]):

- ***Future 1***: Much wetter, large increase in extreme rainfall and hotter.
- ***Future 2***: Increase in extreme rainfall and hotter.
- ***Future 3***: Much hotter and drier with more erratic rainy seasons.

The three climate futures have different implications for food security and livelihoods. The storyline approach to dealing with uncertainty (defined in Box 4.2), can be used to analyse quantitatively key variables affecting yields of key crops. In the context of sweet potato farming in Uganda, for example, this analysis includes total precipitation over the growing season; number of days with temperature between 17°C and 30°C; number of days with temperature above 30°C; monthly average precipitation; and monthly average maximum temperature. By drawing on daily weather data, quantitative climate storylines can be developed, representing the three climate futures and using values as described by Burgin, Rowell and Marsham (2020[51]) (see Table 4.1). These quantitative climate storylines can be inputted to a ***crop network model*** using observed weather data as the baseline.

Table 4.1. Quantitative interpretation of the three climate future storylines for East Africa

	Climate future 1	Climate future 2	Climate future 3
Change in annual temperature (°C)	+ 2	+ 2.5	+ 3.1
Percentage change in precipitation DJFM	+ 17.5	+6.0	+4.0
Percentage change in precipitation AM	+ 27.5	+ 12.0	- 4.0
Percentage change in precipitation JJA	+ 21.0	+ 1.0	- 2.0
Percentage change in precipitation SON	+23.0	+ 2.5	- 8.0

Note: Temperature change is presented as absolute change in degrees Celsius. Precipitation is presented as a percentage change for four distinct periods of the year: December, January, February, March (DJFM); April, May (AM); June, July, August (JJA); September, October, November (SON).
Source: (Burgin et al., 2019[50]).

To simulate the effect of the climate storylines, a model can be developed based on a ***causal inference network.*** This brings together information from different sources, including data, models and expert knowledge to support decision making (Pearl and Mackenzie, 2018[52]). The network summarised in Figure 4.2 sheds light on the links between climatic and non-climatic variables, and how they interact to influence sweet potato crops in Uganda. This information can inform efforts to explore the implications of the different climate storylines in the medium to long term, including for food security, health and nutrition, and the wider economy. As such, causal networks enable relevant climate information to be made meaningful at the local scale. This highlights the benefits of close partnership and dialogue between researchers and local stakeholder communities to improve decision making and outcomes.

Figure 4.2. Causal network of key drivers of sweet potato growth

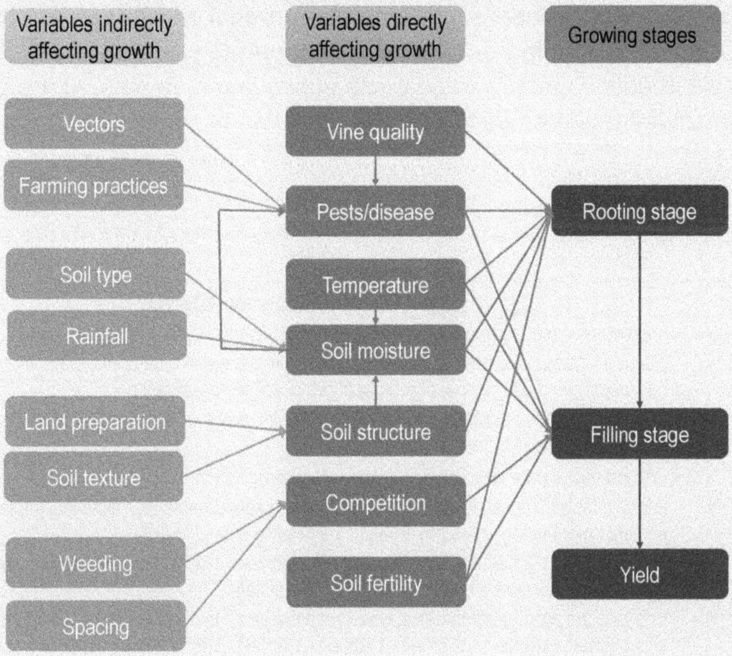

The causal network can inform quantitative analysis focused on a subset of the network for which data and knowledge are available (e.g. temperature, rainfall or the likelihood of pest infestation). To quantify the interactions between the variables, the network can be parameterised as a ***Bayesian Belief Network*** (BBN) [see (Fenton and Neil, 2012[53])]. Within a BBN, the possible states of each node are defined. For example, the amount of rainfall could be categorised as "high", "medium" or "low", with ranges defined for these categories. Conditional probability tables are then produced for each node. These describe the probability of each state of the node occurring, conditional on the values of the parent node. For example, the probability of high soil water content at planting depends on the amount of rainfall in the two weeks prior to planting. The causal structure of the network allows these key interactions to be identified.

The analysis has to be taken a step further to understand how changes to crop yields and prices impact livelihoods. Considerations include the local context; the range of crops grown and their likely response to different climate change scenarios; the relative importance of different crops to different wealth groups within the community; and the various coping strategies these groups can access. The ***Household Economy Approach*** (HEA), widely used by African governments for vulnerability assessments, draws on detailed social and economic data to simulate the impact of yield and price changes on household income and food security (Seaman et al., 2014[54]; Acidri et al., 2018[55]). The ***Integrated Database and Applications for Policymakers*** platform enables storage and analysis of HEA data and provides a platform to link to different models driving impact scenarios (Cornforth, Clegg and Petty, 2021[56]).

A decision-centric framework based on the principles of ***Dynamic Adaptive Policy Pathways*** (DAPP) (see Box 4.2) can be used to select appropriate policy action today in the face of an uncertain future. Here, the policy objective is to prevent an increase in crop failure under the three alternative climate storylines, informed by key intervention points. While this process may be informed by different technical approaches, reliance on local knowledge and practice is central.

When the methodology described above is applied to assess the impact of climate change on sweet potato farming in Uganda it shows that projected crop yields are less vulnerable to rainfall extremes than previously thought. Efforts to control pest infestations (e.g. the sweet potato weevil, *Cylas formicarius*) could offset even the most severe anticipated climate impact. This has implications for the relative emphasis placed on different crops in a changing climate. Unlike engineering or infrastructure options, changes to agricultural policy interventions will likely be gradual responses to changes in the climate. Mechanisms are needed that enable farmers to better respond to climate stresses through, for example, investment in small-scale irrigation and provision of clean planting materials. At the same time, investment should continue in agricultural research into improved varieties of sweet potato (see other policy options summarised in Table 4.2).

Table 4.2. Options for policy action and intervention for sweet potato farming in Uganda

	Policy action and interventions
Local-level interventions	• Improve pest management by provision of clean (weevil-free) planting material. • Reduce water stress: small-scale irrigation, improved system for capture and storage of rainwater (rainwater harvesting), and use of cover crops to improve soil water retention. • Introduce drought-resistant crop varieties or switch crops entirely – such as intensifying sweet potato production in place of maize.
National-level policy actions and interventions	• Provide budgets for large-scale pest reduction/eradication. • Improve farmer access to new scientific knowledge and enhanced technical support to optimise planting dates and take more timely decisions to build their resilience. • Invest in basic agricultural infrastructure and services, including allocating ongoing budget to support agricultural extension – both training and maintaining. • Enhance the agro-meteorological observation network to support localised climate information services for agriculture to provide a full range of advice regarding climate and its impacts on crops. • Long-term investment in agricultural research, developing new crop varieties that will be better suited to the range of climate futures. • Investment in tracking long-term changes at a household level through decentralising data collection and building local capacity to conduct Household Economy Assessments.
Global-level policy actions	• Reduce global emissions of greenhouse gases. • Provide finance, support the development of technical expertise and invest in national-scale networks to provide quantitative information on the social and economic impacts of agricultural infrastructure investments, governance change, local financing arrangements against the backdrop of climate and environmental change. These require global-level commitments and often levels of investment beyond the capability of national governments in developing countries.

4.3. Addressing the urgent challenge of losses and damages

Reducing and managing the risks of losses and damages from climate change requires enhanced focus on the three components of climate risks (i.e. hazard, exposure and vulnerability), the drivers that bring about changes in those components and their interactions, as conceptualised in the Intergovernmental Panel on Climate Change (IPCC) (see Chapter 1). Hazards are the result of the heating effect of previous greenhouse gas (GHG) emissions with complicated influences on regional weather and climate from other pollutants, such as aerosols. Levels of exposure and vulnerability at local, national and regional levels to these different hazards have been shaped by historical, geographical, social, political, cultural and economic circumstances.

However, countries cannot reduce or manage to all risks, whether due to financial, technical or physical constraints resulting in losses and damages (see Chapter 1, Box 1.2). In the face of often devastating or repeated losses and damages, the importance of complementing climate change adaptation with efforts to reduce disaster risks and otherwise limit the creation of hazards and strengthen the resilience of systems has risen on the international agenda (OECD, 2020[57]). A focus on the components of climate risks can be explicit or implicit. An explicit focus, for example, could examine land-use management, agricultural practices and infrastructure standards. An implicit focus might look at livelihoods development, social protection or basic health. Whether explicit or implicit, such a focus may occur *ex ante* or *ex post*. An *ex ante* focus could pro-actively reduce the creation of the hazard or to lessen exposure and vulnerability. An *ex post* focus could lessen the impact of hazards, including emergency relief and longer-term reconstruction to reduce future vulnerability.

Given the pace and extent of climate change, rapid and in some cases transformative changes (Fedele et al., 2019[58]) may be needed, rather than incremental improvements in resilience. Such a transformative approach could aim at fundamentally altering the relationships between the hazard and one or both of the other two components of climate risk. For example, an incremental change – often through technical improvements – could achieve a marginal reduction in exposures or vulnerability. Conversely, in a more transformative response to exposure, a community could be relocated in response to SLR and coastal flood risks (see Section 4.3.3 for other examples). Similarly, large-scale policy interventions targeting pre-existing health or financial inequalities could transform the geography of vulnerability to certain hazards. Given the scale, novelty and frequency of climate-related hazards now and increasingly in future decades, societies will either have to deliberately transform themselves or face unplanned transformation into potentially unfavourable states (Levin et al., 2021[59]).

This section examines the role of policy in addressing each of the three components of climate risk, while Section 4.4 examines the role of policy, governance systems and institutions. The role of finance in reducing and managing risks is discussed in Chapter 5.

4.3.1. Mitigating the climate hazards

The IPCC risk framework emphasises the mitigation of GHG emissions as a central priority to reduce the magnitude of climate hazards. Success in limiting the average global temperature increase is determined by the ability of the international community to achieve timely "net-zero global anthropogenic carbon dioxide (CO_2) emissions and declining net non-CO_2 radiative forcing" (IPCC, 2018[60]). Hence, Article 4 of the Paris Agreement calls for Parties to rapidly reduce emissions "to achieve a balance between anthropogenic emissions by sources and removals by sinks of greenhouse gases in the second half of this century" (UNFCCC, 2015[61]).

In the case of CO_2, such a balance can be achieved through natural "carbon sinks" such as forests and peatland. However, they do not guarantee permanent sequestration of CO_2 in the same way as technologies such as carbon capture and storage. Still, they can simultaneously offer other ecosystem benefits, such as reduced vulnerability of downstream river catchments to flood hazards. Action to reduce CO_2 emissions will also reduce emissions of other pollutants (e.g. methane, nitrous oxide and black carbon) that contribute to climate change. At the same time, additional non-CO_2 mitigation measures (e.g. in agriculture and waste treatment) could help reduce the pace of climate change and limit global average surface temperatures in the short term. These measures could also provide immediate air quality benefits (IPCC, 2018[60]; Harmsen et al., 2019[62]).

Net-zero commitments

Net-zero commitments vary in terms of the definition used; the timeframe; target; status; scope of GHG emissions and sectors covered; as well as governance mechanisms and institutional arrangements adopted. Moreover, many details are currently unclear, especially how countries plan to meet their net-zero commitments, the relative focus on emissions reductions, removals or use of international carbon markets; and the underlying assumptions (e.g. future technologies for direct air capture and land availability) (Jeudy-Hugo, Lo Re and Falduto, 2021[63]).

A survey published in March 2020 found that 124 countries, representing 61% of global emissions, had net-zero commitments in place. Around 40% of these commitments focus on CO_2 emissions, a slightly larger share target all greenhouse gases, with the remaining 14% not specifying which gases are covered (Black et al., 2021[64]). The survey also noted that national commitments are increasingly complemented by commitments put forward by subnational governments and the private sector. Over one-fifth of public companies surveyed in 2020 have net-zero commitments (Black et al., 2021[64]). Of these, only around 20% meet the robustness criteria defined or informed by the UN Race to Zero Campaign (pledge, plan, proceed, publish).

National circumstances will determine countries' net-zero pathways. These circumstances include levels of economic development, resource endowments, and the drivers of emissions by sector or activity. Equally important is the extent to which their emissions reduction pathways focus on reducing demand, as well as decarbonisation of key technologies and infrastructures (OECD, 2017[65]). Some pathways risk not being realised. This includes pathways that exhibit continued growth in CO_2 emissions in the next decade or beyond. They also assume availability and extensive use of carbon dioxide removal (CDR) technologies later in the century. The risk for such pathways is particularly high since most CDR technologies are still at the early stages of development, which contributes to high uncertainties for policy makers.

All sectors will require rapid, far-reaching and unprecedented transitions with deep emissions reductions (IPCC, 2018[60]), but potential for decarbonisation varies. Agriculture and forestry sectors, for example, have more potential for decarbonisation than aviation and heavy industries (Rogelj et al., 2021[66]; OECD, 2017[65]). For the energy sector to achieve net-zero emissions by 2050, two policy shifts are required. First, all new oil, methane gas and coal exploration projects will have to be stopped. Second, gas must be precluded as a "bridge fuel" in the energy transition (IEA, 2021[67]). This sends an important message to policy makers and investors of the inevitable and urgent need to manage the decline of energy based on fossil fuel.

Some of these fossil fuel investments are underpinned by both direct and indirect support. Direct support comes through budgetary aid in financing fossil fuel projects. Meanwhile, fossil fuel subsidies and preferential tax provisions indirectly support fossil fuel production (OECD/IEA, 2021[68]). Support in 2019 for fossil fuel production rose by 30%, primarily recorded in OECD countries (OECD/IEA, 2021[68]). International public finance is also supporting financing for gas expansion in the Global South, which could mean continued operations for several decades (Muttitt et al., 2021[69]). In September 2021, China announced that it will end financing of all overseas coal projects.

Managing trade-offs and synergies with sustainable development

National policies announced or implemented to date fall far short of what is needed to achieve net-zero targets. Policy makers face difficult choices to determine future mitigation pathways. Each choice has implementation challenges, potential synergies and trade-offs with broader sustainable development objectives (IPCC, 2018[60]). The trade-offs, however, are comparatively lower for pathways relying on low-energy demand, low material consumption, and low GHG-intensive food consumption (IPCC, 2018[60]). How policy makers approach these challenging goals will have critically important implications for sustainable development and well-being outcomes, as well as implications for the other two risk components (exposure and vulnerability). As countries seek to recover from the economic aftermath of the COVID-19 pandemic, such pathways also hold greater potential to deliver synergies between climate mitigation and broader sustainable development (or well-being) objectives (Buckle et al., 2020[70]).

The deep transformations required to achieve net-zero globally will be facilitated through fair and inclusive processes for addressing structural change. Such processes must leave no one behind, whether segments of society or across countries (IPCC, 2018[60]). Co-ordinated support in the form of financial or technological know-how will be important for many developing countries. This will allow climate mitigation to be an integral part of development rather than at the expense of it. For example, in the energy sector, developing countries will need to continue to meet the energy needs of growing populations, while reducing emissions. Through international co-operation, the development and implementation of international standards and innovation, countries can pursue these twin objectives in a sustainable manner (IEA, 2021[67]).

Transition strategies that integrate climate mitigation and wider well-being goals will help identify and address trade-offs and enhance synergies between them. This will enhance the benefits and feasibility of mitigation action, making it easier for the population to choose sustainable options (OECD, 2021[71]). At the domestic level, targeted support may still be required for segments of the population directly affected by the transition. These groups may either face loss of employment or higher prices for energy and food (Soergel et al., 2021[72]). Fossil fuel subsidies for production and consumption could be reformed to free up fiscal resources, allowing redistribution of national carbon pricing revenues to these vulnerable groups.

Developed countries carry the primary responsibility to lead the net-zero transition. International climate finance linked to projects that reduce GHG emissions can help accelerate mitigation in developing countries while supporting development. Moreover, targeted finance in large-emitting developing countries can help reduce the risks of losses and damages for all developing countries by lowering the level of hazard. To achieve this outcome, however, emissions must not increase in response to lower hazards, either in the recipient country or elsewhere.

4.3.2. Minimising exposure to weather and climate hazards

Apart from mitigating climate hazards, the IPCC risk framework aims to reduce exposure of lives, livelihoods, economic activities and assets to weather and climate hazards. LDCs, SIDS, and Arctic ecosystems, high mountains and dryland regions are disproportionately exposed to climate variability and change due to their geographic locations and physical characteristics (IPCC, 2018[60]; IPCC, 2019[73]). Exposure is further determined by factors such as demographic change, urbanisation, natural resource management, the availability of livelihoods options and governance arrangements (IPCC, 2012[74]; Duvat et al., 2017[75]). With economic development, people and assets become concentrated in urban centres. As the climate changes, societies might also become exposed to hazards they have not previously faced and to which they might therefore be more vulnerable. For example, climatic changes may extend the range of disease vectors such as mosquitos.

In some countries, increases in exposure may also be correlated with increased vulnerability (see below). This can occur when rapidly growing informal settlements challenge the capacity of local governments both to provide essential services and enforce land-use management regulations (Sudmeier-Rieux et al., 2015[76]). Urban growth may also lead to an expansion of developments into areas that offer a certain lifestyle (e.g. forests, coasts) but also higher exposure to hazards (OECD, 2021[77]).

Climate change itself will alter the intensity, spatial and temporal occurrence of hazards, transcending the range of historic experience in a given location. Such extremes are occurring now, affecting people that may not have considered themselves exposed to such hazards in the past. This was illustrated by the 2021 heatwave over North America. The maximum temperature in Lytton, British Columbia, Canada, was 49.6°C on 29 June, exceeded the previous temperature record by 4.6°C. Similarly, in June 2020, record-breaking temperatures up to 38°C in the Siberian town of Verkhoyansk, caused wide-scale impacts, including wildfires, loss of permafrost and an invasion of pests. Some areas of Siberia exceeded monthly averages by more than 10°C above the 1981-2010 average.

The relative contribution of climate change and other factors in driving exposure varies across contexts and hazards. Both current and future exposure of assets to coastal flooding, for example, are not primarily due to SLR. Rather, rapid urbanisation strains infrastructure and introduces environmental and socio-economic problems (Hinkel et al., 2014[78]; Mason et al., 2020[79]). In comparison, climate change itself is projected to be a stronger determinant of future exposure to heatwaves than demographic change (Jones et al., 2018[80]). Early warning systems (EWS) have played an important role in reducing the exposure of lives (see Box 4.4). However, this does not always reduce vulnerability of livelihoods and assets.

Box 4.4. Bangladesh: Complementing efforts to reduce exposure and vulnerability to hazards

Due to its location, topography and multiple river systems, Bangladesh is exposed to numerous weather hazards, including cyclones, heavy rainfall, floods and drought (Haque et al., 2018[81]; Shakhawat Hossain et al., 2020[82]). Its vulnerability is furthered by high population density and multidimensional poverty. Between 1991 and 2011, it experienced 247 extreme events with an average annual death toll of 824 and financial losses of 1.18% of gross domestic product (GDP) (Nishat et al., 2013[83]). Financial losses went as high as 6% of GDP for some individual events (Haque et al., 2018[81]).

In response, the government has enacted laws, policies and procedures to reduce exposure to such hazards (Haque et al., 2018[81]; Kumar, Lal and Kumar, 2021[84]). This has included a shift in emphasis from disaster relief and recovery to early warning and evacuation, and construction of multi-purpose cyclone shelters. Nature-based solutions, such as planting mangroves and restoring sand dunes, have also lessened the impact of hazards on coastal communities (Rahaman et al., 2020[85]).

In 2018, the government introduced the Bangladesh Delta Plan 2100 that takes an adaptive decision-making approach (see Box 4.2) where policy priorities are adjusted as hazards change. For example, emphasis may shift from improving embankments to building safer ones (Pakulski et al., 2021[86]). This shift in policy has been effective in protecting lives. During Super-cyclone Amphan that hit the Bay of Bengal in May 2020, early warning and evacuation systems led to evacuation of up to 2.5 million people to shelters, limiting the death toll in Bangladesh to 12 (Kumar, Lal and Kumar, 2021[84]; IDMC, 2021[87]).

Nevertheless, Amphan destroyed 150 kilometres of embankments, which led to flooding of infrastructures, agricultural lands and fields that remained inundated for months (IDMC, 2021[87]). Many displaced people could not access evacuation centres and had to shelter in tents or on open embankments (WMO, 2021[88]). While most evacuated people could return home relatively quickly, about 10% were left homeless (UN, 2020[89]; Kumar, Lal and Kumar, 2021[84]). In a survey seven months after the cyclone, respondents said they had reduced their food intake and medical expenses. Nearly 70% had resorted to begging, borrowing or selling household assets (IDMC, 2021[87]).

Amphan is not an isolated case; Cyclone Sidr in 2008, Isla in 2009, and Fani and Bulbul in 2019 all struck the same areas (IDMC, 2021[87]). The impact on livelihoods is expected to worsen as climate change increases. Sea-level rise (SLR) and saline intrusion will gradually contaminate soils and groundwater, adversely affecting agriculture, a main source of livelihood income for the rural population (Khan et al., 2021[90]; Shakhawat Hossain et al., 2020[82]; Clarke et al., 2018[91]). By 2080, 18% of Bangladesh's coastland is projected to be inundated (Khan et al., 2021[90]). Adapting cultivation practices may not be enough (Chen and Mueller, 2018[92]). Extreme floods, cyclones, drought and heat stress could cut yields for rice, wheat and potato by over two-thirds of current levels and in some cases threaten food security (ADB, 2014[93]).

Reduced exposure to hazards must therefore be complemented by reduced vulnerability to the hazards. Sectoral and short- and long-term development policies have focused on this dual approach. In addition, Bangladesh could further protect at-risk populations by strengthening coherence with climate change adaptation (Shamsuddoha et al., 2013[94]; Islam, Chu and Smart, 2020[95]). In 2019, the government initiated a two-year pilot programme to develop a national mechanism on loss and damage. It seeks to i) firmly embed climate change perspectives within policy approaches on disaster risk reduction; ii) address gaps in policy frameworks on climate change adaptation and disaster risk reduction; and iii) design a comprehensive system for a stronger response to losses and damages from climate impacts (Haque et al., 2018[81]).

Following a disaster, decision makers must determine how to respond amid expectations that such events are opportunities for building back or forward better. Experience seems to suggest that the public directly affected by a disaster will often favour policies focused on "building back the same" (Frank, Gesick and Victor, 2021[96]). For people in power, it can be politically difficult to relocate people who have lost everything due to an extreme event. Instead, they are more likely to promise a safe and swift return to previous ways of living. In response to a hurricane, assessments of future risks of similar magnitude at the same location may be sufficiently low to rebuild damaged assets. However, increasing hazards will gradually make this approach less sensible; incentives to reduce future exposure will be urgently needed (Frank, Gesick and Victor, 2021[96]). In other cases, working with nature to reduce and manage climate risks may be an alternative or complementary approach (see Box 4.5).

Approaches to reduce and manage the risks of losses and damages can indirectly contribute to enhanced exposure. Two commonly cited examples illustrate this issue well. First, flood protection measures to reduce vulnerability can indirectly encourage developments on floodplains, increasing exposure. Research from Bangladesh, for example, finds that flood death rates associated with the 2017 flooding were lower in areas with lower protection level (Ferdous et al., 2020[97]). Second, insurance mechanisms play an important role in facilitating the transfer of risks (see Chapter 5). However, in the absence of broader risk management approaches, these mechanisms can unintentionally encourage investments in activities or locations at risk to current or future climatic hazards (Schäfer, Warner and Kreft, 2018[98]; Surminski and Oramas-Dorta, 2013[99]). This does not reduce the potential value of either measure. Rather, it highlights the importance of complementing risk management measures with incentives for economic actors to reduce their exposure to risks and take additional measures to reduce their vulnerability.

Tools to limit exposure to hazards

Decision makers have different tools and mechanisms that can help minimise exposure. The role of EWS in reducing the exposure of people to forecasted hazards has received a lot of political attention in recent years. The Sendai Framework for Disaster Risk Reduction, for example, emphasises multi-hazard EWS (UNDRR, 2015[100]). Despite this recognition for EWS, almost 90% of LDCs and SIDS identify EWS as top priority in their Nationally Determined Contributions to the United Nations Framework Convention on Climate Change (UNFCCC) (WMO, 2020[101]). This focus on EWS points to a potential policy or financing gap. EWS empower individuals and communities to take preventive measures in a timely manner. It has been estimated that they can save assets worth at least ten times their cost. Meanwhile, a 24-hour warning of a storm or heatwave can reduce damages by 30% (GCA, 2019[102]).

EWS also can be effective in communicating the risks and engaging local communities in generating early warning information (UNFCCC, 2020[103]). The overall effectiveness of EWS, however, depends on the capacity of individual stakeholders, as well as the broader national, regional and international systems. When key capacities are lacking or there are gaps in the EWS, the losses can be disastrous. In 2008, a system to forecast tropical cyclones was in place in the North Indian Ocean. However, the Indian Meteorological Department designated to issue official tropical cyclone forecasts and warning did not have a mandate to provide storm-surge forecasts. When Cyclone Nargis hit Myanmar, the death toll exceeded well above 100 000. Over 80% of deaths were related to the storm surge that washed away more than 100 villages (Webster, 2008[104]).

Regional and international mechanisms facilitate exchange of information. This can include, for example, information related to management of cross-border flood risk in river basins or of climate risks across shared terrains or landscapes such as mountainous areas. Regional and international mechanisms can also contribute to enhanced accuracy of the warnings. However, such mechanisms rarely have authority to trigger action (UNDP, 2019[105]). EWS are increasingly also used in the context of disaster risk financing as illustrated by their application in forecast-based financing, discussed in Chapter 5.

Box 4.5. Working with nature to reduce climate risks

Nature-based solutions (NbS) are measures to "protect, sustainably manage or restore nature, with the goal of maintaining or enhancing ecosystem services to address a variety of social, environmental and economic challenges" (OECD, 2020[106]). NbS can help reduce and manage the exposure and vulnerability of lives and livelihoods to climate risks. Protecting and restoring mangroves, seagrass beds and salt marshes, for example, can increase resilience to a range of climate change impacts, such as coastal erosion and flooding due to sea-level rise (SLR) (see Section 4.5). In urban areas, green infrastructure, such as urban forests, can reduce vulnerability to flooding from extreme rainfall events and exposure to heat stress (Seddon et al., 2020[107]).

A long-term perspective is needed for NbS given the time lag between implementation and materialisation of benefits. A 1992 storm caused significant flooding to South Seaside Park in New York. Recovery measures included a focus on building dunes with simple snow fence barriers to catch sand and native grasses to hold them in place (NRC, n.d.[108]). When Hurricane Sandy hit the same area in 2012, the dunes had become 7.5 metres high and 45 metres wide, large enough to reduce vulnerability from the impacts of the storm that devastated neighbouring coastal communities (Smallegan et al., 2016[109]). The success of the NbS projects led Congress to approve allocation of between one-third and one-half of Hurricane Sandy recovery funds to NbS focused on habitat restoration, green infrastructure and community resilience planning (FWS, 2019[110]).

NbS also have potential to mitigate greenhouse gas emissions, with recent estimates suggesting a rate of 10 gigatonnes of CO_2 per year,[1] greater than emissions in the global transportation sector (Griscom et al., 2017[111]). To achieve this potential, scaled-up action is needed to stop the destruction of ecosystems worldwide (Girardin et al., 2021[112]). Despite this potential, there are growing concerns that a focus on the mitigation potential of NbS risks delaying decarbonisation efforts since it enables corporations in particular to claim carbon neutrality without actually cutting emissions (Seddon et al., 2020[107]). The permanence of sequestration in ecosystems is also a concern.

NbS can also have potentially adverse impacts if poorly planned and implemented. Tree planting on natural grasslands and peatlands can disrupt biological and biogeochemical processes. This can reduce soil quality and the ecosystem's ability to store carbon, negatively affecting grassland biodiversity (Friggens et al., 2020[113]). In Cambodia, a large-scale reforestation project for mitigation led to clearing diverse forest landscapes for acacia monocultures, displacing customary land users from access to land and forest resources (Scheidel and Work, 2018[114]). Harvesting and clearing plantations also release stored CO_2 back into the atmosphere every 10-20 years, whereas natural forests continue to sequester carbon for decades (Lewis et al., 2019[115]). The IUCN Global Standard for Nature-based Solutions aims to address the potential adverse impacts of NbS by providing parameters for defining NbS and a common framework for benchmarking progress.

The potential of NbS to help manage climate risks can also be uncertain. Ecosystems change over time, partly in response to pressures (e.g. climate change, pollution, invasive species, habitat loss, over exploitation) that affect their structure and function. This could have significant effects on their projected climate and biodiversity benefits. For example, peatlands that provide valuable ecosystem services through flood management are sensitive to climate change (Shuttleworth et al., 2019[116]).

A focus on risk sensitive land-use planning can also help address increased exposure to weather and climate hazards brought about by development, especially rapid urbanisation. Land management regulations can create both incentives and disincentives in guiding public and private investments. Risk sensitive land-use planning highlights the importance of public policies and institutions in managing the expansion of investments and settlements into areas exposed to hazards (Sudmeier-Rieux et al., 2015[76]).

Similar to EWS, preventive or *ex ante* efforts try to identify and address the drivers of exposure to reduce losses and damages. This may be complemented with targeted support to people and communities temporarily or permanently displaced by weather and climate hazards, or worse, who may need resettlement. In Nepal, for example, risk sensitive land-use planning approaches have contributed to significant growth in the generation of hazard, exposure and vulnerability data. These are essential for understanding the risks and developing complementary land-use plans to reduce and manage those risks (Hada, Shaw and Pokhrel, 2021[117]).

4.3.3. Reducing vulnerabilities to weather and climate hazards

The third component of the IPCC risk framework highlights the importance of reducing the underlying vulnerabilities of human and natural systems to weather and climate hazards. The exposure to hazards takes place in complex social, political and technical contexts within and across countries. Many LDCs, for example, rely primarily on natural resources for their domestic income. Large shares of the population are engaged in outdoor work. In some cases, they have limited financial capacity to adapt to a changing climate and to recover from climate-related hazards (Woetzel et al., 2020[118]).

Within countries, vulnerability is shaped by position in society and the ability to contribute to decision-making processes. Such processes include those that determine access to resources, assets and forms of social protection (Thomas et al., 2018[119]). Groups marginalised by, for example, their gender, race, age, disability, income, class identities, religion or geographic locations are particularly at risk (Eriksen et al., 2021[120]; Winsemius et al., 2015[121]). These contexts determine the ability of different segments of society to access resources that enable them to prepare for and recover from hazards. The resources, both tangible and intangible, include income, time, data and information, awareness and ability to access available resources, among others (Thomas et al., 2018[119]).

Climate vulnerability assessments aim to shed light on who or what is vulnerable to the impacts of climate change. They often focus on the vulnerability of infrastructure (e.g. transport and residential dwellings) and means of survival, and health (e.g. food supply and water). Less emphasis tends to be placed on understanding what determines those vulnerabilities. Issues such as poverty or lack of capacity are highlighted as potential drivers without necessarily being explored in sufficient depth (Ribot, 2014[122]). To address this challenge in the context of broader development, many African governments use the Household Economy Approach (HEA). The HEA aims to shed light on the drivers of vulnerability to poverty and food security (Seaman et al., 2014[54]; Acidri et al., 2018[55]) (as also mentioned in Box 4.3).

The economic, institutional and political drivers of vulnerability

Given the nature of vulnerability, it is important for policy makers to consider the impact of climate change on more intangible factors critical to maintaining social groups and networks. These factors range from social systems and informal networks to cultural knowledge and practices of daily life. The drivers of vulnerability have been categorised into three types of capacities – economic, institutional and political – each requiring tailored approaches (Thomas et al., 2018[119]).

Economic capacity encompasses income diversity and the ability to move between livelihoods or approaches within them. It can determine the impact of a shock on overall household wealth and well-being (Ahmed et al., 2019[123]). Marginalised segments of the population often live in areas more exposed to hazards. In the event of a disaster, then, the share of wealth lost by these segments tends to be relatively larger than for the rest of the population (Hallegatte et al., 2016[124]). In the absence of income diversity, savings or other sources of finance (e.g. insurance or social protection), marginalised households may resort to negative coping mechanisms. However, actions like taking children out of school, cutting consumption or selling productive assets could create poverty traps (Bowen et al., 2020[125]). Others may choose to migrate pre-emptively as an adaptation strategy or in response to climate impacts (see Box 4.6).

Box 4.6. Sea-level rise and migration

Increasingly, people around the world are feeling the impacts of climate change, and this will only grow stronger. In some cases, people will adapt to the impacts through migration; in others, they may be involuntarily displaced. Growing academic and policy interest in the linkages between climate change and human mobility is contributing to a more nuanced understanding of linkages between the two. While some research points towards increased human mobility due to climate change, others suggest vulnerable segments of the population could become less mobile in the face of growing hazards due to political and institutional constraints, lack of means or opportunities, among others (Black et al., 2013[126]). Yet others will be reluctant to migrate due to strong economic, cultural or social ties to a place (McLeman et al., 2021[127]). A focus on the impact of sea-level rise (SLR) on migration can shed light on the multitude of factors influencing these processes.

A large share of the global population resides in coastal areas where SLR will adversely affect well-being (McLeman, 2017[128]). SLR is projected to force millions of people inland if coasts are not protected (Lincke and Hinkel, 2021[129]), which in turn could trigger migration over further distances. Most estimates of global SLR this century fall below 2 metres (see Box 3.2). However, definitions of populations exposed to SLR differ. They include populations living in i) low-elevation coastal zones; ii) 100-year floodplains; or iii) areas that would be inundated under selected SLR scenarios (Hauer et al., 2019[130]). Around 190 million people occupy land below the projected high tide lines for 2100 under a low emissions scenario. This number increases to 630 million people by 2100 under a high emission scenario[1] (Kulp and Strauss, 2019[131]). The number of people exposed to SLR, however, is not the same as the number that will respond to SLR through migration. This is mainly because millions of people are protected against extreme sea levels and SLR. Still, as the climate continues to change, migration is likely to become more widespread (Oppenheimer et al., 2019[132]).

Migration is generally only one outcome that households and communities may choose in response to climate change (McLeman et al., 2021[127]). Similarly, climate change will only be one of a diverse set of factors contributing to decisions to migrate (Hauer et al., 2019[130]). The slow rate of change in SLR, in principle, provides people considerable time to put in place adaptation measures, in addition to efforts to limit SLR through mitigation (McLeman, 2017[128]). The triggering of tipping elements of the Earth system (see Chapter 3) could contribute to non-linear changes in ecological systems and a rapid acceleration of SLR later in the century. Migration patterns would be likely to respond in an equally non-linear fashion (McLeman, 2017[128]).

Although migration in response to SLR could have positive outcomes, it is generally perceived as disruptive to households, and in some cases community well-being as well. A decision to migrate therefore tends to happen in response to broader individual or household contexts. These include changes in assets, food security, or access to formal or informal support (McLeman et al., 2021[127]). Migration can anticipate adverse impacts of SLR or respond to them. Decisions made with greater agency are believed to have greater potential to generate positive outcomes in reducing vulnerability and building adaptive capacity. At the same time, urbanisation, as well as environmental resources and amenities provided by coastal areas, supports coastal developments and encourages migration towards coastal areas (Hauer et al., 2019[130]).

Note:[1] The low emissions scenario is consistent with the IPCC Representative Concentration Pathways (RCPs) 2.6; the high emission scenarios reflects RCP 8.5.

Peoples' vulnerabilities and lack of ***institutional capacities*** can transform hazards into disasters. When Hurricane Katrina hit the western coast of the United States in 2005, it struck an economically disadvantaged region recognised for significant and persistent multidimensional inequality. According to some analyses, the region's status stemmed from discriminatory policies and institutional practices towards Black communities over many years. These policies and practices affected labour markets, housing and mortgages, among others (Henkel, Dovidio and Gaertner, 2006[133]). At the time of Hurricane Katrina, the per capita and median household incomes of Alabama, Louisiana and Mississippi, the states most directly affected by the hurricane, were below the national average. Meanwhile, the share of the population in these states living in poverty was above average (Zottarelli, 2008[134]).

Economic marginalisation and discriminatory policies and practices were mutually reinforcing. The two drivers together meant the exposed population lacked the capacity or resources to take pre-emptive measures to adequately prepare for Katrina. Similarly, it was unable to take protective measures in response, such as by securing safe housing or relocating (Thomas et al., 2018[119]). These vulnerabilities were played out in the context of the built environment. Poorer segments of the population were more likely to settle in cheaper and less desirable coastal locations disproportionally exposed to weather and climate hazards. In terms of recovery, they were also relatively uninsured against floods (Henkel, Dovidio and Gaertner, 2006[133]).

Political capacity in the form of, for example, active participation in decision-making processes plays an important role in determining access to resources, policy approaches and decisions. Adaptation initiatives seek to strengthen the resilience of communities to the impacts of climate change. However, a review of adaptation-related development finance found they often failed to address the underlying drivers of individual or community vulnerabilities (Eriksen et al., 2021[120]). In some cases, adaptation finance inadvertently reinforced, redistributed or created new sources of vulnerability. Priorities determined by local elites, for example, can feed into existing power dynamics and reinforce inequalities. Alternatively, if not carefully managed, a hazard in one community can simply be transferred to different stakeholders (e.g. in the context of water or coastal infrastructure) (Eriksen et al., 2021[120]). Similarly, relocating people or communities can adversely affect social cohesion and sense of place. Decisions to adopt new agricultural practices to sustain production can similarly affect cultural values (Adger et al., 2012[135]).

This discussion highlights the importance of carefully grounding approaches to reduce and manage the risks of losses and damages from climate change in the context of an individual country or community. This process must be guided by a good understanding of the drivers that determine the level of economic, institutional and political capacity. This may not always be through climate-related initiatives. Instead, it could embrace approaches that foster broader sustainable developments, such as education, health or economic development.

Further, local knowledge of the risks and approaches to manage them must guide processes. Local actors, including Indigenous groups, have detailed knowledge on weather and climate hazards, the socio-economic context and local experiences of managing past weather- or climate-related events (ILO, 2017[136]). The UNFCCC recognises the role of Indigenous and local groups in the management of climate risks. The Local Communities and Indigenous Peoples Platform aims to facilitate exchange of experiences of different knowledge systems on climate action. It also seeks to enhance engagement of local communities and Indigenous peoples in the climate process (UNFCCC, n.d.[137]). The Africa Adaptation Initiative and the Least Developed Countries Initiative for Effective Adaptation and Resilience (see Box 4.7) are examples of processes owned and led by such groups at the regional level.

Box 4.7. Ownership and leadership of climate initiatives

Africa Adaptation Initiative (AAI)

AAI, an initiative of the African Union, was launched by African Heads of State at COP21 with three goals. First, it seeks to accelerate efforts to adapt to the adverse impacts of climate change. Second, it aims to strengthen collaboration on adaptation across the continent. Third, it works to galvanise support needed to significantly scale up adaptation efforts.

AAI takes a strategic view by identifying adaptation gaps and connecting regional partners, public and private. In this way, it aims to identify, refine and prioritise activities aligned with the four AAI pillars: i) enhancing climate information services; ii) strengthening policies and institutions; iii) enhancing on the ground action; and iv) climate finance and investments.

Nine guiding principles inform AAI initiatives: i) be stakeholder-driven; ii) be relevant to Africa; iii) build and strengthen new partnerships; iv) support African countries to engage with processes under the UNFCCC; v) promote regional and transboundary co-operation; vi) develop work packages in line with immediate, short, medium and long-term adaptation needs; vii) enhance communication; viii) employ a phased approach; and ix) promote transparency.

The Least Developed Countries (LDCs) Initiative for Effective Adaptation and Resilience (LIFE-AR)

LIFE-AR, led and owned by LDCs, was established in 2018 to develop a long-term vision for delivering a climate-resilient future in LDCs. The LDC Vision is for "LDCs to be on climate resilient development pathways by 2030 and deliver net-zero emissions by 2050 to ensure our societies and ecosystems thrive." LIFE-AR emerged from three beliefs: i) business-as-usual approaches to climate change are not working; ii) the adaptation and local level financing gap in developing countries is wide; and iii) short-term, project-based and sectoral-specific climate responses have limited impact. As such, it seeks to address these challenges and deliver the LDC Vision through long term, multi-sectoral, country led approaches that build country systems, knowledge, and capabilities, with access to predictable and reliable finance – domestic, international, public and private – that reaches the local level.

LIFE-AR is guided by the principles of inclusion, participation, local action, justice, equity and leaving no one behind. LDC governments have made a number of commitments that have been complemented by a set of asks by those governments to the international community as summarised in Table 4.3.

Table 4.3. Commitments and asks of LIFE-AR

Commitments by LDC governments	Ask of the international community
Will work with the whole of society to achieve a low-carbon, climate-resilient future	Provide high-quality, predictable and accessible finance to help LDCs deliver the SDGs and Paris Agreement. Support the LDCs' intention of at least 70% of financial flows supporting local-level action by 2030.
Will develop strong climate finance architecture, with at least 70% of flows supporting local-level action by 2030	Work together to reduce transaction costs and ensure mutual accountability behind LDC leadership.
Will integrate adaptation, mitigation and resilience into national and local development objectives	Work with LDCs in the long term to strengthen national and local institutional capabilities.
Will strengthen climate capabilities, institutions, knowledge, skills and learning	Invest in LDCs' climate-resilient net-zero economies and technology.
Will create more inclusive governance of climate decisions that are centred on gender transformation and social justice	Develop ambitious strategies (in developed countries) for 1.5°C low-carbon climate-resilient pathways by 2020.

Source: https://africaadaptationinitiative.org/; (LIFE-AR, 2019[138])

Gradual vs. transformative change

Actors are addressing their vulnerability in response to growing impacts from climate change. In most cases, this entails gradual adjustments to current practices. At the national level, examples include changes to land-use management, infrastructure development or sectoral strategies. At the individual or household level, livelihood choices can reduce vulnerability to weather and climate hazards. In Uganda, farmers of sweet potatoes are autonomously adjusting their practices to get the best yields possible. To that end, they are planting sweet potato varieties with shorter maturation periods in response to increasing uncertainty about the onset and cessation of the rainy seasons. In other contexts, more drastic, and in some cases transformative, changes are required.

In northern Kenya, some pastoralists have gone beyond adjustments to make more transformative changes. They have replaced cattle with camels that are better suited to the increasingly hotter climate with less predictable rainfall. Camels require less water, eat a wider variety of vegetation and produce up to six times more milk than local cattle species (Salman et al., 2019[139]; Volpato and King, 2018[140]). Over time, the market for camels and camel milk in Kenya has developed, boosting livelihoods and food security (Elhadi, Nyariki and Wasonga, 2015[141]). Like the Kenyan farmers switching from cattle to camels, some farmers in Costa Rica are switching from coffee to oranges. Oranges are better suited to warmer temperatures, and more profitable than coffee that is subject to increasing global competition. These farmers have also observed that oranges are more resilient to droughts, floods, temperature fluctuations, erratic rainfall and higher winds (Tye and Grinspan, 2020[142]).

The changes in Kenya and Costa Rica have occurred autonomously and without any government support. They responded to an evaluation of the suitability of new approaches to different climate futures. For such transformations to be sustainable, however, policy makers must play a more active role in working with the scientific, local and Indigenous communities. Together, they need to identify opportunities for action and develop policies and plans that make available information (including climate information), technical assistance (such as extension services) and financial resources supportive of the transition. In some cases, market policies (e.g. agricultural subsidies) will also have to be adjusted. This adjustment would promote climate-resilient products and approaches and support market creation for emerging products, such as camel milk, as needed (Salman et al., 2019[139]; Volpato and King, 2018[140]). Such adjustments, whether technical or financial, will require time to produce the same level of support as existing measures (Tye and Grinspan, 2020[142]). In the short term, mechanisms should enable individuals and private sector actors to better respond to climate hazards. These mechanisms could include, for example, clear strategic policy guidelines and support mechanisms aligned with those objectives.

4.4. Institutions, governance and norms for reducing and managing losses and damages

Efforts by different stakeholder groups to address the hazard, exposure and vulnerability will be guided by the institutions and governance processes in place. IPCC has identified three ways in which institutions shape and constrain climate policy making and implementation (Somanathan et al., 2014[143]):

- Institutions, whether with formal rules or informal norms, set incentive structures for economic decision making (e.g. in the context of transport investments or behavioural decisions relevant to efficient energy use).
- Institutions shape the political context for decision making, empowering some interests while reducing the influence of others (e.g. as reflected in the energy pricing or broader environmental taxing of some countries).

- Institutions influence how risks are perceived and valued, what risks are prioritised for action, and how they are addressed (i.e. what approaches are included or excluded from consideration and implementation).

Perceptions of climate risks, based on knowledge and previous experience, also guide the prioritisation and management of the risks. They identify which risks are tolerable, which should be addressed, by when and to what extent (Thomas et al., 2018[119]). Approaches to address the components of climate risks therefore are inevitably political, reflecting the diverse and conflicting values and interests of stakeholders. Governments and others in positions of authority may seek to shed light on the risks through policy consultation and co-ordination, research and other means. Individuals and communities will interpret the information and associated guidance mediated by their own perceptions of the risks. These perceptions may not be consistent with wider public concerns (Sudmeier-Rieux et al., 2015[76]). This is equally the case at the global level where countries perceive, experience and respond to global risks, including climate change, in different ways (White and Lawrence, 2020[144]).

Diverging interests and values contribute to delayed climate action. Differences between the economic incentive structures for mitigation action (a global public good) and adaptation (a range of local public goods, common pool resources and private goods) can delay action on climate or lead to inadequate responses. However, diverging interests and values, both nationally and internationally, are also factors. For example, groups with a vested interest in continued fossil fuel consumption have been instrumental in spreading doubt about the credibility of climate science (e.g. through disinformation campaigns).

Growing evidence suggests that climate action does not have to come at the expense of economic development (OECD, 2017[65]; OECD/The World Bank/UN Environment, 2018[145]). However, climate action at the ambitious scale needed to reduce risks of losses and damages will inevitably have winners and losers. At the national level, for example, economic activities may shift towards less fossil-fuel intensive alternatives or to those less vulnerable to weather and climate hazards. Due to this shift, some will lose their jobs, while others will find new opportunities. Similarly, across countries, trade patterns may change as companies seek to reduce their vulnerability to extreme weather events.

A just transition and decent work are becoming political priorities for climate action. Recognising the growing social impacts of climate change policy, decision makers have elevated a just transition of the workforce and the creation of decent work and quality jobs on the political agenda. The preamble to the Paris Agreement, for example, emphasises the "imperative of a just transition of the workforce and the creation of decent work and quality jobs in accordance with nationally defined development priorities" (UNFCCC, 2015[61]).

Policy makers have at their disposal different tools to make climate risks tangible and inform decision-making processes. Some tools raise awareness among different stakeholders on the nature of the risks and solutions for managing them. Others influence incentive structures for decision-making processes, such as one-off compensation, pricing or subsidies. Still others impose regulatory standards or prohibit certain practices such as land-use management or engineering design standards (Baer, Campiglio and Deyris, 2021[146]). The levers can be activated at different levels of governance and across stakeholder groups. The application of different tools, then, must be guided by transparency, a good understanding of the synergies, trade-offs and feedbacks between them. It must also respect the interaction of climate-related impacts with social, environmental and economic drivers across spatial and temporal scales (OECD, 2021[147]).

4.4.1. Governance arrangements for reducing and managing risks of losses and damages

Governance arrangements are central to the management of climate risks. Governance arrangements refer broadly to the structures and processes that steer society and the economy towards common objectives (Ansell and Torfing, 2016[148]). They differ across levels (local, national, regional, global) and modes of governance (market, network, hierarchy) (Jordan et al., 2015[149]). In the context of climate change, governance includes an explicit focus on the management of the hazards. In addition, it includes the broader set of structures and processes that shape the socio-economic context determining exposure and vulnerability of people and assets to different type of climate-related hazards.

As a global problem that depends on collective action to limit the increase in hazards, climate change poses challenges for effective international governance. For example, countries face differential risks. They have different national interests and perceptions of the costs and benefits of mitigation action. They also have large differences in political, economic and technological capacity. These issues have contributed to more emphasis on the risk management component of risk governance (Klinke and Renn, 2019[150]). Risk management approaches emphasise the complexity of and the uncertainties inherent in understanding risk. They also stress the ambiguity or different and sometimes divergent interpretations of the risks and their context (Klinke and Renn, 2019[150]).

Two recent approaches reflect a shift in focus from the distinct processes of risk assessment, risk management and risk communication towards the role of institutions and processes that guide and facilitate the management of the risks. The Sendai Framework for Disaster Risk Reduction identifies strengthened disaster risk governance as a priority for effective and efficient management of disaster risks. It "fosters collaboration and partnerships across mechanisms and institutions for the implementation of instruments relevant to disaster risk reduction and sustainable development" (UNDRR, 2015[100]). For its part, the OECD Council Recommendation on the Governance of Critical Risks also recognises the importance of a fundamental shift in risk governance towards a whole of society effort (OECD, 2014[151]). Table 4.4 summarises the recommendations and proposed areas of action outlined in the OECD Council Recommendation (2014[151]).

Adaptive or iterative approaches to governance of risks place emphasis on the importance of associated governance structures and institutional settings facilitating continuous monitoring, evaluation and learning (Klinke and Renn, 2012[152]; OECD, 2021[147]; Folke et al., 2005[153]). This can be informed by lessons learnt from management of previous or similar risks. It can also draw on emerging understanding of the risks and related technologies as they become available (Klinke and Renn, 2012[152]). Such approaches facilitate a continuous process of characterising risks. This will be critical in informing everything from evaluation of the risks to development, implementation and evaluation of approaches to reduce and manage those risks (IRGC, 2017[154]).

Both climate-related hazards and socio-economic contexts are dynamic and non-linear (see Chapter 2). Consequently, risk governance must assess the different processes and outcomes; their interactions (especially of any feedbacks that may amplify or reduce the effectiveness of measures); and any synergies and trade-offs. Such iterative processes can inform continuous adjustments of approaches based on emerging understanding of the risks and lessons learnt. Box 4.8 summarises the approach promoted by the German Federal Ministry for Economic Co-operation and Development in dealing with disaster and climate risks.

Table 4.4. OECD Council Recommendation on the Governance of Critical Risks

Recommendation	Action
Establish and promote a comprehensive, all-hazard and transboundary approach to risk governance to serve as the foundation for enhancing national resilience and responsiveness.	• Develop a national strategy for the governance of critical risks. • Assign leadership at the national level to drive policy implementation, connect policy agendas and align competing priorities across ministries and between central and local government. • Encourage all government actors at national and subnational levels to co-ordinate a range of stakeholders in inclusive policy-making processes. • Establish partnerships with the private sector to achieve responsiveness and shared responsibilities aligned with the national strategy.
Build preparedness through foresight analysis, risk assessments and financing frameworks to better anticipate complex and wide-ranging impacts.	• Develop risk anticipation capacity linked directly to decision making. • Equip departments and agencies with the capacity to anticipate and manage human induced threats. • Monitor and strengthen core risk management capacities. • Plan for contingent liabilities within clear public finance frameworks by enhancing efforts to minimise the impact that critical risks may have on public finances and the fiscal position of a country to support greater resilience.
Raise awareness of critical risks to mobilise households, businesses and international stakeholders and foster investment in risk prevention and mitigation.	• Encourage a whole-of-society approach to risk communication and facilitate transboundary co-operation using risk registries, media and other public communications on critical risks. • Strengthen the mix of structural protection and non-structural measures to reduce critical risks. • Encourage businesses to take steps to ensure business continuity with a specific focus on critical infrastructure.
Develop adaptive capacity in crisis management by co-ordinating resources across government, its agencies and broader networks to support timely decision making, communication and emergency response.	• Establish strategic crisis management capacities to prepare for unknown and unexpected risks that provoke crises. • Strengthen crisis leadership, early detection and sense-making capacity, and conduct exercises to support inter-agency and international co-operation. • Establish the competence and capacities to scale up emergency response capabilities to contend with crises that result from critical risks. • Build institutional capacity to design and oversee recovery and reconstruction.
Demonstrate transparency and accountability in risk-related decision making by incorporating good governance practices and continuously learning from experience and science.	• Ensure transparency regarding the information used to ensure risk management decisions are better accepted by stakeholders to facilitate policy implementation and limit reputational damage. • Enhance government capacity to make the most of resources dedicated to public safety, national security, preparedness and resilience. • Continuously share knowledge, including lessons learnt from previous events, research and science through post-event reviews, to evaluate the effectiveness of prevention and preparedness activities, as well as response and recovery operations.

Note: Each action area is complemented in the Council Recommendations with suggested approaches or areas of focus.
Source: (OECD, 2014[151]).

Box 4.8. Comprehensive risk management in German development co-operation

The German Federal Ministry for Economic Cooperation and Development (BMZ) promotes an approach to address climate and disaster risks in a comprehensive, integrated manner. BMZ pulls from a wide range of strategies and risk management instruments (see Figure 4.3). It combines both tried-and-tested and innovative instruments from the fields of climate change mitigation, adaptation, disaster risk management and social protection to form a single comprehensive risk management approach. Further, transitional development assistance acts as a bridge to humanitarian aid.

In practice, instruments are chosen specific to the given context. Early warning systems, for example, are implemented as a fundamental component of a preparedness strategy. The combination of adaptation measures such as ecosystem-based adaptation with risk transfer instruments can minimise the risk of losses and damages. Box 5.12 in Chapter 5 highlights the role of risk finance and insurance tools in more detail.

The approach encourages adopting a flexible process. This would be tailored to specific needs, contexts and scales, while also considering potential cascading effects. The comprehensive risk management approach supports both state and non-state actors to factor in all relevant risks when making decisions and implementing strategies and policies.

Figure 4.3. Comprehensive risk management: Strategies and instruments

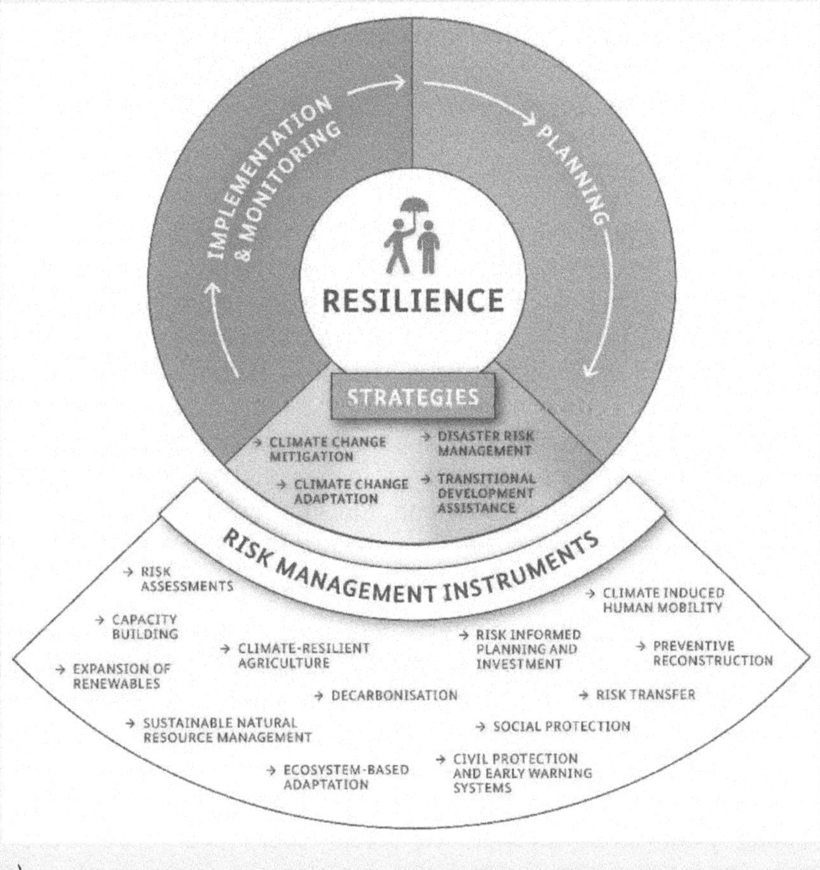

Source: (BMZ, 2019[155])

Engaging stakeholders in an inclusive manner

An iterative approach requires the engagement and consideration of the perspectives of different stakeholder groups – public, private, formal and informal – including local and Indigenous groups. Each stakeholder contributes in a unique and complementary way to understand the risks, and to reduce and manage them according to its respective capacities and accepted functions (Schweizer and Renn, 2019[156]; IPCC, 2012[74]). Different stakeholders will have different resources and capacities to make their voices heard. Consequently, representation and participation on their own do not result in inclusive outcomes (OECD, 2021[147]). Mechanisms must therefore facilitate exchange of information to guide efforts towards a shared understanding of the risks and approaches to reduce and manage them.

For example, in Chile the establishment of a Roundtable on human mobility, climate change and disasters aims to address a governance gap given the increasing relevance of these issues for the country. The Roundtable engages a diverse set of stakeholders from the public, private, academia and civil society. The institutional arrangement facilitates enhanced understanding of the issues and their interlinkages to inform the development of guidelines for subnational governments.

The cascading and uncertain nature of climate risks means that the stakeholder community may not always be well defined. In some cases, it will cross geo-political jurisdictions (UNDRR, 2019[9]). With mounting risks of losses and damages, stakeholders may increasingly also need to make more radical or transformative changes to reduce hazard, exposure and vulnerability. Given climate change does not affect everyone in the same way, such processes must be guided by a widely-shared and robust public understanding of the risks and acceptance of the need for the proposed actions and approaches (UNDRR, 2021[157]). There will also be a political and ethical imperative for the governance system to manage these processes carefully and transparently. This could include careful assessment of distributional implications in advance. It could also include adoption of appropriate complementary compensation measures that can limit the adverse impact of policy measures and other efforts on peoples' well-being (OECD, 2019[158]).

Strategic, operational and technical co-ordination

Countries are increasingly also recognising the benefits of enhanced collaboration and coherence between climate and disaster risk reduction communities (OECD, 2020[57]; Haque et al., 2018[81]). Policy coherence viewed as a process of co-ordination can occur on a continuum – from the strategic to operational and technical levels (OECD, 2020[57]) (see Box 4.9). While increased coherence can improve efficiency and effectiveness, it can also lead to trade-offs between investing in enhanced coherence and enhancing individual policy processes (Dazé, Terton and Maass, 2018[159]). The theoretical rationale for coherence is not always reflected in practice, suggesting actual or perceived mismatches in processes and institutions. Mismatches can be due to several factors. The different institutional histories of the two approaches have contributed to separate institutional structures and funding mechanisms with different operational timescales. The immediate disaster response, for example, may be short term, whereas long-term perspectives are a key element of climate action (OECD, 2020[57]).

Emerging good practice in different country contexts, including the Philippines and Peru, is to establish high-level co-ordination. Such an approach should have the support of political leaders to reach a common understanding of enhanced coherence and how it can be achieved. In practice, key ministries, such as Finance, should ensure that the allocation of resources reflects the allocation of roles and responsibilities. National governments drive efforts to strengthen policy coherence. However, implementation usually occurs at the sector or local level. At these lower levels, capacity may be more limited and the actors in charge will face competing demands. National-level actors must therefore be aware of the burden that planning, implementing and monitoring such processes can place on different stakeholder groups (OECD, 2020[57]).

Box 4.9. Policy coherence: Climate change adaptation and disaster risk reduction

Coherence can be pursued and operationalised: i) horizontally across sectors, ii) vertically by bringing together different levels of government (local, subnational, national, regional and global), and iii) through collaboration across diverse stakeholder groups, from governments and intergovernmental organisations to the private sector, civil society organisations and citizens. These approaches can, in turn, be grouped into three types of coherence:

- ***Strategic (visions and goals)***: Aligned visions, goals and priorities on climate change and disaster risk reduction in national development plans and strategies, providing a framework for pursuing operational coherence. With aligned goals and objectives at the strategic level, the basis for coherence in implementation is strong.
- ***Operational (policy and institutions)***: Policy frameworks and institutional arrangements supportive of the implementation of aligned objectives on climate change and disaster risk reduction, limiting the burden on often stretched human, technical and financial resources. Linking the two agendas at the operational level through the development of effective policies and institutional arrangements can also prevent duplication of efforts, or conflicting activities.
- ***Technical***: Strengthened technical capacities to assess the risks and opportunities, to identify and prioritise climate change and disaster risk reduction measures, and to finance them. For example, adaptation planning can benefit from tools and information already well established in the disaster risk reduction community, such as risk assessments. Conversely, emerging evidence of good practice approaches to climate change can inform disaster risk mitigation measures, reducing the potential for maladaptation.

Source: (OECD, 2020[57]).

4.4.2. Norms and norm entrepreneurs

The role of norms in informing action, including on climate change, is often overlooked. Norms shape preferences, ideas and expectations; they have the potential to also support the integration of international policies and institutions (Galaz et al., 2017[160]). The precautionary principle, for example, calls for action to prevent serious or irreversible damage before harm can be scientifically demonstrated. For its part, the polluter pays principle argues those who pollute should also bear the costs of abating the pollution and preventing associated damages to humans or the natural environment (Munir, 2013[161]). Both principles have become key elements of international environmental law.

Norms are not static but emerge and diffuse until they are adopted by a critical mass of relevant actors (Galaz et al., 2017[160]). Events or triggers can contribute to changes in norms. At the national level, such a trigger could be a devastating extreme weather event or a series of repeated events with widespread losses and damages. Enhanced scientific understanding could also play this role. While some transitions happen relatively rapidly, others take much longer. The pace of change depends on technological, economic, commercial, political and social factors.

The outlawing of ozone-depleting substances (ODSs) is an example of a relatively rapid transition, facilitated by the ready availability of commercially viable substitutes for ODSs in most uses. The Montreal Protocol, which oversees the phasing out of the production and consumption of ODSs, differs from other international environmental agreements. Targets and timelines are complemented with mechanisms that limit incentives for countries to free ride through, for example, trade restrictions (Barrett, 2003[162]). In contrast, institutional inertia in phasing out fossil fuel-based power generation in contexts where the technology has matured and cleaner alternatives are cost competitive illustrates how technological maturity on its own is not enough for transitions to happen. Larger political economy issues may still dominate. In such cases, an explicit focus on the barriers for transition may be needed.

So-called norm entrepreneurs – academics, legal scholars and local and religious leaders to name a few – can help diffuse new norms by identifying the implications of different choices (Otto et al., 2020[163]). For example, with the publication of the encyclical *Laudato si*, Pope Francis used his role within the Catholic Church to highlight the moral imperative for all actors to act on climate change and the ethical implications of failing to do so.

In recent years, young people (individually and collectively) have played a critical role in bringing climate change to the attention of the broader public. They have called on governments to act in accordance with available science, while also highlighting the implications of individual consumption and lifestyle choices (Otto et al., 2020[163]). Over the coming years, members of the youth movement will have the opportunity to engage more directly in the political process, with the potential of bringing about radical change. This points to the important role of education, science and critical thinking in shaping norms. In addition, it highlights the importance of creating institutional structures that give youth and future generations status within policy processes. The Welsh Well-being of Future Generations Act, for example, resulted in the creation of a Future Generations Commissioner.

Time will tell what impact such norm entrepreneurs will have on climate action. However, government officials are increasingly realising the importance of addressing public concerns about the climate. The elections in Australia in 2019 (Colvin and Jotzo, 2021[164]) and Germany in 2017, for example, saw a broader spectrum of political parties include climate change in their programmes.

Civil plaintiffs are taking governments and corporations to court

Public engagement has also contributed to citizens taking governments or corporations to court for failing to take adequate climate action. Plaintiffs have globally brought over 1 500 climate-related lawsuits, with the numbers rising. In most cases, they seek compensation for climate-related losses to compel governments or corporations to take more ambitious climate action (Setzer and Byrnes, 2020[165]). While most claims to date have been unsuccessful, others – such as in Germany and the Netherlands – have influenced change:

- In April 2021, a German court ordered the government to rewrite the climate law. The court ruled that too much of the burden to cut emissions was placed on future generations (LSE, n.d.[166]). In response, the government of Germany adopted an amended Climate Change Act. It includes commitments to reduce GHG emissions by 65% compared to 1990 by 2030 (instead of 55%) and by 88% by 2040 (no prior goal). It also revised the target date for climate neutrality from 2050 to 2045.
- In May 2021, a Dutch court ordered Shell and its suppliers to cut emissions by 45% by 2030 from 2019 levels. The plaintiffs, representing over 17 000 Dutch citizens, argued that Shell's planned emissions reductions of 20% by 2030 violated human rights by fuelling climate crisis (LSE, n.d.[166]). This was the first time a court ordered a large corporation to increase its mitigation efforts. It sets a precedent, giving the public a tool to influence policy outcomes and corporate behaviour (Toussaint, 2020[167]; UNEP, 2021[168]).

In 2020, conversely, the UN Human Rights Committee dismissed a claim by a Kiribati citizen who had argued the effects of climate change displaced the people of Kiribati. The committee ruled that given the rate of SLR, the Republic of Kiribati, with help from the international community, can take "affirmative measures to protect and, where necessary, relocate its population" (UN Human Rights Committee, 2020[169]).

A review of 73 climate-related lawsuits found the evidence submitted often lags behind the state-of-the-art in climate science and that methodologies such as attribution science could inform future cases (Stuart-Smith et al., 2021[170]) (see Chapter 3).

Leadership, partnership and trust

Leadership and partnership are also important in informing change. Partnerships between the scientific and policy communities, for example, can help ensure that science informs approaches to reducing and managing climate risks. It is important to ensure that such partnerships are inclusive to different types of knowledge, including local and Indigenous knowledge. In this way, they can contribute towards a better understanding of the risks and help identify solutions considered legitimate by stakeholders (Cornforth, Petty and Walker, 2021[47]; UNDRR, 2021[157]).

The presence of trust among stakeholders determines whether such partnerships can bring about change. Some argue that stakeholders need to trust that effective public policy will be based on respect in preserving human dignity (Ascher, 2017[171]). Others suggest collaboration will be guided by a diversity of trust processes with affinitive trust playing a central role in the context of climate change (UNDRR, 2021[157]; Coleman and Stern, 2017[172]):

- rational trust, based on expected benefits and risks
- procedural trust, in fairness and integrity of the procedures involved
- affinitive trust, shaped by emotions, charisma, shared identities or feelings but not always longer-term interactions
- dispositional trust, signalling one's predisposition to trust another entity.

With the devastating impacts from climate change becoming increasingly apparent around the world, the emphasis on global solidarity has risen on the political agenda. This has already been written into the international climate process. Examples include: the goal of Paris Agreement to pursue efforts to limit the temperature increase to a range of well-below 2°C and towards 1.5°C above pre-industrial levels; the emphasis on common but differentiated responsibilities that underpins countries' Nationally Determined Contributions; and the requirement that developed countries provide finance and other means of implementation (technology and capacity development support) and lead efforts to reduce emissions. These goals, principles and responsibilities all reflect a sense of international solidarity. They articulate a conviction that collective action to reduce and manage the risks and impacts of climate change benefits all. An emphasis on solidarity in guiding climate action has also risen in the context of the humanitarian community facing increasing pressure to support countries experiencing direct losses and damages from climate change.

4.5. Implications of sea-level rise on policy priorities and decision-making processes in SIDS

This section explores the implications of SLR on decision-making processes and policy priorities in SIDS. It builds on the discussion in Chapter 3 that outlines the impact of SLR on SIDS, as well as on the preceding sections of this chapter. Chapter 3 highlighted that all SIDS are vulnerable to climate change irrespective of their diversity. This is especially true of SLR because the habitable areas are limited to the low-lying coastal zone. SIDS are also disproportionally affected by extreme weather events due to their geographic locations. With relatively undiversified economies and limited natural resources, SIDS risk extensive losses and damages from SLR.

The section first discusses the different types of responses to SLR and their relative strengths and weaknesses (Section 4.5.1). This is complemented with a discussion of potential policy priorities and decision-making processes for addressing SLR in SIDS (Section 4.5.2).

4.5.1. Responses, their strengths and weaknesses

There is no silver bullet to reducing and managing the risk of SLR and associated changes in extreme sea levels, coastal flood hazard, coastal erosion hazard, loss of ecosystems and freshwater resources. There are diverse responses to SLR, each with its strengths and weaknesses. It is therefore useful to consider their complementary roles in an integrated response to SLR. Four fundamentally different types of responses have been identified (Nicholls et al., 2007[173]; Oppenheimer et al., 2019[132]; Wong et al., 2014[174]), each briefly described below. The responses complement the discussion on approaches to address the drivers of exposure and vulnerability to hazards discussed in Section 4.3.

Protection, advance, accommodation and retreat

Protection reduces the chances of coastal hazards (SLR, surges, waves) propagating inland and causing damages to people, their livelihoods and built environment. Protection can be delivered in three ways:

- Hard engineering structures, such as dykes, seawalls and breakwaters, can be built.
- Sediment-based measures can replace eroded sand to nourish beaches and shores.
- NbS can use coastal ecosystems such as reefs, mangroves and salt marshes as buffers.

In this way, NbS can attenuate extreme sea levels (surges, waves); reduce rates of erosion; and raise elevation or create new land by trapping sediments and building-up organic matter and detritus (Pontee et al., 2016[175]; Spalding et al., 2013[176]; Temmerman et al., 2013[177]). The use of seawalls – as one hard coastal protection structure – is widespread in SIDS. These are vertical walls built along the coastline to prevent flooding and erosion (Betzold and Mohamed, 2016[178]).

Advance also aims at preventing the coastal hazard from propagating inland but this time by building new land seawards and upwards. For SIDS, this means reclamation of new land or new islands at higher elevation levels. Land reclamation is widely practised around coastal cities where land is scarce and valuable, including on SIDS. Newly reclaimed land is, however, not necessarily elevated. This may even constitute maladaptation by increasing the exposure to coastal hazards. Globally, about 34 000 km^2 of land has been gained from the sea during the last 30 years. The biggest gains are in places like Dubai, Singapore and China (Donchyts et al., 2016[179]; Martín-Antón et al., 2016[180]). The global area of atoll islands has increased by 62 km^2 from 2000-20, which is roughly twice the size of Tuvalu (Holdaway, Ford and Owen, 2021[181]). The largest increase in land areas of SIDS is found in the Maldives (38 km^2). On the islands of Hulhumalé, for example, land has been reclaimed on a reef flat next to the capital island of Malé. It reaches an elevation about 60 cm higher than Malé to account for future SLR (Brown et al., 2019[182]).

Accommodation, a third approach, refers to a wide array of measures that reduce the vulnerability of coastal residents, their livelihoods and the built environment. As such, it does not prevent coastal hazards from propagating inland. Documented accommodation measures for SIDS include the strengthening and elevation of houses, installation and upgrade of water storage, preservation of food for disasters, a switch to different salinity-tolerant crops, capacity building and awareness raising (Klöck and Nunn, 2019[183]; Mycoo and Donovan, 2018[184]).

Retreat, the fourth response, reduces or eliminates exposure by moving people, infrastructures and human activities out of the coastal risk zone (Hino, Field and Mach, 2017[185]). In Europe and the United States, retreat is often considered to be a coastal adaptation measure. The land retreated acts as a buffer zone attenuating extreme sea levels and, hence, reducing flood risk for the hinterland (Rupp-Armstrong and Nicholls, 2007[186]). Conversely, the literature on SIDS, as summarised in the IPCC Special Report on the

Oceans and the Cryosphere, generally views retreat as loss and damage rather than adaptation. This is because retreat means to give up scarce land or even to abandon entire islands (Oppenheimer et al., 2019[132]). Given the vulnerability of SIDS to disasters, as discussed in Chapter 3, many cases of abandoning islands are documented, including in response to disasters that are not climate-related. Examples include disasters caused by extreme sea levels, such as after the 2004 Indian Ocean tsunami in the Maldives (Gussmann and Hinkel, 2020[187]), volcanic eruptions, such as in Manam in Papua New Guinea (Kelman, 2015[188]), or tectonic land subsidence, such as in northern Vanuatu (Ballu et al., 2011[189]).

All four biophysical response measures are combined with, or initiated through, institutional arrangements that prescribe, recommend or incentivise certain measures (see Section 4.4). Such arrangements have not been the focus of much research on SIDS. Documented institutional responses in SIDS include restriction of access and resource use; efforts to mainstream climate change considerations into national plans and insurance; building codes for flood proofing houses; monetary incentives for risk transfer (e.g. subsidised insurance); or information provision through flood EWS (Klöck and Nunn, 2019[183]; Leal Filho et al., 2021[190]; Robinson, 2020[191]; Mycoo and Donovan, 2018[184]).

Further, research on the risk management experiences of SIDS is far from comprehensive. Recent systematic reviews highlight a focus of the literature on only a small number of SIDS. Pacific SIDS have received the most attention. Research has thereby focused on the main islands at the expense of remote and rural islands (Klöck and Nunn, 2019[183]). Generally, the focus has either been on hard measures or behavioural change. Most responses have been documented as reactive (i.e. after a disaster has occurred). They focus on current extremes rather than future climate change (Klöck and Nunn, 2019[183]). Generally, there is a lack of studies that have evaluated the effectiveness of these responses in SIDS (Gussmann and Hinkel, 2021[192]; Klöck and Nunn, 2019[183]).

Hard vs. soft protection

The question of hard engineering versus soft NbS to protect coasts from extreme sea-level events and SLR has provoked much discussion. Scientific and grey literature often advocates NbS as the solution to coastal adaptation. Conversely, it portrays hard protection measures such as seawalls to be bad, incremental and unsustainable. This is not a useful distinction. Both play complementary roles, and are often combined in so-called hybrid approaches (OECD, 2020[106]).

Hard protection has both strengths and weaknesses. One strength is the need for less space. They are also more reliable and predictable for flood security than many NbS, which vary more over time and space depending on the context (Narayan et al., 2016[193]; Pinsky, Guannel and Arkema, 2013[194]; Quataert et al., 2015[195]). As one weakness, hard protection, in particular on coral islands, interrupts the natural sediment transport from coral reefs onto island shores and surfaces that protect the islands from flooding and erosion in the first place.

NbS provide co-benefits beyond coastal protection such as carbon sequestration, improved water quality, biodiversity, fisheries and other resources (Oppenheimer et al., 2019[132]) (see Box 4.5). Furthermore, NbS can autonomously maintain their effectiveness by naturally adapting to rising sea levels. They can do this through raising land and migrating inland, provided sufficient sediment and inland space is available. In addition, some NbS have been demonstrated to be cheaper than hard measures. Ferrario et al. (2014[196]), for example, found the costs of restoring reefs significantly lower than building artificial breakwaters.

However, many comparisons between the two approaches ignore the opportunity cost of NbS. Opportunity costs of NbS are generally higher, at least in the short term. They often need a lot of space that could be developed into profitable usages of land. In fact, mangrove forests are being destroyed at alarming rates of 4-9% per year (Duarte et al., 2008[197]) primarily because conversion of mangroves into agriculture, shrimp farming or industrial usages is profitable in private terms in the short term (Li et al., 2013[198]).

These strengths and weaknesses mean that different approaches apply in different contexts. For urban and densely populated areas, hard protection has played a central role, and will continue to do so. Many cities around the world, including in SIDS, are protected by hard infrastructure. If there is limited space and large human values are at risk, the continuation of hard protection makes a lot of sense. Even under 21st century high-end SLR, hard protection is highly cost-efficient for cities and densely populated areas (Hallegatte et al., 2013[199]; Lincke and Hinkel, 2021[129]; Tiggeloven et al., 2020[200]). Conversely, rural and sparsely populated islands have more land available and hence may greatly benefit from a focus on NbS.

For coral SIDS, NbS may be favoured for those islands that still have the natural capacity to grow with SLR. These are islands where the natural patterns of sediment production and transport are functioning (see Chapter 3). Introducing hard measures in these environments would ultimately destroy these natural mechanisms, locking the islands into hard development pathways (Duvat and Magnan, 2019[201]). However, NbS may not be recommended for all islands. Islands already heavily modified by humans are nearly impossible to return to their natural morph dynamics. This includes the main and capital islands of many coral SIDS, such as Malé in the Maldives or Vaiaku/Funafuti of Tuvalu. Here, hard protection measures play an important role. However, even urban islands need to maintain a healthy and functioning reef to grow upwards with SLR. These reefs reduce wave energy and heights, making it more affordable and technically much easier to protect the islands against SLR.

Advance vs. retreat

As a general weakness, protection always leaves a residual risk. Both soft and hard protection may fail. Furthermore, extreme sea-level events can exceed protection standards. For that reason, flood damage cannot be completely excluded. In addition, if flood defences are raised with rising SLR, the risk of extreme disasters increases. In the case of defence failure damages will be large due to deep floodplain behind the defence (Hallegatte et al., 2013[199]). The risk of failure can be reduced to almost zero through wide flood defences known as unbreachable dykes (De Bruijn, Klijn and Knoeff, 2013[202]). However, these require a lot of space generally not available for SIDS.

The advance approach offers several strengths. Residual risks can be partially avoided through advance, if newly constructed islands are reclaimed at a sufficiently high level. Under moderate to high SLR, for example, the Maldivian island of Hulhumalé can avoid wave-induced flooding until the end of the century (Brown et al., 2019[182]). As another strength, advance creates new land, which is generally scarce in SIDS. For urban SIDS, advance can help overcome financing barriers. High, up-front investments in the creation of new, better protected land can be recuperated within a few years through real-estate revenues generated from newly created land (Bisaro et al., 2019[203]). The return on investment on such urban advance is shorter and less risky compared to investments in normal coastal protection. This makes it easier to attract finance for advance. Advance also has weaknesses. These include negative environmental externalities and the interruption of natural sediment dynamics, which generally leads to erosion either on the newly created land or in adjacent localities. In atoll islands, new land is often created on the reef flat, which reduces or eliminates its ability to attenuate waves.

With sufficiently high ground available, retreat can avoid residual risks. However, retreat is generally socially and politically contested for several reasons. First, there are vested coastal interests, including tourism and real estate sectors. Second, it raises difficult questions around equity and compensation. Third, there are frequent adverse outcomes, including disruption of livelihoods, loss of culture and identity, and psychological harm (Hauer et al., 2019[130]; Siders, Hino and Mach, 2019[204]).

4.5.2. Policy priorities and decision-making processes

This section presents six complementary policy priorities and decision-making processes that can be considered for addressing SLR in SIDS. It builds on discussions in both this chapter and Chapter 3.

International policy priorities

At the international level, the most important policy priority is mitigation of GHG emissions. Only stringent mitigation can reduce the risk of multiple metres of SLR and its catastrophic consequences on SIDS. SIDS may have more capacity to respond to SLR than often suggested in the media. However, unmitigated climate change and SLR threatens the survival of many SIDS. This is especially true for coral islands with elevations of only 2-3 metres above mean sea levels. These SIDS face the threat of higher and more energetic waves directly hitting the coast and over washing the islands because their natural protection through coral reefs is lost through ocean warming.

A second international policy priority is the need to support SIDS in meeting the cost of adaptation and reconstruction of lifeline infrastructure, assets and livelihoods. No matter the level of mitigation, sea levels will continue to rise, even if the temperature goal of the Paris Agreement is met. This is due to the delayed response of the ocean to global warming (Church et al., 2013[205]; Oppenheimer et al., 2019[132]). Even low-end SLR requires substantial investments in adaptation on SIDS and the risk of losses and damages will grow. Extreme sea levels and other natural hazards impact large fractions of the GDP of many SIDS. This means they have low capacity to finance adaptation and other activities to reduce and manage the risk of losses and damages. Consequently, international efforts to support SIDS are needed (Klöck and Nunn, 2019[183]; OECD, 2018[206]) (see Chapter 5).

Implementation of low-regret measures

From national to local levels, one immediate and generally recognised policy priority is the implementation of no- or low-regret measures. Although their meaning depends on context, no- or low-regret measures include some accommodation and disaster preparedness measures such as emergency planning and EWS. On the plus side, these accommodation measures produce almost immediate net benefits. Multi-hazard EWS have one of the highest benefit-cost ratios. However, these measures alone are only effective for current conditions and small rises in sea level. Hence, they eventually need to be combined, upgraded or replaced with other responses such as coastal protection.

Another low-regret measure is the consideration retreating from individual islands in an archipelago SIDS. Although it is generally disturbing to think of retreat as a no or low regret option, and recognising that what is considered "low regret" will vary across stakeholder groups, there are instances in which retreat may be considered as such. One instance may be in the aftermath of a coastal disaster where reconstruction of livelihoods in their original situation may cost as much as relocation to another island. Experiences after the 2004 Indian Ocean tsunami in the Maldives also show that the affected population may support a retreat under such circumstances (Gussmann and Hinkel, 2020[187]). Relocation may also cause relatively low regret when islands already have small and declining populations. In these cases, people are migrating to seek opportunities in the centre islands of archipelagos (Speelman, Nicholls and Dyke, 2016[207]). In both instances, relocating and concentrating population on fewer islands can bring both development and adaptation benefits; government services and coastal adaptation can be provided more efficiently to a population concentrated on a fewer number of islands.

Finally, some low-regret adaptation measures result from SLR and climate impacts being co-determined by non-climate, local drivers that can be addressed to reduce current and future climate risks. Natural sediment supply and transport processes can be maintained to reduce erosion impacts. Water pollution and tourism activities can be reduced to preserve coral reefs and reduce wave impacts. Mangroves can be preserved to reduce both surge and wave impacts. Finally, sufficient accommodation space can be maintained for mangroves to migrate inland with SLR (Duvat and Magnan, 2019[201]; McLean and Kench, 2015[208]) (see also Chapter 3).

Keeping future options open

Given the large uncertainty about SLR, it is important to keep future options open (Hallegatte, 2009[209]; Hinkel et al., 2019[210]). Long-term decisions that can wait, for example, can be postponed. Many retreat decisions for urban areas in SIDS fall under this category (Oppenheimer et al., 2019[132]). SLR may rise by multiple metres, posing existential threats to SIDS. However, there is also a substantial chance that SLR may stay below 40 cm by 2100 (50th percentile of RCP2.6) if the temperature goals of the Paris Agreement are met. Adapting to the latter amount of SLR is technically feasible in most places and also economically efficient in densely populated and urban areas. Hence, a meaningful strategy for urban areas may be to wait and observe how SLR observations and projections develop over the next decades. This could provide a better basis for an existential decision such as retreat (Hinkel et al., 2019[210]). Such waiting should, however, accompany the two priorities of contingency planning and iterative policy cycles.

Another way of keeping future options open is through flexible options that can be upgraded or changed once more is known about future SLR (see also Section 4.2). This is generally an argument for implementing NbS, including sediment-based measures instead of hard measures. NbS can, to some extent, self-adjust to future SLR. Sediment-based measures provide the flexibility to increase protection by applying more sand as the consequences of SLR unfold. Flexibility can also be built into hard infrastructure. Germany, for example, builds coastal dykes with a wider crest than necessary. This allows dykes to be raised further at low costs if SLR turns out to be higher than anticipated (MELUR-SH, 2012[211]).

Consideration of SLR in decisions that need to be made today

Many long-term decisions must be made today. Given the coastal nature of SIDS, many of these decisions are related to SLR. This includes long-term decisions on critical infrastructure, coastal protection, land-use planning and land reclamation, which can have time horizons of decades to over a century. Many of the urban centres of SIDS, for example, face high population pressures and an associated shortage of land for housing. This needs to be addressed today, and is frequently done by creating new land or islands. Long-term decisions are also needed around spatial planning. It might be beneficial, for example, to decide immediately which areas or islands should be further developed and which should be left undisturbed. This would allow the natural processes, which enable islands to self-adjust to SLR, to prevail.

Factoring in SLR into such decisions is beneficial, but the crucial question is how much SLR to consider. Sea-level science can only give a partial answer. The other part depends on the uncertainty preferences of the stakeholders. Box 3.2 (Chapter 3) highlights decision-making processes related to tolerance of risk and uncertainty. When stakeholders are uncertainty-tolerant and the value at risk is relatively low, the IPCC *likely* ranges provide a good basis for decision making (Oppenheimer et al., 2019[132]). If stakeholders are less tolerant towards uncertainties, then high-end SLR should also be considered. In these cases, there remains a 17% chance that SLR will be above the likely range of the IPCC scenarios. In many urban contexts where number of people and assets exposed to SLR and extreme sea levels is high, people are highly intolerant towards uncertainty. In this case, decision making should consider high-end SLR futures (Hinkel et al., 2019[210]).

Adaptive policy making and monitoring

Another priority is to set up iterative policy cycles for decisions and policies to respond to the extent of changes, together with supportive monitoring systems. This corresponds to “adaptive policy making” or “adaptive planning”, which respond to decision making under uncertainty and ambiguity (Walker, Haasnoot and Kwakkel, 2013[212]; Walker, Rahman and Cave, 2001[213]), as found in the context of SLR (also discussed in Section 4.2). Essentially, such adaptive approaches implement low-regret options and flexible measures today. They then monitor SLR, extreme sea levels and other decision-relevant variables so they can identify when in the future decisions and new policies must be taken. Importantly, a monitoring strategy should help identify needed shifts in policy early enough to allow sufficient time for planning and implementation before negative impacts occur (Hermans, et al., 2017).

Contingency planning for the worst to come

Contingency planning, the final policy priority, goes along with keeping future options open and adaptive. It explores what kind of responses are available and how these could be sequenced in the worst case scenario of high-end SLR. If SLR does follow a worst case trajectory, there may be a future moment in time after which there will not be sufficient time to plan and implement some responses, as these may take decades to plan and implement (Haasnoot et al., 2020[214]). In the context of SIDS, contingency plans include large-scale retreat responses. Retreating whole island states involves many difficult ethical, political, technical, humanitarian and legal aspects (Kelman, 2015[188]; Yamamoto and Esteban, 2014[215]). While many SIDS recognise the possible long-term existential threat of SLR, few countries have so far engaged in contingency planning (Thomas and Benjamin, 2018[216]). In 2014, former president of Kiribati, Anote Tong, initiated a long-term contingency plan to buy land on Fiji for relocating Kiribati's people. However, the plan was later undone by the new president (Kupferberg, 2021[217]).

An inexpensive tool for contingency planning is adaptation pathway analysis (Haasnoot et al., 2013[32]; Haasnoot et al., 2012[218]). This process has gained popularity in coastal contexts with prominent applications for London (Ranger, Reeder and Lowe, 2013[219]), the Netherlands (Haasnoot et al., 2020[214]) and Bangladesh (Government of Bangladesh, 2018[35]) (see also Box 4.2). However, there have been few applications in SIDS. As one possible outcome, the exercise may find that nothing needs to be done now. Instead, it could identify critical decisions to be taken once a certain level of SLR has occurred.

How will policy priorities change over time?

As sea levels continue to rise over the next decades, the policy priorities listed above will change. raising the critical question of if and when SIDS' adaptive capacities will be overwhelmed and they need to switch from a policy mix that combines protect, advance and accommodate to a retreat. Small-scale retreat may play a role in certain circumstances as a low-regret measure today. Large-scale retreat should be considered in contingency planning, but it will in most cases be too early to implement it. However, if sea levels continue to rise unabated, SIDS will eventually need to switch to a large-scale retreat policy (Kelman, 2015[188]).

Efforts to pin down when adaptation limits will be reached or to identify a specific level of SLR have been elusive (Leal Filho et al., 2021[190]; Nurse et al., 2014[220]; Oppenheimer et al., 2019[132]). Some work has conjectured concrete limits, including that most atolls will be uninhabitable by the mid-21st century (Storlazzi et al., 2018[221]). However, these projections have not considered human adaptation responses. Hence, they do not provide a comprehensive assessment. Conversely, assessments that include human dimensions and adaptation have not estimated absolute limits of adaptation in the context of SLR in SIDS (Oppenheimer et al., 2019[132]).

One conclusion that can, however, be drawn is that social, economic and financial limits to adaptation may be reached (long) before technical adaptation limits arise (Hinkel et al., 2018[222]). In principle, there are many technical options available for adapting even to 21st century high-end SLR. These include island raising and construction (Yamamoto and Esteban, 2014[215]); artificial breakwaters substituting the lost protective effects of corals, salt water desalination or import of potable water (Falkland and White, 2020[223]); or even floating islands (Marris, 2017[224]). Implementing these options at significant scales is costly and it is unlikely that SIDS can mobilise and access sufficient domestic and international funds and finance for this (Hinkel et al., 2018[222]; Oppenheimer et al., 2019[132]). Even if SIDS could afford the transformation to such radically different and completely engineered living environments, much of the rich cultural diversity and heritage tied to the natural environment of SIDS would be lost.

References

Acidri, J. et al. (2018), "Uganda – Synthesising evidence for targeted national responses to climate change", *Briefing Note*, No. WIBN0218/01, Walker Institute, University of Reading, United Kingdom, http://dx.doi.org/10.5281/ZENODO.3510110. [55]

ADB (2014), "Bangladesh could see climate change losses reach over 9% of GDP – Report", News Release, 19 August, Asian Development Bank, Manila, https://www.adb.org/news/bangladesh-could-see-climate-change-losses-reach-over-9-gdp-report. [93]

Adger, W. et al. (2012), "Cultural dimensions of climate change impacts and adaptation", *Nature Climate Change*, Vol. 3/2, pp. 112-117, http://dx.doi.org/10.1038/nclimate1666. [135]

Ahmed, I. et al. (2019), "Climate change, environmental stress and loss of livelihoods can push people towards illegal activities: A case study from coastal Bangladesh", *Climate and Development*, Vol. 11/10, pp. 907-917, http://dx.doi.org/10.1080/17565529.2019.1586638. [123]

Ali, G. (ed.) (2021), "Australian voters' attitudes to climate action and their social-political determinants", *PLOS ONE*, Vol. 16/3, p. e0248268, http://dx.doi.org/10.1371/journal.pone.0248268. [164]

Ansell, C. and J. Torfing (2016), *Handbook on Theories of Governance*, Edward Elgar Publishing, Cheltenham, United Kingdom, http://dx.doi.org/10.4337/9781782548508. [148]

Ascher, W. (2017), *Understanding the Policymaking Process in Developing Countries*, Cambridge University Press, Cambridge, United Kingdom, http://dx.doi.org/10.1017/9781108277990. [171]

Baer, M., C. Campiglio and J. Deyris (2021), "It takes two to dance: Institutional dynamics and climate-related financial policies", *Working Paper*, No. 384/386, Centre for Climate Change Economics and Policy/Granta Research Institute on Climate Change and the Environment. [146]

Ballu, V. et al. (2011), "Comparing the role of absolute sea-level rise and vertical tectonic motions in coastal flooding, Torres Islands (Vanuatu)", *Proceedings of the National Academy of Sciences*, Vol. 108/32, pp. 13019-13022, http://dx.doi.org/10.1073/pnas.1102842108. [189]

Barrett, S. (2003), *Environmental and Statecraft: The Strategy of Environmental Treaty-making*, Oxford University Press, United Kingdom. [162]

Betzold, C. and I. Mohamed (2016), "Seawalls as a response to coastal erosion and flooding: A case study from Grande Comore, Comoros (West Indian Ocean)", *Regional Environmental Change*, Vol. 17/4, pp. 1077-1087, http://dx.doi.org/10.1007/s10113-016-1044-x. [178]

Bhave, A. et al. (2016), "Barriers and opportunities for robust decision making approaches to support climate change adaptation in the developing world", *Climate Risk Management*, Vol. 14, pp. 1-10, http://dx.doi.org/10.1016/j.crm.2016.09.004. [30]

Bisaro, A. et al. (2019), "Leveraging public adaptation finance through urban land reclamation: Cases from Germany, the Netherlands and the Maldives", *Climatic Change*, Vol. 160/4, pp. 671-689, http://dx.doi.org/10.1007/s10584-019-02507-5. [203]

Black, R. et al. (2013), “Migration, immobility and displacement outcomes following extreme events”, *Environmental Science & Policy*, Vol. 27, pp. S32-S43, http://dx.doi.org/10.1016/j.envsci.2012.09.001. [126]

Black, R. et al. (2021), *Taking Stock: A Global Assessment of Net Zero Targets*, Energy & Climate Intelligence Unit and Oxford Net Zero, London, https://eciu.net/analysis/reports/2021/taking-stock-assessment-net-zero-targets. [64]

BMZ (2019), *Comprehensive Risk Management: The Approach of German Development Cooperation for Dealing with Disaster and Climate Risks*, German Federal Ministry of Economic Cooperation and Development, Berlin. [155]

Bowen, T. et al. (2020), *Adaptive Social Protection: Building Resilience to Shocks*, Washington, DC: World Bank, http://dx.doi.org/10.1596/978-1-4648-1575-1. [125]

Brown, S. et al. (2019), “Land raising as a solution to sea-level rise: An analysis of coastal flooding on an artificial island in the Maldives”, *Journal of Flood Risk Management*, Vol. 13/S1, http://dx.doi.org/10.1111/jfr3.12567. [182]

Buckle, S. et al. (2020), “Addressing the COVID-19 and climate crises”, *OECD/IEA Climate Change Expert Group Papers*, No. 2020/04, OECD Publishing, Paris, http://dx.doi.org/10.1787/50abd39c-en. [70]

Burgin, L., D. Rowell and J. Marsham (2020), *Possible Futures for East Africa under a Changing Climate: Technical Appendix for HyCRISTAL's Climate Risk Narratives (Version 1)*, Zenodo, http://doi.org/10.5281/zenodo.3620757. [51]

Burgin, L. et al. (2019), *FCFA HyCRISTAL Climate Narrative Rural Infographic and Brief*, Zenodo, http://doi.org/10.5281/zenodo.3257288. [50]

Challinor, A. et al. (2018), “Transmission of climate risks across sectors and borders”, *Philosophical Transactions of the Royal Society A: Mathematical, Physical and Engineering Sciences*, Vol. 376/2121, p. 20170301, http://dx.doi.org/10.1098/rsta.2017.0301. [12]

Chapman, M. (ed.) (2016), “The effectiveness, costs and coastal protection benefits of natural and nature-based defences”, *PLOS ONE*, Vol. 11/5, p. e0154735, http://dx.doi.org/10.1371/journal.pone.0154735. [193]

Chen, J. and V. Mueller (2018), “Coastal climate change, soil salinity and human migration in Bangladesh”, *Nature Climate Change*, Vol. 8/11, pp. 981-985, http://dx.doi.org/10.1038/s41558-018-0313-8. [92]

Church, J. et al. (2013), “Sea Level Change”, in Stocker, T. et al. (eds.), *Climate Change 2013: The Physical Science Basis. Contribution of Working Group I to the Fifth Assessment Report of the Intergovernmental Panel on Climate Change*, Cambridge University Press, Cambridge, United Kingdom and New York, NY. [205]

Clarke, D. et al. (2018), “Prospects for agriculture under climate change and soil salinisation”, in *Ecosystem Services for Well-Being in Deltas*, Springer International Publishing, Cham, http://dx.doi.org/10.1007/978-3-319-71093-8_24. [91]

Coleman, K. and M. Stern (2017), “Exploring the functions of different forms of trust in collaborative natural resource management”, *Society & Natural Resources*, Vol. 31/1, pp. 21-38, http://dx.doi.org/10.1080/08941920.2017.1364452. [172]

Cornforth, R., D. Clegg and E. Petty (2021), *The Integrated Database and Applications for Policymakers (Version v2.0)*, Zenodo, http://doi.org/10.5281/zenodo.5025211. [56]

Cornforth, R., C. Petty and G. Walker (2021), "Supporting climate-resilient planning at national and district levels: A pathway to multi-stakeholder decision-making in Uganda", in *Climate Risk in Africa*, Springer International Publishing, Cham, http://dx.doi.org/10.1007/978-3-030-61160-6_8. [47]

Dazé, A., A. Terton and M. Maass (2018), *Coordinating Climate-Resilient Development Alignment to Advance Climate-Resilient Development. Overview Brief 1: Introduction to Alignment*, NAP Global Network, http://napglobalnetwork.org/wp-content/uploads/2018/08/napgn-en-2018-alignment-to-advance-climate-resilient-development-overview-brief.pdf. [159]

De Bruijn, K., F. Klijn and J. Knoeff (2013), *Unbreachable Embankments? In Pursuit of the Most Effective Stretches for Reducing Fatality Risk*, Taylor & Francis Group. [202]

Donchyts, G. et al. (2016), "Earth's surface water change over the past 30 years", *Nature Climate Change*, Vol. 6/9, pp. 810-813, http://dx.doi.org/10.1038/nclimate3111. [179]

Duarte, C. et al. (2008), "The charisma of coastal ecosystems: Addressing the imbalance", *Estuaries and Coasts*, Vol. 31/2, pp. 233-238, http://dx.doi.org/10.1007/s12237-008-9038-7. [197]

Duvat, V. and A. Magnan (2019), "Rapid human-driven undermining of atoll island capacity to adjust to ocean climate-related pressures", *Scientific Reports*, Vol. 9/1, http://dx.doi.org/10.1038/s41598-019-51468-3. [201]

Duvat, V. et al. (2017), "Trajectories of exposure and vulnerability of small islands to climate change", *WIREs Climate Change*, Vol. 8/6, http://dx.doi.org/10.1002/wcc.478. [75]

Elhadi, Y., D. Nyariki and O. Wasonga (2015), "Role of camel milk in pastoral livelihoods in Kenya: contribution to household diet and income", *Pastoralism*, Vol. 5/1, http://dx.doi.org/10.1186/s13570-015-0028-7. [141]

Eriksen, S. et al. (2021), "Adaptation interventions and their effect on vulnerability in developing countries: Help, hindrance or irrelevance?", *World Development*, Vol. 141, p. 105383, http://dx.doi.org/10.1016/j.worlddev.2020.105383. [120]

Evans, B., D. Rowell and F. Semazzi (2020), "The future-climate, current-policy framework: Towards an approach linking climate science to sector policy development", *Environmental Research Letters*, Vol. 15/11, p. 114037, http://dx.doi.org/10.1088/1748-9326/abbeb9. [43]

Falkland, T. and I. White (2020), "Freshwater availability under climate change", in *Springer Climate, Climate Change and Impacts in the Pacific*, Springer International Publishing, Cham, http://dx.doi.org/10.1007/978-3-030-32878-8_11. [223]

FAO (2021), *The Impact of Disasters and Crises on Agriculture and Food Security: 2021*, Food and Agriculture Organization of the United Nations, Rome, http://dx.doi.org/10.4060/cb3673en. [7]

Fedele, G. et al. (2019), "Transformative adaptation to climate change for sustainable social-ecological systems", *Environmental Science & Policy*, Vol. 101, pp. 116-125, http://dx.doi.org/10.1016/j.envsci.2019.07.001. [58]

Fenton, N. and M. Neil (2012), *Risk Assessment and Decision Analysis with Bayesian Networks*, CRC Press. [53]

Ferdous, M. et al. (2020), "The interplay between structural flood protection, population density, and flood mortality along the Jamuna River, Bangladesh", *Regional Environmental Change*, Vol. 20/1, http://dx.doi.org/10.1007/s10113-020-01600-1. [97]

Ferrario, F. et al. (2014), "The effectiveness of coral reefs for coastal hazard risk reduction and adaptation", *Nature Communications*, Vol. 5/1, http://dx.doi.org/10.1038/ncomms4794. [196]

Folke, C. et al. (2005), "Adaptive governance of social-ecological systems", *Annual Review of Environment and Resources*, Vol. 30/1, pp. 441-473, http://dx.doi.org/10.1146/annurev.energy.30.050504.144511. [153]

Frank, S., E. Gesick and D. Victor (2021), *Inviting Danger: How Federal Disaster, Insurance and Infrastructure Policies are Magnifying the Harm of Climate Change*, Brookings, Washington, DC, https://www.brookings.edu/wp-content/uploads/2021/03/Inviting_Danger_FINAL.pdf. [96]

Friggens, N. et al. (2020), "Tree planting in organic soils does not result in net carbon sequestration on decadal timescales", *Global Change Biology*, Vol. 26/9, pp. 5178-5188, http://dx.doi.org/10.1111/gcb.15229. [113]

FWS (2019), "The Hurricane Sandy Resilience Program: Strengthening Nature for People and Wildlife", (brochure), U.S. Fish & Wildlife Service, Washington, DC, https://www.fws.gov/hurricane/sandy/pdf/Hurricane-Sandy-Resilience-Program-fact-sheet-v4-101019.pdf. [110]

Galaz, V. et al. (2017), "Global governance dimensions of globally networked risks: The state of the art in social science research", *Risk, Hazards & Crisis in Public Policy*, Vol. 8/1, pp. 4-27, http://dx.doi.org/10.1002/rhc3.12108. [160]

Gaupp, F. et al. (2019), "Changing risks of simultaneous global breadbasket failure", *Nature Climate Change*, Vol. 10/1, pp. 54-57, http://dx.doi.org/10.1038/s41558-019-0600-z. [11]

GCA (2019), *Adapt Now: A Global Call for Leadership on Climate Resilience*, Global Commission on Adaptation, Rotterdam, https://cdn.gca.org/assets/2019-09/GlobalCommission_Report_FINAL.pdf. [102]

Girardin, C. et al. (2021), "Nature-based solutions can help cool the planet — if we act now", *Nature*, Vol. 593/7858, pp. 191-194, http://dx.doi.org/10.1038/d41586-021-01241-2. [112]

Goss, M. et al. (2020), "Climate change is increasing the likelihood of extreme autumn wildfire conditions across California", *Environmental Research Letters*, Vol. 15/9, p. 094016, http://dx.doi.org/10.1088/1748-9326/ab83a7. [20]

Government of Bangladesh (2018), *Bangladesh Delta Plan 2100*, General Economic Division, Bangladesh Planning Commission, Dhaka, http://www.plancomm.gov.bd/site/files/fd6c54f6-dfab-4c71-b44a-e983ffd2bdee/-. [35]

Government of the Netherlands (2020), *National Delta Programme 2021: Staying on Track in Climate-proofing the Netherlands*, Ministry of Infrastructure and Water Management; Ministry of Agriculture, Nature and Food Quality; Ministry of the Interior and Kingdom Relations, The Hague, https://english.deltaprogramma.nl/. [34]

Griscom, B. et al. (2017), "Natural climate solutions", *Proceedings of the National Academy of Sciences*, Vol. 114/44, pp. 11645-11650, http://dx.doi.org/10.1073/pnas.1710465114. [111]

Gussmann, G. and J. Hinkel (2021), "A framework for assessing the potential effectiveness of adaptation policies: Coastal risks and sea-level rise in the Maldives", *Environmental Science & Policy*, Vol. 115, pp. 35-42, http://dx.doi.org/10.1016/j.envsci.2020.09.028. [192]

Gussmann, G. and J. Hinkel (2020), "What drives relocation policies in the Maldives?", *Climatic Change*, Vol. 163/2, pp. 931-951, http://dx.doi.org/10.1007/s10584-020-02919-8. [187]

Haasnoot, M. et al. (2020), "Defining the solution space to accelerate climate change adaptation", *Regional Environmental Change*, Vol. 20/2, http://dx.doi.org/10.1007/s10113-020-01623-8. [33]

Haasnoot, M. et al. (2020), "Adaptation to uncertain sea-level rise; how uncertainty in Antarctic mass-loss impacts the coastal adaptation strategy of the Netherlands", *Environmental Research Letters*, Vol. 15/3, p. 034007, http://dx.doi.org/10.1088/1748-9326/ab666c. [214]

Haasnoot, M. et al. (2013), "Dynamic adaptive policy pathways: A method for crafting robust decisions for a deeply uncertain world", *Global Environmental Change*, Vol. 23/2, pp. 485-498, http://dx.doi.org/10.1016/j.gloenvcha.2012.12.006. [32]

Haasnoot, M. et al. (2012), "Exploring pathways for sustainable water management in river deltas in a changing environment", *Climatic Change*, Vol. 115/3-4, pp. 795-819, http://dx.doi.org/10.1007/s10584-012-0444-2. [218]

Hada, C., R. Shaw and A. Pokhrel (2021), "Preparation and adoption of risk sensitive land use plans in the new federal context of Nepal", in *Integrated Research on Disaster Risks, Disaster Risk Reduction*, Springer International Publishing, Cham, http://dx.doi.org/10.1007/978-3-030-55563-4_10. [117]

Hallegatte, S. (2009), "Strategies to adapt to an uncertain climate change", *Global Environmental Change*, Vol. 19/2, pp. 240-247, http://dx.doi.org/10.1016/j.gloenvcha.2008.12.003. [209]

Hallegatte, S. et al. (2013), "Future flood losses in major coastal cities", *Nature Climate Change*, Vol. 3/9, pp. 802-806, http://dx.doi.org/10.1038/nclimate1979. [199]

Hallegatte, S. et al. (2016), *Unbreakable: Building the Resilience of the Poor in the Face of Natural Disasters*, World Bank, Washington, DC, http://dx.doi.org/10.1596/978-1-4648-1003-9. [124]

Haque, M. et al. (2018), "Towards establishing a national mechanism to address losses and damages: A case study from Bangladesh", in *Loss and Damage from Climate Change, Climate Risk Management, Policy and Governance*, Springer International Publishing, Cham, http://dx.doi.org/10.1007/978-3-319-72026-5_19. [81]

Harmsen, M. et al. (2019), "Taking some heat off the NDCs? The limited potential of additional short-lived climate forcers' mitigation", *Climatic Change*, Vol. 163/3, pp. 1443-1461, http://dx.doi.org/10.1007/s10584-019-02436-3. [62]

Hauer, M. et al. (2019), "Sea-level rise and human migration", *Nature Reviews Earth & Environment*, Vol. 1/1, pp. 28-39, http://dx.doi.org/10.1038/s43017-019-0002-9. [130]

Headey, D. and S. Fan (2008), “Anatomy of a crisis: The causes and consequences of surging food prices”, *Agricultural Economics*, Vol. 39, pp. 375-391, http://dx.doi.org/10.1111/j.1574-0862.2008.00345.x. [16]

Healy, A. and N. Malhotra (2009), “Myopic voters and natural disaster policy”, *American Political Science Review*, Vol. 103/3, pp. 387-406, http://dx.doi.org/10.1017/s0003055409990104. [44]

Henkel, K., J. Dovidio and S. Gaertner (2006), “Institutional discrimination, individual racism, and Hurricane Katrina”, *Analyses of Social Issues and Public Policy*, Vol. 6/1, pp. 99-124, http://dx.doi.org/10.1111/j.1530-2415.2006.00106.x. [133]

Hinkel, J. et al. (2018), “The ability of societies to adapt to twenty-first-century sea-level rise”, *Nature Climate Change*, Vol. 8/7, pp. 570-578, http://dx.doi.org/10.1038/s41558-018-0176-z. [222]

Hinkel, J. et al. (2019), “Meeting user needs for sea level rise Information: A decision analysis perspective”, *Earth’s Future*, Vol. 7/3, pp. 320-337, http://dx.doi.org/10.1029/2018ef001071. [210]

Hinkel, J. et al. (2014), “Coastal flood damage and adaptation costs under 21st century sea-level rise”, *Proceedings of the National Academy of Sciences*, Vol. 111/9, pp. 3292-3297, http://dx.doi.org/10.1073/pnas.1222469111. [78]

Hino, M., C. Field and K. Mach (2017), “Managed retreat as a response to natural hazard risk”, *Nature Climate Change*, Vol. 7/5, pp. 364-370, http://dx.doi.org/10.1038/nclimate3252. [185]

Hock, R. et al. (2019), “High mountain areas”, in Pörtner, H. et al. (eds.), *IPCC Special Report on the Ocean and Cryosphere in a Changing Climate*, Intergovernmental Panel on Climate Change, Geneva. [17]

Holdaway, A., M. Ford and S. Owen (2021), “Global-scale changes in the area of atoll islands during the 21st century”, *Anthropocene*, Vol. 33, p. 100282, http://dx.doi.org/10.1016/j.ancene.2021.100282. [181]

IDMC (2021), *The Global Report on Internal Displacement (GRID) 2021*, Internal Displacement Monitoring Centre, Geneva. [87]

IEA (2021), *Net Zero by 2050*, IEA, Paris, https://www.iea.org/reports/net-zero-by-2050. [67]

ILO (2017), *Indigenous Peoples and Climate Change: From Victims to Change Agents through Decent Work*, International Labour Organization, Geneva, https://www.ilo.org/wcmsp5/groups/public/---dgreports/---gender/documents/publication/wcms_551189.pdf. [136]

IPCC (2019), *IPCC Special Report on the Ocean and Cryosphere in a Changing Climate*, Intergovernmental Panel on Climate Change, Geneva, https://www.ipcc.ch/srocc/. [73]

IPCC (2018), *Special Report: Global Warming of 1.5°C*, Intergovernmental Panel on Climate Change, Geneva, https://www.ipcc.ch/sr15/. [60]

IPCC (2014), *Climate Change 2014: Impacts, Adaptation, and Vulnerability. Part A: Global and Sectoral Aspects. Contribution of Working Group II to the Fifth Assessment Report of the Intergovernmental Panel on Climate Change*, Cambridge University Press, Cambridge, United Kingdom, and New York, NY. [4]

IPCC (2012), *Managing the Risks of Extreme Events and Disasters to Advance Climate Change Adaptation. A Special Report of Working Groups I and II of the Intergovernmental Panel on Climate Change*, Cambridge University Press, Cambridge, United Kingdom, https://www.ipcc.ch/pdf/special-reports/srex/SREX_Full_Report.pdf. [74]

IRGC (2017), *Introduction to the IRGC Risk Governance Framework, revised version*, EPFL International Risk Governance Center, Lausanne, http://dx.doi.org/10.5075/epfl-irgc-233739. [154]

Islam, S., C. Chu and J. Smart (2020), "Challenges in integrating disaster risk reduction and climate change adaptation: Exploring the Bangladesh case", *International Journal of Disaster Risk Reduction*, Vol. 47, p. 101540, http://dx.doi.org/10.1016/j.ijdrr.2020.101540. [95]

Jack, C. et al. (2021), "Climate information: Towards transparent distillation", in *Climate Risk in Africa*, Springer International Publishing, Cham, http://dx.doi.org/10.1007/978-3-030-61160-6_2. [45]

Janetos, A. et al. (2017), *The Risk of Multiple Breadbasket Failures in the 21st Century: A Science Research Agenda*, The Frederick S. Pardee Center for the Study of the Longer-Range Future, Boston University, https://www.bu.edu/pardee/files/2017/03/Multiple-Breadbasket-Failures-Pardee-Report.pdf. [15]

Jeudy-Hugo, S., L. Lo Re and C. Falduto (2021), *Understanding countries' net-zero emissions targets*, OECD/IEA Climate Change Expert Group Papers, OECD Publishing, Paris. [63]

Jones, B. et al. (2018), "Avoiding population exposure to heat-related extremes: Demographic change vs climate change", *Climatic Change*, Vol. 146/3-4, pp. 423-437, http://dx.doi.org/10.1007/s10584-017-2133-7. [80]

Jordan, R. et al. (2015), "Citizen science as a distinct field of inquiry", *BioScience*, Vol. 65/2, pp. 208-211, http://dx.doi.org/10.1093/biosci/biu217. [149]

Kelman, I. (2015), "Difficult decisions: Migration from Small Island Developing States under climate change", *Earth's Future*, Vol. 3/4, pp. 133-142, http://dx.doi.org/10.1002/2014ef000278. [188]

Khan, M. et al. (2021), "High-density population and displacement in Bangladesh", *Science*, Vol. 372/6548, pp. 1290-1293, http://dx.doi.org/10.1126/science.abi6364. [90]

Klinke, A. and O. Renn (2019), "The coming of age of risk governance", *Risk Analysis*, Vol. 41/3, pp. 544-557, http://dx.doi.org/10.1111/risa.13383. [150]

Klinke, A. and O. Renn (2012), "Adaptive and integrative governance on risk and uncertainty", *Journal of Risk Research*, Vol. 15/3, pp. 273-292, http://dx.doi.org/10.1080/13669877.2011.636838. [152]

Klöck, C. and P. Nunn (2019), "Adaptation to climate change in Small Island Developing States: A systematic literature review of academic research", *Journal of Environment & Development*, Vol. 28/2, pp. 196-218, http://dx.doi.org/10.1177/1070496519835895. [183]

Kulp, S. and B. Strauss (2019), "New elevation data triple estimates of global vulnerability to sea-level rise and coastal flooding", *Nature Communications*, Vol. 10/1, http://dx.doi.org/10.1038/s41467-019-12808-z. [131]

Kumar, S., P. Lal and A. Kumar (2021), "Influence of Super Cyclone 'Amphan' in the Indian subcontinent amid COVID-19 pandemic", *Remote Sensing in Earth Systems Sciences*, Vol. 4/1-2, pp. 96-103, http://dx.doi.org/10.1007/s41976-021-00048-z. [84]

Kupferberg, J. (2021), "Migration and dignity – relocation and adaptation in the face of climate change displacement in the Pacific – a human rights perspective", *The International Journal of Human Rights*, pp. 1-26, http://dx.doi.org/10.1080/13642987.2021.1889515. [217]

Lau, W. and K. Kim (2012), "The 2010 Pakistan flood and Russian heat wave: Teleconnection of hydrometeorological extremes", *Journal of Hydrometeorology*, Vol. 13/1, pp. 392-403, http://dx.doi.org/10.1175/jhm-d-11-016.1. [13]

Lawrence, J. and M. Haasnoot (2017), "What it took to catalyse uptake of dynamic adaptive pathways planning to address climate change uncertainty", *Environmental Science & Policy*, Vol. 68, pp. 47-57, http://dx.doi.org/10.1016/j.envsci.2016.12.003. [48]

Leal Filho, W. et al. (2021), "Climate change adaptation on Small Island States: An assessment of limits and constraints", *Journal of Marine Science and Engineering*, Vol. 9/6, p. 602, http://dx.doi.org/10.3390/jmse9060602. [190]

Lempert, R. (2019), "Robust Decision Making (RDM)", in *Decision Making under Deep Uncertainty*, Springer International Publishing, Cham, http://dx.doi.org/10.1007/978-3-030-05252-2_2. [29]

Lenton, T. et al. (2019), "Climate tipping points — too risky to bet against", *Nature*, Vol. 575/7784, pp. 592-595, http://dx.doi.org/10.1038/d41586-019-03595-0. [22]

Levin, S. et al. (2021), "Governance in the face of extreme events: Lessons from evolutionary processes for structuring interventions, and the need to go beyond", *SSRN Electronic Journal*, http://dx.doi.org/10.2139/ssrn.3824954. [59]

Lewis, S. et al. (2019), "Restoring natural forests is the best way to remove atmospheric carbon", *Nature*, Vol. 568/7750, pp. 25-28, http://dx.doi.org/10.1038/d41586-019-01026-8. [115]

LIFE-AR (2019), *LDC 2050 Vision: Towards a Climate-resilient Future*, LDC Initiative for Effective Adaptation and Resilience, http://www.ldc-climate.org/wp-content/uploads/2019/09/2050-Vision.pdf. [138]

Lincke, D. and J. Hinkel (2021), "Coastal Migration due to 21st Century Sea-Level Rise", *Earth's Future*, Vol. 9/5, http://dx.doi.org/10.1029/2020ef001965. [129]

Li, Y. et al. (2013), "Coastal wetland loss and environmental change due to rapid urban expansion in Lianyungang, Jiangsu, China", *Regional Environmental Change*, Vol. 14/3, pp. 1175-1188, http://dx.doi.org/10.1007/s10113-013-0552-1. [198]

LSE (n.d.), "Climate Change Laws of the World", webpage, https://climate-laws.org/ (accessed on 11 June 2021). [166]

Marchau, V. et al. (eds.) (2019), *Decision Making under Deep Uncertainty*, Springer International Publishing, Cham, http://dx.doi.org/10.1007/978-3-030-05252-2. [25]

Marris, E. (2017), "Why fake islands might be a real boon for science", *Nature*, Vol. 550/7674, pp. 22-24, http://dx.doi.org/10.1038/550022a. [224]

Marshall, J. and R. Plumb (2008), *Atmosphere, Ocean and Climate Dynamics: An Introductory Text*, Academic Press, Cambridge, US. [6]

Martín-Antón, M. et al. (2016), "Review of coastal land reclamation situation in the world", *Journal of Coastal Research*, Vol. 75/sp1, pp. 667-671, http://dx.doi.org/10.2112/si75-133.1. [180]

Mason, D. et al. (2020), "How urbanization enhanced exposure to climate risks in the Pacific: A case study in the Republic of Palau", *Environmental Research Letters*, Vol. 15/11, p. 114007, http://dx.doi.org/10.1088/1748-9326/abb9dc. [79]

Masson-Delmotte, V. et al. (eds.) (2021), *Climate Change 2021: The Physical Science Basis. Contribution of Working Group I to the Sixth Assessment Report of the Intergovernmental Panel on Climate Change*, Cambridge University Press, Cambridge, United Kingdom. [3]

McLean, R. and P. Kench (2015), "Destruction or persistence of coral atoll islands in the face of 20th and 21st century sea-level rise?", *WIREs Climate Change*, Vol. 6/5, pp. 445-463, http://dx.doi.org/10.1002/wcc.350. [208]

McLeman, R. (2017), "Thresholds in climate migration", *Population and Environment*, Vol. 39/4, pp. 319-338, http://dx.doi.org/10.1007/s11111-017-0290-2. [128]

McLeman, R. et al. (2021), "Conceptual framing to link climate risk assessments and climate-migration scholarship", *Climatic Change*, Vol. 165/1-2, http://dx.doi.org/10.1007/s10584-021-03056-6. [127]

McNamara, K., R. Westoby and A. Chandra (2021), "Exploring climate-driven non-economic loss and damage in the Pacific Islands", *Current Opinion in Environmental Sustainability*, Vol. 50, pp. 1-11, http://dx.doi.org/10.1016/j.cosust.2020.07.004. [21]

MELUR-SH (2012), *Generalplan Küstenschutz des Landes Schleswig-Holstein – Fortschreibung 2012*, Ministerium für Energiewende, Landwirtschaft, Umwelt und ländliche Räume des Landes Schleswig-Holstein, Kiel, Germany. [211]

Mishra, V. (2015), "Climatic uncertainty in Himalayan water towers", *Journal of Geophysical Research: Atmospheres*, Vol. 120/7, pp. 2689-2705, http://dx.doi.org/10.1002/2014jd022650. [19]

Munir, M. (2013), "History and development of the polluter pays principle", *SSRN Electronic Journal*, http://dx.doi.org/10.2139/ssrn.2322485. [161]

Murray-Darling Basin Authority (n.d.), *Climate Variability and Change*, webpage, https://www.mdba.gov.au/basin-plan-roll-out/climate-change (accessed on 29 April 2021). [36]

Muttitt, G. et al. (2021), *Step off the Gas: International Public Finance, Natural Gas, and Clean Alternatives in the Global South*, International Institute for Sustainable Development, Winnipeg. [69]

Mycoo, M. and M. Donovan (2018), *A Blue Urban Agenda: Adapting to Climate Change in the Coastal Cities of Caribbean and Pacific Small Island Developing States*, Inter-American Development Bank, New York. [184]

Naqvi, A., F. Gaupp and S. Hochrainer-Stigler (2020), "The risk and consequences of multiple breadbasket failures: An integrated copula and multilayer agent-based modeling approach", *OR Spectrum*, Vol. 42/3, pp. 727-754, http://dx.doi.org/10.1007/s00291-020-00574-0. [8]

Nicholls, R. et al. (2007), "Coastal systems and low-lying areas", in Parry, M. et al. (eds.), *Coastal Systems and Low-Lying Areas. Climate Change 2007: Impacts, Adaptation and Vulnerability. Contribution of Working Group II to the Fourth Assessment Report of the Intergovernmental Panel on Climate Change*, Cambridge University Press, Cambridge, United Kingdom. [173]

Nishat, A. et al. (2013), *A Range of Approaches to Address Loss and Damage from Climate Change Impacts in Bangladesh*, BRAC University, Dhaka, https://www.weadapt.org/sites/weadapt.org/files/legacy-new/placemarks/files/5555b2dbe48b47069.pdf. [83]

NRC (n.d.), *Dune Restoration, South Seaside Park, NJ*, Case Study, Naturally Resilient Communities:, http://nrcsolutions.org/wp-content/uploads/2017/05/NRC_CaseStudies_Dune-Restoration_South-Seaside-Park_NJ.pdf. [108]

Nurse, L. et al. (2014), *Small islands, Climate Change 2014: Impacts, Adaptation, and Vulnerability. Part B: Regional Aspects. Contribution of Working Group II to the Fifth Assessment Report of the Intergovernmental Panel of Climate Change*, Cambridge University Press, Cambridge, United Kingdom, and New York. [220]

OECD (2021), "Adapting to a changing climate in the management of coastal zones", *OECD Environment Policy Papers*, No. 24, OECD Publishing, Paris, http://dx.doi.org/10.1787/b21083c5-en. [77]

OECD (2021), *Strengthening Climate Resilience: Guidance for Governments and Development Co-operation*, OECD Publishing, Paris, https://dx.doi.org/10.1787/4b08b7be-en. [147]

OECD (2021), *Transport strategies for net-zero systems by design*, OECD Publishing, Paris. [71]

OECD (2020), *Common Ground Between the Paris Agreement and the Sendai Framework: Climate Change Adaptation and Disaster Risk Reduction*, OECD Publishing, Paris, https://dx.doi.org/10.1787/3edc8d09-en. [57]

OECD (2020), "Nature-based solutions for adapting to water-related climate risks", *OECD Environment Policy Papers*, No. 21, OECD Publishing, Paris, https://dx.doi.org/10.1787/2257873d-en. [106]

OECD (2020), *OECD Compendium of Policy Good Practices for Quality Infrastructure Investment*, OECD Publishing, Paris, https://www.oecd.org/finance/oecd-compendium-of-policy-good-practices-for-quality-infrastructure-investment.htm. [42]

OECD (2019), *Accelerating Climate Action: Refocusing Policies through a Well-being Lens*, OECD Publishing, Paris, https://dx.doi.org/10.1787/2f4c8c9a-en. [158]

OECD (2018), "Climate-resilient infrastructure", *OECD Environment Policy Papers*, No. 14, OECD Publishing, Paris, http://dx.doi.org/10.1787/4fdf9eaf-en. [41]

OECD (2018), *Making Development Co-operation Work for Small Island Developing States*, OECD Publishing, Paris, https://dx.doi.org/10.1787/9789264287648-en. [206]

OECD (2017), *Investing in Climate, Investing in Growth*, OECD Publishing, Paris, https://dx.doi.org/10.1787/9789264273528-en. [65]

OECD (2014), *Recommendation of the Council on the Governance of Critical Risks*, https://www.oecd.org/gov/risk/Critical-Risks-Recommendation.pdf. [151]

OECD/IEA (2021), *Update on recent progress in reform of inefficient fossil-fuel subsidies that encourage wasteful consumption*, https://www.oecd.org/fossil-fuels/publicationsandfurtherreading/OECD-IEA-G20-Fossil-Fuel-Subsidies-Reform-Update-2021.pdf. [68]

OECD/The World Bank/UN Environment (2018), *Financing Climate Futures*, OECD Publishing, Paris, http://dx.doi.org/10.1787/9789264308114-en. [145]

Oppenheimer, M. et al. (2019), *Sea Level Rise and Implications for Low Lying Islands, Coasts and Communities*, Oxford University Press. [132]

Otto, I. et al. (2020), "Social tipping dynamics for stabilizing Earth's climate by 2050", *Proceedings of the National Academy of Sciences*, Vol. 117/5, pp. 2354-2365, http://dx.doi.org/10.1073/pnas.1900577117. [163]

Pakulski, I. et al. (2021), *The Bangladesh Delta : A Lighthouse Case Study*, World Bank, Washington, DC, https://openknowledge.worldbank.org/bitstream/handle/10986/35066/The-Bangladesh-Delta-A-Lighthouse-Case-Study.pdf?sequence=5&isAllowed=y. [86]

Pearl, J. and D. Mackenzie (2018), *The Book of Why: The New Science of Cause and Effect*, Penguin. [52]

Pinsky, M., G. Guannel and K. Arkema (2013), "Quantifying wave attenuation to inform coastal habitat conservation", *Ecosphere*, Vol. 4/8, p. art95, http://dx.doi.org/10.1890/es13-00080.1. [194]

Pontee, N. et al. (2016), "Nature-based solutions: Lessons from around the world", *Proceedings of the Institution of Civil Engineers - Maritime Engineering*, Vol. 169/1, pp. 29-36, http://dx.doi.org/10.1680/jmaen.15.00027. [175]

Popper, S. (2019), "Robust decision making and scenario discovery in the absence of formal models", *Futures & Foresight Science*, Vol. 1/3-4, http://dx.doi.org/10.1002/ffo2.22. [40]

Quataert, E. et al. (2015), "The influence of coral reefs and climate change on wave-driven flooding of tropical coastlines", *Geophysical Research Letters*, Vol. 42/15, pp. 6407-6415, http://dx.doi.org/10.1002/2015gl064861. [195]

Rahaman, M. et al. (2020), "Nature-based solutions to promote climate change adaptation and disaster risk reduction along the coastal belt of Bangladesh", in *The Palgrave Handbook of Climate Resilient Societies*, Springer International Publishing, Cham, http://dx.doi.org/10.1007/978-3-030-32811-5_49-1. [85]

Ranger, N., T. Reeder and J. Lowe (2013), "Addressing 'deep' uncertainty over long-term climate in major infrastructure projects: Four innovations of the Thames Estuary 2100 Project", *EURO Journal on Decision Processes*, Vol. 1/3-4, pp. 233-262, http://dx.doi.org/10.1007/s40070-013-0014-5. [219]

Ribot, J. (2014), "Cause and response: vulnerability and climate in the Anthropocene", *The Journal of Peasant Studies*, Vol. 41/5, pp. 667-705, http://dx.doi.org/10.1080/03066150.2014.894911. [122]

Robinson, S. (2020), "Climate change adaptation in SIDS : A systematic review of the literature pre and post the IPCC Fifth Assessment Report", *WIREs Climate Change*, Vol. 11/4, http://dx.doi.org/10.1002/wcc.653. [191]

Rocha, I. et al. (2021), "Typhoons during the COVID-19 pandemic in the Philippines: Impact of a double crisis on mental health", *Disaster Medicine and Public Health Preparedness*, pp. 1-4, http://dx.doi.org/10.1017/dmp.2021.140. [2]

Rogelj, J. et al. (2021), "Net-zero emissions targets are vague: Three ways to fix", *Nature*, Vol. 591/7850, pp. 365-368, http://dx.doi.org/10.1038/d41586-021-00662-3. [66]

Rupp-Armstrong, S. and R. Nicholls (2007), "Coastal and estuarine retreat: A comparison of the application of managed realignment in England and Germany", *Journal of Coastal Research*, Vol. 23/6, http://www.jstor.org/stable/30138541. [186]

Salman, R. et al. (2019), *Transformative adaptation in livestock production systems*, World Resources Institute, Washington, DC, http://www.wri.org/publication/livestock-transformative-adaptation. [139]

Schäfer, L., K. Warner and S. Kreft (2018), "Exploring and Managing Adaptation Frontiers with Climate Risk Insurance", in *Loss and Damage from Climate Change, Climate Risk Management, Policy and Governance*, Springer International Publishing, Cham, http://dx.doi.org/10.1007/978-3-319-72026-5_13. [98]

Scheidel, A. and C. Work (2018), "Forest plantations and climate change discourses: New powers of 'green' grabbing in Cambodia", *Land Use Policy*, Vol. 77, pp. 9-18, http://dx.doi.org/10.1016/j.landusepol.2018.04.057. [114]

Schweizer, P. and O. Renn (2019), "Governance of systemic risks for disaster prevention and mitigation", *Disaster Prevention and Management: An International Journal*, Vol. 28/6, pp. 862-874, http://dx.doi.org/10.1108/dpm-09-2019-0282. [156]

Scott, C. et al. (2019), "Water in the Hindu Kush Himalaya", in *The Hindu Kush Himalaya Assessment*, Springer International Publishing, Cham, http://dx.doi.org/10.1007/978-3-319-92288-1_8. [18]

Seaman, J. et al. (2014), "The Household Economy Approach. Managing the impact of climate change on poverty and food security in developing countries", *Climate Risk Management*, Vol. 4-5, pp. 59-68, http://dx.doi.org/10.1016/j.crm.2014.10.001. [54]

Seddon, N. et al. (2020), "Understanding the value and limits of nature-based solutions to climate change and other global challenges", *Philosophical Transactions of the Royal Society B: Biological Sciences*, Vol. 375/1794, p. 20190120, http://dx.doi.org/10.1098/rstb.2019.0120. [107]

Serpa, S. (ed.) (2021), "Review on socio-economic impacts of 'Triple Threats' of COVID-19, desert locusts, and floods in East Africa: Evidence from Ethiopia", *Cogent Social Sciences*, Vol. 7/1, p. 1885122, http://dx.doi.org/10.1080/23311886.2021.1885122. [1]

Setzer, J. and R. Byrnes (2020), *Global Trends in Climate Change Litigation: 2020 Snapshot*, Grantham Research Institute on Climate Change and the Environment, London, https://www.lse.ac.uk/granthaminstitute/wp-content/uploads/2020/07/Global-trends-in-climate-change. [165]

Shakhawat Hossain, M. et al. (2020), "Climate change impacts on farmland value in Bangladesh", *Ecological Indicators*, Vol. 112, p. 106181, http://dx.doi.org/10.1016/j.ecolind.2020.106181. [82]

Shamsuddoha, M. et al. (2013), *Establishing Links between Disaster Risk Reduction and Climate Change Adaptation in the Context of Loss and Damage: Policies and Approaches to Bangladesh*, Center for Participatory Research and Development, Dhaka. [94]

Shepherd, T. (2019), "Storyline approach to the construction of regional climate change information", *Proceedings of the Royal Society A: Mathematical, Physical and Engineering Sciences*, Vol. 475/2225, p. 20190013, http://dx.doi.org/10.1098/rspa.2019.0013. [38]

Shepherd, T. (2014), "Atmospheric circulation as a source of uncertainty in climate change projections", *Nature Geoscience*, Vol. 7/10, pp. 703-708, http://dx.doi.org/10.1038/ngeo2253. [28]

Shepherd, T. et al. (2018), "Storylines: An alternative approach to representing uncertainty in physical aspects of climate change", *Climatic Change*, Vol. 151/3-4, pp. 555-571, http://dx.doi.org/10.1007/s10584-018-2317-9. [39]

Shortridge, J., S. Guikema and B. Zaitchik (2016), "Robust decision making in data scarce contexts: Addressing data and model limitations for infrastructure planning under transient climate change", *Climatic Change*, Vol. 140/2, pp. 323-337, http://dx.doi.org/10.1007/s10584-016-1845-4. [31]

Shuttleworth, E. et al. (2019), "Restoration of blanket peat moorland delays stormflow from hillslopes and reduces peak discharge", *Journal of Hydrology X*, Vol. 2, p. 100006, http://dx.doi.org/10.1016/j.hydroa.2018.100006. [116]

Siders, A., M. Hino and K. Mach (2019), "The case for strategic and managed climate retreat", *Science*, Vol. 365/6455, pp. 761-763, http://dx.doi.org/10.1126/science.aax8346. [204]

Smallegan, S. et al. (2016), "Morphological response of a sandy barrier island with a buried seawall during Hurricane Sandy", *Coastal Engineering*, Vol. 110, pp. 102-110, http://dx.doi.org/10.1016/j.coastaleng.2016.01.005. [109]

Soergel, B. et al. (2021), "Combining ambitious climate policies with efforts to eradicate poverty", *Nature Communications*, Vol. 12/1, http://dx.doi.org/10.1038/s41467-021-22315-9. [72]

Somanathan, E. et al. (2014), "National and sub-national policies and institutions", in Edenhofer, O. et al. (eds.), *Climate Change 2014: Mitigation of Climate Change. Contribution of Working Group III to the Fifth Assessment Report of the Intergovernmental Panel on Climate Change*, Cambridge University Press, Cambridge, United Kingdom, and New York. [143]

Spalding, M. et al. (2013), "Coastal ecosystems: A critical element of risk reduction", *Conservation Letters*, Vol. 7/3, pp. 293-301, http://dx.doi.org/10.1111/conl.12074. [176]

Speelman, L., R. Nicholls and J. Dyke (2016), "Contemporary migration intentions in the Maldives: The role of environmental and other factors", *Sustainability Science*, Vol. 12/3, pp. 433-451, http://dx.doi.org/10.1007/s11625-016-0410-4. [207]

Storlazzi, C. et al. (2018), "Most atolls will be uninhabitable by the mid-21st century because of sea-level rise exacerbating wave-driven flooding", *Science Advances*, Vol. 4/4, p. eaap9741, http://dx.doi.org/10.1126/sciadv.aap9741. [221]

Stuart-Smith, R. et al. (2021), "Filling the evidentiary gap in climate litigation", *Nature Climate Change*, http://dx.doi.org/10.1038/s41558-021-01086-7. [170]

Sudmeier-Rieux, K. et al. (2015), "Opportunities, incentives and challenges to risk sensitive land use planning: Lessons from Nepal, Spain and Vietnam", *International Journal of Disaster Risk Reduction*, Vol. 14, pp. 205-224, http://dx.doi.org/10.1016/j.ijdrr.2014.09.009. [76]

Surminski, S. and D. Oramas-Dorta (2013), "Do flood insurance schemes in developing countries provide incentives to reduce physical risks?", *Centre for Climate Change Economics and Policy Working Paper*, Vol. 139, http://www.cccep.ac.uk/wp-content/uploads/2015/10/WP11. [99]

Temmerman, S. et al. (2013), "Ecosystem-based coastal defence in the face of global change", *Nature*, Vol. 504/7478, pp. 79-83, http://dx.doi.org/10.1038/nature12859. [177]

Thomas, A. and L. Benjamin (2018), "Policies and mechanisms to address climate-induced migration and displacement in Pacific and Caribbean small island developing states", *International Journal of Climate Change Strategies and Management*, Vol. 10/1, pp. 86-104, http://dx.doi.org/10.1108/ijccsm-03-2017-0055. [216]

Thomas, K. et al. (2018), "Explaining differential vulnerability to climate change: A social science review", *Wiley Interdisciplinary Reviews: Climate Change*, Vol. 10/2, http://dx.doi.org/10.1002/wcc.565. [119]

Tiggeloven, T. et al. (2020), "Global-scale benefit–cost analysis of coastal flood adaptation to different flood risk drivers using structural measures", *Natural Hazards and Earth System Sciences*, Vol. 20/4, pp. 1025-1044, http://dx.doi.org/10.5194/nhess-20-1025-2020. [200]

Toussaint, P. (2020), "Loss and damage and climate litigation: The case for greater interlinkage", *Review of European, Comparative & International Environmental Law*, http://dx.doi.org/10.1111/reel.12335. [167]

Trenberth, K. and J. Fasullo (2012), "Climate extremes and climate change: The Russian heat wave and other climate extremes of 2010", *Journal of Geophysical Research: Atmospheres*, Vol. 117/D17, pp. n/a-n/a, http://dx.doi.org/10.1029/2012jd018020. [14]

Tye, S. and D. Grinspan (2020), "Building a climate resilient future for Costa Rica's coffee farming communities", *Practice Note*, World Resources Institute, Washington, DC, http://dx.doi.org/10.46830/wripn.19.00103. [142]

UK Government (2021), *Thames Estuary TE2100 Plan*, https://www.gov.uk/government/publications/thames-estuary-2100-te2100/thames-estuary-2100-te2100 (accessed on 29 April 2021). [37]

UN (2020), *Flash Update # 2*, 22 May, UN Resident Coordinator for Bangladesh, https://reliefweb.int/report/bangladesh/office-un-resident-coordinator-flash-update-2-22-may-2020-bangladesh-2020-very (accessed on 8 July 2021). [89]

UN Human Rights Committee (2020), *Views adopted by the Committee under article 5 (4) of the Optional*, https://demaribus.files.wordpress.com/2020/02/2728-2016.pdf. [169]

UNDP (2019), *Five Approaches to Build Functional Early Warning Systems*, United Nations Development Programme, New York, https://reliefweb.int/report/world/five-approaches-build-functional-early-warning-systems. [105]

UNDRR (2021), *GAR Special Report on Drought*, United Nations Office for Disaster Risk Reduction, Baltimore, US. [157]

UNDRR (2019), *Global Assessment Report on Disaster Risk Reduction*, United Nations Office for Disaster Risk Reduction, Baltimore, US, https://gar.undrr.org/report-2019. [9]

UNDRR (2015), *Sendai Framework for Disaster Risk Reduction 2015 - 2030*, United Nations Office for Disaster Risk Reduction, Geneva, https://www.undrr.org/publication/sendai-framework-disaster-risk-reduction-2015-2030. [100]

UNEP (2021), *Global Climate Litigation Report: 2020 Status Review*, UN Environment Programme, Nairobi, https://www.unep.org/resources/report/global-climate-litigation-report-2020-status-review. [168]

UNFCCC (2020), *Policy Brief: Technologies for Averting, Minimizing and Addressing Loss and Damage in Coastal Zones*, United Nations Framework Convention on Climate Change, Bonn, https://unfccc.int/ttclear/misc_/StaticFiles/gnwoerk_static/2020_coastalzones/cfecc85aaa8d43d38cd0f6ceae2b61e4/2bb696550804403fa08df8a924922c2e.pdf. [103]

UNFCCC (2015), *Paris Agreement*, United Nations Framework Convention on Climate Change, Bonn, https://treaties.un.org/pages/ViewDetails.aspx?src=TREATY&mtdsg_no=XXVII-7-d&chapter=27. [61]

UNFCCC (n.d.), "Local Communities and Indigenous Peoples Platform", webpage, https://unfccc.int/LCIPP#eq-1 (accessed on 23 June 2021). [137]

Vincent, K. and D. Conway (2021), "Key issues and progress in understanding climate risk in Africa", in *Climate Risk in Africa*, Springer International Publishing, Cham, http://dx.doi.org/10.1007/978-3-030-61160-6_1. [24]

Vincent, K. et al. (2021), "Co-production: Learning from Contexts", in *Climate Risk in Africa*, Springer International Publishing, Cham, http://dx.doi.org/10.1007/978-3-030-61160-6_3. [46]

Volpato, G. and E. King (2018), "From cattle to camels: Trajectories of livelihood adaptation and social-ecological resilience in a Kenyan pastoralist community", *Regional Environmental Change*, Vol. 19/3, pp. 849-865, http://dx.doi.org/10.1007/s10113-018-1438-z. [140]

Wainwright, C. et al. (2019), "'Eastern African Paradox' rainfall decline due to shorter not less intense Long Rains", *npj Climate and Atmospheric Science*, Vol. 2/1, http://dx.doi.org/10.1038/s41612-019-0091-7. [49]

Walker, W., M. Haasnoot and J. Kwakkel (2013), "Adapt or perish: A review of planning approaches for adaptation under deep uncertainty", *Sustainability*, Vol. 5/3, pp. 955-979, http://dx.doi.org/10.3390/su5030955. [212]

Walker, W., R. Lempert and J. Kwakkel (2013), "Deep uncertainty", in *Encyclopedia of Operations Research and Management Science*, Springer US, Boston, MA, http://dx.doi.org/10.1007/978-1-4419-1153-7_1140. [26]

Walker, W., S. Rahman and J. Cave (2001), "Adaptive policies, policy analysis, and policy-making", *European Journal of Operational Research*, Vol. 128/2, pp. 282-289, http://dx.doi.org/10.1016/s0377-2217(00)00071-0. [213]

Webster, P. (2008), "Myanmar's deadly daffodil", *Nature Geoscience*, Vol. 1/8, pp. 488-490, http://dx.doi.org/10.1038/ngeo257. [104]

Webster, P., V. Toma and H. Kim (2011), "Were the 2010 Pakistan floods predictable?", *Geophysical Research Letters*, Vol. 38/4, pp. n/a-n/a, http://dx.doi.org/10.1029/2010gl046346. [27]

White, I. and J. Lawrence (2020), "Continuity and change in national riskscapes: A New Zealand perspective on the challenges for climate governance theory and practice", *Cambridge Journal of Regions, Economy and Society*, Vol. 13/2, pp. 215-231, http://dx.doi.org/10.1093/cjres/rsaa005. [144]

Winsemius, H. et al. (2015), *Disaster Risk, Climate Change, and Poverty: Assessing the Global Exposure of Poor People to Floods and Droughts*, World Bank, Washington, DC, http://dx.doi.org/10.1596/1813-9450-7480. [121]

WMO (2021), *State of the Global Climate 2020*, World Meteorological Organization, Geneva, https://library.wmo.int/index.php?lvl=notice_display&id=21880#.YNxd8ugzbQC. [88]

WMO (2020), *2020 State of Climate Service: Risk Information and Early Warning Systems*, World Meteorological Organization, Geneva, https://library.wmo.int/index.php?lvl=notice_display&id=21777#.YCmtXGhKg2y. [101]

Woetzel, J. et al. (2020), *Climate Risk and Response: Physical Hazards and Socioeconomic Impacts*, McKinsey Global Institute, https://www.mckinsey.com/business-functions/sustainability/our-insights/climate-risk-and-response-physical-hazards-and-socioeconomic-impacts. [118]

Woetzel, J. et al. (2020), "Will the world's breadbaskets become less reliable?", 18 May, McKinsey Global Institute, https://www.mckinsey.com/business-functions/sustainability/our-insights/will-the-worlds-breadbaskets-become-less-reliable. [10]

Wong, P. et al. (2014), "Coastal systems and low-lying areas", in Field, C. et al. (eds.), *Climate Change 2014: Impacts, Adaptation, and Vulnerability. Part A: Global and Sectoral Aspects. Contribution of Working Group II to the Fifth Assessment Report of the Intergovernmental Panel of Climate Change*, Cambridge University Press, Cambridge, United Kingdom, and New York. [174]

World Bank (2021), *Overlooked: Examining the Impact of Disasters and Climate Shocks on Poverty in the Europe and Central Asia Region*, World Bank, Washington, DC. [5]

Yamamoto, L. and M. Esteban (2014), *Atoll Island States and International Law*, Springer Berlin Heidelberg, Berlin, Heidelberg, http://dx.doi.org/10.1007/978-3-642-38186-7. [215]

Zheng, Z., L. Zhao and K. Oleson (2021), "Large model structural uncertainty in global projections of urban heat waves", *Nature Communications*, Vol. 12/1, http://dx.doi.org/10.1038/s41467-021-24113-9. [23]

Zottarelli, L. (2008), "Post-Hurricane Katrina employment recovery: The Interaction of race and place", *Social Science Quarterly*, Vol. 89/3, pp. 592-607, http://dx.doi.org/10.1111/j.1540-6237.2008.00550.x. [134]

5 Finance and financial risks in the face of growing losses and damages

This chapter has two aims. First, it explores the implications of current and future losses and damages from climate change on public finances. These affect the ability of governments to pursue sustainable development and poverty reduction priorities under a changing climate. Second, it examines the critical roles of finance in reducing and managing the risks of losses and damages, namely in risk reduction, retention and transfer. The chapter also provides insights on the landscape of development finance directly or indirectly supporting these efforts, recognising the important role of humanitarian finance in supporting relief.

In Brief

Losses and damages impact fiscal sustainability: Risk financing instruments need to be employed in a comprehensive manner, while ensuring inclusiveness

Climate-related hazards can have large and complex macroeconomic implications with the precise economic effects depending on the type of hazard and the country context. Impacts are already stretching the financial capacity of many vulnerable countries, especially Small Island Developing States (SIDS) and Least Developed Countries (LDCs). The sustainability of the financial sector, which provides tools for risk financing, is also at risk:

- ***Fiscal sustainability*** is impacted through decreasing government revenues and the need to fund disaster response, diverting spending from other priorities (e.g. investment, education, resilience). In the long term, this may weaken the ability to repay debts. Following a disaster, debt financing is likely to be expensive for affected countries. Some may not be eligible for official development assistance (ODA) given their level of development, exacerbating fiscal challenges.
- The ***financial sector*** directly feels the impact from weather and climate events. Damage to household and business assets, for example, can disrupt production processes and value chains through non-performing loans and reduced value of collateral. This, in turn, increases the costs of services supplied by banking and insurance sectors. These increased costs will likely lead to reduced lending and higher insurance premiums, prolonging the recovery period. Some climate events – from slow-onset events to correlations between some extreme weather events and potential tipping points – are likely to challenge financial risk management approaches. Potential financial stability risks merit further attention and may require co-ordinated international action.

Countries, households, businesses and communities use a diverse set of complementary financial mechanisms to reduce and manage the risks of losses and damages from climate change. The different approaches need to be combined in a comprehensive risk financing strategy by national and subnational governments:

- ***Risk reduction***, such as improving the physical durability of buildings, is the first line of defence against the impacts of climate change. It reduces the risks of losses and damages, and provides a basis for managing residual risks. In addition, it covers social protection schemes, which increase the resilience of otherwise vulnerable and marginalised populations.
- ***Risk retention***, such as disaster management funds, can allocate or redirect budgets to help provide quick access to funds in the face of frequent and low-intensity weather events. Credit from international development banks for unforeseen circumstances is more appropriate for medium-frequency, medium-intensity events. The volume of funds needed to better cope with more intense and less frequent hazards usually exceeds the immediately available funds from government budgets.
- ***Risk transfer***, such as catastrophe bonds or climate risk insurance solutions, provide public actors quick access to resources that can support the recovery from losses and damages. These are well suited for low-probability, high-severity events since large funds are most accessible from capital markets. Such risk transfer mechanisms may benefit from further transfer or sharing through risk pooling or enhanced by other types of risk management, in some cases with the support of development finance.

Many countries have gaps in coverage for climate risks. In high-income countries, over half of economic losses and damages from climate-related extreme events are insured; in other countries barely a tenth are covered by insurance. Such gaps are especially prevalent with non-economic losses and damages, such as cultural losses. At the household level, people with limited access to established finance mechanisms may need to resort to alternatives that build resilience in the short term at the expense of the longer term, for example by taking children out of school to help with recovery of the household. At the international level, the potential role of insurance coverage and affordability is increasingly recognised as part of a comprehensive risk financing strategy. Efforts to scale up insurance must reflect the changing nature of the risks to ensure sustainability of the schemes. The gradual emergence of slow-onset events might in the future strain the traditional model for insurance, making diversification of risks more difficult.

Domestic financing needs might be reduced with financial regulation, policy and transparency. Such elements facilitate an enabling environment that incentivises the reduction and management of risks. Government plays an important role in relation to the disclosure, awareness and understanding of climate risks and risk financing options setting expectations for economic actors and for the financial system. These can strengthen the ability of private actors to manage their own risks, increase resilience and highlight priorities for government intervention. Fiscal rules with escape clauses may also provide a tool to facilitate fiscal sustainability.

International development finance also plays an important role in supporting partner countries. These countries are calling (inter alia) for enhanced and simplified access to finance that reflects national circumstances and is aligned with national priorities. Providers of bilateral and multilateral development finance increasingly realise the importance of explicitly taking the risk of losses and damages into account in their strategic and programming approaches. The methodology of this report provides initial insights, though does not yet capture the full complexity and breadth of development finance for reducing and managing the risk of climate-related losses and damages. International development finance needs to ensure that it targets those most at risk. Mechanisms must reflect the nature of those risks to manage fiscal and debt sustainability. Development co-operation may also have to adjust its approach to support provided to countries no longer eligible to ODA. Such countries may remain highly exposed and vulnerable to climate-related hazards. The humanitarian community is playing an increasingly important role in bridging disaster response and preventive action, and such activities can be better co-ordinated with development co-operation efforts.

5.1. Introduction

The adverse impacts of climate-related hazards are stretching the fiscal capacity of many countries affected, as well as impacting people, livelihoods and assets. In 2019, for example, Mozambique was hit by Tropical Cyclones Idai (March) and then Kenneth (April). This pushed government debt to 103% of gross domestic product (GDP) that year. Mozambique was hit again by two major cyclones in January and February 2021; debt was projected to reach 125% of GDP by the end of 2021 (IMF, 2021[1]). Mozambique is not an isolated example. In September 2019, Hurricane Dorian, a Category 5 hurricane, made landfall in the Bahamas causing at least 70 deaths. It also generated losses and damages estimated at USD 3.4 billion, equivalent to around a quarter of the Bahamas' GDP (Zegarra et al., 2020[2]). Dorian was only one of a series of hurricanes to make landfall in the Caribbean in recent years. Parts of Asia are similarly affected by tropical cyclones. These repeatedly occurring disasters affect GDP, often for many years, but they also destroy lives and livelihoods. The attribution of such events to climate change is very difficult for many developing countries because they lack high quality observational data, as highlighted in Chapter 3 and in Hope (2019[3]). However, climate change worsens the adverse impacts of such cyclones: rainfall is more intense and storm surges on coasts higher.

This chapter explores finance in relation to losses and damages from climate change. Section 5.2 surveys the macroeconomic implications of climate change, with a focus on fiscal sustainability. Section 5.3 provides an overview of the roles finance can play with managing losses and damages from climate change, arranged around risk reduction, risk retention and risk transfer. Section 5.4 reports on the current landscape and future trends of the links between development finance and losses and damages from climate change.

5.2. Macroeconomic implications of climate change

Risk of climate-related hazards can have large and complex macroeconomic implications. The economic effects, however, differ across different types of hazards. The immediate economic effects of a hazard will be a shock, with losses or damages of assets (e.g. property or crops in the field) and impacts on labour supply. For example, some climate-related hazards, such as more severe floods and storms, can lead to damages to buildings and infrastructure assets. Others, such as heatwaves, are unlikely to cause as much damage to assets. However, they may have other macroeconomic implications, such as declines in productivity in some sectors (Day et al., 2018[4]).

These implications can disrupt economic output in one or more sectors, which might affect trade, foreign earning and exchange rates. For example, climate risks may affect food security both directly and indirectly. A direct impact could be lower yields, while an indirect impact could be reduced water availability and quality, more pests and disease, and fewer pollination services (Mbow et al., 2019[5]). This, in turn, can contribute to increased food prices locally or even globally. The extent of the price increases will depend on the scale of the adverse impact and the importance of the affected crops in global supply chains (see Box 4.1). Similarly, tourism earnings will be vulnerable to climate risks that may destroy iconic natural attractions (e.g. coral reefs), wash away beaches, destroy resorts and local infrastructure, and reduce freshwater supplies (Wolf et al., 2021[6]). Some losses and damages can be quantified in monetary terms. Others, such as non-economic losses, cannot be quantified. Attempts to quantify such losses may make assumptions that are hard to justify or are not widely accepted. Examples include lives lost, the loss of species, cultural and psychological losses, temporary or permanent impairment of people's mobility and lost opportunities for children and future generations (Tschakert et al., 2019[7]) (see Chapter 2).

Institutions and socio-economic characteristics interact with hazards and some events will have smaller effects because countries already deal with that type of hazard. For example, cold regions will be more vulnerable to high temperatures because houses and infrastructure were built with cold weather in mind, and designed to trap heat. Likewise, hot regions may be more vulnerable to extremely cold days, although such extremes are projected to decrease as climate change progresses (Heutel, Miller and Molitor, 2020[8]). The extreme events of 2021 (e.g. the North American heatwave) demonstrate how the intensity of the extremes is already changing at 1.09°C of warming. Novel hazards are emerging, which may be all the more damaging since countries have no or limited experience with such hazards. Some of these shocks to capital, labour and income may persist over years.

Major impacts or disasters demand an immediate response in terms of support to affected individuals and households. However, such an effort may also increase government deficits, increase public debt levels and limit other productive investments. Subsequent recovery and reconstruction activities are likely to have positive direct and indirect economic impacts. Finance may be attracted if interest rates rise after such a shock, reflecting the need for new capital. Where private (domestic or international) finance does not respond, development assistance will likely need to fill the gap. Capacity constraints may also limit the speed and extent of recovery.

For these reasons, economic activity (GDP per capita) may take a range of plausibly different shapes after a disaster (see Box 5.1 for a methodological overview). Expected growth path will depend on the economic effects of the impact that are assumed to dominate. Potential stylised pathways for GDP per capita are shown in Figure 5.1. Scenarios A and B show no long-term impact on growth pathways. Meanwhile, Scenarios C and D lead to a permanent reduction or increase output per capita, respectively. These effects are perhaps due to biting financial constraints (Scenario C) or the replacement of lost capital by improved technologies (Scenario D). These pathways all have long-run growth rates unaffected by the disaster. This may not always be the case; many future climate projections include frequently recurring or more intense climate-related hazards, already witnessed in many countries. A meta-analysis concluded such extreme climate and weather events have a negative impact on economic growth, with the magnitude varying by disaster and country (Klomp and Valckx, 2014[9]).

Figure 5.1. Stylised pathways for GDP per capita after an extreme weather event

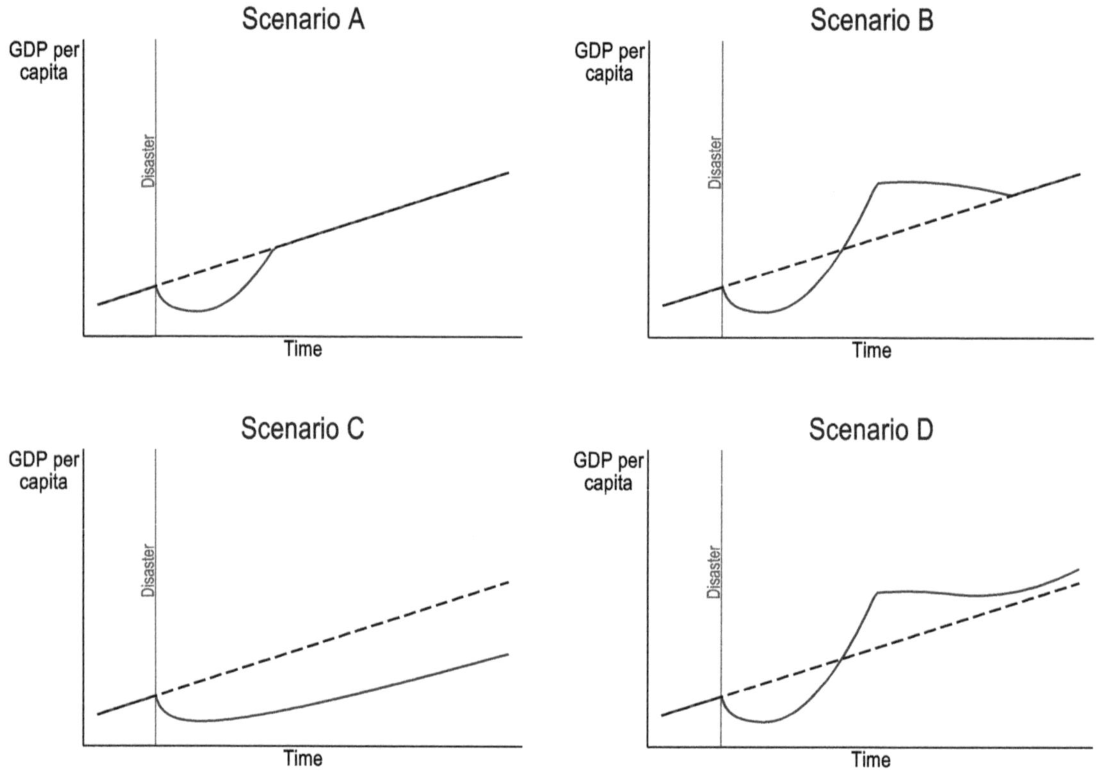

Source: (Chhibber and Laajaj, 2008[10]).

Box 5.1. Understanding impacts of extreme weather and climate events

The macroeconomic implications of extreme weather and climate events have been estimated through a range of different approaches. Some approaches are more suitable for assessing short-term implications (based on no assumed changes to behaviour and production). Others capture the dynamic implications for the economy over longer periods. Typically, in a more long-term approach, different growth models and regional economic models can link the macroeconomic to micro-level losses and damages, perhaps informed by simulation models.

Catastrophe models using geographic information systems are typically used at a range of scales (local to global). They map and then estimate losses and damages to assets (typically property) and affected populations from a range of different hazards. In so doing, they make different assumptions about the frequency and intensity of a specific type of hazard, such as floods.

Such models can be used to price insurance against such risks or to inform cost-benefit analyses of different adaptation interventions and investments. Mechler (2016[11]) finds that cost-benefit ratios to reducing disaster risks *ex ante* are considerable (though varying across context and intervention). Indeed, benefits outweigh costs by a factor of four on average. Agent-based modelling can be used in conjunction with catastrophe models to approximate behaviours of economic actors. This influences disaster preparedness at a local scale, which may lead to significantly lower damage estimates.

Source: (Botzen, Deschenes and Sanders, 2019[12]).

The impact of disasters also depends on the type of losses and damages sustained. Disasters that result in a larger number of lives lost and lives affected (lethal disasters) have a larger negative impact on output growth than those that primarily destroy property and capital. This is because reconstruction of property, especially when covered by insurance, can contribute to a short-term increase in economic growth (Noy and Vu, 2010[13]). Such positive effects of reconstruction on economic growth, however, are unlikely in general (Botzen, Deschenes and Sanders, 2019[12]). Indeed, the effects of weather and climate events on the economy are overwhelmingly found to be negative, sometimes lasting more than a decade (Deryugina, 2017[14]). The finance sector itself is at risk from climate change, see Box 5.2.

The macroeconomic implications are further mediated by a number of country-specific factors:

- ***Geographic location and size***: Financial impacts of climate change are especially felt in countries that are geographically or economically small (IMF, 2019[15]). The average annual cost of disasters in Small Island Developing States (SIDS), for example, is nearly 2% of GDP, more than four times the amount for larger countries (IMF, 2016[16]). This is in part due to their geographic location that exposes many SIDS to extreme events. These range from annual hurricane and cyclone seasons to slow-onset events, such as sea-level rise (SLR) (see Chapters 3 and 4). However, the scale of impacts is also a factor of their relatively small size, adversely affecting the investment, income and revenue base (IMF, 2016[16]).
- ***Socio-economic development:*** Level of socio-economic development can influence the impact of climate events, including factors such as per capita GDP, social protection, trade openness and literacy rates (Botzen, Deschenes and Sanders, 2019[12]). For example, strong property rights enable the development and penetration of insurance markets, which lead to a quicker recovery from extreme events (Kousky, 2019[17]) (see Section 5.3.3). Less diversification and higher levels of agriculture as a share of economic output can amplify the impact of extreme climate and weather events in developing countries (see next bullet). Given that socio-economic development dampens the impacts, Least Developed Countries (LDCs) are and will be among the most affected by climate change. Socio-economic characteristics are also important within countries as well; impacts of

climate-related events differ by sub-national levels of development and other factors (Noy and Vu, 2010[13]).

- ***Composition of the economy:*** Developing countries tend to be more vulnerable because they depend on a few sectors compared to larger or more economically diverse countries (Narain, Rabanal and Byskov, 2003[10]; Joya and Rougier, 2019[19]). Vulnerability is often exacerbated by the relatively dominant role of agricultural products in LDCs, which represent over 15% of GDP, compared to around 1% in OECD countries (World Bank, 2021[20]). Agriculture is a particularly vulnerable sector to changing climate (IPCC, 2018[21]).
- ***Public debt***: Some developing countries already face high levels of public debt – exacerbated by the COVID-19 crisis. This results in less capacity to cope as it constrains their ability to borrow more, including after extreme climate and weather event disasters (see Section 5.2.1). For example, Africa's total debt-to-GDP ratio reached 70% in 2020, more than ten percentage points higher than in 2019 and the recommended level by the African Monetary Co-operation Programme for developing economies (AfDB, 2021[22]). Such high debt levels leave less fiscal space to invest in long-term resilience or even short-term relief.

Different types of climate-related hazards will raise international attention at different levels, which will affect aid flows and ultimately the extent and speed of recovery (Mejia, 2014[23]; Eisensee and Stromberg, 2007[24]). In particular, Caribbean countries are more likely to receive disaster relief following severe tropical storms than following floods (Mejia, 2014[23]). After St. Vincent and the Grenadines was hit by Hurricane Tomas in October 2010, floods followed a few months later. The estimated damages were similar, but the donor response was three times larger for the hurricane (Mejia, 2014[23]; IMF, 2011[25]). Some SIDS, however, are not eligible for official development assistance (ODA) but still face significant climate risks (see Section 5.4.4). The impacts of slow-onset changes such as temperature increase or SLR might be over time even larger than those of extreme events (Kalkuhl and Wenz, 2020[26]; Haer et al., 2013[27]). Hazards also interact. For example, SLR is likely to make coastal flooding following hurricanes more severe (Knutson et al., 2021[28]).

5.2.1. Impacts on fiscal sustainability and domestic remedies

Macroeconomic impacts, such as those discussed above, will make populations more vulnerable. Consequently, governments will likely need to spend more on social protection, and on rebuilding (Burke, Hsiang and Miguel, 2015[29]; Botzen, Deschenes and Sanders, 2019[12]). For example, spending on unemployment insurance is larger in the years after an extreme event (Deryugina, 2017[14]). After Hurricane Katrina, employment in New Orleans fell from over 600 000 to below 450 000 (BLS, 2021[30]). The tax relief after Katrina further reduced tax revenues (Froetsch and Rector, 2005[31]). On the spending side, the cost of the new levees and floodgates of New Orleans alone are estimated at USD 14 billion (Frank, 2019[32]), a considerable sum compared to USD 80 billion annual GDP of the area (US Bureau of Economic Analysis, 2020[33]). Governments often act as guarantors for bank deposits and need to ensure the financial system is viable (Brei, Mohan and Strobl, 2019[34]; Farhi and Tirole, 2017[35]). Consequently, impacts on the financial sector (e.g. non-performing loans, loss of bank capital reducing their ability to make further loans, see Box 5.2) will also affect government finances.

The need for increased spending coupled with lower revenues from less economic activity will put pressure on fiscal sustainability. Sometimes affected countries, like the Bahamas, are not eligible for ODA, giving rise to sovereign debt challenges (discussed in Section 5.4). Evidence suggests *ex ante* measures, such as to reduce risks of losses and damages lead to better macroeconomic outcomes (Catalano, Forni and Pezzolla, 2020[36]). However, fiscal risks can also reduce a government's ability to implement such measures, forcing them to rely on less effective *ex post* measures.

Debt sustainability was, and remains, an issue beyond climate change, but climate change will exacerbate these concerns. Half of the low-income developing countries are in debt distress or at the risk of it, meaning they experience difficulties in repaying their debt (IMF, 2021[37]). Debt servicing was estimated at over USD 3 trillion for developing countries in 2020-21 alone, at a time when revenues are limited (Steele and Patel, 2020[38]). The length and persistence of the effects on debt and debt repayment as a result of climate-related hazards are crucial when assessing debt sustainability. Estimates of repayment of the costs of events range from around two to three years (Ouattara and Strobl, 2013[39]; Mohan and Strobl, 2020[40]) to over ten years (Koetsier, 2017[41]; Deryugina, 2017[14]), depending on institutional settings and socio-economic characteristics of the country. For example, Figure 5.2. shows the debt-to-GDP ratio of Dominica from 1990 until 2020. Horizontal red lines show the occurrence of the major hurricanes with GDP loss. Debt increases sharply after hurricanes. While debt starts to decrease after the hurricanes, they occurred quite frequently so the average level of debt steadily increased (see dashed trend line).

Adverse climate impacts can lead to a vicious cycle. First, countries struggle to repay their debt. Thus, high debt levels limit the possibilities for them to recover and rebuild after the disaster (Fresnillo, 2020[42]). This is of particular concern in LDCs. Fiscal sustainability can therefore constrain the ability of governments to pursue sustainable development (including through adaptation and mitigation activities) and address poverty and other priorities. Money that should have gone to education, health care or infrastructure may get diverted to emergency response, rehabilitation and reconstruction, while access to new finance is limited (Ameli et al., 2021[43]).

Figure 5.2. The effect of repeated cyclones on the government debt of Dominica

Government debt-to-GDP ratio (%)

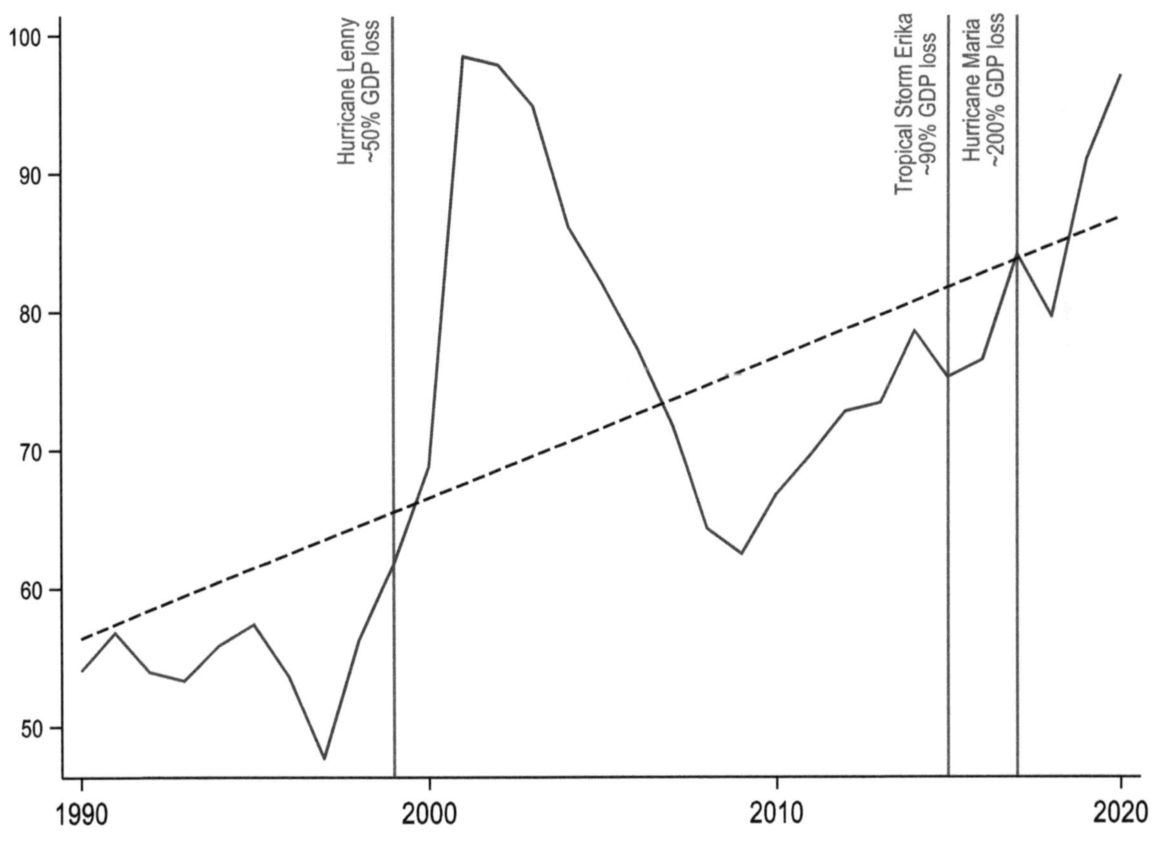

Note: The figure shows the evolution of Dominica's government debt-to-GDP ratio (blue line) against the major extreme events (red vertical lines). Dashed line shows the linear trend.
Source: Based on (IMF, 2021[1]).

Foreign and domestic debt have different implications for debt sustainability, and ideally would be balanced according to the circumstances of the country (Reinhart and Rogoff, 2011[44]; Gros, 2013[45]). In theory, domestic debt could be paid by either raising revenues or decreasing the value of debt. In practice, this approach would create inflation, which may have other damaging consequences. Additionally, domestic debt provides a redistribution within the country, but most funds stay within borders. Therefore, most of the funds to repay the debt will still be available to raise capital for investment in long-term resilience. Foreign debt is almost always denominated in a foreign currency. This makes the debt riskier since governments are exposed to changes in exchange rates. The central bank, in theory, can run out of foreign currency to repay external creditors. This risk may be heightened if the adverse impact reduces the ability of the economy to generate foreign currency earnings (e.g. tourism, agricultural exports). There is also a transfer risk from the imposition of capital outflow controls. For these reasons, foreign debt generally requires a risk premium and presents a larger problem for fiscal sustainability than domestic debt (Gros, 2013[45]).

After an adverse climate impact, the funds needed for reconstruction and social protection tend to be leveraged from foreign sources. This happens simply because domestic investors have less wealth and income to invest. With climate-related hazards that impact on capital assets, interest rates may increase to reflect the higher marginal return on capital (Mohan and Strobl, 2020[40]). Thus, climate change raises debt levels. Moreover, this increase is likely driven by an increase in riskier, foreign debt. For developing countries, international co-operation can also provide an important source of concessional finance. However, in higher-income developing countries not eligible for ODA, this can give rise to sovereign debt challenges as discussed in Section 5.4.4.

Budgeting for fiscal sustainability

In more developed countries, private insurance and central budgetary resources can usually support areas suffering adverse climate impacts; this is not the case in many developing countries. Since the impacts from climate-related hazards cannot be completely eliminated, all countries should adopt measures that reduce the cost of disasters (IMF, 2019[15]). This includes creating fiscal space (e.g. contingent reserves, low debt levels and high insurance coverage), institutional capacity and *ex ante* preparedness. Such actions must be complemented by efforts to strengthen the climate resilience of assets and investments, raise awareness and enhance the capacity of all stakeholders to reduce and manage risks (ADB, 2018[46]). Enhanced financial development also reduces the possible effects of extreme events on public debt (Zhang and Managi, 2020[47]). In the absence of such precautionary approaches, countries risk facing high financing needs at a time when a disaster would have undermined their credit worthiness (IMF, 2019[15]). Governments need to use the different risk management instruments in a complementary way to address the challenges they face, as discussed below.

Traditional fiscal policy approaches, such as fiscal rules, could be important. Fiscal rules are rules that governments need to consider when planning budgets to help ensure fiscal sustainability. Examples for such rules include establishing a debt ceiling or a maximum fiscal deficit. Countries introducing fiscal rules into their constitutions have lower debt and saw improved fiscal sustainability (Asatryan, Castellón and Stratmann, 2018[48]). Such rules might need modification to incorporate the effects of climate change. An escape clause could be inserted in case of severe extreme events (Nakatani, 2021[49]), similar to the "hurricane clauses" in external debt financing (see Section 5.4.4). However, the clause should be clearly defined because vague or flexible applicability hinders stabilisation of debt (Combes, Minea and Sow, 2017[50]). Debt financing will have different effects on debt sustainability depending on whether such debt is domestic or foreign, as discussed in the previous subsection.

Box 5.2. The impact of climate-related hazards on the finance sector

Financial systems (institutions and markets) provide many essential services that could be threatened by climate-related hazards. For example, frequent severe extreme weather events put investment and loan portfolios at risk. Despite this risk, climate-related hazards do not always seem to be considered when pricing financial assets (Ramani, 2020[51]; IMF, 2020[52]). Some financial assets, such as sovereign bonds, are already priced incorporating at least some of the climate risk the country faces (Cevik and Jalles, 2020[53]).

Since financial institutions interact extensively, they form an interconnected system through which financial contagion can spread. Negative effects on one or more independent institutions (depending on their size and connectedness) increases systemic risks for the whole economy (Battiston and Martinez-Jaramillo, 2018[54]; Dastkhan and Gharneh, 2018[55]). Systemic risks may extend across borders, triggering financial crises in other countries, or indeed at the global level (Saha and Viney, 2019[56]). Thus, any material effects on the finance sector can seriously affect the real economy as well. The global financial assets at risk from climate change are estimated at USD 2.5-4.2 trillion and potentially as high as USD 24 trillion (Dietz et al., 2016[57]; Watts, 2015[58]). Consequently, an increasing number of financial regulators, including the insurance regulatory community, are requiring disclosure of climate risks to uncover exposures and vulnerabilities of the financial system (Jones, 2021[59]) (see also Box 5.7).

Systemic financial risks also affect the public budget balances of countries, and vice versa. For example, central governments usually provide guarantees to banks, which means that governments will shoulder some of the costs in a crisis. Additionally, banks are an essential part of the monetary system and critical to the effective functioning of the economy. The potential bail-out of banks by the government encourages banks to take more risks than they would otherwise. On the other hand, the central government may not be considered a creditworthy guarantor; this status will affect banks through multiple channels (Brunnermeier et al., 2016[60]). In case of sovereign default, banks (domestic and foreign) holding sovereign bonds will likely face sudden losses. Additionally, increases in the risks of international debt default may trigger financial contagion. In this case, the debt of countries in similar situations would be repriced to reflect higher perceived risks.

Finally, public debt is used as both asset and collateral by banks and other financial actors. Increase in the riskiness of sovereign debt will affect how easily households, firms and subnational governments can access funds from international financial markets.

5.3. Roles of finance in reducing and managing the risks of losses and damages

This section examines the (actual and potential) roles that finance can play in reducing and managing the risks of losses and damages from climate change. Finance in this context may be public or private, domestic or international. Governments can use different approaches to access funds to reduce and manage the risks. The discussion is structured around three key functions:

1. risk reduction
2. risk retention
3. risk transfer.

Particular financial interventions can be used for more than one of these purposes simultaneously. This may create important synergies but also trade-offs (see discussion of social protection below). An ideal risk management strategy employs and blends these approaches in a comprehensive manner. The approaches have been captured in a stylised way in Figure 5.3 to illustrate the different intervention points for different measures. This is, of necessity, a simplification and abstraction of the dilemmas and options facing decision-makers on different timescales. Each approach has distinct characteristics in terms of timeliness, access and relative costs, as outlined below and summarised in Table 5.1.

Figure 5.3. Stylised illustration of the role of finance in addressing current and future risks of losses and damages

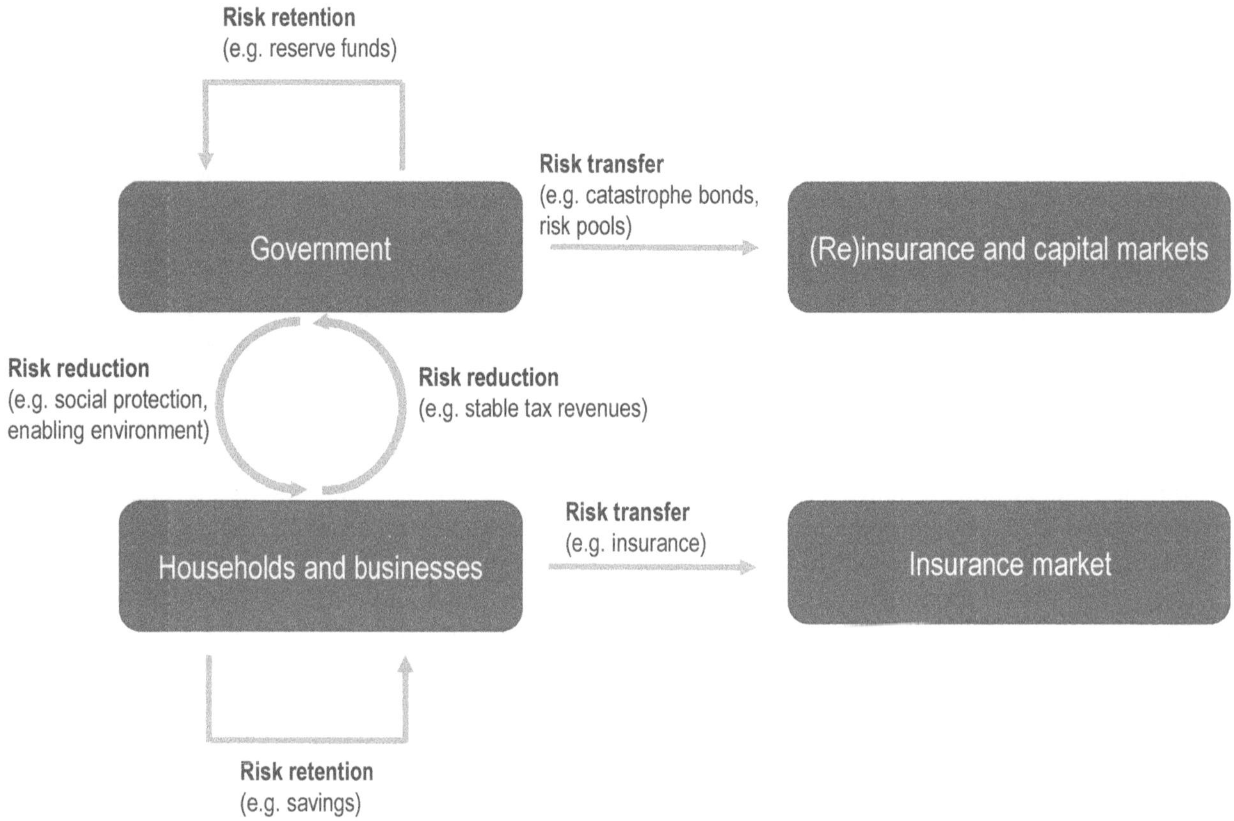

The World Bank recommends a layered approach to funding government contingent liabilities. This would involve risk retention (savings and current funds) for frequent but less severe hazards (e.g. annual flooding/localised drought). Funds would be borrowed for hazards that occur at a medium frequency and with medium severity (e.g. widespread flooding). For less frequent hazards with potentially high impacts, risk transfers are more suitable (e.g. severe droughts or catastrophic cyclones) (Calcutt, Maher and Fitzgibbon, 2021[61]).

Risk management also needs to be embedded into fiscal and public finance mechanisms. This could occur through, for example, risk-sensitive budgetary processes, risk tagging and tracking of budgets, and by integrating risk management into sectoral budgets. The applicability of specific types of financial mechanisms to these current or near-term problems is indicated where relevant throughout the rest of the chapter. The potential role of the different approaches for the recovery and reconstruction phase is highlighted in Box 5.3.

Table 5.1. Options for funding government's climate-related contingent liabilities

	Funding mechanism	Speed of access	Relative cost
Risk reduction	*Social protection:* supporting the most vulnerable segments of society in strengthening their resilience, providing direct relief to affected households following a disaster, and potentially supporting recovery efforts.	Relatively quick, as it is calculated in the budget.	Depends on the opportunity cost related to alternative uses of the allocated funds.
	Providing enabling environment: engaging private sector.	No direct access but important for incentivising action and in some cases mobilising private sector engagement.	Usually small fiscal costs, when raising awareness, potentially larger political and financial costs when designing a regulatory environment.
Risk retention (savings and current funds)	*Dedicated reserve fund for climate risk or contingencies (more generally)*: a set amount of funds allocated annually to address expenses related to climate events or a broader set of contingencies.	Very quick as there is normally no need for additional spending authority.	Depends on the opportunity cost related to alternative uses of the allocated funds.
	Emergency budget re-allocations: funds re-allocated from other spending priorities or uses.	Relatively quick, depending on what additional executive or legislative authorities are required for re-allocation.	Can be relatively high cost as funds will, by definition, be re-allocated from other spending priorities.
Risk retention (borrowing)	*Prearranged contingent credit facilities*: loan facilities that can be accessed based on a climate event.	Very quick, depending on the conditions that must be met to allow access to the fund.	Can be relatively low cost, depending on cost of borrowing. In the case of developing countries, credit facilities can be arranged with development banks and other development partners at low interest rates. Must be repaid – which could lead to debt sustainability risks.
	Debt issuance: the sale of additional government bills or bonds.	Relatively quick, depending on existing access to capital markets and debt issuance experience.	Can be relatively high cost if issued in the midst of a crisis involving heightened credit risk for investors. May have wider debt sustainability consequences.
	Increased taxation: the imposition of new or extraordinary/temporary taxes.	Relatively slow as new executive or legislative authorities are likely to be necessary and it will take time to collect funds from taxpayers.	Likely to be high cost in terms of impact on household and business recovery, particularly if those impacted by climate event face additional taxation.
Risk transfer	*Indemnity insurance for buildings and infrastructure:* insurance coverage for actual rebuilding costs incurred can be acquired from private insurance markets.	Relatively slow as claims payments would only be made once losses are assessed and coverage confirmed, although hybrid products that provide some advance payment could mitigate.	Can be relatively high cost, if damage occurs relatively frequently although suitable for less frequent losses and costs can be reduced through pooling arrangements.
	Financial protection for general government costs (e.g. regional risk pools, catastrophe bonds, parametric insurance): a set amount of financial protection can be acquired to provide a general source of funding for events of a specific level of severity.	Relatively quick as pay-outs are usually based on event characteristics that can be confirmed quickly.	Might be high cost if threshold for pay-out is calibrated for relatively frequent events (more appropriate for less frequent events). There might also be high transaction costs that can be reduced by cost-sharing through regional co-operation. It does not create additional debt sustainability problems, because pay-outs do not need to paid back.

Box 5.3. Recovery and reconstruction

The risk financing strategies in this chapter can also be applied to recovery and reconstruction. Recovery and reconstruction denotes the phases after the immediate humanitarian crisis has been averted. At these stages, basic services can be restored, reconstruction and asset recovery can happen, and restoration of livelihoods can take priority. On occasion, "building back better" might be possible, an effort to reconstruct while increasing resilience. Building back better may decrease the impact of climate and weather events on well-being by around a third (Hallegate, Renschler and Walsh, 2018[62]).

Therefore, while providing relief after a weather or climate event is of utmost importance, it is also crucial to consider the inclusiveness and long-term needs of the society during recovery. For example, following Hurricane Maria in 2017, the government of Puerto Rico permanently closed 250 schools. Most school closures, however, occurred in rural areas. This negatively impacted the rural communities in multiple ways in the long term (Finucane et al., 2020[63]).

Adaptive financing proposes a method to develop more flexible financial instruments, and enable engagement of private finance in recovery. Before the event, a financial instrument (e.g. a loan) is approved in many forms (e.g. size of fund, coverage). Each has different financing requirements (e.g. interest rates). As a climate-related hazard materialises, the instrument can be quickly offered based on preliminary information, which in theory can be updated. Such instruments are usually offered with complementary programmes, such as social protection to enhance and hasten recovery (Hammet and Mixter, 2017[64]).

5.3.1. Risk reduction

Finance is fundamental for enabling and accelerating climate action to reduce and manage the serious and potentially devastating current and future impacts of climate change. As highlighted in Chapters 1 and 4, this requires both climate change mitigation and adaptation, as well as other interventions such as disaster risk reduction, disaster risk finance, and humanitarian assistance. This section focuses on the role of finance in reducing and managing economic losses, i.e. damage to property and loss of income and livelihoods. It understands property as both privately owned buildings and infrastructure, such as homes and businesses. Property also includes publicly owned buildings and infrastructure, such as schools, hospitals, roads and power generation and distribution infrastructure. Risk reduction is focused on reducing current vulnerability and manage risk of future losses. Social protection mechanisms can address both these areas, and are therefore the starting point of this discussion.

Protecting livelihoods, reducing precarity

The role of social protection

Social protection mechanisms can play a critical role in supporting households' immediate needs and ability to recover. This is especially the case where insurance coverage is unavailable or unaffordable to segments of the population. Social protection refers to policies and programmes designed to reduce and prevent poverty and vulnerability to different types of risks (ILO, 2017[65]). Some definitions also highlight the role of social protection in enhancing the social status and rights of marginalised segments of the population, reducing their economic and social vulnerability (Sabates-Wheeler and Devereux, 2007[66]). Approaches with an explicit focus on human rights provide a lens through which to analyse the obligations, inequalities and vulnerabilities of the population and to tackle discriminatory practices that undercut human rights (UNRISD, 2016[67]). Social protection mechanisms can broadly be categorised around four common functions (Devereux and Sabates-Wheeler, 2004[68]):

- ***Protection***: providing direct relief from deprivation in the form of, for example, pensions, unemployment and health insurance.
- ***Prevention***: seeking to avert deprivation as a result of a shock through, for example, cash and food transfers, public works programmes and school feeding programmes.
- ***Promotion***: enhancing income and capabilities to enhance livelihoods, for example, through labour market interventions (job market integration, job benefits and labour standards) and social services (social care, nutrition services and disability services).
- ***Transformation***: addressing concerns of social equity and exclusion.

Social protection programmes can reduce the vulnerability of individuals and households to different types of risks, including climate risks (Costella, Bachofen and Marcondes, 2017[69]; Carter et al., 2019[70]). For example, regular cash transfers to segments of the population based on a set of criteria such as age, income or disability can ensure alternative sources of income. This, in turn, reduces the impact of crop failures on peoples' health. Similarly, cash transfers may reduce pressure on families to resort to harmful coping strategies. In response to climate-related hazards, for example, cash transfers mean they would not have to remove children from school for income-earning activities or to sell their livestock (de Janvry et al., 2006[71]). In many developing countries, social protection interventions, such as food aid and cash transfers (also called "safety nets"), comprise the primary focus of government interventions for vulnerable groups (Calcutt, Maher and Fitzgibbon, 2021[61]).

Complementing the broader notion of social protection, adaptive social protection includes a specific focus on the management of shocks, most commonly in the context of disasters. Such adaptive social protection systems can contribute to climate resilience of communities by directly investing in the capacity of societies to prepare, cope and adapt to the impacts of climate change. They aim to reduce the impact of risks to peoples' well-being by informing and enabling action; preparing for risks through private and public safety net programmes; and by reducing over time the exposure and vulnerability to the risks to build resilience (Bowen et al., 2020[72]). As such, they address current vulnerabilities *and* seek to reduce and manage future risks of losses and damages. Examples include the Kenya Hunger Safety Net Programme, Ethiopia's Productive Safety Net Project and the World Bank's Sahel Adaptive Social Protection Programme. These programmes use climate observations to trigger actions to build resilience. In this way, individuals and communities can better respond to climate-related hazards and other shocks to protect their assets and livelihoods (Daron et al., 2020[73]; World Bank, 2020[74]). Such established programmes contain detailed information on the vulnerability of the population and can adapt their offer of temporary assistance depending on the context. This makes the programmes effective in channelling emergency relief in the context of a shock (Calcutt, Maher and Fitzgibbon, 2021[61]). In some cases, these programmes are supported by development co-operation or the private sector (see Box 5.4).

Adaptive social protection measures could bring about change if they address the inequalities at the root of peoples' vulnerabilities to climate change (Davies et al., 2009[75]). Ethiopia's Productive Safety Net Programme, for example, absorbed an additional 3.1 million people threatened by the 2011 drought in the Horn of Africa and prevented the shock from becoming a humanitarian crisis (Hobson and Campbell, 2012[76]). It has also had a positive impact on food security and asset protection. However, evaluations suggest it has been less effective in protecting participating households from severe shocks, especially drought (Tenzing, 2019[77]). Malawi's Farm Input Support Programme similarly advanced food security by improving agricultural productivity. However, it was less effective in reducing long-term vulnerability to shocks and stresses as demonstrated by 2015 flooding and 2016 drought (Tenzing, 2019[77]).

An evaluation of the World Food Programme's insurance-related programmes revealed similar results. It found that insurance pay-outs enabled households to absorb the effects of failed agricultural seasons through purchasing of food, followed by investments in agricultural or livestock inputs (WFP, 2021[78]). Such insurance products were either delivered through multi-year programmes that could be integrated into broader resilience-building initiatives or as a standalone product. Integrated programmes had a positive impact. In such programmes, insurance was provided with other risk management approaches, such as access to natural capital, information and finance. The synergies created by the different components increased resilience of participants. Conversely, when insurance was provided as a standalone product, pay-outs could help participants absorb the immediate effects of drought events but had no effect on long-term resilience (WFP, 2021[78]).

With increasing climate-related hazards, the risk increases for migration (temporary or permanent, voluntary or involuntary) and displacement (see Box 4.6). As a consequence, it is important to consider the transferability of social protection programmes. For example, decentralised social protection programmes could provide benefits more quickly and effectively than a centralised system, especially in a crisis. A decentralised system would also help make social protection more portable. For example, a decentralised approach in Tanzania proved more cost effective in improving resilience than centralised mechanisms, partly because all stakeholders were involved from the beginning (Greene, 2019[79]).

Climate change may increase pressure on social protection programmes. National governments, for example, may provide high levels of *ex post* financial support for losses incurred by households, businesses or subnational governments. Such losses could have been insured or avoided through proper risk management. Consequently, financial support is likely to reduce incentives to manage or protect against these risks in the future (i.e. moral hazards might emerge). Different domestic and international initiatives should thus be complementary, making the most effective use of scarce resources and avoiding such moral hazards, to the extent possible. Some households, businesses and subnational governments exposed to climate risks have the financial capacity to manage those risks. Governments must ensure all these segments of society have appropriate incentives to manage their own exposures. This includes measures such as risk reduction and risk transfer to insurance markets (see Section 5.3.3).

Box 5.4. Engaging the private sector in strengthening social protection systems: The case of Senegal

The R4 Rural Resilience Initiative delivers integrated risk management services to over 91 000 households in Ethiopia, Kenya, Malawi, Senegal, Zambia and Zimbabwe. It combines several risk management strategies, including risk reduction (improved resource management through asset creation); risk transfer (insurance); risk retention (savings and microcredit); and social protection (through livelihood diversification and building insurance into social safety nets). The insurance interventions help households cope with shocks by providing timely support after an extreme event. In so doing, they allow insured households to meet their basic needs, prevent negative coping mechanisms and smooth incomes. In 2018, for example, low rainfall led to nearly 30 000 farmers in Ethiopia, Kenya, Malawi, Senegal and Zambia receiving insurance pay-outs amounting to USD 1.5 million (WFP, n.d.[80]).

In the case of Senegal, the R4 Initiative worked through the *Compagnie Nationale d'Assurance Agricole du Sénégal* (CNAAS), a public-private insurance company. CNAAS, which specialises in risk insurance solutions for farmers, was supported by a range of development co-operation providers. CNAAS shareholders include the Senegalese government, insurance companies, *Banque Agricole* (a commercial bank) and farmer associations. *Banque Agricole* provides loans and insurance products to micro-, small- and medium-sized enterprises, which are organised around producer organisations, agricultural co-operatives, or groups of micro or individual businesses. These stakeholders sign collective, communal contracts with *Banque Agricole*. The use of such contracts can reduce transaction costs and increase access to credits and financial products to otherwise marginalised stakeholders that largely operate in the informal sector. By contracting this insurance, farmers can take some risks and invest, including in ways that enhance their resilience (e.g. diversifying produce, improving storage facilities, reaching new markets). Unorganised farmers in the informal sector, however, remain excluded from this system, as they are often not part of such producer organisations (Casado-Asensio, Kato and Shin, 2021[81]).

The role of humanitarian assistance

Humanitarian assistance plays an important role in providing relief. This is true in response to both slow-onset changes and extreme events, and in-kind support (including provision of food, water, medicines and tents) (OECD, 2021[82]). While post-disaster humanitarian assistance from donors is a crucial source of funding, the timing and volume can be unpredictable and slow to mobilise (Bowen et al., 2020[72]). In recent years, anticipatory humanitarian assistance has gained traction with experiences in over 60 countries (see Section 5.4.2 with its relation to development finance). This includes programmes by the International Federation of Red Cross and Red Crescent Societies and national societies, the START Network and a number of UN agencies (including the World Food Programme, the Food and Agriculture Organization and the UN Office for the Coordination of Humanitarian Affairs (IFRC, 2020[83]). Other providers are increasingly integrating anticipatory action into existing development (German Federal Foreign Office, 2020[84]; Levine et al., 2020[85]; Kuriyama et al., 2020[86]) and humanitarian programmes (UK Government, 2021[87]).

Anticipatory action refers to a set of actions that help prevent or mitigate potential disaster impacts before a hazard event. It uses weather and other forecasts to trigger funding for pre-determined actions before the hazard turns into a disaster (WFP, 2020[88]). Initiatives that focus on anticipatory action are also referred to as forecast-based early action, forecast-based financing, or early warning and early action. In many developing countries, humanitarian organisations are increasingly integrating forecast-based financing into their approaches to disaster risk management and response. With forecast-based financing, payments before a catastrophe can help beneficiaries prepare for an event, and potentially protect themselves against the impending impact. Vulnerable households in Bangladesh that received forecast-based financing in advance of flooding in 2017 fared better than those that did not receive it. Households with advanced funding reportedly had improved access to food, accumulated less (high-interest) debt and suffered from lower levels of stress during and after the flood (Gros et al., 2019[89]). Enabling actors to take action before an extreme event more effectively mitigates impacts than conventional risk finance instruments, which usually disburse finance following a disaster. These developments closely parallel those in insurance, discussed below. Anticipatory action, however, might have limited applicability with climate-related hazards that are difficult to predict.

Disbursements are often contingent on the monitoring of imminent climate-related hazards, enabling forecast-based financing to contribute to multiple benefits. These benefits include strengthened early warning communication capacity and investments in risk reduction (e.g. to prevent flooding), bridging the gap between climate information to early action (UNFCCC, 2019[90]). The emphasis on *ex ante* prevention also reduces the adverse impact of disasters on development gains (OECD, forthcoming[91]). In Kenya and Sudan, early provision of supplementary livestock feed in anticipation of droughts resulted in lower mortality rates of livestock for beneficiaries (FAO, 2019[92]). Different global initiatives focused on anticipatory action are highlighted in Box 5.5. This aims to provide insights into different initiatives rather than attempting a complete overview. Complementing the initiatives mentioned in the box are a number of different platforms and partnerships that support the scale-up of anticipatory action and promote synergies between the humanitarian, climate and development communities.

Box 5.5. Global initiatives to scale up anticipatory action

The Disaster Relief Emergency Fund and Forecast-based Financing

In 2018, the International Federation of Red Cross and Red Crescent Societies set up the Disaster Relief Emergency Fund to promote forecast-based action through a dedicated financial mechanism (IFRC, 2020[83]). The Fund helps implement anticipatory action by the National Red Cross and Red Crescent Societies and expands its scope. Forecast-based funding builds upon traditional early warning approaches, incorporating impact-based forecasting mechanisms. It does not replace post-disaster response but rather reduces the financial need for coping measures by vulnerable communities after a shock. In Bangladesh, development co-operation providers contribute to a one-off cash transfer to 274 000 households in advance of floods or cyclones to avoid high evacuation costs after disasters (Casado-Asensio, Kato and Shin, 2021[81]). During the 2020 floods in Bangladesh, for instance, the German Federal Foreign Office distributed payments of between USD 61 to USD 3 000 to households, helping those affected to evacuate by boat (German Federal Foreign Office, 2020[84]).

UN Office for the Coordination of Humanitarian Affairs (OCHA) Central Emergency Response Fund

OCHA manages the Central Emergency Response Fund and is undertaking pilots for anticipatory action (e.g. in Somalia to address droughts). The pilots demonstrate how collective anticipatory action can work at scale. For instance, rehabilitation and upgrading of boreholes ahead of a drought can improve household finances, strengthen mental health, keep livestock healthy and reduce disputes related to water (Wittig, 2021[93]). Prior to this, the OCHA-managed Country-Based Pool Funds addressed losses and damages by supporting early action in response to droughts in Afghanistan and Somalia. However, while these pilots focused on rapid response, they were less focused on preparedness, recovery and sustainable development (Willitts-King et al., 2020[94]).

Climate Risk and Early Warning Systems

Climate Risk and Early Warning Systems is a financial mechanism that aims to save lives and livelihoods through the expansion of early warning systems and services in LDCs and SIDS. Established in 2015, it is a collaboration between the World Meteorological Organization, the United Nations Office for Disaster Risk Reduction and the World Bank's Global Facility for Disaster Reduction and Recovery. The initiative focuses on increasing the capabilities of the countries and island states to detect, monitor and forecast severe high-impact weather events. This is complemented by a focus on access to longer-term seasonal predictions and operational early warning and response plans that increase access of vulnerable people to warnings.

Not all anticipatory action has been successful (WFP, 2020[88]). However, it can complement longer-term investment in adaptation, disaster risk reduction and development. These influence the capacity of households and communities to reduce and manage the risks of losses and damages from climate change. Thus, *ex ante* prevention can complement *ex post* disaster risk recovery with a focus on building back better. In this way, anticipatory action is critical for breaking the vicious cycle of extreme weather events turning into humanitarian crises that wipe out development progress. There is scope for governments, humanitarian agencies and development co-operation providers to strengthen synergies between anticipatory financial support and other measures to reduce the risks (Levine et al., 2020[85]). With assistance from Japan, for example, Peru, El Salvador, Fiji and the Philippines received contingency credits and other types of disaster risk financing. At the same time, they developed contingency plans to better prepare for long-term disaster risks (ADB, 2018[95]). The African Risk Capacity similarly emphasis the importance of contingency plans being in place (see Box 5.11). Enhanced collaboration is also needed between those working on climate change adaptation and disaster risk reduction. This may require efforts to harmonise the mandates, interests and priorities of government and development co-operation agencies (Casado-Asensio, Kato and Shin, 2021[81]; OECD, 2020[96]).

Finance in relation to adaptation and mitigation actions

Current levels of exposure and resilience determine the extent of losses and damages after a hazardous event. Effective investment in adaptation will enhance resilience and reduce exposures to future such events. Current resilience and exposures will also determine the domestic resources available to governments, households and firms. Many poorer countries have low levels of resilience and high exposure to hazardous events. This combination can make it difficult for them to overcome a vicious cycle of high levels of losses and damages. Such a cycle leads to lower levels of investment in development and inadequate levels of adaptation spending, increasing vulnerability to future (likely more frequent and intense) hazards.

The vicious cycle can occur despite the high level of returns on many adaptation investments. For example, the Global Commission on Adaptation estimates that a USD 1.8 trillion investment in adaptation could generate USD 7.1 trillion of avoided costs and non-monetary social and environmental benefits (GCA, 2019[97]). Examples of adaptation include early warning systems (EWS), climate-resilient infrastructure, improved dryland agriculture, global mangrove protection and resilient water resources. Countries may need to supplement domestic resources for these costs with international development finance. They will also need to mobilise private finance to the extent possible. Lack of a clear revenue stream to underpin the business case for private investment is a barrier to scaling up mobilisation of adaptation activities.

Private finance as a label hides a large heterogeneity: local producers, international finance corporations and multinationals could all play different roles. Engaging these entities is crucial as the brunt of the losses and damages will fall on private individuals and companies. It can be difficult to raise private finance for approaches that do not have direct revenue stream (e.g. coastal flood management), but good practices are emerging (Hallegatte, Rentschler and Rozenberg, 2019[98]; Casado-Asensio, Kato and Shin, 2021[81]). Even with a tangible revenue stream, the benefits for the wider community are larger than for private actors. A dam, for example, will protect both a factory and surrounding areas. Thus, it is unsurprising (if undesirable) that private sources provided only about 1.6% of adaptation finance in 2017-18 (Tall et al., 2021[99]) (although accounting for all private investments that takes into account climate risks is impossible. As another concern, the regulatory environment is often not well suited for private investments to reduce and manage their risks. Providing an enabling environment can help engage private sources. For example, providing information about climate-related hazards can help private actors manage their own risk (see discussion below).

Incentives for mitigation activities are different. Reducing climate-forcing agents (e.g. the major greenhouse gases (GHGs) that are well-mixed in the atmosphere) contributes to a global public good, with all the risks of under provision and free-riding that this entails. The transparency and review mechanisms of the Paris Agreement are intended to ratchet up the scale of activity over time, but there is little time left to meet the temperature goal of the Agreement. Moreover, governments often see mitigation as a cost in the present with any benefits flowing in the future, which discourages investments. This is a misguided view: mitigation actions could contribute significantly to important improvements in human well-being at the present in relation to the Sustainable Development Goals. By integrating climate action and action on sustainable development, governments can realise early benefits from health improvements and accessibility, as well as job creation, for example. These benefits then enhance the financial and political case for early action on mitigation. Potential trade-offs, such as energy affordability and competitiveness, would need to be identified and addressed to ensure just transition (OECD, 2019[100]).

All countries will need mitigation action to achieve the climate neutrality. However, in practice, the efforts of many poor developing countries with negligible share of global GHG emissions will not significantly affect risks of losses and damages. The main emitting countries will, however, need to make rapid and deep cuts to achieve the goal of the Paris Agreement. Therefore, climate finance to cover the incremental costs of clean technologies for developing countries will be needed to accelerate their mitigation action. Encouragingly, rapid deployment of some clean technologies, such as solar PV and on-shore wind, mean that costs for such technologies have plummeted. In some cases, these price drops have made clean technologies cost competitive compared to fossil fuel alternatives. Such renewable technologies can also enhance energy security and reduce reliance on imported fuels in some countries. Small-scale renewables coupled with energy storage can also provide much-needed off-grid electricity where there is no access to electricity grids. In this way, they can help improve health through the use of clean appliances to reduce indoor air pollution (Obeng et al., 2008[101]).

Development co-operation providers can help partner countries manage the risks of climate-related losses and damages in two ways. First, they can use more predictable and flexible financing to meet immediate humanitarian needs. Second, they can be flexible with programming in response to changing circumstances and future climate risks (Bowen et al., 2020[72]; OECD, 2021[102]) (See Section 5.4).

Choosing the investment portfolio

Governments face a choice when determining investments, commonly using cost-benefit analysis (CBA) to guide decisions. Such analysis estimates the advantages and disadvantages of different options usually in monetary terms. This helps determine which path provides the most benefits net of costs. However, CBAs have been criticised based on ethical and methodological grounds. For example, the IPCC Second Assessment Report valued lives in lower-income countries much less than lives in higher-income countries, which caused controversy (IPCC, 1995[103]; Dennig, 2017[104]; Aldred, 2009[105]).

By their nature, CBAs are useful for illustrating trade-offs between different investments (OECD, 2018[106]). However, they have several limitations when it comes to climate change related to both socio-economic and physical uncertainties. Specifically, the frequency and intensity of future extreme weather events and the unknown long-term trajectory of socio-economic development limit the usefulness of CBA. The range of uncertainties and potentially catastrophic hazards cannot be ruled out even in the relatively near future (see Chapter 3). This underlines the need for caution in placing too much weight on CBA. Their outcomes are heavily determined by a single, unknown and normatively-determined parameter – the discount rate (see Chapter 2).

At times, political, socio-economic or cultural values demand action even in the absence of a CBA – as many countries have done in response to the COVID pandemic. In such cases, there is no reason to compare costs with benefits; the action or project is so vital that the desired benefits must be secured. A more appropriate approach is comparing various plans to ensure the project is carried out at least cost. Typically, a cost-effectiveness analysis is easier to carry out than CBAs because it does not need to monetise every aspect (e.g. lives saved, impact of uncertain catastrophic events) (OECD, 2007[107]). Similar to a CBA, the costs are assessed in monetary terms. However, usually only direct costs are considered (although some do consider co-benefits of mitigation choices). If the impact can be measured without being monetised, the policies might be characterised by their cost-effectiveness ratio (OECD, 2007[107]; Tuominen et al., 2015[108]). Box 6.6 also discusses possible tools for valuing investment options. Any decision-making process should be participatory to ensure consideration of diverse perspectives.

Certain adaptation measures might have unintended or unanticipated consequences that increase risks. Adaptation measures that reduce vulnerability may create short-term incentives not aligned with long-term resilience. For example, the cost of building a sea wall depends on the length – rather than the value of assets – of the exposed coastline. This suggests the need to protect only high-value assets in a limited, well-defined area; low-value assets, or assets spread over a large exposed area, are not worth protecting. Such protection then creates the incentive to relocate or concentrate assets in the protected area, thereby increasing exposure (Gibbs, 2015[109]). Relocation of assets to the area is usually in the interest of local governments as well. More assets provide a larger revenue base, even if additional exposure can be difficult to justify economically (OECD, 2018[110]).

The role of government in facilitating action by others

Governments can reduce their financing needs by providing an enabling environment for the private sector to manage its own risks. Periods of high regulatory uncertainty hinder investment. Investors wait until uncertainty declines or choose to invest in more certain regions or sectors (Baker, Bloom and Davis, 2016[111]; Bloom, 2009[112]). High levels of policy uncertainty also reduce the effectiveness of policies. This is especially the case for sectors most directly affected and in which the investment decisions are the most difficult to reverse (Bloom, Bond and Van Reenen, 2007[113]; Gulen and Ion, 2015[114]). Investment decisions in mitigation and some adaptation are typically difficult to reverse, which makes them especially sensitive to policy uncertainty (Fankhauser and Burton, 2011[115]). This underlines the importance of long-term policy making and a consensus-based vision. A policy that remains relatively unaffected by periods of political uncertainty like election cycles can help mobilise private investment.

Lack of awareness of climate-related hazards is a principal obstacle in reducing and managing the exposure and vulnerability of private actors to these hazards (see Box 5.6 for an example). Perceptions and expectations about risks are among the most important drivers of managing those risks. When unaware households and firms are informed about the climate risks they face, they tend to change their behaviour (Halady and Rao, 2010[116]; Andre et al., 2021[117]). One, undesirable, way to learn about the risks is to experience the impacts first hand. People become more risk averse when impacted negatively by hazards (Sakha, 2019[118]). For example, municipal bonds in California were only priced for disaster risks after the devastating effects of Hurricane Katrina in 2005 because investors required a raise in the risk premium (Fowles, Liu and Mamaril, 2009[119]). Credit rating agencies behave similarly. For example, following Hurricane Harvey, Moody's downgraded Port Arthur from A1 to A2. It referred to its "weak liquidity position that is exposed to additional financial obligations from the recent hurricane damage that are above and beyond the city's regular scope of operations" (Four Twenty Seven, 2018[120]). This is likely to be the case with slow-onset events as well. Farmers, who are typically more vulnerable to changes in the climate than those working outside agriculture, have higher risk perception for changing weather patterns (Schneiderbauer et al., 2021[121]). The financial sector could also be vulnerable to some climate-related hazards (see Box 5.2), which is why central banks and other financial regulators also play a role (see Box 5.7).

Box 5.6. Lack of information leads to overvaluation of properties exposed to floods

Properties exposed to floods or sea-level rise (SLR) are a well-documented example of how lack of information about climate-related hazards creates market failures. In multiple countries, property prices do not fully reflect the cost of flood and SLR inundation risks (Sandink, 2015[122]; Storey et al., 2020[123]). For example, in the United States, the property values in flood plains are overestimated by about 10% (Bakkensen and Barrage, 2017[124]; Hino and Burke, 2021[125]). The most relevant explanation seems to be lack of awareness (Shao et al., 2017[126]). Detailed information on hazards, such as maps, became available relatively recently. Consequently, they may not have been internalised by markets. Lack of awareness can be alleviated through personal experience. Once floods materialise and have a direct impact in the area, risks are priced: the property values decrease and demand for insurance increases (Pilla, Gharbia and Lyons, 2019[127]; Storey and Noy, 2017[128]). Neighbouring localities not directly affected by the flood may experience some of this effect (Gallagher, 2014[129]). Investigations also indicate a gradual fading of the effect, as people tend to forget or decrease their expectations over time (Gallagher, 2014[129]). Therefore, better communication about the risks and possible impacts encourages the property market to price homes appropriately and set the right incentives to move or take up insurance (policies and regulation also play an important role, of course). In France, for example, property sales and rentals are required to disclose risk (OECD, 2016[130]).

Nevertheless, climate change awareness itself is not always enough to spur action. Choosing action also often requires knowledge on context-specific opportunities, institutions and impacts (Dessai and Sims, 2010[131]). Since climate change awareness differs across countries and populations, communication approaches need to be tailored (Lee et al., 2015[132]) (see Chapter 2). Where climate change is deeply political, information about the economic and non-economic benefits of climate action would perhaps be a more fruitful communication strategy than detailing climate risks (Bain et al., 2015[133]). The exact formulation of an awareness campaign depends on the audience and message (Bolsen, Palm and Kingsland, 2019[134]).

Box 5.7. The possible role of central banks

Central banks are one of the most important institutions to provide a safe economic environment for the population. Typically, their mandates include ensuring stability of price levels and employment (Bodea and Hicks, 2014[135]; Blinder et al., 2017[136]; Fontana, 2006[137]). Both of these are affected by climate risks, yet only around one-tenth of the world's central banks have mandates to consider environmental sustainability (Dikau and Volz, 2021[138]). Regulators and supervisors of national (or regional) banking systems and security exchanges have the tools to create an environment that encourages the management of risks. For example, some assets including financial assets are mispriced, as prices do not always reflect the cost of climate risks (IMF, 2020[52]).

Providing disclosure rules for climate sensitivity and making stress tests incorporating climate risk are ways of providing financial stability. Stress tests assume future scenarios, observing how those scenarios would affect individual banks and the financial system based on balance sheets. The Network of Central Banks and Supervisors for Greening the Financial System is one of the main pioneers of assessing physical climate risks on financial risks (NFGS, 2019[139]). Given the nature and complexity of climate change, conducting stress tests for climate risks is challenging. It has only started recently in a few countries (Baudion and Svoronos, 2021[140]). Such tests help identify possible weaknesses of the financial system with respect to climate risks. As such, they could potentially help focus adaptation efforts or highlight areas in need of government intervention.

In 2015, the Financial Stability Board established the Task Force on Climate-related Financial Disclosures (TCFD) to promote and increase consistency in climate-related financial disclosures across countries and companies. The TCFD provides recommendations on disclosures relating to companies' governance, strategy, risk management and metrics. Such transparency contributes to enabling financial markets to price climate-related risks. This, in turn, provides incentives to reduce or manage them, and governments to better target policies (TFCD, 2017[141]; Jones, 2021[59]). Therefore, an increasing number of central banks have started implementing the TCFD guidelines (Bank of England, 2020[142]; European Central Bank, 2021[143]).

5.3.2. Risk retention

Risks can be reduced but unlikely to be eliminated, materialising as losses and damages from climate change. Governments are exposed to losses and damages from climate-related hazards (i.e. contingent liabilities), both as a result of damages to public assets and due to their role as insurer of last resort. For example, Germany recently announced it will provide financial aid to households affected by the 2021 floods, both with and without insurance (Moulson, 2021[144]). Germany is a fiscally disciplined country where insurance is widely available. Moreover, a relatively high share of losses and damages is insured. Yet even in such a country, the government faces large pressures to provide financial aid in the event of a disaster.

A strategy for managing climate risks requires assessment of the potential explicit and implicit contingent liabilities that governments could face in the aftermath of climate and weather events. However, few governments quantify their potential exposures to climate-related contingent liabilities. This is especially true of the implicit liabilities that tend to arise in the aftermath of extreme events where affected parties have limited insurance coverage. Specifically, when the magnitude or scale of risks transcends efforts to reduce them, individuals who may not have insurance or savings to recover losses will absorb the costs. Alternatively, costs will be transferred across levels of governance or stakeholder groups. Examples include the following (Sudmeier-Rieux et al., 2015[145]):

- ***From the private sector to the public sector.*** The former is responsible for large shares of investments that contribute to a country's income. However, these investments also generate many risks to the public sector, which may need to financially support it in response to disasters.
- ***From developing countries to developed countries***. The latter will share the costs, in the form of humanitarian assistance, in response to declared emergencies or development finance supporting low-carbon, climate-resilient development pathways.
- ***From subnational governments to national governments.*** Subnational governments (at the forefront of reducing climate risks through implementation) would transfer costs to national governments (that are ultimately responsible for public safety).

Identifying potential needs for central government financial support for subnational governments remains a key challenge. This is especially the case in countries with decentralised systems of governance. The OECD and World Bank have proposed a framework for managing disaster-related contingent liabilities within public finance frameworks. It involves identification and quantification of potential public finance exposures, and measures to mitigate those risks and to manage remaining residual risks (OECD/World Bank, 2019[146]). Once governments have identified their exposure to climate-related contingent liabilities, they should develop a strategy to ensure that sufficient funding can be accessed to meet spending needs when required. Such a strategy will require the use of multiple instruments including possibly forms of risk retention:

- ***Risk retention – savings and current funds***: Dedicated reserve or contingency funds, such as the national Disaster Management Fund in Mozambique (World Bank, 2019[147]), can absorb climate-related losses within budgetary resources. Such funds could be quickly accessed if need arises. However, setting aside part of the budget for an uncertain future need has both an opportunity cost and a "political" cost. The opportunity cost arises because funds could otherwise be allocated to other spending needs; a political cost is paid if other spending needs are unmet. This political cost also puts reserve funds at risk of diversion to other needs if the funds are not sufficiently protected from political interference. Climate change is likely to exacerbate this challenge. The second option is *ex post* re-allocation of funds, but that also has drawbacks. In case hazard materialises, budget re-allocations can put other priorities at risk. They may require additional legislative approvals, affecting their timeliness.
- ***Risk retention – borrowing***: Prearranged contingent credit facilities are generally well suited for financing medium frequency and intensity hazards that would be costly or politically difficult to address within annual budgets. Several multilateral development banks and bilateral development agencies make contingent credit available to catastrophe-exposed developing countries at relatively low interest rates. Further, they also work with borrowing countries to support risk management in the context of the contingent lending agreements (see Section 5.4). However, this option is also driven by political costs since long tenure make these credits attractive to politicians who are no longer accountable once the credits need to be repaid. In comparison, borrowing or taxation to meet funding needs after an event has disadvantages. Borrowing in the midst of a crisis, for example, might raise fiscal sustainability concerns. Meanwhile, taxation could impose additional burdens on affected households and business, prolonging their recovery. These instruments

should, therefore, only be considered in extreme scenarios where other funding options are not available. Climate change could increase a country's cost of borrowing in the aftermath of a major catastrophe (see Section 5.2.1). For this reason, there have been calls from some countries to include a "hurricane clause" in their debt. Essentially, this is a moratorium on debt repayment when a disaster occurs, making it easier for countries to recover from an extreme weather event (Wigglesworth and Smith, 2019[148]). For example, such clauses were added during the bond restructuring of Grenada in 2015 and Barbados in 2019 (West, 2020[149]) (see Section 5.4).

The different approaches play different roles in terms of an overall strategy for funding contingent liabilities. For example, funds for emergency management and support to households and businesses faced with losses in income or revenue are the priority. Such funds are likely to be needed much sooner than funds for rebuilding (non-essential) publicly owned buildings or infrastructure.

5.3.3. Risk transfer

Insurance coverage can reduce the economic consequences of adverse climate impacts. Higher levels of insurance penetration or coverage have been found to reduce contractions in economic activity after disaster events (Melecky and Raddatz, 2011[150]) or eliminate them in the case of full insurance (Von Peter, Von Dahlen and Saxena, 2012[151]). One recent study examined the economic implications of more than 100 past disaster events. It found that countries with higher insurance penetration recover on average within 12 months. Conversely, those with lower penetration face average recovery periods of four years (Cambridge Centre for Risk Studies and AXA XL, 2020[152]). OECD (2018[153]) identified a similar positive impact on post-disaster recovery from greater use of international property catastrophe reinsurance. In addition to absorbing losses and accelerating economic recovery, the development of insurance markets for climate-related hazards can also help improve risk management.

In many countries, the vast majority of economic losses from climate-related extreme events tend to be absorbed through risk retention (i.e. savings, re-allocation of current income or borrowing). Insurance and other risk transfer arrangements[1] have played only a limited role in absorbing public and private losses and damages. Between 2000 and 2019, approximately 42% of all reported economic losses from climate-related events were insured.[2] This overall figure, however, hides large discrepancies between developed and developing countries. In developed (high-income) countries, 52% of reported economic losses from climate-related events were insured. In developing countries, less than 10% of reported economic losses were insured (see Figure 5.4.). For some especially vulnerable countries, this percentage can be as low as 1-3% (Sheehan, 2021[154]).

Figure 5.4. Insured and uninsured share of climate-related extreme event losses (2000-19)

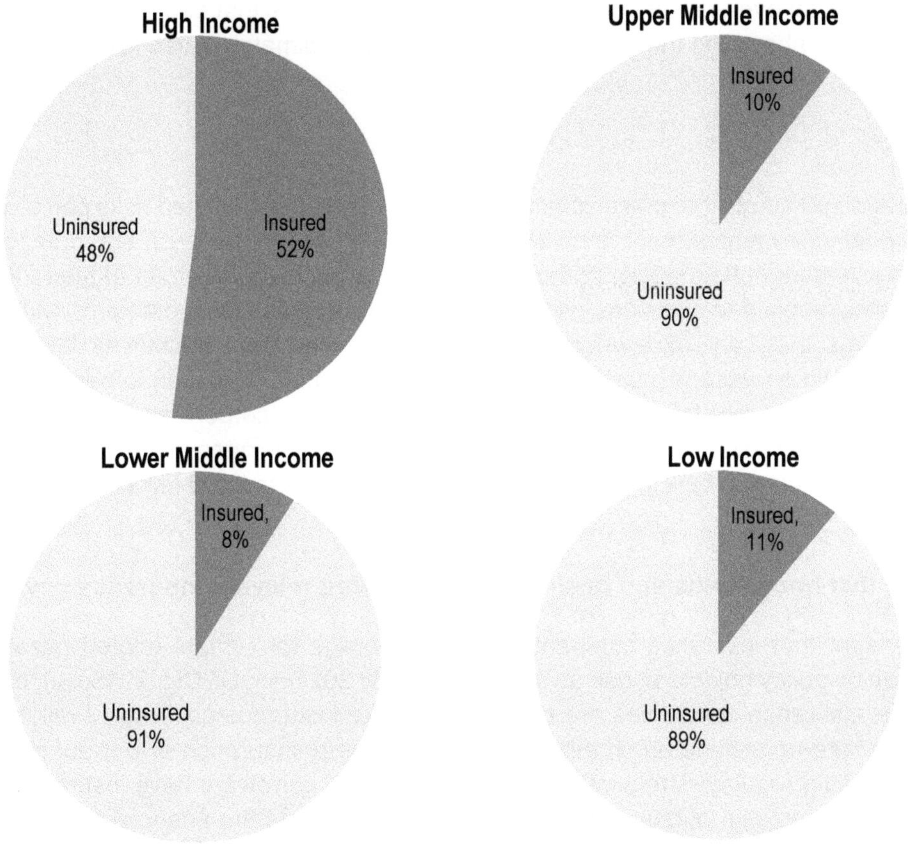

Note: The calculation includes only events with reported economic and insured losses (i.e. events with no reported insured losses were excluded from the calculation). Countries are classified by income level based on World Bank Country and Lending Groups (World Bank, 2021[155]).
Source: OECD calculations based on data provided by Swiss Re sigma and PCS.

Low levels of insurance coverage of climate-related hazards may be due to factors that generate several effects. They could increase the cost of insurance coverage; limit the willingness of insurance companies to offer coverage; or reduce the premium that households, businesses and governments are willing to pay:

- ***Severity of hazards:*** Low frequency and high impact events with high levels of correlation of losses across policyholders are difficult and costly to insure. The higher severity of catastrophe events also requires insurance companies to hold large reserves to cover potential losses or to purchase reinsurance coverage to protect against catastrophic losses. This increases their premiums and possibly leads to affordability challenges (see below).
- ***Consumer behaviour***. For low frequency events, the willingness of policyholders to pay for insurance coverage may be limited. This is because the probability of facing losses may seem remote. They may also expect government compensation for any incurred losses and damages (McClelland, Schulze and Coursey, 1993[156]).
- ***Lack of financial literacy:*** Another reason for limited take-up is lack of understanding of insurance products and markets among the affected population. People who do not understand insurance products because they lack financial literacy will be unable to assess their value and thus will not purchase them.

Measures to increase the contribution of insurance to absorbing climate-related losses

The following provides an overview of policy and regulatory measures that could improve the contribution of insurance markets to absorbing the financial consequences of climate-related losses (Box 5.8).

Box 5.8. The potential risk management benefits of insurance market development

Developed insurance markets that make coverage available for climate-related risks can also contribute to improving overall risk management. Insurance companies use risk assessment tools to underwrite coverage, such as catastrophe models, and to provide probabilistic assessment of future losses. Such tools can be equally applied to decisions on risk mitigation or adaptation investments. Where allowed, insurance premiums that vary by level of risk can provide important incentives for policyholders. Specifically, they could encourage investment in risk reduction and adaptation to benefit from reduced insurance premium costs. For larger policyholders, such as large corporates, insurance companies often offer advice on risk prevention. In addition, insurance companies often play an important advocacy role for land-use planning and building codes to reduce losses on assumed risks.

Ensuring that households and businesses are offered relevant insurance coverage

Measures that ensure that insurance companies make coverage for climate-related hazards available, encourage take-up by policy holders at risk as a result (OECD, 2021[157]; OECD, 2016[158]). In a mandatory offer, for example, insurance companies are required to make insurance coverage available for specific risks. Examples of take-up include automatic inclusion in property insurance or opt-out requirements. In some countries, banking regulators require banks to ensure their borrowers have insurance coverage for relevant risk for properties with outstanding mortgages. This protects the financial system against post-catastrophe borrower defaults. Figure 5.5 shows the level of insurance coverage for past flood-related losses in OECD countries. This is based on differences in requirements on including such coverage in property insurance policies and for having such coverage on properties with mortgage loans. Box 5.9 illustrates the consequences of how insurance is offered based on the experience of India and Myanmar.

Households with higher level of financial literacy are more likely to take insurance in both developing and developed countries (Liu et al., 2021[159]; Weedige et al., 2019[160]). Actors can decide to take up insurance based on similar decisions of others for several reasons. First, some types of insurance are likely to become cheaper as more people buy it because risks can be spread more evenly. Climate hazards like SLR, however, may in the future strain this model, because SLR will happen simultaneously on every coastline, potentially making risk transfer more difficult and costly (Santeramo et al., 2016[161]). Second, a person taking up insurance makes it more likely for others to purchase insurance (Millo and Pasini, 2010[162]). Policy makers are therefore well placed to raise awareness about risk management options and raise financial literacy by offering financial education. Education programmes will likely be more effective if they recognise the differences of individual preferences, circumstances and financial knowledge (Amagir et al., 2017[163]). This would form a basis, not only of insurance, but more generally of climate risk management literacy.

Figure 5.5. Insured share of flood losses by offer or purchase requirement (OECD countries)

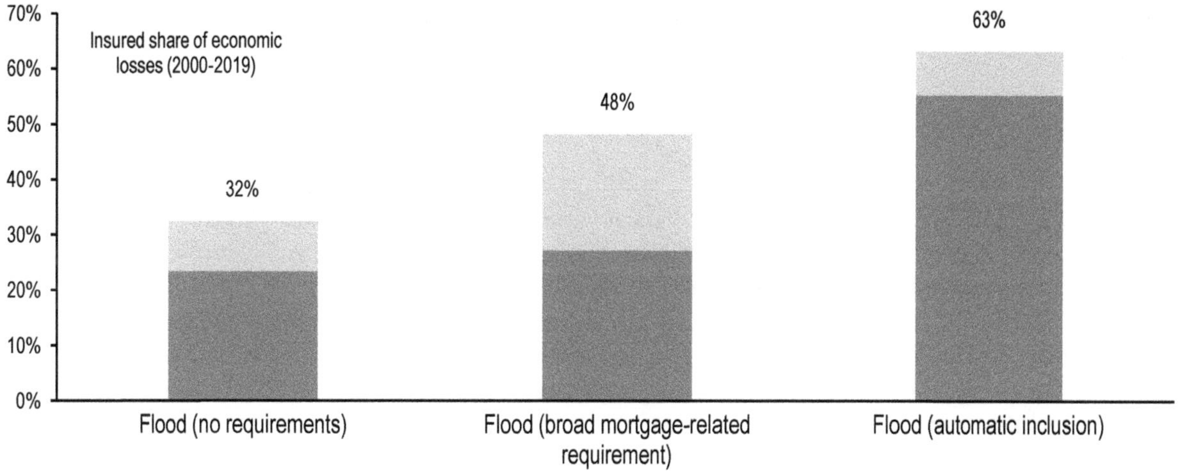

Note: The chart shows two estimates: i) the total share of economic losses insured for all events that occurred between 2000-19; and ii) the simple average of the share of losses insured for each individual event. The figure shown refers to the higher of the two estimates. Information on the form of coverage offer for flood insurance is from OECD (2016[130]). OECD countries are classified as follows: no requirements includes Australia (storm surge), Canada, Chile, Colombia, Czech Republic, Germany, Greece, Italy, Japan, Mexico, New Zealand, Portugal and Turkey; broad-mortgage related requirements includes Ireland and the United States; automatic inclusion includes Australia (rainfall flooding), Belgium, Denmark, France, Poland, Spain, Switzerland and the United Kingdom.
Source: OECD calculations based on data on natural catastrophe losses provided by Swiss Re sigma and PCS.

Box 5.9. Insurance for climate-related catastrophe risks in India and Myanmar

India and Myanmar have similar levels of overall property insurance penetration (property premiums as a share of GDP of approximately 0.06%). However, they have different levels of insurance coverage for climate-related catastrophe hazards. In India, approximately 10-18% of economic losses from floods and storms (including cyclones) between 2000 and 2019 were insured relative to 1-6% in Myanmar. In India, Standard Fire and Special Perils policies offered to commercial/industrial and residential policyholders usually include (automatic) coverage for storm, typhoon, cyclone, tempest, tornado, hurricane, flood or inundation (although policyholders can opt out). As a result, the vast majority of households and business with property insurance also have coverage for damages from storms and floods. In Myanmar, separate coverage endorsements are required for storm, typhoon, hurricane, tempest, cyclone, and flood and inundation. This means that households and businesses with property insurance policies must be offered this additional coverage and choose to acquire it. However, some lending banks do set requirements for adequate insurance coverage for properties with mortgages.

Source: (OECD, 2020[164]).

Addressing insurance affordability challenges

Low insurance coverage highlights the need for governments to address insurability challenges. Government needs to create conditions under which insurance remains a viable option for climate-related hazards. Such challenges are already emerging in several countries (see Box 5.10), possibly due to potential hazards impacting many policyholders simultaneously. The combined impact of hazards decreases the benefits of diversification on which the insurance business model is based. In some cases, hazards might become uninsurable as private insurers refuse to cover them. Private insurance market withdrawals might be temporary. In the United States, for example, private flood insurers are returning to the market because they can better quantify these risks. If the demand for insurance increases, households and business may also be willing to pay the higher premiums to the insurance companies supplying it.

Box 5.10. Insurability challenges of climate-related hazards in the United States

A number of large catastrophic wildfires in recent years has led to insurability challenges within the United States, state of California. Households in areas of high risk of wildfire have faced premium increases and insurer-initiated non-renewals of coverage. In response, the California Department of Insurance has imposed moratoriums on non-renewals (California Department of Insurance, 2019[165]; Insurance Journal, 2020[166]). In addition, it held a virtual investigative hearing in October 2020 to find a solution to the challenges in the insurance sector (Jergler, 2020[167]). There are also recent reports of insurability challenges related to hurricane (wind) coverage in the state of Florida. These include reports of non-renewals by insurers (Insurance Journal, 2018[168]), requests for regulatory approval of large premium rate increases, and an increase in policy count in 2020 and 2021 at Citizens (a publicly owned residual insurer) (Saunders, 2020[169]; O'Connor, 2021[170]).

Premiums based on level of risk to the covered building or infrastructure asset can provide an important pricing signal on risk exposure. This should encourage households and businesses to reduce their risk (i.e. alleviate moral hazards) to benefit from lower insurance costs. The effectiveness of insurance pricing to reduce risks depends on a number of factors. These include the nature of the hazards; the cost of effective mitigation measures; and the ability of insurance companies to measure the risk reduction and offer a lower premium. However, risk-based premiums may be unaffordable for households or businesses facing high levels of risk exposure or limited capacity to pay for insurance coverage. In such cases, various types of catastrophe risk insurance programmes may offer a solution. In one option, insurance companies (or a single public insurer) pool catastrophe exposure to build a diversified portfolio of risks that reduces the aggregate cost of reinsurance coverage. In another, the programmes provide some form of government backstop for extreme losses. Both options ultimately support the affordability of insurance coverage for hazards. The existence of a catastrophe risk insurance programme tends to be correlated with higher levels of insurance coverage of economic losses from hazards. This is especially the case in countries with lower levels of property insurance penetration.[3]

One response to the affordability challenge is a government-backed mandatory insurance scheme or a public insurance provider. Such insurance could be cheaper, than ones provided in a purely private insurance market because insurance penetration – and hence the ability to spread risks – is higher. In theory, a public insurer could be better informed than its private counterpart. As a public body, it could have access to more information about risks facing the insurance holder (such as building codes). It could also integrate insurance policies into the wider climate strategy. However, this information only decreases moral hazards if the insurance premiums are risk-based. This is often considered to be politically unfeasible in case of public insurance schemes (Paleari, 2019[171]). For example, Romania introduced compulsory disaster insurance in 2008 whose premium depends on building quality. This provides some incentive to improve the physical resilience of buildings. However, it does not address other types of moral hazards, such as decreasing exposure or other vulnerabilities (Hanger et al., 2017[172]). Governments might also choose to provide insurance coverage to a selection of citizens. The government of Colombia, for example, included uninsured buildings of the poorest two social groups as a government responsibility (Colombia Ministry of Finance and Public Credit, 2011[173]; Gamper et al., 2017[174]). Despite their shortcomings, mandatory schemes are sometimes preferred to budget re-allocations since the uncertain and *ex post* nature of re-allocations do not provide incentives to decrease moral hazards. According to theoretical investigations, the most efficient and equitable intervention may be a private insurance market partially subsidised by the government. These might include government-backed vouchers or rely increasingly on public-partnership programmes (Hudson, Botzen and Aerts, 2019[175]).

Two additional points are worth making. First, moral hazards might not arise with insurance at all. Insurance holders may be sufficiently risk averse to continue reducing risk, even with insurance coverage (Hudson et al., 2017[176]; Mol, Botzen and Blasch, 2020[177]). Thus, risk aversion of the population is a key ingredient when designing a policy intervention. Second, the uninsurability of assets is not unanimously negative. If assets cannot be insured, there is an incentive to move them from the uninsured location or at least not to place assets in those locations. These incentives themselves, however, are not always enough. In several countries, properties continue to be built in exposed coastal areas or in areas at risk of wildfires. This calls for dissemination of information and raising awareness (see Section 5.3.1).

Maximising access to international reinsurance and capital market capacity

Global reinsurance and capital markets play a critical role in providing an additional layer of loss absorption capacity and diversifying catastrophe risks internationally. This allows for international markets (and some investors) to absorb some portion of the losses from a catastrophic event. It also diversifies the burden away from the domestic financial system. However, several countries impose various restrictions on the transfer of risk to reinsurance and capital markets (and, particularly, for cross-border risk transfer). For example, countries like India and Indonesia limit the amount of risk that can be transferred to reinsurance companies without a local presence. Other countries do not recognise risk transfer to capital markets as an effective way for insurers to reduce the amount of capital they hold (OECD, 2018[153]). As a result, catastrophe (including climate) risks are concentrated in the domestic market or domestic reinsurance companies. This creates risks to the broader economy, limiting the ability of insurance companies to fully capitalise on the benefits of risk transfer to reinsurance markets.

Risk transfer to reinsurance markets provide potentially large benefits. The economy recovered much more quickly in countries where international reinsurance markets absorbed a larger share of losses (OECD, 2018[153]) (see Figure 5.6.). Ultimately, greater access to the capacity available in international reinsurance and capital markets may be necessary. Such access should provide insurance companies with enough protection to manage the expected increase in losses from future climate-related risks.

Figure 5.6. Cumulative loss (or gain) in GDP relative to pre-event projections for different levels of reinsurance coverage

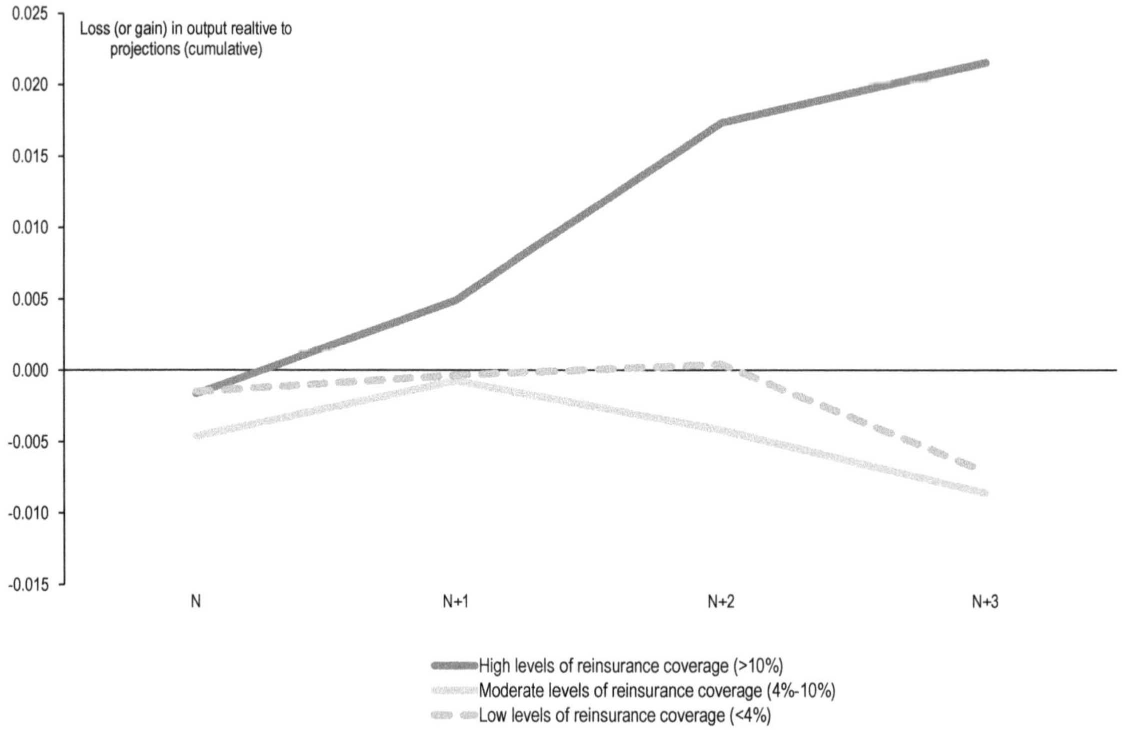

Note: The chart shows actual (post-catastrophe) growth relative to (pre-catastrophe) growth projections at impacted country-level for three categories of catastrophe events: i) those with high levels of reinsurance coverage (where reinsurance covered more than 10% of all reported economic losses); ii) those with moderate levels of reinsurance coverage (where reinsurance covered between 4% and 10% of all reported economic losses); and iii) those with low levels of reinsurance coverage (where reinsurance covered less than 4% of all reported economic losses.

Source: (OECD, 2018[153]).

Insurance for public exposures

Similar to insurance coverage for privately owned buildings, indemnity insurance will normally reimburse most costs incurred to rebuild public buildings and infrastructure to its original form. Some governments (national or subnational) can also acquire financial protection for more general funding needs following a climate-related hazard. This type of financial protection is generally triggered based on the parameters of an event. For example, wind speed or rainfall might exceed a pre-defined level or a modelled-loss might exceed a pre-defined amount. Such protection, known as parametric insurance, provides a quick source of funding and liquidity.

The main advantage of parametric insurance is its simplicity. Coverage can be underwritten based solely on the probability of an event that meets the thresholds for a pay-out occurring at a given location. Further, claims payments are based solely on the occurrence of the triggering event. The main disadvantage of parametric insurance is the potential for significant basis risk. In other words, the coverage might be triggered even if no loss is incurred. Similarly, the policy may not be not triggered when a loss has occurred (e.g. if the specific threshold has not been met). Improvements in the accuracy of risk assessment from new data sources and analytical techniques should reduce this risk over time (ADB and OECD, 2020[178]).

Catastrophe bonds, for example, are a form of debt issued by a "transferor" (a country, for example) through a special purpose entity to transfer risks to capital market investors. If a triggering event occurs, some portion of the funds placed in a special purpose entity is made available to the transferor, and the bond defaults.

Risk pooling may lower the cost of risk transfer tools. Several regional risk pooling arrangements have been established, including in the Caribbean and Central America, the Pacific Islands, in Southeast Asia and in Africa (ARC) (see Box 5.11). These arrangements usually provide a specified amount of quick funding to support recovery needs rather than reconstruction; pay-out is based on some form of parametric trigger. Participating countries benefit from sharing the cost of necessary modelling. They also benefit from more affordable reinsurance coverage based on the diversification benefits achieved by approaching the reinsurance market as a collective. Some programmes like ARC require contributing countries to develop *ex ante* contingency plans on how to use the funds. These define disbursement processes and responsibilities, decreasing uncertainty in case of an event.

Investing in better quality models could improve effectiveness of risk pools as could extending coverage for different types of extreme events. For example, ARC introduced coverage for tropical cyclones in 2020. Other improvement measures are rule-based processes to manage unmet expectations, and possibly including secondary triggers to reduce basis risk. Integrating risk pool disbursements into social protection measures could also improve efficiency, shorten recovery times and help reduce hardship within vulnerable communities. New, sustained support from donors and development banks could further expand risk pools, providing an alternative to sporadic donor funds designated for finance-specific instruments (Martinez-Diaz and McClamrock, 2019[179]).

Governments can also take advantage of economies of scale by pooling the acquisition of insurance coverage for public assets. They can benefit from lower cost access to insurance or reinsurance markets by seeking coverage for a pool of assets (with different risk characteristics). Several countries have established public insurance or compensation arrangements at the national and subnational level. These provide insurance coverage for public assets and subsequently transfer some of the risk assumed to private reinsurance markets.

Challenges for insurance in managing the risks of losses and damages

The growing impact of climate change on the insurance and reinsurance industry is well understood (Krauss et al., 2019[180]). As losses grow, the need for additional funding rises, increasing insurance premiums. One estimate predicts that global premiums collected for property insurance will raise by USD 149 billion to USD 183 billion by 2040 (i.e. an 33-45% growth relative to 2020). This estimate aims to account for the rise in insured catastrophe losses, including as a result of climate change.

Globally linked weather events may also become more difficult to diversify (Herweijer, Ranger and Ward, 2009[181]; Boers et al., 2019[182]). Insurers may also withdraw coverage if the increase in premiums needed to cover losses is greater than the willingness (or capacity) of households and businesses to pay. As a result, insurance will become more progressively expensive, making it difficult for developing countries and poor households to obtain coverage (Duus-Otterström and Jagers, 2011[183]), exacerbating inequalities. This underlines the need for risk reduction to maintain the insurability of climate-related risks by decreasing exposures and vulnerabilities.

Box 5.11. The African Risk Capacity

The African Risk Capacity (ARC) is a regional risk pool established by the African Union. It helps African governments improve their capacities to plan, prepare and respond to extreme weather and climate events through collaboration. To that end, it helps countries harness state-of-the-art technology, as well as gain access to innovative finance mechanisms. While droughts are common across Africa, the ARC assumes they will not likely occur in the same year in all parts of the continent.

In return for an annual premium payment, participating countries can access pay-outs if a pre-determined triggering event occurs. The risk transfer parameters selected by each country determine the pay-out threshold. These parameters include the following:

- ***Deductible/attachment point***: the risk the country wants to retain and manage using other resources.
- ***Exhaustion point***: the maximum modelled drought risk that the country wishes to cover in the insurance policy.
- ***The limit***: the maximum pay-out for a country in case of an extreme drought.
- ***Ceding percentage***: the percentage of the total modelled risk the country wishes to transfer to the pool.

The ARC on average covers USD 30 million per country per season for drought events that occur with a frequency of one in five years or more (though the exact amount varies widely). The ARC makes pay-outs to the national treasury within two to four weeks of the end of the rainfall season. Subsequently, the treasury can use the pay-out to support affected households using a pre-approved contingency plan. The ARC expands climate risk insurance coverage through ARC Replica, an insurance product for the World Food Programme and other humanitarian partners. It aims to improve the effectiveness of emergency humanitarian response in vulnerable African countries prone to climate risks (WFP, 2018[184]).

To be eligible for the ARC, participating governments must develop a contingency plan. This outlines how they will use pay-outs quickly and effectively. It also describes how they will reach those most impacted by the extreme weather event in an efficient and timely manner to protect livelihoods. Whereas the funds ideally should be implemented within 120 days of an ARC pay-out, funded activities should be completed within six months.

Providers of development co-operation, along with participating African Union members, can contribute to the ARC through annual premiums. For example, as part of its COVID-19 Emergency Programme, Germany provided premium payments in 2020 for the ARC to support up to 20 million people in the 2020-21 agricultural season (BMZ, 2021[185]). The United States, the United Kingdom and Switzerland have also supported ARC member states and replica partners with premium financing.

Source: https://www.africanriskcapacity.org.

5.4. Role of development co-operation in supporting developing country approaches to reduce and manage the risks of losses and damages

The challenges outlined in previous sections highlight the importance of access to and use of diverse sources of finance by all stakeholders to reduce and manage the risks of losses and damages. This section explores the role of development finance from bilateral and multilateral providers, including operations linked with climate-related humanitarian assistance. It first lays out the development finance landscape that directly or indirectly supports developing country efforts to reduce and manage climate risks. This is complemented by a short discussion on how providers are integrating risks of losses and damages across their strategic and programming frameworks. Next, it outlines insights on the finance commitments by bilateral and multilateral providers to address the risks of losses and damages from climate change. This analysis builds upon a methodology developed for this report. Finally, the section highlights broader issues that providers need to consider, ending with the role of development finance in the context of fiscal sustainability.

Lack of consensus on a definition of losses and damages politically and in the academic literature (Doelle and Seck, 2020[186]; Toussaint, 2021[187]) permeates to how these concepts are understood in the context of development co-operation. In the broadest understanding, all efforts to curb the global average temperature increase, and to adapt to the adverse effects of climate change, can help reduce and manage the risks of losses and damages from climate change (UNFCCC, 2019[90]). Improved public sector financial management, for example, is not generally defined as climate action. However, it can still help mobilise domestic resources for climate change adaptation (MOPAN, 2021[188]). Other interventions that fall outside the climate sphere may indirectly contribute to adaptation and disaster risk reduction. Examples include education, broader poverty reduction efforts and social protection. Such a broad approach, however, does not shed light on the extent to which providers are considering and addressing the risks of losses and damages in their programming and financing.

A narrower approach informs the analysis in this section, building upon elements discussed and agreed upon through the United Nations (UN) climate negotiations. Article 8 of the Paris Agreement highlights the importance of averting, minimising and addressing loss and damage associated with the adverse effects of climate change. It highlights eight areas of co-operation and facilitation to enhance understanding, action and support (UNFCCC, 2015[189]). It also reaffirms the Warsaw International Mechanism for Loss and Damage (WIM) as the main vehicle for taking these issues forward. Subsequent decisions agreed by countries through the international climate process have further clarified what constitutes different types of losses and damages. Countries are not obliged to separately track or report finance associated with activities for reducing and managing the risk of losses and damages. Instead, support for these activities is partially tracked through established adaptation finance reporting mechanisms such as biennial reports, national communications, biennial update reports and (under the Paris Agreement) biennial transparency reports.

5.4.1. Strategic and programming approaches

Climate-related funds and programmes

The development finance landscape supporting efforts to reduce and manage the risks of losses and damages from climate change includes both bilateral and multilateral providers. This section briefly outlines some key components that fall under the broader heading of multilateral finance, which includes climate-related funds and programmes. The United Nations Framework Convention on Climate Change (UNFCCC) has a number of dedicated financial mechanisms to provide finance for climate action in developing countries. The Green Climate Fund (GCF), an operating entity within the UNFCCC, is mandated to support developing countries take climate action. This includes support to country approaches to avert, minimise and address loss and damage through existing investment frameworks and funding windows (Green Climate Fund, 2021[190]; Kempa et al., 2021[191]). This support reflects decisions made in the context of the climate negotiations. The GCF is also committed to spend half of its resources on climate change adaptation (in grant-equivalent terms).

Other operating entities have been entrusted to the Global Environment Facility (GEF). The GEF Trust Fund, for example, supports enabling activities, notably for reporting on adaptation and other climate change activities under the Convention. The Least Developed Countries Fund supports preparation and implementation of risk assessments and early-warning systems. Meanwhile, the Special Climate Change Fund finances non-LDC pilot or demonstration adaptation activities. In addition, the Adaptation Fund, created under the Kyoto Protocol, supports climate change adaptation projects and programmes in vulnerable developing countries. Finally, the Climate Investment Funds, through the Pilot Program for Climate Resilience, supports the integration of climate risk and resilience into national development planning and implementation.

Different actors play complementary roles in providing climate finance to partner countries. Multilateral and regional development banks often focus on support for larger investments through concessional loans, working with a broad range of partners including from the private sector. Development finance institutions, such as France's AFD or Germany's KfW, also finance large infrastructure projects through concessional loans. Other multilateral and international organisations, such as the UNFCCC financial mechanisms described above, can play different roles, depending on their mandate and financial resources. Bilateral providers of development finance may be relatively well placed to support partner countries in integrating climate change into their national development planning processes. They do this through pilot initiatives, capacity development, technical assistance and technology transfer. Bilateral providers play an equally important role in provision and delivery of humanitarian assistance in response to a climate-related disaster.

Access to finance

The availability of funds does not guarantee access to them. Access is limited by several factors. Accreditation procedures are often complex and differing across funds. Application processes and fiduciary requirements often place a disproportionate burden on institutions in developing countries; yet these countries often have limited administrative and technical capacities. Climate-related funds and programmes are working to address access issues. The GCF, for example, has introduced direct access modality, following the lead of the Adaptation Fund. However, there is growing recognition that more action is needed and that structural issues go beyond the design of individual funds. Environments or credit ratings of individual countries, for example, have also been identified as issues.

In response to these perceived shortcomings of the international development financing architecture (UK Government, 2021[192]; LIFE-AR, 2019[193]), different stakeholders are highlighting the urgent need for enhanced and simplified access to finance to complement the provision and mobilisation of climate finance. To address this challenge, the LDCs Initiative for Effective Adaptation and Resilience (LIFE-AR) seeks to deepen climate knowledge and access to predictable and reliable finance – domestic, international, public and private. Such access would be guided by the principles of inclusion, participation, local action, justice, equity and leaving no one behind (LIFE-AR, 2019[193]). The United Kingdom, in its capacity as incoming COP26 President, has established a Taskforce on Access to Climate Finance. Co-chaired by the United Kingdom and Fiji, the taskforce highlights four principles for effective access (UK Government, 2021[192]): i) national ownership and co-ordination; ii) an aligned, co-ordinated and programmatic response by providers of development co-operation; iii) pragmatism and co-ordination with initiatives; and iv) inclusivity. This is consistent with calls made by the Ministers of Finance of the Vulnerable Twenty Group (V20) for "more robust support and synergistic engagement of the international economic community in support of climate-resilient economies" (V20, 2021[194]).

Strategic and programming frameworks

The focus and approach of development finance providers is informed by increased emphasis of the climate negotiations on Loss and Damage from climate change but also in response to the felt climate impacts of developing countries. One example is the 2021 commitment by the G7 to strengthen support for prearranged risk finance, including through the Centre for Disaster Protection's Crisis Lookout

Campaign. Providers do not use a harmonised terminology. In fact, they often integrate support to reduce and manage the risks of losses and damages into established adaptation, climate resilience and disaster risk reduction initiatives. However, some providers are explicitly referring to losses and damages in their strategic frameworks and programmes:

- The German development agency (GIZ) introduced the *Global Programme on Risk Assessment and Management for Adaptation to Climate Change (Loss and Damage)* in 2013. It aims to support partner countries in developing and implementing measures to "avert, minimise and address" losses and damages from climate change and to mainstream these approaches (GIZ, 2018[195]). Additionally, in its new strategy on climate and energy, the German Federal Ministry for Economic Cooperation and Development explicitly refers to the issue of climate-related loss and damage. The strategy refers to concrete ways to support partner countries, such as promoting climate and disaster risk financing measures; supporting EWS; and providing targeted support to climate risk analyses and management, and capacity- and knowledge-building relating to climate-induced migration and displacement. It also acknowledges the need for a more systematic approach to deal with the vulnerability of partner countries. For example, under the umbrella of the InsuResilience Global Partnership (IGP), KfW Development Bank is supporting a number of relevant funds. These include the InsuResilience Solutions Fund and the InsuResilience Investment Fund. The IGP aims to scale up Climate and Disaster Risk Finance and Insurance solutions in developing and emerging countries (see Box 5.12).
- Denmark's new Strategy for Global Climate Action aims to "contribute to preventing and reducing the risk of losses and damage as a result of climate change, and to help with rebuilding efforts in the wake of climate disasters" through green development co-operation (Government of Denmark, 2020[196]). Denmark, through its Danish International Development Agency (DANIDA) had been helping address climate-related losses and damages before this strategic change. In northern Kenya, for instance, DANIDA supports pastoralists forced to abandon their traditional way of life that includes moving their livestock in search of water and land to graze. It does so through vocational training of herders who have lost their livelihoods, in line with Kenya's National Climate Change Action Plan (Ministry of Foreign Affairs of Denmark, 2020[197]).
- The World Bank's *Climate Action Plan (2021-25)* includes a financing strategy that covers climate change adaptation and losses and damages. It emphasises catastrophe-linked bonds (CAT-bonds) that offer pay-outs when, for example, tropical cyclones meet pre-defined criteria under the bond terms (World Bank, 2021[198]). The World Bank also helped establish programmes such as regional risk pools (e.g. the Caribbean Catastrophe Risk Insurance Facility and the Pacific Catastrophe Risk Assessment and Financing Initiative). In addition, it runs other programmes such as the Global Risk Financing (GRiF) and the Global Facility for Disaster Reduction and Recovery with support from a range of donors. The GRiF aims to pilot and scale up support to strengthen the resilience of vulnerable countries to climate and disaster shocks. To that end, it enables earlier and more reliable response and recovery through prearranged risk financing instruments, including market-based instruments like insurance.

Providers are also using risk assessment to inform responses to climate change. As highlighted in the UNFCCC Suva expert dialogue, this includes the use of risk assessments relevant to averting, minimising and addressing climate impacts. It also includes ongoing work in the areas of open source risk assessment tools to support decision making, national risk profiling and probabilistic risk modelling (UNFCCC, 2019[90]). Climate risk screening tools provide a preventive approach to managing climate and disaster risks by helping to integrate resilience measures into the design of initiatives (World Bank, 2021[199]; AfDB, 2014[200]; ADB, 2014[201]; USAID, 2017[202]; BMZ, 2019[203]). The factors driving climate risks and the associated uncertainties are complex. Consequently, the application of climate risk screening tools faces certain technical challenges (see Chapter 2).

Some providers have developed *ex post* tools to assess needs following climate-related and other hazards. For example, the UN Development Group, the World Bank and the European Union jointly developed the Post-Disaster Needs Assessment (PDNA) in 2008. PDNAs provide a comprehensive assessment to estimate losses and damages, identifying needs of the affected population. They plan the restoration of damaged infrastructure, houses, livelihoods, services, governance and social systems with emphasis on reducing future disaster risks and building resilience. The methodology shapes investment decisions of providers such as the Islamic Development Bank (IsDB, 2019[204]).

Box 5.12. InsuResilience Global Partnership

The InsuResilience Global Partnership (IGP) is an international alliance supporting resilience to climate risks. It aims to help protect the lives and livelihoods of poor and vulnerable people through Climate and Disaster Risk Finance and Insurance (CDRFI) solutions. IGP grew out of the 2015 G7 InsuResilience initiative. It was launched by a group of industrialised countries and members of the G20 and V20 group of vulnerable countries in 2017 at the UNFCCC COP23. IGP works within the international resilience community for mobilising action, raising ambition and fostering coherence of CDRFI contributions across a diverse range of partners. It brings together over 100 members from different stakeholder groups (countries, private sector, multilateral organisations, development banks, civil society and academia).

Since 2017, different actors have met annually through the Partnership Forum, which provides a platform to exchange on best practice, key learnings and future directions of the community on Climate and Disaster Risk Finance and Insurance. Guided by its Vision 2025, presented at the UN Climate Action Summit 2019, IGP enables faster, more reliable and cost-effective responses to climate shocks and disasters, shifting from reactive crisis management to proactive risk management. One of its main targets is to cover 500 million poor and vulnerable people annually by 2025. In 2020, 137 million people in more than 100 countries were reached through 22 implementing programmes under the Forum.

Source: (BMZ, 2021[185]; InsuResilience Global Partnership, 2021[205]).

5.4.2. Humanitarian assistance in response to losses and damages

Humanitarian assistance plays an important role in response to both slow-onset changes and extreme events. It takes the form of relief, as well as in-kind support such as food, water, medicines and tents. While post-disaster humanitarian assistance from donors is crucial, the timing and volume can be unpredictable and slow to mobilise (Bowen et al., 2020[72]). Development co-operation providers can help partner countries manage the risks of climate-related losses and damages in several ways. First, they could use more predictable and flexible financing to meet immediate humanitarian needs. Second, their interventions could adapt to changing circumstances and future climate risks (Bowen et al., 2020[72]; OECD, 2021[102]). Providers are also increasingly integrating anticipatory action into development (German Federal Foreign Office, 2020[84]; Levine et al., 2020[85]; Kuriyama et al., 2020[86]) and humanitarian programmes (UK Government, 2021[87]). Some bilateral and multilateral providers have started to use climate vulnerability indexes to guide investment decisions (see Box 5.13).

Box 5.13. Climate vulnerability indexes and frameworks

Using climate vulnerability indexes may be useful when deploying humanitarian assistance *ex ante* where providers may not have a field presence. The Fragile States Index, for example, highlights social, economic, climate and other vulnerabilities that contribute to the risk of state fragility (The Fund for Peace, n.d.[206]). For its part, the Global Climate Risk Index maps levels of exposure and vulnerability to extreme weather events that countries can use as warnings to prepare for future events (Germanwatch, 2021[207]). The OECD States of Fragility programme helps providers explore approaches to development co-operation so they can achieve greater resilience in fragile and conflict-affected countries. This programme includes the concept of environmental fragility, which encompasses climate-related risks. It shows how providers can factor in these concepts when programming activities in affected countries (OECD, 2020[208]). Such indexes and frameworks help integrate climate-related considerations into regular development co-operation activities, enhancing the contribution of the investments to resilience and sustainable development.

Section 5.3 highlighted the trade-offs governments face when determining the appropriate financing mechanisms in the context of losses and damages (e.g. *ex ante* dedicated reserve funds compared to *ex post* budget re-allocation). Such trade-offs can emerge given the potential risk of diverting resources from broader investments in development. Development co-operation providers face a similar challenge. They must weigh the trade-off between rapid humanitarian assistance and support for recovery versus medium- to longer-term investments to achieve sustainable development (Fanning and Fullwood-Thomas, 2019[209]). Yet development co-operation providers often plan and implement their development interventions, including on climate change, separately from their humanitarian assistance. Different teams or agencies frequently manage the two types of support according to distinct rules, decision-making processes, programming cycles and budget envelopes (OECD, 2019[210]). With mounting losses and damages, the need for greater collaboration across humanitarian and development actors is increasingly recognised (United Nations, 2016[211]). In fact, collaboration between the humanitarian and development co-operation communities will require more synergies. Providers must respond to people's immediate needs, while contributing to their resilience in the wake of both already experienced and projected hazards. They can do this by planning and investing early in preparedness, as noted by the G7 (UK Government, 2021[212]), through their choices of programming, and through early and sustained engagement with local capacities (see Box 5.14).

Box 5.14. Implications of climate change for humanitarian action

Climate-related hazards are among the top drivers exacerbating the need for humanitarian assistance in protracted crises. In addition, the global landscape of humanitarian action has expanded with a proliferation of non-traditional response plans. Humanitarian organisations, local civil society groups and volunteer responders have been on the frontline dealing with the impacts and risks of the climate crisis to communities, lives and livelihoods. The widening gap between need and ability to respond will overwhelm both local and international levels. Therefore, in addition to increased resources, there is an urgent need to adjust the modalities of humanitarian support to contribute directly to global adaptation and community resilience. As input to this process, the United Nations Office for the Coordination of Humanitarian Affairs recommended five ways the humanitarian community can adjust to this growing need:

- ***Act early***: Offsetting the increase in humanitarian need requires getting ahead of the crisis, through preparedness and disaster risk reduction, scaled-up system-wide anticipatory action, and ambitious risk financing and insurance models.
- ***Act long-term***: Long-term action requires long-term funding and programming and an expansion of the humanitarian toolkit to include support, for example, for social protection, effective climate governance structures, climate change adaptation and mitigation. Multi-year funding and programming has lower operational costs and provides a more effective response. This helps develop capacity and enhances resilience at the local level.
- ***Act together***: Addressing increasing fragility, vulnerability and need requires new ways to engage the capacities and expertise of a wider range of actors. Interconnected and co-ordinated networks to reduce climate risk and facilitate climate change adaptation requires time, breaking down systemic silos and forging new, broader partnerships. Networks should include, notably, local-level humanitarian actors, climate science and academic sectors, and the private sector.
- ***Act inclusively***: An equity lens is indispensable to programming, funding and policy making that Does No Harm and addresses the disproportionate impact of climate change and pre-existing inequalities. This requires humanitarian and long-term programmes targeting the most vulnerable and marginalised to go hand in hand. They should ensure equitable access to services that address the unique vulnerabilities of people in need, while empowering them in the process.
- ***Act as translators***: More effective translation of science and research is needed to increase understanding of climate change impacts and adaptation strategies across local communities, governments, sectors and donors. The humanitarian community must equally understand the future threats of the climate crisis. It needs to adapt its operating systems and mechanisms to address expanding demands without increased resources.

Source: UNOCHA (forthcoming), *No Return to Normal: The Growing Humanitarian Climate Crisis*, UNOCHA Policy Branch, New York.

5.4.3. Trends in development finance addressing losses and damages

This section explores trends in development finance for approaches that reduce and manage the risks of losses and damages. The analysis covers ODA commitments by members of the OECD Development Assistance Committee (DAC) and multilateral providers for 2018-19. It draws on the OECD Creditor Reporting System (CRS), a database with project-level information for each development co-operation activity funded by DAC members and multilateral providers. Each project in the CRS is categorised by sector and information on provider and partner countries, financial instruments used and amounts committed, among other fields. The CRS also tracks policy commitments through a system of policy markers, including on climate change, disaster risk reduction, biodiversity and desertification (see Box 5.15).

Box 5.15. The system of markers in the OECD DAC CRS

Since 1998, the Development Assistance Committee (DAC) has monitored development finance flows targeting the objectives of the Rio Conventions on biodiversity, climate change and desertification through the CRS using the "Rio markers". The Rio markers were originally designed to help members prepare their National Communications or National Reports to the Rio Conventions by identifying activities that mainstream the Conventions' objectives into development co-operation. DAC members indicate for each development finance activity if it targets environmental or climate objectives. The Rio markers on biodiversity, climate change mitigation and desertification were introduced in 1998. A fourth marker on climate change adaptation has been applied since 2010. An additional marker to track commitments with a focus on disaster risk reduction was subsequently introduced and data from 2018 onwards are available. In the years following the introduction of a marker, providers usually need to adjust their monitoring systems to fully report against the marker, which could mean that some data are missed.

It is mandatory for DAC members to report on the Rio makers. This is not the case for multilateral providers. Some climate-related funds (e.g. the Green Climate Fund and the Adaptation Fund), however, apply the Rio marker methodology. In contrast, multilateral development banks (MDBs) only report the climate components within projects, based on a joint MDB methodology (AfDB et al., 2020[213]). Some multilateral funds (e.g. the International Fund for Agricultural Development) also apply the climate component methodology for their reporting. Since commitments by multilateral providers can be either reported using the Rio maker methodology of the MDB climate component methodology, the analysis in this section distinguishes between the approach used (i.e. Rio maker or climate component) rather than by provider (i.e. bilateral or multilateral).

The analysis is also based on data on official development assistance (ODA). As such, it excludes analysis of other official flows (OOF), which are defined as official sector transactions that do not meet ODA criteria. OOF include grants to developing countries for representational or essentially commercial purposes; official bilateral transactions to promote development but with a grant element of less than 25%; and, official bilateral transactions, whatever their grant element, that seek primarily to facilitate exports. By definition, this category includes export credits extended directly to an aid recipient by an official agency or institution (official direct export credits); the net acquisition by governments and central monetary institutions of securities issued by multilateral development banks at market terms; subsidies (grants) to the private sector to soften its credits to developing countries; and, funds in support of private investment (OECD, n.d.[214]). The analysis excludes OOF partly because of incomplete reporting by all bilateral and multilateral providers of development co-operation. In addition, OOF flows appear to be less relevant to climate change adaptation or disaster risk reduction type investments. Hence, their exclusion would not alter substantially the conclusions extracted from the data presented here.

The CRS and the policy markers were developed before discussions on losses and damages became salient in the political agenda or appeared in the context of UNFCCC negotiations. This limits the explicit references to project objectives in support of efforts to reduce and manage the risks of losses and damages. Other factors that may limit such explicit references in project descriptions include the following:

- There is no consensus on how to define activities related to losses and damages and no requirement or method to track development finance for this purpose.

- The political focus on losses and damages is relatively recent and has not fully permeated explicitly to the operational level yet.
- Some activities related to losses and damages may use different terminology (e.g. addressing climate impacts) and be partially captured by other elements reported, notably those related to climate change adaptation and disaster risk reduction.
- The CRS records financial commitments for projects and programmes. Conversely, Article 8 of the Paris Agreement and the work streams of the WIM refer to process-based activities, which are more difficult to quantify (e.g. slow-onset events, non-economic losses).

These factors pose challenges for identifying and analysing development finance that directly or indirectly supports efforts to reduce or manage the risks of losses and damages. The CRS still constitutes the most comprehensive database for development finance commitments. As such, it can shed light on the nature of commitments that support these objectives.

Against this background, the analysis in this section is informed by relevant decisions agreed upon by countries in the context of climate negotiations on losses and damages – Article 8 of the Paris Agreement on Loss and Damage and the WIM (see Table 5.2). This guidance informed identification of a set of sector codes in the CRS. When screened against activities that report a focus on adaptation and disaster risk reduction, these codes indicate the scale of commitments for 2018-19 (see Annex 5.A for further information on the OECD statistical framework and the methodology used).

Table 5.2. Sources that informed the quantitative analysis

Article 8	WIM work stream	Guidance available
Early warning systems		See below under comprehensive risk assessment and management.
Emergency preparedness		No official definition (but focus clear).
Slow-onset event	(a) slow-onset events	UNFCCC Decision 1/CP.16 (UNFCCC, 2010[215]); WIM work on slow-onset events (UNFCCC, n.d.[216]); COP17 technical paper under the work programme of loss and damage (UNFCCC, 2011[217]).
Events that may involve irreversible and permanent loss and damage		No official definition.
Comprehensive risk assessment and management	(c) comprehensive risk management approaches (including emergency preparedness?)	WIM work definition (UNFCCC, n.d.[218]).
Risk insurance facilities, climate risk pooling and other insurance solutions		No official definition (but focus clear).
Non-economic losses	(b) non-economic losses	UNFCCC technical paper (UNFCCC, 2013[219]).
Resilience of communities, livelihoods and ecosystems		No official definition.
	(d) human mobility, including migration, displacement and planned relocation	
	(e) enhanced co-operation and facilitation in relation to action and support including finance, technology and capacity building.	

Note: In cases where no official definition was available, the wording of Article 8 and WIM work stream was used to compare CRS purpose codes. These codes were then evaluated on a project-by-project basis to decide whether they were relevant to the losses and damages discussion.

There can be no one estimate of commitments given the lack of an agreed definition of activities related to losses and damages. This report does not put forward such a definition since this falls within the mandate of the UN climate processes. Instead, Figure 5.7. summarises different ranges of development finance commitments that support partner country efforts to reduce and manage their risks of losses and damages from climate change. The analysis is concentrated around three approaches (see Annex 5.A for further details):

- ***Approach 1***: Commitments include a focus on climate change adaptation (using the climate change adaptation marker for bilateral commitments and the climate component methodology for some multilateral providers). Further, they target a defined set of sector codes identified as including activities related to efforts to reduce and manage the risks of losses and damages.
- ***Approach 2***: Commitments include a focus on both climate change adaptation and disaster risk reduction (again using the climate change adaptation marker for bilateral commitments and the climate component methodology for some multilateral providers). They target the sector codes identified as including activities related to efforts to reduce and manage the risks of losses and damages.
- ***Approach 3***: Commitments to three sector codes (disaster risk reduction, multi-hazard response preparedness and immediate post-emergency reconstruction and rehabilitation) that also include a focus on climate change adaptation (using the climate change adaptation marker and the component methodology).

Figure 5.7. Different measurements of losses and damages-related commitments from bilateral and multilateral providers, by reporting method

2018-19 annual average, USD billions, commitments

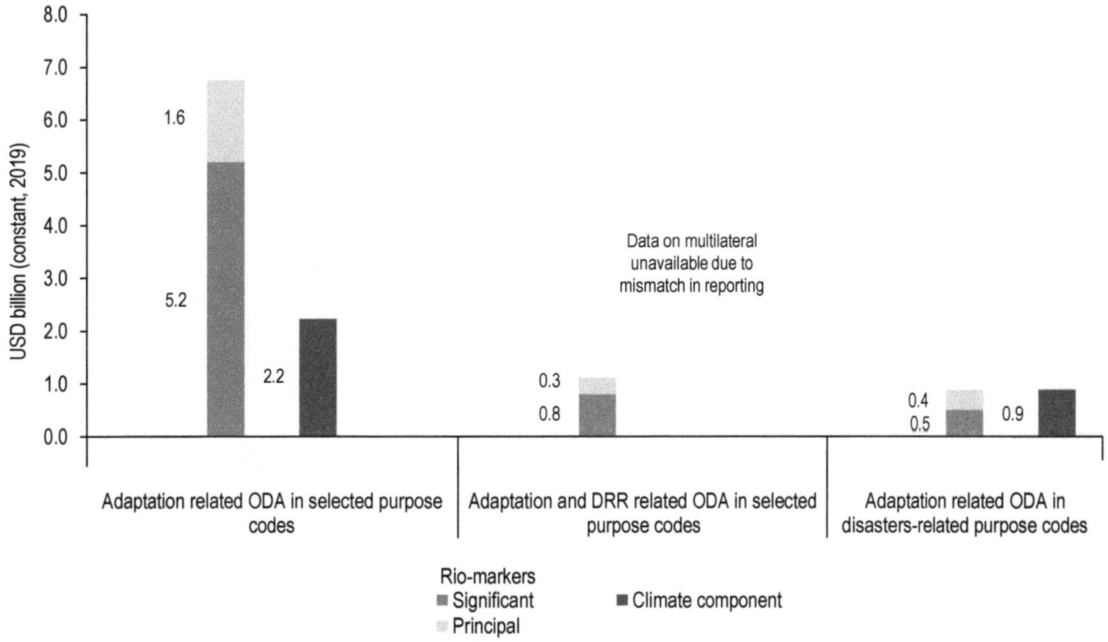

Note: The climate component methodology only takes into account the share of financing allocated for climate change purposes within a specific reported activity. The Rio-markers methodology captures the full face value of the commitment.
Source: (OECD, 2021[82])

The analysis excludes commitments for climate change mitigation despite the need to scale up mitigation overall to limit global average temperature increases and thus avoid losses and damages (see Chapter 1). The CRS only includes mitigation action in developing countries supported by climate-related development finance. As such, it provides an incomplete picture of these efforts by excluding domestic and developed country commitments. At the same time, it focuses on countries that have contributed little to climate change. Box 5.16, however, summarises mitigation-related development finance for ODA-eligible G20 countries. G20 countries account for over 75% of global emissions, which means mitigation efforts in some

Box 5.16. Development finance in support of mitigation in major emitting economies

The IPCC climate risk framework highlights the importance of limiting the creation of climate-related hazards, in addition to reducing the exposure and vulnerability to the hazards. Most developing countries contribute little to greenhouse gas (GHG) emissions. However, a few large emerging economies (and members of the Group of Twenty [G20][1]) account for over 40% of global GHG emissions. These countries do receive support from development providers for climate mitigation objectives. Reducing GHG emissions in these countries, therefore, can have significant impact on future losses and damages.

In 2018-19, mitigation-related official development assistance (ODA) and other official flows (OOF) to G20 ODA-eligible countries from DAC members and other multilateral providers that report with the Rio Marker[2] Methodology reached USD 6.3 billion on average per year (see Figure 5.8). This includes projects with a primary (or principal) focus on mitigation or where it was a significant component. For multilateral providers reporting through the climate component methodology, overall flows (ODA and OOF) amounted to USD 9.6 billion on average in 2018-19, an increase from USD 4.5 billion in 2015-16.

DAC members mainly use ODA, but some multilateral providers resort to concessional financing according to ODA-related criteria (e.g. GCF and other climate funds). Other multilateral providers do not extend concessional finance based on ODA-related considerations. Instead, they provide non-concessional finance based on the income group status of the recipient. In practice, such loans still have favourable terms and conditions compared to the capital market and/or are provided for activities in which the private sector may be reluctant to participate.

Figure 5.8. Climate mitigation ODA and other official flows in G20 ODA-eligible countries, by reporting method

2018-19 annual average, USD billion, gross commitments

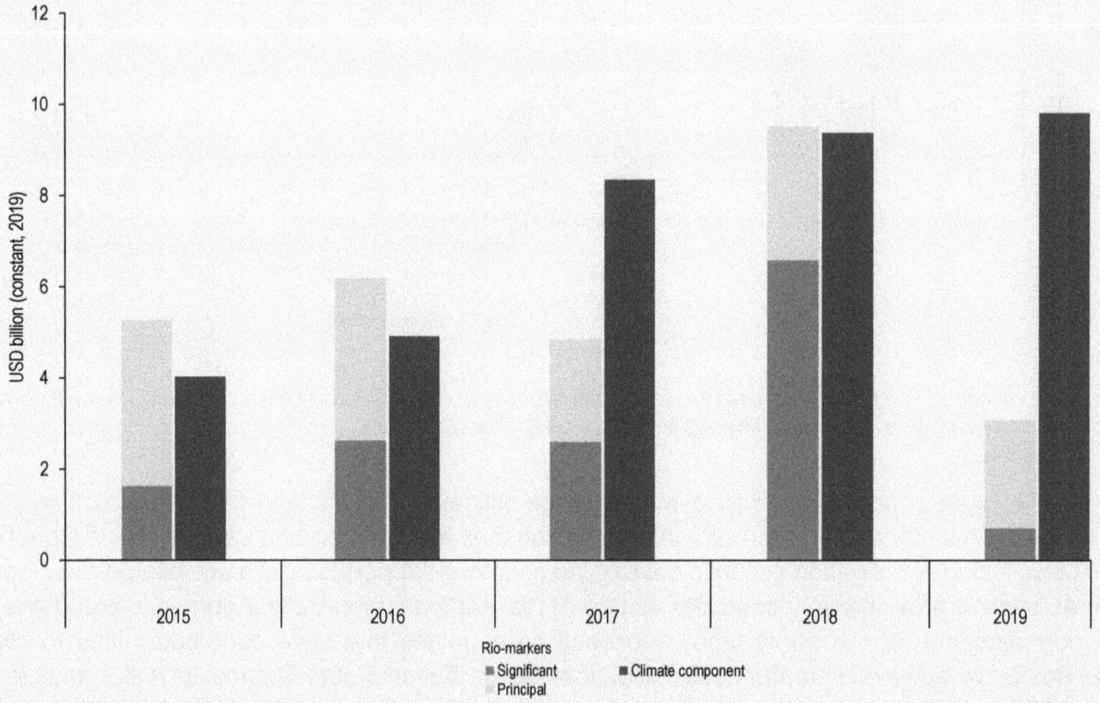

Notes:
[1] ODA-eligible G20 countries include Argentina, Brazil, China, India, Indonesia, Mexico, South Africa and Turkey. The climate component methodology only considers the share of financing allocated for climate mitigation purposes within a specific reported activity. The Rio Markers Methodology captures the full face value of the commitment.
[2.] Multilateral institutions reporting with the Rio marker methodology are Adaptation Fund, Caribbean Development Bank, Climate Investment Funds, the Food and Agriculture Organization, the Green Climate Fund, the Global Environment Facility, the Global Green Growth Institute, the International Fund for Agricultural Development, the Nordic Development Fund and the United Nations Development Programme.
Source: (UNFCCC, 2019[90]; OECD, 2021[82]).

of these countries will contribute significantly to efforts to limit global average temperature increase (Climate Analytics, World Resources Institute, 2021[220]). The same data constraints apply to the rest of the analysis, i.e. it excludes domestic, state and non-state action. However, this analysis focuses on support to developing countries particularly vulnerable to the impacts of climate change.

Approach 1: Commitments for adaptation in selected purpose codes

In 2019, 27% of bilateral ODA (USD 28.6 billion) focused on climate change as either a principal or significant objective, a small increase from 26% in 2018 (OECD, 2020[221]). Climate change adaptation-related commitments *in sectors related to activities for reducing and managing the risks of losses and damages* from DAC members amounted to USD 6.8 billion a year on average in 2018-19. This includes both commitments that integrated climate change adaptation as a principal or significant objective. For multilateral providers, commitments that include a focus on adaptation and the sub-set of sectors identified amounted in 2018-19 to USD 2.2 billion a year (see Figure 5.9.). Note, that multilateral commitments appear in both the Rio-marker and the climate component categories – see Box 5.15 for more details on the markers.

Figure 5.9. Adaptation-related commitments by bilateral and multilateral providers in selected purpose codes, by reporting method

2018-19 annual average, USD billions, gross commitments

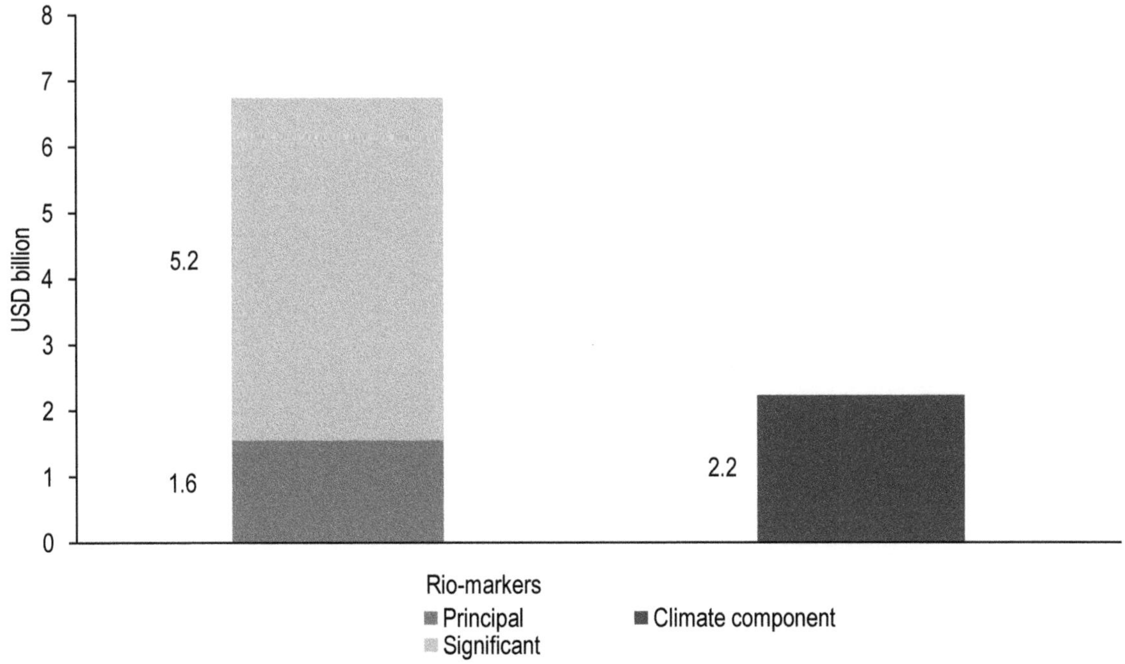

Note: The climate component methodology only considers the share of financing allocated for adaptation purposes. The Rio-markers methodology captures the full face value of the commitment.
Source: (OECD, 2021[82]).

Addressing the vulnerability of developing countries to climate risks that may result in losses and damages, coupled with countries' level of exposure, requires a systemic approach (UNFCCC, 2019[90]). There are several ways to observe how this is achieved. One method is to analyse the level of mainstreaming of climate change adaptation across sectors relevant for losses and damages (see Box 5.17); another is to explore the co-benefits across policy objectives. Providers can use several markers when reporting to the OECD. Doing so may be driven by co-benefits in the implementation of activities. For example, climate-smart agriculture can contribute towards climate resilience, reduced GHG emissions through increased sequestration, and increased productivity and incomes. This analysis shows that 56% (USD 3.4 billion) of bilateral adaptation-related commitments by DAC members in the identified sectors codes in 2018-19 also intersect with other policy markers. Of this share, 40% include a complementary focus on biodiversity, 21% a focus on desertification and 18% a focus on disaster risk reduction.

Box 5.17. Climate change adaptation across sectors relevant for losses and damages

Forestry appears to be the sector where adaptation-related issues are most mainstreamed (75% of all commitments). This is followed by general environment protection (57%), agriculture (56%) and disaster prevention and preparedness (46%). These levels of mainstreaming signal a higher priority and integration of risks and impacts deriving from climate change across activities in these areas. However, this does not reflect volumes. For example, the agriculture sector is only the third sector in terms of mainstreaming but it receives the largest volume of adaptation-related commitments (USD 2 billion) (see right axis of Figure 5.10.).

Figure 5.10. Level of mainstreaming by bilateral providers only in selected purpose codes relevant for losses and damages, by sector

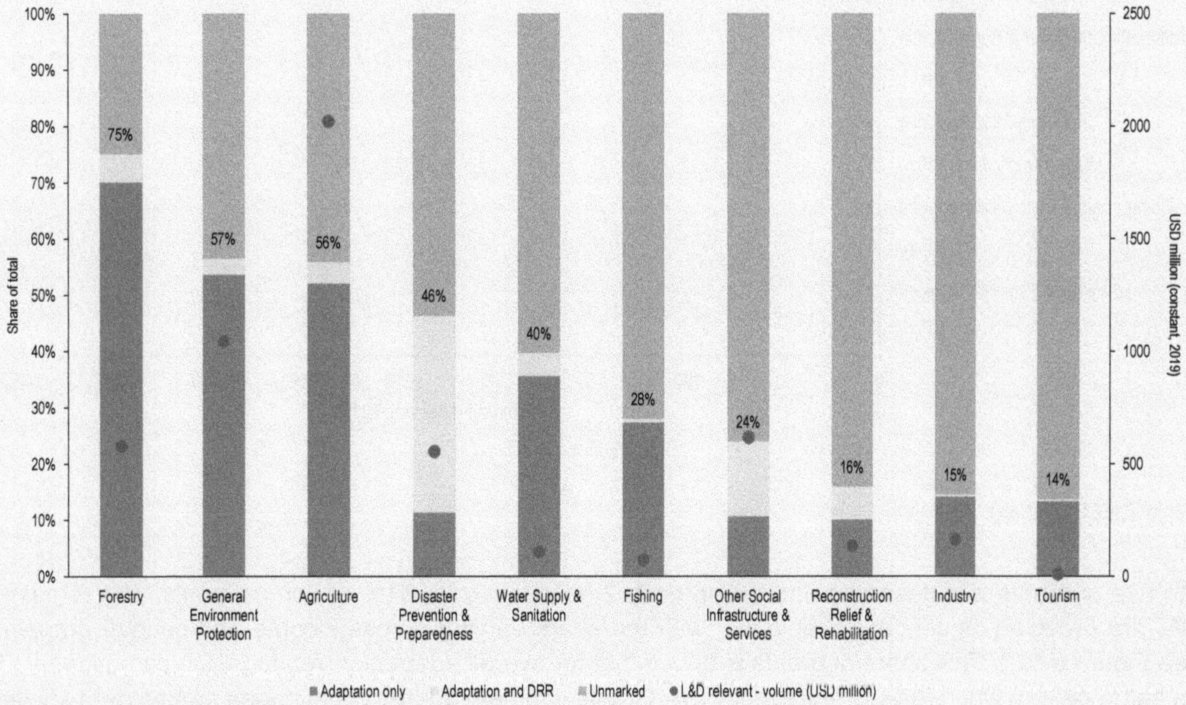

Note: Only losses and damages-relevant purpose codes within each sector were considered (See Annex 5.A.) The purpose code for disaster risk reduction was included under the Sector Disaster Prevention and Preparedness.
Source: (OECD, 2021[82]).

Approach 2: Commitments for adaptation and disaster risk reduction in selected purpose codes

In 2018-19, DAC members committed USD 1.1 billion on average per year for activities that included a focus on both climate change adaptation and disaster risk reduction in the purpose codes deemed relevant for losses and damages (see Figure 5.11.). Similar information on commitments with a focus on disaster risk reduction is not available for multilateral providers given differing reporting obligations to the CRS. The analysis under Approach 2 thus excludes potentially important multilateral commitments; some of these will be reflected under Approach 3. For Approach 2, the most targeted sectors are disaster prevention and preparedness (USD 419 million), other social infrastructure and services (USD 343 million) and agriculture

(USD 138 million). The relatively small dataset means that individual large commitments can influence the overall picture. The relatively large share of commitments provided in loans for Disaster Prevention and Preparedness, for example, was due to a large concessional loan to mitigate urban flood risk provided to a lower middle-income country.

Figure 5.11. ODA commitments by bilateral providers for adaptation and disaster risk reduction in selected purpose codes by sector

2018-19 annual average, USD million, commitment

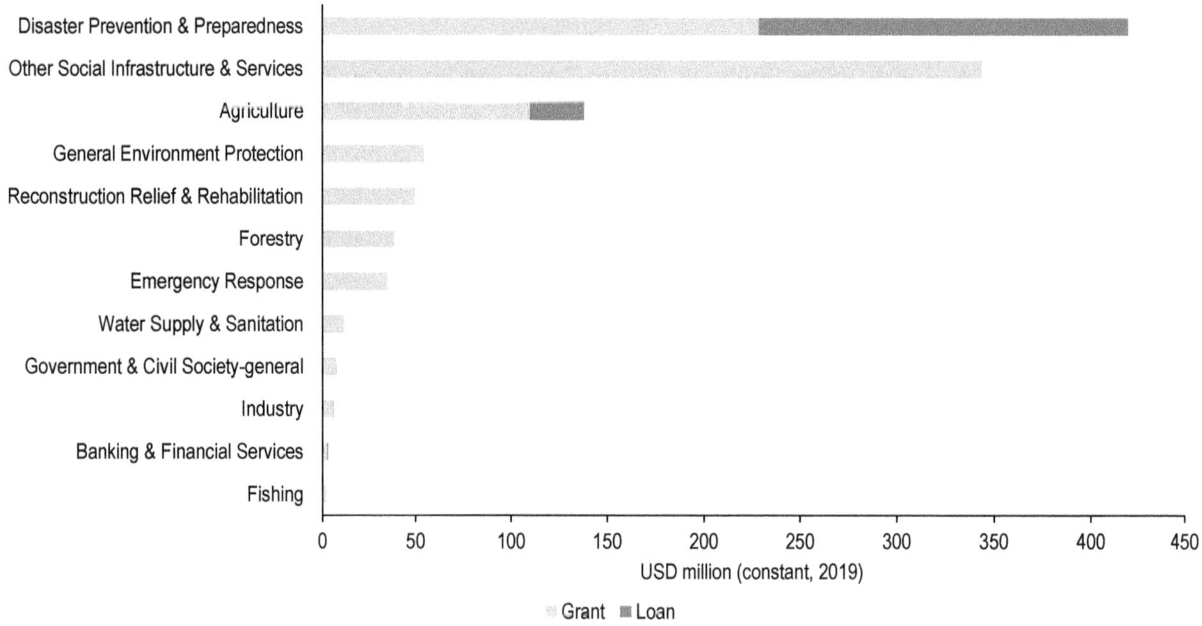

Source: (OECD, 2021[82]).

The use of grants is widespread under Approach 2 accounting for 81% of commitments. The remaining 19% are provided as concessional loans, with the share varying across income and country groupings (see Figure 5.12.). This share of grants is above that for overall adaptation-related ODA commitments for the same period, where grants represent 77%. Grants can help address challenges around debt levels in partner countries in the context of losses and damages (discussed below). They also have potential to catalyse and mobilise further development finance and private sector investment. In addition, grants can play an important role in supporting the implementation of enabling policy environments for climate action, such as National Adaptation Plans; Nationally Determined Contributions; National Disaster Risk Reduction Strategies; contingency plans and related regulatory frameworks. Further, grants can support climate risk and vulnerability assessments and are commonly used to develop risk transfer and pooling mechanisms (OECD/World Bank, 2019[146]) (see example from the Philippines in Box 5.18). Grant-only mechanisms, however, may not offer the rapid, large-scale financing required after certain extreme events, except in some instances, such as grants used to partially subsidise insurance premiums. Another form of grant finance to address losses and damages is humanitarian aid for disaster response and recovery measures, discussed above.

Figure 5.12. Climate adaptation and disaster risk reduction in selected purpose codes by instrument and country grouping

2018-19 annual average, USD million, commitment

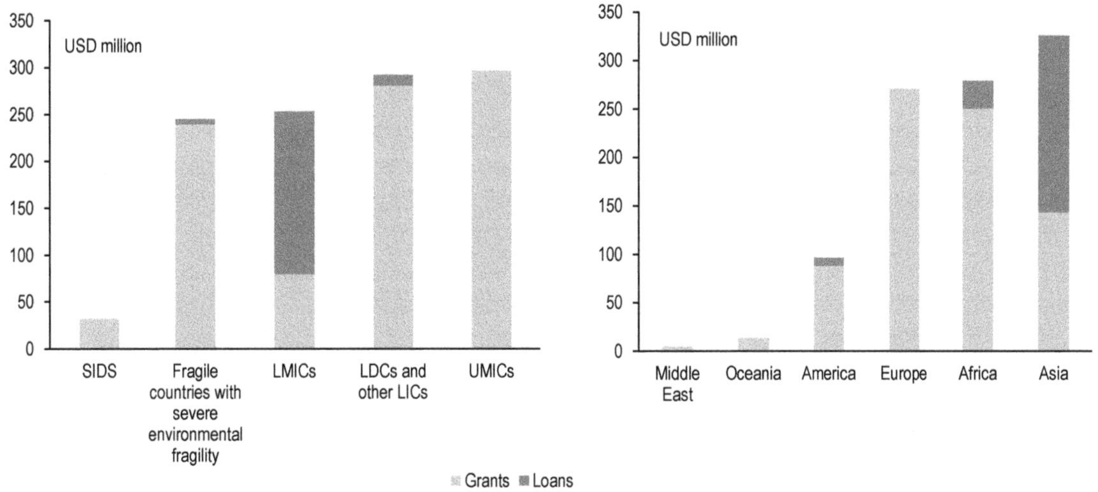

Note: The relatively small dataset means that large individual commitments can influence the overall picture as illustrated with the shares of loans to Low and Middle-Income Countries (LMICs). LDCs=Least Developed Countries; SIDS=Small Island Developing States; UMICs=Upper Middle-Income Countries.
Source: (OECD, 2021[82]).

Box 5.18. Disaster and climate risk management in the Philippines

In 2014, the government of Australia provided a grant of USD 6.6 million to the Philippines, via the United Nations Development Programme (UNDP) for the Disaster and Climate Risk Management initiative (OECD, 2020[96]), an initiative also supported by the World Bank. With a total value of USD 31 million, the initiative aims to develop the capacity of the government's technical agencies in various areas. These include disaster response and monitoring, early warning and forecasting, hazard and risk analysis, climate science and adaptation options to better inform disaster and climate risk management in vulnerable areas. The initiative also involves knowledge sharing between relevant agencies in the Philippines and their Australian counterparts, as well as non-governmental organisations. Some capacity development components have also targeted communities to prepare for and respond to the impacts of disasters. In 2021, Australia and the UNDP agreed to follow up with the initiative *Strengthening Institutions and Empowering Localities against Disasters and Climate Change*. It focuses on strengthening disaster and climate resilience of local government units and communities in the Philippines. Australia will invest USD 14 million in this programme over the next six years (OECD, 2020[96]).

Concessional loans have softer terms and conditions than market rates.[4] Lending at concessional terms can in some cases be suitable for reducing risks through, for instance, investments in climate-resilient infrastructure. Some providers are also piloting novel financial instruments to reinforce this aspect, such as KfW's pilot on shock-resilient loans (KfW, n.d.[222]). These aim to support investments that will bring down investment costs in the long term. Concessional loans, for example, can take the form of Catastrophe Deferred Drawdown Option, the World Bank's Contingency Emergency Response Component and contingent credit lines. Such loans have already been provided to several countries, including Peru and the Philippines (OECD, 2020[96]; OECD/World Bank, 2019[146]). These mechanisms allow for the immediate transfer of financial assistance in response to a disaster that meets pre-defined thresholds (see Box 5.19). Concessional loans have also been used to pay for insurance premiums.

Box 5.19. Reducing vulnerabilities to disasters in Jamaica

The government of Jamaica in collaboration with the Inter-American Development Bank (IADB) and the World Bank developed Jamaica's Strategic Programme for Climate Resilience (PPCR) that aims to strengthen resilience through enhancing adaptive capacity across priority sectors (PPCR, n.d.[223]). In 2016, the IADB approved two initiatives in the country. The Disaster Vulnerability Reduction Project (USD 30 million) improves disaster and climate resilience planning, and risk reduction, including retrofitting of vulnerable key assets and securing coastline. Meanwhile, a Contingency Emergency Response Component supports the country's emergency preparedness and response capacity. These initiatives have helped strengthen the regulatory, institutional and budgetary framework for disaster risk management. Jamaica has also taken steps to strengthen its fiscal resilience to natural shocks and climate impacts. First, it obtained parametric insurance coverage for hurricanes, earthquakes and excessive rainfall events under the regional Caribbean Catastrophe Risk Insurance Facility. Second, it secured a Contingent Credit Facility with the IADB (IADB, 2020[224]).

In 2020, the government received a Fiscal Sustainability and Climate Resilience Development Policy Loan (USD 70 million). This loan seeks to promote fiscal sustainability and inclusion, enhance fiscal and financial resilience against climate and disaster risks, and improve the investment climate for sustainable growth (World Bank, 2020[225]). The loan helps strengthen institutional mechanisms for greater fiscal responsibility, while also increasing sustainability of the social protection system. It supports measures to ensure that resources are available to adequately cope with climate-related hazards. It also improves policies to reinforce the resilience of Jamaica's infrastructure to multiple types of disaster risk. This includes reforms to land titling and to the application approval process for development and building permits, as well as for the effective management and sustainable development of fisheries. Jamaica's portfolio of disaster risk financing instruments is still expanding. In 2021, the World Bank agreed to a catastrophe bond to reduce risk to the insurance sector priced at USD 185 million for 2021-23 to minimise losses from tropical cyclones. Jamaica is the first country in the region to independently sponsor a catastrophe bond to prepare in advance of climate shocks, disasters and crises (World Bank, 2021[226]).

The use of concessional loans, for climate but also for broader development, can overburden countries with the accumulation of debt, even at below market-level interest rates. For instance, contingent loans can be quickly exhausted in the face of climate-related shocks and their recurrent use may add to a country's debt burdens (Bowen et al., 2020[72]). Unsustainable debt levels can threaten the stability of economies of already vulnerable countries, thereby undermining their fiscal resilience against climate-related hazards. This, in turn, could derail what would otherwise look like a clear and robust payback stream. Some even warn against the cost of external finance exacerbating a "climate investment trap" in developing economies (Ameli et al., 2021[43]) (see Section 5.4.4). These dynamics are often observed in SIDS. These countries receive concessional loans as some of them are upper middle-income countries, yet highly exposed and vulnerable to climate-related hazards. Providers therefore need to balance use of concessional loans and grants, especially in vulnerable settings, which is why some donors are piloting new instruments [e.g. (KfW, n.d.[222])]. In some cases, more emphasis on grants may be needed. Moreover, larger grants would be more effective than funding many small projects that do not achieve transformational impact (Ameli et al., 2021[43]) or funding through many channels with relatively small individual pots of grant funding (MOPAN, 2021[188]). While such risks are not evident from Figure 5.12., the data only analysed accounts for a small sub-set of commitments that may support efforts to reduce and manage the risks of losses and damages.

The bulk of commitments at the intersection between adaptation and disaster risk reduction is directed to more vulnerable settings, such as SIDS or LDCs. In LDCs and low-income countries, grants represent 96% of total commitments. In lower middle-income countries, the share of grants is lower at 31%. SIDS receive 100% of financing in the form of grants, while African countries receive 90%. This suggests the bulk of funding for losses and damages is in the form of grants and that providers tend to adjust modalities used depending on the level of vulnerability of partner countries.

Approach 3: Commitments for selected sector codes related to activities for reducing and managing the risk of losses and damages

Among the purpose codes covered by the CRS, three are particularly relevant for losses and damages, namely i) disaster risk reduction; ii) multi-hazard response preparedness; and iii) immediate post-emergency reconstruction and rehabilitation (see Figure 5.13). These mainly focus on climate-related disasters and do not shed light on how providers are responding to the risks of slow-onset events or non-economic losses. Based on application of the climate change adaptation marker in these three purpose codes, ODA from DAC members reached USD 689 million a year in 2018-19. This includes projects that integrated adaptation as a principal or significant component. Multilateral providers committed USD 1.1 billion, USD 886 million reported through the climate component methodology and USD 186 million using the Rio Markers Methodology.

Figure 5.13. Adaptation-related commitments by bilateral and multilateral providers for three sector codes

By reporting method, 2018-19 annual average, USD million, gross commitments

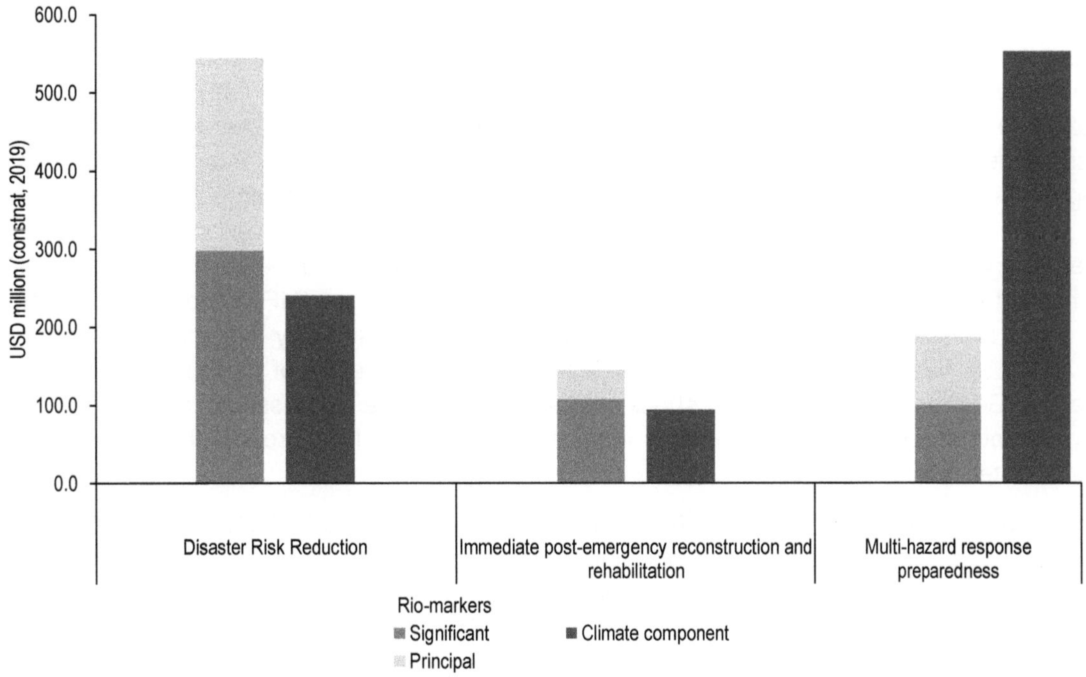

Note: The climate component methodology only considers the share of financing allocated for adaptation purposes. The Rio-markers methodology captures the full face value of the commitment.
Source: (OECD, 2021[82]).

Other sources of development finance

Other sources of development finance need to be closely monitored for future analyses. First, private philanthropy, which increasingly reports to the CRS, is starting to focus on climate change (OECD, 2021[82]). In early 2020, for instance, leading foundations such as the Bill & Melinda Gates Foundation revealed they consider climate change as a top priority; in 2019, the Foundation disbursed USD 150 million towards mitigation and adaptation. However, their reporting to the OECD does not yet reveal that losses and damages or climate change adaptation is an explicit priority.

Second, providers also use official channels, as well as guarantees, to mobilise private finance for development. In the context of climate change, the level of mobilisation has been lower than expected, perhaps reflecting the changing composition of climate finance in aggregate (OECD, 2021[227]). In 2019, private finance mobilised for climate action reached USD 14 billion, a decrease of 4% compared to 2018 (USD 14.6 billion). Private finance mobilised by bilateral public climate finance via direct investment in companies and projects, simple co-financing schemes and credit lines increased; that mobilised by multilateral finance was through guarantees and syndicated loans decreased (OECD, 2021[227]).

Finding more robust ways to work with the private sector in leveraging multilateral and bilateral funds to crowd in private sector funds would help scale up resources, including for climate change adaptation and activities to reduce and manage losses and damages. This goal must recognise, however, that private sector engagement will not be viable in all cases. The insurance sector has a strong competence, for example, in understanding of, and mitigation of risks, expertise that in the right context does not have to be reserved to the sector but can benefit broader decision-making processes.

5.4.4. Fiscal sustainability and development co-operations

Sustainable debt levels in the face of growing climate risks

Debt sustainability is a major concern for many developing countries (see Section 5.2.1), where debt levels reached over USD 8.5 trillion in 2020 (World Bank, 2021[228]) . Providers of development co-operation have started to consider debt sustainability in their activities. In fact, with the ODA reform of 2016, the DAC has explicitly linked its loan policy to compliance with International Monetary Fund (IMF) and World Bank rules for sustainable debt (OECD, 2016[158]). The debt sustainability analyses (DSAs) by the IMF and World Bank assess risk on a scale ranging from "low" to "moderate", "high" or even "over-indebted"; IDA grant-financing is tied to these classifications. By incorporating DSA results in providers' lending process, financing flows can be confined to countries with a public finance position deemed sufficiently sustainable. Moreover, the eligibility conditions have become more favourable for the poorest countries, with the minimum grant element rising from 25% to over 45%. For example, an IMF-World Bank programme in Burkina Faso imposed tighter rules (i.e. a 35% minimum concessionality threshold) (Government of France, 2016[229]). Finally, some providers are directly changing the nature of their loans. For example, as noted earlier, Germany's KfW is piloting shock-resilient loans. These concessional loans include clauses of debt redemption or deferral of instalments in case of an event to limit fiscal burdens and free budget funds for disaster relief (KfW, n.d.[222]).

Compliance with these debt limits is intended to strengthen the debt sustainability framework promoted by the IMF and World Bank in their bilateral loan policies. However, the system may not always capture the consequences of extreme weather and climate events and how they can cause debt distress in developing countries. As noted earlier, Mozambique faced over USD 873 million in damages in 2019 following cyclones Idai and Kenneth when the country was already heading towards unsustainable debt levels. In response to the two cyclones, the IMF agreed to a USD 118 million emergency loan (IMF, 2019[230]). Although the country was in debt distress, climate vulnerabilities were not included in the debt sustainability analysis. Therefore, the country did not qualify for IMF emergency debt relief (Fresnillo, 2020[42]). This affected the concessionality terms that the DAC and other providers could apply to the country, and in turn other resources (including from the private sector) that could have been unlocked to support recovery.

The IMF and other providers of development finance (e.g. the IADB) are aware of these challenges. They are experimenting with novel instruments, including "hurricane clauses" that help mitigate the impact of a disaster on a country's public finances and its debt sustainability [see e.g. (Robinson, 2016[231])]. Broader approaches and types of instruments could also be considered, such as insurance, in the blend of instruments available to governments or promote *ex ante* approaches in the first place.

Against this background, providers can ensure their concessional financing does not worsen debt in partner countries. As one option, they could promote alternative financing instruments such as debt-for-climate or debt-for-nature swaps. Such swaps enable a creditor to reduce its debt in one of two ways. The creditor could convert the debt to local currency, repaying it at a lower interest rate. Alternatively, it could use some other form of debt write-off. Funds saved through this tool can then be used to invest in adaptation, mitigation or biodiversity protection initiatives. As such, the swaps might create more fiscal space for climate, environmental and development commitments. For example, the United States backed a debt-for-nature swap with Costa Rica, trimming off USD 26 million of the country's foreign debt in exchange for tropical forest conservation (OECD, 2019[232]). The United States has developed similar schemes with the governments of Brazil, Indonesia, Guatemala and Jamaica, among others (Sommer, Restivo and Shandra, 2020[233]). While these swaps can lead to high transaction costs and have long timeframes (Cassimon, Prowse and Essers, 2011[234]), they are benefiting from renewed interest by development co-operation providers (Steele and Patel, 2020[38]; Sommer, Restivo and Shandra, 2020[233]; Yue and Wang, 2021[235]). Compared to older schemes, newer swaps set out to help address the debt, climate and biodiversity crises. To that end, the capital saved by partner countries is invested in poverty-reducing climate resilience, climate emissions mitigation or biodiversity protection initiatives, which are key for the COVID-19 recovery (Picolotti and Miller, 2020[236]).

Reinstatement of countries that have graduated from the ODA-eligible status: An option for the future?

Poorer countries are generally more vulnerable to the impacts of climate change. Higher-income developing countries, including some SIDS, can also be very exposed to climate-related hazards. The 2016 hurricanes in the Caribbean, for example, caused a great deal of damage in countries no longer eligible for ODA due to their level of per capita income. This led to calls for some affected territories (such as the British Virgin Islands) to be temporarily reinstated to the list of ODA-eligible countries. This would allow funding for post-hurricane reconstruction to count as ODA (Tew, 2017[237]), which would make access to finance easier.

These calls underscore that climate risks are redefining the traditional ways to understand ODA eligibility. The level of development is no longer only assessed through the level of income (OECD, 2018[238]). Instead, it is increasingly taking into account the level of exposure and vulnerability to climate-related hazards. Some DAC members have agreed to support countries hit by a disaster, even when the countries have already graduated from ODA. For instance, high-income SIDS can still access the European Development Fund (that will be phased out in favour of the Neighbourhood, Development and International Cooperation Instrument). This fund uses an economic vulnerability index in its country allocations formula (Inter-agency Task Force on Financing for Development, 2020[239]). Meanwhile, the International Development Association also has an exemption clause for SIDS, but these flows would not count as ODA. Work is also ongoing in relation to the methodology for updating the DAC List of ODA Recipients (e.g. reinstating countries or territories in case of catastrophic humanitarian crisis) (OECD, 2019[240]). For their part, multilateral processes are discussing how to formalise other measures, such as an interest-free moratorium on debt payments in the aftermath of a climate disaster (Inter-agency Task Force on Financing for Development, 2020[239]).

References

ADB (2018), *Economic and Fiscal Impacts of Disasters in the Pacific*, Asian Development Bank, Manila, http://dx.doi.org/10.22617/tcs189300-2. [46]

ADB (2018), *Mobilizing Contingency Funds for Climate Related Disasters*, Asian Development Bank, Manila, https://reliefweb.int/report/world/mobilizing-contingency-funds-climate-related-disasters. [95]

ADB (2014), *Climate Risk Management in ADB Projects*, Asian Development Bank, Manila, http://www.adb.org/sites/default/files/publication/148796/climate-risk-management-adb-projects.pdf (accessed on 20 September 2021). [201]

ADB and OECD (2020), *Leveraging Technology and Innovation for Disaster Risk Management and Financing*, http://dx.doi.org/10.22617/TCS2000393-2. [178]

AfDB (2021), *African Economic Outlook 2021*, African Development Bank, Abidjan, https://www.afdb.org/en/knowledge/publications/african-economic-outlook. [22]

AfDB (2014), *Climate Screening and Adaptation Review & Evaluation Procedures*, African Development Bank, Abidjan, https://www.afdb.org/fileadmin/uploads/afdb/Documents/Generic-Documents/CSS%20Basics-En_def.pdf (accessed on 25 September 2021). [200]

AfDB et al. (2020), *2019 Joint Report on Multilateral Development Banks' 2019 Climate Finance*, African Development Bank; Asian Development Bank; Asian Infrastructure Investment Bank; European Bank for Reconstruction and Development; European Investment Bank; Inter American Development Bank; Islamic Development Bank; World Bank, https://www.ebrd.com/news/2020/mdbs-climate-finance-in-low-and-middleincome-countries-in-2019-reaches-us-415-billion.html (accessed on 21 July 2021). [213]

Aldred, J. (2009), "Ethics and climate change cost-benefit analysis: Stern and after", *New Political Economy*, Vol. 14/4, pp. 469-488, http://dx.doi.org/10.1080/13563460903288221. [105]

Amagir, A. et al. (2017), "A review of financial-literacy education programs for children and adolescents", *Citizenship, Social and Economics Education*, Vol. 17/1, pp. 56-80, http://dx.doi.org/10.1177/2047173417719555. [163]

Ameli, N. et al. (2021), "Higher cost of finance exacerbates a climate investment trap in developing economies", *Nature Communications*, Vol. 12/4046, https://doi.org/10.1038/s41467-021-24305-3. [43]

Andre, P. et al. (2021), "Fighting climate change: The role of norms, preferences, and moral values", *Discussion Paper*, No. 14518, Institute of Labor Economics, Bonn, http://ftp.iza.org/dp14518.pdf. [117]

Asatryan, Z., C. Castellón and T. Stratmann (2018), "Balanced budget rules and fiscal outcomes: Evidence from historical constitutions", *Journal of Public Economics*, Vol. 167, pp. 105-119, http://dx.doi.org/10.1016/j.jpubeco.2018.09.001. [48]

Bain, P. et al. (2015), "Co-benefits of addressing climate change can motivate action around the world", *Nature Climate Change*, Vol. 6/2, pp. 154-157, http://dx.doi.org/10.1038/nclimate2814. [133]

Baker, S., N. Bloom and S. Davis (2016), "Measuring economic policy uncertainty", *The Quarterly Journal of Economics*, Vol. 131/4, pp. 1593-1636, http://dx.doi.org/10.1093/qje/qjw024. [111]

Bakkensen, L. and L. Barrage (2017), *Flood Risk Belief Heterogeneity and Coastal Home Price Dynamics: Going Under Water?*, National Bureau of Economic Research, Cambridge, MA, http://dx.doi.org/10.3386/w23854. [124]

Bank of England (2020), *The Bank of England's Climate-related Financial Disclosure 2020*, Bank of England, London, https://www.bankofengland.co.uk/-/media/boe/files/annual-report/2020/climate-related-financial-disclosure-report-2019-20.pdf?la=en&hash=5DA959C54540287A2E90C823807E089055E6721B. [142]

Battiston, S. and S. Martinez-Jaramillo (2018), "Financial networks and stress testing: Challenges and new research avenues for systemic risk analysis and financial stability implications", *Journal of Financial Stability*, Vol. 35, pp. 6-16, http://dx.doi.org/10.1016/j.jfs.2018.03.010. [54]

Baudion, P. and J. Svoronos (2021), "Stress-testing banks for climate change – a comparison of practices", *FSI Insights on Policy Implementation*, No. 34, July, Financial Stability Institute, Bank for International Settlements, Basel. [140]

Blinder, A. et al. (2017), "Necessity as the mother of invention: Monetary policy after the crisis", *Economic Policy*, Vol. 32/92, pp. 707-755, http://dx.doi.org/10.1093/epolic/eix013. [136]

Bloom, N. (2009), "The impact of uncertainty shocks", *Econometrica*, Vol. 77/3, pp. 623-685, http://dx.doi.org/10.3982/ecta6248. [112]

Bloom, N., S. Bond and J. Van Reenen (2007), "Uncertainty and investment dynamics", *Review of Economic Studies*, Vol. 74/2, pp. 391-415, http://dx.doi.org/10.1111/j.1467-937x.2007.00426.x. [113]

BLS (2021), *Total Nonfarm Employment, New Orleans-Metairie, LA*, (database), https://www.bls.gov/eag/eag.la_neworleans_msa.htm (accessed on 5 March 2021). [30]

BMZ (2021), "InsuResilience Global Partnership", (brochure), German Federal Minister for Economic Cooperation and Development, Berlin, https://www.bmz.de/resource/blob/57180/ba5d152504bcbb0beeeb3b9e11dde6ea/BMZ_insuresilience_en.pdf. [185]

BMZ (2019), *Comprehensive Risk Management: The Approach of German Development Cooperation for Dealing with Disaster and Climate Risks*, German Federal Ministry of Economic Cooperation and Development, Berlin. [203]

Bodea, C. and R. Hicks (2014), "Price stability and central bank independence: Discipline, credibility, and democratic institutions", *International Organization*, Vol. 69/1, pp. 35-61, http://dx.doi.org/10.1017/s0020818314000277. [135]

Boers, N. et al. (2019), "Complex networks reveal global pattern of extreme-rainfall teleconnections", *Nature*, Vol. 566/7744, pp. 373-377, http://dx.doi.org/10.1038/s41586-018-0872-x. [182]

Bolsen, T., R. Palm and J. Kingsland (2019), “The impact of message source on the effectiveness of communications about climate change”, *Science Communication*, Vol. 41/4, pp. 464-487, http://dx.doi.org/10.1177/1075547019863154. [134]

Botzen, W., O. Deschenes and M. Sanders (2019), “The economic impacts of natural disasters: A review of models and empirical studies”, *Review of Environmental Economics and Policy*, Vol. 13/2, pp. 167-188, http://dx.doi.org/10.1093/reep/rez004. [12]

Bowen, T. et al. (2020), *Adaptive Social Protection Systems, Building Resilience to Shocks*, World Bank, Washington, DC, http://dx.doi.org/10.1596/978-1-4648-1575-1. [72]

Brei, M., P. Mohan and E. Strobl (2019), “The impact of natural disasters on the banking sector: Evidence from hurricane strikes in the Caribbean”, *The Quarterly Review of Economics and Finance*, Vol. 72, pp. 232-239, http://dx.doi.org/10.1016/j.qref.2018.12.004. [34]

Brunnermeier, M. et al. (2016), “The sovereign-bank diabolic loop and ESBies”, *American Economic Review*, Vol. 106/5, pp. 508-512, http://dx.doi.org/10.1257/aer.p20161107. [60]

Burke, M., S. Hsiang and E. Miguel (2015), “Global non-linear effect of temperature on economic production”, *Nature*, Vol. 527/7577, pp. 235-239, http://dx.doi.org/10.1038/nature15725. [29]

Calcutt, E., B. Maher and C. Fitzgibbon (2021), *Emerging Lessons in Financing Adaptive Social Protection*, World Bank, Washington, DC, https://www.financialprotectionforum.org/publication/emerging-lessons-in-financing-adaptive-social-protection?mc_cid=1b791a32e2&mc_eid=2adb4feb83. [61]

California Department of Insurance (2019), “Wildfire insurance crisis leads commissioner to call for first-ever statewide non-renewal moratorium”, 5 December, Press Release, California Department of Insurance, Los Angeles, http://www.insurance.ca.gov/0400-news/0100-press-releases/2019/release092-19.cfm. [165]

Cambridge Centre for Risk Studies and AXA XL (2020), *Optimising Disaster Recovery: The Role of Insurance Capital in Improving Economic Resilience*, Cambridge Centre for Risk Studies at the University of Cambridge Judge Business School, https://axaxl.com/-/media/axaxl/files/optimizing-disaster-recovery.pdf. [152]

Carter, B. et al. (2019), *Social Protection Topic Guide*, Institute of Development Studies, Brighton, United Kingdom, https://gsdrc.org/topic-guides/social-protection/types-of-social-protection/. [70]

Casado-Asensio, J., T. Kato and H. Shin (2021), *Lessons on engaging the private sector in strengthening climate resilience in Guatemala, the Philippines and Senegal*, OECD Publishing, Paris, https://doi.org/10.1787/09b46b3f-en. [81]

Cassimon, Prowse and Essers (2011), “The pitfalls and potential of debt for nature swaps”, *Global Environmental Change*, Vol. 21/1, pp. 93-102, https://www.sciencedirect.com/science/article/abs/pii/S0959378010000981?via%3Dihub. [234]

Catalano, M., L. Forni and E. Pezzolla (2020), “Climate-change adaptation: The role of fiscal policy”, *Resource and Energy Economics*, Vol. 59, pp. 1-19, http://dx.doi.org/10.1016/j.reseneeco.2019.07.005. [36]

Cevik, S. and J. Jalles (2020), “This changes everything: Climate shocks and sovereign bonds”, *IMF Working Papers*, International Monetary Fund, Washington, DC, https://www.imf.org/en/Publications/WP/Issues/2020/06/05/This-Changes-Everything-Climate-Shocks-and-Sovereign-Bonds-49476. [53]

Chhibber, A. and R. Laajaj (2008), “Disasters, climate change and economic development in sub-Saharan Africa: Lessons and directions”, *Journal of African Economies*, Vol. 17/Supplement 2, pp. ii7-ii49, http://dx.doi.org/10.1093/jae/ejn020. [10]

Climate Analytics, World Resources Institute (2021), *Closing the gap: the impact of G20 climate commitments on limiting global temperature rise to 1.5°C*, https://www.wri.org/research/closing-the-gap-g20-climate-commitments-limiting-global-temperature-rise (accessed on 16 October 2021). [220]

Colombia Ministry of Finance and Public Credit (2011), *Contigent Liabilities: The Colombian Experience*, Ministry of Finance and Public Credit, Colombia, http://treasury.worldbank.org/bdm/pdf/Contingent_Liabilities_Colombian_Experience.pdf. [173]

Combes, J., A. Minea and M. Sow (2017), “Is fiscal policy always counter- (pro-) cyclical? The role of public debt and fiscal rules”, *Economic Modelling*, Vol. 65, pp. 138-146, http://dx.doi.org/10.1016/j.econmod.2017.05.017. [50]

Costella, C., C. Bachofen and G. Marcondes (2017), “7 things to know about managing climate risks through social protection”, *Policy Brief*, BRACED, http://www.braced.org/resources/i/?id=394db34f-1a14-4fe5-9daa-d3a1921003fb. [69]

Daron, J. et al. (2020), “Integrating seasonal climate forecasts into adaptive social protection in the Sahel”, *Climate and Development*, pp. 543-550, http://dx.doi.org/10.1080/17565529.2020.1825920. [73]

Dastkhan, H. and N. Gharneh (2018), “How the ownership structures cause epidemics in financial markets: A network-based simulation model”, *Physica A: Statistical Mechanics and its Applications*, Vol. 492, pp. 324-342, http://dx.doi.org/10.1016/j.physa.2017.09.089. [55]

Davies, M. et al. (2009), “‘Adaptive social protection’: Synergies for poverty reduction”, *IDS Bulletin*, Vol. 39/4, pp. 105-112, http://dx.doi.org/10.1111/j.1759-5436.2008.tb00483.x. [75]

Day, E. et al. (2018), “Upholding labour productivity under climate change: An assessment of adaptation options”, *Climate Policy*, Vol. 19/3, pp. 367-385, http://dx.doi.org/10.1080/14693062.2018.1517640. [4]

de Janvry, A. et al. (2006), “Can conditional cash transfer programs serve as safety nets in keeping children at school and from working when exposed to shocks?”, *Journal of Development Economics*, Vol. 79/2, pp. 349-373, http://dx.doi.org/10.1016/j.jdeveco.2006.01.013. [71]

Dennig, F. (2017), “Climate change and the re-evaluation of cost-benefit analysis”, *Climatic Change*, Vol. 151/1, pp. 43-54, http://dx.doi.org/10.1007/s10584-017-2047-4. [104]

Deryugina, T. (2017), “The Fiscal Cost of Hurricanes: Disaster Aid versus Social Insurance”, *American Economic Journal: Economic Policy*, Vol. 9/3, pp. 168-198, http://dx.doi.org/10.1257/pol.20140296. [14]

Dessai, S. and C. Sims (2010), "Public perception of drought and climate change in southeast England", *Environmental Hazards*, Vol. 9/4, pp. 340-357, http://dx.doi.org/10.3763/ehaz.2010.0037. [131]

Devereux, S. and R. Sabates-Wheeler (2004), "Transformative social protection", *Working Paper Series*, No. 232, Institute of Development Studies, Brighton, United Kingdom, https://opendocs.ids.ac.uk/opendocs/handle/20.500.12413/4071. [68]

Dietz, S. et al. (2016), "'Climate value at risk' of global financial assets", *Nature Climate Change*, Vol. 6/7, pp. 676-679, http://dx.doi.org/10.1038/nclimate2972. [57]

Dikau, S. and U. Volz (2021), "Central bank mandates, sustainability objectives and the promotion of green finance", *Ecological Economics*, Vol. 184, p. 107022, http://dx.doi.org/10.1016/j.ecolecon.2021.107022. [138]

Doelle, M. and S. Seck (2020), "Loss and damage from climate change: From concept to remedy?", *Climate Policy*, Vol. 20/6, p. 669, http://dx.doi.org/10.1080/14693062.2019.1630353. [186]

Duus-Otterström, G. and S. Jagers (2011), "Why (most) climate insurance schemes are a bad idea", *Environmental Politics*, Vol. 20/3, pp. 322-339, http://dx.doi.org/10.1080/09644016.2011.573354. [183]

Eisensee, T. and D. Stromberg (2007), "News droughts, news floods, and U.S. disaster relief", *The Quarterly Journal of Economics*, Vol. 122/2, pp. 693-728, http://dx.doi.org/10.1162/qjec.122.2.693. [24]

European Central Bank (2021), "Eurosystem agrees on common stance for climate change-related sustainable investments in non-monetary policy portfolios", 4 February, Press Release, European Central Bank, Frankfurt am Main, https://www.ecb.europa.eu/press/pr/date/2021/html/ecb.pr210204_1~a720bc4f03.en.html. [143]

Fankhauser, S. and I. Burton (2011), "Spending adaptation money wisely", *Climate Policy*, Vol. 11/3, pp. 1037-1049, http://dx.doi.org/10.1080/14693062.2011.582389. [115]

Fanning, E. and J. Fullwood-Thomas (2019), "The humanitarian-development-peace nexus: What does it mean for multi-mandated organizations?", *Discussion Paper*, Oxfam, United Kingdom, http://dx.doi.org/10.21201/2019.4436. [209]

FAO (2019), *The Sudan. Impact of Early Warning Early Action. Protecting Agropastoralist Livelihoods Ahead of Drought.*, Food and Agriculture Organization of the United Nations, Rome, https://www.preventionweb.net/publications/view/65578. [92]

Farhi, E. and J. Tirole (2017), "Deadly Embrace: Sovereign and Financial Balance Sheets Doom Loops", *The Review of Economic Studies*, Vol. 85/3, pp. 1781-1823, http://dx.doi.org/10.1093/restud/rdx059. [35]

Finucane, M. et al. (2020), "Short-term solutions to a long-term challenge: Rethinking disaster recovery planning to reduce vulnerabilities and inequities", *International Journal of Environmental Research and Public Health*, Vol. 17/2, p. 482, http://dx.doi.org/10.3390/ijerph17020482. [63]

Fontana, G. (2006), "The Federal Reserve and the European Central Bank: A theoretical comparison of their legislative mandates", *Journal of Post Keynesian Economics*, Vol. 28/3, pp. 433-450, http://dx.doi.org/10.2753/pke0160-3477280304. [137]

Four Twenty Seven (2018), *Assessing Exposure to Climate Change in U.S. Munis*, May, Four Twenty Seven, San Francisco, http://427mt.com/wp-content/uploads/2018/05/427-Muni-Risk-Paper-May-2018-1.pdf. [120]

Fowles, J., G. Liu and C. Mamaril (2009), "Accounting for natural disasters: The impact of earthquake risk on California municipal bond pricing", *Public Budgeting & Finance*, Vol. 29/1, pp. 68-83, http://dx.doi.org/10.1111/j.1540-5850.2009.00924.x. [119]

Frank, T. (2019), *After a $14-billion upgrade, New Orleans' levees are sinking*, 11 April, https://www.scientificamerican.com/article/after-a-14-billion-upgrade-new-orleans-levees-are-sinking/. [32]

Fresnillo, I. (2020), "A tale of two emergencies – the interplay of sovereign debt and climate crises in the global south", *Briefing Paper*, December, European Network on Debt and Development, Brussels, https://www.eurodad.org/a_tale_of_two_emergencies_the_interplay_of_sovereign_debt_and_climate_crises_in_the_global_south. [42]

Froetsch, T. and R. Rector (2005), *The Economic and Budgetary Effects of the Katrina Emergency Tax Relief Act of 2005*, Heritage Foundation, Washington, DC. [31]

Gallagher, J. (2014), "Learning about an infrequent event: Evidence from flood insurance take-up in the United States", *American Economic Journal: Applied Economics*, Vol. 6/3, pp. 206-233, http://dx.doi.org/10.1257/app.6.3.206. [129]

Gamper, C. et al. (2017), "Managing disaster-related contingent liabilities in public finance frameworks", *OECD Working Papers on Public Governance*, No. 27, OECD Publishing, Paris, https://dx.doi.org/10.1787/a6e0265a-en. [174]

GCA (2019), *Adapt Now: A Global Call for Leadership on Climate Resilience*, Global Center on Adaptation, Rotterdam, https://gca.org/reports/adapt-now-a-global-call-for-leadership-on-climate-resilience/. [97]

German Federal Foreign Office (2020), "Helping Before disaster strikes – anticipatory humanitarian assistance in Bangladesh", 13 October, German Federal Foreign Office, https://www.auswaertiges-amt.de/en/aussenpolitik/themen/humanitaerehilfe/disaster-risk-reduction/2404730. [84]

Germanwatch (2021), "Global Climate Risk Index 2021", webpage, https://reliefweb.int/report/world/global-climate-risk-index-2021 (accessed on 5 August 2021). [207]

Gibbs, M. (2015), "Pitfalls in developing coastal climate adaptation responses", *Climate Risk Management*, Vol. 8, pp. 1-8, http://dx.doi.org/10.1016/j.crm.2015.05.001. [109]

GIZ (2018), *Global Programme on Risk Assessment and Management for Adaptation to Climate Change (Loss and Damage)*, Deutsche Gesellschaft für Internationale Zusammenarbeit (GIZ) GmbH, Eschborn/Bonn, https://www.giz.de/de/downloads/giz2018-en-global-programme-on-risk-assessment.pdf. [195]

Government of Denmark (2020), *A Green and Sustainable World: The Danish Government's long-term Strategy for Global Climate Action*, Government of Denmark, Copenhagen, https://um.dk/en/foreign-policy/new-climate-action-strategy/. [196]

Government of France (2016), "The new rules for official development assistance: What's at stake?", *TRESOR-ECONOMICS*, No. 161, Government of France, Paris, https://www.tresor.economie.gouv.fr/Articles/1b040048-5002-4806-9877-b08143bbedf3/files/ed5e0fd2-0ab1-4a7b-96de-898bdf0b2970. [229]

Green Climate Fund (2021), *Decision of the Board on the Ninth Report of the Green Climate Fund to the Conference of the Parties to the United Nations Framework Convention on Climate Change*, Green Climate Fund, Incheon, https://www.greenclimate.fund/sites/default/files/decision/bbm-2021/decision-bbm-2021-05-bbm-2021-05-decision-board-ninth-report-gcf-cop-unfccc.pdf. [190]

Greene, S. (2019), *Lessons from Piloting the Decentralised Climate Finance Programme, Tanzania*, International Institute for Environment and Development, London, https://pubs.iied.org/g04398?k=Local%20Climate%20Finance. [79]

Gros, C. et al. (2019), *Household-level effects of providing forecast-based cash in anticipation of extreme weather events: Quasi-experimental evidence from humanitarian interventions in the 2017 floods in Bangladesh*, Elsevier Ltd. [89]

Gros, D. (2013), "Foreign debt versus domestic debt in the euro area", *Oxford Review of Economic Policy*, Vol. 29/3, pp. 502-517, http://dx.doi.org/10.1093/oxrep/grt038. [45]

Gulen, H. and M. Ion (2015), "Policy uncertainty and corporate investment", *Review of Financial Studies*, p. hhv050, http://dx.doi.org/10.1093/rfs/hhv050. [114]

Haer, T. et al. (2013), "Relative sea-level rise and the conterminous United States: Consequences of potential land inundation in terms of population at risk and GDP loss", *Global Environmental Change*, Vol. 23/6, pp. 1627-1636, http://dx.doi.org/10.1016/j.gloenvcha.2013.09.005. [27]

Halady, I. and P. Rao (2010), "Does awareness to climate change lead to behavioral change?", *International Journal of Climate Change Strategies and Management*, Vol. 2/1, pp. 6-22, http://dx.doi.org/10.1108/17568691011020229. [116]

Hallegate, S., J. Renschler and B. Walsh (2018), *Building Back Better : Achieving Resilience through Stronger, Faster, and More Inclusive Post-Disaster Reconstruction*, World Bank, Washington, DC, https://openknowledge.worldbank.org/handle/10986/29867. [62]

Hallegatte, S., J. Rentschler and J. Rozenberg (2019), *Lifelines: The Resilient Infrastructure Opportunity*, World Bank, Washington, DC, http://dx.doi.org/10.1596/978-1-4648-1430-3. [98]

Hammet, L. and K. Mixter (2017), *Adaptive Finance to Support Post Disaster Recovery*, Yale Center for Business and the Environment and Yale School of Forestry and Environmental Studies, https://www.weadapt.org/sites/weadapt.org/files/cbey_adaptivefinancing_oct2017.pdf. [64]

Hanger, S. et al. (2017), "Insurance, public assistance, and household flood risk reduction: A Comparative study of Austria, England, and Romania", *Risk Analysis*, Vol. 38/4, pp. 680-693, http://dx.doi.org/10.1111/risa.12881. [172]

Herweijer, C., N. Ranger and R. Ward (2009), "Adaptation to Climate Change: Threats and Opportunities for the Insurance Industry", *The Geneva Papers on Risk and Insurance - Issues and Practice*, Vol. 34/3, pp. 360-380, http://dx.doi.org/10.1057/gpp.2009.13. [181]

Heutel, G., N. Miller and D. Molitor (2020), "Adaptation and the mortality effects of temperature across U.S. climate regions", *The Review of Economics and Statistics*, pp. 1-33, http://dx.doi.org/10.1162/rest_a_00936. [8]

Hino, M. and M. Burke (2021), "The effect of information about climate risk on property values", *Proceedings of the National Academy of Sciences*, Vol. 118/17, p. e2003374118, http://dx.doi.org/10.1073/pnas.2003374118. [125]

Hobson, M. and L. Campbell (2012), "How Ethiopia's Productive Safety Net Programme (PSNP) is responding to the current humanitarian crisis in the Horn", *Humanitarian Exchange* 53, pp. 9-11, https://odihpn.org/magazine/how-ethiopia%C2%92s-productive-safety-net-programme-psnp-is-responding-to-the-current-humanitarian-crisis-in-the-horn/. [76]

Hope, M. (2019), "Cyclones in Mozambique may reveal humanitarian challenges of responding to a new climate reality", *The Lancet Planetary Health*, Vol. 3/8, pp. e338-e339, http://dx.doi.org/10.1016/s2542-5196(19)30131-7. [3]

Hudson, P., W. Botzen and J. Aerts (2019), "Flood insurance arrangements in the European Union for future flood risk under climate and socioeconomic change", *Global Environmental Change*, Vol. 58, p. 101966, http://dx.doi.org/10.1016/j.gloenvcha.2019.101966. [175]

Hudson, P. et al. (2017), "Moral hazard in natural disaster insurance markets: Empirical evidence from Germany and the United States", *Land Economics*, Vol. 93/2, pp. 179-208, http://dx.doi.org/10.3368/le.93.2.179. [176]

IADB (2020), *Corporate Evaluation: Lending Instruments Report*, Inter-American Development Bank, Washington, DC, https://publications.iadb.org/publications/english/document/Lending-Instruments-Report.pdf. [224]

IFRC (2020), *Reducing Risks and Building Resilience – World Disasters Report*, International Federation of Red Cross and Red Crescent Societies, Geneva, https://media.ifrc.org/ifrc/wp-content/uploads/2020/11/IFRC_wdr2020/20201113_WorldDisasters_4.pdf. [83]

ILO (2017), *World Social Protection Report 2017–19: Universal Social Protection to Achieve the Sustainable Development Goals*, International Labour Organization, Geneva, https://www.social-protection.org/gimi/gess/ShowWiki.action?id=594. [65]

IMF (2021), *Fiscal Monitor: Strengthening the Credibility of Public Finances*, IMF Publishing, https://www.imf.org/en/Publications/FM/Issues/2021/10/13/fiscal-monitor-october-2021 (accessed on 14 October 2021). [37]

IMF (2021), *World Economic Outlook Database*, IMF Publishing, https://www.imf.org/en/Publications/WEO/weo-database/2021/April (accessed on 1 September 2021). [1]

IMF (2020), "Climate change: Physical risk and equity prices", in *Global Financial Stability Report: Markets in the Time of COVID-19*, International Monetary Fund, Washington, DC, https://www.imf.org/en/Publications/GFSR/Issues/2020/04/14/global-financial-stability-report-april-2020. [52]

IMF (2019), "Building resilience in developing countries vulnerable to large natural disasters", *Policy Paper*, No. 19/020, International Monetary Fund, Washington, DC, https://www.imf.org/-/media/Files/Publications/PP/2019/PPEA2019020.ashx. [15]

IMF (2019), "IMF Executive Board approves USD 118.2 million Rapid Credit Facility Assistance to the Republic of Mozambique in the wake of Cyclone Idal", 19 April, Press Release, International Monetary Fund, Washington, DC, https://www.imf.org/en/News/Articles/2019/04/19/pr19121-republic-mozambique-imf-exec-board-approves-rapid-credit-facility-assistance-cyclone-idai. [230]

IMF (2016), "Small states' resilience to natural disasters and climate change – role for the IMF", *Policy Paper*, International Monetary Fund, Washington, DC, https://www.imf.org/en/Publications/Policy-Papers/Issues/2016/12/31/Small-States-Resilience-to-Natural-Disasters-and-Climate-Change-Role-for-the-IMF-PP5079. [16]

IMF (2011), *St. Vincent and the Grenadines: Request for disbursement under the Rapid Credit Facility*, International Monetary Fund, Washington, DC. [25]

Insurance Journal (2020), "California issues moratorium on insurers non-renewing or cancelling following wildfires", 5 November, Insurance Journal, https://www.insurancejournal.com/news/west/2020/11/05/589813.htm (accessed on 21 July 2021). [166]

Insurance Journal (2018), "Report: More than 87K Floridians dropped by home insurers last quarter", 12 December, Insurance Journal, https://www.insurancejournal.com/news/southeast/2018/12/12/511652.htm. [168]

InsuResilience Global Partnership (2021), *InsuResilience Annual Report 2020: Climate and Disaster Resilience in a World of Uncertainty*, InsuResilience Global Partnership, https://annualreport.insuresilience.org/. [205]

Inter-agency Task Force on Financing for Development (2020), *Financing for Sustainable Development Report 2020*, Inter-agency Task Force on Financing for Development, https://developmentfinance.un.org/fsdr2020. [239]

IPCC (2018), *Managing the Risks of Extreme Events and Disasters to Advance Climate Change Adaptation*, Intergovernmental Panel on Climate Change, Geneva, https://www.ipcc.ch/site/assets/uploads/2018/03/SREX_Full_Report-1.pdf. [21]

IPCC (1995), *Second Assessment Report*, Intergovernmental Panel on Climate Change, Geneva, https://www.ipcc.ch/site/assets/uploads/2018/06/2nd-assessment-en.pdf. [103]

IsDB (2019), *Disaster Risk Management and Resilience Policy*, Islamic Development Bank, Jeddah, https://www.isdb.org/sites/default/files/media/documents/2021-05/Disaster%20Risk%20Management%20Resilience%20Policy.pdf. [204]

Jergler, D. (2020), "California pledges to protect homeowners from insurer withdrawals due to wildfires", 19 October, Insurance Journal, https://www.insurancejournal.com/news/west/2020/10/19/587154.htm. [167]

Jones, H. (2021), "Financial regulators attempt to align rules on climate risks", 7 July, Reuters, https://www.reuters.com/business/sustainable-business/financial-regulators-attempt-align-rules-climate-risks-2021-07-07/. [59]

Joya, O. and E. Rougier (2019), "Do (all) sectoral shocks lead to aggregate volatility? Empirics from a production network perspective", *European Economic Review*, Vol. 113, pp. 77-107, http://dx.doi.org/10.1016/j.euroecorev.2019.01.004. [19]

Kalkuhl, M. and L. Wenz (2020), "The impact of climate conditions on economic production. Evidence from a global panel of regions", *Journal of Environmental Economics and Management*, Vol. 103, p. 102360, http://dx.doi.org/10.1016/j.jeem.2020.102360. [26]

Kempa, L. et al. (2021), *Financing Loss and Damage: Options for the Green Climate Fund*, Frankfurt School - UNEP Collaboration Centre for Climate and Sustainable Energy Finance, http://dx.doi.org/10.13140/RG.2.2.26829.77285. [191]

KfW (n.d.), *Förderung des Angebots von gegen Naturkatastrophen abgesicherter Darlehen durch die BOAD in Westafrika*, KfW Development Bank, webpage, https://www.kfw-entwicklungsbank.de/ipfz/Projektdatenbank/F%C3%B6rderung-des-Angebots-von-gegen-Naturkatastrophen-abgesicherter-Darlehen-durch-die-BOAD-in-Westafrika-44585.htm (accessed on 29 September 2021). [222]

Klomp, J. and K. Valckx (2014), "Natural disasters and economic growth: A meta-analysis", *Global Environmental Change*, Vol. 26, pp. 183-195, http://dx.doi.org/10.1016/j.gloenvcha.2014.02.006. [9]

Knutson, T. et al. (2021), "Climate change is probably increasing the intensity of tropical cyclones", *ScienceBrief*, Vol. March, pp. 1-7, https://sciencebrief.org/uploads/reviews/ScienceBrief_Review_CYCLONES_Mar2021.pdf. [28]

Koetsier, I. (2017), "The fiscal impact of natural disasters", *Discussion Paper*, Utrecht University, http://dspace.library.uu.nl/bitstream/handle/1874/358659/rebo_use_dp_2017_1717.pdf. [41]

Kousky, C. (2019), "The role of natural disaster insurance in recovery and risk reduction", *Annual Review of Resource Economics*, Vol. 11/1, pp. 399-418, http://dx.doi.org/10.1146/annurev-resource-100518-094028. [17]

Krauss, A. et al. (2019), *Climate Change and the (Re)insurance Implications*, Traub Lieberman Straus & Shrewsberry LLP and Aspen Re. [180]

Kuriyama, N. et al. (2020), "Towards a comparative framework of adaptive planning and anticipatory action regimes in Chile, Japan, and the US: An exploration of multiple contexts Informing tsunami risk-based planning and relocation", *Journal of Disaster Research*, Vol. 15/7, pp. 887-889, https://www.researchgate.net/publication/347773615_Towards_a_Comparative_Framework_of_Adaptive_Planning_and_Anticipatory_Action_Regimes_in_Chile_Japan_and_the_US_An_Exploration_of_Multiple_Contexts_Informing_Tsunami_Risk-Based_Planning_and_Relocation. [86]

Lee, T. et al. (2015), "Predictors of public climate change awareness and risk perception around the world", *Nature Climate Change*, Vol. 5/11, pp. 1014-1020, http://dx.doi.org/10.1038/nclimate2728. [132]

Levine, S. et al. (2020), *Anticipatory action for livelihood protection*, Overseas Development Institute, London, https://cdn.odi.org/media/documents/202006_odi_anticipatory_action_for_livelihood_protection_wp_final.pdf. [85]

LIFE-AR (2019), “LDC 2050 Vision: Towards a climate-resilient future”, (brochure), LDC Initiative for Effective Adaptation and Resilience, http://www.ldc-climate.org/wp-content/uploads/2019/09/2050-Vision.pdf. [193]

Liu, W. et al. (2021), “The effect of financial literacy on rural households insurance participation: Evidence from farmers in southwest China”, *Asia-Pacific Journal of Accounting & Economics*, pp. 1-17, http://dx.doi.org/10.1080/16081625.2021.1915165. [159]

Martinez-Diaz, L. and J. McClamrock (2019), *The future of disaster risk pooling for developing countries: Where do we go from here?*, World Resources Institute, Washington, DC, http://www.wri.org/publication/disaster-risk-pooling. [179]

Mbow, C. et al. (2019), “Food security”, in Shukla, P. et al. (eds.), *Climate Change and Land: An IPCC Special Report on Climate Change, Desertification, Land Degradation, Sustainable Land Management, Food Security, and Greenhouse Gas Fluxes in Terrestrial Ecosystems*. [5]

McClelland, G., W. Schulze and D. Coursey (1993), *Insurance for low-probability hazards: A bimodal response to unlikely events*, Springer, https://link.springer.com/article/10.1007/BF01065317. [156]

Mechler, R. (2016), “Reviewing estimates of the economic efficiency of disaster risk management: opportunities and limitations of using risk-based cost–benefit analysis”, *Natural Hazards*, Vol. 81/3, pp. 2121-2147, http://dx.doi.org/10.1007/s11069-016-2170-y. [11]

Mejia, S. (2014), “Debt, growth and natural disasters: A Caribbean trilogy”*, Working Paper*, International Monetary Fund, Washington, DC, https://www.imf.org/en/Publications/WP/Issues/2016/12/31/Debt-Growth-and-Natural-Disasters-A-Caribbean-Trilogy-41757. [23]

Melecky, M. and C. Raddatz (2011), “How do governments respond after catastrophes? Natural-disaster shocks and the fiscal stance”*, Policy Research Working Paper*, No. 5564, World Bank, Washington, DC, http://dx.doi.org/10.1596/1813-9450-5564. [150]

Millo, G. and G. Pasini (2010), “Does social capital reduce moral hazard? A network model for non-life insurance demand”, *Fiscal Studies*, Vol. 31/3, pp. 341-372, http://dx.doi.org/10.1111/j.1475-5890.2010.00118.x. [162]

Ministry of Foreign Affairs of Denmark (2020), *Strategic Framework, Denmark-Kenya Partnership 2021-2025*, Ministry of Foreign Affairs, Government of Denmark, Copenhagen, https://kenya.um.dk/en/danida-en/denmark-kenya-partnership-policy. [197]

Mohan, P. and E. Strobl (2020), “The impact of tropical storms on the accumulation and composition of government debt”, *International Tax and Public Finance*, Vol. 28/3, pp. 483-496, http://dx.doi.org/10.1007/s10797-020-09622-5. [40]

Mol, J., W. Botzen and J. Blasch (2020), “Risk reduction in compulsory disaster insurance: Experimental evidence on moral hazard and financial incentives”, *Journal of Behavioral and Experimental Economics*, Vol. 84, p. 101500, http://dx.doi.org/10.1016/j.socec.2019.101500. [177]

MOPAN (2021), *Lessons in Multilateral Effectiveness: Pulling Together – The Multilateral Response to Climate Change*, Multilateral Organisation Performance Assessment Network, Paris. [188]

Moulson, G. (2021), "German Cabinet approves some $427 million inf first flood aid", 21 July, Associated Press, https://apnews.com/article/europe-business-government-and-politics-environment-and-nature-floods-a3f662c153903121eb62183427b8d460. [144]

Nakatani, R. (2021), "Fiscal rules for natural disaster- and climate change-prone small states", *Sustainability*, Vol. 13/6, p. 3135, http://dx.doi.org/10.3390/su13063135. [49]

Narain, A., P. Rabanal and S. Byskov (2003), *Prudential issues in less diversified economies*, International Monetary Fund, Washington, DC, https://www.imf.org/en/Publications/WP/Issues/2016/12/30/Prudential-Issues-in-Less-Diversified-Economies-16858. [18]

NFGS (2019), "Guide to climate scenario analysis for central banks and supervisors", *Technical Document*, Network for Greening the Financial System, Banque de France, https://www.ngfs.net/sites/default/files/medias/documents/ngfs_guide_scenario_analysis_final.pdf. [139]

Noy, I. and T. Vu (2010), "The economics of natural disasters in a developing country: The case of Vietnam", *Journal of Asian Economics*, Vol. 21/4, pp. 345-354, http://dx.doi.org/10.1016/j.asieco.2010.03.002. [13]

Obeng, G. et al. (2008), "Impact of solar photovoltaic lighting on indoor air smoke in off-grid rural Ghana", *Energy for Sustainable Development*, Vol. 12/1, pp. 55-61, http://dx.doi.org/10.1016/s0973-0826(08)60419-6. [101]

O'Connor, A. (2021), "Florida regulator nixes citizens' request to remove rate cap on new business", 21 April, Insurance Journal, https://www.insurancejournal.com/news/southeast/2021/04/21/610818.htm. [170]

OECD (2021), *Climate Finance Provided and Mobilised by Developed Countries: Aggregate Trends Updated with 2019 Data*, OECD Publishing, Paris, http://dx.doi.org/10.1787/03590fb7-en. [227]

OECD (2021), *Enhancing Financial Protection Against Catastrophe Risks: The Role of Catastrophe Risk Insurance Programmes*, https://www.oecd.org/daf/fin/insurance/Enhancing-financial-protection-against-catastrophe-risks.htm (accessed on 11 October 2021). [157]

OECD (2021), *OECD DAC Creditor Reporting System (CRS)*, OECD Publishing, Paris, https://stats.oecd.org/Index.aspx?DataSetCode=crs1 (accessed on 1 June 2021). [82]

OECD (2021), *Strengthening Climate Resilience: Guidance for Governments and Development Co-operation*, OECD Publishing, Paris, https://dx.doi.org/10.1787/4b08b7be-en. [102]

OECD (2020), *Common Ground Between the Paris Agreement and the Sendai Framework: Climate Change Adaptation and Disaster Risk Reduction*, OECD Publishing, Paris, https://dx.doi.org/10.1787/3edc8d09-en. [96]

OECD (2020), *Development Co-operation Profiles*, OECD Publishing, Paris, https://dx.doi.org/10.1787/2dcf1367-en. [221]

OECD (2020), *Leveraging the Role of Property Catastrophe Reinsurance Markets: The Case of India, Indonesia, Myanmar, and the Philippines*, https://www.oecd.org/finance/insurance/leveraging-the-role-of-property-catastrophe-reinsurance-markets.htm. [164]

OECD (2020), *States of Fragility 2020*, OECD Publishing, Paris, https://www.oecd.org/dac/states-of-fragility-fa5a6770-en.htm. [208]

OECD (2019), *Accelerating Climate Action: Refocusing Policies through a Well-being Lens*, OECD Publishing, Paris, https://dx.doi.org/10.1787/2f4c8c9a-en. [100]

OECD (2019), "Costa Rica's perspective on Total Official Support for Sustainable Development (TOSSD)", *OECD Development Co-operation Working Papers*, No. 56, OECD Publishing, Paris, https://doi.org/10.1787/94e8be1a-en. [232]

OECD (2019), *DAC Recommendation on the Humanitarian-Development-Peace Nexus*, OECD Development Assistance Committee, Paris, https://legalinstruments.oecd.org/en/instruments/OECD-LEGAL-5019. [210]

OECD (2019), "What is ODA?", (brochure), OECD Publishing, Paris, https://www.oecd.org/development/stats/What-is-ODA.pdf. [240]

OECD (2018), *Assessing the Real Cost of Disasters: The Need for Better Evidence*, OECD Reviews of Risk Management Policies, OECD Publishing, Paris, https://dx.doi.org/10.1787/9789264298798-en. [110]

OECD (2018), *Cost-Benefit Analysis and the Environment: Further Developments and Policy Use*, OECD Publishing, Paris, https://dx.doi.org/10.1787/9789264085169-en. [106]

OECD (2018), *Perspectives on Global Development 2019: Rethinking Development Strategies*, OECD Publishing, Paris, https://dx.doi.org/10.1787/persp_glob_dev-2019-en. [238]

OECD (2018), *The Contribution of Reinsurance Markets to Managing Catastrophe Risk*, http://www.oecd.org/finance/the-contribution-of-reinsurance-markets-to-managing-catastrophe-risk.pdf. [153]

OECD (2017), *Proposal to Establish a Policy Marker for Disaster Risk Reduction (DRR) in theOECD DAC Creditor Reporting System (CRS), DCD/DAC/STAT(2017)26.*, OECD. [242]

OECD (2016), *Financial Management of Flood Risk*, OECD Publishing, Paris, http://www.oecd-ilibrary.org/finance-and-investment/financial-management-of-flood-risk_9789264257689-en. [130]

OECD (2016), "Modernising the Measurement of Concessional Sovereign Loans", OECD Publishing, https://www.oecd.org/dac/financing-sustainable-development/concessional-sovereign-loans.htm (accessed on 23 May 2021). [158]

OECD (2007), *Handbook for Appraisal of Environmental Projects Financed from Public Funds*, OECD Publishing Paris, https://www.oecd.org/environment/outreach/38786197.pdf. [107]

OECD (forthcoming), *Cooling the Hotspots: Climate Finance in Fragile Contexts*, INCAF Financing for Stability Series, OECD Publishing, Paris. [91]

OECD (n.d.), "DAC Glossary of Key Terms and Concepts", webpage, https://www.oecd.org/dac/dac-glossary.htm (accessed on 14 June 2021). [241]

OECD (n.d.), *Other Official Flows*, (database), https://data.oecd.org/drf/other-official-flows-oof.htm#:~:text=Other%20official%20flows%20(OOF)%20are,development%20assistance%20(ODA)%20criteria. (accessed on 27 July 2021). [214]

OECD/World Bank (2019), *Fiscal Resilience to Natural Disasters: Lessons from Country Experiences*, OECD Publishing, Paris, https://doi.org/10.1787/27a4198a-en. [146]

Ouattara, B. and E. Strobl (2013), "The fiscal implications of hurricane strikes in the Caribbean", *Ecological Economics*, Vol. 85, pp. 105-115, http://dx.doi.org/10.1016/j.ecolecon.2012.10.002. [39]

Paleari, S. (2019), "Disaster risk insurance: A comparison of national schemes in the EU-28", *International Journal of Disaster Risk Reduction*, Vol. 35, p. 101059, http://dx.doi.org/10.1016/j.ijdrr.2018.12.021. [171]

Picolotti, R. and A. Miller (2020), "Debt for climate swaps can help developing countries make a green recovery", 13 November, International Institute for Sustainable Development, Winnipeg, https://www.iisd.org/sustainable-recovery/debt-for-climate-swaps-can-help-developing-countries-make-a-green-recovery/. [236]

Pilla, F., S. Gharbia and R. Lyons (2019), "How do households perceive flood-risk? The impact of flooding on the cost of accommodation in Dublin, Ireland", *Science of the Total Environment*, Vol. 650, pp. 144-154, http://dx.doi.org/10.1016/j.scitotenv.2018.08.439. [127]

PPCR (n.d.), "Adaptation Programme and Financing Mechanism", webpage, https://ppcrja.org.jm/adaptation-programme-and-financing-mechanism/ (accessed on 23 September 2021). [223]

Ramani, V. (2020), *Addressing Climate as a Systemic Risk - A Call to Action for U.S. Financial Regulators*, Ceres, Boston, https://www.ceres.org/resources/reports/addressing-climate-systemic-risk. [51]

Reinhart, C. and K. Rogoff (2011), "The forgotten history of domestic debt", *The Economic Journal*, Vol. 121/552, pp. 319-350, http://dx.doi.org/10.1111/j.1468-0297.2011.02426.x. [44]

Robinson, M. (2016), *Introducing Hurricane Clauses: Lessons from Grenada's Recent Experience. A Countercyclical Financial Instrument*, The Commonwealth, London, https://thecommonwealth.org/sites/default/files/inline/Introducing%20Hurricance%20Clauses.PDF. [231]

Sabates-Wheeler, R. and S. Devereux (2007), "Social protection for transformation", *IDS Bulletin*, Vol. 38/3, pp. 23-28, http://dx.doi.org/10.1111/j.1759-5436.2007.tb00368.x. [66]

Saha, S. and B. Viney (2019), "How climate change could spark the next financial crisis", *Journal of International Affairs*, Vol. 73/1, pp. 205-216. [56]

Sakha, S. (2019), "Determinants of risk aversion over time: Experimental evidence from rural Thailand", *Journal of Behavioral and Experimental Economics*, Vol. 80, pp. 184-198, http://dx.doi.org/10.1016/j.socec.2019.03.008. [118]

Sandink, D. (2015), "Urban flooding and ground-related homes in Canada: An overview", *Journal of Flood Risk Management*, Vol. 9/3, pp. 208-223, http://dx.doi.org/10.1111/jfr3.12168. [122]

Santeramo, F. et al. (2016), "Farmer participation, entry and exit decisions in the Italian crop insurance programme", *Journal of Agricultural Economics*, Vol. 67/3, pp. 639-657, http://dx.doi.org/10.1111/1477-9552.12155. [161]

Saunders, J. (2020), "Florida-backed citizens extends moratorium on policy cancellations", 7 August, PropertyCasual360, https://www.propertycasualty360.com/2020/08/07/state-backed-citizens-extends-moratorium-on-policy-cancellations-414-184702/. [169]

Schneiderbauer, S. et al. (2021), "Risk perception of climate change and natural hazards in global mountain regions: A critical review", *Science of the Total Environment*, Vol. 784, p. 146957, http://dx.doi.org/10.1016/j.scitotenv.2021.146957. [121]

Shao, W. et al. (2017), "Understanding the effects of past flood events and perceived and estimated flood risks on individuals' voluntary flood insurance purchase behavior", *Water Research*, Vol. 108, pp. 391-400, http://dx.doi.org/10.1016/j.watres.2016.11.021. [126]

Sheehan, M. (2021), "Weathering climate risk: V20 Group and the IDF call for joint collaboration and international support to strengthen global physical climate risk management capabilities", 20 September, Reinsurance News, https://www.insdevforum.org/weathering-climate-risk-v20-group-and-the-idf-call-for-joint-collaboration-and-international-support-to-strengthen-global-physical-climate-risk-management-capabilities/. [154]

Sommer, J., M. Restivo and J. Shandra (2020), "The United States, bilateral debt-for-nature swaps, and forest loss: A cross-national analysis", *The Journal of Development Studies*, Vol. 56/4, pp. 748-764, https://doi.org/10.1080/00220388.2018.1563683. [233]

Steele, P. and S. Patel (2020), "Tackling the triple crisis. Using debt swaps to address debt, climate and nature loss post-COVID-19", *Issue Paper*, International Institute for Environment and Development, London, https://pubs.iied.org/sites/default/files/pdfs/migrate/16674IIED.pdf. [38]

Storey, B. and I. Noy (2017), "Insuring property under climate change", *Policy Quarterly*, Vol. 13/4, http://dx.doi.org/10.26686/pq.v13i4.4603. [128]

Storey, B. et al. (2020), *Insurance Retreat - Sea Level Rise and the Withdrawal of Residential Insurance in Aotearoa New Zealand*, Report for the Deep South National Science Challenge, https://deepsouthchallenge.co.nz/wp-content/uploads/2021/01/Insurance-Retreat-December-2020-Final-Report.pdf (accessed on 10 July 2021). [123]

Sudmeier-Rieux, K. et al. (2015), "Opportunities, incentives and challenges to risk sensitive land use planning: Lessons from Nepal, Spain and Vietnam", *International Journal of Disaster Risk Reduction*, Vol. 14, pp. 205-224, http://dx.doi.org/10.1016/j.ijdrr.2014.09.009. [145]

Tall, A. et al. (2021), *Enabling Private Investment in Climate Adaptation and Resilience : Current Status, Barriers to Investment and Blueprint for Action*, World Bank, Washington, DC, https://openknowledge.worldbank.org/handle/10986/35203. [99]

Tenzing, J. (2019), "Integrating social protection and climate change adaptation: A review", *WIREs Climate Change*, Vol. 11/2, http://dx.doi.org/10.1002/wcc.626. [77]

Tew, R. (2017), "ODA modernisation: An update following the October 2017 HLM", *Briefing*, Development Initiatives, http://devinit.org/wp-content/uploads/2017/11/ODA-modernisation-an-update-following-the-October-2017-HLM.pdf. [237]

TFCD (2017), *Recommendations of the Task Force on Climate-related Financial Disclosures: Final Report*, Task Force on Climate-related Financial Disclosures, Basel. [141]

The Fund for Peace (n.d.), "Fragile States Index", webpage, https://fragilestatesindex.org/ (accessed on 11 August 2021). [206]

Toussaint, P. (2021), "Loss and damage and climate litigation: The case for greater interlinkage", *Review of European, Comparative and International Environmental Law*, Vol. 30/1, pp. 16-33. [187]

Tschakert, P. et al. (2019), "One thousand ways to experience loss: A systematic analysis of climate-related intangible harm from around the world", *Global Environmental Change*, Vol. 55, pp. 58-72, http://dx.doi.org/10.1016/j.gloenvcha.2018.11.006. [7]

Tuominen, P. et al. (2015), "Economic appraisal of energy efficiency in buildings using cost-effectiveness assessment", *Procedia Economics and Finance*, Vol. 21, pp. 422-430, http://dx.doi.org/10.1016/s2212-5671(15)00195-1. [108]

UK Government (2021), "G7 famine prevention and humanitarian crises compact", *Policy Paper*, 5 May, Government of the United Kingdom, London, https://www.gov.uk/government/publications/g7-foreign-and-development-ministers-meeting-may-2021-communique/g7-famine-prevention-and-humanitarian-crises-compact#iv-scale-up-anticipatory-action. [87]

UK Government (2021), "New G7 action to keep people safer from climate disasters", 13 June, Press Release, Government of the United Kingdom, London, https://www.gov.uk/government/news/new-g7-action-to-keep-people-safer-from-climate-disasters. [212]

UK Government (2021), *Taskforce on Access to Climate Finance: Draft Concept Note*, Government of the United Kingdom, London, https://2nsbq1gn1rl23zol93eyrccj-wpengine.netdna-ssl.com/wp-content/uploads/2021/05/Taskforce-on-Access-to-Climate-Finance-Draft-Concept-Note-May-2021.pdf. [192]

UNFCCC (2019), "Elaboration of the sources of and modalities for accessing financial support for addressing losses and damages", *Technical Paper*, June, United Nations Framework Convention on Climate Change, Bonn, https://unfccc.int/sites/default/files/resource/01_0.pdf. [90]

UNFCCC (2015), *Adoption of the Paris Agreement, COP21 Decision 1/CP.21*, United Nations Framework Convention on Climate Change, Bonn, https://unfccc.int/process-and-meetings/conferences/past-conferences/paris-climate-change-conference-november-2015/cop-21/cop-21-decisions. [189]

UNFCCC (2013), "Non-economic losses in the context of the work programme", *Technical Paper*, United Nations Framework Convention on Climate Change, Bonn, https://unfccc.int/resource/docs/2013/tp/02.pdf. [219]

UNFCCC (2011), *Synopses Series: Slow Onset Events*, United Nations Framework Convention on Climate Change, Bonn, https://unfccc.int/files/adaptation/application/pdf/soe_synopsis.pdf. [217]

UNFCCC (2010), *Report of the Conference of the Parties on its Sixteenth Session, held in Cancun from 29 November to 10 December 2010. Addendum. Part Two: Action taken by the Conference of the Parties at its Xixteenth Session*, United Nations Framework Convention on Climate Change, Bonn, https://unfccc.int/documents/6527. [215]

UNFCCC (n.d.), "Comprehensive Risk Management Approaches", webpage, https://unfccc.int/wim-excom/areas-of-work/crm-approaches (accessed on 11 August 2021). [218]

UNFCCC (n.d.), "Slow Onset Events", webpage, https://unfccc.int/wim-excom/areas-of-work/slow-onset-events (accessed on 16 June 2021). [216]

United Nations (2016), "Too important to fail – addressing the humanitarian financing gap", *Report to the UN Secretary-General*, UN High-Level Panel on Humanitarian Financing, New York, https://digitallibrary.un.org/record/830113?ln=en. [211]

UNRISD (2016), "The human rights-based approach to social protection", *Issue Brief*, No. 2, United Nations Research Institute for Social Development, Geneva. [67]

US Bureau of Economic Analysis (2020), *Total Gross Domestic Product for New Orleans-Metairie, LA (MSA) [NGMP35380]*, (database), https://fred.stlouisfed.org/series/NGMP35380 (accessed on 3 June 2021). [33]

USAID (2017), *Climate Risk Screening and Management Tool*, United States Agency for International Development, Washington, DC, https://www.climatelinks.org/sites/default/files/USAID%20CRM%20Activity%20tool%20%2B%20Annex%202-23-17.pdf. [202]

V20 (2021), "1st Climate Vulnerable Finance Summit Communiqué", 8 July, Vulnerable 20 Group, https://www.v-20.org/activities/ministerial/1st-climate-vulnerables-finance-summit-communique. [194]

Von Peter, G., S. Von Dahlen and S. Saxena (2012), "Unmitigated disasters? New evidence on the macroeconomic cost of natural catastrophes", *BIS Working Papers*, No. 394, Bank for International Settlements, Basel, https://www.bis.org/publ/work394.pdf. [151]

Watts, C. (2015), *The Cost of Inaction: Recognising the Value at Risk from Climate Change*, The Economist Intelligence Unit. [58]

Weedige et al. (2019), "Decision making in personal insurance: Impact of insurance literacy", *Sustainability*, Vol. 11/23, p. 6795, http://dx.doi.org/10.3390/su11236795. [160]

West, O. (2020), "IADB to roll out hurricane clauses as small state please gain traction", 15 October, GlobalMarkets, https://www.globalcapital.com/globalmarkets/article/28mud0joemtvb9q4o3gu8/ssa/iadb-to-roll-out-hurricane-clauses-as-small-state-pleas-gain-traction. [149]

WFP (2021), *Does Climate Insurance Work?*, World Food Programme, Rome, https://docs.wfp.org/api/documents/WFP-0000131314/download/?_ga=2.41432225.2058348918.1631613435-806037866.1627984044. [78]

WFP (2020), *The Evidence Base on Anticipatory Action*, World Food Programme, Rome, https://www.wfp.org/publications/evidence-base-anticipatory-action. [88]

WFP (2018), "ARC Replica. WFP's partnership with the African Risk Capacity (ARC) for the expansion of climate risk insurance", (brochure), World Food Programme, Rome, https://docs.wfp.org/api/documents/WFP-0000063792/download/#:~:text=WHAT%20IS%20ARC%20REPLICA%3F,countries%20prone%20to%20climate%20risks. [184]

WFP (n.d.), "The R4 Rural Resilience Initiative", webpage, https://www.wfp.org/r4-rural-resilience-initiative (accessed on 23 May 2021). [80]

Wigglesworth, R. and C. Smith (2019), "'Hurricane clause' in bonds helps countries struck by disaster", 4 June, FInancial TImes, https://www.ft.com/content/4917e73a-8305-11e9-b592-5fe435b57a3b. [148]

Willitts-King, B. et al. (2020), *Risk-informed approaches to humanitarian funding*, The INSPIRE Consortium, https://cdn.odi.org/media/documents/Risk-informed_approaches_to_humanitarian_funding_using_risk_finance_tools_to_stren.pdf. [94]

Wittig, J. (2021), "UN Central Emergency Response Fund supports anticipatory action in Ethiopia and Somalia", 16 April, United Nations Office for the Coordination of Humanitarian Affairs, New York, https://www.unocha.org/story/un-central-emergency-response-fund-supports-anticipatory-action-ethiopia-and-somalia. [93]

Wolf, F. et al. (2021), "Influences of climate change on tourism development in small Pacific Island states", *Sustainability*, Vol. 13/8, p. 4223, http://dx.doi.org/10.3390/su13084223. [6]

World Bank (2021), *Agriculture, forestry and fishing, value added (% of GDP)*, https://data.worldbank.org/indicator/NV.AGR.TOTL.ZS (accessed on 18 June 2021). [20]

World Bank (2021), *Climate Action Plan, 2021-2025, Supporting Green, Resilient, and Inclusive Development*, World Bank, Washington, DC, https://openknowledge.worldbank.org/bitstream/handle/10986/35799/CCAP-2021-25.pdf?sequence=2&isAllowed=y. [198]

World Bank (2021), *International Debt Statistics 2022*, The World Bank, http://dx.doi.org/10.1596/978-1-4648-1800-4. [228]

World Bank (2021), "Welcome to the World Bank Climate and Disaster Risk Screening Tools", webpage, https://climatescreeningtools.worldbank.org/ (accessed on 2 June 2021). [199]

World Bank (2021), "World Bank catastrophe bond provides Jamaica $185 million in storm protection", 19 July, Press Release, World Bank, Washington, DC, https://www.worldbank.org/en/news/press-release/2021/07/19/world-bank-catastrophe-bond-provides-jamaica-185-million-in-storm-protection?mc_cid=c29830e8a7&mc_eid=2adb4feb83. [226]

World Bank (2021), *World Bank Country and Lending Groups*, (database), https://datahelpdesk.worldbank.org/knowledgebase/articles/906519-world-bank-country-and-lending-groups (accessed on 2 July 2021). [155]

World Bank (2020), "Jamaica First Economic Resilience Development Policy Loan", webpage, https://projects.worldbank.org/en/projects-operations/project-detail/P170223 (accessed on 2 October 2021). [225]

World Bank (2020), "Sahel Adaptive Social Protection Program", webpage, https://www.worldbank.org/en/programs/sahel-adaptive-social-protection-program-trust-fund (accessed on 16 June 2021). [74]

World Bank (2019), *Mozambique: Disaster Risk Management and Resilience Program Project*, World Bank, Washington, DC, https://projects.worldbank.org/en/projects-operations/project-detail/P166437. [147]

Yue, M. and C. Wang (2021), "Debt-for-nature Swaps: A triple-win solution for debt sustainability and biodiversity finance in the Belt and Road Initiative (BRI)?", 1 February, Greenbelt Road and Initiative Center, https://green-bri.org/debt-for-nature-swaps-in-the-belt-and-road-initiative-bri/. [235]

Zegarra, M. et al. (2020), "Impact of Hurricane Dorian in the Bahamas: A View from the sky", *Technical Note*, No. IDB-TN-1857, Inter-American Development Bank, Washington, DC, https://publications.iadb.org/publications/english/document/Impact_of_Hurricane_Dorian_in_The_Bahamas_A_View_from_the_Sky.pdf. [2]

Zhang, D. and S. Managi (2020), "Financial development, natural disasters, and economics of the Pacific small island states", *Economic Analysis and Policy*, Vol. 66, pp. 168-181, http://dx.doi.org/10.1016/j.eap.2020.04.003. [47]

Annex 5.A. Statistical framework and methodology

Methodological considerations

The OECD Development Assistance Committee (DAC) gathers on an annual basis statistics on official development assistance (ODA) and other resource flows to developing countries from bilateral and multilateral development co-operation providers. The data are publicly available in the Creditor Reporting System (CRS) database.

Overview of data coverage in the CRS

Data are collected on individual projects and programmes from bilateral and multilateral providers. Reporting is mandatory for members of the DAC. In their reporting to the CRS, DAC members include information on the purpose of the support provided through the use of sector and sub-sector codes. In reporting on the sector, providers are encouraged to answer the question "which specific area of the recipient's economic or social structure is the transfer intended to foster" [the list of all OECD DAC purpose codes is available at (OECD, n.d.[241])]. Further, the CRS includes a policy marker system that facilitates the monitoring of members' activities in support of the objectives of the 1992 Rio Conventions on climate change, biodiversity and desertification, using the "Rio markers". Reporting on climate change mitigation, biodiversity and desertification became mandatory for members of the DAC in 2006 and on climate change adaptation in 2010. The definition and eligibility criteria for the climate change adaptation marker is summarised in Annex Table 5.A.1. For each activity reported, DAC members (and other bilateral providers) indicate whether it targets the objectives of the Rio Conventions as a "principal" or "significant" objective. Activities marked "principal" would not have been funded but for that policy objective; activities marked "significant" have other prime objectives but have been formulated or adjusted to help meet the policy objective. This differentiation indicates the degree of mainstreaming of environmental considerations into development co-operation portfolios.

Annex Table 5.A.1. Definition and eligibility criteria for the Rio marker for climate change adaptation

Aid targeting the objectives of the Framework Convention on Climate Change: Climate change adaptation	
DEFINITION An activity should be classified as adaptation related (score Principal or Significant) if:	It intends to reduce the vulnerability of human or natural systems to the current and expected impacts of climate change, including climate variability, by maintaining or increasing resilience, through increased ability to adapt to, or absorb, climate change stresses, shocks and variability and/or by helping reduce exposure to them. This encompasses a range of activities from information and knowledge generation, to capacity development, planning and the implementation of climate change adaptation actions.
CRITERIA FOR ELIGIBILITY An activity is eligible for the climate change adaptation marker if:	a) the climate change adaptation objective is explicitly indicated in the activity documentation; and b) the activity contains specific measures targeting the definition above. Carrying out an assessment of vulnerability to climate variability and change, either separately or as an integral part of agencies' standard procedures, facilitates this approach. To guide scoring, a three-step approach is recommended as a "best practice", in particular to justify for a principal score: • Setting out the context of risks, vulnerabilities and impacts related to climate variability and climate change: for a project to be considered as one that contributes to adaptation to climate change, the context of climate vulnerability should be set out clearly using a robust evidence base. This could take a variety of forms, including use of material from existing analyses and reports, or original, bespoke climate vulnerability assessment analysis carried out as part of the preparation of a project. • Stating the intent to address the identified risks, vulnerabilities and impacts in project documentation: The project should set out how it intends to address the context- and location-specific climate change vulnerabilities, as set out in existing analyses, reports or the project's climate vulnerability assessment. • Demonstrating a clear and direct link between the identified risks, vulnerabilities and impacts and the specific project activities: the project should explicitly address risk and vulnerabilities under current and future climate change as identified in the project documentation.

Source: (OECD, 2020[96]).

In 2018, a new policy marker on disaster risk reduction was approved (see definition and eligibility criteria summarised in Annex Table 5.A.2). Reporting on this marker started in 2019 on 2018 flows. In 2018 and 2019, DAC members reported 5 975 ODA-eligible activities using this marker. The number of marked activities increased by 38% over 2018-19. In 2018, three members (United Kingdom, Belgium and Hungary) did not report any activity against this marker, while they did in 2019. Several countries also substantially increased the number of initiatives reported over this period. These increases are unlikely to highlight a change in policy priorities (or a large disaster in that period) that could have triggered a renewed focus on these issues. Rather, the changes reflect the usual trajectory for new markers: it may take a few reporting cycles for a marker to reflect the policy focus.

Annex Table 5.A.2. Definition and eligibility criteria for the policy marker on the Sendai Framework for Disaster Risk Reduction

Aid targeting the objectives of the Sendai Framework for Disaster Risk Reduction	
DEFINITION An activity should be classified as related to disaster risk reduction (DRR) (score Principal or Significant) if:	It promotes the goal and global targets* of the Sendai Framework to achieve substantial reduction of disaster risk and losses in lives, livelihoods and health and in the economic, physical, social, cultural and environmental assets of persons, businesses, communities and countries.
CRITERIA FOR ELIGIBILITY	The activity contributes to the prevention of new disaster risk, and/or the reduction of existing disaster risk, and/or the strengthening of resilience through the implementation of integrated and inclusive economic, structural, legal, social, health, cultural, educational, environmental, technological, political and institutional measures that prevent and reduce hazard exposure and vulnerability to disaster, and increase preparedness for response and recovery with the explicit purpose of increasing human security, well-being, quality of life, resilience and sustainable development. The activity will score "principal objective" if it directly and explicitly contributes to at least one of the four Priorities for Action of the Sendai Framework: • Priority 1: Understanding disaster risk. • Priority 2: Strengthening disaster risk governance to manage disaster risk. • Priority 3: Investing in disaster risk reduction for resilience. • Priority 4: Enhancing disaster preparedness for effective response and to "Build Back Better" in recovery, rehabilitation and reconstruction.
EXAMPLES OF TYPICAL ACTIVITIES	Support for design, implementation, and evaluation of strategies, policies, and measures to improve the understanding of disaster risk, DRR considerations integrated into development policies, planning and legislation, fostering political commitment and community participation in DRR, multi-hazard risk mapping, modelling, assessments and dissemination, decision support tools for risk-sensitive planning, early warning systems with outreach to communities, developing knowledge, public awareness and co-operation on DRR, inclusion of DRR into curricula and capacity building for educators, disaster risk management training to communities, local authorities, and targeted sectors, DRR considerations integrated with the climate change adaptation, social protection and environmental policies, legal norms for resilient infrastructure and land use planning, disaster financing and insurance, disaster preparedness planning and regular drills for enhancing response, protective infrastructure and equipment, and resilient recovery planning and financing

Source: (OECD, 2017[242]).

Activities may qualify for more than one marker; this needs to be considered when aggregating data across the markers. In this chapter, aggregate figures for climate change adaptation and DDR-related development finance have not been added up in order to avoid double counting. In general, statistical presentations should either be prepared for one marker at a time (without adding up the resulting totals) or the overlap should be presented and treated to avoid double counting. This analysis considers the overlaps across markers to avoid double counting.

The methodology described above applies to DAC members but not to all multilateral providers of development co-operation. Climate-related funds (e.g. the Green Climate Fund and the Adaptation Fund) apply the Rio marker methodology. However, multilateral development banks (MDBs) only report the climate components within projects, based on a joint MDB methodology (AfDB et al., 2020[213]). While multilateral providers in theory could report against the disaster risk reduction marker, only 618 activities from four organisations (Asian Development Bank, Global Green Growth Institute, Green Climate Fund and World Health Organization) were reported in 2018-19. Multilateral providers are therefore excluded from the analysis that covers the disaster risk reduction components in loss and damage sectors.

Methodological considerations

The statistical analysis focuses on all adaptation-marked activities (including the overlapping elements with biodiversity, mitigation, desertification, environment and disaster risk reduction markers). Given the disaster risk reduction marker was only introduced in 2018, the analysis is centred on 2018-19 commitments. Data for 2020 will be available in late 2021.

The analysis focuses on bilateral providers, i.e. the 30 OECD DAC members that report aid flows to the CRS at the activity level and apply the Rio Marker Methodology. This includes Australia, Austria, Belgium, Canada, Czech Republic, Denmark, European Union, Finland, France, Germany, Greece, Hungary, Iceland, Ireland, Italy, Japan, Korea, Luxembourg, Netherlands, New Zealand, Norway, Poland, Portugal, Slovakia, Slovenia, Spain, Sweden, Switzerland, United Kingdom and the United States. While Korea is listed in the list of UNFCCC Non-Annex I countries, it is a DAC member and thus included in this analysis. The CRS includes data from 30 other bilateral providers of development co-operation beyond the DAC. However, the use of the Rio Marker Methodology is limited across these members. They have therefore been excluded from this analysis.

In addition, several multilateral development banks and a few climate-specific funds and programmes report project-level data on their climate-related development finance to the OECD. These are the Adaptation Fund; African Development Bank; African Development Fund; Asian Development Bank; Development Bank of Latin America; Caribbean Development Bank; Climate Investment Funds; European Investment Bank; Food and Agriculture Organization of the United Nations; Green Climate Fund; Global Environment Facility; Global Green Growth Institute; Inter-American Development Bank; IDB Invest; International Fund for Agricultural Development; Islamic Development Bank; Nordic Development Fund; UNDP; International Bank for Reconstruction and Development; and International Development Association. For analyses going beyond ODA, information also includes data from the Asian Infrastructure Investment Bank, the Council of Europe Development Bank and the European Bank for Reconstruction and Development. As noted, not all of these use the Rio Marker Methodology. The group that uses this methodology is distinguished from those that use the joint methodology (using separate bars for DAC members and multilateral providers that use different methodologies).

The analysis is based on a number of relevant purpose codes that can help address losses and damages, using the UNFCCC process definitions as guidance to define these codes (i.e. Article 8 of the Paris Agreement, the five work streams of the WIM and agreed COP definitions). A manual revision of these codes (and excluded codes that at first glance appeared to be relevant given the definition of the purpose code in the OECD DAC statistical guidelines) helped narrow down the list to codes most relevant to losses and damages (see Annex Table 5.A.3). This analysis will help approximate the extent to which providers are including considerations related to the reduction and management of the risk of losses and damages from climate change in their development finance.

Annex Table 5.A.3. Losses and damages-relevant purpose codes

Article 8	WIM work stream	Relevant purpose codes
Early warning systems		
Slow-onset event	(a) slow onset events	Biosphere protection – 41020 Biodiversity – 41030 Forestry development – 31220 Forestry policy and administrative management – 31210 Basic drinking water supply – 14031
Events that may involve irreversible and permanent loss and damage		Material relief assistance and services – 72010 (73011 and 73012) Emergency food assistance – 72040 Reconstruction, relief and rehabilitation – 730 (73010) Emergency response (720) (excluding relief co-ordination and support services – 72050)
Comprehensive risk assessment and management	(c) comprehensive risk management approaches	Disaster prevention and preparedness – 740 (including 74020) Disaster risk reduction – 43060 Social protection – 16010 Social protection and welfare services policy, planning and administration – 16011 Multisector aid for basic social services – 16050
Risk insurance facilities, climate risk pooling and other insurance solutions		Financial policy and administrative management – 24010 Formal sector financial intermediaries – 24030 Informal/semi-formal financial intermediaries – 24040 Agricultural financial services – 31193
Non-economic losses	(b) non-economic losses	
Resilience of communities, livelihoods and ecosystems		Rural development – 43042 Employment creation – 16020 Agricultural development – 31120 Agricultural land resources – 31130 Agricultural water resources – 31140 Agricultural inputs – 31150 Food crop production – 31161 Fishery development – 31320 Fishery education/training – 31381 Fishery research – 31382 Fishery services – 31391 Tourism policy and administrative management – 33210 Small and medium-sized enterprises development – 32130
	(d) human mobility, including migration, displacement and planned relocation	Facilitation of orderly, safe, regular and responsible migration and mobility – 15190
	(e) enhanced co-operation and facilitation in relation to action and support including finance, technology and capacity building	Technological research and development – 32182 Telecommunications – 22020 Information and communication technology (ICT) – 22040 Meteorological services – 15143 Education and training in water supply and sanitation – 14081 Agricultural extension – 31166 Agricultural education/training – 31181 Agricultural research – 31182 Fishery education/training – 31381 Fishery research – 31382 Environmental education/training – 41081 Environmental research – 41082 Forestry research – 31282

Source: (OECD, n.d.[241])

Notes

[1] Insurance and other risk transfer arrangements also involve costs for household, business and government policyholders. They pay a premium for the coverage provided, which is usually meant to be sufficient to cover expected losses.

[2] Estimate based on data provided by Swiss Re sigma and PCS. The calculation includes only events with reported economic and insured losses (i.e. events with no reported insured losses were excluded from the calculation).

[3] Between 2000 and 2019, about 58% of economic losses from floods were insured in OECD countries with a catastrophe risk insurance programme covering flood compared to about 31% in countries without a programme. For storms, about 59% of economic losses were covered in countries with programmes relative to 50% in countries without them. In Spain, a public insurer provides coverage for a broad range of hazards. As a result, the share of economic losses covered by insurance is significantly higher than in other countries with similar levels of property insurance penetration (Greece, Italy, Mexico).

[4] While non-concessional loans are provided at, or near to, market terms, concessional loans are provided at softer terms. To help distinguish ODA from other official flows, a minimum grant element of 25% has been specified. See OECD (n.d.[241]) for further information.

6 Technology for reducing and managing losses and damages

Technology is essential for effective risk governance, especially for the complex and potentially systemic hazards stemming from climate change. An understanding of the risks and current and future impacts of climate change is needed before developing and implementing approaches to reduce and manage the associated risks of losses and damages. Observation and modelling of the climate system and forecasting capabilities can inform the characterisation of risks. Technologies will provide the underpinning for evaluating risks, as well as developing approaches to reduce and manage those risks. As risks are always evolving, an iterative process of monitoring, evaluation and learning can inform both understanding and management of the risks over time.

In Brief

Technology is critical to all stages of understanding and managing the risks of losses and damages from climate change

Technologies are fundamental to reducing and managing the risks of losses and damages from climate change. When decisions are made under uncertainty, a risk governance process must facilitate continuous monitoring, evaluation and learning. Such iterative processes can be guided by i) clear characterisation and ii) evaluation of the risks, complemented by iii) development and implementation of approaches to reduce and manage the risks. Technology is vital for each of the three components of risk governance. This chapter highlights some such technologies without trying to be comprehensive.

Technology for characterisation of the risks

Understanding climate variability and change is a complex scientific challenge. Development in technologies such as space observation equipment, high computing power, mapping software and telecommunication systems has provided tools essential for improving understanding of the climate system and characterising the risks. Inclusive stakeholder engagement – including Indigenous and local knowledge – can complement scientific knowledge on the drivers of risks that data observations may miss. Globally, such collaboration can facilitate the sharing of data, information and modelling capacities that may not be available to individual countries.

Weather and climate information services (WCIS) are essential for identifying and assessing options for reducing and managing the risks of losses and damages, and for monitoring their performance. Early and sustained engagement with different users of the services can help ensure that data and information are decision-relevant. Improved data assimilation, such as deterministic forecasts of cyclone trajectories, can play a vital role in improving decision making. There is, however, a significant gap in the WCIS in many Least Developed Countries (LDCs) and Small Islands Developing States (SIDS). Furthermore, while weather services are well established, those to inform actions on longer timescales are less common, despite major progress in recent years. Continued improvements in provider-user engagement and the way in which information is conveyed are needed to ensure that such climate services are demand-driven and are both usable and useful.

Understanding exposure and vulnerability to climate-related hazards requires granular socio-economic data and an understanding of how risks impact on people's livelihoods, health and their communities at large. Much of these data may not be easily quantifiable. In evaluating exposure to climate-related hazards, technologies are needed to facilitate the provision of high-resolution data on the characteristics of the natural and built environments. Geospatial technology and data products can provide insights on the overlaps of hazard, exposure and vulnerability. Such products provide improved granularity and relevance of risk assessments for specific locations and socio-economic groups over time. Surveys and predictive analytics (e.g. modelling, machine learning and data mining) coupled with the use of social media can also provide valuable information about the diversity and intensity of risk perceptions, concerns and potential impacts.

Technology for evaluation of the risks

Information from risk characterisation can inform the evaluation of the risks, allowing decision makers to identify actions in reducing and managing emerging risks. For example, WMO Global Producing

Centres for Annual to Decadal Climate Predictions draw on scientific expertise and computer modelling from world-leading climate centres to produce actionable information for decision makers.

Technologies for monitoring and modelling the climate system will also be essential for characterising how hazards may evolve over time and space. This can inform early warning systems and contribute to an understanding of the multiple, and potentially cascading, impacts of climate change. This will be particularly important in the face of emerging hazards should one or more climate tipping points be triggered. Evaluation of risk tolerance on different timescales will be challenging, going far beyond evaluation of individual climate-related disasters familiar in the current climate.

Technology for development, implementation and evaluation of approaches to reduce and manage the risks

Decisions on which risks to address, how, to what extent and when will be political or personal. However, implementation of those choices may sometimes depend on availability of technologies and technological capacity (e.g. infrastructure or skills). For example, to limit the creation of hazards, deep and rapid reductions in greenhouse gases are required. Low-emissions pathways must scale up the use of low-carbon technologies and redesign systems to limit the growth in energy and materials demand. This will avoid risky reliance on technologies to remove carbon dioxide from the atmosphere later this century. Such technologies might put at risk other goals (food security, reversing biodiversity loss). Technologies for limiting exposure and reducing vulnerability to climate-related hazards include early warning for climate hazards, among others. Such systems must consider a range of timescales and potential hazards. These include slow-onset changes, extreme events and the potential triggering of climate tipping points, even at levels of warming likely this century.

Technologies also underpin innovations that can reduce losses and damages in the event of a disaster. For example, they can accelerate financial payments to help individuals, communities and countries to recover through parametric insurance. In addition, blockchain technologies have the potential to reduce costs of remittances.

The availability of technologies will in many cases rely on local, regional, and international co-operation to address diffusion challenges and capacity constraints. Closer co-operation across countries, regions and at the global level on major investments such as high-performance computers, satellites and state-of-the-art modelling and forecasting capabilities is particularly important. International support is also important in addressing capacity constraints (financial, technical and organisational) and in supporting technology development and innovation in many developing countries. Partnerships and international initiatives can support the collection and sharing of observational data, climate monitoring and modelling and weather forecasting needs. Local community inclusion is needed in the decision making process to understand local context and capacity for improved technology diffusion.

6.1. Introduction

The identification and effective implementation of approaches to reduce and manage the risks of losses and damages from climate change relies on different types of input. This includes local and Indigenous knowledge, data and information from natural and social sciences, and a diverse stakeholder engagement process. Chapter 4 highlighted the need for risk governance processes that recognise the importance of, and include, mechanisms that facilitate continuous, monitoring, evaluation and learning when decisions are made under uncertainty (Klinke and Renn, 2012[1]), such as climate change. This process can either be informed by lessons learned from the management of previous or similar risks, or by drawing on emerging understanding of the risks and related technologies as they become available. Such iterative processes to managing risk can be guided by three closely linked components:

- characterisation of the risks
- evaluation of the risks
- development, implementation and evaluation of approaches to reduce and manage the risks.

These components are closely aligned with the National Adaptation Plan process established by the United Nations Framework Convention on Climate Change (UNFCCC). The process highlights the important steps of first acquiring information, then reviewing preparatory elements for planning design, before developing long-term implementation strategies (UNFCCC, 2012[2]). Each component is supplemented by a number of cross-cutting elements, including transparent and inclusive communication and accounting for the societal context.

The management of risk governance should be guided by a transparent and inclusive process that facilitates the engagement of different perspectives to understand the risks (Schweizer and Renn, 2019[3]; IRGC, 2017[4]). Decision making must consider the broader social, institutional, political and economic contexts. The organisational capacity of key actors – government, businesses and individuals – affects levels of risk tolerance and trust in the process. Therefore, decision making must recognise the capability of key actors within the risk governance framework to fulfil their roles (IRGC, 2017[4]).

This chapter discusses the role of technology in relation to the three components of the risk governance process. It recognises that technology is only one determining factor that guides the process. The chapter also highlights how technologies can support cross-cutting aspects of governance, such as stakeholder engagement and communication. In this context, technology refers to both a physical piece of equipment (such as a satellite) and more broadly a technique, practical knowledge or skill needed to support a particular activity (Boldt et al., 2012[5]).

The rest of this chapter is structured around the three components of the risk governance process summarised above. Section 6.2.1 explores the role technology can play in informing the characterisation of risks. Section 6.2.2 focuses on the role of technology in evaluation of risks and subsequent decision-making processes that determine what risks are addressed, how, when and to what extent. Section 6.2.3 then examines the role of technology in the development, implementation and evaluation of approaches to reduce and manage the risks. Section 6.2.4 reviews important criteria for creating an enabling environment for technology diffusion. Table 6.1 summarises key issues and highlights considerations when exploring the role of technology in Small Island Developing States (SIDS) and Least Developed Countries (LDCs).

Table 6.1. The role of technology in supporting risk governance processes in relation to losses and damages

Component	Approach	Technological underpinning (including scientific infrastructure)	SIDS and LDC considerations
Characterisation – Risk and stakeholder assessments	Hazard assessment	• Weather and climate information services: Earth observation and predictive modelling capabilities (e.g. for cyclones, storm surge and flooding). • Long-term observational datasets facilitate identification of variability and change, facilitating attribution. Satellite measurements and in-place monitoring of key elements of climate system (e.g. Antarctic ice sheets). • Climate modelling (general circulation model) on high-performance computers; data assimilation and machine learning; climate research, forecasting. • Global observational meteorological networks, paleoclimate records contextualise current change and variability and understand some potential tipping elements in climate system.	• Developing countries may have incomplete observational data, technological and modelling capabilities that regional or global collaboration can partly address. • Studies of extreme events in lower income countries are rare, reflecting weak observational records, differences in extreme event impact reporting mechanisms and climate models are less good at simulating tropical climate. • Indigenous knowledge can complement scientific knowledge on the drivers of risks that established data processes may miss. • Level of technological capabilities and access to finance will (among other factors) determine the level of uptake of these technologies.
	Exposure and vulnerability assessment	• Large-scale datasets on spatial characteristics of exposure and vulnerability to different types of climate-related hazards by socio-economic status. Technology can facilitate this through big data, rapid surveys using satellites or UAVs* and communication with exposed communities. • Surveys and assessments, such as through crowdsourcing and use of data analytics, and gauging risk perceptions and other concerns through social media.	• Quality of data, access to functioning infrastructures and communication technologies may be weaker or less available in some regions. • Indigenous knowledge can provide insights that established data processes may miss. • The concerns of Indigenous communities in remote areas and other minorities may be underrepresented.
Evaluation – Knowledge characterisation	Evidence-based, risk profile, conclusions and risk reduction options	• Characterisation of how climate-related hazards may evolve over time and space through, for example, technologies for monitoring and modelling the climate system. This can inform early warnings and an understanding of the multiple and potentially cascading impacts of emerging climate-related hazards (e.g. tipping points).	• Incomplete observational records will impact monitoring and modelling. • Climate models perform less well in tropical regions due to complex interaction of convection and variability.
Evaluation – Risk evaluation	Value-based, judging the tolerability, acceptability and need for risk reduction measures	• Real-time measurement and forecasting capabilities, including the use of Earth observation and surface-based sensors, inform projections on climate-related hazards in relation to assessments of exposure and vulnerability. • Risk assessment tools, such as digital risk maps, can include participatory approaches to provide more details on exposure and vulnerability.	• Scarcity of data on extreme events and impacts, lack of time series data for climate variables, exposures and changes in vulnerability. • Capacity constraints in relation to forecasting capacity.
Developing, implementing and evaluating approaches – Development	Option identification and generation, evaluation and selection	• Physical infrastructure, network connectivity, institutional technical capacity, are examples of factors that influence technology diffusion and dissemination.	• LDCs and SIDS lack technological capabilities and access to finance (among other factors), which can impact the level of uptake of certain technologies.

Component	Approach	Technological underpinning (including scientific infrastructure)	SIDS and LDC considerations
	Decision support tools	• Advanced algorithms and visualisations have improved decision making tools: cost-benefit analysis, cost-effectiveness analysis and multi-criteria analysis. • Computational models coupled with policy exercises, such as social simulation tools, can inform decision processes that involve complex social interactions.	• Development co-operation can support LDCs and SIDS in identifying suitable approaches for risk assessments that can reduce and manage the risks of losses and damages.
Developing, implementing and evaluating approaches – Implementation	Reducing climate-related hazards	• Efforts to reduce global emissions (mitigation): scale-up of key technologies, e.g. renewables, energy storage, smart grids and redesign of systems to reduce energy and materials demand.	• Some LDCs and SIDS lack stable electricity, which can limit their ability to uptake mitigation technologies.
	Minimising exposure and vulnerability	• Financial disaster recovery technology, e.g. blockchain technology for remittances, weather risk index and artificial intelligence risk scoring for insurance underwriting. • Weather monitoring and forecasting capabilities to trigger financial payments to assist disaster recovery.	• The application of some (including pilot) technologies may depend on access to finance for SIDS and LDCs that in some cases will rely on international finance.
	Minimising exposure and vulnerability	• Early warning systems: Earth observation capabilities, advanced weather forecasting, monitoring of key potential hazards in the climate system (e.g. ocean salinity, Antarctic ice sheets, permafrost melt). Capabilities to communicate and respond to early warning signals, such as mobile communications, internet.	• Ability to generate early warnings will be subject to technological capacities (modelling, monitoring). • Technological and infrastructural weaknesses in some regions can undermine effective use of early warning.
Developing, implementing and evaluating approaches – Monitoring and review	Monitoring, control and feedback from practice	• Machine learning techniques can create inventories of extreme events and impacts to improve understanding of risks.	• National inventories can shed light on the factors influencing exposure and vulnerability across regions.
Cross-cutting	Communication	• Information communication technologies underpin social media, focus groups, and predictive analytics to improved understanding of risks. • Information communication technologies allow access to early warnings and other relevant information.	• Draws awareness to and strengthens dialogue on the concerns of losses and damages faced by LDCs and SIDS.
Cross-cutting	Stakeholder engagement	• Survey applications, focus groups and predictive analytics (e.g. modelling, machine learning and data mining) coupled with use of social media can provide valuable information about the diversity and intensity of risk perceptions, concerns and potential socio-economic impacts, from different stakeholders.	• Satellite communications technology increases resilience of communications with international agencies, local and regional stakeholders, to communicate information from climate-related hazards to disaster reduction response.

Notes: *UAVs are unmanned aerial vehicles.
Sources: Informed by (Schweizer and Renn, 2019[3]; IRGC, 2017[4]; Arendt-Cassetta, 2021[6]).

6.2. Technology for understanding, reducing and managing the risks of losses and damages from climate change

This section examines the three components of the risk governance approach summarised in Section 6.1. For each component, it highlights the role technology can play in supporting these risk governance approaches. The application of technology will be most effective when complemented with transparent communication, ongoing engagement with stakeholders and capacity development.

6.2.1. Technology for characterising the risks of losses and damages

Understanding the climate, let alone climate variability and change, is a complex scientific challenge (see discussion in Chapter 2). Improving understanding of the atmosphere and its interdependencies with the other components of the climate system can help prepare for, manage and reduce risk effectively. Development in technologies, such as space observation equipment, high computing power, mapping software and telecommunication systems, has provided tools essential to improve understanding of the climate system, and to advance observational data collection and climate modelling. Such technological developments have been fundamental to understanding the nature of climate change and climate-related hazards. They will continue to underpin further improvements in understanding and responses. Large volumes of data generated by Earth observation technologies, such as satellites and remote sensing, have become increasingly available and are growing exponentially (Reichstein et al., 2019[7]).

Engagement with stakeholders can help policy makers learn about their risk perspectives and how climate-related hazards adversely impact their livelihoods. This will contribute to a comprehensive analysis that will inform the characterisation of the risks for a given location or community. Such analysis reveals how those hazards play out in the socio-economic context with the aim of informing decision-making processes on whether and how to reduce and manage resulting risks. As set out in Chapter 1, climate risk is a function of hazard, the exposure of people and assets to the hazard, and their vulnerability to that particular hazard. This section discusses how technology can support such assessments, exploring in turn hazards, exposure and vulnerability.

Hazard assessment

Hazard assessment is the process of identifying hazards and evaluating their risk. Hazard data constitutes the input needed to make estimates about the magnitude and frequency of meteorological events. The weather and climate information services (WCIS) value chain (Figure 6.1.) must deliver high-quality knowledge for accurate information on trends and projections. This section highlights some prominent elements of this process without attempting to be comprehensive.

Figure 6.1. Weather and climate information service value chain

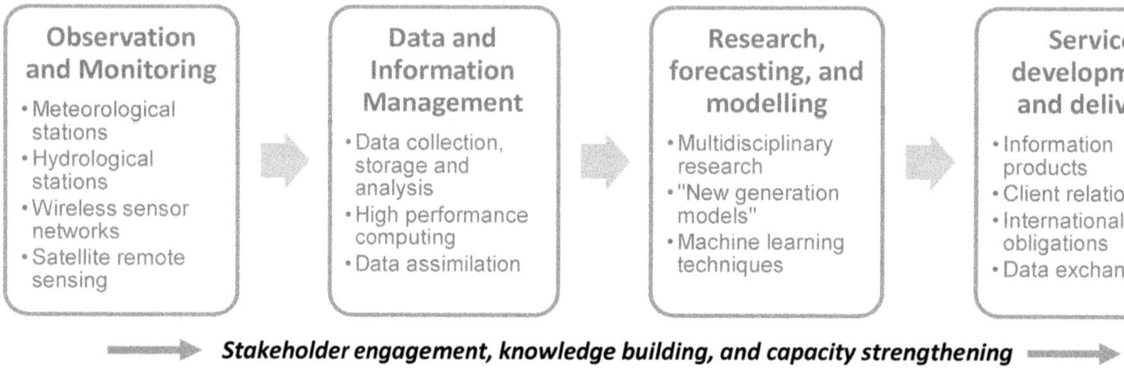

Source: Adapted from (WMO, 2015[8]; CIF, 2020[9]).

WCIS are critical to decision making (Allis et al., 2019[10]), providing the necessary information on past, present and future states of the atmosphere across different timescales. They provide the information needed for assessing the potential impacts of hazards for a particular geographic area. Aspects of the underpinning infrastructure include data gathering instruments; systems to collect, preserve and manage data; and processes for developing and delivering weather and climate services. Research suggests that weather services are well established, but climate services to inform actions on longer timescales are less so, despite major progress in recent years (Hewitt et al., 2020[11]). This has contributed to calls for the continued need to improve provider-user engagement and ensure information is both usable and useful for end-users.

WCIS can improve understanding of weather and climate hazards, enabling government, businesses, and individuals to better anticipate and implement actions to reduce and manage risks. For instance, data on tides, wind and atmospheric pressure interacting with coastal features can improve understanding of hurricane and flooding hazards (Alley, Emanuel and Zhang, 2019[12]). Millions of people already live in flood-prone basins across the globe. Improved weather forecasting can help track the scale and intensity of the hazard events to lessen the harm, and potential losses and damages to people in such exposed areas (Zhang and Weng, 2015[13]).

Components of the WCIS value chain comprise diverse sets of stakeholders and service platforms. They include activities in meteorological and hydrological observation stations; data and information management and research; forecasting and modelling products; and service development and dissemination (WMO, 2015[8]). Each component generates value, connecting production of services to stakeholders' decision-making processes. Reliability and accuracy of weather observations will only be beneficial if systems can translate them into information that can inform decisions-making processes (WMO, 2020[14]). Therefore, continued investments in the WCIS value chain are necessary to ensure reliability and delivery of weather and climate information products. Such products must remain relevant, accessible and credible to a wide audience of decision makers, clients and communities (WMO and GFCS, 2019[15]).

Observation and monitoring

At the most fundamental level, a network of weather stations provides direct measurements of key meteorological variables at a sufficiently granular level. This is critical for establishing reliable time series to climatic variability and change, including the frequency and occurrence of extreme events, and for calibrating models and the outputs of remote sensing instruments. However, the current network is sparse, particularly in developing countries. For example, air temperature is a key variable to assess climate change. However, observations of air temperature are only available from a limited number of weather stations distributed mainly in developed countries (WMO, 2015[8]). Furthermore, observations – particularly in developing countries – often have gaps in time and space, reporting time series with missing variables. Satellites, conversely, can measure temperature from land surface more continuously. In this way, they can develop a dataset in which air temperature is predicted from land surface temperature (Hooker, Duveiller and Cescatti, 2018[16]).

A range of technologies beyond standard meteorological instruments can inform a better understanding of climate-related hazards (UNCTAD, 2021[17]). For example, precipitation measurements are vital input for hydrological and ecological models. Gauge observations can measure precipitation at the Earth's surface. However, they can be incomplete in aerial coverage because of limitations of surface stations (see Chapter 2 and Box 6.3). To improve accuracy, gauge observations can be combined with satellite observations, for example, which are more spatially homogenous (Sun et al., 2018[18]). Data from air- and seaborne sensors and space satellites also provide a wealth of information that can shed light on changes, such as to Arctic sea ice. Many of these instruments can provide nearly real-time data to monitor the atmosphere, oceans and land surface, including the effects of climate variability and change.

Earth observations from satellites play an important role as a global tool for forecasting weather and observing climate change. Observations of climate rely on a complementary mix of satellites and surface-based measurements to provide the needed coverage. The ability of satellites to monitor the environment from space can support developing countries that may lack their own monitoring capacity. For instance, the World Meteorological Organization (WMO) Global Observing System (GOS) encompasses both surface- and space-based observations, essential for enhancing understanding the Earth system and facilitating production of WCIS. Satellite data from the WMO GOS provide 90% of the data for Global Numerical Weather Prediction, which underpins most Earth system modelling approaches (ITU, 2020[19]).

Wireless sensor networks (WSNs) are sensor nodes that can collect real-time data on the surrounding environment, such as temperature, water pressure and smoke-impacted geographical areas (ADB/OECD, 2020[20]). With the Internet of things (IoT),[1] for example, WSNs can be deployed in urban environments to detect and measure levels of greenhouse gas (GHG) emissions and air pollution, which can then be used for environmental monitoring (Khan, Gupta and Gupta, 2020[21]). In the agricultural sector, they can monitor water quality or soil moisture (ITU, 2016[22]). For example, in Rwanda, tea plantations are distressed from drought, flooding, soil erosion, pests and diseases. WSNs provide tea farmers with a cost-effective alternative, compared to expensive space technologies, to monitor soil conditions (e.g. humidity, acidity) and the surrounding environment. These WSNs are powered through solar panels and the data are transmitted wirelessly (ITU, 2016[22]).

Data and information management

The different data collected on the Earth system come from various sources and can range in time and spatial scales, data type and physical processes. With the plethora of data available, there is ample opportunity to advance scientific discovery. As such, the management of data is essential to research, forecasting and climate modelling. Data management from various centres all bear responsibilities for the stewardship of data to serve the GOS for the climate (WMO, 2015[23]). These include international data centres, national centres, real-time monitoring centres, delayed-mode analysis centres and reanalysis centres. Improved climate monitoring depends on better data management capacity (i.e. tools, methods and infrastructure). Improved capacity would support the storage and exchange of data, allowing the regular flow of data to the user community, monitoring of data streams and provision of long-term preservation of data for future use (WMO, 2015[23]). Box 6.1 discusses the importance of National Meteorological and Hydrological Services (NMHSs) in this context.

Box 6.1. Strengthening National Meteorological and Hydrological Services

National Meteorological Hydrological Services (NMHSs) are the primary source of weather, water and climate data and information in many countries. Their mandate often includes design, operation and maintenance of national observation, monitoring, modelling and forecasting systems. Further, it entails data processing, management, exchange and dissemination of related products (OECD, 2021[24]).

Hydro-meteorological information plays a significant role in supporting different stakeholders affected by climate risks (e.g. agriculture, energy, transport, health and water). NMHSs can, for example, support early warnings and land-use planning. With increasing demand for NMHSs, the need for additional investments is rising. Such investment is needed, for example, to obtain comprehensive and high-quality observation network, efficient data collection and management, state-of-the-art computing facilities, sophisticated data-analysis schemes, improved research and efficient dissemination (WMO, 2015[8]).

NMHSs are publicly funded entities. Having to compete for state budgets, NMHSs in many developing countries are often relatively poorly resourced. This adversely affects technological and human capacity (both in terms of the number of staff and their technical skills to maintain equipment and process data and information) (OECD, 2021[24]). While there are various ways to strengthen processes of NMHSs, depending on the regional or country context, recommendations include the following (Hewitt et al., 2020[11]; Bruno Soares, Daly and Dessai, 2018[25]; WMO, 2015[8]):

- ***Improve*** collaboration with sectoral partners and key stakeholders to coproduce tailored services on impacts, risks and strategies. International collaboration can inform knowledge sharing to countries that may face similar climate challenges.
- ***Develop*** a portfolio of funding from diverse investors to support necessary resources and scientific and technical developments. This will require co-ordination and working closely with donors and development banks to avoid fragmented implementation.
- ***Support*** LDCs with better access to climate models, observational data and advanced computational power, enabling their NMHSs to provide better forecasts at the granularity needed for informed decision-making approaches.
- ***Create*** better communication strategies to show the benefits of NMHSs. This can justify public expenditure for secured and sustained public investments through, for example, valuation studies to show potential returns on investments.

Advanced data assimilation techniques and computing resources permit assimilation of large, high-resolution observations of environmental flows from remotely sensed sources on the ground. These flows can then be analysed and forecasted in climate models (Zhang and Weng, 2015[13]). Consistently and continually running models over time with diverse observations has revolutionised predictions of hazard events. There are now more timely and accurate weather forecasts in hazards, including hurricanes, blizzards and flash floods (Alley, Emanuel and Zhang, 2019[12]). A hurricane, for instance, is a large-scale event. However, it depends strongly on smaller-scale processes that are nonlinear and harder to observe and predict. The assimilation of high-resolution, remote sensing observations of the characteristics of the hurricane's structure provide a more realistic vortex in modelling for improved deterministic forecasts (Zhang and Weng, 2015[13]). Another example is the assimilation of high-resolution radar reflectivity of cloud properties obtained from remote sensing data. These data combined with satellite data improve modelling of forecasts for catching early developments of storm events (Jones et al., 2015[26]).

Supporting the provision and application of climate services, data management tools can help countries with less advanced technological and digital capacities. Such tools include open source and cloud-based systems for data collection, storage, processing and forecasting. Only 3 of 28 major modelling groups contributing to the international climate modelling inter-comparison project (CMIP6) are from developing countries: the People's Republic of China (hereafter "China"), India and Thailand (CIF, 2020[9]). Access to open source databases will not require license extensions going forward, which makes it easier to systematically access data and information to feed as inputs into models. This is especially beneficial for researchers and government institutions in LDCs and SIDS that may have limited institutional and technical capacity to collect and model data. Despite the enthusiasm for open source data in developing countries, ownership, co-authorship and location of data holdings might raise propriety concerns (Brönnimann et al., 2018[27]).

Several of these databases and platforms are available to researchers and decision makers. The European Space Agency's Earth Observation for Sustainable Development, for example, provides a large database of open access Earth observation data. It also provides users with access to a library of tools and software resources to visualise, analyse and process observational data (ESA, n.d.[28]). The Copernicus Climate Change Service (C3S) is a regional and global resource that offers open access to climate data and tools, such as Application Programming Interface (API) reference library and tutorials for various applications (Copernicus, n.d.[29]). The Oasis Loss Modelling offers open-source catastrophe modelling that unites multinational public-private-partnerships from insurers, reinsurers, businesses and weather modellers to make insurance modelling more accessible and transparent to the public. The platform is designed for developing countries to provide insights to modelling and improve interoperability (Oasis, 2021[30]).

Climate research, forecasting and modelling

To understand important features of the Earth's climate quantitatively, physical theories and observations must be turned into models to represent key features and interactions. The sheer complexity of the system means that some fundamental dynamics need to be approximated and biases corrected. In addition, the spatial and temporal scales of the chosen model must be in line with the capacities of the computer, which may be constrained. Some key processes on smaller scales than the model resolves (such as cloud formation) therefore need to be described by estimated parameters rather than by explicit calculation. These features may affect important aspects of model behaviour, resulting in widely differing projections for some climate phenomena in some regions (Shepherd, 2014[31]; Bony et al., 2015[32]).

Understanding the uncertainties arising from the availability of observational data (Chapter 2) can help improve performance of climate models. Advances in machine-learning approaches can identify model uncertainties and provide key insights of spatial-temporal features from very large, evolving and complex datasets of the Earth's variables. Uncertainties related to seasonal or inter-annual variations, which can vary considerably by region and over time (see Chapter 2), are one challenge for climate models. Machine-learning techniques, such as artificial neural network, can filter out the noise in data and predict seasonal variations. For example, such techniques may be able to extract patterns of respiration in the spring due to root growth, leaf expansion and high soil moisture. Such features were formerly not well represented in carbon cycle models (Papale and Valentini, 2003[33]).

Deep learning, a machine-learning approach, can be used to extract features and insights from large and complex datasets to classify, identify and predict weather patterns from spatial and temporal details (Reichstein et al., 2019[7]). For example, it can be used to detect hurricanes by extracting spatial features based on their characteristics (e.g. pressure levels, spatial shapes, spiral flows) to define and classify the type of extreme event (Liu et al., 2016[34]). Accurate characterisation of extreme events in climate simulations and observational data archives is important to understanding trends to detecting extreme events across geographic scale (Reichstein et al., 2019[7]). Deep learning has also been applied to modelling short-term regional sea-level variability by exploiting key ocean temperature estimates. This can provide a promising tool for anticipating sea-level changes for near-term decision-making processes (Nieves, Radin and Camps-Valls, 2021[35]).

Building data science capacity, along with theory-based knowledge, is a necessary skill to handle and interpret observational data. While machine-learning applications present opportunities, they could be limited due to a number of challenges. These include interpretability; dynamic and changing physical variables over time; and uncertainty and complexity of observational data. For example, deep-learning approaches can be accurate when applied to modelling. However, predictions are only as good as the quality of observational data provided to the algorithm (UNCTAD, 2021[17]; Reichstein et al., 2019[7]). The training dataset that is used to train an algorithm to predict an outcome can be derived from observations that are not a true representation of the model, especially if the training set is small (Karpatne et al., 2017[36]). If there is bias in the training dataset, machine-learning models may end up replicating those biases. Furthermore, due to changing climate dynamics and physical processes, long-term predictions may be implausible (Karpatne et al., 2017[36]). New approaches to analyse scientific datasets combining theory-driven knowledge, physical modelling and algorithms that can learn from biased labels, will be key to extracting value from observational datasets of the Earth system (Bergen et al., 2019[37]).

Developing climate models is resource-intensive, requiring multiple actors to develop and make available critical data and information. The WMO Global Data-processing and Forecasting System has several integral components. The WMO, for example, has designated Global Producing Centres for Long-Range Forecasts (GPCLRFs) across the globe (WMO, n.d.[38]). These centres support WMO Regional Climate Centres (RCCs), as well as NMHSs. For example, the European Centre for Medium-Range Weather Forecasts provides global forecasts and climate analysis and datasets that can support different users' needs. These data can be complemented by the Global Producing Centres for Annual to Decadal Climate Predictions that. These centres draw on expertise from renowned climate scientists and recent computer modelling from world-leading climate centres to produce updates on actionable information for decision makers across the globe (WMO, 2020[39]). The RCCs organise Regional Climate Outlook Forums to achieve consensus – from national, regional, and international climate experts – on relevant climate outlook products, such as regional climate outlooks. These forums support co-ordinating operations for seasonal forecasts and tailored products to support country-level service delivery by NMHSs. They ensure consistency in the access to, and interpretation of climate information (WMO, n.d.[40]).

Service development and delivery

Effective WCIS can help decision makers reduce and manage the risks of losses and damages. Society has yet to benefit optimally from the available WCIS for better informed decisions (Hewitt et al., 2020[11]). WCIS are most useful when tailored to the needs of decision makers and society, and deliver relevant, accessible and credible information (WMO and GFCS, 2019[15]). However, it is hard to identify users and determine how to engage with them, which makes active and rigorous user engagement difficult (Hewitt et al., 2020[11]). Reducing vulnerability and exposure of lives and livelihoods to weather and climate hazards requires a good understanding of the socio-economic context. As such, fostering interdisciplinary teams of researchers, communication specialists and social scientists that bring different expertise can deliver WCIS appropriate for specific institutions and sectors. This can bring value to service development and delivery by accounting for diverse social structures, behaviours and contexts, while considering the technical capabilities of users (Shove, 2010[41]).

Investments in human skills can promote understanding of climate processes. This investment can manifest through education, training and mentoring in multidisciplinary topics such as science, data analytics and artificial intelligence. Climate science and information tend to produce outputs that are complex to interpret. Non-scientists may lack both the technical capacity to interpret outputs and the predictive skills to support decision making (Bruno Soares, Daly and Dessai, 2018[25]). The capacity to manage climate-related risks for relevant countries and sectors will require improved climate literacy, access to climate information and the capacity to interpret WCIS. Exploiting such capacities could then help improve climate-smart decision making, modelling and risk management options (WMO, 2015[8]).

Capacity constraints for characterising the risks of losses and damages from climate change

WCIS can be an effective tool for climate risk governance for several reasons. First, it can help protect lives by, for example, supporting early warning systems (EWS). It can also enable anticipatory and preventive action to reduce and manage losses and damages (Hallegatte, 2012[42]). However, a significant gap in WCIS exists in LDCs and SIDS, which are also the most vulnerable to the impacts of climate variability and change (WMO, 2020[14]). Space technologies and *in-situ* instruments can be very costly for many LDCs and SIDS. Moreover, many lack the supporting infrastructure, governance and digital capacity to implement and operationalise observation and monitoring equipment. For example, countries in sub-Saharan Africa lack access to stable electricity and basic telecommunication network coverage. In such situations, simpler resources may prove more cost effective (ITU, 2016[22]). Section 6.2.4 discusses in further detail the challenges of technology dissemination.

Global partnerships and international collaboration are key to exchanging and helping obtain high-quality observational data for countries with limited domestic capacity. Blending data from the national observation network with satellite and climate reanalysis, and elevation maps, can enhance availability of data. For example, this process helped produce spatially complete time series of 30 years of rainfall and 50 years of temperature at a 4-km grid across Africa. These time series significantly improved the characterisation of climate risk information at local scales (Dinku et al., 2017[43]).

Artificial intelligence can support efforts to blend data from different sources (Gil et al., 2018[44]). The International Research Institute for Climate and Society initiated the Enhancing National Climate Services initiative to help African countries improve the gaps and quality of observational data. This could then improve time series data. Box 6.2 lists similar initiatives that both support data production and help build knowledge of climate risks through various risk assessment tools.

Notwithstanding, local-level data availability remains a challenge. Understanding local-level impacts is especially critical as communities may be facing a rise in different types of climate-related hazards occurring one after the other (e.g. heavy floods followed by droughts) (Mohanty, 2020[45]). Scarcity of local-level risk data prevents localised risk assessments, which hinders informed planning and strategies to reduce the scale of losses and damages. Datasets of climate variables from organisations such as the World Bank, European Centre, National Oceanic and Atmospheric Administration and NatCatService are most often available in meta or spatial format. This format is complex, requiring technical skills in data analysis or use of geospatial software to inform risk assessments. Mohanty (2020[45]) describes a methodology used in India for creating micro-level gridded hazard data, or a *climate risk atlas*. This can identify risk at high resolution to enhance preparedness and enable effective climate policies. Decadal analysis using micro-level hazard mapping can inform the compounded impacts that occur in specific local regions and reveal any shifts in microclimate zones.

Box 6.2. Risk assessment tools

Several platforms address the challenges of building capacity for quantitative risk assessments at the regional and country level. Such platforms can empower decision makers through improved understanding of the climate risks and approaches to manage them (GFDRR, 2016[46]). Examples include:

- ***The Integrated Database for African Policymakers (IDAPs)*** cumulates relevant datasets related to climate, crops, hydrology and livelihoods on a cloud-based platform. The information translates hazard scenarios to the projected impact on people's livelihoods in a format that is easy for non-specialists to understand (Cornforth, Petty and Walker, 2021[47]). IDAPs allows local decision makers to create and explore their own scenarios in adaptation planning.
- ***The Netherlands Red Cross 510*** offers digital risk assessment tools and impact-based forecasting that predicts impending disasters that may affect vulnerable communities to implement anticipatory action plans (Red Cross 510, 2021[48]).
- ***Pacific Catastrophe Risk Assessment and Financing Initiative (PCRAFI)*** programme provides disaster risk assessment tools to help understand, model and assess risk for 15 Pacific Island countries with information available for regional assessments. PCRAFI collects, processes and develops georeferenced data of hazards and socio-economic information for risk modelling. The data are stored and accessible through the Pacific Risk Information System (PCRAFI, n.d.[49]).
- ***Central American Probabilistic Risk Assessment*** provides tools to Central American government institutions, academics and practitioners for strengthened capacity in assessing, understanding and communicating disaster risk. The platform provides specialised software applications, consultancy, advisory services and training to support risk management and risk financing strategies (CAPRA, n.d.[50]).
- ***World Bank Urban Risk Assessment*** provides a flexible approach for city managers to identify cost-effective measures to assess a city's risks. The project focuses hazard impacts assessments, institutional assessments and socio-economic assessments (Dickson et al., 2012[51]).

Lack of hydro-meteorological observations can have implications at regional and global scales. Global efforts, such as the WMO's Global Framework of Climate Services, aims to address and reduce the data gaps in LDCs and SIDS. However, they can also have positive benefits for the rest of the world. As part of this initiative, the Indian Meteorological Department has shared its weather prediction technology and advisory service with many vulnerable countries that lack hydro-meteorological services (Biswas, 2016[52]). The Alliance for Hydromet Development has also successfully united international development, humanitarian agencies and finance institutions to improve weather, climate and related environmental information services. The Alliance's partnership with numerous institutions, such as the Climate Investment Funds, Adaptation Fund, Asian Development Bank and Green Climate Fund, share approaches to co-ordinate and design investments to support vulnerable countries. Their collaboration and diagnostic tools help support the operating environment of NMHSs by improving capacity, developing high-quality weather forecasts, EWS and climate information (Alliance, 2021[53]). The Alliance also supports the WMO's Systematic Observations Financial Facility to help countries generate observational data critical for improved weather forecasts and climate services (see Box 6.3).

Box 6.3. World Meteorological Organization, Systematic Observations Financial Facility

Gaps in global surface-based data-sharing reduce the accuracy of weather forecasting and climate analysis from the local level to global levels. Small Island Developing States (SIDS) and Least Developed Countries (LDCs) lack the capacity to operate and maintain observation infrastructures. Improved quality of weather forecasts from LDCs and SIDS will improve medium- to long-range forecasts globally; and inform better informed climate action in those countries.

The Global Basic Observing Network (GBON) established by the World Meteorological Organization (WMO) requires WMO members to collect and share internationally surface-based observational data with a minimum level of spatial resolutions and time frequency. A fully implemented GBON in SIDS and LDCs requires around 2 300 functioning network of surface-based stations. In order to meet this requirement, 2 000 observations stations will need to be rehabilitated or installed. Furthermore, strengthened capacity coupled with substantial and continued investments will be needed to help operate and maintain weather and climate services.

The WMO created the Systematic Observations Financial Facility (SOFF) to help close the capacity gap on high-quality weather forecasts and climate services. It will provide long-term financing and technical assistance to help vulnerable countries meet internationally agreed metrics required by GBON. In its first five years, SOFF aims to help 68 SIDS and LDCs become GBON-compliant and access improved weather and climate information. Ultimately, this will scale up 10 times more observations generated from upper air stations and 20 times more data from weather stations to be shared globally. Improved observations from across the globe will benefit local forecasting and climate analysis in any given location.

Source: (WMO, 2020[14]; WMO, 2020[54]).

Exposure and vulnerability assessment

In addition to technologies for observational data collection and monitoring, technologies for the collection of data on exposure and vulnerability also help build a comprehensive picture of climate risks. In many cases, data on hazards are more available and accessible than those on exposure and vulnerability. This suggests that vulnerability and exposure assessments must be complemented by stronger identification of the socio-economic context (OECD, 2021[24]). Several elements should guide vulnerability and exposure assessments. These include knowledge; bottom-up qualitative approaches, such as *causal inference network* in the storyline approach (Chapter 4); and stakeholder engagement, which can inform quantitative processes to support exposure and vulnerability assessments.

Understanding societal vulnerability requires granular socio-economic data and assessments of the impact of risks on people's livelihoods, health and their communities at large. Much of this is often not directly quantifiable. Adverse impacts will disproportionately affect the most vulnerable segments of society, magnifying social inequalities. For example, people on limited income in coastal areas may have limited opportunities for relocating or rebuilding their homes after a disaster (Bell et al., 2021[55]). Using geospatial technology and data products allows for overlaps of hazard, exposure and vulnerability data. These insights can improve the granularity and relevance of risk assessments for specific locations and socio-economic groups over time. As an example, a study combined data on surface urban heat stress intensity (SUHI) with georeferenced census data. It found that in major American cities an average person of colour and those living below the poverty line lived in areas with higher SUHI (Hsu et al., 2021[56]; Chakraborty et al., 2020[57]). Remote sensing and geospatial information systems data can be combined with mobile phone network data to create a predictive poverty map that is more timely than census-based methods.

Smartphone technologies can be leveraged to crowdsource granular vulnerability data in a cost-effective manner; such data are difficult to capture with traditional methods (e.g. Earth observations) (Salvati et al., 2021[58]). Smartphone ownership has increased in all countries, allowing more opportunities for people to help collect relevant data. For example, data on the physical characteristics of buildings (e.g. construction material or location) are needed to monitor their vulnerability to climate-related hazards. Such data provide input to the development and implementation of local climate and civil protection plans (Salvati et al., 2021[58]). The Italian city of La Spezia, for example, is exposed to a number of geo-hydrological hazards including floods, flash floods and landslides. By drawing on data crowdsourced from smartphones, researchers gathered information on the physical characteristics of buildings that could help assess their vulnerability to geo-hydrological events (Salvati et al., 2021[58]).

Mobile apps may also allow people to upload photos and report damages on infrastructures to gain insights on flood risks in a given location. These can be used for subsequent flood management and geo-localised water assessments (Frigerio et al., 2018[59]). Such crowdsourced data can improve accuracy in identifying areas impacted by hazards. This can be used to provide benefits for products that rely on vulnerability and exposure data for forecasting. For example, a global study involving the application of an algorithm to social media posts developed real-time and historic database of flood events. This can be used to validate flood risk models; task satellites (allowing for collection of remote sensing data of exposures to individual events); improve early warning and situational awareness to reduce impacts of extreme floods; and improve applications that depend on historical data (e.g. forecast-based financing schemes) (de Bruijn et al., 2019[60]).

Data with high resolution and coverage on characteristics of the natural and built environments can assist in various components of climate risk management. Advanced remote sensing methods, such as Light Detection and Ranging (LiDAR) and Synthetic Aperture Radar (SAR), can penetrate cloud cover to identify building and construction materials, building heights and topographic features (ADB/OECD, 2020[20]). LiDAR and SAR scanners have been used to produce high-resolution hazard maps because they can collect data at a very fine resolution. Such maps can then can be used for preparedness and mitigation strategies (Yu, Yang and Li, 2018[61]). For example, in the Philippines, LiDAR scanners were used to identify structural damage from flooding in rapidly urbanising areas of low-lying land (Bragais et al., 2016[62]). They also helped detect transport network obstruction after Hurricane Katrina in the United States to help emergency crews (Kwan and Ransberger, 2010[63]). SAR data can be used for preparedness strategies such as flood risk reduction planning and flood disaster management (Rahman and Thakur, 2018[64]).

Airborne sensors can capture aerial imagery at finer resolutions and supply real-time situational information to respond to hazardous events. Such events include detecting areas exposed to forest fires, as well as helping characterise the hazard by size and proximity from inhabited areas, among other areas. Aircrafts equipped with infrared sensors can detect hotspots at low elevation, record the data and transfer them directly to firefighters on the ground (Marder, 2019[65]). The data collected can be used to improve and develop protocols and strategic plans, including development of real-time maps for future fire risk management. They can also be used as an advanced level tool for detecting fine cracks and damages in structures for post-disaster assessments (Sarker et al., 2020[66]).

Unmanned aerial vehicles (UAVs or drones) can be more cost effective than aerial images from aircraft. UAVs can collect ground surface data at high resolution, and make them more accessible to different stakeholders (Minges, 2019[67]; ADB/OECD, 2020[20]). UAVs can carry various types of sensors, including cameras, videos, infrared, radiation sensors and weather sensors. In Tanzania, for example, UAVs periodically survey urban neighbourhoods to create detailed maps for local governments on exposure of flood risk (Ackerman and Koziol, 2019[68]). Farmers have used UAVs with digital cameras attached to monitor the health of crops, as well as detect damage done by drought, hailstorms and floods (Michels, von Hobe and Musshoff, 2020[69]). In the United States, during Hurricane Florence in 2018, researchers used underwater UAVs to measure ocean heat that was fuelling the hurricane. This filled in gaps in satellite images, improving hurricane modelling (Minges, 2019[67]).

Deciding how to respond to climate-related hazards will require a good spatial and temporal understanding of both exposure and vulnerability. This will require the sorts of geospatial data, analysis and visualisation tools described above. They will need real-time capabilities to monitor the exposure of people to a given hazard and to facilitate communications between responsible authorities and the affected population. The technologies discussed above – mobile communications, social media and the use of satellite imagery and UAVs to carry out rapid assessments – will be of particular value. The latter will require advanced data processing capacities. High-resolution geospatial data on the patterns of exposure and vulnerability coupled with artificial intelligence capabilities will also help guide the choice of response and its implementation. Issues of data confidentiality and trust will need careful consideration when using mobile communications applications, including for data collection in affected populations (Arendt-Cassetta, 2021[6]).

Inclusive stakeholder engagement for informing risks

Stakeholder engagement is a cross-cutting component of the risk governance process. It recognises that stakeholder groups will have different values, concerns and views of risk, both within and across countries. This may be due to their socio-economic situation; past experience of risks; or differences in their perception of the cause and nature of the hazard and its consequences. Differences may also be due to political and wider public discourse about the risk; a person's social networks; an individual or group's ability to influence outcomes (e.g. through social media); or broader attitudes and views towards nature (Brody et al., 2007[70]).

Public or individual perceptions may be as, or more, important as scientific risk assessments in motivating action to address risks. Social circumstances may exclude vulnerable communities from discussions on the evaluation of risks. Policy makers may therefore have to engage with them deliberately to ensure that their views can inform decision-making processes. For example, local and Indigenous knowledge may provide valuable insights to complement observational data on widespread risks that communities have dealt with over generations (see Box 6.4). Private sector representatives can provide an alternative perspective of the risks that can inform research, technology development and communication of the risks, among others.

Survey applications, focus groups and predictive analytics (e.g. modelling, machine learning and data mining) coupled with use of social media can provide valuable information about the diversity and intensity of risk perceptions, concerns and potential socio-economic impacts. The use of geographic information systems and spatial analysis can also shed light on how vulnerability and exposure influences perceived risks (Brody et al., 2007[70]). These technologies can be combined with stakeholder engagement processes to inform their perspective or risks. Such approaches may be highly relevant for assessing options because perceptions are likely to affect willingness to support policy interventions. They may also influence exposure and vulnerability, such as the likelihood that stakeholders will build a house in a high-risk zone.

Box 6.4. Local and Indigenous knowledge

Local knowledge refers to the understanding and skills developed by the individuals and the populations, specific to a given place. Indigenous knowledge refers to the understanding, skills, and philosophies developed by societies with long histories of interaction with their natural environment (IPCC, 2019[71]). Many communities have well-established traditions of responding to changes in the environment that are passed down over generations through oral history (Granderson, 2017[72]).

In the Pacific island of Vanuatu, Indigenous knowledge in observing and forecasting climate variability has been practised and passed down orally for generations. In combination with science, Indigenous knowledge on bioclimatic patterns enhanced climate monitoring and modelling of hazards. For example, it provides insight into the links between cloud formation, wind direction, tides and other environmental conditions with changes in plant and animal behaviour (Granderson, 2017[72]).

In the United States, firefighters in California are engaging with Native American tribes, who have practised techniques for thousands of years to protect their land and prevent wildfires from spreading across mountains (Sommer, 2020[73]). In the Hawai'ian islands, a project to create hazard maps used a participatory modelling approach with rural community members, incorporating expertise from *kupuna* (elders). In this way, Indigenous knowledge of communication networks informed spatial adaptation planning (Baudoin et al., 2016[74]).

6.2.2. Technology for evaluating the risks of losses and damages

Acceptability of different risks is often determined by stakeholders' understanding of those risks. As described in Chapters 2 and 3, the level of knowledge varies. It can depend on the type of hazard considered, as well as understanding of related exposures and vulnerabilities, timescale and what is at stake. This section highlights some technologies that inform risk governance, such as developments in climate monitoring and modelling, predictive analytics and evaluation tools. The process of assessing the tolerability and acceptance of risks can be structured into two distinct components that separates the evidence-based (knowledge characterisation) component and the value-based (risk evaluation) component for making necessary judgments.

Knowledge characterisation

Climate risks are complex and can take on different dimensions, influencing approaches to reduce and manage them. The knowledge acquired during the risk characterisation phase can help categorise understanding of the risks on a decision-making spectrum (see Section 4.2). The extreme ends of the spectrum are defined as full certainty or total ignorance. In between are levels of uncertainty ranging from a clear future; a few possible futures relatively well understood; many plausible futures; or unknown futures. Given the characterisation of hazards, and thus how to address them, can vary widely.

Climate monitoring and modelling, as well as weather forecasting, can show decision makers how hazards may evolve over time. This, in turn, can inform strategies to reduce and manage losses and damages of systems at risk. The risk is characterised in a multidimensional profile before its acceptability is assessed (discussed below). The characterisation of risks can change over time as understanding of the hazards evolves. This highlights the importance of approaches to decision-making under uncertainty that perform well under different climate futures as discussed in Chapter 4.

Forecasts of weather and climate-related hazards have long aspired to be seamless across the range of relevant timescales (Shukla et al., 2010[75]). Hoskins (2012[76]) argues there can in principle be predictive power on all timescales. Indeed, he argues this can occur despite the chaotic nature of the atmosphere and the transfer of uncertainty from the smallest scale to the global scale. There are well-developed monitoring systems for short-term forecasts of hazards (e.g. up to a week). These have been extensively discussed above and need no further elaboration here.

Models on slightly longer timescales (e.g. up to a month) do not predict hazards well because they fail to adequately represent the tropics (both in terms of convection and patterns of climate variability). Such models, nonetheless, are crucial for many developing countries and SIDS. On a seasonal timescale, the powerful El Niño Southern Oscillation (ENSO) provides predictive power to models for timescales up to a year ahead. It can do this because ENSO evolves slowly on a monthly timescale and its influence on regional weather across the globe is well understood – though not deterministic (Hoskins, 2012[76]). The inertia in sea-surface temperatures and the persistence of some modes of variability over several years could provide a basis for forecasts up to a decadal timescale. There is also hope for predictive power beyond decadal timescales. Key factors include external conditions like changes in solar energy flux hitting the Earth; volcanic aerosols and projected human-caused GHG and aerosol emissions; and persistent oscillatory modes in the Atlantic and Pacific oceans (Hoskins, 2012[76]).

A World Climate Research Programme Grand Challenge aims to improve multi-year to decadal climate predictions and their usefulness to decision makers for near-term planning activities (e.g. urban planning, agriculture). Researchers must consider different underlying drivers from both climate projection and climate prediction. While climate projections carry out global mean of anthropogenic-forced climate starting from the past, climate predictions are initialised using the current climate system. Together, they enable multi-year decadal climate predictions and regionally-specific information (see Figure 6.2) (IPCC, 2013[77]). WMO Global Producing Centres for Annual to Decadal Climate Predictions now draw on scientific expertise and computer modelling from world-leading climate centres to produce actionable information for decision makers around the world (WMO, 2021[78]). As discussed in Chapter 2, the different sources of uncertainty are likely to contribute differently to different climate-related hazards.

Part of knowledge characterisation is understanding ambiguity stemming from divergent perspectives on a given risk. For climate change, the ambiguity (and controversy) stemming from differing economic and ethical perspectives is well known. The IPCC's latest statement is tremendously important in that context. According to the IPPC, "(i)t is unequivocal that human influence has warmed the atmosphere, ocean and land. Widespread and rapid changes in the atmosphere, ocean, cryosphere and biosphere have occurred" (IPCC, 2021[79]). Ambiguity also stems from the uncertainty in projections of extreme events by climate models, as discussed extensively in Chapter 2. Approaches for acting in the face of such uncertainties are discussed in Chapter 4; successful approaches need to be dynamic, adaptive and iterative.

Monitoring efforts to reduce climate-related hazards, such as GHG emissions, contributes to a global public good. Monitoring reduces the scale of climate-related hazard faced by everyone, whether a country, company, community or individual. Furthermore, it quantifies the potential release of GHG emissions more effectively. This will improve researchers' understanding of how emissions contribute to observed changes in major ecosystems, as well as to where future tipping points might lie (Lenton et al., 2019[80]). The incentives for each type of action are therefore different.

Technologies that can support effective measuring, reporting and verification of efforts to reduce GHG emissions will tend to encourage greater co-operation. Examples include Earth observations to detect and monitor GHG emissions and associated land and ocean carbon sinks globally. Japan's Greenhouse Gases Observing Satellite, for example, senses infrared radiation reflected and emitted from the surface of the Earth and atmosphere. This provides global coverage over a three-day period, complementing ground and air-based measurement networks (Stokke and Young, 2017[81]; Faiyetole, 2018[82]). The Group on Earth Observations is an intergovernmental partnership working to improve availability, access, and use of global observation systems to support the implementation of the Paris Agreement including in relation to national reporting (GEO, 2018[83]).

Figure 6.2. Climate prediction: The interplay of natural variability and climate change

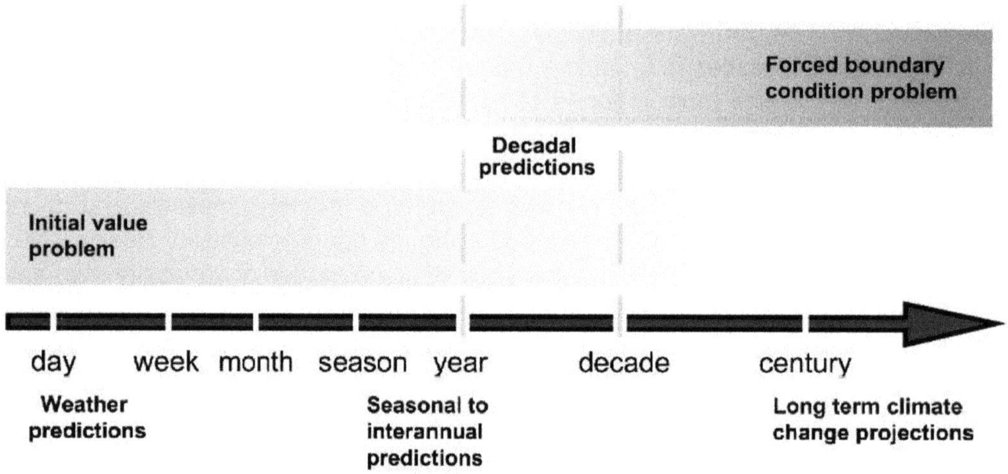

Note: Decadal predictions need to consider both initial conditions of the climate system, as well as the evolution of long-term forcing.
Source: (IPCC, 2013[77]).

The evaluation of risks for reducing and managing losses and damages must consider both slow-onset changes and extreme events. A deeper knowledge of past extreme events and related factors influencing them could inform understanding and preparedness for future extreme events and help quantify losses and damages (Clarke, Otto and Jones, 2021[84]). Further, evaluation of the risks must also consider the possibility of the abrupt, nonlinear and cascading high-impact phenomena of tipping points. Once an irreversible global tipping point has been passed, the system cannot revert back to its original state, despite lessoning and reversing strategies (Lenton et al., 2019[80]). Many systems are near their tipping points or will reach them. Examples include the loss of ice sheets in the West Antarctic, the shutdown of the global Atlantic Meridional Overturning Circulation (see Chapter 3), disappearance of alpine glaciers or the die-off of coral reefs. Understanding the proximity of reaching the crucial threshold for different systems will require improvements in process-based understanding of the risks each system face (Swingedouw et al., 2020[85]).

Technologies to support understanding, measuring and monitoring tipping elements

The possible crossing of thresholds that will trigger climatic tipping points must be part of risk management (IPCC, 2021[79]). The impacts (globally and regionally) of such tipping points may significantly reduce the effectiveness of adaptation measures to address exposure and vulnerability to climate-related hazards projected in the absence of such tipping points. Technologies for better monitoring and modelling of the climate system, in addition to modelling and data assimilation techniques (Section 6.2.1), will be essential. These need to characterise how climate-related hazards may evolve over time and space and when the system will approach a less habitable climate state. High-quality scientific data on an appropriate frequency are key to understand, monitor and perhaps even achieve early warning for these tipping elements. These include observational data on abrupt climate changes in the geological past to improve the ability of models to capture couplings and feedbacks in the Earth system (Lenton et al., 2019[80]). Deciphering statistical characteristics of variables from hundreds of years of variations can help provide more insights into the probability of reaching threshold level in various systems (Swingedouw et al., 2020[85]). However, detecting early warning signals is challenging and there may be limited ability to predict some of these critical transitions (Ditlevsen and Johnsen, 2010[86]; Lenton, 2011[87]; Swingedouw et al., 2020[85]; Bury, Bauch and Anand, 2020[88]; Rosier et al., 2021[89]). Indeed, the prediction of tipping points remains difficult, mainly due to the need to assess the interaction between natural variability and anthropogenic forcing (Swingedouw et al., 2020[85]).

Remote sensing observations from various sources in combination with longer Earth time series observations of key variables have contributed to the knowledge of different tipping elements in the biosphere, oceans and cryosphere (Swingedouw et al., 2020[85]). Remote sensing observations are crucial for identifying anthropogenic forced variations from natural variability, which improves the modelling of systems. For example, remote sensing tools for ocean network monitoring, such as the Argo Network, use autonomous floats to measure the ocean's salinity, temperature and strength of gravity of the upper ocean to measure ocean current stability. More than 3 000 free-drifting robot floats operate in the upper 2 000 metres of the ocean (NOAA, n.d.[90]). In order to explain the response of marine species composition and communities from crossing large-scale biodiversity or ecosystem changes, methods to enable quantifiable predictions of space and time patterns with ecological theories will be needed to investigate long-term impacts (Beaugrand et al., 2019[91]).

Techniques for improving the understanding of the proximity of reaching tipping points of various systems are still in their infancy. The state at which tipping points are crossed is difficult to predict. Driving parameters often experience only incremental changes before the state of the system makes sudden or persistent transitions. Early warning indicators (EWI) are one method to help detect early loss of system resilience (Gsell et al., 2016[92]). EWI are statistical metrics that can quantify the loss of temporal or spatial resilience of systems to detect a "regime shift". In this way, they can signal the proximity to crucial thresholds. Another method is a machine-vision approach to automatically detect edges, which reveals abrupt shifts in climate state and extreme climate events in climate datasets (Bathiany, Hidding and Scheffer, 2020[93]). This approach can quantify the abruptness, provide details to help understand the causes of the shift and assess some uncertainties of climate events. Better monitoring technologies are needed to improve high-level observation of disturbances in spatial patterns related to fragile transitions in systems. An international scientific programme focused on monitoring, modelling and developing potential EWI for a range of tipping elements would have significant global public benefits. Progress in this direction seems to be underway. In early 2021, for example, the ESA Climate Office convened a forum on Remote Sensing of Tipping Points in the Climate System; the forum was hosted by the International Space Science Institute (ESA, n.d.[94]). In addition, the Future Earth AIMES project hold discussion series that brings together representatives of diverse natural and social science communities to advance knowledge about tipping elements, irreversibility, and abrupt changes in the Earth system (AIMES, n.d.[95]).

Risk evaluation

Risk evaluation assesses whether the risk under consideration is acceptable to the decision maker and stakeholders. This is often determined by stakeholders' understanding of the risks, which includes their values and perspectives. The risks can be analysed at different levels of granularity or on a combination of probability of how likely the risk will occur and its possible impact should it take place. The international community, for example, has decided that the risks posed by climate change are not acceptable and that both mitigation and adaptation measures should be implemented to reduce the risks to a tolerable level. The temperature goal of the Paris Agreement might be seen in this context. It indicates the level of climate change at which the risks are so great that they should be avoided. Figure 6.3 illustrates the different judgements on the acceptability of the risk: acceptable, tolerable and intolerable. The figure displays the combinations of likelihood and extent of consequences that might lead a decision maker to classify a given risk as *acceptable* (no formal intervention necessary); *tolerable* (associated benefits are worth the risk but should be complemented with appropriate risk reduction measures); and *intolerable* (change must simply be prohibited or substituted because risk cannot be avoided) (IRGC, 2017[4]).

Figure 6.3. Risk evaluation

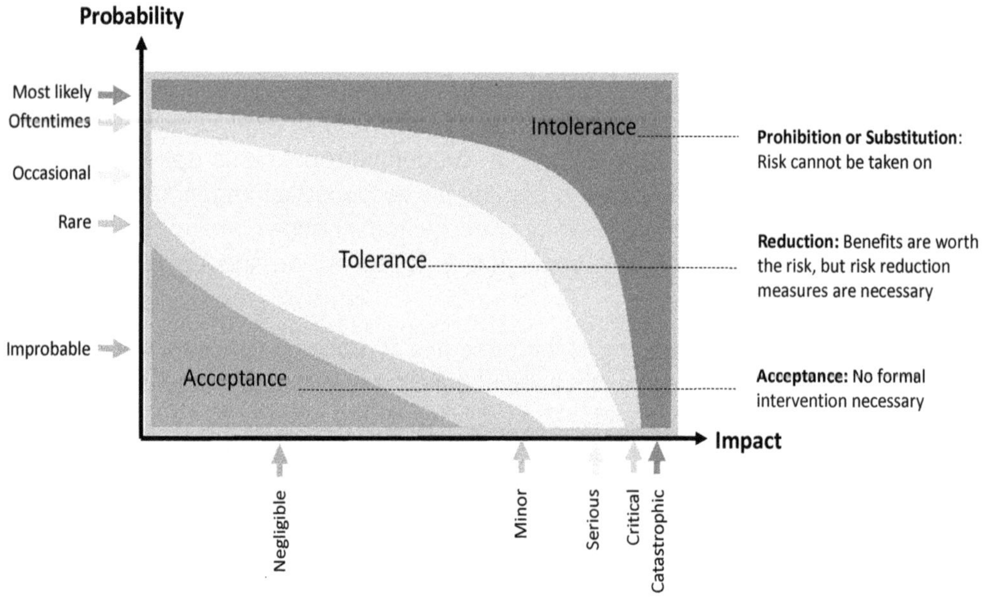

Source: Adapted from (IRGC, 2017[4]).

At the global level, the nature of climate change means the behaviour of individual large-emitting countries will determine whether the goals of the Paris Agreement are met. The level of climate change associated with the Paris Agreement temperature goal has implicitly been agreed as tolerable, provided risk reduction measures are implemented (e.g. mitigation, decarbonisation, enhancing adaptive capacity). However, vulnerable countries may not be in the position (financially, technologically or in terms of capabilities) to implement the necessary measures. Efforts will therefore be needed to reduce the exposure of people and assets to hazards and to reduce vulnerability through approaches discussed in Chapter 4.

Individual risks at a smaller spatial scale and shorter timescale will need a similar assessment process. Some risks, almost by definition, will have extremely serious consequences but may not be avoidable (see Box 1.1). These could include extreme events such as landfall by a major hurricane or cyclone in a highly populated area. In such cases, an effective early warning system and evacuation plan could be prioritised to minimise exposure of people to the hazard. While this may reduce or even eliminate loss of life, it cannot fully prevent economic and psychological losses and damages. As sea level continues to rise, SIDS may well face difficult decisions about whether the risks of losses and damages from climate change remain tolerable (see Chapter 4).

Risk evaluation involves a broader value base, including societal values, economic interests and political considerations, which can influence the judgement of risk. Participatory approaches to, for example, the creation of community risk assessment tools, are critical in risk evaluation. They build a meaningful exchange of information that makes decision makers aware of how society judges risks and bring to light the communities' perspective of increased climate risks to livelihoods and systems (van Aalst, Cannon and Burton, 2008[96]). The methodology may involve a range of tools, including risk mapping, focus group meetings, surveys and discussions, and interviews.

As an example, digital community risk maps can are easy to share, update, and integrate into other digital applications. The approach facilitates risk-knowledge co-generation and evaluation that can inform adaptation and disaster risk reduction measures. For example, the Risk Geo-Wiki portal established by the International Institute for Applied Systems Analysis, provides a two-way information exchange between local knowledge and expert-sourced knowledge of the risk (Geo-Wiki, n.d.[97]). It incorporates a community-based participatory mapping process where community members provide, for example, existing or hand-drawn maps of the locations of critical infrastructures, emergency shelters, community resources. The information is then digitalised and can be further developed by local stakeholders. Furthermore, the digitalised maps can be overlaid upon satellite imagery to better visualise and aid in planning, designing and developing initiatives. This portal have been used in communities in Nepal, Peru, Mexico (Mechler et al., 2018[98]).

Advances in geospatial technologies have allowed for the input of qualitative local knowledge to be translated into mathematical models to evaluate quantitatively the potential outcomes, such as restoration and protection projects of impacted communities (Hemmerling et al., 2019[99]). The process can map localised knowledge into usable datasets, where it can combine with existing datasets and serve multiple purpose in the planning process. Such quantification can, for example, be utilised to identify and reduce the risk of disproportionate impacts on particular social or cultural groups, and further provide geographically targeted evidence-based planning strategies. This allows policy makers to make informed decisions, whether aimed at a budget, or adoption of new adaptation and resilience plans (Cornforth, Petty and Walker, 2021[47]).

6.2.3. Technology for developing, implementing and evaluating approaches to reduce and manage the risk of losses and damages

This component of the process decides on the most appropriate approaches for climate risk management based on the risk evaluation discussed in Section 6.2.2. The legitimacy and effectiveness of any risk governance process will depend on many non-technical factors, including the trust of stakeholders in the process. Chapters 4 and 5 examined how the risks of losses and damages from climate change can be reduced and managed. This section focuses on how strategies, options and approaches to reduce and manage the risks depend on specific technologies or require technological capacity (e.g. infrastructure or skills). It describes how understanding the risks can help determine a suitable decision-making approach.

Developing management options

The development of approaches to reduce and manage the risks of losses and damages can benefit from a review of the information generated from the different components of the risk governance process, such as risk characterisation and risk evaluation. In the context of climate change, decisions will often be made in the context of uncertainty. In such circumstances, iterative processes to manage the risks will be important. These processes should be informed by continuous monitoring, evaluation and learning, and complemented by adaptive decision-making approaches (see discussion in Section 4.2). Selection of the management option should consider the broader socio-economic.

Decision support tools

As defined in Section 6.1, technology means both a physical piece of equipment and, more broadly, a technique to carry out an activity. Here, decision support tools help evaluate risks to determine priorities for decision-making approaches. Translating information from risk assessments into operationalisation of goals or strategies require good understanding of the broader context, including the various affected systems. This will help limit transfer of risks from one area to another. Decision makers may struggle to navigate the data and information available to assess the risks and formulate actions. Development co-operation can play a valuable role to help vulnerable communities identify suitable approaches. One example is the AGRICA project summarised in Box 6.5.

Box 6.5. Climate risk analysis for identifying and weighing adaptation strategies

The Climate risk analysis for identifying and weighing adaptation strategies in sub-Saharan Africa (AGRICA) project is implemented by the Potsdam Institute for Climate Impact Research in co-operation with the German Development Agency on behalf of the German Federal Ministry for Economic Cooperation and Development. Sub-Saharan Africa has limited access to reliable information on climate risks and impacts to inform decision making and adaptation strategies. AGRICA projects focus on the agriculture sector, providing aid to countries in sub-Saharan Africa for identifying adaptation strategies with costed adaptation scenarios.

AGRICA models the full agricultural impact chain and potential adaptation strategies that will support efforts in the sector to cope with a changing climate. The individual climate risk studies are comprised of assessments on impacts. These include examining the interplay of a changing climate, changing water availability and resulting climate impacts on the agriculture sector. Then, based on the impact assessment, suitable adaptation strategies are determined using biophysical, cost-benefit and socio-economic analyses.

The project aims to support governments and development actors in the case study countries. The results of the climate risk analyses, in turn, can feed into national and subnational planning processes, such as Nationally Determined Contributions and National Adaptation Plans. Further, the results can guide development co-operation, both in terms of identifying national priorities but also in limiting exposure to climate risks.

Source: (PIK, n.d.[100]) discussed in (OECD, 2021[24]).

Decision support tools, such as cost-benefit analysis, cost-effectiveness analysis and multi-criteria analysis can be used to screen different options (see Box 6.6). The tools help determine what approaches are cost effective and equitable in reducing and managing the risks of losses and damages given the assumptions. Advancements in techniques and algorithms have improved software capacity to integrate and analyse data from various sources, and add spatial and temporal functions. These improve the ability to visualise and compare different options. Such capabilities provide the evaluation of the performance of different options against various uncertainties and future hazard scenarios. This allows for the measurement of effectiveness of risk reduction options, providing transparent and consistent analysis to support decision making (Newman et al., 2017[101]). Another example of decision support tools to aid in evaluating complex problems involving multiple actors are policy exercises, such as social simulation tools called “serious gaming”. This combines computational models and participation of real actors, to inform different perspectives in situations when decision making requires management of complex social interactions (Mechler et al., 2018[98]).

Box 6.6. Tools for valuing options

Cost-Benefit Analysis (CBA) is focused on economic efficiency of a particular strategy or option. It compares costs associated with the option against benefits to calculate the net present value. Ultimately, CBA strives to maximise social welfare against identified climate change impacts. CBA, however, does not consider important aspects of risks, such as levels of uncertainty and ambiguity, distribution and equity, or stakeholder value judgements of projects (see discussion in Section 5.3.1 for the limitations in CBA). Given the long-term scales of some policy measures, CBA applies most to shorter-term options that are straightforward with simple risks.

Cost-Effectiveness Analysis (CEA) compares the attractiveness of different approaches or options through comparison and ranking to achieve a pre-defined target. While costs are assessed in monetary terms, CEA allows benefits to be valued in non-monetary terms. It is most useful when assessing short-term options that are simple, non-technical or "soft", such as capacity building. CEA requires in-depth work to ensure policies are implemented together to factor in elements that previous assessments may not have considered. This makes it applicable to addressing characteristics of ambiguity.

Multi-criteria Analysis (MCA) uses relative scoring or ranking of different options depending on assessment criteria. MCA considers elements to be weighted based on relative importance. As such, it can be used in cross-sectoral analyses for assessment of strategies that contains a broad range of objectives that are hard to quantify, for example, acceptability, equity, urgency, or co-benefits. The approach works with scenario planning of individual events, which can include options on how to perform against uncertainty. It may also be most suitable for encouraging stakeholder participation in decision making to combine expert judgement and preferences.

Source: (Econadapt, n.d.[102]).

Reducing climate-related hazards through mitigation

Rapid and deep cuts in GHG emissions, including from land-use change, are the most effective action to limit the scale in frequency and intensity of climate-related hazards (IPCC, 2021[79]). The ability to achieve stringent mitigation targets such as those implied by the Paris Agreement fundamentally depends on technology. Indeed, solar, wind and hydro technologies have achieved rapid reductions. These results, alongside the subsequent scaling-up of renewable deployment and generation, are one of the bright spots to achieve rapid and far-reaching emissions reductions. Even here, however, efforts need to be accelerated (IEA, 2021[103]). Moreover, emissions reductions are required right across the economy, even in hard-to-abate sectors such as food production and freight transport. Otherwise, CO_2 emissions will need to go net-negative to offset any remaining emissions from such sectors.

This may require the use of carbon dioxide removal (CDR) technologies. The most promising of these technologies is the combustion of biomass with the capture and long-term geological sequestration of resulting CO_2 emissions through carbon, capture and storage (CCS) technologies. Atmospheric CO_2 concentrations could be reduced over repeated cycles of biomass growth, harvesting and combustion. The required scale of deploying CCS technologies alone in such scenarios would be extremely challenging. Box 6.7 describes the global net CO_2 emissions for four pathways. It shows that even if CCS technologies are achievable at large scale, they may still raise concerns for reducing net emissions.

Box 6.7. The technological implications of global emissions pathways

Scenarios with high levels of future energy demand show lower levels of CO_2 emissions reductions to 2030; this is in line with the "P4" scenario in Figure 6.4 and IPCC (2018[104]) To achieve a 1.5°C target, such scenarios would require cumulative negative emissions over the century of some 1 200 gigatonnes of CO_2 – roughly the equivalent of 30 years of pre-COVID (2019) annual energy-related CO_2 emissions (IPCC, 2018[101]). This would require carbon dioxide removal technologies, such as Bioenergy with Carbon Capture and Storage (BECCS), as well as protection and – if possible – enhancement of natural carbon sinks. BECCS is seen as the most plausible technology and modelling approach. The P4 scenario projects that some 7.2 million square kilometres of land would be needed by 2050 for bioenergy crops. This is more than 30 times the area required for the lower demand scenario (moving towards "P1" on the left hand side of Figure 6.4) (IPCC, 2018[104]) and equivalent to almost 15% of the world's total agricultural land.[2]

The acceptability of large-scale BECCS deployment, and its technical feasibility on its own, raises significant doubts about the credibility of large-scale CDR. This, in turn, raises more doubts as to whether high-demand scenarios, such as "P4", are credible potential pathways to achieve the Paris temperature goal. Even if CCS deployment on such a scale were achievable, the sheer scale of land-use for bioenergy in such pathways raises major issues around the competition for land and the potential impacts of climate mitigation on food security and biodiversity loss. Simultaneously ensuring food security and protecting biodiversity will be easier through pathways with low future growth in demand for energy and other resources.

Figure 6.4. Breakdown of contributions to global net CO_2 emissions in four illustrative model pathways

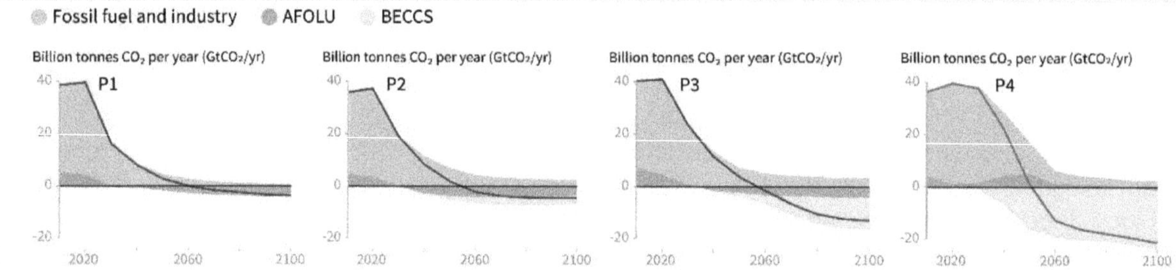

Note: Final energy demand increases from left (P1) to right (P4). These different mitigation strategies can all limit global warming to 1.5°C with no or limited overshoot. All pathways use carbon dioxide removal, but the amount varies along with the relative contributions of Bioenergy with Carbon Capture and Storage and removals in the agriculture, forestry and other land use sector. P1 is a scenario with low-energy demand (Grubler et al., 2018[105]) and reflects literature with a stronger focus on demand-side measures; P2 is a sustainability-oriented scenario (based on SSP1) developed with the AIM mode (Fujimori et al., 2017[106]) I; P3 is a middle-of-the-road scenario (based on SSP2) developed with the MESSAGEGLOBIOM model (Fricko et al., 2017[107]); and P4 is a fossil-fuel intensive and high-energy demand scenario (based on SSP5) developed with the REMIND-MAgPIE model (Kriegler et al., 2017[108]). A description of the different SSP scenario narratives can be found in O'Neill et al. (2017[109]).
Source: IPCC Special report on 1.5°C (IPCC, 2018[104]).

Deep emission reductions will require further technological innovation, development and deployment (e.g. for large-scale energy storage and CCS). They will also require changes in the systems in which technologies are embedded. In this way, they can create dynamic linkages between supply and demand (e.g. through smart grids) but also radically change system design to reduce the energy and materials intensity of economies (Buckle et al., 2020[110]). IPCC (2021[79]) notes that pathways with very low or low

GHG emissions would have rapid and sustained effects to limit human-caused climate change compared with scenarios with high or very high GHG emissions. They would also give the best chance of doing so without further undermining the well-being of humans and natural systems.

Reducing exposure and vulnerability to climate-related hazards

Exposure and vulnerability are complex and multidimensional characteristics of socio-economic systems. For example, some types of exposure may only be alterable by interventions on long timescales (e.g. infrastructure or agricultural land). Other types of exposure may be more flexible, even on the scales of hours or days, such as human exposure to extreme events. Technologies and systems underpinning early warning and response systems can reduce exposure of individuals to hazards such as storms, floods and heatwaves through physical relocation. This section examines the role of technology in supporting a small subset of approaches to reduce the exposure and vulnerability of people and livelihoods to climate risks: EWS, sectoral resilience and disaster recovery. An extended discussion on the role of technology in strengthening resilience, including technology transfer and needs assessments, is provided in OECD (2021[24]).

Early warning systems (EWS)

Reducing and managing the risks of losses and damages from climate change requires approaches that protect and prepare communities. Effective preparedness is a long-term, integrated approach to risk governance. In designing strategies for adaptation, deciding how to respond to weather and climate hazards will therefore require a good spatial and temporal understanding of both exposure and vulnerability. The increasing risks of weather and climate hazards makes surveillance imperative. This will require the sorts of geospatial data, analysis and visualisation tools described in Section 6.2.1. This includes real-time capabilities to monitor the exposure of people to the hazards and facilitate communications between authorities responding to a hazard and the affected population.

EWS are integrated systems of hazard monitoring. EWS provides warnings and communicate the risks to the public, government and businesses to inform timely action. Improvement in weather, water and climate observation, as well as in modelling and forecasting capabilities, plays an important role in monitoring hazards, in particular extreme events (e.g. heavy rain, storms, cyclones, heatwaves). Earth observation satellites provide fast and accurate early warning data through dissemination methods and geographic information system mapping tools (UNCTAD, 2021[17]). Technological developments in Earth observations and monitoring (e.g. atmosphere, land and oceans, and elements such as temperature, precipitation, pressure and wind) have enabled the detection of real-time weather and hazard events (e.g. storms, floods, droughts) (Guo, Zhang and Zhu, 2015[111]). For example, the Earth observation-based Information Products for Drought Risk Reduction at the National Level project by the Centre for Remote Sensing of Land Surfaces in Germany provides early warning risk information on drought hazards in South Africa and Ukraine (ZFL, 2021[112]). Earth observation-based methods monitor soil moisture, precipitation and vegetation to assess drought risk (UN, 2021[113]).

Technology advances have also contributed to increased optimisation and accuracy in EWS co-ordination. However, longer-term hazard forecasting (rather than weather forecasting or climate projections) needs more operational capacity. Observational monitoring of key systems affecting hazards at these longer timescales (e.g. Antarctic ice shelves, permafrost melt and ocean circulation) is also needed both remotely and *in-situ.* EWS may also be feasible for some climate tipping points (Lenton, 2011[87]); see Swingedouw (2020[85]) for a discussion of the use of Earth observation in providing early warning for such tipping points.

Different countries have different capacities and needs to deliver EWS effectively. Examples from different country contexts include:

- In ***Ethiopia***, the semi-subjective climate modelling methodology was replaced with a new objective approach based on climate science. This allows improved seasonal forecast to help the country advance in mitigating and anticipating losses from extreme climate events (WMO, 2020[114]).
- In ***Mongolia***, extreme climate conditions have caused many herding households to lose their livestock. A joint partnership between the government and FAO-WFP Crop and Food Security Assessment allowed overlaying monitoring and forecasting with socio-economic indicators to help target vulnerable families to provide anticipatory action (WMO, 2020[114]).
- In ***Nepal***, early warning delivered to the community was not well received due to poor radio connectivity and a gap in the community's understanding of the level of flood severity. Working closely with community members in co-designing EWS helped ensure that messages are suitable and well understood by the community (Shrestha et al., 2021[115]).
- In ***Japan***, a centralised platform for EWS delivers information regarding safety and security details, evacuation plans and post-disaster recovery. This approach distributes the same information to all stakeholders, including the media, municipality and utility companies (GFDRR, 2019[116]).

With EWS, it is essential to engage with community stakeholders, especially marginalised or vulnerable segments. Reaching marginalised and vulnerable members can be challenging due to physical location, social norms or technological barriers. For instance, in some cultures, women are not encouraged to participate in capacity building training (Shrestha et al., 2021[115]). Creative methods to increase inclusion of all stakeholders should be part of plans to ensure delivery of EWS protocols. In some rural communities with little to no communication infrastructures, information comes from members within the community. In Sri Lanka, for example, many communities are situated in remote locations. In response, EWS capacity building through assigning leadership roles empower community members to inform vulnerable groups about hazard risks (Baudoin et al., 2016[74]).

The role of technology in financing disaster recovery

Vulnerability arises from a range of factors. These include levels of development, inequality and geographic location alongside individual characteristics (gender, age, health, social status, ethnicity and class). These factors influence levels of access to assets and income, where people live and their access to essential services, including housing and health care. Chapter 5 discusses financial mechanisms, including social protection and insurance programmes. Such programmes support individuals, households or businesses to reduce the risks of losses and damages from climate-related hazards, as well as to manage exposure and vulnerability to climate risks. Technological innovations underpin many of these financial services. Box 6.8 illustrates the potential for blockchain technologies to significantly reduce the costs of international remittance payments from family members, which globally far exceed the value of official development assistance.

Box 6.8. Remittances and blockchain technology

Remittances play an important role in development, amounting to over three times the level of official development assistance in 2018. They provide low- and middle-income countries with a stable source of finance. However, transferring remittances is expensive, with a global average cost for sending them to low-and middle-income countries of 6.9% of the remittance value (Rühmann et al., 2020[117]). The cost of South-South remittances reaches 18.7% on average within sub-Saharan Africa, three times higher than the global average (Rühmann et al., 2020[117]).

Blockchain offers an innovative approach to sending and receiving remittances faster and cheaper, and to reach areas underserved by formal financial systems. Blockchain is based on a distributed ledger technology that provides a way to record data across multiple ledgers, which are maintained and controlled by a decentralised (distributed) network of computer servers (Rühmann et al., 2020[117]). The technology offers an approach to send and receive remittances in digital forms of money through a novel payment infrastructure, cutting out intermediaries, to enable peer-to-peer transfer. Blockchain can offer quicker and more affordable cross-border payments than traditional cash transfer systems and help ensure payments are made for their intended purposes. Blockchain technology may be more accessible to users through smartphone technology (World Bank, 2019[118]). In low-income countries where many adults do not have access to banking services, smartphones offer an alternative to receiving payments. In Latin America and the Caribbean, for instance, 90% of adults who do not have banking services have mobile phones (World Bank, 2019[118]).

However, Rühmann et al. (2020[117]) outline several limitations, including data privacy issues, regulatory uncertainties and last-mile delivery in cash. Blockchain use is unlikely to solve the last-mile problem as converting digital currency to cash can be difficult, even large banking institutions have failed to deliver cash conversions.

Insurance can provide vital access to finance to households adversely impacted by climate change (see discussion in Chapter 5). Emerging technologies and innovations offer opportunities for more effective target insurance products. Such technologies provide new sources of data on hazard, exposure and vulnerability (e.g. Earth observation, crowdsourced imagery) and tools for analysing them (e.g. artificial intelligence, machine learning). In this way, they expand the availability of affordable coverage for climate-related hazards. New technologies and tools, for example, can be used to reduce the cost of insurance underwriting, a process that typically accounts for as much as 20-25% of gross premium cost. For instance, an insurance company integrated risk scoring with artificial intelligence in assessing wildfire risk. It found secondary factors that decrease households' risk, such as landscaping and fire-resistant buildings, in addition to distance from high-risk vegetation, lowered the cost of insurance for those living in high-risk fire zones (Sams, 2020[119]). These same technologies can also be applied to claims settlement and contribute to lower loss adjustment expenses. Online insurance distribution and innovations such as smart contracts could potentially provide further efficiency gains (Goldby et al., 2019[120]).

These innovations in financing disaster recovery could play a particularly important role in addressing gaps in commercial catastrophe modelling coverage. This, in turn, would allow insurance companies to make coverage available in countries where data and risk analytics tools are more limited. For example, in Zambia, a partnership between the national bank and an insurance institution has led to a creation of an affordable property insurance coverage for micro, small and medium enterprises. It insures against storm, fire and flood by leveraging a digital software-as-a-service platform to underwrite and price coverage (Inclusivity Solutions, 2020[121]). These technologies and innovations can also expand the ability of insurance companies to offer innovative insurance coverages such as parametric insurance or weather-based insurance (Box 6.9).

Box 6.9. Machine learning for weather risk insurance

Smallholder farmers are vulnerable to climate shocks. Weather index insurance is a financial risk transfer product that can overcome the problems of traditional insurance schemes. Traditional crop insurance schemes typically pay out to farmers after the growing season for verifiable loss. Conversely, weather index insurance uses an index composed of rainfall patterns, temperature and other indicators. These work as a proxy for risk and translate extreme weather fluctuations as an indicator for crop failure (Bettini, Gioli and Felli, 2020[122]). This provides farmers pay-out tied to risk instead of individual losses. Because neither the farmer nor insurer can manipulate rainfall measurements, the weather index approach reduces issues of information asymmetry. Losses are no longer tied to payments, which eliminates the moral hazard problem as farmers will not gain anything if their crops fail. It also eliminate home visits to verify insurers' crop loss. In this way, premiums are kept more affordable (Bettini, Gioli and Felli, 2020[122]).

Technology has helped overcome several unresolved problems associated with weather index. Weather index requires a dense network of weather stations, which are sparse in many parts of the world. This is especially the case in developing countries where smallholder farmers will benefit most from weather index insurance. Although satellite data have become more available, weather index insurance can benefit more for local-level observations. To overcome this, several countries have adopted different strategies.

- In ***Tanzania*** and ***Mozambique***, machine learning was used to build a dynamic index that links local meteorological records with user-generated weather observations, farmers' reports on crop yield losses and global market prices data. This provides a more refined crop loss and risk management strategies (Biffis and Chavez, 2017[123]).
- In ***Rwanda***, solar-powered weather stations collect weather data every 15 minutes. Data are aggregated and compared with historical weather data at the end of the growing season. Payments are then calculated and sent, along with weather information, via mobile phones. This reduces delivery and administrative costs (ITU, 2016[22]).
- In ***Kenya***, InsuResilience Solutions Fund and the Kenyan Ministry of Agriculture, Livestock and Fishery have partnered on a climate-smart insurance strategy for smallholder farmers. It combines two technological innovations in climate risk insurance: soil moisture index and a picture-based loss verification tool, which minimises the cost of loss verification. Versatile climate-smart advisory services to farmers and decision support also complemented the insurance programme (InsuResilience, 2021[124]).
- In ***Bangladesh***, ***Nigeria*** and ***Sri Lanka***, use virtual sensing technique with commercial microwave links to collect ground-level measurements. Commercial microwave links are ground-level radio connections used in mobile telecommunication networks. During rainfall, the signal strength can be analysed and converted to accurate rainfall measurements. This essentially turns mobile networks into a virtual network of rain gauges. (Raithatha and Tricarico, 2019[125]).

Monitoring and review

Adaptive or iterative approaches of risk governance call for mechanisms that facilitate continuous monitoring, evaluation and learning when decisions are made under uncertainty. Monitoring and review are needed in all components of risk governance. Capacity and governance processes must be continuously strengthened to create a systematic practice to deliver knowledge among key organisations, private and public entities, and decision makers. Furthermore, transferring knowledge compatible with the capacities of intended users will support their understanding of the issues, and in turn their confidence in utilising climate risk information to act (Weaver et al., 2017[126]; Butler et al., 2015[127]; Street et al., 2019[128]).

Inventories of extreme weather events and impacts can provide useful information and exploration of unprecedented events. It identifies damaging hazardous events, and the vulnerabilities and exposure characteristics associated with those hazardous events over time. This allows the exploration of lessons learned from past events that may inform policy processes in response to similar events in the future or benefit other regions that may encounter similar situations. However, even the most comprehensive and systematic hazard databases are not designed to understand the factors influencing the severity of past disasters (including exposure and vulnerability) nor to quantify losses and damages related to an event in part or wholly caused by anthropogenic climate change (Clarke, Otto and Jones, 2021[84]). Clarke, et al. (2021[84]) set out a framework for recording the details of high-impact events on a national scale. Underpinning the development of such database requires collating vast amount of data from various sources, data analysis, machine learning techniques, in addition to best practices and methodologies.

6.2.4. Creating an enabling environment for technology diffusion

Climate risk management relies on the functionality of technologies (i.e. equipment and skill) and their ability to diffuse. In many cases, technology could be developed, available and effective to one context (country, society, socio-economic), but produce different diffusion results in another (OECD, 2021[24]). Failed attempts of technology diffusion are partly due to lack of understanding of local needs. Simply put, access to technology will not ensure local actors have the capacity or the skills to absorb and use the technology. In some cases, the intended user may not fully comprehend how the new technology will benefit risk management. Understanding and accessing the societal context and availability of local resources needed are critical to supporting adoption and absorption of technology. Table 6.2 lists some criteria to consider when selecting specific technologies to underpin risk governance processes. This is followed by a discussion on approaches to address barriers to diffusion to effective implementation and development of technologies.

Table 6.2. Examples of criteria for technology diffusion

Criteria	Examples
Economic and financial	Access to finance, cost of capital, financial opportunity, financial viability, economic incentives
Market	Market infrastructure, even playing field, adequate sources of increasing returns, market demand
Policy, legal and regulatory	Sufficient legal framework, trade policies, political stability, data access and sharing, bureaucracy
Network	Connectivity between actors and communication framework
Institutional and organisational capacity	Increase professional institutions, institutional capacity and trust in organisations
Physical infrastructure	Investments in underpinning infrastructure to support technological capabilities
Human skills	Adequate training, mentorship, human skill development, multidisciplinary research
Social, cultural and behavioural	Consumer preferences and social norms, traditions, dispersed settlements, social behaviour
Information and awareness	Support dissemination capabilities to increase information awareness and benefits of technology application, incorporate a framework to receive feedback
Technical	Technical competition, standards and codes, operation and maintenance, reliable product
Other	Environmental impacts, geophysical factors, scalability

Source: Adapted from (Boldt et al., 2012[5]).

Accessibility

The losses and damages from climate change will continue to worsen. Access to technologies can support countries in reducing and managing the risks more effectively. Without such access, vulnerable communities may have to implement largely imitation-type technologies (Homberg and McQuistan, 2018[129]), or choose other means that are simple, non-technological and more affordable (Dechezleprêtre et al., 2020[130]). For example, crowdsourced data might be more cost effective in collecting local data for flood maps compared with satellites and remote sensors. However, they are not as reliable for collecting continuous observations. Failure to address this technology gap leads to an incomplete understanding of local exposure and vulnerability to risks. Even though technologies initially may be expensive, they can become more cost effective over time if they benefit from sufficient dissemination (OECD/IEA, 2003[131]). The Santiago Network, established at COP 25 as part of the Warsaw International Mechanism, aims to support developing countries in addressing losses and damages through technical assistance (UNFCCC, n.d.[132]). Developed countries will need to provide financial support to ensure the network can serve developing countries effectively.

Data access might in some cases be restricted by government regulation or commercial copyright, such as privacy protection, data localisation requirements (ADB/OECD, 2020[20]). As such, government investments in data collection infrastructures such as NMHS (see Box 6.1) or initiatives that encourage collaboration between public and private entities could support data needs. Some developing countries may require support in access to data processing and analytical capacity to improve risk management.

Inequality gap

International patent registrations show that innovation in adaptation is concentrated in high-income economies and China (Dechezleprêtre et al., 2020[130]). This suggests that diffusion of innovation and technology is driven by the ability of countries to absorb the technology or innovation (Dechezleprêtre et al., 2020[130]). Some countries most vulnerable to climate change, including LDCs and SIDS, often lack institutional and financial capacity. This leads to limits in research and development opportunities, knowledge sharing and new innovation to address climate risks and the risks of losses and damages (Izumi et al., 2019[133]). Improvements in technological capabilities and infrastructures to uptake and develop technologies in developing countries can be scaled up, ensuring inclusion of vulnerable communities. This will provide society with the backbone needed to prepare for the onset of technological developments to tackle climate risks.

Digital divide

Action such as improving telecommunication networks and infrastructure can help reduce the digital divide. This, in turn, can improve capabilities for countries to uptake technology. Building the physical infrastructure will support uptake of specific technologies and facilitate their diffusion and adoption through various channels over time. For example, the expansion of infrastructures for information communication technologies to improve broadband coverage in developing countries can support observational data collection, early warning communications or facilitate the transfer of financial support via mobile devices in the case of a hazardous event. In Latin America, Brazil, Chile and Colombia have proposed nationwide Wi-Fi access hot spots to ensure digital inclusion (OECD et al., 2020[134]).

Instituting policy and finance mechanisms that support business models that enable a changing technological landscape, can support future technological adaptation. This could include training programmes for individuals and businesses on digital tools available and a focus on strengthening their technical capacity. Supporting climate technology incubators and accelerators can support entrepreneurs in developing business strategies, market connections, and provide sources and procedures to access finance (UNFCCC, 2020[135]).

Technology transfer

Governance arrangements should facilitate inclusive access to technologies and knowledge to reduce and manage losses and damages. International partnerships, trade policies and special trade agreements can provide support for dissemination of technologies across borders (Boldt et al., 2012[5]). For instance, South-South[3] and triangular cooperation[4] can play a vital role in accelerating climate action and supporting technology and knowledge transfer amongst developing countries. Technologies originating from developing countries may be more suitable and cost-effective for other developing countries as they tend to be attuned to similar local conditions (UNFCCC, 2017[136]). As one strategy, technologies that support climate risk management could be linked with sustainable development strategies and National Adaptation Plans to align technology transfer with broader development goals.

Another option is to tap into new markets or exploit existing markets where developing countries can manage and absorb developing technology (Homberg and McQuistan, 2018[129]). International technology transfers are critical for closing the technology gap between developed and developing countries, including for climate change. However, this approach requires caution. Such increased investments may lead to commercial models that could have disadvantages for SIDS and LDCs (Hewitt et al., 2020[11]). Closer co-operation across countries, regions and at the global level can provide economies of scale to major investments such as high-performance computers, satellites and state-of-the art modelling and forecasting capabilities in LDCs. Such co-operation creates opportunities for learning.

International co-operation

International co-operation and collaboration can support LDCs and SIDS in building their capacity – financial, technical and organisational – to produce WCIS and to develop and adapt approaches to reduce and manage the losses. Development co-operation, for example, can support LDCs and SIDS through capacity development initiatives focused on the collection of observational data, or by sharing data, methods and tools. Further, international partnerships can support governments in integrating climate change considerations – and those related to reducing and managing the risks of losses and damages – into broader development and sectoral policies and practice. International community members may have knowledge and insights of the risks and how technologies were used to address them, information they can share with the countries they are collaborating with. This will increase national capacity to better understand the risks and reduce and manage those risks effectively. It will also create value in climate services, which justifies new investments in those services in different sectors.

Funding

Technological development and dissemination can be supported through funding possibilities within various technology mechanisms. These include the Climate Technology Centre and Network, UNFCCC Technology Executive Committee, South-South and Triangular Co-operation or the Santiago Network for Loss and Damage (part of the Warsaw International Mechanism). These programmes provide expertise and support for vulnerable countries and LDCs through a variety of means. Examples include technical assessments related to technology needs; development and transfer; provisions of funding, training, management; and identification of technology barriers (UNOSSC, n.d.[137]; UNFCCC, n.d.[132]; CTCN, n.d.[138]; UNFCCC, n.d.[139]). Supporting technology diffusion and technological innovation in many developing countries is essential to reduce and manage the risks of losses and damages.

References

Ackerman, E. and M. Koziol (2019), "Tanzania Builds a Drone Industry From Local Know-How and Bamboo", webpage, https://spectrum.ieee.org/robotics/drones/tanzanias-homegrown-drone-industry-takes-off-on-bamboo-wings (accessed on 30 April 2021). [68]

ADB/OECD (2020), *Leveraging Technology and Innovation for Disaster Risk Management and Financing*, Asian Development Bank, Manila, http://dx.doi.org/10.22617/tcs200393-2. [20]

AIMES (n.d.), "Analysis, Integration, and Modeling of the Earth System", webpage, https://aimesproject.org/ (accessed on 18 Oct 2021). [95]

Alley, R., K. Emanuel and F. Zhang (2019), "Advances in weather prediction", *Science*, Vol. 363/6425, pp. 342-344, http://dx.doi.org/10.1126/science.aav7274. [12]

Alliance (2021), "Country Hydromet Diagnostics", webpage, https://alliancehydromet.org/country-hydromet-diagnostics/ (accessed on 15 September 2021). [53]

Allis, E. et al. (2019), "The future of climate services", No. 68, WMO Bulletin, World Meteorological Organization, Geneva, https://public.wmo.int/en/resources/bulletin/future-of-climate-services. [10]

Arendt-Cassetta, L. (2021), "From digital promise to frontile practice: New and emerging technologies in humanitarian action", *Policy Brief*, UN Office for the Coordination of Humanitarian Affairs, New York. [6]

Bathiany, S., J. Hidding and M. Scheffer (2020), "Edge detection reveals abrupt and extreme climate events", *Journal of Climate*, Vol. 33/15, pp. 6399-6421, http://dx.doi.org/10.1175/jcli-d-19-0449.1. [93]

Baudoin, M. et al. (2016), "From top-down to 'community-centric' approaches to early warning systems: Exploring pathways to improve disaster risk reduction through community participation", *International Journal of Disaster Risk Science*, Vol. 7/2, pp. 163-174, http://dx.doi.org/10.1007/s13753-016-0085-6. [74]

Beaugrand, G. et al. (2019), "Prediction of unprecedented biological shifts in the global ocean", *Nature Climate Change*, Vol. 9/3, pp. 237-243, http://dx.doi.org/10.1038/s41558-019-0420-1. [91]

Bell, A. et al. (2021), "Migration towards Bangladesh coastlines projected to increase with sea-level rise through 2100", *Environmental Research Letters*, Vol. 16/2, p. 024045, http://dx.doi.org/10.1088/1748-9326/abdc5b. [55]

Bergen, K. et al. (2019), "Machine learning for data-driven discovery in solid Earth geoscience", *Science*, Vol. 363/6433, p. eaau0323, http://dx.doi.org/10.1126/science.aau0323. [37]

Bettini, G., G. Gioli and R. Felli (2020), "Clouded skies: How digital technologies could reshape 'loss and damage' from climate change", *WIREs Climate Change*, Vol. 11/4, http://dx.doi.org/10.1002/wcc.650. [122]

Biffis, E. and E. Chavez (2017), "Satellite data and machine learning for weather risk management and food security", *Risk Analysis*, Vol. 37/8, pp. 1508-1521, http://dx.doi.org/10.1111/risa.12847. [123]

Biswas, P. (2016), "India's Met model for world: Bhutan, 7 others to replicate tech-based advice", 16 October, The Indian Express, https://indianexpress.com/article/india/india-news-india/indias-met-model-for-world-bhutan-7-others-to-replicate-tech-based-advice-3729310/. [52]

Boldt, J. et al. (2012), *Overcoming Barriers to the Transfer and Diffusion of Climate Technologies*, TNA Guidebook Series, Risø DTU National Laboratory for Sustainable Energy, UNEP Risø Centre on Energy, Climate and Sustainable Development, https://unepdtu.org/publications/overcoming-barriers-to-the-transfer-and-diffusion-of-climate-technologies/. [5]

Bony, S. et al. (2015), "Clouds, circulation and climate sensitivity", *Nature Geoscience*, Vol. 8/4, pp. 261-268, http://dx.doi.org/10.1038/ngeo2398. [32]

Bragais, M. et al. (2016), "Vulnerability assessment using Lidar data", *The International Archives of the Photogrammetry, Remote Sensing and Spatial Information Sciences*, Vol. XLI-B8, pp. 1397-1401, http://dx.doi.org/10.5194/isprs-archives-xli-b8-1397-2016. [62]

Brody, S. et al. (2007), "Examining the relationship between physical vulnerability and public perceptions of global climate change in the United States", *Environment and Behavior*, Vol. 40/1, pp. 72-95, http://dx.doi.org/10.1177/0013916506298800. [70]

Brönnimann, S. et al. (2018), "A roadmap to climate data rescue services", *Geoscience Data Journal*, Vol. 5/1, pp. 28-39, http://dx.doi.org/10.1002/gdj3.56. [27]

Bruno Soares, M., M. Daly and S. Dessai (2018), "Assessing the value of seasonal climate forecasts for decision-making", *WIREs Climate Change*, Vol. 9/4, http://dx.doi.org/10.1002/wcc.523. [25]

Buckle, S. et al. (2020), "Addressing the COVID-19 and climate crises: Potential economic recovery pathways and their implications for climate change mitigation, NDCs and broader socio-economic goals", *OECD/IEA Climate Change Expert Group Papers*, No. 2020/04, OECD Publishing, Paris, https://dx.doi.org/10.1787/50abd39c-en. [110]

Bury, T., C. Bauch and M. Anand (2020), "Detecting and distinguishing tipping points using spectral early warning signals", *Journal of The Royal Society Interface*, Vol. 17/170, p. 20200482, http://dx.doi.org/10.1098/rsif.2020.0482. [88]

Butler, J. et al. (2015), "Integrating top-down and bottom-up adaptation planning to build adaptive capacity: A structured learning approach", *Coastal Management*, Vol. 43/4, pp. 346-364, http://dx.doi.org/10.1080/08920753.2015.1046802. [127]

CAPRA (n.d.), "CAPRA Probabilistic Risk Assessment Platform", webpage, https://ecapra.org/ (accessed on 17 August 2021). [50]

Chakraborty, T. et al. (2020), "A spatially explicit surface urban heat island database for the United States: Characterization, uncertainties, and possible applications", *ISPRS Journal of Photogrammetry and Remote Sensing*, Vol. 168, pp. 74-88, http://dx.doi.org/10.1016/j.isprsjprs.2020.07.021. [57]

CIF (2020), *Strengthening Weather and Climate Information Serices: Highlights from PPCR Supported Projects*, Climate Investment Funds, Washington, DC, https://www.climateinvestmentfunds.org/sites/cif_enc/files/knowledge-documents/ppcr_resilience_series_weather_and_climate_information_services.pdf. [9]

Clarke, B., F. Otto and R. Jones (2021), “Inventories of extreme weather events and impacts: Implications for loss and damage from and adaptation to climate extremes”, *Climate Risk Management*, Vol. 32, p. 100285, http://dx.doi.org/10.1016/j.crm.2021.100285. [84]

Copernicus (n.d.), “Copernicus Key Products and Services”, webpage, https://climate.copernicus.eu/ (accessed on 26 July 2021). [29]

Cornforth, R., C. Petty and G. Walker (2021), “Supporting climate-resilient planning at national and district levels: A pathway to multi-stakeholder decision-making in Uganda”, in *Climate Risk in Africa*, Springer International Publishing, Cham, http://dx.doi.org/10.1007/978-3-030-61160-6_8. [47]

CTCN (n.d.), “About the Climate Technology Centre and Network (CTCN)”, webpage, https://www.ctc-n.org/about-ctcn (accessed on 22 September 2021). [138]

de Bruijn, J. et al. (2019), “A global database of historic and real-time flood events based on social media”, *Scientific Data*, Vol. 6/1, http://dx.doi.org/10.1038/s41597-019-0326-9. [60]

Dechezleprêtre, A. et al. (2020), *Invention and Global Diffusion of Technologies for Climate Change Adaptation: A Patent Analysis*, International Bank for Reconstruction and Development/World Bank, Washington, DC. [130]

Dickson, E. et al. (2012), *Urban Risk Assessments: Understanding Disaster and Climate Risk in Cities*, World Bank, Washington, DC, https://www.worldbank.org/en/topic/urbandevelopment/publication/urban-risk-assessments. [51]

Dinku, T. et al. (2017), “Enhancing National Climate Services (ENACTS) for development in Africa”, *Climate and Development*, Vol. 10/7, pp. 664-672, http://dx.doi.org/10.1080/17565529.2017.1405784. [43]

Ditlevsen, P. and S. Johnsen (2010), “Tipping points: Early warning and wishful thinking”, *Geophysical Research Letters*, Vol. 37/19, http://dx.doi.org/10.1029/2010gl044486. [86]

Econadapt (n.d.), “Econadapt Toolbox, Methods”, webpage, https://econadapt-toolbox.eu/methods (accessed on 21 September 2021). [102]

ESA (n.d.), “Earth Observation Information Discovery Platform”, webpage, https://earth.esa.int/eogateway (accessed on 4 June 2021). [28]

ESA (n.d.), “Remote Sensing Of Tipping Points In The Climate System”, webpage, https://climate.esa.int/en/news-events/remote-sensing-tipping-points-climate-system/ (accessed on 18 Oct 2021). [94]

Faiyetole, A. (2018), “Potentialities of space-based systems for monitoring climate policies and mitigation of climate process drivers”, *Astropolitics*, Vol. 16/1, pp. 28-48, http://dx.doi.org/10.1080/14777622.2018.1436329. [82]

Fricko, O. et al. (2017), “The marker quantification of the Shared Socioeconomic Pathway 2: A middle-of-the-road scenario for the 21st century”, *Global Environmental Change*, Vol. 42, pp. 251-267, http://dx.doi.org/10.1016/j.gloenvcha.2016.06.004. [107]

Frigerio, S. et al. (2018), “Hands-on experience of crowdsourcing for flood risks. An android mobile application tested in Frederikssund, Denmark”, *International Journal of Environmental Research and Public Health*, Vol. 15/9, p. 1926, http://dx.doi.org/10.3390/ijerph15091926. [59]

Fujimori, S. et al. (2017), "SSP3: AIM implementation of Shared Socioeconomic Pathways", *Global Environmental Change*, Vol. 42, pp. 268-283, http://dx.doi.org/10.1016/j.gloenvcha.2016.06.009. [106]

GEO (2018), *Geo Work Programme and The Paris Agreement*, UNFCCC, Geneva, https://unfccc.int/sites/default/files/resource/2.30%20GEO-WP.pdf. [83]

Geo-Wiki (n.d.), "Risk Geo-Wiki", webpage, https://geo-wiki.org/branches/risk/ (accessed on 18 Oct 2021). [97]

GFDRR (2019), *Information and Communication Technology for Disaser Risk Managment in Japan*, World Bank, Washington, DC. [116]

GFDRR (2016), *Solving the Puzzle: Innovating to Reduce Risk; Written Contributions*, World Bank, Washington, DC. [46]

Gil, Y. et al. (2018), "Intelligent systems for geosciences", *Communications of the ACM*, Vol. 62/1, pp. 76-84, http://dx.doi.org/10.1145/3192335. [44]

Goldby, M. et al. (2019), "Triggering innovation: How smart contracts bring policies to life", *Emerging Risks Report 2019*, Lloyd's and Centre for Commercial Law Studies, London, https://assets.lloyds.com/assets/pdf-triggering-innovation-how-smart-contracts-bring-policies-to-life/1/pdf-triggering-innovation-how-smart-contracts-bring-policies-to-life.pdf. [120]

Granderson, A. (2017), "The role of traditional knowledge in building adaptive capacity for climate change: Perspectives from Vanuatu", *Weather, Climate, and Society*, Vol. 9/3, pp. 545-561, http://dx.doi.org/10.1175/wcas-d-16-0094.1. [72]

Grubler, A. et al. (2018), "A low energy demand scenario for meeting the 1.5 °C target and sustainable development goals without negative emission technologies", *Nature Energy*, Vol. 3/6, pp. 515-527, http://dx.doi.org/10.1038/s41560-018-0172-6. [105]

Gsell, A. et al. (2016), "Evaluating early-warning indicators of critical transitions in natural aquatic ecosystems", *Proceedings of the National Academy of Sciences*, Vol. 113/50, pp. E8089-E8095, http://dx.doi.org/10.1073/pnas.1608242113. [92]

Guo, H., L. Zhang and L. Zhu (2015), "Earth observation big data for climate change research", *Advances in Climate Change Research*, Vol. 6/2, pp. 108-117, http://dx.doi.org/10.1016/j.accre.2015.09.007. [111]

Hallegatte, S. (2012), *A Cost Effective Solution to Reduce Disaster Losses in Developing Countries: Hydro-Meteorological Services, Early Warning and Evacuation*, World Bank, Washington, DC, https://openknowledge.worldbank.org/bitstream/handle/10986/9359/WPS6058.pdf?s. [42]

Hemmerling, S. et al. (2019), "Elevating local knowledge through participatory modeling: active community engagement in restoration planning in coastal Louisiana", *Journal of Geographical Systems*, Vol. 22/2, pp. 241-266, http://dx.doi.org/10.1007/s10109-019-00313-2. [99]

Hewitt, C. et al. (2020), "Making society climate resilient: International progress under the Global Framework for Climate Services", *Bulletin of the American Meteorological Society*, Vol. 101/2, pp. E237-E252, http://dx.doi.org/10.1175/bams-d-18-0211.1. [11]

Homberg, M. and C. McQuistan (2018), “Technology for climate justice: A reporting framework for loss and damage as part of key global agreements”, in *Loss and Damage from Climate Change, Climate Risk Management, Policy and Governance*, Springer International Publishing, Cham, http://dx.doi.org/10.1007/978-3-319-72026-5_22. [129]

Hooker, J., G. Duveiller and A. Cescatti (2018), “A global dataset of air temperature derived from satellite remote sensing and weather stations”, *Scientific Data*, Vol. 5/1, http://dx.doi.org/10.1038/sdata.2018.246. [16]

Hoskins, B. (2012), “The potential for skill across the range of the seamless weather-climate prediction problem: A stimulus for our science”, *Quarterly Journal of the Royal Meteorological Society*, Vol. 139/672, pp. 573-584, http://dx.doi.org/10.1002/qj.1991. [76]

Hsu, A. et al. (2021), “Disproportionate exposure to urban heat island intensity across major US cities”, *Nature Communications*, Vol. 12/1, http://dx.doi.org/10.1038/s41467-021-22799-5. [56]

IEA (2021), *Financing Clean Energy Transitions in Emerging and Developing Economies*, IEA, Paris. [103]

Inclusivity Solutions (2020), *Hollard Insurance and FNB Zambia Unveil New Insurance Product to Protect Small Businesses from Economic Shocks*, https://inclusivitysolutions.com/hollard-insurance-and-fnb-zambia-unveil-new-insurance-product/. [121]

InsuResilience (2021), “Crop Insurance Program for Smallholder Farmers in Kenya”, webpage, https://www.insuresilience-solutions-fund.org/news-events (accessed on 15 September 2021). [124]

IPCC (2021), *Climate Change 2021: The Physical Science Basis. Contribution of Working Group I to the Sixth Assessment Report of the Intergovernmental Panel on Climate Change*, Masson-Delmotte, V. et al. (eds.), Cambridge University Press, Cambridge, United Kingdom, https://www.ipcc.ch/report/ar6/wg1/downloads/report/IPCC_AR6_WGI_Full_Report.pdf. [79]

IPCC (2019), *Climate Change and Land: an IPCC special report on climate change, desertification, land degradation, sustainable land management, food security, and greenhouse gas fluxes in terrestrial ecosystems*, Intergovernmental Panel on Climate Change, Geneva. [71]

IPCC (2018), *IPCC Special Report Global Warming of 1.5 °C*, Intergovernmental Panel on Climate Change, Geneva. [104]

IPCC (2013), *Climate Change 2013: The Physical Science Basis. Contribution of Working Group I to the Fifth Assessment Report of the Intergovernmental Panel on Climate Change*, Cambridge University Press, Cambridge, United Kingdom, https://www.ipcc.ch/report/ar5/wg1/. [77]

IRGC (2017), *Introduction to the IRGC Risk Governance Framework, revised version*, EPFL International Risk Governance Center, Lausanne, http://dx.doi.org/10.5075/epfl-irgc-233739. [4]

ITU (2020), *Space Science for Achieving the Sustainable Development Goals*, International Telecommunication Union, Geneva. [19]

ITU (2016), *Harnessing the Internet of Things for Global Development*, International Telecommunication Union, Geneva, https://www.itu.int/en/action/broadband/Documents/Harnessing-IoT-Global-Development.pdf. [22]

Izumi, T. et al. (2019), "Disaster risk reduction and innovations", *Progress in Disaster Science*, Vol. 2, p. 100033, http://dx.doi.org/10.1016/j.pdisas.2019.100033. [133]

Jones, T. et al. (2015), "Simultaneous radar and satellite data storm-scale assimilation using an Ensemble Kalman Filter approach for 24 May 2011", *Monthly Weather Review*, Vol. 143/1, pp. 165-194, http://dx.doi.org/10.1175/mwr-d-14-00180.1. [26]

Karpatne, A. et al. (2017), "Theory-guided data science: A new paradigm for scientific discovery from data", *IEEE Transactions on Knowledge and Data Engineering*, Vol. 29/10, pp. 2318-2331, http://dx.doi.org/10.1109/tkde.2017.2720168. [36]

Khan, A., S. Gupta and S. Gupta (2020), "Multi-hazard disaster studies: Monitoring, detection, recovery, and management, based on emerging technologies and optimal techniques", *International Journal of Disaster Risk Reduction*, Vol. 47, p. 101642, http://dx.doi.org/10.1016/j.ijdrr.2020.101642. [21]

Klinke, A. and O. Renn (2012), "Adaptive and integrative governance on risk and uncertainty", *Journal of Risk Research*, Vol. 15/3, pp. 273-292, http://dx.doi.org/10.1080/13669877.2011.636838. [1]

Kriegler, E. et al. (2017), "Fossil-fueled development (SSP5): An energy and resource intensive scenario for the 21st century", *Global Environmental Change*, Vol. 42, pp. 297-315, http://dx.doi.org/10.1016/j.gloenvcha.2016.05.015. [108]

Kwan, M. and D. Ransberger (2010), "LiDAR assisted emergency response: Detection of transport network obstructions caused by major disasters", *Computers, Environment and Urban Systems*, Vol. 34/3, pp. 179-188, http://dx.doi.org/10.1016/j.compenvurbsys.2010.02.001. [63]

Lenton, T. (2011), "Early warning of climate tipping points", *Nature Climate Change*, Vol. 1/4, pp. 201-209, http://dx.doi.org/10.1038/nclimate1143. [87]

Lenton, T. et al. (2019), "Climate tipping points – too risky to bet against", *Nature*, Vol. 575/7784, pp. 592-595, http://dx.doi.org/10.1038/d41586-019-03595-0. [80]

Liu, Y. et al. (2016), "Application of deep convolutional neural networks for detecting extreme weather in climate datasets", *Computer Vision and Pattern Recognition*, https://arxiv.org/abs/1605.01156. [34]

Marder, J. (2019), "NASA Tracks Wildfires From Above to Aid Firefighters Below", webpage, https://www.nasa.gov/feature/goddard/2019/nasa-tracks-wildfires-from-above-to-aid-firefighters-below (accessed on 21 June 2021). [65]

Mechler, R. et al. (2018), "Supporting Climate Risk Management at Scale. Insights from the Zurich Flood Resilience Alliance Partnership Model Applied in Peru & Nepal", in *Loss and Damage from Climate Change, Climate Risk Management, Policy and Governance*, Springer International Publishing, Cham, http://dx.doi.org/10.1007/978-3-319-72026-5_17. [98]

Michels, M., C. von Hobe and O. Musshoff (2020), "A trans-theoretical model for the adoption of drones by large-scale German farmers", *Journal of Rural Studies*, Vol. 75, pp. 80-88, http://dx.doi.org/10.1016/j.jrurstud.2020.01.005. [69]

Minges, M. (2019), *Disruptive Technologies and their Use in Disaster Risk Reduction and Management*, International Telecommunication Union, Geneva, https://www.itu.int/en/ITU-D/Emergency-Telecommunications/Documents/2019/GET_2019/Disruptive-Technologies.pdf. [67]

Mohanty, A. (2020), *Preparing India for Extreme Climate Events: Mapping Hotspots and Response Mechanisms*, Council on Energy, Environment and Water, New Delhi, https://www.ceew.in/sites/default/files/CEEW-Preparing-India-for-extreme-climate-events_10Dec20.pdf. [45]

Newman, J. et al. (2017), "Review of literature on decision support systems for natural hazard risk reduction: Current status and future research directions", *Environmental Modelling & Software*, Vol. 96, pp. 378-409, http://dx.doi.org/10.1016/j.envsoft.2017.06.042. [101]

Nieves, V., C. Radin and G. Camps-Valls (2021), "Predicting regional coastal sea level changes with machine learning", *Scientific Reports*, Vol. 11/1, pp. 358-361, http://dx.doi.org/10.1038/s41598-021-87460-z. [35]

NOAA (n.d.), "Argo Center", webpage, https://www.aoml.noaa.gov/phod/argo/ (accessed on 21 September 2021). [90]

O'Neill, B. et al. (2017), "The roads ahead: Narratives for shared socioeconomic pathways describing world futures in the 21st century", *Global Environmental Change*, Vol. 42, pp. 169-180, http://dx.doi.org/10.1016/j.gloenvcha.2015.01.004. [109]

Oasis (2021), "An Open Source Catastrophe Modelling Platform", webpage, https://oasislmf.org/ (accessed on 7 May 2021). [30]

OECD (2021), *Strengthening Climate Resilience: Guidance for Governments and Development Co-operation*, OECD Publishing, Paris, https://dx.doi.org/10.1787/4b08b7be-en. [24]

OECD et al. (2020), *Latin American Economic Outlook 2020: Digital Transformation for Building Back Better*, OECD Publishing, Paris, https://dx.doi.org/10.1787/e6e864fb-en. [134]

OECD/IEA (2003), *Technology Innovation, Development and Diffusion*, OECD Publishing, Paris, https://www.oecd.org/env/cc/2956490.pdf. [131]

Papale, D. and R. Valentini (2003), "A new assessment of European forests carbon exchanges by eddy fluxes and artificial neural network spatialization", *Global Change Biology*, Vol. 9/4, pp. 525-535, http://dx.doi.org/10.1046/j.1365-2486.2003.00609.x. [33]

PCRAFI (n.d.), "Pacific Risk Information System Community", webpage, http://pcrafi.spc.int/ (accessed on 17 August 2021). [49]

PIK (n.d.), "AGRICA - Climate Risk Analyses for Identifying and Weighing Adaptation Strategies in sub-Saharan Africa", webpage, https://www.pik-potsdam.de/en/institute/departments/climate-resilience/projects/project-pages/agrica/agrica-sv-giz-climate-project (accessed on 25 September 2020). [100]

Rahman, M. and P. Thakur (2018), "Detecting, mapping and analysing of flood water propagation using synthetic aperture radar (SAR) satellite data and GIS: A case study from the Kendrapara District of Orissa State of India", *The Egyptian Journal of Remote Sensing and Space Science*, Vol. 21, pp. S37-S41, http://dx.doi.org/10.1016/j.ejrs.2017.10.002. [64]

Raithatha, R. and D. Tricarico (2019), *Mobile Technology for Rural Climate Resilience: The Role of Mobile Operators in Bridging the Data Gap*, GSMA AgriTech Programme, London, https://www.gsma.com/mobilefordevelopment/wp-content/uploads/2019/10/GSMA_AgriTech_Climate_Report.pdf. [125]

Red Cross 510 (2021), "510.Global", webpage, http://510.global (accessed on 4 June 2021). [48]

Reichstein, M. et al. (2019), "Deep learning and process understanding for data-driven Earth system science", *Nature*, Vol. 566/7743, pp. 195-204, http://dx.doi.org/10.1038/s41586-019-0912-1. [7]

Rosier, S. et al. (2021), "The tipping points and early warning indicators for Pine Island Glacier, West Antarctica", *The Cryosphere*, Vol. 15/3, pp. 1501-1516, http://dx.doi.org/10.5194/tc-15-1501-2021. [89]

Rühmann, F. et al. (2020), "Can blockchain technology reduce the cost of remittances?", *OECD Development Co-operation Working Papers*, No. 73, OECD Publishing, Paris, https://dx.doi.org/10.1787/d4d6ac8f-en. [117]

Salvati, P. et al. (2021), "Acquiring vulnerability indicators to geo-hydrological hazards: An example of mobile phone-based data collection", *International Journal of Disaster Risk Reduction*, Vol. 55, p. 102087, http://dx.doi.org/10.1016/j.ijdrr.2021.102087. [58]

Sams, J. (2020), "Not all homes in wildfire zones are uninsurable. Here's how insurers can tell", 22 May, Insurance Journal, https://www.insurancejournal.com/news/national/2020/05/22/569684.htm. [119]

Sarker, M. et al. (2020), "Disaster resilience through big data: Way to environmental sustainability", *International Journal of Disaster Risk Reduction*, Vol. 51, http://dx.doi.org/10.1016/j.ijdrr.2020.101769. [66]

Schweizer, P. and O. Renn (2019), "Governance of systemic risks for disaster prevention and mitigation", *Disaster Prevention and Management: An International Journal*, Vol. 28/6, pp. 862-874, http://dx.doi.org/10.1108/dpm-09-2019-0282. [3]

Shepherd, T. (2014), "Atmospheric circulation as a source of uncertainty in climate change projections", *Nature Geoscience*, Vol. 7/10, pp. 703-708, http://dx.doi.org/10.1038/ngeo2253. [31]

Shove, E. (2010), "Beyond the ABC: Climate Change Policy and Theories of Social Change", *Environment and Planning A: Economy and Space*, Vol. 42/6, pp. 1273-1285, http://dx.doi.org/10.1068/a42282. [41]

Shrestha, M. et al. (2021), "The last mile: Flood risk communication for better preparedness in Nepal", *International Journal of Disaster Risk Reduction*, Vol. 56, p. 102118, http://dx.doi.org/10.1016/j.ijdrr.2021.102118. [115]

Shukla, J. et al. (2010), "Toward a new generation of world climate research and computing facilities", *Bulletin of the American Meteorological Society*, Vol. 91/10, pp. 1407-1412, http://dx.doi.org/10.1175/2010bams2900.1. [75]

Sommer, L. (2020), "To manage wildfire, California looks to what tribes have known all along", 24 August, NPR, https://www.npr.org/2020/08/24/899422710/to-manage-wildfire-california-looks-to-what-tribes-have-known-all-along. [73]

Stokke, O. and O. Young (2017), "Integrating Earth observation systems and international environmental regimes", in *Satellite Earth Observations and their Impact on Society and Policy*, Springer Singapore, Singapore, http://dx.doi.org/10.1007/978-981-10-3713-9_16. [81]

Street, R. et al. (2019), "How could climate services support disaster risk reduction in the 21st century", *International Journal of Disaster Risk Reduction*, Vol. 24/March, pp. 28-33, http://dx.doi.org/10.1016/j.ijdrr.2018.12.001. [128]

Sun, Q. et al. (2018), "A review of global precipitation data sets: Data sources, estimation, and intercomparisons", *Reviews of Geophysics*, Vol. 56/1, pp. 79-107, http://dx.doi.org/10.1002/2017rg000574. [18]

Swingedouw, D. et al. (2020), "Early warning from space for a few key tipping points in physical, biological, and social-ecological systems", *Surveys in Geophysics*, Vol. 41/6, pp. 1237-1284, http://dx.doi.org/10.1007/s10712-020-09604-6. [85]

UN (2021), "UN-Spider.org", webpage, https://www.un-spider.org/projects/evidenz/background-information (accessed on 31 May 2021). [113]

UNCTAD (2021), *Exploring Space Technologies for Sustainable Development*, United Nations Conference on Trade and Development, Geneva, https://unctad.org/system/files/official-document/dtlstict2021d1_en.pdf. [17]

UNFCCC (2020), *Policy Brief: Technologies for Averting, Minimising and Addressing Loss and Damage in Coastal Zones*, United Nations, Bonn. [135]

UNFCCC (2017), *South–South cooperation and triangular cooperation on technologies for adaptation water and agriculture sectors*, UNFCCC, Bonn. [136]

UNFCCC (2012), *The National Adaptation Plan Process: A Brief Overview*, United Nations Framework Convention on Climate Change, Bonn, https://unfccc.int/files/adaptation/application/pdf/nap_overview.pdf. [2]

UNFCCC (n.d.), "About the Santiago Network", webpage, https://unfccc.int/santiago-network/about (accessed on 22 September 2021). [132]

UNFCCC (n.d.), "Technology Executive Committee", webpage, https://unfccc.int/ttclear/tec (accessed on 22 September 2021). [139]

UNOSSC (n.d.), "About South-South and Triangular Cooperation", webpage, https://www.unsouthsouth.org/about/about-sstc/ (accessed on 22 September 2021). [137]

van Aalst, M., T. Cannon and I. Burton (2008), "Community level adaptation to climate change: The potential role of participatory community risk assessment", *Global Environmental Change*, Vol. 18/1, pp. 165-179, http://dx.doi.org/10.1016/j.gloenvcha.2007.06.002. [96]

Weaver, C. et al. (2017), "Reframing climate change assessments around risk: Recommendations for the US National Climate Assessment", *Environmental Research Letters*, Vol. 12/9, http://dx.doi.org/10.1088/1748-9326/aa846a. [126]

WMO (2021), "New climate predictions increase likelihood of temporarily reaching 1.5 °C in next 5 years", 27 May, Press Release, World Meteorological Organization, Geneva, https://public.wmo.int/en/media/press-release/new-climate-predictions-increase-likelihood-of-temporarily-reaching-15-%C2%B0c-next-5. [78]

WMO (2020), *2020 State of Climate Services: Risk Information and Early Warning Systems*, World Meteorological Organization, Geneva, https://library.wmo.int/doc_num.php?explnum_id=10385. [114]

WMO (2020), "New climate predictions assess global temperatures in coming five years", 8 July, News Release, World Meteorological Organization, Geneva, https://public.wmo.int/en/media/press-release/new-climate-predictions-assess-global-temperatures-coming-five-years. [39]

WMO (2020), "The Systematic Observations Financing Facility: How will it work?", *Information Brief*, World Meteorological Organization, Geneva, https://library.wmo.int/doc_num.php?explnum_id=10378. [14]

WMO (2020), "The value of Surface-Based Meteorological Observational Data: Costs and benefits of the Global Basic Observing Network", *Information Brief*, World Meteorological Organization, Geneva, https://library.wmo.int/doc_num.php?explnum_id=10376. [54]

WMO (2015), *Status of the Global Observing System for Climate*, World Meteorological Organization, Geneva, https://library.wmo.int/doc_num.php?explnum_id=7213. [23]

WMO (2015), *Valuing Weather and Climate: Economic Assessment of Meteorological and Hydrological Services*, World Meteorological Organization, Geneva, https://library.wmo.int/doc_num.php?explnum_id=3314. [8]

WMO (n.d.), "Global Producing Centres for Long-Range Forecasts", webpage, https://community.wmo.int/global-producing-centres-long-range-forecasts (accessed on 23 September 2021). [38]

WMO (n.d.), "Regional Climate Outlook Forums", webpage, https://public.wmo.int/en/our-mandate/climate/regional-climate-outlook-products. [40]

WMO and GFCS (2019), "2019 State of climate services", *Working Paper*, No. 1242, World Meteorological Organization, Geneva, https://library.wmo.int/doc_num.php?explnum_id=10089. [15]

World Bank (2019), "Blockchain: How the Fourth Industrial Revolution can help accelerate progress towards development", 24 January, World Bank, Washington, DC, https://www.worldbank.org/en/news/feature/2019/01/24/blockchain-como-asegurarse-que-cada-dolar-llegue-a-quien-lo-necesita. [118]

Yu, M., C. Yang and Y. Li (2018), "Big data in natural disaster management: A Review", *Geosciences*, Vol. 8/5, p. 165, http://dx.doi.org/10.3390/geosciences8050165. [61]

ZFL (2021), "EvIDENz", webpage, https://www.zfl.uni-bonn.de/research/projects/ (accessed on 7 June 2021). [112]

Zhang, F. and Y. Weng (2015), "Predicting hurricane intensity and associated hazards: A five-year real-time forecast experiment with assimilation of airborne Doppler radar observations", *Bulletin of the American Meteorological Society*, Vol. 96/1, pp. 25-33, http://dx.doi.org/10.1175/bams-d-13-00231.1. [13]

Notes

[1] IoT is the convergence of networks of physical objects, such as software, sensors and other Internet-connected devices used to exchange and monitor information in real-time e.g. temperature, water quality, emissions, smoke, humidity.

[2] Using FAO's figure of around 5 billion hectares of agricultural land globally – see www.fao.org/sustainability/news/detail/en/c/1274219/.

[3] South–South cooperation is a "broad framework of collaboration among countries of the South in the political, economic, social, cultural, environmental and technical domains. Involving two or more developing countries, it can take place on a bilateral, regional, intraregional or interregional basis. Developing countries share knowledge, skills, expertise and resources to meet their development goals through concerted efforts" (UNOSSC, n.d.[137])

[4] Triangular cooperation is "collaboration in which traditional donor countries and multilateral organizations facilitate South–South initiatives through the provision of funding, training, management and technological systems as well as other forms of support" (UNOSSC, n.d.[137]).

www.ingramcontent.com/pod-product-compliance
Ingram Content Group UK Ltd.
Pitfield, Milton Keynes, MK11 3LW, UK
UKHW051457290926
15471UKWH00008B/1246

9 789264 344396